To Dave

Tony Martin:

TARGET OF POLICE CONSPIRACY

by

Brian Pead

with

Tony Martin

Foreword
by
Sir Henry Bellingham, MP

to Bruno, Daniel and Otto: because, like me, you had your lives turned upside down

to the memory of Anne Frank, because she, too, lived in fear and in fear of burglary, should she and her family be discovered in hiding
TONY MARTIN

for my daughter and grandchildren and nephews so that they might learn the Truth and come to see the lies perpetuated by the police about me were but an echo of the lies perpetrated against Tony Martin and those perpetrated by the police throughout the Hillsborough Disaster
BRIAN PEAD

A special thanks must go to Christopher Schooling of the *Tony Martin Action Group* for his invaluable contribution.

first published in England 2016   ISBN 978-0-995475-50-2

revised edition 2019   ISBN 978-0-9957847-2-7

Copyright   © Brian Pead & Tony Martin
Photographer   Kerry Bensley
Photographs   © The Sorrel Press

The moral rights of the authors have been asserted.

All rights reserved. No part of this publication may be reproduced or transmitted in any form or by any means, electronic or mechanical, including photocopying, recording, or any information storage or retrieval system, without prior permission in writing from the publishers:

The Sorrel Press, Unit 2, 66 Goodwins Road, King's Lynn, Norfolk, PE30 5PD

The most dangerous man to any government
is the man who is able to think things out for himself,
without regard to the prevailing superstitions and taboos.
Almost inevitably he comes to the conclusion
that the government he lives under
is dishonest, insane and intolerable.
Henry Louis Mencken, 1880 - 1956

also by Brian Pead:

Football
Liverpool: A Complete Record 1892- 1986	1986
Liverpool: A Complete Record 1892- 1988	1988
Liverpool: A Complete Record 1892- 1990	1990
Liverpool: Champions of Champions 1990	1990
Ee Aye Addio – We've won the Cup!	1993

Education
National Curriculum Homework Sheets (with Ann Armin)	1999

True Crime
from Hillsborough to Lambeth 2012 (with Michael Bird)	*(currently banned)*	2012
Framed! (under the name William Brian Freeman)		2013
10 Prisons, 12 Weeks (under the name William Brian Freeman)		2014
TONY MARTIN: THE TRUTH		2016
from Hillsborough to Lambeth, second edition		2017
BLUEPRINT FOR ABUSE		2017
MY COUNTRY DECLARED WAR ON ME		2017

In preparation
Letters to my Grandchildren

How Stupid Are You?

To My Daughter, Sorrel

TONY MARTIN: THE COURAGE TO BE FREE

CONTENTS

	Foreword	7
	Introduction	9
	Methodology	11
1	The early years	18
2	1964-1988	27
3	1988-1999	57
4	The Sheridan murders	87
5	January – May 1999	98
6	A shooting incident or two	107
7	Saturday 21 August 1999	153
8	The alleged crime scene	196
9	Following the discovery of the body	212
10	Sunday 22 August 1999	222
11	Ongoing 'investigation'	243
12	"Legal engineering"	515
13	The defence of self-defence	518
14	The trial	523
15	Judge's summing-up	559
16	Jury verdicts	579
17	After the trial & prison	590
18	Appeal against conviction	623
19	the Court of Appeal	636
20	Release from prison	659
21	Diary	674
22	Petition	792
23	Index	794

BLUEPRINT FOR ABUSE

shines a spotlight on State-controlled child abuse in modern Britain

There are some things so far removed from the lives of normal, decent people as to be simply unbelievable by them. The calmest, simplest statements of fact are almost beyond the comprehension or belief of most men and women who have no contact with the dark and hideous secrets of 'an underworld' where child abuse is created and allowed to flourish by the UK government.

Children's homes, special units and boarding schools are not always what they appear to be. The ordinary person can scarcely believe that the abuse of children is often State-controlled, highly organised and hidden in plain sight in collusion with the intelligence services, the police and the Church.

This book provides a detailed history of child abuse in the UK which has been perpetuated by the government for a variety of reasons.

Soft cover, 500+ pages

Foreword
by Sir Henry Bellingham, MP

EVERYONE who is old enough remembers the day that John F Kennedy was murdered. Likewise the vast majority remember waking up on the morning Diana, Princess of Wales, died in the Paris car crash. The majority of people also have vivid memories of the infamous shooting incident at Tony Martin's home.

The events of that fateful evening struck a chord with the whole country – but why was this? The reasons are many and complex but, above all else, there was a tidal wave of public sympathy for a lone farmer who had been abandoned by the Police, trying to protect his own home. Although some people were sympathetic to the young Fred Barras and his grieving family, the overwhelming majority of people in this country felt that he should have never been there in the first place. Instinct also told them that Tony Martin was quite entitled to take all necessary steps to defend himself and his property.

I remember thinking at the time that it was extremely unlikely that the Police and CPS would charge Tony Martin with anything more serious than possession of an illegal shotgun. Anyway, if they did put in place such charges, then no jury in Britain would ever convict him.

After all, it was pitch black and Tony Martin was obviously absolutely petrified. He had heard the intruders but could not see them. He had no idea whether or not they were armed, and he would have been most mindful of a neighbour of his murdered by burglars a few years before. How on earth do we know from the comfort of our homes exactly what was going through Tony Martin's mind that night? What we do know is that one of the intruders shone a bright torch at Tony Martin, and shortly after that he opened fire and deliberately tried to fire low.

I was personally staggered that the Police and CPS decided to charge him with murder. It was also particularly shameful the way Norfolk Constabulary tried to explain away their own abject failings in their lack of rural policing that prevented people like Tony Martin receiving the necessary support. From the word go they seemed to hurl the proverbial book at the Norfolk farmer.

What followed was one of the most extraordinary trials in this country's history. For a start, why on earth was it held in Norwich when there had been warnings that the jury was likely to be intimidated? Also, why on earth did the Judge allow various members of the extended Barras and Fearon families to go on attending Court where it was obvious they were trying to stare at members of the jury?

The final verdict was nothing less than a total shock to those of us who believed that decency and common sense would prevail. However, whilst the trial in some ways showed the worst in human nature, the public response was truly amazing – so pressure grew for an appeal based on diminished responsibility and quashing of the murder conviction. Eventually Tony came out of prison and was able to get on with his life. But, of course, scars have been immense, and it is little wonder he has never moved back into Bleak House.

However, he can be very proud of one legacy, namely the changes in the law that have since taken place. I was fortunate enough to be involved in a number of Private Members Bills where we were attempting to change the balance between the householder and the intruder, so that the former would be able take whatever steps they deemed to be reasonable and proportionate in the circumstances. So, in other words, we were going to move from the previous test which was much more objective, to one where the Police, CPS and the jury all had to ask themselves what the householder actually thought was reasonable given every possible factor.

Eventually Parliament did make the long overdue changes, but why oh why did it require the Bleak House tragedy to bring it about?

Brian Pead's book on this whole saga is I believe the fourth one of its kind, and Brian's second. It is innovative, brave and thought provoking. I believe it is a very important contribution to the debate that has raged ever since. Furthermore, Brian has uncovered a great deal of startling new evidence, which had it been available at the time, might have resulted in a very different outcome. I understand from Brian that Tony Martin's Appeal has now been accepted by the Criminal Cases Review Commission and I, and I expect the whole nation, avidly await their deliberations.

I would like to congratulate Brian on his very well-researched volume, which I am sure will be a great success.

Introduction

Everyone over the age of 40 will have had some experience of the Tony Martin murder trial. The basic facts as made known to the great British public were that the farmer was an eccentric who lived alone in a remote part of northwest Norfolk on the border with Cambridgeshire.

It was said that on the night of 20th August 1999, two burglars from Newark in Nottinghamshire were driven down to Emneth with the specific intent of robbing the farmer.

It was said that they smashed their way into his farmhouse (how many "burglars" make so much noise?) and woke him.

The farmer stated that he ventured downstairs into the darkness and, having had a torch shone in his eyes in the darkness, he fired off a warning shot or two.

The official police narrative was that he intentionally seriously wounded one "burglar", Brendon Fearon, 29 and killed another, Fred Barras, 16. Yet the ballistic evidence didn't match the injuries had the farmer fired from the stairs, so the CPS claimed that the farmer had lied.

No-one thought to challenge the official version. No one thought to ask why dozens of statements were not entered into court. Or why crucial witnesses were not called before a jury.

For the first time ever, this book publishes those statements which never made their way into court. It provides the evidence unlawfully kept hidden from the jury and the public. It shows how 60 million people were swept along on an emotional tide – caught up in an argument about a person's right to defend himself. Caught up in the emotional whirlpool surrounding the death of a teenaged "burglar". Caught up in the propaganda about an "eccentric loner". Caught up in a murder trial designed to divert the public's attention away from the nastiness perpetrated by the Blair government. Caught up in thinking "What if I had been invaded?" Caught up in questioning whether the law would really protect you.

Sometimes two events that seem related in time or place aren't really related as cause and event. In other words, just because Tony Martin fired his gun and just because two men sustained gunshot wounds it doesn't necessarily follow that Tony Martin shot them.

That is what you were *meant* to believe. The evidence – much of it police evidence – points to the fact that Bleak House was invaded by an unknown number of intruders and, as a consequence, the most famous farmer in England fired his shotgun. The evidence also points to the fact that the so-called "burglars" never made it to the house, that they were shot on a track leading to a house and that they were shot *after* Tony Martin had left his property having fired his pump-action Winchester shotgun.

The Police sold you – and 60 million others – a false narrative:

> "...in the big lie there is always a certain force of credibility; because the broad masses of a nation are always more easily corrupted in the deeper strata of their emotional nature than consciously or voluntarily; and thus in the primitive simplicity of their minds they more readily fall victims to the big lie than the small lie ... they would not believe that others could have the impudence to distort the truth so infamously..."

And the Truth *was* distorted as this book shows:

> "...If you tell a lie big enough and keep repeating it, people will eventually come to believe it. The lie can be maintained only for such time as the State can shield the people from the political, economic and/or military consequences of the lie. It thus becomes vitally important for the State to use all of its powers to repress dissent, for the truth is the mortal enemy of the lie, and thus by extension, the truth is the greatest enemy of the State..."

Many, many people told lies in the Tony Martin murder trial. Police officers of all rank, prosecution witnesses, barristers ... even the judge ... and the only person who told the truth about the events of that night as he knew them to be was the beleaguered farmer. And much of what he knew to be true was lost to him for years, buried beneath an avalanche of State corruption and bullying. He, too, had fallen for the fallacy. And yet he had admitted the following:

1. that he had been woken from his sleep by "burglars" making an extraordinary amount of noise (how many "burglars" make so much noise, especially when the owner's car is parked at the front of the house?)
2. that he had seen reflections in the shoes of the intruders (the "burglars" were wearing trainers);
3. that he had never seen anybody when he fired his shotgun into the darkness from the hip and on the stairs;
4. that he had heard nobody call out either before he fired or afterwards;
5. that he had seen no blood on the window pulled out of its opening;
6. that he had seen no pellets embedded in it or furniture in that room;
7. that he had seen no blood trail in the breakfast room;
8. that he had seen no car tracks on the lawn to the rear of the house;
9. that he had seen no footsteps in the heavy dew on the lawn and yet the police claimed the "burglars" had escaped out of the rear window.

The reality is that why Tony Martin did not think he had hit anybody when he fired his gun was *because the police's own evidence was that he could not have hit anybody*. The ONLY reason that he eventually came to believe that he shot Fearon and killed Barras was *because the police told him so* and *because his own barrister conspired with the CPS to ensure that a guilty verdict would be delivered*. The angle from the stairs did not match the men's injuries. Yet, instead of questioning the obviously fabricated police evidence, the farmer was keen to go along with it so that he could "stand tall" in his own mind and in the nation's hearts.

The farmer – a fierce advocate of right and wrong - couldn't comprehend that the police could lie to him on so large a scale.

And then his ego kicked in and he lived out the fantasy that he was the "nation's hero for standing up for all our rights." Yet the police had simply used his own character against himself and he fell for the propaganda because he could finally be heard after years of having no voice and after decades of people (including the police) not listening to him. At last he had a platform – a national and even international platform – upon which to expound his views on society. And yet that platform came at a great cost to the man himself – his belief in the fantasy that the police had created for him and the nation got in the way of his forensically examining his own case. His over-inflated ego cost him dearly. He lost good friends – friends who would write to him in prison and tell him that he was living out a fantasy, friends who wanted to bring him back down to earth to focus on the case itself, and the wrongful allegations that he was a murderer. Yet this naïve and innocent farmer trusted the wrong people – those who would help him to feed his fantasy because they had an ulterior motive of their own which he was too gullible to even see. The farmer swiftly dropped true friends in favour of self-seeking publicists, hangers-on and those who would defraud various charities and support groups of monies sent in by the public to assist the farmer in his days of need against State bullying. And the farmer – who instinctively knew that he had been fitted up for a crime which he didn't commit – spent so long on feeding the "hero" status thrust upon him, that he took his eye off the ball and failed to ever look at the fabricated evidence against him.

Two decades later he complains of being "lonely" and yet fails to comprehend how he contributed to his own loneliness – his own downfall, his fall back into mediocrity.

Two decades after firing his gun, he STILL believes that he shot two "burglars" because it feeds his fragile ego, despite all the police evidence pointing to the fact that he *couldn't have shot them*.

His ego refuses to allow him to consider that for two decades he was wrong to believe the narrative the police were happy to let him believe because it extricated them from their own wrong-doing (and shield the *real* murderer), it refuses to allow him to consider that he was never a "hero", it refuses to allow him to accept that his own myopic character contributed to his foolishness in believing the police account over his own.

For more than half a century he had repressed his feelings, his own voice and too often trusted the words of others. And, when the chips were down, and he really needed to listen to his own inner voice, he merely repeated his own history – of failing to listen to his own internal critic and believing the words of corrupt police officers and "friends" who were wolves in sheep's clothing: out not to help the man but to feather their own nests (at great cost to the farmer). But he lacked the wisdom to see it. And the police stood back, allowed his ego to grow unfettered towards self-destruction and on a path to eventual loneliness in his 70s. I have had the privilege of meeting and interacting with the man for more than six years and I have borne witness to his many moods so that I was able, as a counsellor as well as an author, to form a psychological profile of the ordinary man who – urged on by vultures posing as friendly pets - tried to clothe himself in the mantle of greatness but who lacked the emotional and intellectual depth to wear it.

TONY MARTIN: TARGET OF POLICE CONSPIRACY is the first book to highlight the farmer's truth as he saw it (and forgot it) and the State's denial and repression of that truth.

It was Joseph Goebbels, Hitler's Minister for Propaganda, who wrote:

> "The essential English leadership secret does not depend on particular intelligence. Rather, it depends on a remarkably stupid thick-headedness. The English follow the principle that when one lies, one should lie big, and stick to it. They keep up their lies, even at the risk of looking ridiculous."

Tony Martin had steadfastly maintained his innocence whilst the government lied big and kept up their lies and continued to look ridiculous. When a man believes his own hype – aided and abetted in that process by the government – he is on the path to self-destruction and loneliness. And when a man casts aside his own instincts and his own truth and adopts the false police narrative simply so that he can be a "national hero" to bask in the false and undeserved glory, he has lost sight of who he is, he has lost his values, his moral compass, his direction in life.

On the basis of the police's own evidence, it was not only the police and the government that looked foolish, but also the very target of the police conspiracy against him, who had been easily seduced into believing that he was not only a "hero" but that he had shot two "burglars" in his house in spite of the overwhelming weight of evidence against that possibility which I reproduce in this book.

Methodology

It has been necessary to occasionally add punctuation or to correct typing errors in the transcripts of police interviews and witness statements for the sake of making them easier to read and for grammatical accuracy, but the transcripts have not been altered in any other way. They are, therefore, essentially the very same documents that the police entered into court in the Used Material file or which they did not enter into court in the Unused Material file.

In every criminal case, under the Criminal Procedure Rules, the prosecution is obliged to provide the defence with *all* of the documents which it intends to rely on in court, and also provide the defence with *all* of the documents which it has decided not to use, even where that documentation may completely weaken the prosecution's case against the defendant. Both Tony and I believe the rules around disclosure need to be addressed because the system is currently heavily weighted against defendants in all types of cases.

This problem is further exacerbated if the defendant is unfortunate enough to have a poor defence team who have not been diligent in reading through the minutiae of the paperwork.

However, this book is not the most appropriate forum in which to discuss such a major change in the rules so that they more accurately reflect the notion of Justice. That said, it is important for the reader to know that some of the documentation supplied to Tony Martin after the trial and after his eventual release from prison was, in our view, inadequate, improper and incomplete to the point where it renders his original trial a miscarriage of justice and all subsequent trials based on those fundamental flaws in the original trial also a miscarriage.

With regard to the various ranks of police officers, I have used abbreviations wherever possible to reduce the number of pages and to make the text flow more easily. I felt, for example, it was easier on the eye to read 'ACC' rather than keep reading 'assistant chief constable' and I have provided a list of the most frequent abbreviations below.

I refer throughout this book to the HOLMES 'murder book'. This is a large A3 size book which is essentially a line-by-line log of all of the decisions taken by the police in the murder inquiry – it shows the 'lines of inquiry' that they are taking and the results of those lines of inquiry. HOLMES is an acronym for Home Office Large Major Enquiry System.

Northamptonshire Police provide the following description of the national HOLMES computerised system which provides administrative support for major police investigations:

It was created as a result of the 'Yorkshire Ripper' enquiry in the 1980s, when it became evident that a standardised computer system (for usage by all police forces) was an essential investigative tool. The Yorkshire Ripper, Peter Sutcliffe, was interviewed several times by different forces, but the necessary links, which led to his eventual capture and arrest were lacking. Prior to this each force had its own system which was incompatible with other forces. Today, HOLMES manages thousands of individual data such as DNA, fingerprints, physical descriptions and offender profiles which is shared with other forces for their enquiries.[1]

You will also see information boxes and I'll explain them now:

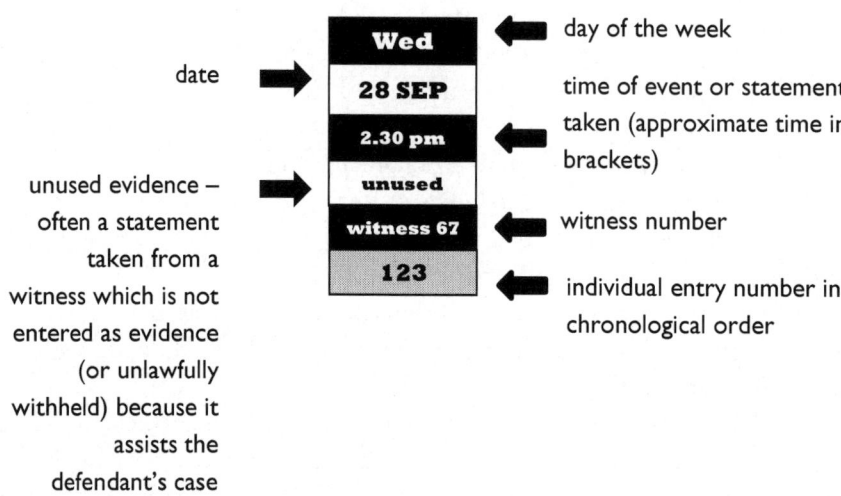

- date
- unused evidence – often a statement taken from a witness which is not entered as evidence (or unlawfully withheld) because it assists the defendant's case
- day of the week
- time of event or statement taken (approximate time in brackets)
- witness number
- individual entry number in chronological order

Other evidence that I read through included hundreds of witness statements, official court documents such as the list of witnesses, list of all evidence entered into court, police intelligence files, newspaper reports, solicitors' papers, letters and cards.

I cross-referenced everything with the HOLMES book and found literally hundreds of discrepancies (even *within* the HOLMES book itself) – some of which were, I feel sure, simply errors in the way in which fallible human beings record things, particularly names: for example, I saw PC 1048 Paul Bassham frequently spelled as 'Bassean' and 'Bassan' and other variations.

Often police constables marry one another and it was sometimes a task to differentiate between the male PC Hooper and the female PC Hooper, for example.

All of that said, I found a disturbingly large number of witness statements which had "disappeared" from the official records. I found a reference in the HOLMES book to a named police officer and his or her statement but no statement was to be found in the boxes and boxes of paperwork that I trawled through in order to prepare this book.

---

[1] http://www.northants.police.uk/page/investigations-holmes.

There is, of course, a world of difference between human error (a civilian typist inputting 'Bassean' instead of 'Bassham' for example) and the deliberate, corrupt and unlawful tampering and destruction of evidence. Furthermore, I came across a significant number of police witness statements in which they said they *hadn't* been at Tony's farm on the night of, or in the early hours following, the shooting. It smelt of desperation: "I wasn't there, honest guv!" Who would make a statement saying you weren't where the official police computer aided dispatches had placed you rather than stating where you were unless you were attempting to create an alibi – and a false one at that? There were more than half-a-dozen such statements of police officers claiming that they hadn't been at Bleak House after all. In fact, did those (usually junior ranked) officers actually make those statements at all? – they weren't signed, were not witnessed, no mention of the officer to whom they were made was recorded, and often no time or location specified. You do not have to be an Einstein to smell a rat in such circumstances. You just have to have – like Tony Martin has often said – "common sense" and it became obvious to me as I read deeper and deeper into the case that something was seriously wrong and that Tony had been "fitted up" for murder.

Now, why would the police have fitted him up for murder? You can be sure that they did and I provide the evidence in this book.

A senior Scotland Yard detective once told me that if you look at *any* crime and trace it right back to its root source, it'll often have its origins in child abuse. If you look at the high-profile child abuse cases in Rochdale, Rotherham, Oxford, Telford and elsewhere (no town in this country is exempt from organised child abuse) you'll find that many of the *victims* of child abuse had been convicted of petty crimes such as shoplifting or underage drinking or drugtaking and yet the core criminal activity had been the child abuse. (For a much deeper analysis of this subject, I refer you to my book *Blueprint for Abuse*.)

Not many people know that Tony Martin suffered child abuse at the hands of his Headmaster at Glebe House School in Hunstanton, Norfolk and at the hands of a well-connected son of a vicar – all explored in forthcoming pages.

Tony would tell all and sundry about the abuse – even complete strangers whom he'd met for the first time (you'll read about one such person. That statement, of course, did not get entered as evidence at court.)

Those in authority who perpetrate such abuse do not like those who refuse to be silent about the abuse. You will read how I have been unlawfully imprisoned because I refused to be silent about the abuse that I and my two brothers (and hundreds of others) suffered at the Highfield Oval children's home in Harpenden, Hertfordshire between 1955 and 1960. But the abuse had been going on much longer before we arrived and it continued long after we left.

Tony Martin does not like homosexual men – not because he is homophobic but because so many men (and women for that matter) hide behind the mask of homosexuality and lesbianism in order to abuse children. Indeed, at one period in recent history, Islington Council in London would only employ homosexual men in its children's homes. They weren't, of course, merely homosexual, but paedophiles masquerading as having only an interest in men.

In the children's home in which I resided, the 'sisters' often perpetrated sexual abuse. They also groomed and procured children for clergymen, justices of the peace, police officers, local councillors and others. I suggest that you can have very little idea of what *really* goes in such institutions and why a national network was *really* established in the first place (it wasn't an altruistic act.)

Tony Martin calls them perverts – not "ordinary" homosexuals – but those who hide behind that label in order to abuse children. We should understand that this hatred of such people is deeply ingrained into his psyche, for very understandable reasons. It is this back story upon which the shooting at Bleak House sits and the reasons that the decent, law-abiding innocent farmer was fitted up for murder.

You will also come across what I have called 'corruption alert' boxes. These perform two main functions – the first is to highlight definite corruption with clear proof beyond all reasonable doubt and the second is to show what is probably corruption with some proof, but not beyond all reasonable doubt.

LIST OF FREQUENT ABBREVIATIONS

ACC	assistant chief constable
ARV	armed response vehicle
CCRC	Criminal Cases Review Commission
CID	Criminal Investigation Department
CPS	Crown Prosecution Service
DC	detective constable
DCI	detective chief inspector
DCS	detective chief superintendent
DI	detective inspector
DNA	deoxyribonucleic acid
DS	detective sergeant
DSupt	detective superintendent
MP	Member of Parliament
PACE	Police and Criminal Evidence Act 1984
PC	police constable
PNC	police national computer
PS	police sergeant
QC	Queen's Counsel
SAO	senior administration officer

ILLUSTRATIONS

Page 16 – a view of Bleak House from the front;
Page 25 – cottages from the rear;
Page 26 – across a cornfield towards the Hungate Corner with the Leets' bungalow on the left;
Page 57 – Bleak House to the rear with Tony Martin's bedroom window on the upper floor to the right;
Page 76 – signpost at the Hungate Corner;
Page 87 – Bleak House and adjoining field;
Page 97 – long grass silhouetted against gathering storm clouds;
Page 98 – gravel drive leading to Bleak House;
Page 107 – a wooden box marked A.R. Garner of Emneth Hungate. This was Tony's uncle, farmer Arthur Garner;
Page 152 – the front of the cottages (some 150 yards or so from Bleak House itself);
Page 196 – the front of Bleak House from the right hand corner (also showing the garage);
Page 212 – an example of steel plating over all the doors and windows;
Page 222 – high hedges around Foreman's Bungalow on the Smeeth Road;
Page 243 – apple trees in the front orchard adjoining the Smeeth Road;
Page 439 – an echo of happier times sitting in the garden drinking tea and watching tennis on the nearby court;
Page 516 – Bleak House to the rear from which alleged burglars escaped without leaving footprints on the lawn or a trail of blood;
Page 519 – the last vestiges of a tennis court to the rear of the house;
Page 524 – empty produce crates littering the landscape;
Page 560 – Bleak House from the right-hand corner;
Page 580 – Titkill Bridge at the junction of the Smeeth Road and the lane running to Bleak House – the bridge was built in 1776;
Page 591 – an oil lamp;
Page 624 – ladders in trees to the rear of Bleak House to aid with cutting off branches;
Page 637 – an echo of Tony's uncle (Arthur Garner) when he farmed at Three Holes, near Wisbech;
Page 660 – the Hungate Corner from Tony Martin's land – Eileen Sutton's bungalow is behind the tree on the right;
Page 676 – the orchard towards the Smeeth Road;
Page 793 – the rear of Bleak House (an alleged crime scene).

The early years

Part 1: the early years

Anthony Edward 'Tony' Martin was born on Saturday 16 December 1944 to Hilary (née Mitcham) and Walter Martin, of March, Cambridgeshire. They already had one son, David Robin, aged 6, born on Saturday 3 December 1938. The family were farmers and were, if not wealthy, then extremely comfortable by the standards of the day, owning a car when such a thing was a rarity.

Tony describes his early years as "reasonably happy" but a major change in his life occurred when in 1952, at the age of 8, he was sent away to board at Glebe House School in Hunstanton. He felt that he was being abandoned by his own family as they sought to grow and develop their farming business, mainly through the mother due to the fact that Walter was – as described by Tony – "a lover of drink who would often take to lying in bed all day." Without any form of judgment, it therefore fell to Hilary to become more of a provider than a nurturing mother and I believe this is the first major example in Tony's life when he was not listened to or when he did not receive the care and attention that he craved – that all children crave, in fact:

> We didn't get on, my father and me. He'd lie in bed all day after his nervous breakdown and so my Uncle Henry (who was 16 years older than my father) ran the farm and made it all pay.
>
> My father was aloof; he drank heavily, smoked a lot and died at the age of 67. When my brother was born, Uncle Henry gave him a farm."

David – always known as Robin (and I will continue to refer to him throughout as Robin) – was 14 and able to lend a hand around the farm in a way that the eight-year-old Tony could not.

"I was propelled into a different world," is how Tony describes being sent to Glebe House. The seeds of emotional distance and parental isolation were being sown just as easily as the seeds in the wheat fields farmed by his parents:

> On the first day I arrived, I saw boys crying and I would have liked to have cried myself, but I kept a stiff upper lip for the sake of my mother. I developed stoicism. I didn't want to go to boarding school at all, but I was determined to show that it wasn't a problem – that I could cope."

Glebe House School was founded in 1874 and sits just a few hundred yards from the sea in an idyllic location. Mr Howard Cambridge Barber was headmaster for 40 years. Part of the site was originally rented from the Church, hence the name 'Glebe', a piece of land serving as part of a clergyman's benefits and providing income to support the role. Barber wished to provide a preparatory boarding school for boys which would be a 'feeder school' for public schools and Royal Navy Schools. It did not become co-educational until the mid-1980s.

Its motto is "sicut aquilae" ("as eagles") which is taken from Isaiah 40 v 31 – "(They who wait upon the Lord) will soar on wings like eagles; they will run and not grow weary, they will walk and not be faint."

It is an impressive and inspiring motto: that the pupils who pass through its doors will acquire knowledge and develop a spiritual, moral, social and cultural outlook as they 'soar like eagles' through life. But Tony Martin had his wings clipped by the actions of another male role model who, like his father, failed to live up to expectations.

During our many conversations, Tony repeatedly told me the story of how the Headmaster at Glebe House, Major Bailey, would reprimand certain boys:

> Major Bailey ... If you weren't good at a subject ... you would be called to the study where he would lecture you. He would smack you around the head several times, perhaps half a dozen times. He would clout you with his giant hands ... it was like a ritual ... he would get you to drop your trousers ... then your pants ... Then he would bring out a hairbrush which was leather-lined to prevent bruising. He would smack your bare bottom until it stung ... I tried not to cry through the throbbing pain ... then he would sometimes hug you."

Tony Martin's description of this abuse is shocking, sad and anger-provoking. No teacher has – or ever had - the right to treat his or her pupils in this way. These numerous incidents of abuse – emotional, physical and sexual – obviously had a severe impact on the young Tony Martin. The shadow of Major Bailey's perverted and sadistic acts still looms large in Tony Martin's psyche some 60 years or more later:

> When one of the teachers, Mr Coghill, died, Major Bailey came along. Nurse Dawson was supposed to be Coghill's girlfriend and I can't help but think that she must have known that there was something abnormal going on in that school. When I found out that she was about 90 and in a nursing home, I thought, 'How can I put that woman through all my questioning?' So I left it alone."

Notice how Tony thought about the feelings of the elderly former nurse at Glebe House.

"When my mother used to visit the school at the end of term and so on, she would ask how I liked it. I covered up my true feelings so as not to upset her" which shows that Tony was very good at hiding his feelings, in line with the Victorian type of upbringing that he had had. He was living out a pattern of behaviour in which he would cover up his feelings in order to please others. As a counsellor as well as an author, I'd say this was a recipe for disaster – because one day those feelings would have to be expressed in one form or another.

Like everything in life, it's rare that something is all good or all bad and Tony had some enjoyable moments:

> One of the teachers – a Miss Godfrey – was strange to my way of thinking. She had a drinker's nose and was a heavy smoker. She wore glasses and drove a green Ford Popular car. She taught me to read and write in just 10 weeks. I was 8½ years old at the time."

It would seem that Tony was something of a late developer in terms of being able to read and write, but was apparently very good at sport at Glebe House:

> I won the Victor Ludorum for running and jumping. One summer I had a sore throat but still won the obstacle race. In my third year there I won all the events on sports day."

I took Tony at his word and didn't check out his sporting successes – my remit meant that other research was far more pressing.

But his abuse at school was not one isolated incident:

> I used to be fearful of Maths and English because of Major Bailey. I enjoyed History and Geography and learning about Ethiopia and the Spanish Civil War. I learnt discipline and diction at Glebe House. My mother had sent me there because she didn't want me to be a 'Fen Johnny' – an uncouth person.
>
> Many people who meet me today think I'm a toff because of the way I speak, but I'm not, it's just a throwback to Glebe House where great emphasis was placed on clear diction. I often listen to the diction in the film *Dial M for Murder*.
>
> Throughout my time there, Major Bailey behaved this way towards me. I was caned at school because I was told I was thick."

But the abuse did not just begin and end at Glebe House. Tony tells the story of a family friend, Rodney Townley:

> One day when I was about 9 years old, we were driving home to March and Rodney and I were in the back of my father's Jaguar; my parents in the front. He put his hand on my leg, but then he tried to get his hand inside the leg of my short trousers, but he couldn't ... the leg was tight ... but this exacerbated the problem. It seemed to make him even more determined. I was in a state of shock ... I couldn't believe that men could act in this way ... I was frightened, but I said

nothing because I did not think that I would be believed. My mother thought that Rodney was a cut above other people. He wasn't."

[Author's note: He was very well connected, and mixed with MPs, bishops, high-ranking police officers and it's possible that he was part of a VIP paedophile ring. He was a paedophile masquerading as a homosexual and he even got married in later life as a cover for his sexual interest in young boys.]

Again, this incident was not an isolated one involving Mr Townley:

> We had a two-bedroom house in March, one for mum and dad and one for us two boys. My parents slept apart. My brother and I had two separate beds in the big bedroom. My parents put a mattress on the floor of our bedroom for Rodney to sleep on one night. When he came to stay, I tucked my sheets in really tight, but it made it worse. I didn't want that kind of attention. Why didn't I tell my parents? When you're younger, fear comes into it. You can get fed up with fear, you know."

Thus it is clear that the young Tony encountered sexual, physical and emotional abuse as a child and these encounters undoubtedly helped to shape the man he was to become. I think it is fair to say that they left him with deep emotional scars which manifested themselves in sometimes odd or apparently bizarre behaviour:

> When I come into contact with people, I get people to say hello to me first, otherwise I feel they don't want me to talk to them because I'm odd or a pervert."

People who are survivors of child abuse (in all its forms, but primarily sexual) can often grow up believing that they are at fault for the abuse, that they somehow deserved it. Guilt can often play a large part in their psychological makeup. Tony appears to have interpreted the sexual abuse as happening because *he* was the perverted one, not the perpetrator. This is not uncommon in survivors of abuse.

These incidents had a profound impact on Tony Martin. He began to develop a deep-seated distrust of authority figures in general and of homosexual men in particular. The male role models whom all young boys aspire to become were absent from Tony's life and those who were around him abused him, sexually, physically and emotionally.

These seeds were sown in the young man's mind and there they germinated until his view of relationships with women in particular became slightly narrow amid a complex web of psychological belief systems which had little to do with the reality of life in general but a lot to do with the reality of life for Tony Martin. We need to step inside Tony's shoes and talk a walk around before we can say that we know a little about him.

Tony Martin undoubtedly blamed himself for the abuse, as most survivors do. He began to hate himself. He thought that there was something wrong with him because if there had not been, these men would not have been attracted to him. This cycle of self-loathing has never left Tony. It remains to this day and I have witnessed it on many occasions. His lack of self-esteem, especially around women, is sometimes over-compensated with a bombastic nature in which he makes comments which are carefully designed to elicit a response.

I imagine that most people who encounter Tony do not possess counselling skills or lots of patience and are thus frustrated or annoyed or feel 'pushed away' by him. I do not condemn them for their response – I merely think that it is a pity that they have failed to see so many other aspects to his personality and that he has failed to allow them. Yet their rejection of him is what he has set up on an unconscious level – he sets up the game so that *he* rejects them before *they* can reject him. This way – on his terms – he retains the power in the relationship that he craves after lacking such power in his early relationships with his parents, an uncle and a teacher:

> " In my mid-20s, I'd got through the stage of going out with girls, one-night stands and so on. I always reproached myself, which is a form of guilt ... It was unwarranted, but I began to think that I had become a molester like the molesters I encountered as a child. When I went to a party I kept away from people because of a lack of self-esteem ... If anybody rejected me, I'd always go down the same mental road - that they'd rejected me because they thought I was a pervert.
>
> I assumed that Rodney Townley and Major Bailey did what they did to me because they thought I was queer and then I began to believe that everybody thought I was 'queer' ... I don't mean homosexual, but a 'pervert' ... In the background, there's still this something ... constantly nagging away, that anything that I do ... for some unknown reason ... (although it never happens with you, Brian) ... I think people are polite to me but in the background I feel they are just being polite but that they think I'm queer or a pervert ...
>
> Had I not been sexually abused, it makes me wonder whether I would have had such mental turmoil or whether life would have been nice and simple."

These are clearly the words of a man in torment – a torment caused by adults who ought to have known better. But I think the following paragraphs provide us with even more insight into the mind of an abused person:

" A few years before my mother died, I told her I was happy, but it was a lie. I wasn't happy. I've been watching the film *Rebecca* lately ... There are things in that film that I never really entertained as a youngster. Joan Fontaine asks, "We are happy, aren't we?" but he said, "That's a difficult one - I don't know what happiness is."

I don't know what happiness is, either. Things happen in your life that take it away. When I got to Bleak House, I was still very depressed after being on the oil rigs in Scotland to try to forget yet another failed romance. I found a hellebore in my garden and it uplifted me. All my life I have looked for things to give me a reason to live. A sense of purpose to continue. I had gone to Scotland to get away from my depression and from the girl. I should have married her, but I didn't because I couldn't have walked up the aisle without thinking that people would think I was a pervert. I can't show emotion because people might think I'm a paedophile like those who abused me.

I would have liked children, but I can't give them emotion and it wouldn't be fair on them. I'm very stoical and keep my feelings to myself. If we had a proper police service and had right and wrong in this country, I wouldn't have ended up as I did."

As a counsellor I have worked with several survivors of abuse and I, too, am a survivor of abuse in a children's home in Harpenden, Hertfordshire. I have heard many stories of crippling emotional turmoil, but I found myself appalled at the cost that the abuse has had on Tony Martin. I think of the man he might have become – a husband, a father and grandfather - but for the abuse. I think of what loving sustenance he might have enjoyed from a woman, and I think of the family connectedness he might have had but for the abuse.

As he became a teenager, Tony moved to Pierrepont School in Frensham, Surrey. The school was a private country house residence prior to becoming a boys-only educational establishment for day pupils and boarders. It became a listed building in 1973 – large houses were to become a feature of Tony's life.

The building contained a large stone fireplace, timbered ceilings, panelling throughout, large, stone windows, and an armorial stained glass window.

Pierrepont House School was founded in 1947 as an independent school for boys by its first headmaster, Thomas Joyce Parry. The following year Parry established a school Combined Cadet Force, with himself as its commanding officer, and became known in the school as 'Major Parry'. He had served in the British Army in both the 1st and 2nd World Wars.

The school's aim for its boys was to give them a good all-round education while developing character through sports and other outdoor activities, and its syllabus included adventure training, leadership, and personal survival. Like most British independent schools, it was divided into houses, all with names recalling military history: Agincourt, Trafalgar, and Waterloo. From 1955 to 1962, the headmaster was NA Dromgoole.

Founded in 1957 by Francis Brown, at the heart of the school is an early 18th-century Grade II listed Queen Anne style country house. The original roll consisted of just 14 boys. The school is set in 150 acres of parkland and there is also a chapel in the grounds. I believe that the young Tony Martin soaked up the wide open spaces, the listed building and the furniture and décor and took this forward into his adult life, where he lived in hundreds of acres of Norfolk farmland, inherited an old house and collected antique furniture: "Show me the boy and I'll show you the man."

Cokethorpe lists notable former pupils on its website as Martin Edwards, a former Manchester United chairman, Richard and Michael Hills, twins and both successful flat racing jockeys in the UK, Toby Sebastian, a professional actor starring in the hit series *Game Of Thrones* and Tony is described as "an English farmer who was imprisoned for fatally shooting a burglar."

Whilst his alma mater might well remember him, Tony only mentioned Cokethorpe once to me and that was to say that he had attended it.

Tony continues the story of life after school:

> I've slept with several girls but I didn't want to see them anymore because I'd defiled them. In the Barossa Valley in South Australia, I was working with a girl and then 'the sun came out.' She had a bright look about her and I could tell she wanted to sleep with me. I initially left her alone, but after a few drinks ... I couldn't understand what the setup was ... she asked me if I wanted to meet her aunt ... but I thought no, her aunt might think I'm a pervert.
>
> And other possibilities escaped my grasp because of my past. I create a lot of my disappointments. Forty years ago I had a good relationship with a woman but I was absent emotionally."

I have observed Tony Martin over a long period of time and in close proximity. It is difficult not to feel sympathy for a man who has a lot to offer people but who is held back because of his past. I believe that he became diminished *emotionally*, but not that his *responsibility* was diminished. I am left in no doubt that the years of abuse and family emotional deprivation have left a lasting legacy on Tony Martin and that – I believe – the outward expression of his emotional landscape did not become as broad as it might otherwise have done.

> I would have liked marriage, but I find sex too personal – it's like an assault on the other person. A woman told me she was in love with me but was it just a sexual calling of nature? When she approached me, it was as if *she* was the molester."

And that paragraph tells us so much about the torment that Tony went through as a younger man and it's something he still carries to this day.

Andrew Fountaine (1918-1997)
It would be remiss of me not to include a section on one of Tony's uncles, Andrew Fountaine, with whom Tony had some contact throughout his formative years.

Fountaine was an activist involved in the British far right. After military service in a number of conflicts including the second Italo-Abyssinian war, the Spanish Civil War (fighting on the side of Franco) and the second world war, Fountaine joined the Conservative Party and was selected as a parliamentary candidate until his outspoken views resulted in his being disowned by the party.

He was subsequently involved with a number of fringe rightist movements before becoming a founder member of the National Front in 1967. He had several roles within the party and was involved in a number of internal feuds until he left in 1979. He briefly led his own splinter party before retiring from politics to concentrate on growing trees on his estate near Swaffham.

Despite Fountaine's past fighting in various conflicts and his access to guns, we must be extremely careful not to directly link this to the Tony Martin case. I have included this section simply to provide a historical record of the fact that Fountaine was Tony's uncle. It does not follow that Tony Martin used a shotgun to protect himself from intruders in the dead of night simply because he was Fountaine's nephew. On 15 July 2018, I asked Tony about his famous uncle. He told me that he saw him "usually only at Christmas" and that his (Tony's) views were his own formed from his own experiences of life and not passed on to him by his uncle. He described links between his uncle and the shooting at Bleak House reported in the press as "nothing but lazy journalism".

I think the last word in this chapter should rest with Tony, because I believe that when you read the following paragraphs spoken by Tony, there is nothing I could add to further describe the striking poignancy of his words:

> My mother passed away in June 2011: I never really told her about all the pain that I have endured throughout my life, most of which stems from the abuse I suffered.
>
> Then there was this shooting and I felt that this was the final insult. I knew I was innocent, but everything around me was crowding in. I was labelled a murderer and so many lies were told about me. I wondered how much further they were going to push it. Our laws are dreadful in this country.
>
> I no longer recognised myself. I was no longer the man I used to be."

1964—1988

Part 2: 1964 -1988

> " When I was a young man I used to do things on the farm that other people wouldn't do; I would be up to my arms in chickenshit to recover a spanner when others would just leave it; I hated to see money wasted. I was brought up amongst animals and they didn't worry what I looked like; I'd be amongst the chickens – we had around 6,000 or so - and I made everything work; but I knew it was not sustainable without me; I was about 17 or 18 when I walked into the snow to Haddenham to escape my family; I knocked on a policeman's door and they took me to Fulbourn Mental Hospital for the night; I realised you couldn't live in that environment – my family – it was madness. I loved my hair, but one day just cut it all off. I was self-destructive."

I think this passage provides us with an indication of some of the torment endured by Tony Martin. What is clear to me is that his philosophy of life was completely at odds with those closest to him – his family – and that he never really felt accepted by them.

The Tony Martin who was leaving his adolescence behind as he emerged into adulthood was, it seems to me, acutely aware of his family's shortcomings in working as a cohesive unit and this, coupled with his sexual and emotional abuse, lent itself to a young man who was tormented yet strikingly brave and who, at times, was wonderfully carefree. Not everyone who has been abused and part of a dysfunctional family has the wherewithal to break free and strike out alone, and yet Tony possessed such strength. I believe we should admire him for this. He had his values and principles in life and he did not want to compromise these, even for the sake of his family. He would rather be on his own and live life according to his own conscience than forego his principles just to be part of a family unit.

Having left school and with several unsuccessful relationships with young women behind him like most young men of his age, Tony set sail alone for Australia in his late teens with the Shaw Savill and Albion Steamship Company.

He worked his passage and after arriving in Sydney, he went travelling round that vast country, and worked as a sheep shearer in Dubbo, some 250 miles north-west of Sydney in New South Wales.

Whilst working on sheep farms, the young and energetic Tony Martin would jump hurdles easily and his robust, muscular frame became honed with hard work.

Tony also told me about life at sea on prawn fishing boats for the Craig Mostyn company in the Gulf of Carpentaria working out of the port of Karumba in the Gulf Country region of Queensland. The prawn industry expanded in the 1960s and Tony happened to be in the right place at the right time as the expansion brought much work. He also sailed in the Arafura Sea, between the coast of New Guinea and the Northern Territories. Seventeen exotic varieties of prawns including banana and tiger were the prizes to be gained from harvesting the seas.

Tough times for tough men and women. Being in this environment and amongst these people, Tony could not help but imbibe their tenacity, their strength and their resourcefulness, their resilience and their bloody-mindedness.

Tony then moved on to New Zealand, calling initially at Auckland:

> Immediately after I went ashore in Auckland, I felt that it was wonderful. I ended up in a club and the girls loved that I was English. I met one and she took to me and I told her that I was illegal, but she didn't mind and said she'd find me somewhere to live. I ended up in Waimana in the Bay of Plenty between Whatakane and Opotiki. But they eventually caught up with me and put me in prison, though they didn't lock the door. Shaw Savill took me home."

So, we have a man who, by the age of 21, had been used to rural Cambridgeshire – his family farming near March – and who had experienced being sent away to boarding school in Norfolk where he was abused, sailing to Australasia and working on sheep farms and prawn fishing boats. This is a man of the earth, a rugged man shaped by his environment – tough, living-in-the-moment, worldly-wise.

All of these experiences helped to shape the man we came to know as Tony Martin, the farmer who fired his shotgun when intruders smashed their way into his house. In most cases, all of us are shaped by our experiences and we learn from them and they mould us into becoming the adult that emerges from childhood and adolescence like a butterfly emerging from the stages of being a caterpillar and a chrysalis.

Yet even this seemingly-idyllic lifestyle was tainted by his youth:

> Because of what happened to me in Glebe House and with Rodney Townley, I felt dirty amongst people. I felt dirty to even admit to myself that a woman would want me – I felt that I was assaulting them. I couldn't help but feel they thought that I was a pervert like Major Bailey and Townley."

Thus, at a time in his life when he could have been experiencing more of the joys of being human, the abuse he suffered as a child contaminated what should have been a momentous time in his life. In his mid-twenties, Tony returned to England to make fresh acquaintances.

home address of John 'Robbie' Auger, Outwell
Dial House, an old, sprawling farmhouse in Outwell, was invaded by three men wearing stockings and balaclavas over their faces. The owner, John 'Robbie' Auger, a wealthy fruit farmer, was beaten to death with an iron bar, his safe was dragged out and put into his truck, which the killers drove away.

Auger's wife had been bound and gagged during the attack, and the crime was discovered when Auger's daughter Audrey, aged 33, returned home to find her stricken father and helpless mother. She alerted a neighbour, saying, "Come quickly, Dad's been attacked."

Mr Auger was found bound and gagged at the edge of an orchard near his home by his daughter, Audrey, shortly after 11pm. He had been battered to death. The weapon used on Mr Auger was a clawed case opener and the police wanted to interview three men, all with Fen accents – so they were assumed to be local men.

As well as tying up the farmer with a thick wagon rope, the intruders, wearing nylon stocking masks, used considerable force in tying and gagging Mr Auger's wife, Isabella, aged 59.

The *Lynn News* reported[2] that "Immediately a full-scale manhunt was swung into operation, every available policeman from Norfolk Constabulary and the Mid-Anglia forces being used. Two senior Scotland Yard officers, DSupt Wallace Virgo and DS Thomas Parry, together with Supt Reginald Lester of the regional crime squad are leading the investigations."

On the Saturday following the killing, DSupt Virgo appealed for witnesses and police appealed to farmers to look around fields and drains for the safe which weighed between 2 and 3 hundredweight. The safe was stolen from the house and driven away in Mr Auger's Volkswagen pick-up truck. Nothing was taken from Mr Auger's collection of porcelain and Dresden china, which had an estimated value of £50,000 or approximately £850,000 at 2018 values.

Audrey raised the alarm with a neighbour, 55-year-old Arthur Atkins, who worked for Mr Auger. Atkins tried in vain to revive his employer by using artificial respiration. After untying the farmer, Arthur Atkins carried him into the house with the aid of his son, 18-year-old Terry and Mr Leonard Jermey. Inside the house he continued the artificial respiration for about ten minutes.

Outwell is approximately 3½ miles from Emneth, using the Fendyke Road. Tony Martin was 23 years old at the time and this vicious murder of a fellow

---

[2] The *Lynn News*, 14 July 1967, front page.

farmer weighed heavily on his mind. It is impossible, I suggest, to tell the story of the 1999 shooting without greater reference to the killing of Robbie Auger because of certain parallels beyond that of them both being farmers.

Fri 17 MAR 1967 2

***Lynn News* – Murder hunt police seek 2 more men**
The newspaper carried a photo of a safe being winched out of a dyke in an orchard in Meadowgate Lane, Wisbech. It had been found by Adrian Carlisle, a nurseryman of Outwell and his son-in-law E. Hempson and brother-in-law W. Hempson. The search followed a television appeal to all farmers to make an inspection of their dykes.

The *Lynn News* reported that "Police revealed on Wednesday 12 March that they believed that five men – not three – may be able to help them in their inquiries into the murder of John 'Robbie' Auger last Friday.

Meadowgate Lane is a backway route to Waterlees Road where Mr Auger's abandoned pick-up was found on Saturday. This led the police to believe that the murder was the work of local men.

On Wednesday morning it was stated that more police officers were to be drafted into the murder HQ.

The inquest into the death of the fruit farmer, whose home was at The Woodlands, Wisbech Road, Outwell, was formally opened at Lynn police station on Tuesday morning by Lynn District Coroner, Mr A. Bantoft.

Dr GA Gresham, consultant pathologist at Addenbrooke's Hospital, Cambridge, said he went to Mr Auger's home at 6:40am on Saturday and saw the body. He conducted a post-mortem at Addenbrooke's that morning.

He produced a report to the Coroner, who stated that the cause of death was cerebral contusion followed by traumatic fractures of the skull.

Brian Auger, of Manor Farm, Walpole Highway, said he went to the mortuary at Lynn on Sunday and identified the body of his father. He said his father was 62. He had last seen his father alive the previous Sunday afternoon.

The Coroner said he did not think he could issue a certificate as the pathologist had still to make further inquiries. 'This is an unusual case and I must see that all steps are taken,' he added.

He adjourned the inquest to a date to be fixed."

Lynn News – "Crime on Doorstep" says police chief
Superintendent D.W. Beamis, head of Downham division, said at Swaffham last Friday that a war was being fought not only for road safety, but against crime. "Don't let us get any ideas about Norfolk being quiet – for it isn't. We have got it right on our doorstep."

Supt Beamis was speaking at a dinner of Lynn sub-area of the Road Haulage Association: "I do say to you in all sincerity, and from the bottom of my heart as a citizen and a policeman, if you feel there is anything you see which in conscience is not right, please do not pass on the other side of the road – do something yourself even to the extent of dialling 999. It is here for all of us to tackle."

Lynn News – Murder dragnet is spread wider
Inquiries into the murder of Robbie Auger are now being spread outside the Wisbech area and DSupt Virgo of Scotland Yard said yesterday that a .410 gun was being sent from Luton to Wisbech for examination.

"Tracker dogs[3] and a group of 10 policemen made a thorough search of the main road from Outwell to Waterlees Road in Wisbech on Saturday. They covered the area from where Mr Auger's body was found to where his van was abandoned.

Commenting on a claw case opener found beside Mr Auger's gagged and bound body, DSupt Virgo said that it was a type widely used by fruit growers to open apple boxes and crates, that it had been broken at one end and repaired by a blacksmith.

Up until yesterday, police claimed to have taken more than 1,000 statements from members of the public."

Lynn News – Two witnesses help police in murder hunt
Detectives leading the inquiries into the murder of 62-year-old Outwell farmer, John 'Robbie' Auger, swooped on two houses at Wisbech early on Tuesday evening (21 March).

---

[3] Compare the use of tracker dogs in this case with the alleged non-deployment of tracker dogs at Bleak House in 1999 which should have been used to search for the body of Fred Barras.

"In a search, DSupt Virgo of Scotland Yard and DSupt Lester, head of Norfolk CID were accompanied by 20 other detectives. While men stood outside, others went inside the houses. A steady growing crowd saw various items of equipment taken into one of the houses.

STOP PRESS – MURDER CHARGE TODAY

Supt F. Calvert, head of the Lynn Police division, issued the following statement last night: 'A man has been detained in custody at my divisional headquarters. He will be charged with the murder of Mr Auger tomorrow morning'."

Tue 28 MAR 1967 5

Lynn News – Three men remanded on murder charge
Three men have made appearances at special sittings at Terrington St Clement Magistrates' Court on charges alleging the murder of John Robert Auger at Emneth. David Warden, of Wisbech, is charged with the murder and Barrie Cooper, of Sutton St Edmund and Patrick Collins of no fixed address were both charged with being concerned with others in murdering Mr Auger.

Warden and Cooper appeared at the court on Thursday evening and Collins appeared on Saturday evening. They were all remanded in custody to appear at the court on Friday.

DSupt Virgo said that members of the public who were coming forward as witnesses had been threatened and intimidated.

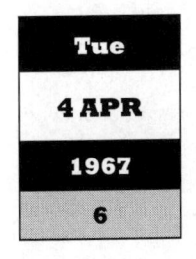

Tue 4 APR 1967 6

Lynn News – Further remands on murder charge
The three men accused of the murder of Robbie Auger made a two-minute appearance at Terrington Magistrates' Court on Friday.
They were all further remanded into custody to appear at Taverham Magistrates' Court, Norwich on Thursday. DSupt Virgo said it was anticipated that further remands would be asked for on April 6, 13 and 20, and the committal proceedings could begin on 29 April.

Mr K. Land (Southwell, Dennis and Land, Wisbech) who is representing the men, said that as only further remands would be asked for at the next hearing it could be a waste of public money for him to go to Taverham court.

The three men arrived at Terrington court in a coach. They stood during the short hearing, each handcuffed to a police officer.

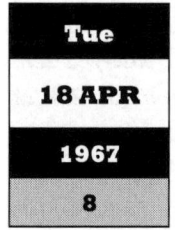

Lynn News – Murder charge: "Interference with witnesses"

The three men accused of the Fenland murder of 'Robbie' Auger were further remanded in custody for seven days at Taverham Magistrates' Court in Norwich yesterday. During their brief appearance, DSupt Virgo, of Scotland Yard, told the court "There has been some interference with witnesses in this case and I am sure if these men are given bail, witnesses will be intimidated."[4]

Collins – one of the three men – told the Bench: "I have pleaded not guilty to the charge. I strongly deny it."

The three men, each handcuffed to a prison officer, were led from the court and returned to Norwich Prison.

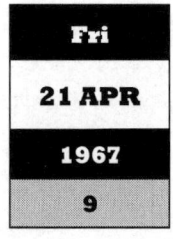

Lynn News – Mr Auger's porcelain to be shown

Pieces of porcelain from the collection of Mr Auger, the Fenland farmer, are to go on show at the Wisbech and Fenland Museum.

About 400 pieces – almost two-thirds of the total collection – have been lent to the museum by Mr Auger's widow and his daughter, Miss Audrey Auger.

The collection is now being catalogued, but it will be several weeks before it is on view to the public. The museum committee hopes that the collection will remain on loan for some years.

Mr Auger owned one of country's finest private collections which he kept in a special room built on to his home at 'Woodlands', Wisbech Road, Emneth.

Lynn News – Three men remanded again

When they appeared at Taverham Magistrates' Court in Norwich yesterday, the three men charged with the murder of the fruit farmer were remanded in custody to Terrington Magistrates' Court next Thursday.

---

[4] Imprisoning people "to prevent interference with witnesses" is a tactic often used by the Police to actually prevent innocent suspects from meeting with people or conducting their own research into the case against them. With a suspect in prison, the Police are, of course, free to interfere with witnesses themselves and create a false narrative that the general public will buy into. In 1999 and 2000, Tony Martin was often held in prison "for his own safety" – in reality the Police prevented him from meeting with family, friends, supporters and possible witnesses for the defence.

| Thur 27 APR 1967 10 | **Lynn News – Farmer received repeated blows to the head**
John 'Robbie' Auger received repeated blows from a blunt instrument and suffered numerous skull fractures according to Christopher Bourke, prosecuting for the Director of Public Prosecutions at the Terrington St Clement Magistrates' Court. |

The *Lynn News* dated Friday 28 April 1967 gave over almost its entire front page to a report of the trial. In disturbing echoes of the Tony Martin murder trial, there were indications of police corruption, witness intimidation and allegations of evidence having been 'planted' and – in shades of Hillsborough in 1989 – witness statements having been fraudulently created by the police.

| Mon 1 MAY 1967 11 | **Lynn News – Three men sent to trial at Crown Court**
On the third day of the Magistrates' Court hearing, the case was sent from Terrington St Clement to the Norwich Assizes and a new date of 23 May was set.
Through their counsel, Mr Christopher Lewis, the three defendants said they had no connection with the events at 'Woodlands' on 10 March and they denied the charges against them. |

Mr Lewis said they would reserve their defence and they did not wish to give evidence or call witnesses.

The chairman of the magistrates, Mr W. Lane, said the Bench found there was a case against the accused and they would be remanded in custody. The magistrates granted defence certificates for each of the men.

DS Dennis Grant, of the Regional Crime Squad stationed at Basildon in Essex, told the Magistrates that on 25 March he travelled in a car from Birmingham with one of the accused, Patrick Collins, and claimed that Collins had asked "Has my arrest got anything to do with the Outwell murder?" This is yet another echo of the Tony Martin case with regard to the police's use of 'unsolicited comments' which will be revealed later in this book.

During the second day's hearing at the Magistrates' court, three people were treated as hostile witnesses and it is evident from reading the report in the *Lynn News* that there was far more to this case than the police were letting the public know about – further shades of the Tony Martin shooting.

One of the 'hostile' witnesses, Kenneth Holman from Wisbech, said that he'd been arrested at night, taken to the police station, denied access to his solicitor who had gone to the station, and told he couldn't see his solicitor unless he signed a statement first.

Mon
3 JUL
1967
12

Lynn News – Murder trial allegation
One of the three defendants in the Fenland murder trial was alleged at Hertford Assizes – the fifth day of the trial – to have said: "If only I could turn the clock back, I would not have done what has been done." DS James Brakewell said he arrested Patrick Collins on 23 March at Birmingham on a house-breaking charge.

DS Brakewell alleged that Collins was "getting under a double bed" when he entered a room in his parents' house. When he was being arrested on a house-breaking charge, Brakewell said Collins said: "Thank God for that – I thought you had come about something else." DS Brakewell added: "He also said, 'If only I could turn the clock back I would not have done what has been done'."

DC Peter Valleley claimed that he had never heard defendant David Warden ask for a solicitor at any time.

The entire report in the *Lynn News* was focused on the police claiming that the defendants had implicated themselves upon arrest – but in reality it was nothing more than unsubstantiated hearsay. This became a feature of the Tony Martin case some three decades later.

Thur
6 JUL
1967
13

Lynn News – "I always fixed an alibi" said defendant
Barrie Cooper of Sutton St Edmund, admitted in the Fenland murder trial at Hertford Assizes that he was an "idle layabout" who lived by crime. He said he had broken into 60 premises in six months and was caught only twice.

Mrs Doris Lynn of Bath Road, Wisbech told the court that she was unable to distinguish between defendant David Warden and his twin brother.

CORRUPTION ALERT   *Detectives accused of manufacturing evidence*

In an interesting historical detail, defence counsel said it was a pity that the Treasury did not provide the police with tape recorders after DS Parry said that he had written down the questions and answers when defendant Cooper was interviewed by DSupt Virgo.

Cooper's defence counsel called into question the veracity of the police records of the interview. For his part, DSupt Virgo – the last of nearly 30 prosecution witnesses – said he was "appalled" at a suggestion that he invented a remark allegedly made by Warden which placed him at the scene of the crime.

DSupt Virgo said that 35 sets of fingerprints found at The Woodlands were cleared on April 14 and that none of the prints belonged to the three accused.

DSupt Virgo denied saying that if Cooper made a statement he would get off with five years.

Answering James Comyn, defence counsel for Collins, DSupt Virgo said that The Woodlands had been broken into twice before the murder, that crimes of violence had been "very bad indeed" in the Wisbech area and people had armed themselves with shotguns.

Although some 32 years prior to the Tony Martin case, this trial provides us with an excellent insight into the prevailing zeitgeist in the 1960s which continued unabated into the 1990s and the new millennium. In fact, as the number of police officers and police stations was reduced year-on-year by successive governments, the crime rate increased exponentially. Indeed, it could be argued that the government of the day actually *assisted* the increase in crime by significantly reducing the number of police officers on the beat. We should be in no doubt that Tony Martin – at times an incredibly astute and intuitive (and much misunderstood) man – was observing all these political and social undercurrents and noting their impact on his local community and the wider farming and countryside communities.

Mon 10 JUL 1967 14

Lynn News – Son's letter to mother
Fenland murder trial defendant David Warden wrote a letter to his mother which read: "I have done nothing wrong, so I have got nothing to worry about."

On the tenth day of the trial at Hertford Assizes, Leslie Boreham, Warden's defence counsel, said that Warden had written the letter to his mother from Norwich Prison.

The letter contained the following: "When the police arrested me they would not let me see a lawyer. They wrote things down I never said. Still, they always have their say." Warden's father told the court that his son was at home on the night of the murder.

In connection with Cooper's allegations against the police, prosecutor Owen Stable said: "You are a lying layabout who loathes the police and would do anything to discredit them." (These claims of the defendant being a liar and hater of the police, were mirrored in the Tony Martin case as we shall see in due course.)

During the trial, Warden informed the judge that he had been the driver on a job to steal turkeys in Suffolk.

Thur
13 JUL
1967
15

Lynn News – Murder trial 'Not Guilty'

The three men accused of murdering the Emneth farmer, John Auger, were found not guilty at Hertford Assizes.

But the jury found them guilty of manslaughter and burglary. The jury took one hour and 50 minutes to reach their verdict.

Barrie Cooper, 26, was sentenced to 15 years imprisonment with five years concurrent for the burglary.

David Warden, 22, was sentenced to 12 years with five years concurrent for the burglary.

Patrick Collins, 28, was sentenced to 12 years with five years concurrent for the burglary.

The judge, Mr Justice Glyn-Jones, said Cooper was the organiser of the raid and that Warden was the one who used violence on Mrs Isabella Auger.

He said he took into consideration that on Cooper's own admission he was an habitual criminal and "a grave menace to society." The judge said that it was one of the worst manslaughter cases to come before him.

Asked if he had anything to say, Collins maintained that he had been "verballed" by the police and he would keep saying it.

The jury retired early in the afternoon to consider their verdicts on the 13th day of the trial. The judge, who began his summing up on Wednesday afternoon and continued today, gave the jury several warnings to exercise caution when considering certain evidence.

The judge said that if the defence were correct, ten policemen had entered into a criminal conspiracy by fabricating evidence and supporting it by perjury.[5] He added that if certain allegations against Inspector Trevor were true, they would have no bearing on this case.

The judge said that DS Thomas Parry had been accused by Cooper's defence counsel, Hugh Griffiths, of corruption, conspiracy and forgery. DS Parry took notes at a question-and-answer session between defendant Cooper and DSupt Wallace Virgo and DSupt Reginald Lester. "If you see no reason to doubt these three officers, then Cooper made an admission," said the judge. He added that there was "practically nothing" against Collins and nothing to connect him with the crime except an alleged oral admission of complicity.

---

[5] The Hillsborough inquiry eventually showed that more than 10 officers had been involved in a conspiracy, in fabricating evidence and committing perjury. The implication in the Auger case was that it stretched credulity too far because alleged corruption would have involved ten policemen and that's too high a number for the reasonable person to accept. In reality, of course, many high-profile cases have shown us that the police as an organisation is inherently corrupt, particularly at senior levels. See also *Blueprint for Abuse*, op. cit.

On page 7 of the *Lynn News* dated Friday 14 July 1967 there were some fascinating parallels with the Tony Martin case: Leslie Boreham – defence counsel – said that there was a head-on clash with defendant Warden and certain police officers. He asked if it was likely that Warden would have confessed in a Wisbech betting shop to DC Peter Valleley – certain police officers took a dislike to Tony (with the help of his brother) and, in my view, fitted him up for murder.

Defence counsel said there was no question of remorse on Warden's part because he was not at The Woodlands on 10 March – Tony would be accused of showing no remorse at the death of Fred Barras. None of the defendants was known to have used violence – again, a parallel with Tony.

CORRUPTION ALERT *Police integrity called into question by judge and defence counsel*

Perhaps the most disturbing element of this trial was the address to the jury by James Comyn, counsel for Collins:

"I hope if this case establishes anything that it will get rid of oral admissions and I hope that we will have some untamperable means of court recording in the future.

This sort of nonsense has gone on long enough and the police oral evidence in this case is all there is.

The greatest tribute to the police is the way they entered into these inquiries. But we have to be careful about trial by police. We have to be careful about the police going into the witness box and saying: "He admitted it to me. I am an honourable man."

"We would be coming," continued Mr Comyn, "to the stage when a defendant would be damned before he started.

If these admissions were made spontaneously, then it is astonishing. Or were they made after a series of mental proddings and cross-examinations?

It is easy to say of the defendants: 'They are a bad lot, society can do without them for a long, long time' but please put that prejudice, however rational it may be, out of your minds. The more you dislike people, the more your duty is to be fair. Prejudice, dislike and distaste can very easily run away with you.

There is no evidence of any kind against my client and no evidence that connects him with the scene of the crime. These three men are only small time amateur crooks. Do you think they were capable of planning this crime on military lines and leaving no clues?"

Even from a distance of more than half a century, we would be wise to listen carefully to those words which I found extremely disturbing. Apart from the not-so-hidden subtext about police perjury and corruption, I was concerned to learn of Mr Comyn's use of the phrase "planning this crime on military lines and leaving no clues". There is the possibility that the police themselves were involved in the robbery and murder and if that sounds too fanciful I offer you two compelling reasons for that assertion:

Reason number one – I refer you to a former Flying Squad commander, John O'Connor, writing in 2011:[6]

CORRUPTION ALERT *Scotland Yard detectives accused of endemic corruption by one of their own*

"Scotland Yard is facing its worst corruption crisis since the 1970s, when senior police officers were found to be controlling London's pornography industry. The investigation and subsequent purge left many detectives out of a job and in some cases serving prison sentences. The gloom that surrounded the Yard in those days is similar to the atmosphere that pervades it today. Each day reveals more details of misconduct by the press and the police."

That from a former Flying Squad commander. Corruption is endemic within the police and government ministers are clearly not beyond reproach following the MP allowances scandal. O'Connor added in his article that "Nobody in authority was prepared to recognise the endemic nature of this corruption and each case was dealt with as a stand-alone incident." He continued in his condemnation of his former employers:

"At risk is the reputation and integrity of the service. It cannot afford to get it wrong again. The problem is that senior officers did not recognise the extent of the corruption. [...] They must accept their responsibility for what has happened. It is astonishing that with so many resources being spent on anti-corruption, they could not see it when it was right under their noses."

There is no magic in the uniform. Police officers of all ranks are human beings and lie, cheat, steal and commit offences like anybody else might.

---

[6] Source: *The Independent on Sunday*, 10 July 2011, 'The suspects are in charge of the case'.

Reason number two: just a fortnight prior to the killing of Robbie Auger, the police had been to his house and conducted a 'Home Protection' visit in which they learnt a great deal about the movements of the entire Auger family, their wealth and possessions. Obviously you'd like to think that the police could be trusted with that information but not if one or more of the officers was corrupt.

It was alleged that the safe contained between five and £15,000 but when it was discovered it was said to have contained only two coins. Where did the money go? And given that at 2018 values, the money was worth somewhere between £85,000 and £250,000, it is likely that the police learnt about this small fortune during their Home Protection visit.

And if that still sounds too fanciful to be true, I offer you the following:[7]

"Since the Metropolitan Police was founded in 1829 there have been two complete reorganizations of its detective department. Both were provoked by massive corruption scandals leading to criminal trials exactly one hundred years apart, in 1877 and 1977. In each scandal Freemasonry played a dominant role.

Scotland Yard's first 'Detective Force' was set up in 1842. It consisted of only two inspectors and six sergeants. By 1869, 180 detectives were dealing with minor crime in outlying divisions but serious investigations in London were left to only 27 officers out of 9,000. In the 1870s most of this squad was itself a criminal conspiracy in which not only were the prime culprits Freemasons; Freemasonry was what brought them together.

In 1872 a confidence trickster named William Kurr was running a bogus betting operation. Like any shrewd small-time criminal with big ideas, he saw that the way to make real money was to bring policemen into the racket. Bribing detectives after you get caught is costly and uncertain. Far better to cut them in on the profits beforehand and avoid arrest altogether. The one safe place where Kurr could proposition policemen was his Masonic lodge.

At a lodge meeting in Islington, Kurr made friends with just the man: Inspector John Meiklejohn. In return for £100 - nearly half his annual pay - Meiklejohn agreed to give Kurr advance warning of any police action against him or his betting racket. At first the corrupt officer kept the payoff to himself but as the racket expanded, he involved three chief inspectors in the Detective Force whom he also knew as brother Masons."

The *North Otago Times* (New Zealand)[8] reported that Meiklejohn had received more than £5,000 from the conmen over a 5-year period [equating to approximately £540,000 in 2018.] A look back at history and a useful knowledge of human nature tells its own story. Men and women in uniform are not beyond

---

[7] Article entitled "A firm in a firm: Freemasonry and police corruption", Short, M., <http://freemasonrywatch.org/true_blue.html>
[8] Volume XXVI, Issue 1702, 3 October 1877, p.2.

reproach and the higher up the chain of command they go, the more corrupt they often become.

That glimpse into history over, we now return to Tony's life. For the remainder of the Sixties and throughout the Seventies, Tony continued working on the family farm and there were "girls again, and sex, but I always had the same problem – I felt that I had violated them."

Clearly relationships for Tony were a major problem in his life, but one particular relationship with a woman – his aunt and godmother Gladys Garner – was always positive and enriching. In the many conversations that I have been fortunate to have had with Tony, it seems that she somehow inherently understood her nephew, recognised his torment, and said the right things to soothe him. He felt emotionally close to her.

A will had apparently been written leaving Bleak House (more properly called Cowcroft Farm) to Robin, but Gladys complained saying, "Whoever wrote that will out?" before going over to March to sign a hastily re-written will leaving all to Tony. Herein lay a seed for a family feud which was to come to the attention of the police over a number of years.

Sat 29 NOV 1969 16

***The Times*: "London policemen in bribe allegations"**
The article alleged that three South London detectives had taken bribes, given false evidence in exchange for money and had "allowed a criminal to pursue his activities."

This story was to engender three major inquiries into corruption in the Metropolitan Police, producing in turn five major trials of London detectives. One of the most senior detectives was Commander Wallace Virgo – the man who put away the alleged murderers of Robbie Auger.

Following his "success", Virgo was made up to the rank of Commander and became head of the Obscene Publications Squad, where he was later charged with 33 counts of bribery and corruption. However, in 1970 he was head of CID at Scotland Yard and in charge of the Met's specialist crime squads. In that role Commander Virgo appointed Detective Chief Superintendent Bill Moody as his senior investigating officer into police corruption. Moody was receiving tens of thousands of pounds in bribes from Soho's porn barons. Virgo has been described as "head of the Dirty Squad" and Moody as "the most corrupt officer in the history of the British police service.[9]

---

[9] For a more detailed analysis of the scale and depth of corruption endemic in Scotland Yard, visit the excellent site: <https://manyvoicesBlog.wordpress.com/2013/10/18/frank-williamson-the-fall-of-scotland-yard>

Wallace Virgo was later sentenced to 12 years in prison. He later had his convictions quashed, not on the basis of any innocence, but simply because "the judge's summing up had been unduly harsh and the jury misdirected".

According to the *Guardian* dated 21 July 2011, Virgo – who was said to have been receiving £2,000 a month (approximately £22,000 in 2018) in bribes from Soho pornographer Jimmy Humphreys - died "a few years after his appeal".

death of Aunt Gladys

In 1984, with Tony now aged 40, Gladys Garner died, and her death was to have such a significant impact on him that his life was never the same again:

> The death of my Aunt Gladys was a great shock to me. What was, is now nothing. When something is really hurting me, I tend to block it out and instead of firing on all four cylinders, I was now just running on one or two."

The phrase 'What was, is now nothing' was almost poetic from this rugged man and it expressed beautifully the classic feelings experienced by those coping with bereavement. It became clear to me during our many conversations that Tony had had no-one in his life at these crucial moments with whom he could talk about his feelings.

Upon his Aunt's death, Tony inherited the farm and a modest, yet beautiful, red-brick Victorian farmhouse in a secluded part of west Norfolk.

He set about with relish the task of making the farm pay and it is evident from reading the accounts of numerous farmers and neighbours that Tony was hard-working, always willing to learn, and not afraid to try out new ideas. This led to him sometimes being described as 'eccentric', but we might say the same about Einstein and his theory of relativity. Being eccentric, of course, is not a crime.

According to Tony, Robin Martin did not like the idea that Cowcroft Farm was left entirely to his younger brother. There was already ill-feeling between the brothers when Robin was left their parents' much larger farm:

> Robin tried to get Bleak House for himself. Aunt Gladys had a lifetime's interest in it, which meant that she could live there until she died and then it was to be left to me, but Robin didn't like this at all. He swindled my aunt out of £17,500 and bought a Bentley, and when I challenged him about this he said, 'It's no good you asking me for the money because I've spent it.' Robin is jealous of everyone. My brother is dishonest, has convictions for receiving stolen goods and I want nothing to do with a dishonest man."

This feud was known to the police and others. The local village bobby, Rodney Gooderson, used to "keep an eye on Tony" and was constantly monitoring the situation.

I believe that you should have access to three secret intelligence reports which demonstrated the feud between the Martin brothers, the lengths the police were going to in order to monitor it, and how the interventions of the police actually made matters worse – whether by accident or design. Someone, somewhere was keeping a watchful eye on this feud and, it seems, wanted to profit from it.

Thur
31 MAR
1988
17

Swaffham police station, Norfolk

The first report was authored by PC 320 Neil Mackley stationed at Swaffham and the intended recipient was the Chief Superintendent of 'D' division. The report was headed 'Domestic Dispute: Martin & Martin'.

[Author's note: we should be aware of the level at which this 'domestic dispute' was being monitored and ask ourselves why.]

"On Tuesday 29 March, 1988 I saw Robin Martin who lives at the Red Lion public house, Swaffham. He told me that his brother Tony had been to see him at lunch time concerning the 1300 acre farm that their father left only to Robin. They have been in dispute for years. When they left the Red Lion he made a veiled threat.

Robin Martin is concerned as he says his brother is mentally unstable and is the type that could cause another Hungerford.

Both DC 329 Matthews and myself heard from different sources in February this year that Tony was in possession of a sawn off shotgun. He was seen by his local beat officer PC Rodney Gooderson. Tony admitted saying he had one, that it was all verbals just to keep people away from his home. PC Gooderson believes that he would not carry out the threats he has made, (at least he never has done up to now.)

What concerns me is what Robin Martin tells me about incidents in the past.

1: 10 years ago an incident occurred at Wisbech St Mary involving a .45 Webley Mk IV revolver (which he may still have) and a female. A Mr Colin Desborough was a witness.

2: Within the last three months Tony discharged a shotgun through a window in a snooker room[10] when a car of the same make and colour as his

---

[10] Tony informed me in a conversation on 1st January 2015 that the snooker table in that room had come from Narford Hall, a listed grade I large country mansion built to an irregular plan of carrstone with ashlar dressings under a slate roof. The original block, built in c 1702 for Andrew Fountaine of Salle, lies to the south-west and is mainly of

arrived. A Mr Clive Giddens, 108, Willsey Rd,[11] Whittlesey was in this car and witnessed the incident.

I accept that Robin Martin may be 'gilding the lily' in his favour. However, he does give names of witnesses and if there is truth in these allegations I feel some concern as to whether Martin is a suitable person to retain a shotgun certificate. He owns a white Mini index number OMK139P in rough condition.

Tony Martin is described as 5' 10", plumpish build, dark hair, greying, untidy appearance. Wears dark blue anorak, dark trousers, green wellies.

I ask that this report be forwarded to the Chief Super for his consideration."

The report was submitted and on 29 March 1988 the police recorded that they kept a 'continuous watch' on the Red Lion public house in Swaffham.

You may find it interesting to note that information came to me from a police officer that PC Mackley actually used to drink at the Red Lion in Swaffham when he was off duty. We must bear this in mind when reading the report. Have his social habits interfered with his judgment, or has he produced a balanced report? Is the information I received even true? I leave you to decide.

The copies of these secret intelligence reports that I obtained show that notes were added by more senior officers in the chain of command and it is evident from these notes that the intention was to revoke Tony's shotgun licence.

It is worth considering that – certainly at this stage – the police had taken everything that Robin had said as being true and that Tony had not been engaged in conversation about these matters. This apparently one-sided report forces us to question the validity of such 'police intelligence.' I suggest that a one-sided report is no report at all.

Notwithstanding my comments, it is clear that the police were taking this family feud seriously. So much so, that PC Rodney Gooderson was asked to submit his report, being the local beat officer with what we might describe as something of an 'intimate' knowledge of Tony Martin.

| Thur 2 JUN 1988 18 | **Outwell police station, Norfolk**
I reproduce PC Gooderson's report below. It's rather long but provides us with much necessary detail so that we might better understand not only the Martin brothers' feud, but also the way in which the situation was being monitored by very senior police officers whose jurisdiction did not extend to 'domestic' disputes: |

---

two storeys with a seven-bay facade.

[11] I could find no such road. I think the typist meant Whittlesey Road, Whittlesey, near Peterborough.

"After liaising with Inspector Horn (Downham Market) re PC Mackley's report, I have made lengthy enquiries into the matter and report as follows.

The two main persons involved are:

Anthony Edward Martin, 43, (16.12.44). No recorded convictions.

David Robin Martin, 50, (03.12.38). List of previous convictions attached.

I know nothing about David Robin Martin other than the facts revealed during my enquiries. However, I have had numerous contact and dealings with Anthony Edward Martin over several years, mainly owing to him having been the victim of theft and burglary.

During this time he has developed into a quite useful source of information and has very strong views on crime and punishment. He is known to most of my beat colleagues by virtue of the above. I would describe him as eccentric, having rather peculiar personal habits regarding dress, cleanliness and business management. He often tends to shut himself off from the public for lengthy periods of time and drives battered/well-used motor vehicles which attract attention from various sources.

He is prone to lengthy verbal outbursts if one of his pet subjects comes under discussion. As a result of the criminal attacks on his property he has employed various forms of booby traps in his dwelling and farm buildings as a deterrent. He verbally publicises this fact towards anyone he considers suspect. As a result of his habits and appearance he has become known locally as 'Mad Martin.' He has until now given no cause for police concern, although knowledge of how to approach him has always been beneficial. He has made it known to myself and other officers that he is not too fond of his brother, but tends to ramble on as to the cause which was obviously a family rift. This dispute has to my knowledge been going on for years over what he claimed to be unfair distribution of family land between them. He never made the facts very clear and I did not consider it a police matter.

On 6th February 1988, DC Matthews of Swaffham contacted DS Farnham at Downham Market regarding Anthony Martin - possession of a sawn off shotgun. A photocopy of the relevant intelligence book entry is attached. As a result of this I saw Anthony later that same day. Photocopy of my intelligence book entry also attached. The matter being on hearsay only I had to introduce it into conversation during what I purported to be a welfare visit/social call. I informed him that rumour suggested he was in possession of this type of weapon. He laughed it off, openly inviting me to search his home, buildings and vehicles if I so wished. He then went on as is typical of him to say words to the effect, "If I had one, you don't think I'd be daft enough to put it anywhere where you could find it and if I haven't got one it's easy enough to get one or make one if I wanted to." Knowing Martin (who likes to throw down this type of challenge), I did not waste my time pursuing his invitation or taking the matter further. I pointed out to him the consequences he would face if ever found in possession of this type of weapon and advised him that if he did possess or have access to one to destroy it. He was made aware that in view of the rumour he may well find that he was being subjected to vehicle stop checks by other officers. I considered this to be the only way to tackle the matter, (prevention being better than cure). The source of the information was never guessed by Martin and the Swaffham connection was not raised or his brother mentioned.

On receipt of PC Mackley's report I made tactful enquiries with numerous members and close friends of the Martin family, none of whom wished to become officially involved and agreed to speak to me 'only in the strictest confidence.' As a result I was able to obtain a fairly concise history of the whole Martin family, including personal habits and financial status. These facts are all contributory to the dispute between Anthony Edward and David Robin Martin, but are not relevant to the points raised of police interest. However, all gave a fairly consistent story and shared the same views which I summarise as follows:

Summary of dispute between the Martin brothers

The dispute between the two Martins in question is basically over division of family assets and land after the deaths of other interested relatives, resulting from conflicting verbal agreements and transactions made prior to the deaths against the terms of the relevant wills of the deceased. The dispute has been furthered by the two disagreeing with each other's personal life styles and business methods.

The mother, Hilary Martin, has been left as mediator between her two sons which often finds her in direct conflict with both whilst attempting to protect each one's interests and her own financial position. The dispute has been going on for years. Both of those involved are described as equally hot headed and volatile under the right circumstances. Anthony Martin has been threatening to shoot his brother for years, but it is felt that if he was ever going to, he would have done so by now and that this is just one of his typical verbal outbursts. On the other hand it was felt that David Robin Martin was equally capable of shooting or harming Anthony under the right provocation and of the two he was more likely to carry this out being more of a man of action than words.

However, all felt that the chances of either actually harming the other were extremely remote and everybody had come to accept that the dispute was likely to continue unresolved for the foreseeable future and they had all come to learn to live with it. All were aware of the revolver and shotgun incidents referred to in PC Mackley's report, (which I shall explain in detail later) but considered them to be internal family matters past and now considered dead and buried. It was generally felt that any attempt to resurrect these matters or to revoke Anthony Edward Martin's shotgun certificate may well stir up more trouble than it solved. This was based on the fact that once he learned that the matter had been brought up by his brother (which he undoubtedly would during legal proceedings) it would be like a red rag to a bull. All were equally anxious that he did not find out that enquiry into his personal affairs had been made with the family 'behind his back.' I reassured them as best as possible that I would try to prevent this from happening and that identities would not be revealed. All felt that police action was not necessary at present and that the matter could be satisfactorily controlled and maintained at family level in the future, as in the past. It was agreed that there was no harm in the police having a background history on record for future reference if necessary. I can now go into more detail regarding the firearms incidents raised.

Firstly the revolver:
This incident involved a female acquaintance of Anthony Edward Martin. I have traced and spoken to this lady who did not wish to be identified or become officially involved by making witness statements etc. She now holds quite a respectable position in society and did not wish for her past private life to be open to public scrutiny in any proceedings involving Martin. She agreed to reveal details of the incident on the understanding that she would remain anonymous and was very co-operative towards me. She gave a full account of her past association with him, summarised as follows:

She first met Martin some 17 years ago when he returned to England from a long stay in Australia. They became very friendly during 1972 and 1973 and had what appears to have been an intimate relationship. Martin's interest in the woman then seems to have declined and they parted.

The woman, although initially somewhat upset at the break-up of the relationship soon came to terms with it and decided she wanted nothing else to do with him. Martin went abroad again, but returned to England some time later, believed early 1976. Purely by chance, during the early part of that summer Martin and the female met again in a public house. Martin immediately attempted to renew their relationship but she firmly declined.

Martin then became obsessed by her and started to follow her everywhere she went socially, pestering her to renew the relationship.

She continued to repel his advances which only had the effect of making him more determined. Up to this point Martin had not been aware of the woman's current place of employment, but this was inadvertently revealed to him when he visited mutual friends, the Desboroughs.

the Desboroughs
For continuity their joint versions of what occurred are as follows: Colin and Ann Desborough, 'Chasford', High Road, Wisbech St Mary.

Martin visited them at about 7:15am on 29 June 1976. (Ann Desborough remembers the date vividly as it was the morning of one of her children's birthdays). He rambled on to them about how much he loved the other woman and how desperate he was to renew the relationship. He then learned from them her place of employment. Martin then got up and went out to his car and came back into the house carrying a revolver. He waved it about in his hand declaring to the Desboroughs "If I can't have her, nobody will." He then left in his motor vehicle.

The Desboroughs declined to make witness statements about the incident and did not want the matter raised again (a) for the sake of the woman involved, (b) they considered it so long in the past it could be forgotten about. [Author's note: When asked to make a statement in 1999 following the death of Barras, the Desboroughs again declined to make a statement about the alleged incident with Tony and the revolver.]

Patricia Ann Masters
Returning to the account of the woman involved, she arrived at her place of work early that same morning, (29 June 1976) to find Martin waiting there for her. He immediately began pleading with her to renew their relationship again. To save any embarrassment in front of her colleagues, the woman agreed to meet him that evening and discuss the matter. Martin then calmed down and left the premises.

During that day the Desboroughs contacted her and warned her that Martin was in possession of a hand gun. However, she decided that she would still see Martin that evening in an attempt to finally convince him that he was wasting his time pursuing her.

As arranged, Martin collected the woman from her parents' home and drove her to an orchard he owned at Wisbech St Mary. The relationship was discussed. Martin then said to her, "I've got a gun you know," reaching across from the driver's seat to the glove box, from where he produced the revolver. She attempted to laugh this off saying words to the effect, "It isn't loaded; put it away, it's not a real gun" etc. to which Martin responded by saying he would prove it to her, got out of the car and shot and killed a wood pigeon in one of the trees. He then got back into the vehicle and returned the weapon to the glove box.

The woman stated that she had then become very concerned and feared for her safety, although she was adamant that Martin never made any verbal threats or pointed the weapon towards her. She attempted to persuade him to take her home and after some time he agreed to do so.

On reaching her home, Martin did not stop and carried on with the woman to one of his relative's homes about a mile away. Again he parked up and attempted to talk her into renewing the relationship. She refused – asked to be taken home, but the car would not start. She got out and started to run towards her home. Martin pursued her on foot but she managed to beat him to her home and locked him out.

This incident, the whole of which occurred in the Cambridgeshire area, was not reported to the police.

Apparently, (unknown to the woman at the time) Martin spent the whole of that night up a tree in her garden and the next morning once again followed her to her place of work, remained outside in his vehicle most of the day, once attempted to enter the premises but was intercepted by a work colleague, who after being badgered by Martin about his obsession with the woman persuaded him to leave.

Martin continued to hound her and on several occasions she returned home or to her vehicle to find evidence of him having entered both: notes and small gifts having been left and evidence of her bed having been slept in in her absence. On two occasions he was actually found by her inside her parents' home and she established that he had gained entry with a duplicate key he had stolen on previous entry via unsecure window. (He never made any threats towards her, but his mere presence intimidated her and she became increasingly anxious about his activities and constant harassment). As a result, all exterior door locks were changed (about September 1976), but the woman learned that Martin still gained access by use of skeleton keys.

Finally in desperation she went to Wisbech Police which resulted in Martin being visited by two CID officers and warned off.[12] This was believed to have been late January/early February 1977 and the woman has not seen Martin since. I have been unable to trace any record of this matter via Wisbech or the identity of the CID officers who visited him. The woman states that she never did lodge any official complaint and the matter seems to have been dealt with under, 'The Ways and Means Act'.[13]

She did mention that Martin had, prior to visiting Australia, been an in-patient at Fulbourn Mental Hospital, Cambs. (believed voluntarily), for a recurring mental disorder.[14] He had also been treated for this disorder by his GP - Dr Lodge - now retired and living at Townsend Road, Wisbech. I have made no attempt to obtain medical history from either of these sources as I feel that this would be denied on ethical grounds.

Having liaised further with Inspector Horn we both shared the view that it was of paramount importance to locate the whereabouts of the revolver possessed by Martin during the 1976 incident. This proved to be a very sensitive and delicate task, but with the aid of a well-meaning member of the family the weapon has been surrendered into my possession under an unofficial amnesty -

---

[12] Tony has told me that this never happened at all and that it is a figment of his former lover's imagination, that of certain Wisbech police officers, or Rodney Gooderson's.

[13] There is no such act. It is a phrase often used by police officers to describe that there are 'ways and means' by which to achieve a result without always resorting to the courts.

[14] Tony only ever spent one night in Fulbourn (see previous chapter) and certainly does not have, nor ever had, "a recurring mental health disorder".

without this I feel that the weapon would not have been traced so long after the event. I am assured that it has not been in Anthony Edward Martin's possession since shortly after the incident in question. I was informed by my contact that the history of the weapon is as follows: Originally it was a First World War British service revolver, issued to a now-deceased member of the family. It has never been subject to a Firearms Certificate for authorised possession. On the death of the original holder it passed to other members of the family who apparently regarded it as a sentimental heirloom and the fact that it was a Part 1 Firearm was not appreciated. The weapon in question is of Spanish manufacture and is currently held at Downham Market police station pending destruction or other disposal as directed.

The shotgun incident:
The witness Giddens has been seen, but refused to make a statement (see report of PC 939 Keith Jones, Whittlesey, Cambs. dated 25 April 1988, which is self-explanatory).[15] From my enquiries I established that the incident occurred just before Christmas 1987, at Ripes House, Wisbech St Mary, which David Robin Martin refers to as his home. However, this property is now owned and occupied by the mother, Hilary Martin. By virtue of the dispute and financial difficulties previously referred to, I have visited Mrs Martin and discussed the whole matter with her - again in confidence.

Mrs Martin was initially and quite understandably very protective towards both her sons, not wishing to say anything which would land either in trouble or promote ill feeling between them. Once I had managed to 'break the ice' with her, she was fairly forthcoming and verified much of the family background already outlined, referring to each of her sons as Tony and Robin. She stated that each was equally volatile under provocation and she was their go-between in the dispute, both being far from what she considered perfect. She stated that Tony legally owns and farms several acres of farmland at Ripes House, the rest being farmed by Robin. Consequently each son has cause to regularly visit the farm and her home.

On the date of the shotgun incident Tony was on the farm, visited her and she mentioned the dispute with his brother to him with another suggested resolution. Tony disagreed with the proposal and flew into one of his rages, shooting both barrels of his 12-bore shotgun, which he had under his arm at the time through the snooker room window. This room is not part of the dwelling but is a conversion at one end of a garage block in the farm yard. Mrs Martin stated that both she and Tony were aware that the room was not occupied at the

---

[15] In 1999, following the shooting of Fearon and Barras, Clive Giddens was approached by police to make a statement about the alleged shooting in the snooker room. He again declined.

time. I believe that this building is part of the property subject to dispute between the two brothers. The incident was not reported to the police.

Mrs Martin did not wish to make any complaint about it and had considered the matter private and closed. When asked about Tony's mental problems she denied that he was mentally unstable, but agreed that he had undergone medical treatment for chronic depression several years ago.[16] She, like everyone else involved, felt that any official intervention between her sons would cause more trouble, not prevent it. She also shared the view that although Tony was verbally aggressive and appeared strange at times, Robin was the one most likely to promote trouble and become physically violent. She regretted the fact that Robin had involved the police, but wished that we could persuade him to stop pressurising Tony to accept his terms of resolving their dispute, although she understood we could not intervene in civil matters.

Towards the end of my enquiries, on 10 May 1988, I went to the Red Lion in Swaffham and there saw David Robin Martin. He did not wish to make any official complaint against his brother. When questioned re the alleged threats to kill, mentioned by PC Mackley, he stated that on Tony's last visit to the public house to discuss the points in dispute they had again failed to agree. Apparently on leaving the premises Tony said to Robin's common-law wife, (not in his presence), "It's a lovely day", to which she replied, "Yes." Tony going on to say, "But there won't be many more of them for you." She had regarded this as a threat, but had since accepted it as just another verbal outburst. I took a short witness statement from David Robin Martin to clarify the points raised, (attached).

Witness statement of Robin Martin
Strangely, David Robin Martin quoted his date of birth to me as 07.03.38. However, his mother is adamant that this is in fact 03.12.38. This may have been an attempt by him to cover up his previous convictions, but does not warrant further pursuit. (I have amended the heading of his statement to show the correct date of birth).

We now come to the point of this whole enquiry. Revocation of Anthony Martin's shotgun certificate. Obviously I cannot commit myself and say that he is or is not a fit person to hold one, but would like to underline several points:

(i) he has no known convictions;

(ii) there are persons with considerable criminal records still authorised shotgun certificate holders;

(iii) it appears that David Robin Martin is, of the two, more likely to resort to violence. If we combine this fact with his criminal record,

---

[16] In my view, this depression would have been directly linked to the child abuse perpetrated against him at Glebe House School, Hunstanton.

	should we not also consider revocation of his firearm and shotgun certificates - although obviously this is a Cambs. police matter;
(iv)	we have no willing witnesses or real evidence, only hearsay and no access to medical history;
(v)	in the event of revocation, knowing Martin, I feel that he would lodge an appeal. In view of (i) and (iv) above we would have nothing to bring forth as justification;
(vi)	there is no guarantee that we would be able to recover the shotguns in his possession;
(vii)	in the event of revocation/appeal etc. Martin would undoubtedly discover that the matter was initially instigated by his brother. This would probably produce a result completely contrary to that which we desire. Maybe this is a classical case where it is best 'to let sleeping dogs lie' and just monitor the situation and be ready to step in should the need arise.
(viii)	David Robin Martin spends lengthy periods of time in Spain. (He states normally 2 weeks in England then 2 or 3 abroad). There is little threat to him from his brother when he is not in the country;
(ix)	a lot of the trouble appears to be initially provoked by David Robin Martin, against the advice of his mother and other members of the family;
(x)	it would be bad for public relations if we appeared to be taking sides or were being "used as a lever in a civil dispute."

In conclusion I must apologise for the length of this report. This has been a rather complex matter and I have attempted to condense the facts as best as possible without omitting any of the relevant points. I have had to adopt a very low key attitude during the enquiry to achieve the information and co-operation obtained. Without this, I feel that I would have been faced with a rather impenetrable brick wall.

Report submitted for your information and any further action deemed necessary."

Before I provide you with a third report in this particular matter, let's take a look again at some of the points in PC Gooderson's report.

Robin Martin had a list of convictions which could be summarised as follows: receiving stolen goods, leaving the scene of a road traffic accident and assault. His lifestyle came under scrutiny by his younger brother who was a fierce advocate of right and wrong and in behaving morally and ethically. Tony regarded him as "a greedy person" and told me that in all of Robin's business dealings he always wrote contracts that ensured he would "come out on top." But that was merely one sibling's view of another.

Rodney Gooderson confirmed that Tony *had* reported numerous thefts and burglaries at Bleak House – the police were later to claim that Tony had made a lot of these up in an attention-seeking pattern of behaviour.

It was Mr Gooderson who first wrote about Tony as being 'eccentric' and – like most labels – once they have been attached, they become extremely difficult to throw off. Yet the village bobby wrote that Tony had never given the police any cause for concern and that everything said about Tony was mere 'hearsay.'

PC Gooderson confirmed that no family member or close friends of the family wanted to make official statements about Tony. Indeed, when PC Gooderson visited the Red Lion pub in Swaffham, Robin Martin – who, it seems, was the puppet-master to the police – also refused to make anything official, yet he was defaming his younger brother at every possible opportunity.

The report also stated that of the two brothers, it was Robin who was more likely to carry out any threat to shoot, since he was a man of action, not of words, and because he had criminal convictions for assault.

PC Gooderson confirmed that Tony's former girlfriend also did not want to make any official statement to the police. You might like to ask why, particularly when the Outwell bobby was unable to find evidence of any involvement with Wisbech Police as she had suggested.

Mr Giddens, who apparently witnessed the shooting in the snooker room, also did not want to make an official statement to the police – the list of people who were happy to talk to the police on an 'unofficial' basis grew ever longer. You might like to ask yourself why.

PC Gooderson noted that Robin Martin referred to his mother's house as his own, but it was not. Hilary Martin legally owned the property. Furthermore, Rodney Gooderson stated that there was no real evidence against Tony Martin, that everything the police had been told was mere hearsay, that the investigation had been instigated by Robin Martin behind Tony's back and that the older brother was the initiator of trouble.

Objectively, I thought the report was balanced, though I do feel that PC Gooderson ought to have considered the role of Robin Martin in this more closely – unlike his counter-part, PC Mackley, he appears to have overlooked how the older brother may have been 'gilding the lily' in his own favour and to Tony's detriment.

Sun
12 JUN
1988
19

Downham Market police station, Norfolk

And so to the third report, authored by Inspector Horn of Downham Market and again intended for the Chief Superintendent. I suggest we ask ourselves why someone at this level of the police was involving himself in a family dispute – what did he have to gain from such an intense interest in this civil matter?

"PC Gooderson has liaised with me several times during the course of his investigations. It may, on the face of it, seem to have taken quite a long time to complete this enquiry. However, it has been very difficult and sensitive and the contents of PC Gooderson's comprehensive report have only been obtained with some difficulty and in the belief that the information has been given on a strictly confidential basis.

There are ample indications that Anthony Martin is not a suitable person to hold a shotgun certificate. His actions with a hand gun nearly 12 years ago and much more recently 'the window incident' clearly underline this.

Whilst there are ample indications, there is very little evidence. If Anthony Martin's certificate was to be revoked then there is a very real possibility that he would appeal. At this present time we have little evidence on which to oppose an appeal and it is very unlikely that we would get more.

I think it is relevant to say that had Anthony intended to carry out threats to cause physical harm then he has already had ample opportunity to do so.

There is clearly a dispute between the Martins over property and it may be that David [Robin] intended from the outset to draw the police into this affair perhaps to benefit his own ends. As the file raises doubts about Anthony's suitability so it must about David's.

The decisions to be arrived at are not easy ones to make in this case but my suggestion is that on the basis of the evidence available we do not revoke Anthony's shotgun certificate nor offer any recommendation that David's certificates are revoked either.

Whilst liaising with PC Gooderson it was apparent that the slight possibility existed of the police obtaining possession of a hand gun, probably the one used as described. It was quite plain that had we pursued the recovery of this weapon on a formal basis we were on a 'non-starter.' Rightly or wrongly, rightly I believe, I told PC Gooderson that I would like to see the weapon out of circulation if at all possible and asked him to get it even though it was on a surrender basis which would result in no further action. The weapon had obviously laid somewhere and has not been used or handled for some time as it was seized up. I suggest it be destroyed by forwarding it together with a copy of this report to Headquarters."

And that was that – neither brother had their certificates revoked. Note how Inspector Horn stated that there were 'ample indications' that Tony was not a suitable person to hold a shotgun certificate, but equally that there was no evidence to warrant its revocation.

Note, too, how the Inspector stated that the police were unlikely to gather evidence that would support the revocation of Tony's licence.

But we must pay close regard to the following sentence in the report: "It may be that David [Robin] intended from the outset to draw the police into this affair perhaps to benefit his own ends."

Sensational new book shines a spotlight on everything rotten about policing and criminal justice

10 PRISONS 12 WEEKS provides a unique insight into prison life as seen through the eyes of an innocent author, Brian Pead, whose book exposing child abuse in Lambeth is banned at the High Court. A permanent gagging order is sought against him by the Council before his arrest by armed police.

Unlawfully estranged from his beloved daughter and grandchildren in a move designed to break him emotionally, he is ghosted between **10 PRISONS** in just **12 WEEKS** and held incommunicado in an attempt by corrupt agents of the State to silence him.

This book shines a spotlight on the lengths to which the agencies of State will go in their attempts to cover up child abuse and police and judicial corruption.

Soft cover, 490 pages

1988—1999

Part 3: 1988 - 1999

In this section, I will introduce the saga – and make no mistake, it was a saga – of Tony Martin's shotgun certificate. It would be mentioned at trial that the farmer did not have a valid certificate, but there are highly unusual circumstances surrounding the fact that he did not have one which I'll explain here.

And we'll see how he led various Chief Constables of Norfolk a merry dance, so that the Constabulary almost beg Tony to take his guns back out of the police armoury!

I believe that all of the following events you'll read about in a decade-long battle between the farmer and the police help us to learn more about the character of Tony Martin and also help us see how the police took isolated snippets of information about the farmer's life and wove them into a poisonous narrative before feeding them to the media and an unsuspecting British public. Make no mistake that you were deceived by the very authorities meant to tell you the truth and protect you. Definite shades of Hillsborough.

As always, I hope that you will be able to form your own conclusions from the available evidence and then ask yourself "Should Tony Martin have ever been on trial for murder?" and "Were my tax pounds spent wisely on taking him to trial?"

If we, as a nation, are to learn anything from the débâcle that was Hillsborough, then we must ask ourselves these questions whenever someone is taken to trial, whether a run of the mill case or a high-profile murder trial.

With the reports on Tony collected in, further investigations were carried out, as they should have been because, up to now, it was all nothing more than hearsay from people with an axe to grind against the farmer.

| Thur 10 APR 1988 20 | **Robin Martin statement to police**
Tony's older brother, Robin (landlord of the Red Lion public house in Swaffham) had previously declined to make a statement, but changed his mind and made one to the police at Swaffham, in which it appears that he was setting up his brother for future problems: |

"With reference to my conversation with PC Neil Mackley on 29 March 1988, concerning my brother Tony. To clarify certain points I will state the following: there has been friction between Tony and myself for many years concerning tenancy of land and distribution of family assets. During this time, Tony has often threatened to kill me. However, I have never felt that he had the intention of doing so as he is subject to outbursts of verbal fantasy. When I mentioned this to PC Mackley, I was not making any official complaint to the effect of believing he intended to kill me. I do not wish to make a complaint of threats to kill.

Tony is in my opinion very unstable and could at a later date become dangerous. This is why I felt it was my duty to bring the matter to the notice of the police, more as a safeguard for the future and so that the situation could be maintained and there were certain relevant facts on record in the event of something occurring in the future. I do feel at the moment that if any action was taken against Tony it would probably tend to create more problems than it solved. My only concern is that the police are aware of the situation as a safeguard for the future. I understand that there is a civil remedy in the event of Tony continuing to cause me harassment. The incidents I quoted to PC Mackley regarding the shooting of the snooker room windows and his possession of a revolver were simply to underline his erratic behaviour.

None of these incidents were reported to the police at the time and I understand that it is pointless trying to pursue them without a proper complaint and witnesses to the facts. I would appreciate it if the local police could keep the facts on file so that they could be ready to act and be fully conversant with the history of the dispute if necessary. This is the only reason for my mentioning anything about it."

This entire statement could be interpreted as Robin Martin attempting to curry favour with the police and deflect their attention away from him. He said that he wanted something "on the record for the future" and this could lead us to believe that he had conspired against his brother using other family members or anyone else to assist him, including potentially gullible police officers. Of course it would suit his purposes if his brother was "officially" recorded as being a danger to the public and "mentally unstable". Of course, we do have to consider that the police have a job to do to protect the public from mentally unstable people with shotguns and, to cover their backsides, they're going to have to be seen to be doing something.

It would appear from this statement that PC Mackley had suggested to Robin that he might wish to make an official complaint of Threats to Kill against his brother, but the older brother declined to do so.

It's worth noting the reasonably high level at which this was being overseen – Chief Inspector and Chief Superintendent. Let's not forget that it is, essentially, a family dispute, a civil matter and therefore nothing to do with the police. So, I argue, we ought to be asking why such senior police officers were involved – what did they have to gain from such a close attachment to a relatively innocuous argument between two brothers?

Mon
25 APR
1988
21

Whittlesey police station, Cambridgeshire

PC 939 Keith Jones sent a Cambridgeshire Constabulary memo to the Chief Superintendent regarding a telephone message received at Whittlesey on 19 April 1988, from PC Gooderson requesting that a statement be obtained from Clive Giddens, of Eastrea, detailing his relationship to his distant cousins Tony and Robin Martin.

"It is alleged that some 3 to 4 months ago a shotgun was discharged through a snooker room window by Tony Martin, who is in dispute with Robin Martin, over some land.

At 9pm on Wednesday 20 April 1988, I visited Mr Giddens, who is a distant cousin of the Martins and Robin is also his father-in-law. Giddens refused to make any statement and wished to be 'off the record', when he confirmed that there is a dispute over land between the Martins and also that Tony discharged a shotgun through the snooker room windows of Robin's house. He said that no one was inside at the time and that he had seen the 'event' as he arrived at the house in his car.

Giddens' refusal to make a statement is based on his fear of possible retaliation from Tony Martin towards him and his family - although he has never been threatened himself and is sure that the dispute is confined to Tony and Robin Martin."

Note that Mr Giddens would only speak "off the record". In this event, he could have been saying anything or he could have been telling the complete truth.

In a later chapter we will return to the Giddens family who took Tony to court in a dispute over some land in May 2016.

Tue
26 JUL
1988
22

Norfolk Constabulary minute sheet

In a Norfolk Constabulary minute sheet entitled Martin Family Dispute, CI Finbow informed the Chief Superintendent of 'D' division that the police had no evidence on which to base the successful revocation of either Tony or his brother's firearm and shotgun certificates.

Finbow added that the incidents involving the younger brother would not be known to the police had it not been for the confidence and anonymity acknowledged by PC Gooderson to those members of the family to whom he had spoken. Finbow took the view that to further sour family relations by attempting to take any official action in respect of the illegal possession of the revolver, the two past incidents or attempted revocation of certificates would not serve any useful purpose whatsoever.

Although the two incidents may have led to the revocation of Tony's certificate, Finbow felt it fair to say that on neither occasion did he actually endanger human life, nor was there any record that he had ever done so. Furthermore, the younger sibling had no criminal record.

Finbow suggested that PC Gooderson should remain alert to Tony's conduct and that the surrendered firearm be destroyed as "the original owner is now deceased."

Hopefully you're now beginning to see that the police are somewhat painting themselves into a corner. Make no mistake that Tony Martin understands all of this because he is at least one step ahead of them.

Wed 24 AUG 1988 23

Norfolk Constabulary minute sheet
In another minute sheet also entitled 'Martin Family Dispute', PC Gooderson informed Inspector Horn that two days previously he had met with Tony's GP, Dr Hall-Smith, who told the constable on an unofficial basis that he seldom saw Tony Martin and that it had been several years since he was last consulted.

The doctor did not consider the farmer unsuitable to hold firearms from the information he had on record.

On the same Minute sheet, Inspector Horn commented: "This is rather a tricky one. We could be wrong whatever is done. It does seem that Anthony Martin's certificate should be revoked, but we have no clear evidence; the lady does not wish to be identified; incidents go back to 1976 and to top it all the doctor says unofficially he does not consider Anthony unsuitable from the record. I recommend we take legal advice on the matter as revocation seems difficult in the circumstances."

In a Norfolk Constabulary memo, the county solicitor, CG Harding wrote to Charles Fretwell of the Firearms Department and described the report by PC Gooderson as "full and helpful", but that "in the absence of anybody who is prepared to testify in court to these incidents, then there is insufficient (almost non-existent) evidence to justify the Deputy Chief Constable's decision to revoke Anthony Martin's certificate."

The county solicitor added that whilst he appreciated the worry that this case caused Norfolk Constabulary, in cases of civil proceedings such as this that were decided on the balance of probabilities: "you do need some evidence, and *that does not exist here*." [Author's emphasis]

Wisely in my view, Harding added that another concern was that Robin Martin could have been using this as a cover for any defensive action he might take in the future: "We have to recognise that Tony Martin may have a legitimate and different view as to how the incidents arose. The prospect of Robin Martin acting in haste could not be ruled out given his background, but similarly we have no real evidence to revoke his certificate either. My conclusion is therefore reluctantly, no further action as to revocation of firearms certificate."

Notice that Mr Harding highlighted the fact that no-one was prepared to testify in court, that Robin Martin could have been using this as a precursor to any action he might take, and that he might have acted in haste. Surely the single most damning piece of evidence against the Constabulary was this sentence: "it is my view that there is insufficient (almost non-existent) evidence on which the Deputy Chief Constable could have based a decision to revoke Mr Martin's certificate."

You will have your own views about this on-going saga carried out at considerable public expense. And you will definitely have your own views about what happened just three days later which 'miraculously' assisted the police in their endeavours to revoke Tony Martin's certificate.

Thur
15 SEP
1988
1.35 pm
24

Ripes House, High Road, Wisbech St Mary

We now move on to Ripes House which had been a Grade II listed building since 23 June 1952. At this point in our narrative, the house was owned by Tony's mother, Hilary.

Some four months after Robin Martin's statement to the police warning them about his "aggressive brother", constables 575 David Brammer and 13 John Balmforth attended Ripes House to speak with Robin, who showed the constables a 1-inch cut to the right shin, a bruise on his left elbow and he complained of a wrenched shoulder. He said the injuries were inflicted by his brother.

I decided to take a deeper look into this incident because it seemed to me too 'convenient'. The police appeared to have overlooked the fact that Robin was a farmer and could easily have sustained such simple injuries in the normal course of his work.

The brothers' Aunt Betty - Mrs Elizabeth Chadfield – provided a statement to the police in which she said that at lunchtime she had been in the kitchen of Ripes House with her sister Hilary and Robin. She stated that "Tony walked into the kitchen and had a very angry and aggressive look about him." According to Betty, Tony said to Robin, "What are you doing about this farm?" and Robin was supposed to have replied, "Mind your own business."

Betty Chadfield stated that she got up out of her chair and put down a cup and saucer she had been holding because she felt very vulnerable as she "knew that Tony is very unpredictable and prone to violent outbursts. He kept shouting at Robin concerning the farm business."

She described how "Tony then moved round the kitchen in a very aggressive manner towards Robin who was seated at this time. As Tony reached Robin,

Robin stood up. Tony started flailing his fists at Robin and I saw Robin take hold of Tony's arms to restrain him. Tony was struggling violently and lashed out with his fists and feet."

She described how Robin managed to get Tony down on the ground and then released him but Tony got up straight away and began attacking Robin again, lashing out with his feet and fists.

During this struggle - according to her account - the fighting brothers fell against the kitchen table which broke. She then took hold of Tony's jumper and tried to pull him off Robin and called out to him to stop.

They eventually parted and Tony kept "ranting and raving until the police arrived." He then left. She concluded her account by stating that at no time did Robin incite Tony or use excessive force against him and that she was willing to attend court if necessary.

Robin Martin's view of the incident was that he was at home in the kitchen with his aunt, Mrs Elizabeth Chadfield and his mother. Tony walked straight into the kitchen with a woman (this was not mentioned in Betty Chadfield's statement, you'll notice.) A fight ensued and the description of it followed almost to the letter that which Mrs Chadfield had told the police.

Robin added that the police were called by their mother and everyone awaited their attendance with the brothers continuing to bicker at each other until their arrival. He also stated that he was willing to attend court as a witness if required.

Let's pay regard to two important aspects of this incident: (i) Tony Martin took a woman to this alleged incident – why did the police not take a statement from her? (ii) the errant boys' mother also did not make a statement, yet an aunt has supported Robin.

Fri
16 SEP
1988
7.30 am
25

Bleak House, Emneth, Norfolk

At 7:30 the next morning, Tony was arrested by PC Balmforth and taken to Wisbech police station where he was charged with Actual Bodily Harm (ABH) on his brother contrary to section 47 of the Offences against the Person Act, 1861.

Tony remained in police custody to appear at Peterborough Magistrates' Court on the following day (the 17th).

His fingerprints were taken and a list of his previous convictions was noted. For the record this consisted of him 'deserting ship' on 28 September 1965 in Auckland, New Zealand. He was detained and deported on 3rd November 1965 - that was the extent of his "convictions".

> **CORRUPTION ALERT** *Police failed to interview all available witnesses*

The police failed to interview half of the people present at the scene of the alleged assault: Hilary Martin, Aunt Rosemary (whose presence Aunt Betty and Robin Martin somewhat conveniently failed to mention in their statements) and Helen Lilley, whom Tony had taken to meet his mother.

Was he treated fairly?

At 9:30am, Tony Martin was interviewed by constables Brammer and Balmforth. Let's take a look at the interview, a record of which was produced not by tape recorder but by way of notes taken at the time by the constables – this is another echo of the Robbie Auger case that we have read about.

PC Brammer cautioned the farmer, who gave no reply. From a legal point of view, this was perfectly acceptable and many would say, extremely wise. Tony was asked if he understood the caution and again there was no reply.

Police interview

Brammer: Robin has complained to us that you went to the house and assaulted him in the kitchen. Is this correct?

Martin: There's no answer to that is there?

Brammer: I believe that leading up to the incident there was some argument about a pile of wood on your land. Is that right?

Martin: You're telling me this is what somebody told you. What can I do about it? Why haven't you guys gone down to Maurice Daley's and got my gates back that Robin took off my farm?

[Author's note: Tony felt aggrieved that the police should listen to hearsay from third parties without speaking with him and he was still annoyed that the police had failed to deal with his gates, stolen – he says – by his brother.]

Police interview continued

Brammer: So you were both fighting?

Martin: Yes.

Brammer: Who threw the first punch or kick?

Martin: Basically, I always let someone else hit me first.

Brammer: So you're saying Robin hit you first?

Martin: He grabbed me, I pushed him over and he did what he normally does – he scratched me. There's the scratch mark.

Brammer: When the fight started, had you approached Robin while he was sat in his chair?

[Author's note: I'm surprised that the constable didn't follow up on the fact that Tony said Robin had thrown the first punch and that Robin scratched him. There's a strong case to say that Robin should have been the brother in court.]

Police interview continued

Brammer: So you're saying, are you, that the fight was his fault?

Martin: The fight came about because I asked him a civil question and he flew into a rage as he normally does, like he does with everybody if he can't get his own way. That's why he's been done for GBH.

Brammer: So you're saying that he got up and grabbed hold of you?

Martin: He got off his chair and grabbed hold of me. He got off his chair and grabbed hold of me.

Brammer: Did you, before the fight started, walk across to Robin aggressively so that he may have had the impression that you were going to attack him?

Martin: That's something you would have to ask the witnesses about as far as I'm concerned. I stood there for about 10 minutes. It depends on how people take things as to whether I was aggressive. He is always intimidating and is always trying to intimidate me.

Brammer: Do you agree that this interview has been conducted fairly?

Martin: A matter of opinion – it depends on what people think. But it depends whether or not the police believe me or my brother, who is a convincing liar.

I don't think that it was a completely fair interview because it seemed designed to try to get Tony Martin to implicate himself and because the constables didn't appear to develop their line of questioning from Tony's responses in order to delve deeper and to try to ascertain the truth. I don't know about you, but this all seemed rather too contrived to me and too one-sided. There appears to have been no consideration given to Robin's role in this 'assault'. It's possible from Robin's statement about living in fear of his life that he was further seeking to discredit Tony and perhaps work towards gaining control of Tony's farm.

Tony was let out on bail, with three conditions: that he should keep away from his older brother – a somewhat difficult proposition given that Tony used to go to Ripes House to visit his mother and Robin was also living there on an ad hoc basis; that his weapons should remain surrendered and that he should reside each night at Bleak House.

I found Tony completely honest and candid about this incident. He didn't deny that there was great animosity, but his version is that both brothers hated each other as much as the other.

He added that the other aunt present was Aunt Rosemary and that he took a female friend – Helen Lilley, owner of the Marmion Hotel in Wisbech, a favourite haunt of Tony's at the time – to his mother's. Yet the police did not take statements from Hilary Martin (their mother), Aunt Rosemary or Helen Lilley. Three of those present did not make statements – that is hardly fair.

And then we come to an amazing 'coincidence' – I asked Tony why his Aunt Betty would make a statement against him, why she would choose one nephew over the other. It did not make sense to me until Tony told me that Clive Giddens was Betty's son – and that he was in business with ... Robin Martin.

Tony added that Clive Giddens' father was a tenant of some 700 acres who could no longer afford to farm and Clive said he'd finance the running of around 300 acres in partnership with Robin, who'd farm the remaining 400 acres.

> "But Robin spotted a weakness in Clive and he decided he wanted to farm the whole 700 acres. Clive met and had a relationship with Robin's daughter, Nicola, but found out they were cousins and so didn't marry. Robin issued Clive with an ultimatum – 'I'll control the farming of the entire 700 acres – take it or leave it.'
>
> But this was Robin's downfall because he got greedy. In 1984 allowances on machinery were coming to an end and in 1985 the crops failed and Robin owed money everywhere.
>
> Basically, Robin was greedy and over-extended himself. I'm far more conservative and not flash at all. I've always lived within my means and he was jealous of that. I was making a success of Bleak House and the farm and he didn't like it."

Sun 9 OCT 1988 26

Norfolk Constabulary minute sheet

In a Minute sheet Inspector Horn informed Superintendent Reeve of Tony's arrest, that he had to surrender his firearms as a condition of bail and that a fresh look would be taken in the light of evidence as to his suitability to hold a certificate.

Now a relatively simple story becomes ever more complicated by the involvement of the police. Is this mere coincidence – that at the very time the police are attempting to take Tony's certificate from him, he was involved in a dust-up with his brother and that this dust-up now put his possession of a firearms certificate in jeopardy?

When I asked Tony whether he felt Robin was in league with some rogue police officers, he replied:

> **"** I will never know if what happened in the kitchen was accidental or on purpose. I merely wanted to know whether my brother had sub-let my land or whether he had unlawfully sold it to raise cash when it wasn't his to sell.
>
> You see, he had stolen a lot of chemical spray from Johnny Clark's farm and hid it up in our chicken shed. When I found it, I thought that it belonged to him and that he'd hidden it so that it wouldn't be stolen, but he went round the local pubs in Guyhirn and a copper overheard him saying he had a load of cheap spray for sale.
>
> So Robin was arrested and convicted of theft. He is just very greedy. My mother thought he was just 'a naughty little boy' and she tolerated him to excess. He could never understand why I was righteous, but I don't believe in thieving.
>
> With regard to the fight ... well, he raised his hand to me and that set me off. I had to defend myself.
>
> As for Aunt Rosemary, several years later she told me that Robin had tried to stitch her up in business with a land deal, and she turned round and told me, 'Tony, I'm sorry. You're not the problem, he is. I see it differently now.'
>
> Many years later – in 2014 – Clive Giddens tried to get 3½ acres off me over at Wisbech St Mary. He called me a thief, but that land was left to me and it's mine. Robin told the police that my orchard was his orchard. He is a very crooked man and knew some very shady people. My problem is that I get caught up in the demise of other people."

Wed 9 NOV 1988 27

Wisbech Magistrates' Court
The case was transferred from Peterborough to Wisbech Magistrates' Court but, in a piece of 'legal engineering', on 9th November 1988 sentencing was withdrawn and Tony was bound over to keep the peace for 12 months and pay a fine of £100.

Was this justified, given all of the facts involved? My concern is that not all of the facts were considered by the bench and that three important witnesses were never even interviewed by the police. And PC Brammer failed, in my opinion, to give consideration to Tony's account that his brother had struck the first blow and scratched him. If we haven't had all of the evidence in court, how can we ever arrive at a reliable verdict?

And I'd like you to consider these facts: one - this case had taken almost two months to get to the Magistrates' Court; two – Tony's shotgun licence was due to expire on 15 November 1988, less than a week after the hearing.

If we study the chronology of these facts, do you think this was the reason for the delay in bringing the case, so that Tony's attention would be distracted and his certificate expire whilst his attention was on farming and the case itself?

Fri 2 DEC 1988 28

Norfolk Constabulary minute sheet
Inspector Horn informed the Chief Superintendent that one of the consequences of the binding over was that Tony's firearms would have to be surrendered.

Perhaps the reader is now better able to understand Tony's extreme frustration at the parlous state of policing in Britain.

Notice that this entire report was based on a possible fallacy – that Tony Martin was guilty of an assault on his brother. From the evidence I have read, this was never investigated properly by the police and Robin Martin had provided no medical evidence that the injuries he claimed to have sustained had been caused on that particular day and in the manner he described. After all, it was recorded that Robin had a bruise on his left elbow and yet the alleged fight had taken place only an hour or so before the police were called. Bruises, of course, usually take longer to develop. Yet this alleged incident had become a 'fact'. And that 'fact' was being used by the police to create a plausible, yet inaccurate, narrative. This has remarkable overtones of Hillsborough – which occurred just a few months later on 15 April 1989.

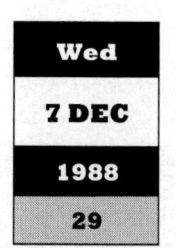

Wed 7 DEC 1988 29

Norfolk Constabulary minute sheet
Five days later, Finbow minuted that the obvious "on-going hostility between the two brothers points to real potential for escalating violence: we have now reached a point where revocation of Anthony's shotgun certificate could be a distinct possibility and I recommend the views of the county solicitor are sought to this end."

A copy was sent to the Firearms Department at police headquarters.

Fri 6 JAN 1989 30

Police headquarters, Martineau Lane, Norwich, Norfolk

At great public expense – money which might better have been used to employ a constable or two or properly detect crime – the Chief Constable sought advice from barrister Simon Barham of Wensum Chambers in Norwich.

The salient points of Barham's written advice included the opinion that Tony's shotgun certificate should *not* be revoked. Barham further advised that if it were to be revoked, Tony's appeal would be likely to succeed.

Essentially, Barham's reasons included the fact that the two incidents with firearms did not put people at risk and that all of the police intelligence was actually hearsay unless there were witnesses to support the claims made and, as we know, no witnesses were prepared to come forward.

Barham also noted that it was possible that Robin Martin had brought this matter to the attention of the police for his own ends and that a lot of the ill-will resulted from Robin Martin trying to pressurize his brother into accepting plans for the resolution of the dispute between them.

The barrister added that a binding over did not constitute a conviction and, should the shotgun certificate matter go to court, witnesses would need to be called and Barham believed (and I'm inclined to agree with him) they would not attend. He did not consider that the alleged fight would be sufficient to justify the revocation of a shotgun certificate. Appreciating that it was the last of a number of incidents, he said the fight on its own was not particularly serious and did not involve the use of a shotgun or firearm. According to Barham, *any appeal by Tony Martin would be likely to succeed.* [Author's emphasis]

Barham suggested that the constabulary should keep a record of any complaint, whether by a member of the family or otherwise, that Tony Martin had threatened anyone or behaved irrationally or violently.

Objectively, it would appear that Norfolk Police were unable to take a more detached view of what was really going on in that family. I do not say this because I have any particular allegiance to Tony Martin, but because of my knowledge of family dynamics. What were the police doing in giving this any credence? Well, Tony Martin was, as we know, a fierce critic of government cutbacks and reductions in police numbers and the closure of police stations. This might be reason enough to gather any kind of information (it does not have to be true), officially record it as 'genuine' and then use it against their critic when the time arises: "The very concept of objective truth is fading out of the world. Lies will pass into history." This was not to be the first time that lies about Tony Martin would be recorded as 'fact' and become part of the false narratives with which governments attempt to shackle their citizens.

If a person makes a statement to the police, in my opinion they ought to be willing to make it official and to go to court to substantiate their claims. Aunt Betty and Robin Martin actually ended their witness statements by saying that they were prepared to go to court. And yet the matter was mysteriously dropped at the Magistrates' Court in favour of a bind over which meant that these witnesses would never be called. The police had what they wanted: a bind over, court papers to put in the file and another 'fact' of violence giving them a 'legitimate' reason to seize Tony's shotguns.

Had this matter gone to court – Robin Martin and Aunt Betty might have been exposed as possibly colluding and the other Aunt (Rosemary) and Helen Lilley would surely have been called as witnesses by Tony's defence. The easiest route out of this mess? A bind over.

Perhaps now the reader will have a greater understanding of the meaning of Tony Martin's phrase "legal engineering."[17] In my view, it is a perfect summation of the bastardisation of the rule of law to suit political purposes. And I include the police in my use of the word 'political'.

Some five months after the altercation in the kitchen, Tony's local beat officer sent yet another report to the Chief Superintendent on 26 February 1989. I've reproduced extracts from it below because I think it makes for interesting reading in the next episode of this costly soap opera.

In his report, PC Gooderson explained that following advice from the county solicitor on 12 September 1988, no action was taken and it had been decided to sit on the matter and monitor Tony's behaviour. The constable then included information about the ABH by Tony – however PC Gooderson interestingly referred to it as an 'alleged' ABH.

Fri 24 FEB 1989 8.25 pm 31	**Bleak House** *The local beat officer (Rodney Gooderson) was going to arrange for the return of Tony's shotguns, only to find that the certificate had expired, so he attended Bleak House[18] with the intention of having Tony complete the necessary renewal form.* *The farmer then related in detail the dispute between himself and Robin resulting in the official action by Wisbech police.*

---

[17] To be clear: the phrase 'legal engineering' belongs (at least in this book) to Tony Martin. We have discussed this phrase on many occasions and, during those discussions, I adapted it to become 'illegal engineering' because there simply is nothing legal about what the police and the courts do in perverting the course of public justice.

[18] Note that despite the late hour on a dark February night at which PC Gooderson attended the house, he was clearly able to find it. However, 10 years later – and with a helicopter flying overhead with a powerful searchlight and heat-seeking equipment on board – Norfolk Constabulary claimed that they were "unable to locate the house."

He was obviously annoyed with the police, feeling the action biased and unfair and added that on several occasions, complaints by him against his brother at Wisbech police station regarding action in their area had never been investigated. Gooderson advised him on his rights and the action he should take if he felt he had been the victim of a crime. Tony replied, "It's not worth the time and trouble involved."

Tony was invited to complete the application form for the renewal of his certificate so that his weapons could be returned, but he declined, saying:

> If Wisbech police took my guns away in the first place, they must feel that I'm not safe to have them so I don't think I should have them back at the moment either."

The constable asked him if he was prepared to surrender them for disposal or destruction, but Tony replied:

> No, I didn't mean I *never* want them back. But while you've got them, at least they won't get stolen will they?"

Gooderson advised Tony to reconsider his attitude and that any lengthy delay in renewing his certificate might jeopardize this and then he'd need to apply for the grant of a fresh certificate instead. It was also suggested that Tony think his actions over and the policeman said he'd call back at a later date.

PC Gooderson noted that he felt that Tony was trying to make some act of protest and suggested that given a few weeks to accept the facts, he would eventually agree to renew the certificate and accept the return of his shotguns.

The report concluded: "In the meantime it appears that the situation has backfired on us somewhat and we shall have to retain his weapons until the matter is resolved."

So here we have a remarkable twist in the tale – Tony is now refusing to take back his shotguns for a number of reasons, not least because he is angry at the treatment he received from Wisbech police (and who can blame him?), and the police have now painted themselves into a corner because they have been informed by barrister Barham that they don't have any grounds on which to revoke his certificate.

I cannot stress too strongly enough the cost to the public purse of all this. I ask the reader to take a detached view – forget that this drama is about the national icon known as Tony Martin and his dysfunctional family and instead just think of the person-hours involved. Yet the police constantly bleat in the media about the lack of officers and other resources at their disposal: can we honestly say that our tax pounds were wisely spent on this entire case? I, for one, don't think so. I think my taxes were squandered by egotistical superior officers out to prove a point against a stubborn farmer feeling betrayed by public servants. This could have been dealt with far more efficiently and cost-effectively by other, more human, means. We ought never to lose sight of the fact that throughout this episode, rural crime was escalating; even the police (who like to massage such figures) did not disagree.

Mon 27 FEB 1989 32

Norfolk Constabulary minute sheet
Inspector Horn's minute sheet to the Chief Superintendent showed that he was concerned that the police now had a situation whereby Tony refused to take back his weapons and at the same time declined to renew his certificate.

Horn's attempt to solve this conundrum was to send a letter to the farmer to tell him that a failure to renew his certificate within a specified period would mean he would have to eventually pay a 'grant' cost should he decide he wanted a certificate. He should also be told, the Inspector added, that he must make arrangements for either the storage or disposal of the weapons: "I do not see that we can clutter our armoury up with unnecessary guns."

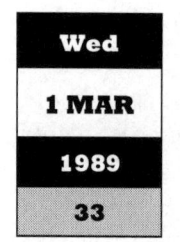

Wed 1 MAR 1989 33

Norfolk Constabulary minute sheet
CI Finbow added the following note: "Papers returned as discussed in order that Rodney Gooderson can make another visit to Martin within the next four weeks when it is anticipated the matter can be brought to a satisfactory conclusion. The Firearms Department at HQ are aware of the position."

Five days later, Brian Martin (no relation), the SAO for the Chief Constable, sent a note to the ACC: "Martin's shotgun certificate expired on 15/11/88. Suggest we write to Martin stating that he must arrange for a dealer or another certificated holder be identified to collect/store his shotguns. If he fails to do so, we will apply for a court order to dispose of them; also, if he should require a shotgun certificate in future, he will have to apply for the grant of one."

It seems that the police have realised that they have been outmanoeuvred by the farmer and so start to wield the big stick again. I detect a worrying absence of emotional intelligence.

Fri
10 MAR
1989
34

office of the Assistant Chief Constable, Norfolk
In this continuing saga, the office of the ACC wrote to the inscrutable farmer under the Firearms Act, saying that he had been invited to renew his shotgun certificate and refused to do so. Tony was now given 21 days from receipt of the letter to collect his guns, or the Chief Constable would apply for an order to destroy them.

Wed
15 MAR
1989
35

Bleak House
Five days later, Tony composed a thoughtful and intelligent response to the Assistant Chief Constable:

> You have been informed incorrectly. I have not refused to renew my shotgun certificate. The officer who called by my house happened, I understand, to hold a form for the return of my firearms but then realised he had come without the renewal form for my gun licence which I understand has run out. I would not know this as you have my certificate. In passing conversation, I had wanted to know what right anybody had to take my guns in the first place.
>
> I also told the officer I do not use my guns very often except for killing rats around the grain drier and pigeons in my rape crop if they become too destructive and felt that my guns were far safer in a police station and would fetch them when required. I say 'safer' - my house and farm building and garage have been broken into on numerous occasions. Many of these I have not reported. I found not only were thieves a waste of time, but without offence, calling the police in was as well.
>
> If you don't believe me come down this way and talk to the locals. Some people I have met dare not leave their homes.
>
> I would like a reply to this letter so I know what needs to be done.
>
> PS: I have had my house shot and a dog shot at. I would like to hear your views on this matter. I would also like to say that I have no criminal record and safely say I know of nobody who would accuse me of being violent except Wisbech police. I think it better not to write on paper what I think of Wisbech police. The truth often offends."

I think we can safely say that in this letter we have all the ingredients for the 1999 shooting: Tony's complete dissatisfaction with the police, the constabulary not listening to him and continually trying to wield the big stick as their only answer to a situation they have largely created for themselves. Note Tony's invitation to the ACC to pay a visit to Emneth. Sadly some members of Tony's community chose not to see him as a concerned crusader who was looking out for their safety as well as his own but rather as a mad man instead. The ACC, in any event, didn't take up Tony's offer to visit.

Fri 24 MAR 1989 36

Norfolk Constabulary minute sheet
PC Gooderson reported to the Chief Superintendent that he had met with Tony and that the farmer had completed the application form for renewal of his certificate.
The constable added a note to the effect that he would arrange the return of Tony's weapons and ammunition with the certificate.

A further note was added saying that it was agreed that the police would follow PC Gooderson's recommendations.

Mon 3 APR 1989 37

Norfolk Constabulary minute sheet
On the same minute sheet, a further note was added by the Chief Superintendent to the effect that: "The matter now appears resolved. I suggest action as recommended above."

But the matter was far from concluded. At additional cost to the innocent taxpayer, Tony's guns had been moved from Wisbech (his nearest police station) to Downham Market and then on to King's Lynn in anticipation of his collecting them.

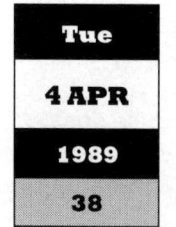

Tue 4 APR 1989 38

office of the Assistant Chief Constable, Norfolk
In a letter from the ACC, Tony was advised that if he was not prepared to arrange for the removal of his weapons from the armoury, the police would have no alternative but to charge for storage at a rate of £5 per month, plus VAT, commencing from 1st May 1989.

If Tony could arrange for the weapons to be stored with a Registered Firearms Dealer or another shotgun certificate holder prior to that date, no charge would be made. And then a classic riposte from the ACC to the landowner who had complained that the police were useless: "With regard to your comments regarding your concern over the safety of your person and property, you should ensure that any such incidents are reported to your local police station so that they may be properly investigated."

Wed
5 APR
1989
39

Bleak House
On his application form for the renewal of a shotgun certificate, Tony stated that he was bound over by Wisbech Magistrates' Court and that he had no other convictions except jumping ship 25 years ago. The question: "Do you suffer from any form of mental disorder or defect?" was answered with a "No." At no stage was this assertion ever challenged by the police.

Mon
10 APR
1989
40

office of the County Solicitor
Now someone else gets involved and the cost to the taxpayer increases too. Alison Ings, the county solicitor, wrote quite forcefully to the ACC to the effect that as Tony had now renewed his certificate, he was "perfectly capable of collecting his guns".

She suggested that he be given 14 days from receipt of the letter to collect them or they would be destroyed. Note the unnecessarily punitive tone from a public servant.

A resolution was finally achieved when Tony's cousin, Edward Martin, a car salesman and firearms holder, agreed to store the guns. But the resolution was only temporary. There would be yet further twists in this remarkable affair.

Thur
16 NOV
1989
41

Firearms Department, Norfolk Constabulary
The shotgun certificate was renewed on 16 November 1989 and that very action must have meant that the police had confidence in the fact that Tony was (a) not a danger to anyone and (b) not mentally impaired in any way to prevent him from owning and using shotguns.

The counter-signatory to the application was Nelson Lewis, manager at the National Westminster Bank in Wisbech, who stated that he had known the applicant for 4 years.

Tony informed the police that he kept the guns in a large safe. He declared a Victor Sarasqueta 12-bore double barrel shotgun, a Foreign .410 single shot, a Webley 9mm single shotgun and a Webley Sportsman 9mm single shotgun.

The fee of £11 was duly paid, a receipt numbered 203668 was issued and the form was processed by PC 805 DA Davidson of Downham Market police.

| Sun 26 NOV 1989 42 | **Firearms Department, Norfolk Constabulary** *Form SG103/1 was completed internally by the police. Question 1 asked: Is the applicant of good character and fit to be trusted with firearms? The form had been completed with a YES – he was suitable. Question 4 asked: "Has applicant been invited to surrender shotguns?" The form had been completed with 'NO'.* |

The form was signed by PC 468 Gooderson and two days later it was countersigned with a signature I was unable to read. So, in light of the alleged mental instability of Tony Martin portrayed by his older brother to the police, there was actually no evidence of this on official police forms.

EMNETH 1¼
OUTWELL 3

ST JOHNS HIGHWAY 5

~ 5 Years Later ~

Sun 23 OCT 1994 11 am 43

Bleak House orchard

The story now moves from the summer of 1994 to the autumn. Tony has had his latest shotgun certificate since November 1991, but it is just coming up for renewal again.

His apple trees are heavily laden with fruit and on Sunday 23rd October he finds a man trespassing in his orchard and stealing some of his crop.

In order to research this episode in our narrative, I interviewed Martin Hollis, a cousin of Tony's living in Heacham on the Norfolk coast. A keen cyclist, the ruddy-faced, slim 61-year-old was clearly extremely fit. I learnt that he kayaks, hang-glides and is a qualified pilot. Yet his demeanour was one of humility – he was measured in his words, not at all boastful or given over to profanity or exaggeration. He was well-spoken and had been educated at a minor private boarding school. Mr Hollis was clearly an example of the perfect kind of witness you would want to interview – articulate, intelligent, measured. I will let him tell you the story of the gunshot fired in the apple orchard in 1994:

"It was a glorious sunny day and I decided to swing by Tony's house as he had not long had his rottweiler puppies and was keen for me to meet them. He let them out of the cottages where he kept them and they were delightful creatures.

Tony and I have always got on well, although we are different in our personalities. We had been chatting away for about fifteen or twenty minutes when we saw a 4x4 drive off the Smeeth Road and straight on to the orchard. We looked at one another in disbelief – neither of us was quite sure that what we had just seen was real.

We decided to walk down to the orchard and we found the vehicle in the middle, amongst all the apple trees. The male driver had two young girls with him and they each had a carrier bag which they were filling with apples.

We had the dogs with us as we approached the man. I stood about six feet back from Tony and observed what was played out.

The exchange was becoming more heated as Tony asked the man who he was and the man then asked Tony who he was. Tony told him that he was the landowner and that he had not given permission for the man to come on to his land and told him to leave. The man refused initially.

The dogs were well-behaved and offered no harm to anyone, but I could see that they were sensing the conflict. I've always had dogs myself – I love dogs – and all the time I was thinking that the dogs know what's happening here.

Throughout this exchange, the man and the two girls continued to fill the plastic bags with Tony's apples.

Eventually the girls got back into the vehicle and the driver followed. Then he drove at us. I got behind a tree. Tony stood his ground. Thankfully, the trespasser drove off after a couple of goes at us.

Tony said to me, "He'll be back!"

We both walked back to the house. Tony collected a shotgun because he feared reprisals. We then both walked down to the end of his drive, where it meets the Smeeth Road.

After a short while, the 4x4 came along, driving with some purpose. The man had dropped the two girls off somewhere and now he had returned. He then drove straight towards the dogs and it was clear to me that he intended to harm them. The dogs were aware and took evasive action, but the man came two or three times at them.

Tony fired a single shot low to the ground in the direction of the rear tyre. At no point did he aim the gun at the driver or the vehicle itself. It was merely a defensive shot because the driver had first tried to drive at us and then at the dogs. The driver clearly had the intention of causing us and the dogs harm and Tony took the most appropriate preventative measures in the circumstances.

Once the driver had left after the single gunshot, we went back to the house again and Tony immediately called the police. We waited down on the Smeeth Road and it was quite some time before they arrived. It was not an armed response vehicle, but an ordinary marked police car. The constables didn't even bother to get out of the vehicle. They just spoke through an open window.[19]

Tony told them exactly what had happened and he mentioned that I was a witness, but they never spoke to me about the incident either there and then, or by visiting me at my home on a later date. I found this most unusual. It seemed to me that if the police wanted to investigate the matter properly, they ought to have taken a statement from me in the interest of justice. But they never did.

This was in stark contrast to five years later when, after the Barras shooting, detectives visited me on no less than four occasions trying to get me to make a statement against my cousin. Now, I'm not the sort of man who wouldn't make a statement against a cousin if he or she had done something wrong, but in my opinion, Tony didn't do anything wrong that night. The death of Fred Barras is deeply regrettable, but Tony did not kill him.

I refused to incriminate Tony and the detectives wanted me to speak to them about the gunshot in the orchard as if it had anything to do with the shooting of Barras and Fearon.

---

[19] Official records show that the constables who failed to perform the duties expected of them by the public were 32-year-old PC 78 Lindsey Wakefield and 46-year-old PC 868 Neil John Thompson.

They had never bothered to seek my version of events in 1994 and here they were some five years or so later trying to get me to incriminate Tony. On the fourth occasion, they walked to the beach as I was coming out of the sea with my kayak and I told them I wanted nothing to do with them and that I wouldn't make a statement.

At the age of 26, I nearly died in a hang-gliding accident when I was testing out equipment, and Tony, who is ten years older, helped me recover from that dreadful experience. I think that what happened to Tony was dreadful and that he should never have been treated the way he was by the State. I am proud that he is my cousin."

This account puts a completely different complexion on the orchard incident and one that the general public (and jury) never got to hear about. Now, we have to understand that the shooting in the orchard incident was mentioned at the murder trial as the prosecution sought to gain an advantage by portraying Tony Martin as a man who would resort to firing his shotgun at every conceivable opportunity, whether it was justified or not.

I found Mr Hollis to be a highly credible witness, mainly because he struck me as a man who would tell the truth no matter what. If he thought that his cousin had committed a crime, he would have said so.

The next obvious question to ask Mr Hollis was whether the defence team ever called him to give evidence on Tony's behalf. The prosecution had made tentative steps to claim him as their own witness when the police asked for a statement – but, as we have seen, he declined to assist them. This therefore left the way open for defence counsel. "No, I was never approached by Tony's defence team. I found this most strange, as I had a different account from that which the prosecution was putting forward and surely a jury should hear both sides of an argument. But they never approached me, despite the fact that I was willing to be a witness."

From the evidence we have before us, I am inclined to think that Norfolk police did persecute Tony Martin over a sustained period of years. Not taking a statement from a major witness is reprehensible. Then trying to revoke his licence on the basis of Tony having fired a single downward shot at a rear wheel when you know you haven't been fair and even-handed by taking a statement which might throw a different light on events is also reprehensible.

Then trying desperately to "round up" just about anyone who might have something bad to say against the farmer shows a despicable attitude, in my opinion, not only towards Tony Martin, but also towards policing itself. We would do well to remember, at this point, that policing in England and Wales is supposed to be *by consent only*. Little wonder that the public's perception of policing in this country is at an all-time low and little wonder that Tony Martin felt let down by the police. The evidence shows that he was.

Wed
16 NOV
1994
44

Firearms Department, Norfolk Constabulary

At significant cost to the taxpayer, the saga continued to roll on. On Wednesday 16 November 1994, police records show that Tony's shotgun certificate (number 51644) expired. On 14 December, the same police records show that he was sent a second reminder to renew his certificate. (The first had apparently been posted to his address eight weeks previously.)

Sun
18 DEC
1994
45

office of the Chief Constable, Norfolk

PC 300 Hardstaff is alleged to have sent the following note directly to the Chief Constable: "Fearing for his own safety, Mr Martin armed himself with his shotgun and fired a round at the rear of the intruder's vehicle. No injuries were caused. The intruder has declined to make a complaint. Although the public at large, particularly in the Fenland area may have considerable sympathy for Mr Martin, we must demonstrate that this sort of action is not acceptable. Unfortunately, the criminal has now become the victim but he will not make a statement of complaint. Suggest revocation."

The criminal has now become the victim? He first attempts to steal apples, then drives at Tony and his cousin and then the dogs. He then returns to the farm for a second attempt. Since when was he ever a victim?

But note the use of the phrase "*Fearing for his own safety,*[20] Mr Martin armed himself with his shotgun and fired a round..." We would do well to recall this phrase in the light of the Barras incident, but let's not get ahead of ourselves. After Hardstaff's memo to the Chief Constable, things started to move fast.

Wed
21 DEC
1994
46

Firearms Department, Norfolk Constabulary

Charles Fretwell of the Firearms Department sent a note to Brian Martin, SAO to the Chief Constable: "On reading the file submitted by PC Hardstaff, and taking into account Martin's file shows two previous incidents where he has resorted to the use of firearms in attempts to impose his will on others, I recommend revocation: danger to the public safety or to the peace."

Brian Martin then sent a note to the ACC recommending revocation. And the single word 'Revoke' is ordered by a higher ranking officer whose signature is indecipherable, but is probably the ACC's.

---

[20] Author's emphasis.

Thur 29 DEC 1994 — 47

office of the Assistant Chief Constable, Norfolk

Thus, without any evidence, Tony Martin's shotgun certificate was unilaterally revoked by the police. The letter was personally served on him by PC 300 Hardstaff on direct instructions from the ACC.

Upon receiving the letter, records show that Tony responded with, "You could have told me this over the phone."

So we have a uniformed officer playing postman and delivering a letter at public expense rather than having him reducing crime in the community in which he was supposed to serve.

The letter - signed on behalf of the ACC – arrogantly stated: "You may wish to appeal this revocation. Should you decide to appeal, you would be well advised to consult a solicitor." You probably don't need me to point out that, as we have seen, the police were well aware that should Tony Martin appeal, they had been advised by counsel that he was likely to win his appeal based on the fact that the police had no evidence against him.

From my perspective, I think this is an appalling waste of public money which is going on every day throughout all police forces in the land. I still can't help thinking that the cost of all of this could have been put to better use by increasing the number of constables on the beat.

Fri 27 JAN 1995 — 48

King's Lynn police station

PC Hardstaff sent a fax to PS Keith Manship at King's Lynn informing him that Tony Martin's certificate had been revoked and that notice had been served the day before. The weapons were held in the armoury. PC Hardstaff added the following comment: "I don't think we have heard the last of Mr Martin."

How very prescient of him, since he had played a significant part in this saga. And, significantly, he had withheld evidence by failing to mention in his note to the Chief Constable that there was a witness to the incident in the orchard who had not been interviewed by the police.

Mon 13 FEB 1995 — 49

Norfolk Constabulary headquarters

Norfolk Police received notification from Tony that he wished to appeal the revocation of his licence.

On the same day, his cousin Edward Martin collected Tony's weapons from the armoury at King's Lynn.

Still the saga would not end.

Thur
2 MAR
1995
50

office of director of legal services

Director of legal services, Anthony Vittadini, stated in a letter to Brian Martin, SAO, that having carefully read the papers and discussed the case with his colleague John Bates, he was regretfully of the opinion that the court would not uphold the ACC's decision.

Vittadini added that the problems which occurred in 1988 were before the most recent renewal of Tony's certificate: "Although the incident when considered against the background of the case shows willingness on Mr Martin's behalf to be threatening and when threatened to resort to use of his shotgun, the court are likely to be sympathetic to Mr Martin given that it is over six years since he was in any 'trouble' with the police."

Remarkably, Brian Martin telephoned Mr Vittadini and asked him to instruct counsel for a second opinion. More public money being spent on a futile exercise by egotistical public servants.

In this seemingly never-ending feud between Tony Martin and the Chief Constable of Norfolk, Richard Daniel of Sackville Chambers, Norwich, sent a copy of his advice to Nicholas Hancox, a director of legal services.

This advice, dated 12 April 1995, from barrister Daniel throws a completely different light on the idea that Tony Martin was "a nutter with guns."

Daniel stated that he did not dissent from the previous view of Simon Barham in that "it is far too late to try and go back and rely on any of those incidents in connection with any proceedings now involving this appellant's fitness to hold a shotgun certificate."

Daniel then referred to the orchard incident and stated that far from being apologetic and withdrawing from the land, Aldin became threatening and abusive and the appellant, claiming that he was in fear that Aldin was going to run over one of his dogs, discharged a shot at the rear wheels of Aldin's substantial vehicle, an Isuzu Trooper.

"Furthermore," continued Daniel, "what I regard as highly significant is that Martin himself, within half an hour, rang through to report the incident to the police. When Aldin was seen he accepted that he had been in the wrong and declined to make any complaint." Daniel added that the appellant had the right to require Aldin to leave his land and (if it became necessary) to use no more force than was reasonably necessary to secure that ejection.

"Whilst the discharge of the shot at the vehicle wheel might well be considered an excessive response, the inescapable fact is that it has not produced a complaint from the vehicle owner and there have been no criminal proceedings out of the incident.

There is no suggestion of any threat to go after Aldin, nor any other incident in which we can lead evidence to suggest misuse of the shotgun.[21] I am driven to advise that, in my professional judgment, there is insufficient material to sustain a revocation and that this appeal is likely to succeed. Furthermore it is the sort of case in which a successful appeal might be followed by an order for costs against the Chief Constable."

Clearly, this throws a completely different light not only on the 1988 incidents, but also the shooting in the orchard and – ultimately – on the trial for the alleged murder of Frederick Jackson Barras.

It is significant, I feel, that Daniel made mention of the fact that he had relied on the very detailed report of PC Gooderson, and we have already seen that much of that police 'intelligence' was effectively created by Robin Martin and other family members who appear to have conspired against Tony Martin in order to further their own ends – family members who, we should remember, were always willing to provide the police with information only on the basis that it was "off the record" and therefore unofficial.

Mr Daniel made mention of the previous advice to the Chief Constable authored by Simon Barham in 1989. Here we are, some *six years later* with the office of Chief Constable still trying to pursue the revocation of Tony Martin's shotgun certificate at great cost to the public purse. No doubt the very same Chief Constable who would complain that his budget was cut and he was "appalled" that he was forced to close police stations and reduce the numbers of "bobbies on the beat." Readers might like to send a Freedom of Information Act request (free of charge on *www.whatdotheyknow.com*) and ask their current Chief Constable exactly what percentage of his or her overall annual budget is spent on legal fees and court cases and how many "bobbies on the beat" that money would provide. I think the information you receive back will simply stagger you.

Again, if we fast-forward to the 1999 shooting and the 2000 trial, had this been dealt with properly, the jury could have had a completely different perspective on this incident. The police and CPS fed the baying press hounds a lot of disinformation about the shooting in the orchard. Barrister Richard Daniel had stated that the farmer was quite within his rights to use a gun against the

---

[21] Determined to find *anything* to pin on Tony, the police interviewed Aldin on 26 August 1999. However, Aldin told the police: "I left my children with my wife, got a baseball bat put it in the truck and drove straight back to the orchard. I was going to beat the dogs. I pulled into the farmyard; the men were nowhere in sight. I swung my 4 wheel drive round so it was facing back down the lane and I got out, the dogs all came round again. I hit one with the bat - it yelped and ran off; the other two were still near me and I was trying to get them." This pre-meditated determination by Aldin to injure Tony's dogs was not only justification for the farmer to fire at the vehicle's tyres, but also the reason why the police made sure that this statement was not entered as evidence at the murder trial.

trespasser by shooting downwards and not directly at the individual who had refused to leave the land and who was becoming increasingly aggressive.

I found Mr Daniel's advice to have been well-presented, professionally detached and eminently sensible. I conclude that this whole sorry (and expensive) saga was nothing less than a witch hunt against a farmer whom various Chief Constables of Norfolk had misspent thousands of pounds of public funds on pursuing and attempting to defame him as 'mentally unstable'.

I was once sectioned under the Mental Health Act in 2014 after informing a police doctor that I had reported child abuse in Lambeth. I was released after 24 hours since it was obvious to all concerned that I was far from mentally unfit, and no danger to myself or others, though a great danger to corrupt State officials. The next day, news about significant child abuse in Lambeth was front page news across the broadsheets and redtops.

Throughout history, governments and police forces have tried to claim that campaigners and critics are 'mentally unfit' and then seek to create 'evidence' to substantiate their erroneous claims.

I suggest that Mr Daniel's advice to the Chief Constable was not too well received at police HQ, and that Tony Martin was being heavily monitored in order that they could 'drum something up' against him. I further submit that the burglaries and thefts from his property were not just random acts, but a concerted effort perpetrated against him in order to frighten him, drive him 'mad', make him snap and leave the land.

Despite Mr Daniel's concerns that he regarded the chance of success as 'minimal', the obsessive and egocentric ACC still wished to defend the appeal and instructed counsel. Thus, despite strong advice to the contrary, Norfolk police were *still* going to use public funds to fight Tony in court.

Tue
18 JUL
1995
51

office of director of legal services
Vittadini wrote to the Chief Constable: "I enclose a copy of [assistant chief constable] Mr MacIntyre's statement incorporating the amendments suggested by Mr Daniel.

I would be grateful if you would ask him to sign the statement if he is content with the additions."

Two days later, ACC William MacIntyre made the following statement:
"Anthony Edward Martin was granted a shotgun certificate no.51644 on 16/11/84 which was subsequently renewed, expiring on 16/11/94.

On 23/10/94, Martin was involved in an incident which resulted in him discharging his shotgun at a vehicle. As a result of reports concerning this incident and previous incidents involving Martin, I came to the conclusion that he could no longer be entrusted with a shotgun without danger to the public safety or to the peace and, therefore, revoked his shotgun certificate."

Is it possible that the police were determined to take his guns off him so that he would be left vulnerable and so that one day we would be reading about a dead farmer killed in a burglary in a remote farmhouse in Emneth?

Nor should we overlook the fact that had Tony Martin not called the police after he discharged the gun at the vehicle's rear wheels, none of this could have happened. It was only because he was honest – some might say too honest – that the police had any ammunition with which to attack him. Tony had held a shotgun certificate for 10 years without any danger to the public whatsoever.

Sat
18 APR
1998
witness 109
52

Methwold village hall

According to official records, PC 837 Douglas 'Danny' Cracknell, usually stationed at Downham Market, was present at Methwold village hall with PC 9094 Sally Hawkins "and three special constables" during a police surgery. The public-spirited Tony Martin attended, spoke briefly with the officers to ask them what the police were doing to prevent the rising tide of crime in the area and left.

There are three versions of this seemingly innocuous event which was later to feature in one of the most famous murder trials in British history.

Tony's version is that he was the only member of the public who turned up all the while he was there, that he asked about the police's policy on combatting crime, that he didn't receive a sensible reply from PC Cracknell and so left "within four or five minutes".

PC Cracknell allegedly made a statement dated 1 November 1999 – some nineteen months after the event – which differed significantly from the farmer's version. This statement was entered into court and, indeed, PC Cracknell was listed as having been sworn in to give evidence on Monday 10 April 2000. The constable claimed that he attended the surgery along with PC Hawkins and three special constables who were operating in that area. He added that Methwold was some distance from Emneth and that it was "out of Mr Martin's parish".

The constable claimed never to have seen the farmer before, adding that Tony asked "Where are the senior officers?", or words to that effect.

The constable claimed he replied, "Well, that's not the purpose. The purpose of the surgery is for local police officers to meet local people."

Cracknell then claimed that Tony said, "I got the impression that he thought that there would be senior police officers present" and that when the farmer realised there were not, he then "became abusive about the police service, but not abusive of me and he added that he wasn't happy with the way the police dealt with crime. He described how there had been a milk float stolen and that it had been left on his land. When eventually somebody had come to collect the milk float he said the police were not there. He was asked if he had told the police and he said he had not but he said the police were no use whatsoever. He went on to say 'There are better ways of dealing with criminals. What should happen is that criminals should surrounded with barbed wire fences and there should be a machine gun which could be used upon them. Drive them all in there and then you could shoot them all.' The police, he said, and the court system were in general terms useless."

According to PC Cracknell, Tony Martin was "there in all for an hour and a half despite there being no senior officers there. At times he would be apparently very, very calm and other times not so calm. He came across as an educated man of the world and I was a bit bemused especially when I learned that this man was not from what I call his parish. He did mention that the police had done nothing to help when things had been stolen."

Thus we have a significant difference as to the length of time Tony stayed at the village hall – either a few minutes or an hour and a half.

According to HOLMES, PC Sally Hawkins made a statement on 16 December 1999 about this meeting, but I have been unable to find it. HOLMES shows that it was not entered as evidence into court but it should, nevertheless, have been entered in the Unused Material file and it wasn't. It seems to have simply 'disappeared'. Furthermore, the statement attributed to PC Hawkins is shown in HOLMES as being of a meeting dated Sunday, 18 April 1999, not 1998. It could just be, of course, a simple typing error. Tony's recollection – some 20 years later – was that the meeting was "just before the shooting in August."

CORRUPTION ALERT — *Inadmissible hearsay evidence used against Tony*

At trial, PC Cracknell admitted that he had not made a statement from notes in his pocket notebook because he never made any notes at the meeting. In other words, his entire testimony against Tony was nothing more than mere hearsay and, as such, ought never to have been allowed into court. The constable ought never to have been allowed to give evidence because his statement was inadmissible.

Had Tony's barrister been doing his job properly, he would have called PC Hawkins to court. It seems likely that her account differed significantly from that of Cracknell's which is probably why it went 'missing'.

PC Cracknell would later join Tony Bone in the Farmwatch business.

The Sheridan murders

Part 4: the Sheridan murders

Sun

10 JAN

1999

53

home address of Constance & Janice Sheridan, Upwell
It is, I argue, impossible to tell the true story of Bleak House without recourse to a double murder a little more than 3 miles from Tony's farmhouse and just seven months prior to the shooting.

Constance and Janice Sheridan were brutally murdered not far from Bleak House and Tony became aware of it almost immediately.

We have read about the murder of wealthy fruit farmer John 'Robbie' Auger [see entry 1] and this was in the dark recesses of Tony's consciousness – not something he'd dwell on on a daily basis, but there nonetheless, never too far from the forefront of his mind. He still regularly mentions it to me to this day.

I'll pause Tony's story to provide you with information about these double murders because – although ostensibly separate – they are, in fact, inexplicably bound up with the shooting at Emneth.

The victims were Janice Sheridan, aged 45, and her mother Constance Sheridan, aged 79. The daughter was a successful dog breeder and she and her mother lived with more than twenty whippets in their isolated cottage in the village of Upwell, on the border of Norfolk and Cambridgeshire, at the end of a winding narrow driveway.

Their bodies were found partly clothed, with multiple stab wounds, and Janice was bound with black masking tape. The police believed that the bodies had lain in the house for some days, and the murder weapon was never found. Janice Sheridan was last seen by witnesses the previous Thursday walking her dogs. The bodies were discovered on Sunday, 10 January 1999.

The Sheridans had been burgled two years before, and the daughter Janice was involved in a dispute with travellers, who she wished to prevent moving into the village. At first it was thought that the motive might be connected to these, or to her success in the dog-breeding circuit.

The police described the murders as ruthless and determined, and the binding of daughter Janice suggested that either she was kept alive after her mother was murdered, or else that she was restrained while the killer waited for the mother to return home.

The Independent ran an article dated 23 January 1999[22] entitled 'Nowhere to run, nowhere to hide - the murder of two women in a quiet village has revealed violence and tension in the Norfolk Fens.'

---

[22] http://www.independent.co.uk/arts-entertainment/nowhere-to-run-nowhere-to-hide-1075622.html

It provides a fascinating backdrop to the Tony Martin case and I suggest that we would ignore it at our peril because it has, in my view, so many parallels with Tony's case and even that of Robbie Auger:

"They'll never solve it, never," says Mally, the local coalman, sitting with a bottle of brown ale in the corner of The Globe Inn in Upwell, Norfolk. "How can they? They've got no evidence."

He is talking about the brutal double murder of a spinster dog-breeder and her ageing mother which shocked this Fenland community when it was discovered two weeks ago this weekend. The women were repeatedly stabbed with a six-to-eight-inch knife, and left lying on the floor of their front parlour at their home on the outskirts of the village. It was up to three days before they were discovered.

Outside the room, 14 of the prized pedigree whippets bred by Janice Sheridan, 45, had been left to pine for their dead mistress. Nothing of value had apparently been taken.

Even though about 70 police officers are working on the case, Mally's fatalistic view is shared by many of the locals. Such attitudes speak volumes about the women and the place where they lived and died.

Strangely, few people seem that bothered by the event. "It sounds terrible, but it's like it never happened," says Duncan, the Globe's landlord, a former Royal Navy sailor from the area. "I tell you, if it hadn't been on the telly and in the newspapers, no one would even know about it."

Jan lived with her mother Connie, 79, in almost total seclusion. Their nearest neighbour, also a dog-breeder, says she was probably their best friend, and was the last person to see them alive. But she admits that she knew nothing of their personal lives. The murders were discovered only after Jan failed to turn up for work two days running at the local kennels where she used to help out.

The general view was that the murderer had some kind of grudge against Jan Sheridan, and that her mother was killed as a potential witness. Whoever it was had now slipped back into the normal rhythm of village life or left long ago.

The story, then, is a real murder mystery, worthy of the PD James crime novels set in this eerily flat part of the country. It is in the dark undercurrents of the place itself that clues as to how all this could have happened, and why it may never be solved, can best be found.

Upwell, and the adjoining village of Outwell, are known for being the longest settlement in the country. For anyone brought up in a remotely hilly part of the UK, this is an astonishing place to see. Upwell lies exactly 3ft above sea level. Three Holes, a couple of miles south, is also 3ft above the waves.

Above this area of huge, black, fertile fields arch enormous skies - one day a soul-lifting, piercing blue, the next a grey-black canopy. They emit either pink sunsets or driving, unremitting rain.

The Rev Robin Blackwall says: "There is a sense of shock and distress that such a tragedy should take place within our village community." Special prayers were said for both women at services last Sunday.

Graham Mallet, chairman of the parish council and a society steward at the local Methodist church, is also shocked. "It is a terrible blot on the reputation of the village," he says. "I can't remember anything of this sort of scale happening here before. Violence like this is unheard of."[23]

On paper, at least, this is true. The last murder in the village was in the Seventies, when a local farmer was bludgeoned to death during a burglary, and it was quickly solved.[24] The son of a former Globe landlord (coincidentally called Sheridan, but no relation) was also killed, about 20 years ago, by a drug-crazed flatmate in Peterborough.

But current Globe regulars paint a very different picture of village life. Where once you knew everybody, they say, many people are now strangers. Wisbech, just four miles up the road, was recently said to have the highest per capita crime rate in the country, outside London and Liverpool.[25]

"It's gun law round here. Lots of people have got guns - handguns, shotguns, sawn-offs," said one.[26]

Duncan tells of an occasion when someone was in the bar recovering from shotgun wounds, and a group of eight men came charging across the bridge outside, intent on dealing out more punishment.

On New Year's Day, a gang of local travellers set about a man with baseball bats because he had threatened to 'glass' one of their daughters. The police did arrive in force, but no complaint was made and no one was arrested or charged.

Behind it all is the grievance that the police presence here is almost non-existent.[27] One officer does live in the village, but all the local stations close at night. "The coppers are bloody hopeless. If you ring them up they will arrive six weeks later," says a local.[28]

---

[23] One can only conclude that Mr Mallet had not heard of the killing of Robbie Auger.
[24] This is inaccurate – the murder of Robbie Auger was, as we have seen, in 1967. [See entry 1].
[25] Tony Martin was highly attuned to this crime wave. Many of his neighbours – some of whom were keen to rush to judgment of him as either 'mad' or 'eccentric' – lacked the awareness of what was happening right under their noses.
[26] The journalist didn't say it, but the subtext was that many of these guns were unlicensed. Tony maintains the view to this day that "Britain is awash with guns."
[27] This journalist is reiterating all that Tony had said about crime in the area and the lack of police response to the needs of the locals trying to live in peace.
[28] These words might well have been those of Tony Martin, but they were not. Nonetheless, these were very much his sentiments and remain so to this day.

Another local resident even arms himself. "If you want to go out round here, you have to go tooled up, because if you get into trouble there is no one to help you," he says, producing a 6-inch-long flick knife to prove his point.

A sense of lawlessness prevails.[29] The policeman trying to solve the current murders is Detective Superintendent Steve Swain, head of Norfolk CID. Clearly exhausted after many late nights on this case, he still has few leads.

"Usually you can tell right away why a murder happened. But at this stage we can't see an obvious motive," he says. "It doesn't appear to have been a burglary; it doesn't appear to be because someone was disturbed. It seems that it was either a person known to them or a person who had a legitimate reason for being there and being let in."

Many of his hopes seem to be pinned on forensic tests conducted at the murder scene, yet to be processed. One early line of inquiry was that the murders might have had something to do with professional jealousy in the dog-breeding world. Jan was well known in this community, had been a dog-show judge, and had qualified for an entry to Cruft's this March. But a trip by officers to a whippet show over the weekend found only people saying nice things about her, apart from her having an occasional bad temper.

The nearest thing to a lead that *The Independent* turned up was a shopkeeper who said that in the days before she was killed Jan appeared to have had a dramatic change of character.

"Normally she could be, well, almost rude. But on that day she was all smiles and chat. It was very different. It is the only conversation I remember having with her," he says. "Maybe she thought she was on to something good, which turned out wrong."

Another theory was that Jan may have had a secret lover. One story did appear last week, but even that was about a supposed relationship that finished four years ago. 'At the moment, no significant current relationships have been unearthed,' says DSupt Swain.

And so the investigation continues. In the meantime, life in Upwell goes on as normal - or something that passes for it."

I have made dozens of visits to Upwell and Outwell. At first glance, they represent chocolate-box type scenes – especially with scores of colourful boats and barges moored up along the banks of the meandering canal.

But pause, stand back and take a closer look and you'll come across burnt out cars, derelict buildings and numerous signs of criminal damage. The chocolate-box cover photograph is nothing but an illusion, a myth. And Tony Martin knew this. He longed for peace, he dreamt of being left alone to get on with running his farm and he hoped (in vain) for a greater police presence.

---

[29] This sentiment was regularly voiced by Tony and many other locals and farmers in the Fens – but ignored by the police.

Everything that Tony had been saying about lawlessness, the lack of police and the underlying tensions and fears abounding in the remote area were highlighted and brought sharply into focus by the double murder of the Sheridans.

Norfolk Constabulary claimed [30] to have solved the murder when Kevin Cotterell, 33, was found guilty at Norwich Crown Court, a case overseen by Judge Owen – who was to take charge of Tony's case a week later.

The *Lynn News*[31] carried the following story on 5th April 2000:

"Pentney man Kevin Cotterell was given two life sentences yesterday for the terrifying murders of a 79-year-old Upwell woman and her 45-year-old daughter.

Now police are investigating the possibility that he could have been responsible for other crimes – and are looking for help from the public. The former salesman changed his plea to guilty[32] in a surprise move when his trial at Norwich Crown Court was due to start. The length of time he will serve in jail has yet to be announced by the judge. Mr Cotterell (33), of Crossways, Narborough Road, Pentney, admitted killing Constance Sheridan, and her daughter Janice at their isolated home at Zealmyre, The Pingle, Upwell, between January 6 and 11, 1999.

The dog breeders had lived there for around ten years. Mr Justice Owen said: "These were terrible and terrifying offences. How they came to be committed is not clear but that they were committed and committed by you is abundantly clear, and there is only one sentence possible, or immediately appropriate, and that is life imprisonment in each case and I pass that sentence."

The judge added he would also have to make a recommendation as to the period of time Mr Cotterell would serve in jail. "It is important as I see it, that I should ensure my horror at what happened does not compromise the fairness of approach that is necessary, no matter how terrible the offences are. I shall be considering that over the next few days and if you wish anything more to be considered by me, I will of course consider it," he told Mr Cotterell. Mr Justice Owen told the jury that nobody knew Mr Cotterell would plead guilty until yesterday.

---

[30] This claim was rebutted at <http://www.justjustice.org/salesmen.html>

[31] https://www.lynnnews.co.uk/news/two-life-sentences-for-murderer-1-526636

[32] Many innocent people change their plea to 'guilty' at the last minute because they fear that, though innocent, the system will find them guilty and so they plead guilty in order to get a reduced sentence. I make no comment in respect of Mr Cotterell because I have not investigated his case. We should remember that the Birmingham Six were beaten into confessing to bombing pubs in Birmingham and that, 17 years later, they were finally released because they were so obviously innocent. I have been fortunate to have met Paddy Hill, one of the six.

Prosecutor Andrew Munday QC said Constance and her unmarried daughter came to live in the area about ten years ago. They kept themselves to themselves and Constance was rarely seen by anyone while Janice would regularly be seen taking her whippets for a walk. At the time of her death there were 22 whippets at the house and Janice, who was known as the whippet lady, had an arrangement with fellow dog breeder Poppy Becker, who lived nearby, to pick up a copy of *Dog World* magazine from Upwell Post Office each week.

There was also an arrangement when if either of them was going to be away, they would call the other and let them know because there had been a burglary in the area about 18 months previously, said Mr Munday.

Janice had last been seen alive when she called at the post office on Thursday 7 January, between 2pm and 4pm to collect her mother's pension.

Mr Munday said during the course of that week a local man was working his land opposite the Sheridan's home when he saw a strange car come over the bridge and along The Pingle. When he did not see it return he went to investigate and saw a light-coloured vehicle parked next to Zealmyre. He memorised the number as G567PVF and later wrote it down and gave it to police.

About 8:30pm on 7 January the Boyce family, who live about 500 metres from Zealmyre, at Pingle Lodge Farm, remembered one of their dogs barking at the window after hearing some disturbance outside, the court heard.

Mrs Boyce went to investigate but could not see anything, though she heard the barking of whippet dogs coming from Zealmyre before returning indoors.

The following morning, about 9am, Dale Boyce, one of the sons, was driving along Pingle Road and noticed a G-registered light coloured vehicle coming towards him. Mr Munday said this could have been a return visit or it was possible that the vehicle had remained at the Sheridan's overnight.

Mrs Becker phoned the Sheridans' home on 8 January to say she was going out and phoned a similar message on 9 January to ask if Janice had collected *Dog World* because she had not seen her about. Each time the answerphone cut in, Mr Munday said.

On 10 January dog breeder John Bromiley and his girlfriend Miss Sylvia Flatt called the police to Zealmyre after Janice failed to arrive for work at Mr Bromiley's kennels as usual. Miss Flatt had been to the house and called Mr Bromiley there when the back door was found unlocked. The couple used their expertise to control the dogs while police entered the house.[33]

When they reached the front room they found the door had been blocked by a statuette and a settee. Police discovered the bodies of Janice and Constance in that room, Mr Munday told the court. Forensic scientists carried out comprehensive sampling in the room. Constance had suffered bruising on the skull and eight separate stab wounds to the front of her chest, also one to the

---

[33] In due course, compare the use of dog experts by the police in Tony's case.

stomach and one to the left forearm. The stab wounds had gone through the clothed body with enough force to penetrate the breast bone and fracture some ribs, said Mr Munday. There were also injuries to her hand indicative of fending off the assault. "It's likely she received her wounds in that location," said Mr Munday.

Janice Sheridan was found with her back on the floor and her feet raised on an armchair with her head pointing towards the hearth. The front of her jumper had been cut in a ragged way from the bottom to the top and then either pulled or fallen to the side. Her bra had been undone and pulled over her head so it was behind her neck. She was wearing no trousers or skirt. Her knickers were down and inside-out and her ankles were bound with thick, black adhesive tape. On moving the body there was found to be a wound between the shoulder blades. The wound to the front of her chest had been inflicted after the cutting of the clothing and its removal to one side, said Mr Munday.

He added it was obvious to the forensic scientists at the scene that not only had her feet been bound but also at some stage her wrists had been bound, presumably with similar tape.

Post-mortem examinations also revealed faint bruising to the shins, hand, back of the head and a series of stab wounds. It was the pathologist's view that some of the injuries to the hands were consistent with defensive actions, said Mr Munday.

He added blood splashes were found on the hearth and it was considered the wounds would have been inflicted in the position where the body was found. Blood spots were found on nearby photographs and fingerprints found on the mounts of them, and a thumb print was discovered on the hearth.

"It is clear that the defendant, having killed both the Sheridans, left the premises, locking them and taking with him the keys," said Mr Munday. [Author's note: Notice how this contradicts the evidence of Sylvia Flatt who discovered the back door *unlocked*.] Extensive police inquiries were carried out and everyone living in the immediate area was questioned and re-questioned to see if any additional facts might be revealed, Mr Munday said.

All those who had been to the premises were sought, found and interviewed. Among those was Mr Cotterell. The court was told that in 1996 the Sheridans had the front windows of their home replaced by Anglian Windows. In 1998 one of the Anglian Windows employees called to make another sale and an appointment was made, and Mr Cotterell, who was working as a salesman, visited the house on 3 June 1998.

He told the police that he had only gone to the kitchen and middle room where the windows were to be replaced and no other room. In April 1999 at the time of his arrest, the defendant was claiming jobseekers' allowance but also on occasions working for Kleeneze supplying materials. When police examined his home they found two items of more than "passing interest", said Mr Munday.

They found a Kleeneze bag which contained the catalogue for customers which appeared to have blood on it, which was examined. There was also on the top of a wardrobe, on newspaper, a Swiss Army knife, which was also examined. But Mr Munday stressed that could not have been the murder weapon, which had never been found.

Also at the Pentney house was the defendant's car with the plate G567HVP. Mr Munday said the print on the hearth was a direct match with that of Mr Cotterell and the fingerprint on the mounts of the photographs which had been splattered with blood were also found to be Mr Cotterell's.

Footprints found in the dust on the hearth matched the sole belonging to him and were also found at his address. Blood on the Kleeneze bag matched that of Janice to the extent that there was a 1 in 43 million chance of it being anybody else. There was also a 23 million to 1 chance of the match with Constance's blood on the Kleeneze bag being that of anyone else. Mr Munday said the Swiss Army knife could have been used to cut the tape, there was blood and cell material on the hinge of the blade which was a mix of that from Janice, Constance and Mr Cotterell. Swabs taken from Janice's breasts again showed a mixture of DNA. The defendant was interviewed and agreed that he had visited their house in late May or early June of 1998 for the window manufacturer but that he had not returned there since. Mr Munday said Mr Cotterell had given a statement saying he had gone through the kitchen and into a room to measure a window. But he later changed his tune and said because of the dogs in the house he had not gone into that room at all but measured the window from the outside.

During further questioning after more material had been given to the police and he had been told his fingerprints had been found, he said he might have entered other rooms, including the lounge, to measure the windows. But he denied being in the house at any time since June 1998, or being involved in killing either of the Sheridans.

Mr Munday said the defendant had been before the court on one previous occasion on 8 November 1983 at Swaffham Magistrates' Court when he appeared for two offences of burglary committed in July that year for which he received a 12-month probation order.

Mr Munday said it appeared that during one of the burglaries the defendant had ejaculated on the bed and at the other he had scattered around women's underwear.

In mitigation, Mr Graham Parkins QC said his client had shown no history of violent incidents or psychiatric disorders. He told the court he could not answer the question as to why it had happened.

DI Paul Chapman, speaking after the hearing, said: "Kevin Cotterell is wicked and evil beyond belief. We cannot begin to imagine the pain and suffering he inflicted upon Constance and Janice in their own home. Our thoughts at this time are with their family and friends.

"I would like to take this opportunity to thank everyone living in and around Upwell for their co-operation and patience during what was a long and, at times, difficult inquiry. I would also like to pay tribute to my colleagues and the forensic science service who worked tirelessly to bring the investigation to a successful conclusion. This was an outstanding team effort."

He added that professionals (criminal psychologists) think it is a huge step from burgling a house to killing two women. "Therefore I am clearly interested in the intervening period between 1983 and 1999 and would like to speak to anyone who can tell us more about him."

He said the Sheridans' family had been very angry that they had not had the chance to hear why the two women had been murdered. "The difficulty from day one was a clear motive," he said. "There was an inference that it was sexual but no real proof and now officers hope Mr Cotterell will talk about why he killed them."

Describing Mr Cotterell as being "confident and arrogant" during interviews, Mr Chapman said there were still questions which remained unanswered."

It is not within the remit of this book to analyse or investigate that murder, but there were a number of issues I discovered in that case which called the police 'investigation' into question.

The police had apparently been looking for a green car with the number plate of G567PVF and yet Cotterell's was a silver Rover, with the number G567HVP.

And no apparent motive? The women had been burgled some 18 months previously and burglars would have noted what treasures lay within if they had not taken everything with them that they wanted.

Two: travellers would often go 'knocking' in the area asking if the householder wanted to sell any antiques.

Three: Janice Sheridan had vociferously opposed a travellers' site being allowed in the village.

Four: Janice Sheridan had just had a dog entered at Cruft's and perhaps someone – another whippet owner, perhaps – wanted her dead so that the dog could not be shown.

Five: a possible spurned lover.

Six: a possible adulterer – was Janice Sheridan going to reveal the name of someone having an extra-marital affair?

Seven: theft of a dog. Pedigree whippets command good money.

Eight: Whippets are often used in hare coursing, an activity in which huge sums of money often change hands.

Nine: a will – who would benefit from their deaths?

Ten: Janice Sheridan took photographs in her spare time – was she in possession of any compromising ones which someone didn't want circulated?

There are at least ten possible motives and yet Norfolk Constabulary were allegedly floundering around trying to establish *any* kind of motive.

Just three or four days before this double murder, Tony Martin suffered a burglary at Bleak House and when he got to hear of these murders, his fears for his own safety increased dramatically, as did that of many other locals.

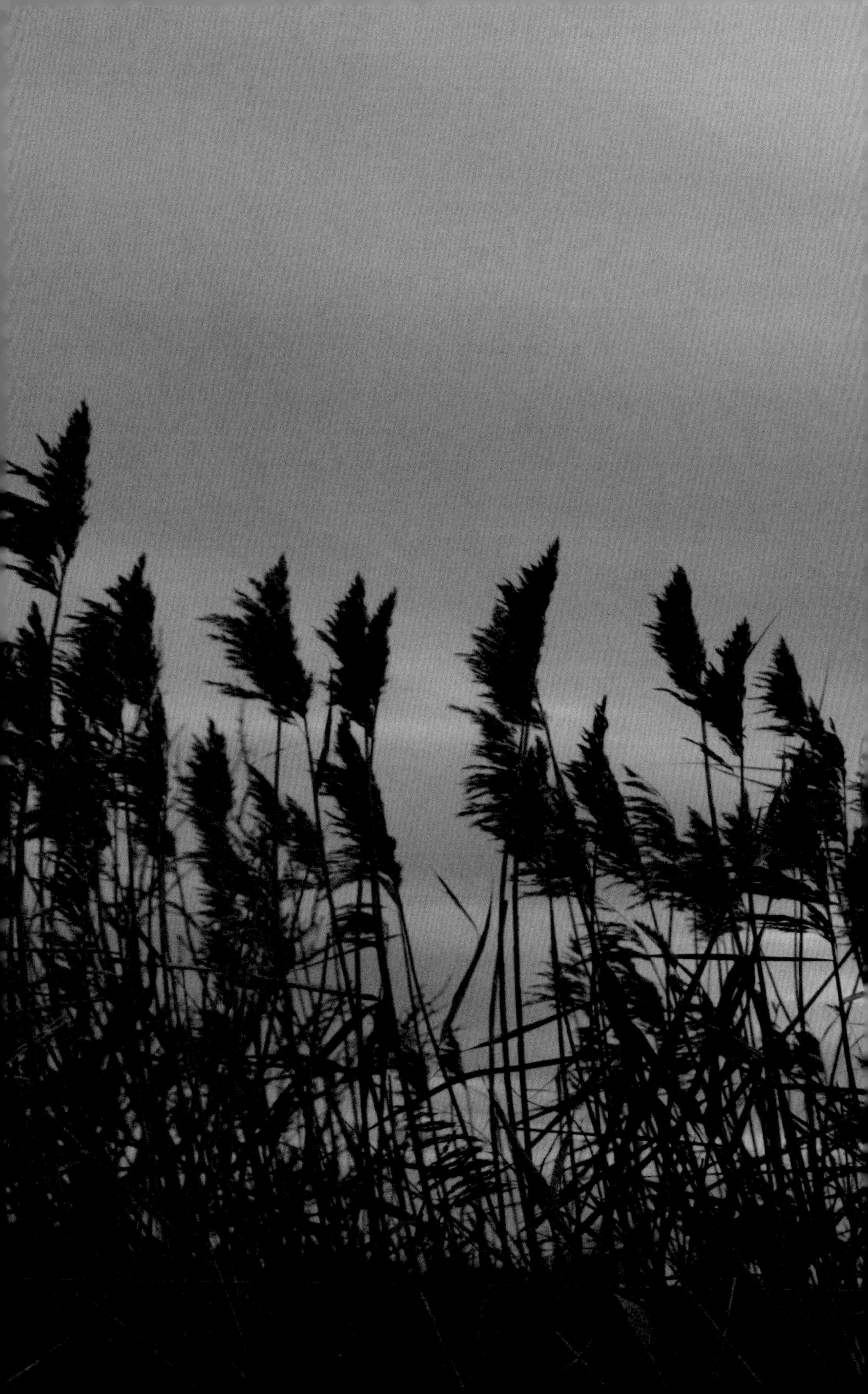

January–May 1999

Part 5: January – May 1999

We now turn to the fact that Tony had been burgled on two previous occasions in 1999 prior to the August shooting incident: in January and May. In the January, items which meant a great deal to him including photographs of his grandparents and other relatives were stolen. I've been privileged to have seen some of these photographs and it was obvious to me from the emotion in his voice just how much these photos and the people in them meant to him.

> **❝** I didn't bother reporting it, because experience had taught me that the police did nothing. Sometimes they even laughed at me, or said, "Oh no, not you again!" I was on medication for the blood clot on my lung at the time, and the burglary was yet another inconvenience I really could have done without.
>
> When I got home, I saw that there was extra daylight to be seen in the hallway and I realised that it was because the tall grandfather clock had been stolen. I was also employing contract labour at the time because of the blood clot on my lung and it crossed my mind that it might have been any one of them who had stolen the antique clock."

This was another in a long line of thefts and burglaries from Bleak House and the farm. It weighed heavily on Tony's mind.

Tue
23 FEB
1999
7 pm
54

Rod Herbert's engineering works, King's Lynn
After being informed at the last minute that a meeting of Farmwatch (www.farmwatchltd.co.uk) was ostensibly taking place for the benefit of farmers, Tony decided to attend. Strictly speaking, he had not been invited. The meeting was held in the canteen of Rod Herbert's engineering company and was run by a former firearms police officer known as Anthony 'Tony' Bone, who was accompanied by colleague Derek Stuart.

Thur
18 MAR
1999
6.30 pm
55

home address of Hugh Ward

Following the double murder of Janice and Constance Sheridan, the police were conducting house-to-house inquiries and fingerprinting all villagers over the age of 13 who were willing to submit to that process.

One of the villagers in Upwell was Hugh Ward, a very good friend of Tony's. While the police were at Mr Ward's house, Tony happened to arrive. Here's the witness statement of DC 417 Ian Abel, not made until 12 October 1999:

"At 6:30pm on Thursday, 18 March 1999, I was on duty in plain clothes with DC 105 Platt[34] at Baldwin House, Baldwins Drove, Outwell.

I was at the address for a pre-arranged meeting with the occupant, a Mr Hugh Ward. This was to obtain details and fingerprints of Mr Ward on the Sheridan murder enquiry.

I was there as part of a house-to-house enquiry team to obtain details and fingerprints of any person over the age of 13 years, with their consent, who lived within a 3 mile radius of the scene.

DC Platt obtained details of Mr Ward. After completing this, I took the fingerprints of Mr Ward. We were standing at the kitchen worktop by the side of the rear door, which was full glass. During the time I was taking the fingerprints, I was aware of a person standing outside the door. It was dark at the time. However, because of the close proximity, I could see the male person.

He raised his arms as if he was holding a rifle or shotgun. There was nothing in his hands. He said "Bang, bang – it would be as easy as that."

The man was invited in by Mr Ward who obviously knew the man and called him "Tony."

I cannot remember the initial conversation; however, it was obvious both Mr Ward and Tony were friends. We were identified by Mr Ward as police to which Tony stated he realised and was aware what we were doing from media publicity.

Tony I would describe as a male, white, approximately 55 years old, 5'7" tall, greyish, unkempt hair, thinning. He was wearing warm winter work type clothing. From conversation Tony had an unusual accent which from certain words was Australian, however very mixed.

Early during the conversation I asked for Tony's details which he refused on more than one occasion. We remained in conversation for some time. I cannot be specific what was said.

During conversation Tony mentioned that he had lived in Western Australia.

---

[34] DC Abel's statement refers to DC Platt. However, HOLMES has this person listed as DC Flatt. In order to keep the integrity of DC Abel's witness statement, I have left it as Platt. Please also note that a Sylvia Flatt visited the Sheridans' property on 10 January 1999 where it was claimed she discovered the back door unlocked.

However he had lived back in England for 20 years. The police in Australia had different ways of dealing with crime and criminals. Tony considered them to be harder and from the conversation was anti-British police. Tony related when he had farm machinery stolen, his contact with police was they could not help which he considered not appropriate.

I explained the reason for our attendance at Baldwin House and the fingerprint procedure. Tony again would not give any details but stated he lived beyond our catchment parameters. Tony had no information with regards to our enquiries. Prior to leaving he wished us well with our enquiries and hoped for a speedy conclusion.

On leaving Baldwin House, parked on the verge, gate area was a grey coloured Nissan Bluebird estate, C460APW, motor vehicle. This was not there when we had entered the house.

On returning to our office I completed various paperwork including a message form. I was not happy with Tony - however I could not do any more at that time.

Having completed a message form and obtained details of who I thought Tony was, I requested follow up enquiries to be done by officers already involved with the enquiry, action teams."

The statement attributed to DC Abel was dated some two months after the August shooting and *seven months* after the visit to Hugh Ward's house.

The statement attributed to his colleague DC 105 Paul Flatt was dated 27 September 1999, so it pre-dated DC Abel's version. They were practically word for word.

Wed
12 MAY
1999
evening
56

Bleak House
Less than three months after the Farmwatch meeting and four months after the Sheridan murders, Tony was burgled again in May 1999. It was this second burglary of that year which played on his mind more than any other because of what was stolen – sentimental possessions that had once belonged to his Aunt Gladys (who, according to Tony, left him the farm in her will) and his grandmother.

As in the January burglary, items such as irreplaceable photographs had been removed from the property – and we are forced to ask ourselves why. They had no extrinsic monetary value – but to Tony they were of inestimable worth.

Did the burglars specifically target these items? Were they privy to inside information that the theft of such items would cause Tony considerable emotional distress? Or were they just randomly removed, along with other far more valuable items? Was Robin Martin somehow involved? And was Tony Martin being set up to fail by – if not Norfolk Constabulary in its entirety - then certain rogue officers within that force?

Whilst this might sound somewhat far-fetched, or part of a grand conspiracy against Tony Martin, let's hear what he has to say next:

> I went out to Wisbech the night I was broken into: 12 May 1999. I have often wondered whether people were watching my home to see when I would leave it.
>
> A few days later a man named 'Smithy' who worked for Fred Deptford's opposite my place, found some photographs and tapes in a dyke six miles from here at Marshland St James and when he began to play the tapes he recognised my voice and brought the photos and tapes back to me. I was grateful to him for that. The police had done nothing.
>
> I am not anti-police, but I do feel that people in this country deserve a much better deal. I think the police are in denial. I want a public inquiry into policing in this country – it's inadequate and unprofessional and driven by statistics, not based on common sense or humanity or decency. Where is the morality in all this?
>
> And then, of course, there have been issues of police corruption with Hillsborough, Plebgate and the Stephen Lawrence inquiry. It's all wrong and I believe that the Great British Public deserves a much better police force based not on corruption, but on integrity and decency."

It is evident that Tony was feeling let down by Norfolk Constabulary and that he was treated differently from others who'd reported crime. He had made numerous complaints to the police and his main concern was that they failed to listen to him or even record the thefts and provide him with a crime number.

It also seems apparent that this lack of assistance from the police was having a negative impact upon his emotional state of mind at a time when his physical prowess was declining. Throughout his life, he had been involved in jobs which required a high degree of physical exertion and, although not a particularly big man in terms of height or his physical frame, he is, nevertheless, a solid man with a robust physique developed over several decades of manual labour. At his age – 55 – he was aware of his middle years and the lack of physical agility that was inexorably descending upon him. The blood clot on his lung had taken its toll of both his physical and emotional health.

I believe that this 'drip-drip' effect of a lack of action from Norfolk police in the rural outposts was causing Tony Martin great emotional stress. Farmers and country folk in general were becoming alarmed at the rapid rise in crime in rural areas which coincided with the closures of police stations and the significant reduction in personnel.

From what we have seen in this chapter, it is evident that Tony Martin – like so many others in rural communities – was the victim of crime.

On 12 May 1999, Bleak House was targeted again. One of those involved was said to have been Christopher Webster who had been traced because of a dropped cigarette end which Tony had discovered in the house after the burglary and the DNA from that butt allegedly led to Webster.

Just before midnight, Tony called the police to report the burglary. [See also entries **181** (Pauline Webster) and **260** (DS Paul Watson).]

Thur
10 JUN
1999
2.10 pm
57

Bleak House
The witness statement below is attributed to King's Lynn-based PC 656 Jim Welham.[35]
We would do well to note that it was created after the shooting incident in August and not written immediately after his visit to Bleak House in June as we might reasonably expect.

"On Thursday 10 June 1999 I was attached to the CID. At 2:10pm that day, as a result of a written message from PC Wells, I went to Bleak House.
I had great difficulty finding the premises, although I was in the right area. The house stood in the middle of what appeared to be a solid mass of trees and vegetation.[36]

I saw a male person dressed in a green beret wearing sunglasses and overalls standing in the undergrowth watching me.

I asked him if he was Mr Martin.

He refused to answer.

I introduced myself and said that I had come at his request.

He then agreed that he was Anthony Martin and spent a considerable time making anti-police statements about pension schemes, ill health benefits, early retirements, bad management and anything else he could think of that might offend me.

It was a pleasant sunny day and I sat on the bonnet of my car waiting for him to finish his tirade[37] which after about an hour he did.

We then had a more sensible conversation about him being a product of Glebe House School, Hunstanton which he described as a breeding ground for homosexuals.[38]

---

[35] Dated 23 August 1999, three days after the shooting incident.
[36] Notice how PC Welham claimed that he couldn't find the house in the afternoon in June. Yet in earlier reports (entry **31**), PC Gooderson had found it easily enough *at night*.
[37] At public expense.

He seemed to have a particular dislike of criminals, in general, and gypsies in particular.

He mentioned several times a suspicious white transit van, and a burglary at his house where property had been recovered at Wisbech and a cigarette end that had been dropped in his house. He said it must have been dropped in his house by a burglar as he had not dusted his house for years and did not smoke.

I was not sure whether he was talking about a genuine burglary or if it was just a figment of his imagination.[39]

His conversation would be disjointed and he would talk about putting gypsies in one of his fields surrounded by barbed wire then machine gun them,[40] and then said how he stank like a polecat because he was eccentric.

He returned several times to talking about a transit that had been on his land a month before the burglary, and that a similar one was just up the road.

I asked him where it was and he said that I would have to find it myself. After a while he changed his mind and at his request I drove him to a nearby house where he pointed out a carpet seller's transit as being similar, but not the same.

He showed interest in the Sheridan's murder, and said that although their location was described as isolated, it was nothing like as isolated as his.

I was unable to glean any real information about the burglary which had happened several weeks previously. I eventually left Bleak House with no idea of what he had wanted.[41]

I searched the crime system but could find no trace of the burglary. I later discussed the matter with SOCO DC Aldous."

What this adds to our knowledge

PC Welham appeared to have little grasp of the role of a police constable and seemed particularly inept about the burglary in May – he seemed uncertain as to whether it had even occurred. He stated that he could find no record of it on the crime system – yet Tony had reported it on the night of the crime having occurred: 12 May 1999 and that call *had* been recorded (according to the police).

---

[38] Tony insists that he mentioned child abuse that he suffered there and it would appear that PC Welham (or a senior officer) has diluted the statement to omit this.
[39] That sentence is complete nonsense. He admitted that he had attended Bleak House after being asked to by PC Wells because Tony had reported a burglary.
[40] Where was the evidence that Tony had ever said this? Tony refutes it. Did the constable note it down in his pocket book? If so, why did he not produce it?
[41] Surely this shows the inadequacies of the constable's ability to communicate with members of the public.

It was this sort of ineptitude, mis-reporting and downright lies from constables that infuriated Tony and many others in the area.

Yet, at this time, the police failed to properly investigate this second burglary of the year, leaving Tony Martin with the only option left to a reasonable person – to take the law into his own hands.

When I spoke with Tony about this visit he remembered it well. His view was that PC Welham was "three sheets to the wind" and he had told the farmer that he had just returned from sick leave.

Thur
13 MAY
1999
11.35 am
58

Bleak House

Official records show that a statement was made by King's Lynn-based SOCO DC Rick Aldous about this burglary, but not until 21 September 1999 (four months after the event and a month after the shooting incident):

"At 11:35am on Thursday 13 May 1999, I was on duty and attended at Bleak House. The house is in a very remote location and completely hidden by trees.[42] Entry believed gained via the front door. The front door was partially open and an item of furniture, believed a chest of drawers or similar, had been abandoned in the doorway. I was taken by a Mr Martin, into a ground floor room, where a chest of drawers had been stolen from. *The house was in a very dirty run down condition.*[43] I seized a cigarette end from the floor of the room, exhibit RA/1.

At 2pm the same day, I placed the cigarette end in the freezer in the scenes of crime office at King's Lynn police station."

What this adds to our knowledge	DC Aldous would ordinarily have made a statement in relation to this burglary soon after the crime itself – not some 4 months later and – rather conveniently for the police – after the August incident. Note that there was no mention of DC Aldous or anyone else taking fingerprints but it is clear from PC Wells' statement dated **27 August 1999** that Tony had told him someone had taken fingerprints.

---

[42] The house was not (and is not) "completely hidden by trees". This is a deliberately engineered and misleading statement designed to bolster the police's false claims that they couldn't find the house on the night of 20 August 1999 and, as a consequence of which, Fred Barras had died.

[43] Author's emphasis. This sentence was completely irrelevant and serves no purpose as far as the burglary was concerned. It had been included to serve the false narrative being created by the police.

Tony had found the cigarette end and taken a great interest in the crime. He was not – and is not – the sort of man to "leave it up to the police".

Tony told me that when Aldous arrived at the house, the SOCO told the farmer that the butt was a "waste of time" and "could have been caught up in someone's shoe from King's Lynn." Aldous was based in King's Lynn and, annoyed at such nonsense, Tony's account is that he insisted that the SOCO take the butt away for forensic analysis, which is what eventually happened. Tony was incensed at the SOCO's "couldn't-care-less attitude to policing and crime". The farmer was not alone in also thinking that "the police seemed to be covering up for the criminals and they'd do anything *not* to conduct an investigation or make an arrest."

Norfolk Constabulary – particularly the Chief Constable, Kenneth Williams - were later to claim that Tony had not engaged with them and not reported crimes. Clearly he had reported this one because even DC Aldous admitted to having turned up at Bleak House and seen the forced entry via the front doors.

The question remains why nobody was promptly arrested.

A. R. GARNER

CMNETH HUNGATE

A shooting incident

Part 6: A shooting incident, 20 August 1999

Fri 20 AUG 1999 6 pm — 59

Wisbech St Mary & Emneth
Tony went to his mother's in Wisbech St Mary at around 4 o'clock and she offered to cook him a nice piece of salmon for his tea. He turned down her offer because it was getting late and, feeling that he ought to be getting back to Bleak House before it got too dark, he stayed until approximately 6pm. At this time, Hilary Martin (born 11 March 1918) was 81 years of age.

Fri 20 AUG 1999 (7 pm) — 60

Newark, Nottinghamshire
According to official records – which we do not have to believe - unemployed Darren Bark and 'career criminal' Brendon Fearon prepare to leave Newark to drive down to burgle Bleak House of its 'smalls'. It was said that they intended to pick up 16-year-old traveller Frederick Jackson Barras, who has just been released from Newark police station with a Bail Notice in his back pocket.

Fri 20 AUG 1999 8.10 pm — 61

Balderton, Newark, Nottinghamshire
Approximately 2½ miles to the southeast of Newark, the village of Balderton lies between the B6326 and the A1 and is close to the start of the alleged burglars' journey that night. In a statement attributed to PC 2030 Andrew Knight of Nottinghamshire Constabulary,[44] he explained why he allegedly stopped the car said to have been driven by Bark en route to Bleak House:

"At 8:10pm on Friday 20 August 1999 I was on uniformed mobile patrol in a fully liveried Volvo patrol car registration number P341HRB. At this time I was on Main Street at Balderton near Newark. I saw a white Ford Granada saloon car registration F98LHJ travel along London Road (from Newark town centre towards Balderton) and then turn left onto Main Street. I followed the vehicle containing three males which then turned left onto Warwick Road.

I illuminated the blue beacon lights fitted to the patrol car and I caused the vehicle to stop. I alighted from my patrol car and approached the driver of the Granada; I recognised the driver to be a man called Darren Bark. In the front passenger seat was a black male whom I know to be Brendon Fearon. In the rear

---

[44] According to official records, this statement was made on 21 August 1999.

seat of the vehicle was a younger white male of slim build, aged approximately 18 years with short cut dark brown hair, tall with casual clothing. I believed this male to be called Fred Barras.[45]

I carried out a check of the vehicle before issuing the driver Bark with a form HORT/1 to produce his documents at Newark police station. The form was also issued to Bark for a defective tyre. He produced his driving licence to me at the roadside."

Now, we should consider that the time of 8:10pm had been supplied by PC Knight. As far as I have been able to tell from all the documents in this case, that time has never been confirmed. Although I believe we would do well to challenge the time, for the purposes of this book and the narrative that unfolds, I continue to use it as the starting point for all subsequent timings on the night of the shooting based on official records (in which I have little faith).

We would do well to consider that PC Knight didn't provide a reason for stopping the car – he told us that he issued a form about a defective tyre after he had carried out a check. In light of other evidence which you'll come to read, I challenge his real reason for stopping the car and I also challenge the time.

The official list of Exhibits at trial did not contain this alleged HORT form and thus it was not shown to the jury as proof that it even existed. However, according to his statement dated 28 September 1999, DS Peters took possession of this form. If this is true, why wasn't it entered into evidence in court? DC Peters' statement is listed in HOLMES at line S14e.

Fri
20 AUG
1999
(8.15 pm)
62

Balderton, Newark
According to official records, Fearon, Bark and Barras leave town at approximately 8:15pm on their way to Emneth. This assumes that they were stopped at 8:10pm and detained by PC Knight for no longer than five minutes. However, if this time is correct, then it would mean that they could not have arrived in Emneth any earlier than 9:45pm and this time becomes critical.

The following account has been produced from various documents regarded as "official" but which clearly show that there was something seriously amiss with that "official" narrative.

As you will read, Tony fell asleep and shortly afterwards was awoken by an unknown number of intruders smashing their way into his home. Note my use

---

[45] This 'fact' is challenged (entries **63** & **183**) by a sighting of Barras with a group of lads in Eton Road, Newark at between 8:15 and 8:30pm. If true, then he could not have been in the car at the time it was stopped by PC Knight.

of the word 'intruders' and not 'burglars' because the distinction needs to be pointed out.

His neighbours, the Leets, down at the Hungate Corner, said he'd called round to theirs "sometime between 9:30 and 9:45pm" *after* he'd discharged his shotgun at the 'intruders'.

According to Tony this was his *second* visit to their bungalow that night, so that would put the time that he fired his shotgun at anywhere between 8pm and 8:30pm (it taking him about three or four minutes to drive from his house to the bungalow.) But – according to the farmer's own account –he had also performed a number of other activities after firing his shotgun from the stairs which I have calculated to take about 32 minutes before driving to the Leets' bungalow. We need to factor all this in to provide a realistic timescale.

And the reason this causes the authorities great difficulties is that – according to the "official" documents, the 'burglars' didn't arrive at the track leading to Tony's house until 9:45pm *at the very earliest*. This would mean, of course, that according to the official evidence, Tony could not have shot the 'burglars' because he'd already fired his shotgun and called round to the Leets.

Fri 20 AUG 1999 (8.15 - 8.30 pm) 63	**Eton Road, Newark** *According to witness John Dolan, an uncle to Fred Barras, he saw his nephew Fred walking along Eton Road, Newark at about this time. "He was with about four or five younger lads who I didn't know. Fred wasn't carrying anything and I could see that he smiled at us. I waved to him and Fred waved back. As I drove on I watched Fred in my rear view mirror and saw him waving to us as we drove out of view."*

If this statement is true (and not an uncle covering something up), then this changes everything we were told about the shooting. If Fred Barras was still in Newark between 8:15 and 8:30pm, he could not have arrived in Emneth until 9:45pm at the very earliest. Which means that Tony Martin could not have shot him because, as already pointed out, the farmer had called round to the Leets around 9:30pm having already fired his shotgun inside his house and undertaking several other activities over a half-hour period.

If true, this statement suggests that Barras must have been killed by someone other than Tony Martin and possibly elsewhere. Which means that the farmer was always innocent of the crimes alleged against him.

If this statement has been fabricated to place John Dolan and/or Fred Barras up in Newark around 8:30pm and not elsewhere (such as in the Emneth area), then this also serves the farmer well because it is fraud and fraud negates any trial and any verdicts arising from that trial.

Yet, having this statement in their possession, the police and the CPS did not call Mr Dolan to trial for obvious reasons – there could be no trial with it.

However, Tony's barrister ought to have called Mr Dolan as a witness and his failure to do so shows that he acted against his client at trial.

Fri
20 AUG
1999
(8.32 pm)
64

Foreman's Bungalow,[46] **Hungate Corner, Emneth**
According to Tony Martin, he called round at the Leets' home about this time after having fired his shotgun when intruders smashed their way into his house. As you will read in future entries, the Leets claim that they were not in when he first called round to them that night, and you'll also read wildly different timings from this point onwards as the police sought to create a false narrative.

As you will read in a later entry (**273**), a Mrs Christine Clarke believed that she heard shots at no later than 8pm but after 7:30pm. *There were two distinctive shots about 1-2 seconds apart."* Mrs Clarke's statement was unused. Tony's barrister failed to call her as a witness in support of his client.

Fri
20 AUG
1999
(8 - 8.30 pm)
65

Bleak House, Emneth
For the first time ever, this is Tony Martin's account of an unknown number of intruders smashing their way into his farmhouse and of his firing his shotgun. We should note that he said that he had called at the Leets' house twice *that night and that they were either out or failed to answer the door when he first called round:*

> **❝** I drove home from my mother's, but was feeling rather tired and emotionally drained. I had had a blood clot on my lung a few months earlier and at this time I was on medication – Warfarin - for it. I was feeling tired because of all the rain we'd had (unusual for August) which might affect my harvest. This played on my mind a lot and, although I had always been a man whose work was based on physical activity, I was not in the best of health in August 1999, either physically or emotionally. My home had been broken into in the January and again in the May and the failure of the police to investigate caused me great concern. I couldn't

---

[46] The police refer to Foreman's Cottage throughout their records. There is a sign in a window referring to 'Foreman's Bungalow'. It is a bungalow and so I continue to call it this throughout, except in police statements (in order to maintain their integrity.)

understand where the world of the 1950s and '60s had disappeared to. When honour and integrity meant something. When people respected each other's property and when folk would look out for one another. I was born into a world of a civilised lifestyle and it's gone. I think it's gone forever and I mourn for its return.

When I got back home, I went to my bedroom on the first floor. I had a copy of *Farmers Weekly* with me and lay on my bed to read it, knowing that sooner or later I would fall asleep.

I was fully dressed and still had my boots on. Contrary to popular opinion, and what was put out by the media (especially by ITV in their error-strewn documentary called *A Shot in the Dark*), I did not have a shotgun at my side. It was on the floor under the bed, weighed down by two large piles of heavy newspapers. Until the burglaries, I had never had a gun in the house. My guns were locked away in a large safe in the garage, some way from the house itself."

I didn't particularly like the way I was living, but it suited my needs at that time. I wanted to clear my house of furniture because of the dust that had accumulated from knocking down walls and so on, so I removed a lot of furniture to other locations.

I'm not sure how long I'd been asleep when I was suddenly woken by loud noises downstairs. I had effectively secured all the points of entry into the house and felt like something of a prisoner in my own home. I didn't realise it at the time, of course, but my lifestyle was a precursor to prison life. I went down the blacksmith's, David Patrick at Martin Works in Wisbech, to order steel straps to bolt across the inside of the main external doors so that I couldn't use them anymore and my animals could no longer use them. I felt that I couldn't have anybody in my own house any more. I even said to myself, 'Tony, this isn't a home any more, it's more like a prison'."

The noises seemed to me as though the end of the house had fallen down; I also considered whether a dog was in there but that didn't make sense to me as there was so much banging and crashing and the sound was too loud. I then thought it might have been a cat, but that wasn't a sensible idea either, so I ended up returning to my original thought that it must be intruders. When I heard that crashing noise, I instinctively knew in that precise moment that I had serious problems. I tried to cushion the blow: could it be this, or could it be that, but I had told myself to listen to my brain, to trust my initial gut reaction ... and I heard a lot of banging and crashing which meant in my mind that I had intruders again – for the third time in just eight months.

I had no idea of the number of intruders, though at least three[47] had been involved in the burglary in May, so my first thoughts were that there must be at least three again this time and that perhaps the same people had come back to rob my home again. But I could not be sure about the number of intruders and to this day I still don't know how many there really were inside or outside my house that night.

I just couldn't understand why I had intruders. Who would do such a thing? Why would anyone want to do such a thing? I was living my life and not interfering with anyone else and I just wanted to get on with my life and farm my land.

My silver Nissan car was parked on the drive, so anyone coming up the drive to burgle Bleak House must surely have seen my car there. Bruno, one of my three rottweiler dogs, was patrolling the grounds around the house, but he did not start barking until after the loud noises that woke me up. The intruders must have been aware of Bruno, and, although I didn't think this at the time, upon reflection, they must have known that someone would be around to feed him or take him in at night. Anyway, I got it in my mind that the intruders knew I was in the house at that moment in time and I couldn't understand what they were doing in my house.

All of these thoughts were going through my mind as I lay on my bed. As strange as it may sound, one part of me just wanted to turn over and go back to sleep. Perhaps it was a defence mechanism.

I felt like I was a prisoner in my own home, which is laughable – how can anyone be a prisoner in their own home? Why should anyone have to go through what I kept going through? I was still struggling to get over the devastating experience of the burglary in May. The only difference between prison and your home is that someone else locks and unlocks your door. At home you lock yourself up at night to keep yourself safe and that is what I thought I had done.

Immediately my body went into a state of 'High Alert' at the noises in the dark below. I realised that I had an unknown quantity in my house. This fact alone places a person under immense stress and when you are under such intense danger and the fact that it was at night time, every sound becomes considerably magnified.

From a distance, I heard the sound of muffled voices, but they sounded foreign to my ears. I didn't recognise what they were talking about. I had employed foreign workers on the farm the previous year to pick the apple harvest and the thought crossed my mind that they might have returned to burgle me. They had made remarks about my property

---

[47] In a subsequent entry you will read that one of the burglars on that job said that the team was much larger than three.

being run-down and I thought, "What's that got to do with you?" The thing is, at such moments of great stress, hundreds of thoughts cross your mind. I had visions that the intruders would hit me with a piece of broken brick which they could use to smash me in the face. This was a fear of mine.

I decided to leave the sanctuary of my bedroom and go out on to the landing to try to assess the situation. Obviously I wanted to make as little noise as possible because the floorboards, being old, were very creaky. I crept out of my room and on to the landing. Even this relatively simple manoeuvre was fraught with danger because, once outside of my bedroom, I had to go through my bathroom and then into the hallway at the top of the stairs.

There is a recess in the wall of the hallway and anybody might have been standing there ready to ambush me. As I made my way towards the top of the stairs, I listened intently to the noises below, and I was very careful on the landing so as not to give my position away. I didn't want a confrontation. The voices grew slightly louder but still sounded foreign to me; at any rate the voices were not on my wavelength and they were largely unintelligible to me. Other people might have heard the voices differently, but to me they were unintelligible and this caused me further concern. A sense of panic and terror flooded over me. I knew I was alone. I knew I was isolated. I knew I was outnumbered. You are faced with an unknown quantity in your own home in the middle of the night with your nearest neighbour at least a quarter of a mile away.

This frightened me, but my fear increased significantly when suddenly I heard the clink of metal. This sound of aluminium scared me. My heart jumped. My throat became instantly dry. My body stiffened. It also confirmed what I had suspected when I first heard the crashing noises that had awoken me: I had intruders who were moving about in my home. In my mind, the clinking sound of metal had only one meaning: that the intruders were at the bottom of my stairs where I had placed an aluminium ladder in the shape of a letter 'M' to temporarily replace the rotten treads and risers on that part of the staircase. I later learnt at trial that the police claimed that this was a booby trap, but in my view booby traps are hidden and this ladder was in plain sight and used by me to climb up and down my stairs.

I decided that my best course of action was to retreat to my bedroom. As slowly and as quietly as I could, I inched my way through the darkness, from the landing to the bathroom and from the bathroom to my bedroom. All the time I moved away from the landing and back to my bedroom, the fear in the back of my mind was that the intruders might be planning to come up the stairs behind me, and this increased my previous burglary.

As my mind leap-frogged from one apparently unconnected thought to another and as funny as it might sound now, thoughts about the harvest were also racing around my head. The wheat was ready to harvest and I was worried because it had already started to chit with all the rain we'd had in the past month. I remember thinking 'I must sort that out tomorrow and get the harvest in, even if I have to put it in the drying shed.' My mind pushed thoughts about the harvest to one side, and my survival instinct took over again.

I was vying with different problems and different solutions. I was alone. It was dark. I was living in a remote part of the country. There was an unknown number of intruders in my house. I did not know if they were armed. I did not know how many there were. I did not know if they would kill me. I had no idea about their intentions that night.

I overcame my fear and decided to get the gun. Overcoming my fear gave me the courage to walk into the unknown. I scrambled around under the bed and was confronted by two large piles of old newspapers. Layer upon layer of out of date papers, all on top of one another. Paper can be very heavy when there is a lot of it piled up and I struggled to lift the papers up and take out the gun, which was lying on the floor. I eventually managed to work my hands and arms underneath the layers of papers to what I could tell was the gun, so I pulled that out. My intention was simply to protect myself.

I had no malice aforethought. It was not pre-meditated. I had a carrier bag of shotgun cartridges but I don't even know how I got the cartridges into the chamber, or even how many I put into the gun. I felt like an automaton and my conscious mind was focussed on my survival, and not on counting the number of cartridges.

I left my bedroom with the loaded gun in my hand, but although I had the gun, I still didn't want a confrontation; I didn't actually want to use it.

My mind leap-frogged back to the sound created by the aluminium ladder. My brain had already associated the clink of aluminium with the ladder at the bottom of my stairs which, to my mind, meant that the intruders might be coming up the stairs after me.

I panicked. My mind raced away with the thought that the intruders were on the ladder and coming up the stairs.

My mind was focused on the ladder at the bottom of the stairs and so I had the realisation that I had to go down the stairs. I was trying to understand what was happening down there. I moved out of my bedroom, through the bathroom and onto the landing.

At this point, the blood was rushing at great speed through my body and the sound of it rushing through me is a sound that has stayed with me to this day, because it's not something you normally hear, of course. My heart was pounding furiously. There were rushing noises in my head. I considered stopping on the landing at the top of the stairs and let them come up to me, but I didn't like that option and I quickly dismissed the idea.

As I moved towards the stairs, I saw a light. Yet the light was strange – it was like a goldy colour, like the light from a car's headlights. How many people there were and how many torches there were I don't know. This only served to make me feel more confused and disoriented. I thought I had the advantage but when I realised that I didn't have the advantage, I was in a frantic situation once again.

I went two or three steps down the staircase, just enough for me to crouch down and peer into the breakfast room. I had a torch, but it didn't come on. It was difficult walking down the stairs with a torch and a shotgun in my hands. Although it didn't come on, I didn't dare drop the torch because that would have made a noise and alerted the intruders. This was all happening in a split second. Time became distorted again. It was as if I was in some kind of time-warp with time racing at the speed of light and also being funereally slow.

I saw some reflection in some feet[48] and there looked a lot of feet to me and I had also heard this murmuring. It wasn't audible speech – at least to me. Suddenly, and without any prior warning, a flashlight shone in my face, temporarily blinding me and my instant reaction was to pull the trigger but when I pulled it nothing happened and I became frantic. Then I found that the gun wasn't cocked. Realising that it was a pump-action shotgun, I pumped it, and it fired. I do not recall the number of times I fired. I heard no noises. No voices. No shouts. Everything was still pitch-black. Now that I had fired the gun, I hoped that whoever was in there would go and never return.

Then there was complete silence. It was tranquil. It was as though the place had been cleansed.

I turned round and went back upstairs. I went to the bedroom and I seemed to be in a state of turmoil. I took my hat off and threw it on the bed. I wanted to lie down; I was physically and emotionally exhausted.

I sat on the bed, and thought about going back to bed, but reasoned that I couldn't, so I put my hat back on again and decided to go downstairs.

I couldn't see what had happened or what was in the breakfast room. I then went outside into the car and got another torch.

I went back inside the house and then shone the torch around the

---

[48] Having seen "some reflection in some feet" suggests, of course, polished boots. Tony wouldn't have seen a reflection in the trainers worn by any 'burglars' that night.

breakfast room. I noticed that the intruders had removed the window in the breakfast room.

As I turned away from the window, I kicked over some bricks and bottles and cans.

Not far from an old Welsh dresser, I found a holdall bag. I thought I'd look inside it. With my mind in turmoil, I didn't really know what had happened. I thought I'd better be careful because I'd have to involve the police again since I'd had yet another break-in. The intruders had already taken some small items of silver out of a cupboard and put them into the holdall. I had personally bought these items – mustard pots, sugar bowls and cream jugs - from various auctions.

I then went out to the car. I was still frantic and couldn't find my car keys. Then I noticed that they were actually in the car. I took the gun with me and put it in the car for safekeeping.

As I drove down the driveway looking for any intruders, I had visions of people appearing from behind the bushes or trees and throwing things at me, like bricks or bottles.

I manoeuvred out across the field and went down the drove at the back of my house. I couldn't see anybody there. I reversed out because I couldn't go any further forward down the lane because of the horses on my land. I wondered whether the people who put the horses there without my permission were the same people who had broken in.

I went round the back through the yard, down the side of the orchard and round down the bottom where I saw the conker nut tree, as far as the other end of the garden.

I turned round and got up the other end to where the house is. I sat in my car on the lawn with my headlights on and looked at my house with a window missing in the breakfast room. It already felt as though it was no longer my home.

I have been told by the police that the gaping hole where my window had been was where the intruders had not entered my house but where they had exited from.

I had my car at a slight angle, facing the bushes, with my headlights full on because I was worried that intruders might be hiding in the bushes, but I saw nobody.[49]

I told the police in my second interview that as I drove around I could see there was a heavy dew on the ground and yet wherever I went I couldn't see any footprints and I couldn't see any tyre marks on the grass.

---

[49] These are the very bushes in which the Police claimed they found Barras, with his legs sticking out of the bushes and with white trainers on his feet. Had he been there, it is inconceivable that Tony would not have seen him.

I didn't think of it at the time, but if the intruders came out of the window like the police claimed, why were there no footprints across the lawn? Obviously any intruders would leave footprints if they ran across my lawn but I definitely didn't see any, and I'm a tracker from my time in Australia – I notice things like that whereas most people wouldn't.

I drove around for a few minutes longer – I'm not sure exactly how long – but then I suddenly wanted somebody to talk to. I decided to go and see my nearest neighbours, Paul and Jacqueline Leet, because I knew that they'd had at least one break in during daylight, and Paul had told me about it and said, "If anybody had been in the house, the big lump of concrete which had been thrown through the bedroom window could have damaged somebody."

But the first time I went round there, they didn't answer the door, so I assumed they weren't in.

As I told the police in my interview, I was just going down to the Hungate corner when I saw a car coming fast so I turned around. I thought I'd chase it and it didn't actually act as though it felt that it was being chased this car, but he was going a fair speed down there. I got closer and closer to it and it was a sort of paley blue car and I think there was a single person in it but I'm not sure. I decided not to pursue it any further because I wanted to get back to the house.

I don't know how many times I went round the lanes. All this time I had the shotgun in my car and I was nervous because I knew that I had no licence for it.

I know I went round the garden once and then I went down to the Hungate corner again to see if the Leets were in.

This time they were in and I spoke with Paul Leet on his driveway. I told him that intruders had smashed their way into my house, that I didn't know how many there were, that I had fired off my shotgun to scare them away and that I'd been around my place and the lanes looking to see if anybody was still about.

While I was standing there talking to Paul Leet, I heard a noise and I thought 'What's that?' and then I heard a noise again, I said to him, "Can you hear that, Paul?" and he said, "Well, that's coming from the little orchard over there" and I thought 'Well, that's a long way over there.'

After leaving the Leets', I went driving round again for a few minutes before going to my mother's. I'm not sure of the exact time, but I got to my mother's about 10:30pm. She was getting ready for bed and I took the gun into the house and said something like: "I'll just drop this off for your safekeeping." I stood the gun in the kitchen dining area and left. I don't suppose I was in the house much more than 10 or 15 minutes though I might have been. I can't really be sure because of the terror I had just faced in my own home. From my mother's house, I then drove to Wisbech to see Helen Lilley at the Marmion House Hotel.

When I was in Bleak House I didn't use to feel any dirt or filth; it was my inner refuge where nothing hurt me. But all that calmness and tranquillity were stolen from me that night.

I was robbed of my home that night, too. A bedroom, to me, is like a badger's sett: it's a place of tranquillity, a place of safety, a refuge. I used to regard my bedroom as a retreat, but now it has come to be my last retreat from Bleak House. I've never lived there since ..."

There are a number of issues in Tony's account of that night which I believe need to be highlighted and discussed in greater detail in the interest of justice.

Surely the most important point in Tony Martin's entire account is that he states that he was terrified by an unknown number of intruders who smashed their way into his home and, in fear of his life, he felt forced to fire off a warning shot or two – just as he had done five years previously in the orchard.

Whether the intruders were (as some evidence suggests) police officers in a tactical operations exercise or Fearon and Barras or any of their accomplices actually matters little in respect of intent. If the intruders were police officers on an unlawful exercise, then he had every right to defend himself against such an unwarranted attack in any manner he saw fit. If the intruders were Fearon and Barras (as the police narrative ran) then Tony still had every right to defend himself by shooting low and not *at anybody*.

We also need to be mindful that Tony tells us that he was on medication for a blood clot and this played on his mind. He was frightened that he might have a stroke or heart attack because his body went into a state of 'High Alert' as he describes it. He envisaged people coming into his bedroom and this created terror; the terror and the panic attack were causing him immense emotional pain and stress, and this added to his fear that he might have a stroke. It was a vicious circle from which he felt there was no escape.

He tells us that his bedroom was his 'inner refuge' and that when he knew there were intruders in the house he immediately felt that he had been violated, a word used by many victims of burglary or rape.

He tells us that he had a gun concealed under his bed and that he overcame his inner fear when he decided to pick up that gun. In his own words he became courageous but still did not want a confrontation. Not wanting a confrontation surely suggests a lack of intent to commit murder or to wound. We should consider that the concurrence principle is particularly relevant here (as it is in *all* criminal trials actually): this means that the *actus reus* (the alleged criminal act) and the *mens rea* (the 'guilty mind' or intent) <u>must</u> coincide in time. According to Simester, Spencer, Sullivan and Virgo[50] this principle has an ancient pedigree.

---

[50] Simester and Sullivan's Criminal Law: Theory and Doctrine, Hart Publishing, 2010.

As long ago as 1798, Lord Kenyon described it as:

> "a principle of natural justice, and of our law, that *actus non facit reum nisi mens sit rea* (the act is not culpable unless the mind is guilty). The intent and the act must both concur to constitute the crime."

Needless to say, Tony's barrister at trial failed to get the jury to thoroughly consider the mental element of the charge of murder.

Tony was already tired prior to the encounter with the intruders and, in fact, he says they woke him up and I suggest that his thought processes were not as sharp as normal. Whose are when you've just woken up?

Then we come to the issue of the stairs. He firmly stated that he was on the stairs when he fired the shots. When he was on the stairs he says he was momentarily blinded by a light being shone in his face and in that moment he pulled the trigger. Does that suggest to you an intent to murder *anybody* – whether police officers or burglars? Or does it suggest that it was more like an automatic reaction to having a light shone in your face in the middle of the night by an unknown number of intruders in an unlit space?

Tony says he fired at least one further shot, but could not recall the precise number of shots he had fired. Are you concerned that he cannot recall how many shots were fired? I suggest not. Given the extreme fear that he was experiencing, given his focus on survival, given the fact that there was an unknown number of intruders inside his home, should we be concerned that he cannot recall precisely how many shots he fired? It seems more likely to me that he is telling the truth *because* he cannot recall the number of shots. Surely, if he was able to remain cool enough to recall the number of shots fired, that would lean towards him being cold and calculating and possessing, perhaps, a 'murderous intent'.

Now that you have read Tony Martin's account in his own words, do you believe it? Is it plausible? Is there anything about his account that doesn't seem to 'ring true' to you?

You may ask why he had a gun in the first place since there are many other ways to protect oneself. Since he didn't like shooting animals, it would seem that he kept the gun in the event that he would one day face intruders in his house. So, do you think he kept the gun so that he would one day cause serious injury or kill intruders, or just as a weapon to fire off warning shots?

I put forward the notion that his intent was exhibited by his firing in a *downward* trajectory. The issue of *intent* is of paramount importance: do you believe *beyond all reasonable doubt* that he intended to cause harm, or are you of the opposite opinion?

Perhaps before you come to such a conclusion, it's best we wait to consider the account given by Brendon Fearon, who survived the shooting. Note that I do not say "who survived the shooting *by Tony Martin*" because in my view, he was not shot by the farmer, but by others as I will reveal in forthcoming entries.

Fri 20 AUG 1999 (8.40 pm) 66

Bleak House, Emneth
According to his statement to the police under caution, having gone back upstairs after firing his gun to gather his thoughts, Tony then went to his car to get a torch. He's told us that he then went into the breakfast room where he found some of his silver mustard pots in holdalls which did not belong to him.

While this was going on *inside* the house, the official version is that Brendon Fearon and Fred Barras had exited the house via a rear window. Barras, having been shot in the leg as well as a lung, allegedly[51] collapsed into some small bushes just 15 feet (5 metres) from the house and to the left of the exit window. He was wearing white trainers.

Fearon, it is alleged, despite having around 200 shotgun pellets in his legs and groin, and blood pouring out of a large hole in his knee, managed to crawl through the rear garden, through the orchard and into a cornfield, where he collapsed. Do we believe that Fearon went on such an epic journey across Tony's farmland once he had sustained such serious injuries to his legs? There is, in fact, an alternative scenario once we meet John Spalton, the "Fenland eelman."

Fri 20 AUG 1999 (8.50 – 9.15 pm) 67

Bleak House, Emneth
Having seen a 'swag bag' in the breakfast room, Tony then left his house and drove around his land looking for any sign of the intruders as he struggled to make sense of the invasion to his property and a possible attempt on his life. He had the shotgun in his car, but removed a single cartridge from the gun which fell to the floor.

As we have read from his own account, Tony Martin drove to the rear of his house and saw that a window had been removed by the "burglars" as they fled the house. For obvious reasons, he didn't leave the safety of his car. According to official sources, the injured Barras, wearing white trainers, was lying just a few

---

[51] I use the word 'allegedly' because this is where the body was said to have been found. It does not necessarily follow that if he was found in the bushes he died there. He may well have been moved there.

feet away in some bushes with his legs sticking out.

So, if we are to believe the official version, why didn't the farmer see footprints belonging to the escaping burglars in the dew on his lawn and why didn't he see Barras's legs – with white trainers on his feet - sticking out of the bushes at the rear of Bleak House?

The following times are our best estimates based on Tony Martin's own account of his actions immediately after firing his gun. No-one (not even Tony Martin himself) can be completely sure of these timings but they are nonetheless critical to the case. I have based them on Tony firing his gun at 8:30pm (you will recall that Christine Clarke said "no later than 8pm"), but I have taken 8:30pm as an arbitrary time. I have also been extremely conservative in my time estimates. I believe that some of the activities undertaken would have taken slightly longer than I have allowed for.

In the interest of justice, and although I do not believe that he did, we should consider that Tony Martin may have lied about his activities after firing the gun.

Approx. time of day	Approx. length of time	Action as described by Tony Martin
8.30 pm	2 minutes	Fires gun; waits, walks back upstairs to bedroom
8.32 pm	2 minutes	Throws hat on bed; sits on bed, considers going back to bed; gets up and walks downstairs
8.34 pm	1 minute	Arrives in breakfast room; too dark to see; needs torch
8.35 pm	2 minutes	Goes to car, gets torch, back to breakfast room
8.37 pm	3 minutes	Back in breakfast room, looks around. Sees window removed. Sees no blood or pellets embedded. Kicks over bricks and bottles. Finds holdalls – looks inside. Decides to go back to car.
8.40 pm	30 secs	Back to car. Puts gun in car.
	30 secs	Drives down gravel driveway.
	2 mins	Drives down to drove. Sees nobody. Reverses out.
	2 mins	Drives down side of orchard to conker nut tree.
	1 min	Drives to back of house. Sits in car on lawn with headlights on. Looks at missing window.
	4 mins	Drives round again for 3-4 minutes.
	2 mins	Drives to Leets.
8.52 pm	90 secs	Pulls up. Gets out. Knocks on door. Waits. No answer. Gets back in car.
8.53.30 pm	90 secs	At Hungate Corner sees pale blue car driving fast – chases after it, then returns to house
8.55 pm	3 mins	Drives around lanes 3-4 minutes;
	2 mins	Goes round garden again,
	2 mins	Decides to return to Leets
9.02 pm		Arrives at Leets for second time. (Leets tell police Tony Martin called round to them between 9:30 and 9:45pm)

NOTES

1. If we accept that Tony fired his gun at 8pm, then he would have completed these tasks by 8:32pm.
2. If we accept the Leets *latest* time estimate of 9:45pm and deduct the 32 minutes from that, then Tony fired his gun at 9:13pm. On the police's own evidence, the "burglars" were still on their way down to Emneth and so the farmer could not have shot them.

Fri
20 AUG
1999
(9.45 pm)
68

Bleak House

The drive from Newark to Wisbech takes approximately 1½ - 2 hours by car at that time of day. According to all available records which I continue to challenge throughout this book, at approximately 9:45pm (although other evidence shows that it was later), it was alleged that Darren Bark,[52] Brendon Fearon and Fred Barras arrived in the Smeeth Road at the bottom of the track leading to Bleak House.

According to Bark and Fearon's witness statements (which we'll read in due course), Bark dropped Fearon and Barras at the bottom of the farm track and he went to park up on Moyse's Bank, a turning to the left off the Smeeth Road which faces Bleak House, though I must stress that the house could not be seen from the road because it sat some 400 yards away across a cornfield and in a clearing behind a copse of trees which shielded it from the road. I should also make it clear that, although the house could not be seen at all, any gunshots would carry on the still August night air because there was little noise pollution such as you'd get in a town or city.

Fri
20 AUG
1999
(9.30 - 9.45 pm)
69

Foreman's Bungalow, Hungate Corner, Emneth

According to statements attributed to Paul and Jacqueline Leet, Tony Martin called round to their home at "somewhere between 9:30pm and 9:45pm" to tell them that he had fired "at three burglars". Tony Martin says he didn't mention a specific number of intruders. In any event, the timing causes the police significant problems because it means that Tony fired at an unknown number of intruders BEFORE the alleged burglars had arrived in the area. The police, of course, tried to push the time of the shooting of Fearon and Barras towards this time so as to incriminate Tony for the shooting.

---

[52] This claim is challenged by two witness statements: one by Bark himself (see entry **118**) and his girlfriend Dawn Jepson (entry **189**).

Fri
20 AUG
1999
(10.30 pm)
70

Bleak House, Emneth

Records show that Brendon Fearon had allegedly crawled halfway across the cornfield and, exhausted and in need of urgent medical assistance, fallen on to his back to take a short rest before gathering up all his strength to continue towards the light in the Leets' bungalow.

And then something remarkable happens – something that was never mentioned in court for reasons which will become obvious.

Whilst lying on his back and looking up into the dark night sky – and remember, there is little light pollution out in the country – Fearon claimed to have seen a police helicopter fly across the cornfield and hover over Bleak House, its searchlight illuminating the farmhouse.

Why is this remarkable? According to Paul Leet, he claimed that neither he nor his wife called the police because, in his view, Tony was "eccentric" and his having fired his gun when there were intruders in his house was probably "just something and nothing."

So, if we believe him when he says that he didn't call the police, and if we believe Fearon when he says he saw a helicopter, how the heck did it get there?

Surely we are driven to conclude that either Leet was lying (why would he – what has he got to gain by lying?) or Fearon was lying (why would he – what has he got to gain by lying), or that their statements have been altered or that *someone else called the police*. If so, who called them? And why?

And we ought to at least consider (if only to reject it) that the police might well have been "in on the job" and knew that shots had been fired and so ordered up a helicopter. If the alleged burglars' car was really stopped en route at Balderton by the police, was this actually part of a police operation in which rogue officers were working alongside the burglars?

In my view, we have a major problem because a police helicopter doesn't suddenly appear in the sky without a process having taken place to put it there. Someone has to make a call to the police, someone within the police has to authorise the use of a helicopter because it's an expensive piece of kit, the machine has to be scrambled, and it has to fly from RAF Wyton (or elsewhere) to Emneth Hungate, a flying time of approximately 15 minutes. At the very least, that entire process would take 20 minutes. If, as Paul Leet said, Tony had called on him around 9:30 - 9:45pm, and if Tony's actions after the shooting had taken him about 32 minutes, then that would give us an approximate time of somewhere between 9 and 9:15pm when Tony fired his shotgun.

But that doesn't work because PC Knight said he stopped the alleged burglars' car at 8:10pm. If his encounter took at the very least 5 minutes, that would mean the drive from Newark to Emneth took only an hour. I don't believe it's possible. I've made that journey on a lot of occasions and it's a horrible one to make because of the amount of traffic and – particularly at that time of day and at that time of year – you almost always encounter a lot of farm traffic, which slows you down. No, something about the timings isn't right. But surely the simplest way to prove this is by ensuring that PC Knight attend court to show the HORT form that he claimed to have issued to Darren Bark and also to produce his pocket notebook.[53]

But the helicopter that Fearon claimed to have seen whilst lying on his back in the cornfield bothers me (for reasons you'll read about later). At this point, I ask you to think about who made the call that got the machine in the sky.

And, if it *was* there around 10:30pm, why didn't Paul Leet mention the helicopter in his statement to the police? Surely, since it's such a rare event at that time of night in the countryside, it's not something you'd omit?

So, I draw your attention at this point to four major problems: (1) the timings, (2) the helicopter, (3) the possible alteration of witness statements, and (4) the possibility that there were *two* separate helicopter flights that night.

Fri 20 AUG 1999 (10.30 pm) 71	**Redmoor House, Friday Bridge** *Timing is everything – particularly in a murder trial. After leaving the Leets', Tony drove back to Bleak House to let his dogs out. With two smashed windows, he knew he would not be able to sleep in his home that night. He then drove to his mother's house and left the shotgun in her kitchen for safekeeping. In a statement made the day after the shooting – so you would think it would be clear in her mind – Hilary Martin told police that Tony called round "about 10:30pm".*
Fri 20 AUG 1999 (10.50 pm) 72	**Moyse's Bank** *Fearon, having allegedly emerged from the cornfield into Moyse's Bank, claimed to have been knocked over by a van[54] driven by "eel fisherman" John Spalton.* *It is uncertain as to exactly how he arrived at the bungalow on the corner of Moyse's Bank and the Smeeth Road – the home of the Leets' – as discussed in future entries.*

---

[53] In the event, PC Knight produced neither the HORT form nor his pocket notebook at trial and Tony's barrister failed to ensure that due process was followed.

[54] This incident was told to me by Brendon Fearon himself in a telephone conversation in 2016. Within a month, I was unlawfully held in Norwich prison. There is no official record of this collision happening. See also Spalton's statement (entry **240**) for his statement which was entered into evidence in court. See also entries **522, 613**.

Fri	**Foreman's Bungalow, Hungate Corner, Emneth**
20 AUG	*Fearon, having apparently crawled through the cornfield, arrived at the Leets' bungalow at approximately the same time as Tony Martin was leaving his mother's. We are told that Jacqueline Leet made a 999 call at 10:53pm.*
1999	
10.53 pm	
73	

Tony put me in possession of a transcript of that call. It becomes a very important transcript for reasons which I'll explain as the narrative unfolds.

According to a statement which we'll read later, an ambulance arrived from Wisbech within four minutes. According to several police statements, no helicopter arrived. So now we must ask why an ambulance turned up and yet no police helicopter as a result of Mrs Leet's call. And, just as importantly, we are forced to ask how on earth an ambulance allegedly made the journey from Wisbech ambulance station to Tony's farm in four minutes – it's simply not possible, even exceeding the speed limit on blues and twos.

Clearly, if the helicopter Fearon claimed to have seen was flying around 10:30pm, then just how did it get airborne *before Fearon arrived at the Leets' house*? Or was Fearon lying? But if he was lying, what on earth did he have to gain by lying? Or had his statement been altered?

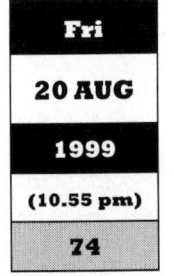

Fri	**armed response vehicle, King's Lynn town centre**
20 AUG	*According to official records, PC 485 Barry James Gotts and PC 338 Paul Derek Cant in their Norwich-based armed response vehicle (ARV) received a radio message about the shooting in Emneth at approximately 10:55pm whilst they were allegedly on duty in King's Lynn. According to their statements, they were ordered to remain in King's Lynn [see also entry **88**].*
1999	
(10.55 pm)	
74	

But, if this is true, who gave the orders for them to remain in King's Lynn and not drive straight to the crime scene which – at that time of night – was only about 15 - 20 minutes away? Operationally, surely that decision was a complete disaster because two alleged burglars had still to be found and who knew whether they were armed?

Fri	**Tilney St Lawrence, Norfolk**
20 AUG	*According to official records,*[55] *PS 3093 Richard Andrew Davidson claimed he was on general supervisory duties in uniform in a marked*
1999	*police vehicle in Tilney St Lawrence when he received a radio message of a person outside Foreman's Cottage with gunshot wounds. Driving*
10.57 pm	*from Downham Market*[56] *via Terrington St John police station, where he*
75	*claimed to have collected PC 543 Richard William Mann, they allegedly arrived together at the Hungate Corner at 11:06pm.*

"I saw an ambulance parked in the front drive of Foreman's Cottage and an ambulance crew treating an injured male person who was writhing around on the grass front lawn and screaming in agony. I instructed PC Mann to assist the ambulance crew and try to ascertain what the injured male could tell them about how his injuries were sustained.

I established from the Leets that Tony Martin had attended Foreman's Cottage earlier in the evening alleging that three people[57] had attempted to break into his house and he had fired a gun at them. The Leets stated they were afraid, and had advised Tony to return home and contact the police. A short while later, the injured Fearon turned up in their front garden."

What this adds to our knowledge	From this information, it seems we can be sure that the police were aware *on their own evidence* that there were (at least) three intruders involved in a shooting incident as early as 11:06pm (if we believe the police timings). Now, given this information, and given the fact that they have an injured man in front of them with serious gunshot wounds, wouldn't you think that their main priority would have been to find that man's accomplices?

Joined by PC Mann in the house, PS Davidson (according to his statement) instigated a scene log to be kept, established landline communications, tried to ascertain further and fuller details of Tony Martin and *briefed further* [unnamed] *officers* arriving as to what had allegedly occurred and organised their deployment to protect the Leets and their own colleagues. The emphasis is mine: Davidson's statement informs us that he briefed other officers about the circumstances of

---

[55] Davidson's witness statement of 22 August 1999.

[56] Note that previously in this same statement, PS Davidson had said he was in Tilney St Lawrence and not Downham Market.

[57] This is the second occasion on which the police had supposedly been told that there were "three burglars" at Bleak House – the first was in the 999 call made by Mrs Leet and she has now allegedly confirmed this to PS Davidson in person. Yet the police were later to claim that they never knew there was a "third" person.

the shooting (as far as they were aware) and that, of course, involved the issue of there being "three burglars" at Bleak House. We are surely immediately forced to ask why a thorough search of the area (and particularly in the immediate vicinity of Bleak House) was not conducted to find the other two, who may or may not have been wounded. Given that at least one of them (Fearon) was badly wounded, was it not reasonable to assume that the others might also have been injured and, in any event, it would have been good practice to at least establish whether others were injured and in need of medical assistance. But there is no mention in PS Davidson's statement that such a search was a priority for the police. Barras, we should remember, was allegedly lying wounded just yards from Bleak House and an ambulance was said to have been close by.

Given that PS Davidson claimed to have been on duty in Emneth until just after 7am, and given that it was him who instigated the Crime Scene Log, I am also puzzled as to why he made no mention in his statement of the helicopter flying over Bleak House. I believe that that would have been a significant event – at such a time and particularly with its powerful searchlights lighting up the area. It would have been part of the operational response to the shooting and surely worthy of mention, unless his statement had been altered by senior officers.

PS Davidson said that he was accompanied by PC Mann, so we ought to look at the 53-year-old Mann's statement, made on 3rd September 1999, at a time and place unknown to us because it was not recorded. You might wonder why.

Mann stated that he attempted to interview Fearon but "because of his deteriorating condition the ambulance crew insisted that he had to go to hospital immediately."

Mann claimed that he remained at the house and on instruction from PS Davidson opened and maintained the 'Scene Log' and manned the telephone communication. He claimed to have left the scene at 7:20am the following day.

Again, there is no mention of the urgency to establish a search of the grounds of Bleak House or, indeed, of the house itself to establish whether any other people were injured. Nor is there mention of a helicopter flight.

But there was mention in PC Mann's statement of something which never came out in the trial or in the media and yet which, I suggest, provides a more accurate narrative about what really occurred at Bleak House that night: "I asked the injured man [Fearon] what had happened and he said, "*Went down land somewhere and man shot me twice.*"

So, it would seem, there were early indications that the police were aware that Fearon and Barras weren't shot *inside* Bleak House at all, but *on farmland*. Which means, of course, that Tony Martin, shooting from the stairs *inside* the house, couldn't have shot them *inside* the breakfast room at all because they never made it as far as the house according to evidence in the possession of the police.

The mystery deepens. And it deepens yet further when we study the

Computer Aided Dispatch (CAD) report from Norfolk Constabulary's own records because this shows that PC Mann was dispatched to the scene at 10:56pm *on his own* and that he arrived at 11:31pm *on his own* in car DR05A. The same CAD report shows that PS Davidson was sent to Bleak House *on his own* at 10:57pm and that he arrived *on his own* at 11:06pm in car DZ01. Yet, on both officers' statements, they claimed that they *had arrived together in the same vehicle.* It would appear that those statements have been fabricated or significantly altered. Or the CAD report. Or all three.

According to the CAD report, PS Davidson was the first police officer to arrive at 11:06pm, followed by PC 9056 Tamsin Jane Raines at 11:14pm in car DR07 and PC 935 Patricia Josephine Hooper at 11:23pm in car DR08.

Fri	
20 AUG	**Foreman's Bungalow, Emneth Hungate**
10.59 pm	*According to statements made by 51-year-old paramedic Derek Sands (who had been in the job for 20 years) and driver Mick Kiff, the ambulance arrived at 10:59pm. Sands and Kiff claimed to have always worked together and took turns to drive. It is claimed that upon arrival at the scene, they immediately attended to Fearon. So let's hear from driver Mick Kiff:*
evidence	
76	

"At 10:55pm we received a call from ambulance control directing us to Moyse's Bank, Emneth Hungate. The message stated that someone thought they had been shot. We immediately made our way to the location on blues and twos from Wisbech. I was driving whilst paramedic Derek Sands was preparing himself. We arrived at 10:59pm."

I'll interject into Mick Kiff's statement at this point to draw attention to the speed with which the ambulance arrived at the scene – just four minutes. Even at that time of night, that's pretty impressive driving over the distance covered. So impressive that it's actually impossible. But back to Mr Kiff:

"Upon arrival we were waved down by a man who I presumed to be the owner of the bungalow where the victim was. Derek got out of the vehicle, whilst I reversed the vehicle onto the driveway.

The victim, who I now know to be Brendon Fearon, was laid on the front lawn of the bungalow. He was slightly on his right side with a light coloured blanket[58] over him. Derek removed the blanket and examined the boy's[59] injuries.

---

[58] This innocuous object – the blanket – becomes an important piece of a jigsaw which shows that many statements (if not all) were created falsely by senior police officers in

I could see that his left upper thigh had a very large open wound. His right upper thigh was bloody and I could see it was peppered with pellets.[60] I dressed the left thigh whilst Derek got the stretcher. Fearon was wearing dark coloured track suit bottoms, but I cannot recall what he was wearing on his upper half.

We asked Fearon what had happened. He told us that *he had been shot twice* [author's emphasis]. He wouldn't say who by. He did say that he had been looking for work when he had been shot. He also wouldn't tell us whereabouts it was where he was shot.

Both Derek and myself presumed that the shooting must have occurred *very near to Moyse's Bank because the nature of his injuries wouldn't have allowed him to walk far.*[61] At this point on the lawn Fearon would not give us his details. Whilst we were tending to his wounds, the police arrived.

After placing Fearon in the back of the ambulance, we were approached by a male officer[62] who asked Fearon for his details. This is when I found out Fearon's name. He gave his name, address and date of birth to the officer who actually got into the back of the ambulance to note these details. The officer also asked him what happened. Fearon gave the same reply to the officer as he had to us a short while earlier. Once the officer had finished and left the ambulance, we transported Fearon to the Queen Elizabeth Hospital, King's Lynn. I was driving whilst Derek was tending to his legs. We left the scene at 11:15pm and arrived at the hospital at 11:35pm.

To clarify – when I first saw Fearon, Derek had already cut his bottoms from the wounds in order to examine them further. I would say that the whole time I was with Fearon he was in a total state of shock.

At no point whilst we were treating and transporting Fearon did he ever mention that he was with anyone else [author's emphasis]. If he had done so, we would have made the police aware and informed our control also."

---

the case and that Tony Martin was taken to trial (and found 'guilty' of murder) based on nothing more than false documents.

[59] Why would Mr Kiff refer to the 29-year-old Brendon Fearon as a 'boy'? There is surely more than a suggestion that Fred Barras was also seen by the ambulance crew.

[60] Notice that Mr Kiff did not say that the left thigh contained any pellets.

[61] I suggest you pay close regard to this piece of information – that Fearon would not have been able to walk far after he sustained such major leg injuries. The police were asking the public to believe that Fearon was shot by Tony Martin inside Bleak House and that he then walked more than a quarter of a mile to Foreman's bungalow.

[62] According to the official Norfolk Constabulary CAD report, this could only have been PS Davidson, since no other male officer had allegedly arrived by the time the ambulance left.

> **What this adds to our knowledge**
>
> Records show that that statement was made at 6:30pm at the Wisbech ambulance station to DC 751 Paul Cross on 31 August – some 11 days after the event. I question why it took the police so long to take a statement from Mr Kiff. But I also ask further questions because I'm not entirely happy about the authenticity of this statement.

I want to draw your attention to the fact that driver Mick Kiff told the police that Fearon had told him that he had been shot *twice*. I think we can safely assume that nobody coerced Fearon to say how many times he had been shot and so I believe that it is highly likely that he's telling the truth. This became a very important issue at trial which you'll read about later.

Turning to the statement[63] of paramedic Derek Sands, he said:

"I automatically checked the patient's pulse by feeling his right wrist, and I asked him what had happened and where he hurt. He replied, "I've been shot in the legs. There were two shots."

So, according to the paramedic and the ambulance driver, the injured person told them he had been shot twice. Not three times, but twice. It seems pretty conclusive that that there were only two shots, but do we trust the authenticity of these statements?

Sands' statement added:

"I saw that the left upper front thigh had a wound consistent with shotgun wounds and gave the appearance of a large piece of flesh having been scooped out leaving a blackened and gaping wound with edges that had collapsed into it.

I immediately cut off the left trouser leg of his track suit bottoms and we dressed the wound to prevent infection. *The wound was not bleeding which is common with shotgun injuries.*[64]

The man then complained about pain in his inner right thigh, so I again cut open the leg of his trousers and saw a peppering of shot covering most of the inner right thigh. As this was not bleeding I did not dress it but covered the patient with a blanket.[65]

---

[63] There is an official statement said to have been made to DC Buxton on 31 August 1999 at 6:30pm taken at Wisbech ambulance station.

[64] The emphasis is the author's, not Mr Sands'. The Leets and eel fisherman John Spalton were later to describe in their witness statements how Fearon was bleeding profusely.

[65] We should ask ourselves 'Why would he cover Fearon with a blanket when according to Paul Leet, *he* had covered Fearon with a blanket?'

I then removed his jacket which was a leather material and held together by a broken zip. This was to enable access to the patient's arms for any necessary treatment etc.

We placed him on the bed and loaded him into the rear of the ambulance.

By this time, a police officer had arrived on the scene[66] and he requested permission to speak to the patient. He then sat in the back of the vehicle and I was present when the police officer asked the patient some questions.

He asked his name and what he was doing. I heard the patient say, '*I was just walking along the road looking for some work when I heard someone call out and the next thing I knew was I had been shot.*'[67]

The police officer then left and we proceeded to the Queen Elizabeth Hospital at King's Lynn.

There was no further conversation between the patient and I about what had happened and the only other information I learnt from him was his name, date of birth and his address."

Which all sounds pretty accurate. But what do you make of this:

"At no time did the patient say anything about anyone else having been shot nor did he give any more information about the incident."

Do we believe that, or has Mr Sands' statement been altered? And:

"During the journey, there was nobody else in the ambulance apart from the patient, myself and Mick Kiff who was driving."

Why would Mr Sands say that (if, indeed, he did?) You see, Fearon was convinced that there was someone else in the ambulance, though he couldn't be sure who.

---

[66] Notice that Sands refers to a single police officer arriving on the scene, whereas official police statements claimed that two officers (PS Davidson and PC Mann) arrived together.
[67] Again, we have evidence gathered by the police which indicates that Fearon had told others that he had been shot *outside* and not *inside*. There is no doubt at all that Tony Martin fired his shotgun *inside* the house whilst on the staircase but there is contradictory evidence to suggest that he didn't actually hit anybody and certainly not Fearon or Barras.

Fri	**Foreman's Bungalow, Emneth Hungate**
20 AUG	*According to statements by PS Davidson and PC Mann, they were the first to arrive on the scene.*
11.06 pm	
77	As I have shown earlier, these accounts differ significantly from the CAD report and depart significantly from the truth.

Fri	**Foreman's Bungalow, Emneth Hungate**
20 AUG	*According to statements by PC 9056 Tamsin Raines*[68] *and PC 935 Patricia Hooper,*[69] *they arrived on the scene at this time.*
11.10 pm	*PC Raines stated that she was on duty in Downham Market when, at approximately 10:55pm she received a radio message to attend Foreman's Cottage.*
78	

She claimed that she collected PC Hooper from the police station and upon arrival in Emneth Hungate, travelling along Edge Bank, she observed a car travelling down Moyse's Bank. She stated that she could see the vehicle's head and rear lights as they turned into Moyse's Bank. A few seconds later at approximately 11:10pm she said that she could no longer see this vehicle. She made no mention of the type or colour of car that she allegedly saw. She claimed that she parked her vehicle in front of Foreman's Cottage, just as the ambulance was leaving.

She claimed that she and PC Hooper entered the bungalow to liaise with the Leets and PS Davidson and PC Mann. The statement attributed to PC Raines added that during the early hours of Saturday 21 August 1999, she obtained original notes from Jacqueline Leet which were completed at 3am.

Again, no mention of the helicopter. Nor does her statement include the time it was made, nor the location. What it tells us, however, is that – according to the police narrative - by approximately 11:10pm (two or three hours or so after Tony Martin fired his gun) there was one police sergeant on the scene, along with three constables. Fearon was allegedly in an ambulance on his way to hospital, Barras was allegedly lying on the ground outside Bleak House. Bark, the alleged getaway driver, was said to have been in his car in Moyse's Bank outside Foreman's Bungalow. And Tony Martin, having been to his mother's house to drop off the shotgun for "safekeeping", was now on his way to the

---

[68] A statement attributed to PC Raines was made on 25 August 1999. We do not know to whom the statement was made, at what location it was made, or the time it was made because none of this usual information was recorded.

[69] A statement attributed to PC Hooper was made on 25 August 1999. We do not know to whom the statement was made, at what location it was made, or the time it was made because none of this usual information was recorded.

Marmion House Hotel.

As with the other "official" police statements, PC Raines made no mention of any degree of urgency to find other alleged burglars.

> **CORRUPTION ALERT** — *Discrepancy between policewoman's statement and official CAD report*

PC Raines claimed that she collected PC Hooper from Downham Market police station en route to Emneth and that they both arrived together in the same vehicle. If this was true, why does the Computer Aided Dispatch (CAD) report show that Hooper arrived in a separate vehicle nine minutes after Raines?

Both constables had been dispatched to Emneth at almost the same time (10:56:55, Raines, and 10:56:59, Hooper).

In a separate statement,[70] Inspector David Chilvers (based at Hunstanton) stated that he "first became aware of the shooting incident" at this time. If this is true, why had it taken almost 15 minutes for him to become aware?

"I had a number of conversations by radio and telephone with PS 3093 Davidson who informed me he was at Emneth.

Following these conversations over a period of two hours approximately, I made arrangements and supervised the deployment of police resources.

About 1:20am on Saturday 21 August 1999, I left King's Lynn police station in company with PC 1025 Bavin and drove to Emneth, arriving at Hungate Corner about 1:43pm.[71] [72]

There I saw a number of police officers including PC 935 Hooper who was standing beside a parked white Ford Granada saloon car. In the driver's seat was a male person who I understood to be Darren Bark.[73] I spoke to PS Davidson and together with him supervised the deployment of officers in the area.

On my arrival, I saw a helicopter circling the area and using a searchlight. Also present at my location on my arrival was CI Curtis.

---

[70] Dated 1 September 1999. We do not know to whom the statement was made, at what location it was made, or the time it was made because none of this information was recorded.

[71] Note the use by Inspector Chilvers of the word 'about' twice within the same sentence when referring to alleged times.

[72] Why would you go to the Hungate Corner if you had been informed that there had been a shooting at Bleak House?

[73] If Bark had been arrested by this point in time, why was he sitting in his own car?

Shortly after 2:45pm Supt Hale attended my location and undertook overall command of the officers present.

During the period I was present, a police inspector from Cambridgeshire constabulary[74] arrived and spoke with Supt Hale and CI Curtis. Each of these officers left a short time after. I remained at Hungate Corner.

DC Peters arrived,[75] spoke with the man I believed to be Darren Bark[76] and they then left together in an unmarked police vehicle. I remained at Hungate Corner until about 6:08am when I left again in company with PC 1025 Bavin.

All other officers[77] present, except PS Davidson and PC 543 Mann, left about the same time. The white Ford Granada saloon was still in the position it had been, adjacent to Foreman's Cottage, when I arrived."

What this adds to our knowledge

Firstly, we must consider the fact that the statement was not signed, there was no location or time recorded on it and we do not know to whom it was made. Are you concerned?

Chilvers was adamant that the helicopter was flying in the early hours of Saturday morning and not late on Friday night.

The official CAD report showed that the helicopter arrived at 1:06am which means that it had been and gone by the time Inspector Chilvers claimed to have arrived at the scene. Furthermore, the CAD report provided to Tony Martin by his legal team at the original trial has a crucial page missing – between 1:04am and 1:14am on 21 August 1999. Additionally, we ought to consider the possibility that there were *two* helicopter flights over Bleak House that night...

CORRUPTION ALERT *Statements do not match official records*

Note that Chilvers claimed that when he left the scene, PS Davidson and PC Mann were still on duty.

However, the CAD report showed that Davidson and Mann also left the scene at 6:08am.

---

[74] Why is this police inspector not named?

[75] Note that Inspector Chilvers did not provide the time at which DC Peters allegedly arrived.

[76] Believing it to be Darren Bark isn't the same as *knowing* it was Bark. Note the possible (mis)use of language by the Inspector.

[77] Why are these "other officers" not named?

Fri 20 AUG 11.15 pm 79	**Foreman's Bungalow, Emneth Hungate**

According to official records, acting DI Sharman arrived at King's Lynn police station and took charge of the investigation.

Strangely, I could find no substantive statement or report from him except a brief statement attributed to him about a visit he paid to Bleak House on 15 September – [see entry **261**], and another brief statement made on 1 October - [see entry **307**].

Also at this time, official records show that the ambulance left the scene with Fearon on its way to the Queen Elizabeth Hospital in King's Lynn.

Fri 20 AUG 11.24 pm 80	**Foreman's Bungalow, Emneth Hungate**

According to their statements, PCs 155 Mark Beer and 364 David Cole arrived in Emneth at the junction of the Smeeth Road and Moyse's Bank and stopped Bark who was said to have been driving down Moyse's Bank in the direction of the Smeeth Road:

"I am Mark Beer, a serving traffic officer stationed at King's Lynn. At approximately 10:52pm I was on uniform patrol in company with PC Cole on Friday 20 August 1999, when as a result of a radio call, we attended Moyse's Bank, Hungate Road, Emneth following a report of a person having been shot.

At 11:24pm on arrival at that location I saw the lights of a vehicle approaching us along a lane which runs from Moyse's Bank to join Smeeth Road at Hungate Corner. We caused the vehicle to stop and found it was a white Ford Granada motor car index no. F98LHJ. The driver I now know to be Darren Bark of Newark.

Bark stated that at about 10pm that evening, whilst at his home address, a call was received[78] from a male who he knew,[79] who had stated he and a mate had broken down near to Wisbech. He then gave me a description of the male which I recorded - he stated he was possibly with a male called Fearon and again provided a description.

A supervisor was already present at our location and I was informed by Sgt Davidson that a male had been conveyed to hospital with gunshot wounds.

I informed him of Bark's story and was advised to remain with Bark until a CID officer attended.

I then remained at that location with Mr Bark with other officers.

---

[78] It would, of course, have been easy to have verified whether a call was received by Bark at this time. There was no record that this has been investigated and verified.

[79] In his statement, Bark was to claim that he did not know who the call was from.

I also assisted in a vehicle check along Smeeth Road when it was ascertained we were looking for a vehicle believed to be owned by a Tony Martin which was not resident at his home address.

At 4:41am I was relieved and returned to King's Lynn police station."

Now, even if we believe PC Beer's statement that they asked Darren Bark whether there were any accomplices with him, and even if Bark did say that there weren't, it's nonsense *because the police's own evidence shows that Paul Leet claimed that Tony Martin had allegedly said there were three* and they've only got one of them (Fearon). Bark had told the police he'd been in Newark at 10pm and, if that's true, then Barras (the "third man") was still unaccounted for.

But what do you make of this: the official Norfolk Constabulary CAD report recorded that PCs Beer and Cole were dispatched to the Hungate Corner at 11:24pm and arrived *one second later* in car TC11. Further mystery surrounding the attendance of officers that night.

Fri 20 AUG 11.30 pm — 81

King's Lynn police station
According to his statement, dated 25 August 1999, Chief Inspector Richard Curtis was on duty in King's Lynn police station when he "first became aware of a shooting incident."

Isn't it odd that a chief inspector didn't "become aware" of the incident for more than ½ an hour after constables in their cars?

Fri 20 AUG (11.30 pm) UNUSED — 82

Marmion House Hotel, Lynn Road, Wisbech
Having left his mother's house in Friday Bridge, Tony Martin arrived at the Marmion House Hotel, ironically about 100 yards from Wisbech police station. The owner of the hotel, 57-year-old Helen Lilley, was shown as having made the very first statement to the police in their 'investigation' on 22 August 1999 to DS 3132 Thomas Neill at her home address. The statement was unused:

"I have known Tony Martin for many years. He was very supportive when my husband died about 13 years ago and we became very close friends. He is also very close to the remainder of my family. He visits us at the hotel on an almost daily basis; he is like a surrogate uncle to my grandchildren.

He has suffered many burglaries at his home over the years and I know this has made him feel very nervous about living in his own house. His house is very isolated and set well back from the road behind an orchard and I know that he has valuable antiques in the house.

Sometime between 11:30pm and midnight on Friday 20 August 1999, Tony arrived at the hotel. He seemed upset and said there had been an incident and the police would probably call for him. He said there had been another break in.

The relationship between Tony and I is one where he would not put me in any awkward situation by telling me something which I did not need to know and I would not delve into his business.

He had a cup of tea and I went off to bed. Before I did so, he gave me the keys to the house and the contents of his pockets to pay someone's wages and deal with other matters for him.

The next thing was about 6am the following morning when the police made contact with me and subsequently arrived and arrested Tony.

About 9:30am that morning I received a telephone call from Tony [who was then in the police station] asking me to arrange insurance for his house and security as they had got into the house and pulled a window out. He also asked me to arrange clothes for him and to lock the dogs up."

We should take note of the following: Tony Martin did not try to flee the area as a guilty man might well have done. Instead, he merely drove to a place of safety, to a place where he felt himself to be 'part of the family.' He did not stay the night at his mother's or his brother's but chose instead the Marmion House Hotel.

We should note that Helen Lilley told the police that Tony suffered many burglaries over the years and had felt very nervous about living in Bleak House.

Mrs Lilley confirmed Tony's approximate time of arrival and this seems to fit with his chronology.

But now we must pay particular attention to the fact that Tony gave her his keys – she, in turn, would have given them to the police.

And we must also note the fact that Mrs Lilley said that Tony had asked her to arrange to have the dogs locked up – this simple fact is of huge significance in the entire case against Tony, as we will see in future entries.

With Tony safely ensconced in the Marmion and sleeping on a sofa, our attention now turns to Brendon Fearon, allegedly in an ambulance speeding its way to the Queen Elizabeth Hospital near King's Lynn (though there is some doubt about the police chronology as you will read).

Fri
20 AUG
11.35 pm
83

Queen Elizabeth Hospital, King's Lynn
According to official records, the ambulance carrying Brendon Fearon arrived at the Queen Elizabeth Hospital at this time. Fearon was said to have arrived at 11:35pm and was seen by 35-year-old Dhananjay Kumar, working as a Senior House Officer in the A&E department. He had qualified as a doctor from Ranchi University in India in 1990.

Dr Kumar made a statement to the police on 2nd September 1999 according to the official police records. However, I must point out that there is no indication on the statement of which officer it was made to, where it was made, or at what time it was made. Additionally, the statement was not witnessed. All of this, of course, is contrary to normal police protocol and makes it inadmissible as evidence in court.

It was claimed in Dr Kumar's statement that he called for x-rays of both of Fearon's thighs – "I could not see any bony lesion in those x-rays but there were multiple small foreign bodies seen." (These would have been shotgun pellets.)

Photos of the wounds were also taken before Dr Kumar handed Fearon over to the Orthopaedic team led by Mr Mandal in the resuscitation room.

Now, to avoid any charges of being labelled a conspiracy theorist because I called the authenticity of Dr Kumar's statement into question, I'm afraid that I'm now going to throw yet another spanner in the works because I came across a statement allegedly made by Narayanan Vinodkumar. In this statement, Dr Vinodkumar is described as a Senior House Officer who first saw Fearon (described as being conscious) before passing the patient on to the Registrar. Apparently this statement was made on 23 September 1999 – some 3 weeks after that made by Dr Kumar. Again the statement doesn't provide the location at which the statement was made, or the time or the name of any officer who took the statement. Slipshod work – or something more sinister?

Now, if Fearon *was* conscious do we still believe that he didn't mention Barras to anyone?

I am of the opinion that these statements are false or that at the very least they have been altered to edit out any references Fearon made about Barras. If you think that's a bit far-fetched, you may come to revise that view in further paragraphs.

Records show that Fearon was passed to 34-year-old Shantanu Mandal, Orthopaedic Staff Grade. Before I divulge what the statement revealed, I need to inform you that, although it is dated 14 *September* 1999 (a month after the shooting), there is no record of the location, the time it was made, the name of the police officer to whom it was made and neither is there a witness signature:

"At approximately 11:50pm, I received a telephone call from the Accident and Emergency department about the presence of a 29-year-old male who had sustained gunshot injuries to both his legs. Within 5 minutes, I saw Mr Fearon in the Resuscitation Room of the A&E department.

He was in a lot of pain and his description of the incident was sketchy. I could gather that *he had sustained gunshot wounds in the farmland.*[80] There were

---

[80] This is yet another reference to the fact that Fearon and Barras were shot *outside* and not *inside* and that Tony Martin, firing from the stairs, could not possibly have shot them *outside*.

some dogs in the vicinity and the patient had dragged himself through a field. *He was hit from a distance of about 20-30 yards.*[81] No other details of the incident were available."

Mandal described Fearon as "conscious" and added that "examination of both groin and thighs revealed multiple pellets embedded in the skin and tissue of his thighs." There was no loss of sensation or movement in his toes.

Mandal added that "the underlying muscles were exposed on his left thigh and he had skin loss. *The muscles were contaminated with corn cobs.*[82] The surrounding skin had multiple pellets embedded. There was no loss of sensation or movement in his toes or foot. The left knee was not swollen and had full range of movement.

The x-rays showed no fractures and so Fearon was passed on to the consultant on call, Mr Anil Chakrabarti.

Fearon was given antibiotics in the form of Cefuroxime and Metronidazole and he received a tetanus injection and 3 units of blood. The wounds were photographed before being cleaned and dressed prior to him being taken to the operating theatre."

---

[81] According to Fearon's statement, he actually said he'd been shot after *walking* 20-30 yards along a track and not that he'd been hit *from a distance* of 20-30 yards. These are not the same thing at all.

[82] Author's emphasis.

Fri
20 AUG
11.35 pm
84

Queen Elizabeth Hospital, King's Lynn

According to official records, the 29-year-old PC 9130 Clare Smith and PC 1282 Jonathan Miller[83] attended the Queen Elizabeth Hospital at the same time that Fearon had allegedly been brought in.

However, according to PC Miller's statement,[84] he and PC Smith didn't attend the hospital until 0:10am.

He added that PC Smith was asking questions of Fearon about how he came to be shot while he (Miller) was making "hand written notes on a piece of unmarked white A4 paper". As you probably know, police officers are supplied (free of charge by the taxpayer) with pocket notebooks. Why didn't he use this? I suggest that this statement has been re-written to edit out details of the shooting that the police didn't want the public finding out.

The statement then went on to say that he was called to another part of the hospital due to "operational demands" and that he left his notes with PC Smith.

According to PC Smith's statement, she and Miller arrived at 11:35pm (not the 0:10am stated by Miller[85]) and found Fearon in Resuscitation Room 1. She added that she seized Fearon's clothes at 11:45pm and then questioned the patient about how he came to be shot. What was recorded is reproduced below:

"I was dropped off because he was going a different way to where I wanted to go. I wanted to know where a pub was, so I went to ask at the house. A dog came towards me and then I saw a man. I said to the man, 'Watch your dog. The man shot me. I heard two shots.' I then said to Fearon, "Why did you get dropped off there?" He said, "I was getting a lift." I then asked if he was hitchhiking and he said, "Yeah." Fearon then said, "I can't talk anymore, I'm in too much pain."

At 1:40am on 21 August 1999, Fearon was taken to the x-ray department, prior to going to theatre. I was able to wait outside the door. Nurse Chris[tine] Rumble came out to me and said, "He's just told me the farmer shot him because he thought he was stealing from him." I wrote this down straightaway.

---

[83] On 29 January 2014, I was arrested by PC Miller (then crewed with PC 400 Adrian Girton's wife, Karen). However, this was an unlawful arrest because he failed to inform me of the reason for arrest at the point of arrest. I later learnt that the arrest had been for allegedly "impersonating a barrister". This arrest came within 6 months of (i) my meeting Tony Martin and (ii) Lambeth Council banning my book *from Hillsborough to Lambeth* and seeking a permanent gagging order against me for having reported child abuse, racism and bullying when I worked as the Head teacher of a pupil referral unit for extremely vulnerable 14-16 year old pupils.

[84] Apparently PC Miller made two statements: one on 23 August 1999 (to which this entry refers) and a second one on 27 September 1999 (see relevant entry). Neither was entered into evidence at the trial as they ought to have been.

[85] The official CAD report has PCs Smith and Miller arriving at the hospital at 11:37pm.

A few minutes later Fearon was taken up to the theatre at approximately 1:50am. I spoke to him on the way and asked: "Why did the farmer shoot you?" He replied, "I wasn't stealing anything."

At approximately 2:30am, I returned to King's Lynn police station and booked Fearon's clothing into the Property Subject to Enquiry book. I placed each item of his clothing into a brown paper bag as it was heavily bloodstained.[86]

These are my original notes made at King's Lynn police station on 21 August 1999 at 3:30am."

What this adds to our knowledge	I don't believe that these are her original notes at all. Surely he would also have mentioned seeing a helicopter if he had done so and surely he would have mentioned having been knocked down by the eelman in his van.

Who gave the order (if anyone did) for PC Smith to return to King's Lynn police station rather than search Bleak House for the injured Barras? – after all, the clothes could easily have been processed another day. Surely the priority was finding Barras, unless the police already knew where he was.

PC Smith also stated (if we believe the official document) that she wrote down what the 41-year-old staff nurse Christine Rumble had told her but doesn't say whether this was recorded in her pocket notebook or on another piece of random A4 paper.

Having noted certain subtle discrepancies between the statements of both police officers, I then referred to the statement of staff nurse Rumble. Even that exercise raised suspicions, because official records show that there were *two* statements attributed to her: the first on 14 September 1999 (almost an entire month after we were told she'd attended to Fearon) and a second statement dated 20 October 1999 (two months after the shooting incident):

"I spoke to the patient at one point and asked him what had happened. He said, 'I was dropped off, walked up this drive to ask for directions and was shot at' – or words to that effect. I asked if he was attempting to burgle the house at the time and he replied, 'No.'

I did not speak to him anymore, except to ask questions about his welfare in relation to his injuries."

This first statement was allegedly made at the hospital at 10:40am to DC Buxton. Strangely, a second statement was authored a month later:

---

[86] You will recall that paramedic Derek Sands said in his statement dated 31 August 1999 that Fearon's wounds had not been bleeding.

"Further to my previous statement, I would like to add that whilst I was in the x-ray department with Brendon Fearon, he said, "The farmer shot me because he thought I was stealing from him."

I asked him if he was stealing and he replied, 'No'.

I later passed this information on to PC Clare Smith."

I can see no difference between the statements so we are then forced to ask why a second statement was ever made by the staff nurse (if it was).

I cannot but help think that this second statement was either falsely created or altered in some way. It appears to me to have been engineered so as to fit nicely with PC Clare Smith's statement, but what do you think?

**Fri
20 AUG
11.45 pm
85**

home address of DS Peter Colin Newton
According to his witness statement dated 31 August 1999, DS Peter Newton was called at home by acting DI Matthew Sharman.

DS Newton was to be the senior officer when Tony was interviewed under caution.

"As a result of this call I immediately attended King's Lynn police station. I was made aware of a shooting incident at Bleak House, Emneth Hungate, the home of an Anthony Martin.[87]

I established that the victim was Brendon Fearon from Newark.[88] I was then engaged in the logistics of the criminal investigation.

At 3am on Saturday 21st August 1999 at King's Lynn police station, I saw PC Smith and took possession of clothing belonging to Brendon Fearon (exhibits CAS/1 to CAS/10 inclusive). I retained these items.

At 8:50am the same day, together with DC 8 Aldous I put exhibits CAS/1 and CAS/5 to CAS/9 inclusive in a dryer at the SOC department in King's Lynn police station. The dryer was then sealed.

At 10:30am the same day I saw PC Hemeter at King's Lynn police station and took possession of exhibits BT/1 and MJW/1 to MJW/4 inclusive. These relate to Anthony Edward Martin."

This statement raises a number of interesting questions, if it's true. What was DS Newton doing between the time he was allegedly called on duty at 11:45pm to 3am when he allegedly took possession of Fearon's clothes from PC Smith?

---

[87] Notice the description of "a shooting incident". It does not follow that this was the incident in which Tony Martin fired his gun.
[88] Notice that Brendon Fearon was the victim of "a shooting incident". It need not follow that Tony Martin shot him.

What was he doing between 3am and 8:50am (mostly daylight hours in August), when he allegedly put some clothes in a drier in the SOC office, and between 9am and 10:30am when he claimed to have taken possession of exhibits from PC Hemeter?

Would we be correct in thinking that DS Newton was at Bleak House, the scene of the crime to which he'd been called out to? And, of course, had he gone there (as the reasonable person might expect), he'd surely have seen the body of Barras lying, according to the police, just 15 feet from the house. And he'd have seen the body long before the public was told and long before he interviewed Tony Martin.

Fri
20 AUG
11.50 pm
UNUSED
86

Foreman's Bungalow, Emneth Hungate

According to official records, authorised firearms officers PC 400 Adrian Girton[89] and PC 852 Paul White – in a King's Lynn-based armed response vehicle – arrived at Foreman's Bungalow.

Let's see what the 33-year-old PC Girton (normally based at King's Lynn) had to say in his unused statement dated 2 September 1999[90]:

"At 9:33pm on Friday 20 August 1999, I was on duty in uniform in the King's Lynn based armed response vehicle with PC 852 White when, acting on information received, we attended Hillington Square, King's Lynn for a suspected firearms incident.

Whilst engaged on that incident, at approximately 10:56pm, I heard a radio message concerning another firearms incident at Emneth, where it was believed a male had been shot. After being briefed by the Control Room we were released from the King's Lynn incident and attended Hungate Corner, near Emneth, arriving at 11:50pm.[91] We were later joined by the Norwich-based armed response vehicle, crewed by PC 338 Cant and PC 485 Gotts. Also at the scene was a King's Lynn based Traffic vehicle, crewed by PC 155 Beer and PC 364 Cole, and several other divisional mobiles in attendance. We were located at the junction with Moyse's Bank.

---

[89] I (who was not armed) was once arrested by PC 400 Girton (who was armed at the time and not in full uniform) on 1st August 2013 for alleged criminal damage to a car. There is, of course, a significant back-story to that arrest, details of which can be found in my books *from Hillsborough to Lambeth*, *Framed!* and *10 Prisons, 12 Weeks*.

[90] This statement was dated 2 September 1999. If it was a bona fide record, why had it taken PC Girton *13 days* to provide an account of his movements on the night of the shooting? Additionally, his partner that night – PC White – was said to have made a statement on 21 August but didn't mention attending Bleak House at all, though he did in a second statement dated 9 September 1999.

[91] The official CAD report had him arriving at three seconds past midnight.

After being briefed by the local units, I understood the situation to be that a male had come to the bungalow, at our location, with gunshot wounds to his legs. He had come across a cropped field from a copse of wood, some 300 yards distance. In the copse of wood was a farmhouse owned by a Mr Tony Martin.

Along with the other divisional units was a male sitting in a vehicle, on Moyse's Bank, who was waiting and looking for a friend who had broken down in a red Ford transit.[92] In my understanding, this male was believed to be with the male who had been shot.

The surrounding area was in total darkness due to there being no street lighting. Both ourselves and the other ARV crews viewed the copse through some night viewing devices, but were unable to see any buildings in the copse, or signs of movement. *The suspect who had fired the weapon was unknown to us.*[93]

CI Curtis and the ARV crews discussed the options available concerning locating the premises, locating vehicles, persons involved, safe approaches and protecting the unarmed officers and the public.

At approximately 1:05am on 21 August 1999, the Cambridgeshire Police helicopter arrived above the scene and commenced a search of the location.

PC Cant was in radio communication with the crew of the helicopter, informing them of what we required from them. A search was then commenced by them, using the thermal imaging device and night sun spotlight.

The helicopter crew informed us that there was no movement or heat sources, except for two dogs, in the area of the wood. *We also had difficulties in identifying the exact location of the farmhouse itself, even with the help from local residents.*[94]

The situation was re-discussed and it was decided that the two ARVs, a dog handler and CI Curtis would approach the building along the entrance track, whilst phoning the property to attempt to make contact with the occupant, either by phone or visually. Whilst doing this, the helicopter remained overhead to monitor the surrounding area for signs of movement, etc. On our approach to the buildings there was no reply to the telephone calls and, even on the scene, we couldn't identify the location of the farmhouse from the track. It was decided to withdraw to our original position to re-assess the situation. Following further discussion, the two ARVs took up positions either side of the entrance track to monitor vehicle movement and have a more flexible response to any further incident or movement.

We remained in these locations until we were relieved by other ARV crews. We then left the scene and returned to King's Lynn."

---

[92] This red transit van – said to have broken down – was, it appears, owned by Joe Price, a known accomplice of Bark, Fearon, Christopher Webster and others (see later entries).
[93] Author's emphasis. This has been written in order to get people thinking that Tony Martin was responsible for the shooting of the two intruders.
[94] Author's emphasis.

I don't believe that statement for one moment. To suggest that they couldn't find Bleak House is, in my view, palpable nonsense. The house was remote, but is it at all realistic that with the sophisticated thermal imaging equipment and strong spotlight available to them, the police were unable to find Bleak House in a clearing in the middle of a copse? PC Rodney Gooderson had managed to find it on a dark February night. From as long ago as 1888, Bleak House was clearly marked on Ordnance Survey maps. I believe the police did find the house and that this statement had been created to cover up that fact.

Let's see what the 36-year-old PC White had to say in his statement dated 9th September 1999. It was, in effect, word-for-word the same as PC Girton's statement made a week earlier but for two important differences:

"On being released by the central control room inspector we attended Hungate Corner, Emneth arriving at 11:50pm,[95] where some divisional and traffic officers were already on the scene.

I saw PC 155 Beer and PC 364 Cole had stopped on Moyse's Bank a Ford Granada colour white with a male driver.

I spoke to the male driver of the Granada and said, "*Is there anyone else in there?*[96] The male replied, "I don't know, I'm here looking for a mate who has broken down."

We then had a conversation regarding the type of vehicle and who might be driving it; the male was very evasive and even when told that someone had already been shot stuck to the story about a broken down transit van.

About 0:34am on Saturday 21 August 1999, the second ARV crewed by PC 338 Cant and PC 485 Gotts arrived on the scene with CI Curtis.

The copse area was very dark and we viewed the area with night viewing aids. I could see no movement/light or vehicles in the copse area.

CI Curtis and the ARV crew discussed the options available regarding locating the premises which could not be seen from our location, locating Mr Martin's vehicles, locating Mr Martin, safe approaches, protecting unarmed officers and public and our action plans. It was decided more resources were required before taking further action safely.

About 1:05am the same day contact was made with the Cambridgeshire police helicopter which then proceeded to search the location. The helicopter reported two heat sources which moved about and were dogs and stated it was difficult to identify the exact location of the farmhouse.

---

[95] According to the official Norfolk Constabulary computer aided dispatch (CAD) record, which lists all of the officers deployed to the crime scene, Girton and White were dispatched to Emneth at 11:49pm and arrived at 00:00. The same record shows that they were cleared to leave the scene at 5:19am on Saturday 21 August 1999.
[96] Author's emphasis.

The officers present re discussed our options and it was decided the two ARVs *followed by PC Claxton in the dog van would approach the buildings along the main drive*[97] whilst CI Curtis would attempt to make contact with the farmhouse via the phone, the helicopter would remain overhead to monitor the area. I was informed as we entered the track that no contact was made via the phone and I could not identify the farmhouse from the track. We withdrew from the track as this was too vulnerable a position.

Following further discussions the ARVs took up a position either side of the track to monitor vehicle movement; we positioned ourselves 150 metres to the King's Lynn side of the premises until relieved by the early turn ARV."

The two main distinctions between the statements of Girton and White are that the latter stated that he asked Bark if there was anyone else at Bleak House and that dog handler PC Claxton was apparently deployed.

Let's take the question to Bark first. Why would any police officer need to ask such a question when by all other accounts (and by way of Jacqui Leet's 999 call) they always knew that there were at least 3 alleged intruders? They had Fearon (in the hospital) and they had Bark (sitting in a car), so there really was no need to ask such a question of Bark. It appears to me as though this has been created – added in to the statement - to try to get the public thinking that the police *didn't* know there were other injured people, to get the public thinking that Bark was the 'getaway driver', and that nobody had mentioned the presence of Barras.

But what do we make of the fact that White has stated that Claxton was deployed? If you re-read Girton's statement, you'll see that he briefly made a reference to a "dog handler" (no name provided, despite his earlier paragraph in which he'd listed everyone else present).

Yet here White informs us that Claxton was indeed deployed, as we might reasonably expect. If I'm in charge of this incident, and we've been given sufficient information that other injured parties have yet to be found, I'm going to deploy a dog handler (or two) at the scene. I'm going to make the rounding up of Tony's dogs a priority and get searching the house and immediate surroundings.

---

[97] Author's emphasis.

Fri **20 AUG** 11.54 pm 87	**request by Norfolk Constabulary to surrounding forces** *According to the official CAD report, the Norfolk police control room put out a request to Lincolnshire and Nottinghamshire constabularies to be on the lookout for an 'R' registration red transit van with a full length roof rack driven by a Joe Price.*

Fri **20 AUG** 11.57 pm 88	**armed response vehicle, King's Lynn** *According to the CAD report, Inspector Jones telephoned the control room stating that Chief Super Sandall had requested that an ARV from King's Lynn returns to the police station to collect CI Curtis before driving to Emneth. This task fell to PCs Gotts and Cant. They had first become aware of the shooting – or so the records show – at 10:55pm.*

Do we really believe that an ARV would sit around waiting in King's Lynn for an hour and a quarter rather than be deployed at the scene of a shooting?

I have been unable to find a statement from Superintendent Sandall and neither he nor Inspector Jones were mentioned in the HOLMES database.

Fri **20 AUG** 11.58 pm UNUSED 89	**Foreman's Bungalow, Emneth Hungate** *According to official records, dog handler PC 31 Andrew Claxton[98] was deployed to report to a 'firearms' incident at Emneth at "about 11:58pm on 20 August 1999."* *He claims to have arrived about 0:20am on Saturday 21st at a bungalow situated at Hungate Corner where he liaised with Sergeant Davidson and the ARV teams.*

"I had no direct involvement in any search and police dog 'Solo' – a German shepherd general purpose dog – was not deployed. My involvement was as part of a containment of the area in conjunction with armed units. I was stood down at 6:09am."

---

[98] In a statement dated 23 August 1999. We do not know to whom the statement was made, where it was made or at what time it was made. This statement is listed at line S62 in HOLMES despite earlier entries being dated *after* PC Claxton's statement. In other words, all the evidence supports that this statement has been documented out of chronological order which leads, I suggest, the reasonable person to conclude that it is a false statement and has simply been created to distance the constable from the scene.

> **CORRUPTION ALERT**
>
> *Police dog handler allegedly not deployed*

Here is yet another police statement in which the officer is distancing himself from any involvement in a search – but note that he actually used the word 'search'. According to other police statements, there was no search. Why was he called on duty as a specialist police dog handler if he wasn't used?

The Norfolk Constabulary CAD report tells an entirely different story from that put forward in this statement. Claxton was dispatched at 11:58pm and was recorded as having arrived at 2:34am. It also shows that he was cleared to leave the crime scene at 6:08am – so what was he doing in those 3½ hours?

And, furthermore, what was he doing between having been called on duty at two minutes before midnight and allegedly arriving at 2:34am?

Saturday 21 August 1999

Part 7: Saturday 21 August 1999

Sat
21 AUG
0.09 am
90

call from Nottinghamshire Constabulary
According to the official CAD report, Norfolk Constabulary central control room received a call from Nottinghamshire police requesting further information on why they were asked to stop a vehicle and whether firearms were involved.

This suggests that the vehicle stopped by PC Knight was not as the result of anything the constable had seen, but that he had been tasked with stopping the vehicle as part of a pre-planned and pre-meditated police operation. Now, why would that be?

Sat
21 AUG
0.10 am
91

response from Norfolk Constabulary
According to the CAD report, Norfolk Constabulary informed Nottinghamshire police that at this stage it was not known whether firearms had been involved, that they were still doing enquiries and that when any further information became available, they would be contacted again.

How on earth could Norfolk Constabulary claim that they did not know whether firearms had been involved? Why would Norfolk police mislead their counterparts in Nottingham?

Sat
21 AUG
0.10 am
92

control room request to Lincolnshire police
According to the CAD report, Norfolk Constabulary requested that Lincolnshire police hold Price "under obs" – observation.

Given his alleged activity on the night, why wasn't Price arrested or called to trial by Tony's barrister to be questioned?

| Sat 21 AUG 0.13 am 93 | **Chief superintendent requests helicopter**
According to the CAD report, Chief Superintendent Sandall requested that a helicopter be deployed "to look for the outstanding person". |

This evidence demonstrates the police corruption in the case. At all times, and using evidence from their own control room, the police were always aware of an "outstanding person" – and later claims from Norfolk Constabulary that they never knew the existence of "a third person" until the body of Barras had been "found" were nothing more than lies, clearly created to deceive the public. Tony Martin ought never to have been taken to trial and the fact that he was is anathema to justice.

| Sat 21 AUG 0.34 am 94 | **Foreman's Bungalow, Emneth Hungate**
According to official records, CI Curtis and PCs Cant and Gotts arrived at Foreman's Cottage having left King's Lynn at 0:09am and met with PCs White and Girton (also an armed response team) who were already there.
The following is PC Gotts' account: |

"I also was aware that it was possible the injured man was an intruder at the premises and had accomplices with him who may also have been injured. It was clear more resources were needed to achieve any of the earlier options considered in safety so a request was made to arrange for further support. As this support would take a considerable amount of time to assemble it was decided to also request air support with specialist equipment. We maintained our positions and waited the arrival of the Cambridgeshire Police helicopter.

When this arrived it was able to make a comprehensive aerial sweep of the area surrounding the premises using firstly heat seeking equipment, then powerful spotlight equipment."

| **What this adds to our knowledge** | That's at least four constables sitting in their cars and not searching for the missing injured male if we are to believe the statements attributed to them. Official records show that PS Davidson and PC Mann were allegedly still at the Leets' house, as were PCs Raines, Hooper, Beer and Cole. I make that ten police officers at the scene doing very little and certainly not searching for "the outstanding person" if we can believe the official records. |

Sat
21 AUG
1.01 am
95

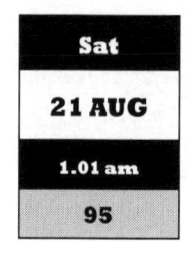

call from helicopter to control room
The CAD report stated that the Cambridgeshire Constabulary helicopter had called to say that it was on its way and that its estimated time of arrival (ETA) was five minutes hence. Apparently the helicopter also asked the control room to ensure that cars on site activate their blue lights to assist the helicopter in its search.

How on earth could Norfolk Constabulary later claim that they couldn't even find Bleak House?

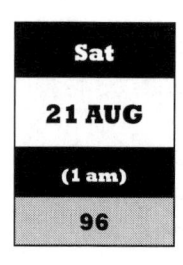

Sat
21 AUG
(1 am)
96

Bleak House
According to official records, CI Curtis claimed that the helicopter arrived "about 1a.m."; (note the lack of accuracy in the timing from a senior police officer - this is reminiscent of concocted statements written by senior police officers in the Hillsborough tragedy).

He added "I watched it circle Mr Martin's farm on several occasions, and received information from them that the only heat sources that they could see were animals."

The only heat sources were animals? Do you believe this nonsense? Even if Barras had died by this time, his body would have been warm enough (it was, after all, August) to have been picked up by the thermal imaging cameras.

Notice how this statement reflects the statements of low-ranking PCs Girton and White which we have previously seen. It is clear that the statements could have been true, or that collusion has taken place, or that the statements of Girton and White have been re-written by senior officers (as occurred at Hillsborough). There is, of course, an easy way to establish the truth – obtain the log of the helicopter flight over Bleak House that night.

Sat
21 AUG
(1.05 am)
97

Bleak House
PC Girton claimed in his unused witness statement that the helicopter arrived at this time (which seems to corroborate what Chief Inspector Curtis had stated.)

PC Cant in his statement also said that the helicopter arrived at this time.

Sat
21 AUG
1.15 am
98

control room attempts to contact Commander Thacker
According to official records, the Control Room attempted to make contact with Commander Thacker but he was said to have been "not available".

Sat
21 AUG
1.20 am
99

King's Lynn police station
Official records show that Inspector Chilvers left King's Lynn in a car driven by PC 1025 Graham Bavin.

In a witness statement attributed to him, Chilvers stated that he became aware that a helicopter "with thermal-imaging equipment was on its way to the crime scene".

However, this contradicted the timing provided by CI Curtis and PC Cant. I could find no mention in the CAD report of PC Bavin as having been dispatched to the scene, but see entry **173**.

Sat
21 AUG
1.25 am
100

Bleak House, Emneth
PC Cant claimed in his statement that the helicopter ceased its search of the area at this time, having only found "two dogs". PC Cant added that he and his partner remained in their car outside Foreman's Cottage until 4:10am and that PCs Girton and White were parked outside the barn at Bleak House for a similar length of time.

Sat
21 AUG
1.40 am
101

Queen Elizabeth Hospital, King's Lynn
According to official records, Brendon Fearon was taken to the x-ray department prior to being operated on.

Sat
21 AUG
1.43 am
102

Bleak House, Emneth
Records show that Inspector Chilvers and PC Bavin arrive at the scene.

We're now up to a dozen officers at the scene (that we know of from the "official" statements.)

Sat
21 AUG
1.45 am
103

Bleak House, Emneth

The statement of Inspector Chilvers shows that the Cambridgeshire police helicopter arrived at this time, circled the area and used its searchlight and heat-seeking equipment. PC 960 Andrew Plumb (assigned to the Air Support Unit at RAF Wyton) stated that the helicopter arrived at 1:45am in an unsigned witness statement.

What this adds to our knowledge

Clearly this timing is significantly different from that provided by CI Curtis and others. Wouldn't you think it was pretty simple to record the time of a helicopter flight (since it's recorded in the log book of all flights)? [See also entry dated 23 August 1999].

Sat
21 AUG
1.45 am
104

Queen Elizabeth Hospital, King's Lynn

According to official records, Brendon Fearon was taken to the operating theatre.

At this time, Tony Martin was in a light sleep on a sofa in the Marmion House Hotel in Wisbech.

Sat
21 AUG
1.46 am
105

control room instructions to police

According to official records, the Control Room requested police in the area to keep Tony's car under observation only and that it was likely to be found at the Marmion House Hotel.

Sat
21 AUG
2 am
UNUSED
106

home address of PC 322 Philip Clarke

According to his statement, PC 322 Philip Clarke was called on duty from his home and tasked to attend the Emneth shooting with PC 1088 Mark Gray. That's now at least 14 police officers of varying rank at the scene of the crime and yet – according to all their statements – not one of them has been to Bleak House.

Strangely, according to the statement by PC Gotts, he and PC Cant were not relieved by Clarke and Gray until 4:10am. If this is true, then what were Clarke and Gray doing during those two missing hours?

So, if Clarke had been called on duty at 2am, why did he not arrive at Bleak House (according to his statement)[99] until 4am? In fact, the CAD report stated that the two officers arrived at 4:30am, having been dispatched at 3:27am. Then, despite not having been cleared to leave the scene, the CAD report has the two officers arriving *again* at 5:20am before being cleared to leave the scene at 6:08am. Aside from the missing two hours unaccounted for, note this comment:

"On the Smeeth Road we relieved two officers from their point: PC 400 Girton and PC 852 White. This point was on the Smeeth Road about 150 metres on the Marshland St James side of the driveway to Bleak House.

We were on this point from 4:00am to 6:00am. *Not at any time did we drive into the driveway of Bleak House.*"

What this adds to our knowledge	The emphasis is mine. Here is yet another police statement in which an officer is distancing himself from having entered the driveway to Bleak House or being anywhere near its immediate environment. Now, I ask again, why would a police officer make a statement to say he *hadn't* done something?

Furthermore, PC Clarke claimed that he and Gray had relieved PCs Girton and White at 4am, but the CAD report shows that Girton and White were still on the scene at 5:19am.

And, I ask again, was this a true statement written by PC Clarke or had it been re-written à la Hillsborough by senior officers to cover their tracks for the death of Barras who *hadn't* been shot by Tony Martin?

I could find no statement from PC Gray.

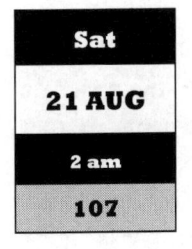

Sat	**operating theatre, Queen Elizabeth Hospital**
21 AUG	*Fearon was re-examined with Mr Anil Chakrabarti*[100] *joining Shantu Mandal*[101] *and Ashish Prabhudesai,*[102] *Senior House Officer in Orthopaedics (who apparently didn't make a statement until 26 September 1999 – but we don't know where the statement was made, at what time, to whom, though it was apparently witnessed by a Julie Berry, though there is no signature.)*
2 am	
107	

---

[99] There is a statement attributed to PC Clarke dated 27 August 1999. There is no time recorded, no mention of to whom the statement was made or even where it was made. There was no signature nor, of course, a witness to the statement.
[100] Anil Chakrabarti was prosecution witness number 49.
[101] Shantanu Mandal was prosecution witness number 47.
[102] Ashish Prabhudesai was prosecution witness number 48.

The blood supply to both legs "remained satisfactory" despite there being "a 10 cm x 10 cm heavily contaminated wound on the left thigh."

All of the wounds were left open and dressed appropriately. Several pieces of shot were removed and given to theatre practitioner Karen Whittleton. [Author's note: I could find no statement from Ms Whittleton].

We now turn to the 36-year-old Anil Chakrabarti's statement made on 3rd September, a fortnight after the incident.

This statement also doesn't provide any note of where it was made, at what time it was made or to which officer it was made. It was not signed or witnessed.

"Upon my arrival in the theatre, the patient was already anaesthetised, prepared and draped on the operating table with both legs exposed and his genitalia covered."

And then the rest of the statement reads almost word for word as that of Shantanu Mandal's. However, Mr Chakrabarti added that on 23 August, Fearon gave his verbal and written consent for "bullet swabs and other material" being used as forensic evidence together with photographs of his injuries, he was again taken to theatre where his wounds were redressed under a general anaesthetic. The statement added that also in attendance were DC Trevor Buxton and SOCO Laura Bishop. It was explained to Fearon that he would require plastic surgery to his thighs and skin grafts.

Bizarrely, in my view, Dr Prabhudesai's final sentence in his (unsigned) statement read: "This description is consistent with the account given by Mr Mandal."

How would he know?

I am not at all satisfied that any one of these statements is bona fide on a number of levels. And do we really believe that Fearon didn't mention Barras to a single one of these people examining him?

If we subscribe to the view that these statements are not bona fide and that they have been altered in some way, the question arises: why would the police do that? What would they have to gain by changing witness statements (if they were, indeed, changed?) Well, Hillsborough taught us that almost 200 witness statements were changed *by the police in collusion with their lawyers* and many were completely re-written. The motivation of senior police officers was, as we have now learned, to cover-up their own inadequacies. For more on that subject (and I was there as a Liverpool supporter on 15 April 1989), I refer you to the work by Professor Phil Scraton of the University of Belfast who writes extensively about the police corruption in the Hillsborough tragedy. Who on earth would imagine that police corruption was confined only to Hillsborough?

We've already learnt that – according to Brendon Fearon's statement dated 23 August 1999 – he saw a helicopter flying over Bleak House whilst lying on his back to rest after stumbling and crawling through a cornfield towards the Leets' bungalow. The fact that he was moving through a cornfield appears to have been confirmed by the medical statements that we've just read because pieces of corn were found in his wounds. But can we trust the authenticity of those medical statements, or have they been altered by senior police officers to place Fearon in the cornfield after having allegedly escaped Bleak House?

I'll continue with the chronology of the police operation that I pieced together from reading tens of dozens of witness statements:

Sat 21 AUG 2.20 am 108

St John's, Fen End
Official records show that PCs Cole and Beer left the scene to drive to St John's, Fen End to speak with Edward Martin, a cousin of Tony's, with regard to trying to locate the farmer.

There is no record on the CAD report, however, of the officers ever having been cleared to leave the scene to drive to St John's, Fen End.

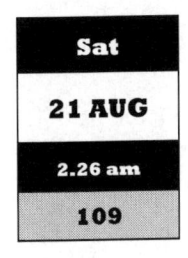

Sat 21 AUG 2.26 am 109

Bleak House
The official Norfolk Constabulary CAD report recorded: "Tony Martin's in darkness. Phone call to the premises – no reply" at 02:26:43.

That simple line in the CAD report causes the police several problems: (i) it is not possible to establish that the house was in darkness unless you had been there, (ii) if you had been there, then the statements by several constables that they couldn't find the house have all been fabricated, (iii) that the house *couldn't have been in darkness because Tony Martin left his bedroom light on day and night*, (iv) that he didn't turn the light out when he left his house, and (v) that if *he* didn't turn the light out before driving to his mother's, then who did?

It is at this point in the story that I ask you to seriously consider the notion that the intruders who smashed their way into the house, waking the farmer, were not burglars at all but people staging a scene to make it look as though a burglary had been taking place and that the farmer had shot them. In my opinion, only a fool would *automatically assume* that the farmer had shot men because (A) he had fired his gun and (B) men were found with gunshot injuries.

A plus B created, I suggest, a false conclusion that Tony Martin – who admitted to having fired his shotgun - had shot Fearon and Barras whereas, in fact, it was impossible for him to have shot them from the stairs. And if I am wrong in that analysis, why are there so many inaccuracies in the police statements, why won't the police release a list of all 999 calls made that night, why won't the police release the flight logs of the helicopter(s) flying over Bleak House, why did the police claim that they didn't know of the existence of Barras, why did the police claim they couldn't find Bleak House even though it had been clearly marked on ordnance survey maps for more than 100 years, why did they claim that they couldn't find Barras because of Tony Martin's dogs and why did so many police officers make statements in which they denied that they had been anywhere near Bleak House even though the official CAD report had placed them there? And why, if Barras had died as the police claimed at around 10pm on *the Friday night,* was he still "in full rigor mortis" according to the pathologist some 41 hours later at 3pm *on the Sunday afternoon* when according to nature's own immutable clock, the body would have returned to its flaccid state?

Sat 21 AUG 2.30 am 110	**Bleak House** *According to her witness statement dated 21 August 1999,* PC *Clare Smith returned to King's Lynn police station to process Fearon's clothing. However, as we have seen, the official Norfolk Constabulary* CAD *report has her placed at the hospital between 11:37pm and 3:56am.*

It is surely not possible for her to (a) have been at the hospital and (b) to have taken Fearon's clothes from the hospital to King's Lynn police station without first having been cleared to leave the scene. All of which leads us to conclude that her statement and/or the CAD report must be false.

Sat 21 AUG 2.41 am 111	**Marmion House Hotel, Lynn Road, Wisbech** *Official records show that the police had identified Tony's car outside the hotel at this time.* This would indicate that Tony was inside the hotel and not still at Bleak House as a possible "lone gunman threat" to the police or others.

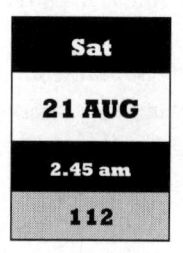

Sat 21 AUG 2.45 am 112	**Bleak House** *Official records show that with several junior ranked officers away from the scene, Superintendent John Richard Hale arrived.* [See also entry **285**]

Sat
21 AUG
3 am
113

Hungate Corner

PCs Cole and Beer are said to have returned to the scene from St John's, Fen End, having apparently ascertained that Tony was not with his cousin Edward. Records show that acting Inspector Robert Linley Turner of the Cambridgeshire Constabulary arrived and spoke with Supt Hale and CI Curtis.

According to the CAD report, Inspector Turner met with Supt Hale and an unnamed Chief Inspector at the Marmion House Hotel car park at 3:30am where they saw Tony's car. We ought to question why Tony wasn't arrested for another 2½ hours according to the official records.

Sat
21 AUG
3.33 am
114

Marmion House Hotel, Lynn Road, Wisbech

Official records show that the unnamed Chief Inspector, an unnamed Superintendent and Inspector Turner (the duty inspector at Wisbech) arrived at the hotel.

Why, we might ask, didn't they arrest Tony Martin at this point? I could find no record of where these police officers went after having arrived at the hotel or for how long they apparently stayed.

Sat
21 AUG
4.10 am
115

Bleak House

Having allegedly been relieved by Clarke and Gray, official records show that PCs Gotts and Cant left the scene and returned to Norwich.

The CAD report showed Gotts and Cant as having arrived in a car with a call sign of TC01 and yet they were cleared to leave the scene in a car with a call sign of TC70.

Two officers with collar numbers of 70 (PC Coller) and 17 (PC Maxwell) left the scene in TC01 yet there is no mention of these two officers as having even been dispatched to the scene in the CAD report provided to Tony Martin although, significantly I believe, there are further pages missing. Why would Tony's barrister not have ensured that his client was provided with a complete and *bona fide* copy of the CAD report?

Do you still think that Tony Martin shot Fearon and Barras? Do you still think he was guilty of murder, manslaughter or wounding with intent or do you believe from the evidence thus far that he was the victim of a police "stitch-up" and deserves to have his convictions quashed?

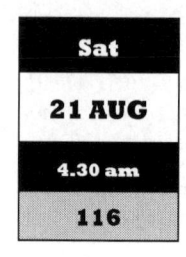

Bleak House

Sat 21 AUG 4.30 am 116

*Official records show that PCs Cole and Beer went off duty. According to his statement, PC 17 Duncan Craig Maxwell, 36, attended in his capacity as a firearms officer. He was said to have manned a checkpoint at Hungate Corner until 6am before returning to King's Lynn at "about 6:30am" (note the lack of accuracy). [See also **234**].*

By my Maths, I make it at least 20 police officers (that we have been told about) who attended the scene and yet still no-one had found Barras?

Bizarrely, the Norfolk Constabulary CAD report shows that all of the officers deployed that evening were dispatched to the Hungate Corner and *not to Bleak House* the alleged scene of the shooting of Barras and Fearon. Now, why would all the officers be sent to the bungalow at the Hungate Corner and not to Bleak House? What was occurring at Bleak House that senior police officers didn't want discovered?

King's Lynn police station

Sat 21 AUG 4.30 am 117

In a witness statement dated as late as 1st October 1999, Detective Sergeant Peter Colin Newton stated that "at 4:30am on Saturday 21st August 1999 PC 9130 Smith handed me two sheets of paper containing rough notes, one exhibited as CAS/11 & the other as JM/1. I retained these exhibits."

Let's turn to the exhibit JM/1 first. It was, as stated, an A4 piece of white paper. It has the exhibit number JM/1 in the top right-hand corner. The name 'Brendon Fearon' is spelled out in capital letters in the middle of the page, together with his address and date of birth. This is what Fearon told the Police before they Police before they decided to change his narrative for their own:

"I pulled into the drive to ask where to put my van and a dog came towards me. I saw the owner and told him to watch his dog and then he shot me.
 I remember two SHOTS" - (in capital letters in the original).

PC Miller then added the following:

- wounds to both legs (thighs)
- left thigh possibly dog wound
- right thigh serious gunshot wound.

PC Miller also added the telephone number of the ambulance station. This statement was obviously not used because it completely undermined the entire case against Tony Martin. According to these notes, Fearon was driving a van. There was, it seems, no "getaway driver".

The fact that Fearon got out to ask where to put his van suggests that he had a pre-arranged appointment to pick up something: perhaps antiques, drugs, or money. This was the world in which Fearon moved.

Apparently a dog went towards Fearon and the owner came outside. Fearon told him to "watch your dog" and, as he walked away, he was shot. Fearon remembered two shots.

None of this, of course, matches the police narrative of Tony Martin shooting "burglars" inside his house. Then we turn to PC Miller's additional comments: that Fearon had sustained wounds in both legs, and that the one on the left thigh was *possibly caused by a dog*. The constable had added that the wound to the right thigh had been caused by a "gunshot" and not a shot gun. There is a subtle, but important, difference.

The police and the CPS would claim that Fearon's comments were lies – that he had concocted a story to avoid a burglary charge. But if that were true, why would the CPS deliberately choose to airbrush this statement and exhibit out of the trial, out of history?

It seems that the comments made by Fearon were true – that he had driven down to Emneth and pulled into a driveway and been perhaps bitten by a dog and shot outside. This would mean, of course, that Tony Martin could not possibly have shot him.

But notice that Fearon didn't mention Fred Barras in these comments to the police. Was this a man covering up for the young tearaway, or was the truth that Barras was lured elsewhere and shot elsewhere or at a different time from Fearon?

CORRUPTION ALERT *Constable's statements and exhibit not used at trial*

PC Miller's two separate statements were never used at trial. His exhibit – the piece of paper on which was recorded Fearon's original statement – was not entered as evidence.

Any defence barrister in the country would have called PC Miller as a witness to tell the jury what Fearon had originally told the police as to how he had become injured. That Scrivener did not call PC Miller supports the notion that this case was not being handled by the judiciary but by Ministers of the State. Other evidence will later substantiate this view.

Now that we know that PC Miller's two statements and exhibit were not used at trial, we are forced to ask why the CPS would airbrush these documents out of history. Clearly they contained information that someone did not want the jury or the public to know.

Furthermore, we must note that DS Newton *was aware of Fearon's account prior to his interviewing Tony Martin.*

We now turn to exhibit CAS/11. This also suggests corruption. There are three statements attributed to PC Clare Smith, dated 21 August (in which she painstakingly and correctly listed Fearon's clothing as exhibits 1-10 but makes no mention whatsoever of exhibit 11), 27 September (still no mention of exhibit 11) and a second statement also dated 27 September in which exhibit CAS/11 is then mentioned.

In what was allegedly her *third* statement, PC Smith stated:

"Further to my last statement I would like to add, that on 21st August 1999, I made notes on a piece of paper, concerning names of people involved in the treatment of Brendon Fearon, whilst at the Queen Elizabeth Hospital, King's Lynn. I also made additional notes on the paper. I can exhibit this piece of paper as CAS/11. On the same day at approximately 2:15am, I received from PC 1282 Miller a piece of paper, which were his original notes of the conversation with Brendon Fearon. I took possession of the paper, and passed it along with my exhibit CAS/11 to PS Newton 4:30am."

Quite why it had taken *three* statements for PC Smith to allegedly recall these notes defies belief. But also notice another sleight-of-hand: the notes made by PC Jonathan Miller on the night (and therefore *his* exhibit) have allegedly been passed to DS Newton by PC Smith, not Miller.

In his *first* statement, PC Miller claimed: "I could see that Fearon had wounds to both of his legs. PC 9130 Smith asked Fearon several questions relating to how Fearon had sustained his leg injuries, and I made hand written notes on a piece of unmarked white A4 paper in my own handwriting, recording his reply.

Due to operational duties I then was diverted to another task at the A&E department and handed my handwritten notes to PC 9130 Smith before leaving. This statement is from my original notes."

This again could lead the reasonable person to smell a rat. More than a month had passed between PC Miller making notes by Fearon's bedside and the *second* statement attributed to him. Surely the constable would have mentioned these notes – fundamental to his being at Fearon's bedside – in his *first* statement.

Sat	**Terrington St John police station**
21 AUG	
4.50 am	
UNUSED	
118	

Terrington St John police station

According to official records, the 33-year-old Darren Bark was interviewed at this time by DC Peters.

The CAD report shows that Bark was being transferred from Terrington St John beat base police station to divisional headquarters at King's Lynn at 5:02am.

Given the length of this statement, I don't believe that Bark was processed at Terrington, interviewed and into a car to King's Lynn all within 12 minutes. Again, I call into question the veracity of these statements.

"I have lived at my present lodgings for the past 5 years. For the past two weeks I have been staying at my girlfriend's. She is Dawn Jepson who lives in Newark with her dad.

I have lived in Newark most of my life and I know a lot of people there. I know a number of the travellers who live on the Tolney Road site and I know a good few of the Nottinghamshire knockers. One of these is a lad called Brendon Fearon whom I have known for about 8 years. I have never done any knocking with him or any other work and I have never committed an offence with him.

The last time I saw Brendon was on Thursday 19 August 1999 when I took him to the dentist's at Long Eaton in Derbyshire. On that day Brendon phoned me up on my mobile phone and asked me to take him. I picked him up from his home at around 12 noon and we drove there in my white Ford Granada F98LHJ. We got there in plenty of time and had to wait for the appointment.

After Brendon had been to the dentist's, I took him back to Newark and dropped him off at his girlfriend's in Devon Road. I don't know her name. *I made no arrangements to see Brendon again.*

Brendon told me that he was currently working as a bouncer at Lighting Jacks about 3 nights a week.

After dropping Brendon off I went back to Dawn's and stayed there the rest of the night. I did not get up until about 11am on Friday morning. Dawn made me a cup of tea and then I went out on my own in my car for a drive around. I drove around Mansfield and Chesterfield. I did not call anywhere. I arrived back at Dawn's at about 5.30 to 6pm that evening.[103]

I watched a video (Jungle Book) while Dawn made me some tea. We sat in her room watching the television until a mate of mine called Eddie called round. He had a load of shirts for sale which he had in a hire car he was driving - I

---

[103] We would be wise to consider that Bark had had ample time to drive to Bleak House and back. I do not necessarily dispute his claims to have been elsewhere, but if, as others claimed, he had set up a planned burglary of Bleak House, it is possible that he went there to finalise any details.

think it was a Mercedes from Hampsons.

I sat and talked to Eddie for about an hour and then went back indoors. At about 10pm I got a phone call. I think the call was made from a phonebox[104] to Dawn's home phone. I don't know the number of Dawn's phone but I had it written down and I had given it to a number of my friends, including Brendon.

I answered the phone which was in Dawn's room. The caller said, "Are you alright Daz? Is that you?" 'Daz' is my nickname. I did not recognise the caller's voice and the caller seemed out of breath and excited. I said, "Yeah, it's me. What do you want?"

The caller said, "We've got some trouble, me and Brendon. Can you come and pick us up straightaway?"

I said, "Where are you?" He didn't say what trouble he and Brendon were in but he asked me to get there as quick as I could and gave me directions.

I left Dawn's immediately and travelled down to Wisbech and then took the directions I had been given. I couldn't find Brendon or his mate and I drove along every route that I could see; once I came out onto a main road and then turned back around and drove back into the countryside.

I drove slowly like this for about half an hour until I drove into a dead end, then I put some petrol in my car from a can I had in the boot and it was while I was doing this I saw an ambulance go to a house nearby.[105] I saw a police car arrive about the same time as the ambulance.[106] I drove towards where I had seen the ambulance and it was then I got stopped by the police.

The police told me that someone had been shot and later I was told that it was Brendon Fearon who had been shot. To start with I told the police a lie: I said I was looking for my mate Joe who was driving a red transit and had broken down. This was not true. I made this up because I was frightened by what was happening. I really do not know the name of the lad who phoned me up and obviously he did not tell me what had occurred because I would not have come out and got involved had I known what was happening.

I cannot remember the number of my mobile phone or Dawn's number. I have owned the Granada for about a week. I bought it off Joe. I paid him £250

---

[104] In his police interview dated 23 August 1999 (according to official records), Tony informed the officers that there was a phonebox on the Hungate Corner at the time of the shooting. Other locals confirmed this. It has since been removed.

[105] If Bark left Newark immediately after the phonecall at 10pm, he would have arrived at the Hungate Corner at sometime between 11:30pm and midnight. He could not, therefore, have seen the ambulance which took Fearon to the hospital, because *that* ambulance was arriving at the hospital in King's Lynn if we believe the official records. If his statement is true, however, was this a *second* ambulance collecting Barras and if so, was Barras still alive at this point?

[106] According to the CAD report, no police car was on the scene when the ambulance arrived at 11:01pm. The first police car is said to have arrived at 11:06pm.

for the car. It's registered in the name of the bloke that Joe bought the car from. All I know about him is that he is the landlord of The Cardinal's Hat pub.

I have been asked to speculate as to who the caller was who rang me on Friday evening might have been. It was definitely not Brendon - I know his voice well. The only lad I know who goes about with Brendon quite a lot is Roy Bowers. The last time I saw Roy was last Saturday in the Old Market Pub; he was with Brendon at the time. The only other people who I have given Dawn's telephone number to are Eddie, Mick and my landlord and landlady. I do not know where Roy Bowers lives, but when I spoke to him last Saturday he said that he was going knocking in London.

If I knew the identity of the person who phoned me I would say his name."

> **What this adds to our knowledge**
>
> The emphases are the author's. This potentially changes everything and would explain a lot of re-writes of statements around the timing of the alleged burglary. Alternatively, it could simply have been an elaborate narrative created by Bark to extricate him from any involvement in a prospective burglary.

However, it might actually be based in truth. For this present discussion, let's assume that it's true and that Bark did receive a call from someone saying: "We've got some trouble, me and Brendon. Can you come and pick us up straightaway?"

Surely the phrase "me and Brendon" immediately suggests that Fred Barras made the call. Or was it Fearon who called and Bark was, at this point, covering up for him?

Alternatively, it might have been a third party altogether – perhaps another prospective burglar. You'll read in due course about a villager who said she saw two cars speeding away from the direction of Bleak House. This would mean, then, that Bark wasn't necessarily the getaway driver which begs the question: "If it wasn't Bark, then who was it?"

Bark claimed that he thought that the call had been made from a phonebox so, if that's true, then it probably wasn't the injured Barras or Fearon, unless Barras had called *prior to being shot*. But, if it wasn't Bark, Barras or Fearon, then it *must* have been someone else, another member of the prospective burglary team or perhaps a rogue police officer.

If the call was really made, and if we subscribe to Bark's timings, he would have arrived at Hungate Corner between 11:30pm and midnight. That's completely possible, so we might be wise to re-assess our notion that the original getaway driver was Bark. I will return to this point in subsequent entries, because we will gain more important information about this in due course.

I'm also interested in the claim that Bark topped up his car with petrol from a can. If true, this could suggest that he did, in fact, receive a call and race down to Emneth without stopping to fill up the car. From another angle, perhaps he had been parked up in Emneth all along and added petrol simply because he wanted some sort of alibi to watch what was happening further down Moyse's Bank outside the Leets' bungalow.

Surely the simplest way to investigate Bark's claims would have been to have obtained the phone records of Dawn Jepson, and I could not find that this had been done. This leads me to conclude that not obtaining or producing those records suggests a cover-up of some sort.

Although we should bear in mind that this whole statement is nonsense, some of the issues raised in it will not go away.

Flipping the coin, we are forced to explore the notion that Bark *was* the getaway driver and had dropped off Fearon and Barras somewhere between 9:45pm and 10:15pm. Crucially, by this time, Tony had *already fired his shotgun at an unknown number of intruders and he had already called round to the Leets*.

Bark admitted owning a mobile phone. The police told him they recovered two from the Granada after his arrest. So, if he had a mobile phone, and if he was the original getaway driver and knew that gunshots had been fired, why did he not call the police and ask for an ambulance? Of course, you might say that he would not call the police at this point because he could make good his escape and not be implicated. But he must have known that there was no sight of Fearon or Barras and surely anyone would have called the police and asked for an ambulance in those circumstances. Honour amongst thieves is all well and good in Hollywood movies, but when there have been shots fired, surely your first course of action is to get some medical help. But before we might be inclined to condemn Bark for not taking what we might feel would have been appropriate action in the circumstances, we must be patient because, like most things in this case, all is not as it seems...

Sat 21 AUG 5.54 am 119

Marmion House Hotel, Lynn Road, Wisbech

Acting Inspector Robert Linley Turner then played his part when, at 5:50am on Saturday 21 August 1999, he returned to the Marmion with other officers and spoke with Helen Lilley. She led them through to a lounge area, where they saw Tony lying on a settee. According to the official records, Tony was arrested at 5:54am on suspicion of the attempted murder of Brendon Fearon.[107] He was then cautioned, but made no reply before being escorted about one hundred yards from the hotel along the Lynn Road to Wisbech police station.

---

[107] In all of our conversations, Tony has consistently told me that he was arrested on suspicion of wounding Fearon, not for attempted murder.

Tony Martin was processed and put in police cell number four. Meanwhile, the agencies of State were swiftly moving into action. It would seem from all the available evidence that senior officers were gathered round creating a story that would implicate this most awkward of critics against police ineffectiveness and against sexual abuse in a private boarding school. Having been at Hillsborough, I see remarkable echoes in Tony's case of what the South Yorkshire Police did immediately after the gate was opened – they sprang into action to provide a story that a gullible British public would buy into and one which would (a) defame the innocent Liverpool fans and (b) extricate the police from their own wrong-doing.

Denial and blaming others for your own wrong-doing is the default position of constabularies, local authorities, the Church and all other agencies of State.

Sat 21 AUG 6.08 am 120

Bleak House
According to official records, Inspector Chilvers left the scene and was driven away by PC 1025 Bavin.

In the statement attributed to Chilvers, it stated: "All other officers present, except PS Davidson and PC Mann, left about the same time."

Can you believe this? The "third person" – presumed to be injured – has allegedly still not been found and dozens of officers leave the scene. Who took that ludicrous decision, and why? But is it even true, or have these statements been falsely created? As previously stated, I could find no direct reference to PC Bavin on the CAD report.

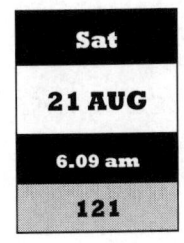

Sat 21 AUG 6.09 am 121

somewhere in Cambridgeshire
According to official records, an unnamed male was arrested in Cambridgeshire. The official CAD report added: "No weapon found".

The CAD report did not contain any further mention of who this arrested person was, but he was presumably linked to the incident and, it would seem, it was thought that he might have been armed. Again, we are forced to ask why Tony's barrister at trial didn't seek this information.

Sat
21 AUG
7.08 am
UNUSED
122

Hungate Corner, Emneth
According to a statement,[108] PC 1267 William George arrived on the scene to replace PS Davidson. The CAD report shows that PC George left at 7:09am – just one minute later.

PC George's statement – unused at trial - can be found on 25 August 1999 [see entry 125).

Sat
21 AUG
7.14 am
UNUSED
123

Hungate Corner, Emneth
According to the Norfolk Constabulary CAD report, PC 9078 Carmel Ann Fitzpatrick, 27, was dispatched to the Hungate Corner at 7:14am, arriving one second later and was cleared to leave the scene at 8:03am. In her unused statement dated 26 August 1999, she is alleged to have said: "About 7:15am on Saturday 21st August 1999 I was on duty in full uniform on mobile patrol at King's Lynn. I never attended Emneth that day and was dealing with another incident in King's Lynn totally unrelated to the Emneth enquiry."

She did not state what the "other incident" in King's Lynn was about and nor did she provide any evidence that she was at King's Lynn. [See also entry **203**]

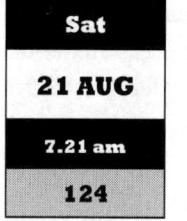

Sat
21 AUG
7.21 am
124

arrest of Darren Bark
According to official records, Darren Bark was arrested at this time "on suspicion of involvement in the burglary."

At this point, of course, no burglary had been proven.

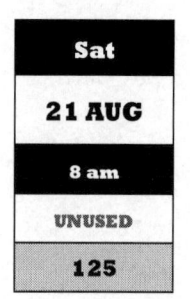

Sat
21 AUG
8 am
UNUSED
125

Bleak House
According to an unused statement,[109] on Saturday 21 August 1999, the 37-year-old PC 86 Ian Thexton was on duty at King's Lynn police station in full uniform, working an early shift, 7am to 3pm.

He claimed to have arrived on the scene to replace PC 1267 William George:

---

[108] See 25 August 1999.

[109] Recorded as allegedly having been made on 11 November 1999 – some three months after the shooting incident.

"At about 7:30am, as a result of information received, I went to Bleak House, Emneth where, overnight, a firearms incident had occurred. My purpose for attending was to secure the scene and relieve the night duty officer, Will George.

Upon attending I was informed that an incident had occurred *in the grounds of Bleak House*,[110] and that I was to prevent anyone having access to the house and grounds from Smeeth Road. I remained at the junction of the access road from Smeeth Road to Bleak House. I completed a log of callers to the premises,[111] although no access was given.

I was also informed by the night duty officer that three rottweiler dogs were roaming the grounds.[112] I remained at my given location and was advised by local residents to beware of the dogs, as they were very vicious.[113]

Later I was advised that persons unknown may attend the premises[114] and attempt to remove the firearm, which was still unaccounted for.

I relocated my police vehicle to just outside the main grain barn, opposite a field on which farm machinery was parked. On numerous occasions one or more of the dogs approached me at my location.

I was later joined by officers from a search team, who carried out various searches locally.[115]

Arrangements were made for dog wardens to attend and capture the wandering dogs.

A male friend[116] of the owner attended and assisted to round up the dogs, which were known to him. He had with him a large bag of animal bones to use.

A while later[117] the male assisting the search team to capture the dogs returned to my location, in company with PC 9059 Nichola Louise Marshall.

I was informed that a male's body had been discovered in the grounds of Bleak House. Various other members[118] of the police force later attended the scene, and the area was secured by officers.

Throughout, while I was present at Bleak House, I completed a log detailing those who attended and left the scene. Each entry made by me was signed and

---

[110] Author's emphasis. Notice how this is supported by Fearon's first statement to the police and doctors in that he claimed to have been shot whilst walking up a track.
[111] I have been unable to locate the existence of this log.
[112] How would they know this if the helicopter only located two dogs (allegedly)?
[113] When I met local resident Eileen Sutton on 13 January 2019, she told me that one of the dogs was a frequent visitor to her house where her husband would stroke it.
[114] Who advised him and who were these persons supposed to be?
[115] Who were these officers, at what time was this, and where did they search? All of the answers to these questions ought to have been in his statement.
[116] This was possibly Roger Putterill. See his separate statements.
[117] Notice the absence of an accurate time – a feature of all of the police statements.
[118] Notice the absence of named officers.

timed.[119]

I was relieved by other officers,[120] and handed the log to a night duty constable at 11:10pm.[121]

One of the dogs remained at the location as those milling were unable to capture it."

> **What this adds to our knowledge**
>
> I believe that that statement is an appalling indictment of Norfolk Constabulary's "investigation" into this murder case. It is full of inconsistencies and alarming holes where full details ought to have been recorded.

I do not trust the truthfulness of this statement and I am deeply concerned that it was not authored (allegedly) until 11 November 1999 – some 3 months after the shooting incident.

According to his statement, PC George arrived at Bleak House to replace PS Davidson. Yet here PC Thexton is claiming he replaced the night duty officer Will George at 7:30am. Clearly, PC George couldn't have been the night duty officer if he didn't arrive on the scene until 7:08am. Furthermore, if it's true that PC George *did* arrive at 7:08am, and was cleared to leave the scene at 7:09am, how could he have been replaced at 7:30am if he'd already gone? It clearly doesn't make sense and I suggest that these statements have been fraudulently created and/or altered.

Furthermore, why didn't PC George mention in his statement that he was crewed with PC Cook? That's a strange omission don't you think? And why would PC Cook say in his statement "On Friday the 20th of August 1999 I was on duty, and crewed with PC 1267 George on mobile patrol in King's Lynn and at no time during that duty did we attend at the incident at Emneth"?

Even more worryingly, there is no mention of PC 86 Thexton in the official constabulary CAD report. In other words, officially he wasn't even there...

---

[119] I have been unable to locate this log.

[120] Again unnamed.

[121] If PC Thexton was working the 7am-3pm shift, how was he able to hand over the log at 11:30pm, given that he didn't mention that he worked overtime?

Sat
21 AUG
(8 am)
witness 3
126

Bleak House

Around 8am, Roger Putterill, a friend of Tony's and son-in-law to the owner of the Marmion House Hotel, Helen Lilley, went to Bleak House and offered to round up Tony's dogs for the police. Putterill claimed to have heard about the shooting on the radio, knew the dogs well and had turned up with a bag of bones.

The police apparently sent him away. Now - why would they do that? Why wouldn't the police want Putterill moving around the area immediately surrounding Bleak House? Notice that in the previous entry, PC Thexton didn't say that they had sent Mr Putterill away and his statement was written in such a way that Tony's friend had stayed on the farm throughout the morning and until early afternoon.

We will return to this incident a little later.

Sat
21 AUG
9.10 am
UNUSED
127

Wisbech police station

According to his witness statement dated 9 September 1999, SOCO officer 6653 Brian Taylor of the Cambridgeshire Constabulary said that at 9:10am on Saturday the 21st August 1999 he attended the Wisbech police station custody suite at the request of Cambridgeshire Constabulary force control room.

"I met with Mr Martin and used a Forensic Science Service gunshot residue or explosive sampling kit no. 3297, following the instructions on the outer packaging, and also the written instructions from inside the kit, in the correct sequence, and part completed the form from inside the kit. On completion I handed the kit with the partially completed form to PC 1149 Hemeter of Norfolk Constabulary at 9:30am."

Bizarrely, this gunshot residue evidence was apparently never entered into evidence at Tony's trial. Nor were his clothes, also taken from him at 6:30am in the cells at Wisbech police station, by PC 961 Michael Judge.

Given that this trial was about the farmer having used his shotgun to "kill and wound burglars", weren't his clothes and the gunshot residue kit of *paramount importance* to prove that the farmer had actually fired his gun?

In notes he made at trial, Tony Martin wrote; "Did anyone test my bedroom, my sheets for gunshot residue? If not, why not? I went to lay on my bed after firing my gun."

He made a good point – no-one had tested these most obvious of items (as far as we were led to believe).

SOCO Brian Taylor apparently made a third statement (all of them unused) as late as 5 November 1999 in which he stated: "Further to my statements of the 9th September, 1999. Relating firstly to my attendance at Wisbech police station at 9:10am, Saturday 21 August, 1999. The explosive sampling kit no. 3297 should now be known as BT/1, gunshot residue kit no. 3297.

Secondly, the photographs of the bar and lounge area of the Marmion Hotel, Lynn Road, Wisbech, which I took on 22 August 1999, at approximately 12:30pm, and exhibited as BT/1, should now be known as BT/1A, photographs."

Not for the first time, exhibits in the Tony Martin trial would be re-labelled and eventually disappear from the case.

Sat 21 AUG 9.25 am 128

Wisbech police station
According to the witness statements of PCs Scott Hemeter (witness 115) and Stuart Kevin Hooper (witness 116), Tony made a call to his friend, Helen Lilley, in which he was alleged by the constables to have said, "They were in the house. I don't know who they were but they pulled a window out. There are tools in the grain shed on the slats that need taking away."

A decision was taken to transport the prisoner from Wisbech to King's Lynn and PC 1149 Scott Hemeter and PC 816 Stuart Hooper were tasked to take Tony to Norfolk, despite his arrest in Cambridgeshire. Geographically in Norfolk, any crime at Bleak House came under the jurisdiction of that constabulary.

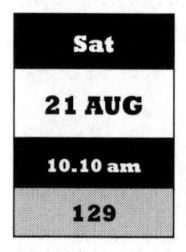

Sat 21 AUG 10.10 am 129

King's Lynn police station
According to official records Tony, upon arrival at King's Lynn police station and before being placed in cell number 4, allegedly said to the desk sergeant in the presence of Hemeter and Hooper: "If the judges locked them up, they wouldn't have to lock people like me up for what I've done like they will."

Both PCs Hemeter and Hooper included that unsolicited comment in their witness statements. Somewhat conveniently in my opinion. In my view, the process of the police fitting Tony up had already begun. See also entry **15** regarding the subject of police officers making uncorroborated statements (uncorroborated, that is, apart from other corrupt officers) in which they claim that a defendant has either directly incriminated himself or made comments which go some way to supporting the prosecution's and police case. By and large this practice still exists but is mostly done in the form of the police creating evidence (using Photoshop or similar tools) which will often bear the (false) signature of the defendant.[122]

Tony denied making any such statement and I have to say that grammatically it certainly doesn't sound like Tony.

| Sat 21 AUG 10.15 am 130 | **police briefing, Downham Market police station**
We learn from police records that a briefing in relation to a search to be carried out at Bleak House (allegedly) took place at Downham Market police station at 10:15am on Saturday 21 August 1999. |

| Sat 21 AUG 10.15 am 131 | **search of Bleak House**
According to official records, a search team was gathering at Bleak House under the command of POLSA Inspector Paul Rush. The team leader was PS 3065 Ian Fletcher. POLSA, which stands for Police Search Adviser, is a British police qualification and also a national educational qualification at City and Guilds level. |

At 11:15am, PC 248 Russell Peter Brett[123] was said to have conducted a search of the outbuildings and barns which are situated between 50 and 100 yards from Bleak House. The statement attributed to PC Brett said: "During the search, and also at the scene, *I did not seize anything from the area.*"[124]

PC 802 Graham Alan Keeley[125] was said to have been part of the search team and in his witness statement he said that it was not until 11:50am that a search started of various outbuildings.

---

[122] See HILLSBOROUGH – THE TRUTH by Professor Phil Scraton, Mainstream Publishing, 2016.

[123] According to official records, PC Brett didn't make a statement about his involvement at Bleak House until 26 October 1999 – some 11½ weeks after the incident. What reasonable explanation can there be for such a lengthy delay? The statement does not show to whom it was made, where it was made or at what time it was made. This causes me considerable concern and it is possible that this statement had either been altered by senior officers or entirely created by them.

[124] Author's emphasis. Note that this is yet another statement from a police officer in which he stated that he *didn't do something* rather than what he *did* do.

[125] Dated 24 August 1999. It was unsigned and no location had been recorded.

Sat
21 AUG
11.30 am
witness 120
132

Bleak House

According to official records, acting DI Sharman claimed in his statement that he visited the scene along with Inspector Rush and a search team. Sharman claimed that he did not get out of his car.

Realistically, as the senior investigating officer at this time, do we really believe that he didn't get out of the car to search the house and gardens? Isn't that the *very least* that the senior investigating officer would do, particularly since the police CAD report had recorded *a full 12 hours previously* that "there may be other injured parties in the orchard and evidence relating to the injuries sustained by [Fearon]"?

Sat
21 AUG
12.25 pm
133

call for Council dog warden to attend

According to official records, acting DI Sharman requested that the three dogs at the scene be dealt with by the council dog warden.

Is it not bizarre that this request had not been made much earlier – or is this request part of the false narrative being created minute-by-minute by the police?

Sat
21 AUG
1.15 pm
134

Bleak House

According to official records, acting DI Sharman returned to King's Lynn police station, presumably to supervise the interviewing of Tony Martin.

So, what had he been doing sitting in his car since 11:30 that morning? Do you subscribe to this police narrative?

Sat
21 AUG
1.54 pm
UNUSED
135

King's Lynn police station

With dozens of police officers allegedly searching the farm, official records (which we do not have to believe) show that Tony was taken from cell 4 to Interview Room One at six minutes before 2pm to be interviewed by DS 3135 Peter Newton and DC 356 Stuart Peters.[126]

Due to my research into child abuse and miscarriages of justice, I have been in many police interview rooms (see my books

---

[126] In yet another example of corruption, this interview is shown in HOLMES as having been used as evidence. It wasn't. At trial, Judge Owen made a shocking and unlawful ruling that it shouldn't be used as evidence and that the jury shouldn't see the transcript.

Framed! and *10 Prisons, 12 Weeks*) and they are all usually bare and uninviting places containing a table and up to four chairs, audio recording equipment and increasingly often video recording equipment. Unless you have a legal representative present, you are automatically outnumbered (since there are usually two interviewing officers) and thus placed in a 'down' position. This is all part of the system which is designed not to exonerate you on the presumption of innocence, but to process you towards a conviction.

Lack of legal representation

We need to note that Tony fended for himself, having elected not to have legal representation. I need to issue a word of caution here to all would-be defendants. Most people arrested on criminal charges do not have a solicitor who they can contact, so the police will 'play the game' and offer you a 'duty solicitor' – someone 'on call' from a list of solicitors in the area. Most defendants, usually a little frightened, opt for legal representation from the list of duty solicitors. The game as it is played is that you think you will get a totally independent lawyer *who will be on your side from the minute he or she walks into the interview room*. Rarely is that the case – most 'duty' solicitors work alongside the police and the CPS and most are rarely independent. I fully accept that the police and 'duty' solicitors will disagree but just ask any prisoner how they got on with the 'duty' solicitor, especially those lawyers who "happened to be in the police station as you were brought in." The legal profession is far from noble – it is infested with corrupt lawyers or those acting on specific instructions from the Home Office. You may well believe that you live in a free society with an independent police service and legal profession, but it is nothing but a myth. If you're challenging the "authorities", and particularly about child abuse, and holding them to account, see how quickly your human rights are tossed aside as the full force of the State is brought to bear against you. This is what happened to Tony. And also to me.

We should bear in mind that prior to interviewing the farmer, both officers had been to Emneth that night and morning and that they both knew of the comments made by Fearon in the hospital when first discussing the shooting.

From the start of the interview, DC Peters - to cover his back - ensured that Tony signed the appropriate form stating that he wished to forego legal representation. It is likely that the interviewing officers would have been delighted that Tony had no-one sitting alongside him in the interview room, so that they could then hopefully get him to incriminate himself.

Reason for arrest

DCP: The offence for which you have been arrested is attempted murder but let us just specify what it is you have been arrested for in simple terms. Last night a man was discovered with gunshot wounds who said he had been shot in the Emneth area. This man was later taken to hospital and has undergone some surgery for wounds that he has received. This man is not local to this area and he has no knowledge of who or how he became so injured. Because of the seriousness of his injuries we have not had chance to interview him and what we want to do, right now, is to ask you, because we believe you're the person that shot him. What, in your words, happened yesterday? Can you tell us please? Just quite simply, however you want to tell us, you tell us what took place.

I should point out that Tony had the option of saying nothing at all – he could have given what's called a 'No Comment' interview, literally answering 'No Comment' to any questions. He would have been quite within his rights to answer in this way and I feel that he ought to have done so, given his precarious state of mind at this point in time.

DCP: Whereabouts were you asleep?

AM: You're on your own ... I was up in my bedroom.

DCP: Where did you hear the noises?

AM: I dunno - I just live in one room and err - there were so many noises. It's horrendous. I never felt so afraid in all my life. I hate ... I'm - I don't know if it's a failing to say that, but I really felt absolutely terrified. And I really don't want to discuss it anymore today, thank you very much.

"I felt absolutely terrified"
We must note that Tony said that he felt he had never been so afraid in all his life – this is a critical point given the charges he was about to face: it provides an early indication of his state of mind, the fear that he experienced and his need to defend himself against an unknown number of intruders.

Notice how he said, "I don't know if it's a failing to say, but I really felt absolutely terrified." I could not but help hear the stoical young Tony on his first day at Glebe House School – wanting to cry but keeping a stiff upper lip so as not to upset his mother. There is no shame in admitting that you might be terrified when encountering intruders who have smashed their way into your remote farmhouse in the dead of night and knowing that you're outnumbered and not knowing whether they are armed and intent on murder.

Tony had made it clear that he didn't want to discuss the incident at that point in time. He had had little sleep since the shooting and was feeling overwhelmed by everything that had happened since the intruders smashed their way in.

But when DS Newton insisted that the matter must be discussed at that time, Tony replied: "No, I don't want to discuss it anymore. I'm a man who minds my own business. I get on with my own work."

DC Peters claimed that the police were just trying to find out what happened and that they couldn't speak to Fearon because he had not long been out of surgery. But we know – although Tony had no way of knowing – that the police had in fact already spoken to the injured Fearon.

DC Peters and DS Newton were – as perhaps you'd expect – working together to get Tony to engage with them. However, whilst the police have a job to do, it is noticeable that Tony's state of mind was not at all conducive to talking about anything, let alone re-living what he has called a nightmare. There is clearly a battle going on: Tony doesn't want to talk about it at all - at least at this time – but the police officers have been tasked to interview him.

But listen in to what the senior interviewing officer says about Fearon:

DSN: But what he just said is that *he approached your house*[127] - your dogs came out; he asked you to get hold of them and as he turned to walk away you shot him. You shot him in the leg.

AM: Which part?

DSN: Upper part of the leg.

AM: Well, if you want to believe that, you believe it.

Newton and Peters remained focused on their aim – to try to engage Tony in conversation about the shooting. Clearly not well emotionally, he replied:

> " I don't want to discuss it anymore today. I just want - I want solace. I've wanted it for so long. I can't get any peace…"

This was plainly a cry for help. Wearing my counsellor's hat, it seems to me that the solace Tony was craving was something he'd sought for many years, and was not related entirely to this incident. We have to recall the dysfunctional family he had grown up in, his long list (on his own admission) of failed relationships with women, his adversarial character and his inability to trust others. With such a perspective on the world, it is likely that he rarely felt at peace and it's clear that he lives with inner turmoil on a daily basis, though in the 6 years or so that I've known him, I've seen him mellow somewhat as he learns more about the way the world around him *really* works, not how he'd *like* it to work.

But the police officers completely ignored Tony's mood. He had just told

---

[127] Author's emphasis. This is yet another reference in evidence *supplied by the police* that Fearon and Barras were shot *outside of Bleak House.*

them that he wanted some solace. He had been through a traumatic experience and saw this as the culmination of a two-decades long struggle against trespass, thefts and burglaries in which he had felt – and was right - completely unsupported by the police whom, he said, often mocked him.

Yet for all his bluster, one of Tony Martin's weaknesses is that he will talk to just about anyone who'll listen as he seeks connection to others and the detectives soon get him to open up, asking him to tell them where he lives. As soon as Tony mentioned that he lived "down a pea gravel drive with lime trees", DC Peters seized upon this by saying, "Now a pea gravel drive means that if vehicles or persons come along the pea gravel drive, and you've got three rottweilers and there's yourself and you're fairly observant and alert to things, you would hear somebody coming down at some stage - yes?"

And this was the start of the rot. DC Peters wanted Tony to say that yes, he could have heard anyone coming up that drive. It doesn't follow that you would hear someone walking up that drive because the drive stops short of the house and there's competition from other countryside noises and a television on in Tony's upstairs bedroom at the rear. We would do well to remember the role of the police at this point – they are supposed to remain impartial and investigate, not jump in as Peters has done and try to create a narrative that did not happen.

Tony asked: "Why did the man want to come down my driveway in the first place?" which is, of course, an appropriate question.

DC Peters claimed not to know, which was a lie. Tony asked another question: "Where did they come from?" but DS Newton responded with: "We're asking the questions."

Suddenly DC Peters seized upon Tony's last comment: "When you say 'they', what do you mean by 'Where did *they* come from?' We've only got one man - what do you mean by '*they*'?"

This was another lie – "We've only got one man." We know this is a lie because the police know about Fearon – who is in the hospital, of course – and they also have Bark under arrest. Indeed, it was Peters himself who arrested Bark at 4:54 that very morning at Terrington St John police station (if the statement attributed to Peters is to be believed).

But Peters had mentioned this in order to try to draw Tony out – to get him talking by challenging him. Tony unfortunately took the bait.

He told them that he heard 'people' talking and so he immediately knew he was outnumbered. He said they were inside his house and that he had not invited them there. He added that nobody goes into his house, not even his best friend:

> I have many, many friends, and you can ring them all up and nobody ever comes in my house. There is a reason for it."

The police failed to ask the reason.

Then Tony was asked to describe the events of that day; he readily acquiesced to that request but then started stuttering and showing classic symptoms of someone experiencing a trauma and struggling to gather his thoughts. In my view, the interview ought to have been stopped and held on another day because by continuing with it at this time, the police were surely laying themselves open to a suggestion by an astute defence counsel that anything Tony said at this time was not valid since he was obviously in great discomfort and mental anguish and that the interview was oppressive. But Newton and Peters continued unabated. I regard this as an attack on Tony; you may well take the view that they were only doing their job. I'd reply by saying that it is clear he was in no fit emotional state to be interviewed, he was in custody and not going anywhere and so the interview could have been conducted on another day.

Tony told them he was worried about all the rain in August and his harvest, and DC Peters seized upon this and asked, "So is it fair to say you're a bit depressed by conditions about the weather and stuff like that at the moment?"

Notice how Peters - with an apparent ulterior motive - introduced the element of a mental issue for the first time. This was to have great significance in the coming months.

But Tony replied:

> " No. I'm depressed about something I really don't want to talk about today."

DS Newton retorted: "Well I think, Mr Martin, we've really got to get a bit closer about what happened last night. The noise you heard downstairs inside the house – well, what did you do?"

"I really don't want to talk about it; it's so horrendous."

Again Tony used the word 'horrendous' when describing the experience he had had. He said that he didn't want to discuss it at that moment in time, but Newton pressed on regardless.

DS Newton then said to Tony: "I've got a statement here from Mrs Leet. We are in the process of taking a statement off Paul Leet. He remembers you driving into his driveway. He said he met you at your car and that you got out and walked towards him." Now this is what he says you said: 'I've just caught three blokes in my house and shot at them.' Did you say that to Mr Leet?"

> " As I've said, I've had such a horrendous experience I just don't want to talk about it, I'm afraid."

Notice Tony's use of the word 'horrendous' once again.

I've spoken with Tony about this interview and he says that with the knowledge he has now he would always make only a "No Comment" interview. You'll understand why as you read on:

AM: My life's a nightmare.

DCP: It's probably the most distressing thing that's ever happened to you in your life. I know that.

AM: I've had a lot of nightmares in my life. I've had a lot of things pull me right down but I tell you what, this is something I...

DCP: Well, tell us about this.

AM: I just can't handle it. I just don't - I just don't want to – I'd just rather go back and stay in the cell and read Winston Churchill [a biography].

And then DS Newton came out with the classic 'we're-good-guys-really' bullshit:

DSN: "No – we're not here to just lock you up - we need to know what is right to do - not just for you but for everybody else. We're not saying we are going to do everything right for you 'cos it might not work out exactly right for you, but it'll be fair."

AM: No, I haven't come across any fairness for a long while.

Signs of emotional trauma
At this stage in the interview, Tony was continuing to stutter, he was holding his head in his hands, his eyes were shut, he was shaking his head. These are, of course, all the usual signs of someone suffering considerable emotional trauma and yet these obvious signs were ignored as the officers ploughed on relentlessly. DS Newton decided to cover his backside by asking:

DSN: Mr Martin - would you like to speak to a solicitor? Would you like some legal advice?

AM: I just want some peace.

DSN: Mr Martin, you have been seen by the doctor today and he says that you are quite ... that there is no problem with you being in custody here.

There is, of course, a great deal of difference between being fit enough to be held in custody and being fit enough emotionally to be interviewed on a charge of attempted murder. DS Newton knew this and so asked Tony whether he wanted legal advice. But listen to what DC Peters then said:

DCP: Try and wake yourself up while we are interviewing you and go to sleep

	when you're in the cells. You've been in the cells…
AM:	Alright, if you want to start being sarcastic.
DCP:	No, we're not being sarcastic…
AM:	That's the end of this conversation!
DCP:	I just want to make one other…
AM:	I wannagoback!

Notice how Tony was displaying all the signs of tiredness (and of course he would be since he had hardly slept in 48 hours) and also the effects of trauma by just wanting to go back to his cell and lie down. The "Iwannagoback" sounds like a man near to a breakdown. But still the police – who have already admitted that Tony is obviously very tired – continued with trying to get Tony to implicate himself.

Oppressive interview

I believe this to have been an oppressive interview throughout, but certainly at this point. Once the police have acknowledged his physical and mental condition, I am of the opinion that they ought to have stopped the interview and carried on another day.

Then DS Newton reminded Tony of "the burglary of 13 May 1999." (It was, in fact, on 12 May – Tony reported it just before midnight on 12 May and the call went over into 13 May.)

"Do you recall saying that 'they had left the chest of drawers outside, they may be back for that and if they do, I'll blow their heads off. Know what I mean?' Do you remember saying that over the telephone to the controller?"[128]

"I do remember saying that, yes."

"What happened last night wasn't the heads was it? It was a leg Mr Martin, wasn't it?"

---

[128] It was never proven that Tony said this to the controller. [See entries **181** (communications officer Carol Woods) and **260** (PS Paul Watson).] However, he consistently admits to me that he did, in fact, say that as a means of drawing police attention to his suffering so many thefts and burglaries – "If you mention guns, Brian, they'll usually be down within minutes." Whilst I acknowledge his logical reasoning, the police were to use that strategy against him at trial. Nevertheless, despite claiming to record all calls, bizarrely that call was not recorded that night because "the equipment was faulty". (All other machines in the control room were working that night.) This leads me to conclude that Tony also mentioned child abuse at Glebe House – one of his most talked about subjects – to the controller that night. She "could not remember that call".

> May I say, Sir, that it's known in our area that the police do not respond to us when we are in difficulties and things and it's well known that if you want to get a response from the police you just glibly say a remark like that and they'll be down straightaway."

Nightmare

DS Newton, the senior detective, told Tony that he was going to have to tell them his account of the shooting but Tony replied:

> No, I don't have to do anything. I've had - just had enough of it. It's a nightmare. It's dreadful."

DS Newton asked what Tony meant by his use of the phrase "It's a nightmare" and the farmer replied: "You wouldn't know what a nightmare was."

DC Peters asked Tony why he felt the need to use his gun when intruders broke into his house and he replied:

> I've told you before, I was terrified. I don't want to go any further. I've told you. I was terrified. I am terrified. And I don't think you appreciate how terrified some people are."

It's clear at this point that Tony Martin had been frank and transparent – he was terrified, he repeatedly said. This has important ramifications later in our story, not only on the issue of diminished responsibility which we will discuss in forthcoming chapters, but also on the issue of self-defence.

Tony reiterated that the whole experience had been a 'nightmare' and that he'd had some horrendous experiences whilst living on the farm. DC Peters asked the farmer to tell him about the nightmare, about the experience, but Tony replied:

> I can't tell you now because you'll turn it and you'll twist it."

Despite displaying many of the signs of still being traumatised, Tony was astute enough to know that the police do twist things that you tell them. I have been on the receiving end of this myself and know from personal experience.

DC Peters claimed that the police wouldn't twist anything, but clearly the police can – and do - twist things: Hillsborough, the Birmingham Six, the Guildford Four. The list is extremely long.

"Put a bullet in my bloody head!"

And then Tony reached the point of mental meltdown:

> Take me up to the court. Take me to Norwich Prison. Get rid of me out the way. I wish I was in China. Put a bullet in my bloody head and I'll be finished and out the way. I don't want to discuss it anymore…"

It is evident that Tony was extremely emotionally fragile at this point in time – his language was bordering on suicidal ideation and I am of the opinion that the interview ought to have been concluded, if not before this point, then certainly at this point. Tony was in custody and there was time enough to resume the interview on another day.

He reiterated that he didn't want to re-live the nightmare – certainly not at this point. Listen carefully to DC Peters' reply:

DCP Is living a nightmare living in a house that is almost derelict with trees right up to the walls that can hardly be found with - with these rottweilers patrolling round it and heaps of old machinery - is that your nightmare? Has it become such an intolerable life?

And with those words, Tony then told them that the interview was over. The detectives tried to engage Tony in the interview, but he continued to sit with his head in his hands, his eyes closed, shaking his head. He was clearly traumatised, emotionally frozen and felt threatened by the tone of the police questioning.

However, the police questioning raises some very important issues for us, as DS Newton said:

DSN: This guy said last night that all he was doing was walking up to your land asking for directions. "I'm lost, sir. Can you tell me…?"
You let your dogs on him. He says "Control the dogs!" and you shoot him. He's saying you came out there and blew him away on purpose. Just for being … [on your land]

We should note that the senior interviewing officer has told Tony that Fearon's first statement to the police was that he was shot on the land and that the shooter "came out" of a building to shoot him. This is, obviously, a completely different scenario from the notion that he and Barras broke into Bleak House and were shot inside. Clearly, we should bear in mind that Fearon could have invented this scenario to extricate himself from any burglary. Alternatively, it could very well be the truth. Oftentimes, the first thing people tell the police turns out to be the truth when compared with their subsequent statements.

DS Newton again: "But the problem is that they're not likely to admit being in your house. They might - well they might admit being on your land…"

This could be a case of the police knowing that Fearon was shot outside of the house by someone other than Tony and providing a ready-made excuse for Fearon not to place himself *inside* the house.

DSN: You're just sitting there shaking your head and closing your eyes... Are you serious? You don't want to say anything more? Mr. Martin? You looked very surprised when I told you exactly what the bloke was saying - what the man said and just sitting there shaking your head and closing your eyes, I'm sorry, isn't good enough. Is it?

Tony was clearly perplexed. He was trying to process what the police were telling him and weighing that up against what he knew, or *thought that he knew*. What he did know was that (a) he had had people smash their way into his house, (b) he had fired his gun an unknown number of times from the top of his stairs, (c) he had heard no shouts from any intruders that they had been struck, (d) he then returned to the safety of his bedroom, and (e) when he went down the stairs into the breakfast room, he saw no blood or shotgun pellets and certainly no people in there. All he saw was that a window had been pulled out and that some of his silverware had been placed in a holdall.

All of this does not prove that when he fired his gun he actually hit anybody, and so it is completely possible that Fearon and Barras were never in the house and that they could not have been shot by Tony. It is equally possible that they *were* shot outside on the land as they walked to the house intending to burgle it but not actually doing so.

Before we conclude this section, let's pause and read what DS Newton asked about a shooting *on the land*:

DSN   Do you perceive that shooting at someone who is trespassing on your land, do you think that that is a terrible wrong?

and

DSN   Did you have anybody on your land last night?

and

DSN   This guy said last night that all he was doing was walking up to your land asking for directions...

and

DSN   Well ... did you shoot anybody?

DSN   Did you discharge a firearm at somebody in or near your house?

DSN   Well did you shoot anybody last night? Did you discharge a firearm at somebody last night? A shotgun?

DSN   Well is it a nightmare because you shot somebody?

Notice the disingenuous use of language by DS Newton. You can discharge a firearm without shooting *at anybody* – indeed, Tony had done that in the 1994 shooting incident in the orchard. The senior detective is trying to get Tony to think a certain way ... to sell him the notion that he did shoot someone when he discharged his gun.

There is already sufficient doubt as to the exact scenario of how Fearon and Barras came to be shot and yet this doubt – this *reasonable doubt* – never made its way into the courtroom at trial. What on earth were the judge and Tony's barrister doing by keeping this from the jury?

DC Peters assisted his colleague in the attempted deconstruction of Tony's emotional wellbeing:

DCP: You told Mr Leet you shot somebody last night. Or you shot at them and all we want to know is what did you use to shoot at them and who were "them" and where were "them" when you shot them and what - why did you shoot at them? I mean that is it in a nutshell, that's what we want to know and you're the best placed person to challenge that because you're the person with the gun pulling the trigger.

DS Newton continued:

DSN: Come on, you're a man of the world. You're a man of principles. And now you've let yourself down. Haven't you? You've become something that you despise. Haven't you really Mr Martin? Will you look at me? Okay, fine.

Notice how DS Newton used the phrase "You've become something you despise." He hadn't yet heard Tony's full defence to the allegations and yet was attempting to sow such negative statements in his mind. I cannot see any justification to suggest to Tony that he had become something he despises, but it does seem to me that the police officers were psychologically trying to break Tony's resolve down, to *deconstruct* his perception of himself whilst simultaneously *constructing* a false police narrative about how the men from Newark came to be shot. And all of this State oppression compounded the horrendous ordeal the farmer had been through.

Sat	
21 AUG	
2.29 pm	
136	

Bleak House

According to official records, an unnamed dog warden arrived on the scene at this time. The official CAD report had recorded that a containment had been sought as early as 1am by CI Curtis "because of dogs running about".

The question has to be asked: why did it take so long for a dog warden to attend the scene and why did the Police claim that they didn't deploy their own dog handler who was allegedly on site hours earlier? [See also entry **89**].

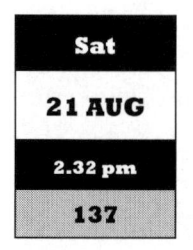

Sat	
21 AUG	
2.32 pm	
137	

Bleak House

According to the official CAD report, the body of Fred Barras was found at this time, some 16½ hours after he had been shot (if we are to believe the official records).

The body was allegedly found in some bushes just fifteen feet from the rear window of Bleak House.

Records show that PC 248 Russell Brett was deployed to search outbuildings and barns with PC 396 Andrew Harrison. At 2:30pm, PC Harrison was ordered to search the garage adjacent to Bleak House when the search operation was suddenly suspended.

With the clock apparently showing 2:32pm,[129] outside of the oppressive interview room, according to the statement made by PC 248 Russell Brett to which I have previously referred, the search was halted "due to a discovery by fellow officers of a male body at the rear of the main house", as the result of one of Tony's dogs taking officers to the body – more of which later. Thus, whilst Tony was being interviewed on suspicion of the attempted murder of Fearon, the body of Fred Barras, now deceased, was allegedly being found for the first time – by one of Tony's dogs. You will recall that PC Claxton and dog Solo were (allegedly) not deployed to search the grounds hours earlier. You will recall that CI Curtis had allegedly asked for assistance to round up the dogs at 1am – some 13½ hours previously.

The body was found, we are told, just fifteen feet (5 metres) from the rear exit window, but this does not mean, of course, that Barras actually died there. He may well have died elsewhere on the land and his still-warm body partly hidden in bushes by the police, to ensure that he would not be discovered "too soon". If that idea appears to be too fanciful for you, read on.

---

[129] Note the 10-minute time difference between PC Brett's statement and the official CAD report.

> **What this adds to our knowledge**
>
> I am concerned that the search would commence with 'various outbuildings' when a third person had allegedly not been accounted for. I am not saying, of course, that a thorough search of the area ought not to have been conducted, but it seems that the priority ought to have been to find Barras. He might have been in the barn, of course, but surely the priority ought to have been a search of the house itself and the immediate curtilage. Surrounding the house was (and still is) a pathway of 'crazy paving' which is 8 feet (approximately 2.44 metres) wide allowing easy access all the way around. And yet no-one found the body of Barras so close to the house?

There really seems to have been no appetite for finding Barras, though I put forward the view that the police knew exactly where he was and his condition. According to official records, the first search of Bleak House commenced at 6:52am, having been authorised by Inspector James. The result of that search was not minuted in the CAD report and Inspector James apparently made no statement to the police about it (or, if he did, it went 'missing' and wasn't supplied to Tony). James did make a statement on 27 September but didn't mention anything about organising a search – isn't that a startling omission?

At 11:15am – some 13¼ hours after the police time of the shooting – a second search allegedly occurred. Again, the CAD report does not provide any evidence of this search and the only evidence we have is provided by the witness statements of police officers – that is, in my view, of considerable concern.

According to the CAD again, Inspector Rush (the POLSA) attended the scene at 14:41 and within a minute the body of Barras was allegedly found! There was no mention of the body being found by Roger Putterill, so we are forced to conclude that he didn't find the body at all – despite his claims to have done so in his *second* statement to the police.

But, see again entry **132** in which DI Sharman claimed that Inspector Rush had been with him at the front of Bleak House at 11:30 that morning – there was no mention of him being there at that time in the CAD report.

Sat 21 AUG 2.36 pm 138

King's Lynn police station

According to official records, the 42-minute interview was concluded at 2:36pm and Tony was returned to the custody of PS Middlebrook and placed back in cell 4.

Tony continued to read an autobiography of Winston Churchill, a person the farmer admires.

In my view, that entire interview ought never to have taken place. It actually served little purpose because of Tony's reluctance to speak about the shooting so soon after it. I believe that, given Tony's fragile mental state so soon after the shooting, that this was an oppressive interview which indicated the police's partiality and determination to obtain a conviction, not achieve justice. You may well believe it to have been within acceptable boundaries.

Sat 21 AUG 2.46 pm 139

Norfolk Constabulary control room
According to the CAD report, Assistant Chief Constable Fraser was informed about the dead body.
According to official records, five minutes later Supt Hale was informed. Three minutes later, Supt Steve Thacker, Divisional Commander, was also informed.

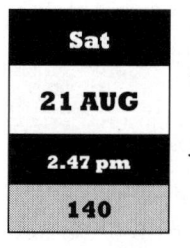

Sat 21 AUG 2.47 pm 140

King's Lynn police station
At 2:47pm, DS Peters entered cell number 4 and arrested Tony on suspicion of the murder of an "as yet unidentified male[130] found dead from gunshot wounds." Tony was cautioned and then asked whether he wished to say anything.
He replied, "No."

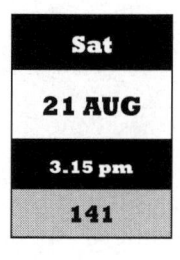

Sat 21 AUG 3.15 pm 141

Norfolk Constabulary control room
According to the CAD report, Mel Lacey from the Constabulary's Press Liaison was paged.
Note the speed with which the Constabulary was preparing to control the flow of (false) information fed to the public.

---

[130] We are forced to ask how Barras have been 'unidentified' when he had in his back pocket a bail notice with his name and address on it. I accept that the bail notice may not have applied to him, but it would have been simple to have identified him via his family. [See also the statement of PC Stephenson dated 30 September 1999 (entry **305**) in which he stated that he had "formally identified the body to pathologist Dr Heath."]

Sat 21 AUG 3.20 pm 142

King's Lynn police station
According to official records, DI Sharman requested that the police surgeon be called out. This was apparently Dr John Skinner from Swaffham.

Isn't it odd that almost another hour is wasted before calling out a police doctor? And why not call out a pathologist?

Sat 21 AUG 3.51 pm 143

King's Lynn police station
According to official records, Detective Superintendent Christopher R. Grant[131] and DCI Martin Wright attend King's Lynn police station as the senior CID officers in the case.

Sat 21 AUG 4.07 pm 144

Bleak House
*Official records show that Dr John M. Skinner of the Campingland Surgery, Swaffham attended Bleak House at 4:07pm. He was said to have donned protective overalls, overshoes and gloves before going to the location of the body. At 4:16pm it was said that he confirmed that the body of "a young, white male" was dead. [See also **350**].*

Sat 21 AUG 4.56 pm UNUSED 145

King's Lynn police station
According to a transcript which Tony's barrister was put in possession of prior to the trial, Darren Bark was interviewed on this day by DS Peters and DC Buxton at 4:56pm in the presence of his solicitor, Christopher Toms, of Ward Gethin in King's Lynn. Bark claimed that his first statement to the police had been a lie.

---

[131] Confusingly (and perhaps deliberately), there are *three* 'Grants' referred to in this case – Supt Christopher R. Grant; DCI Grant, and Inspector Grant. Various police constables (and others) refer to these individuals, but they might be one and the same. I did not conduct the research – I merely replicated the rank referred to in the various statements in order to maintain the authenticity of the scripts. The HOLMES database mentions only *two* – the Supt (who allegedly made a statement on 11 November 1999 and who was referred to as of that rank by pathologist Michael Heath) and DCI (as referred to by PC Stephenson, who may have been mistaken as to Mr Grant's rank.)

The 'lie' was that Bark had told officers that he was in the area looking for his mate Joe Price, who'd broken down in his red transit van. The 'truth' was that he'd been in the area all along, having dropped off Fearon and Barras at the track leading from the Smeeth Road to Tony's farm. You will read much more about these different versions as the narrative unfolds.

DC Peters said to Bark, "Now, as a result of this *alleged* shooting incident, officers like myself were called out around about the midnight time and I arrived around about 1am at Emneth."

So, Peters had been to the scene (though there is no mention of him in the official CAD report) but had apparently failed to find Barras. Did you notice Peters' use of the word "alleged" shooting? There *had* been a shooting incident, so it was hardly an "alleged" shooting. The only thing "alleged" about the shooting, in my view, based on all the available evidence was that Tony had shot Fearon and Barras.

And, during the interview, Bark said that Billy Price and Robert Carlisle had sent Chris Webster and Owen Hirrel on a job there "a while ago." [Author's note – the May burglary for certain, possibly others.]

Bark also claimed that when Webster had been arrested at Sutton Bridge with a van load of antique furniture from Bleak House, the police let him go because the stolen items had not been reported. Yet they had – on the police's own admission, Tony had called them the same night and it was said that Webster hadn't been stopped *until the following day*. So the police ought to have known about the stolen items of furniture.

The transcript of this interview was given the exhibit number of SJP/9. It was never used at trial and yet it ought to have been.

| Sat
21 AUG
9.39 pm
UNUSED
146 | **King's Lynn police station**
According to official records, Bark made a statement at 4:50am and was then interviewed from 4:56pm until 5:21pm and from 5:59pm until 6:17pm; Christopher Toms, from Ward Gethin solicitors in King's Lynn, was recorded as having been present throughout.
    At 9:39pm, the record shows that Bark was offered a deal read out by DS 3132 Thomas Neill. DC Buxton and Mr Toms were also said to have been present: |

"You have been interviewed on tape about your involvement in a burglary. It is clear that you are also a witness in relation to a murder inquiry.

We are inviting you, on tape, to make a witness statement in relation to a murder. We want to make it clear before you make your decision, that your decision to make or not make a statement will not influence how you are dealt with for the burglary.

You can have an assurance which has been agreed with the Crown Prosecution Service that a statement made with regard to the murder will not be tendered in any subsequent burglary inquiry."

According to the official record, Bark apparently made no reply and the interview concluded at 9:42pm. But note that no specific burglary had been mentioned. The assumption, of course, is that it was the intended burglary of Tony Martin's farmhouse, but it is dangerous to make such assumptions. Particularly when there had been so many burglaries and the murder of the Sheridans in the area over a period of just a few months...

Sat 21 AUG 10 pm 147

King's Lynn police station
According to official records, at 10pm Bark made another witness statement which was significantly different from his others and consisted of 11 pages in total.

We have to bear in mind on the one hand that, if he was directly involved in conspiracy to burgle, he is likely to produce an account which will reduce his involvement so that a likely prison sentence is reduced. We also ought to consider on the other hand that the entire statement is fictitious and had been created in order to support the false narrative that the police were creating against an innocent farmer.

Bark claimed that the burglars arrived at Bleak House about 9:30pm or a little afterwards. (Straightaway the police have a problem – Tony had called round to the Leets' bungalow prior to this time, so he *couldn't have shot Fearon or Barras when he fired his gun inside his house.*)

After dropping off Fearon and Barras at the end of the track to Tony's farm, he parked up in Moyse's Bank, the agreed rendezvous point. Bark told police that he never entered the property – "Check my boots, there's no mud on them" is offered as evidence – but in reality, he could have had a spare pair of boots with him in his car and disposed of any muddy pair prior to his arrest.

Bark stated that he was quite prepared to attend court to give evidence. *So, why did the prosecution not call him to trial?*

And, perhaps more importantly, why did Tony's barrister, Scrivener, not call Bark as a witness to examine him about the role he was alleged to have played in the alleged burglary and the time he claimed to have arrived at the farm?

The alleged crime scene

Part 8: the alleged crime scene

The narrative that has so far been created by the authorities was that Tony Martin fired his shotgun at an unknown number of intruders and that Fearon and Barras were two of the intruders who got shot by the farmer. But it does *not automatically follow* that because a farmer fired his gun and because two people were shot in the area, that the farmer shot them. That is the false narrative that you and about 60 million other people were sold in the media. You were sold the story so often that you began to believe it and that is precisely what the authorities wanted you to do. But you were deceived and in this chapter – apart from all other chapters – you'll discover why I say that, on the evidence provided *by the police*, Tony Martin *could not have shot Fearon and Barras.*

For several years there has been a plethora of detective programmes on the television and so I imagine that many readers will be familiar with the usual protocol after a body has been discovered – the first step usually being to call in the pathologist who'll then take the two most important steps of (a) estimating the time of death and (b) suggesting the cause of death *from what the body tells the pathologist* and not whatever scenario the pathologist unilaterally imposes upon the body. In other words, the body is evidence and it has its own secrets. In this chapter, you're about to embark upon a scientific journey and become acquainted with some of the most important aspects of the pathologist's role.

In the following paragraphs about the role of a pathologist, establishing and securing a crime scene and obtaining forensic evidence, I have referred to the website www.exploreforensics.co.uk and I am indebted to that organisation for allowing me to use their copyright material throughout this book.

So, what exactly is a crime scene?
In short, it's any location at which a crime has taken place and a location that may yield physical clues as to the nature of the crime and the person or persons responsible for it.

Once a police officer has determined the area to be regarded as a crime scene he or she must make it inaccessible to all but authorised personnel such as other police officers, Scenes of Crime Officers (SOCO) and a police doctor - or pathologist. *It is important that the integrity of a crime scene is maintained wherever possible so as not to contaminate any evidence that may be available.* [Author's emphasis].

If the crime scene is located outside then the officer may find it necessary to place a cloth or waterproof sheeting over anything that he or she might consider to be evidence. It is also important to note at this point that anything can be evidence - from the largest item to the smallest thing such as a cigarette end[132] or piece of tissue.

The police may also erect tents or tarpaulins to minimise the view of a crime scene to both press and public and also so that a police doctor or pathologist can carry out a cursory examination of a corpse before it is moved for autopsy. It is necessary that a corpse is examined at its current location so that no claims of bruising or post-mortem injury can be made.

A pathologist would normally carry out a cursory examination of a corpse before it is moved for autopsy. [Author's emphasis].

Once a crime scene has been established it is important that all evidence is collated, catalogued and recorded for further reference. This task is normally performed by the SOCOs and is carried out using a variety of methods. We'll now take a look at some of these methods.

Evidence that is loose and perhaps lying on the ground should be bagged up and catalogued; each piece of evidence is given an individual identification number so that it can be cross-matched against corresponding investigative reports. The evidence is bagged in clear plastic bags, which are sealed airtight to prevent contamination.

Each of these bags is accompanied by a 'custody chain' document; this document is to be filled out by any officer who wishes to use or view the evidence. This is necessary to reduce the loss of evidence and/or cross contamination by individuals who should not have contact with it.

The area is photographed in meticulous detail and any signs of injury such as bloodstains are marked, numbered and photographed. These photographs are often important in the piecing together of an event so that officers who were not able to attend the scene can get an understanding for how it looked. Video cameras are also used to record the nature of the scene. SOCOs may also make audio recordings as to their findings while they go. Fingerprints are taken where possible and if the crime scene is outdoors the area is marked out and searched.

It is sometimes necessary for dogs to be used at a crime scene; this is done so that evidence that may not be visible to the naked eye can be detected.

Internal crime scenes are photographed, blood spatter patterns are measured and documented, and *bloodstains on carpets and floors are measured for radius.*[133]

Regardless of the location of a crime scene it is imperative that all of those personnel involved in the recording and preserving of it are dressed correctly in protective clothing.

---

[132] The reader will recall that some of those responsible for the May burglary of Bleak House were apparently traced because of a dropped cigarette end.

[133] According to all the available police evidence that Tony put at my disposal, this was never done by the police. The reason, I suggest, is obvious – that there was no blood spatter on the floor of the breakfast room because Tony didn't shoot anybody when he fired his shotgun on the stairs.

According to official records, the dog handler, PC Claxton, had arrived at Bleak House at twenty minutes past midnight. We would do well to remember that the police dog Solo was taken to the crime scene but allegedly not used. You'll remember that Solo was a "general purpose dog" and not a "sniffer" dog – usually a spaniel. PC Claxton made no mention in his statement of his having used a sniffer dog. And, of course, if you're looking for a body, you're far more likely to use a sniffer dog than a general purpose dog. I suggest, therefore, that we cannot trust the truthfulness of the statement attributed to PC Claxton.

What is a pathologist?

A pathologist is the senior doctor responsible for the performance of autopsies and for determining how an individual died. This particular role within the forensic science sector is a demanding and sometimes harrowing job, which is not for those faint of heart. A pathologist will often be called upon not just to perform autopsies but to offer expert advice to law enforcement agencies as well as supervise the running of the pathology laboratory and those individuals who are employed there.

Pathologists are also responsible for the supervising of a crime scene and the evidence collection process that takes place there. This is all geared towards providing the relevant authorities with as much information as possible.

A pathologist will often have to juggle more than one investigation at a time and supervise teams who are charged with collating information, samples, blood and tissues. During these investigations the pathologist will have to attend inquests and give expert advice to both juries and counsel alike; breaking down complex medical jargon and putting it across in such a way that it is accessible and understandable to all.

The pathologist will also have to discuss the nature of autopsies performed, his or her findings, and ultimately offer their opinions as to the nature of how death occurred.

While the crime scene is the realm of the police, the pathologist has the ultimate say in what happens with the body. Even though the crime scene has its own secrets to reveal, the body is the most important piece of evidence in any crime and the pathologist is the individual responsible for unlocking the corpse's secrets.

Responsible for the overseeing of everything from the removal of the corpse to the ultimate returning of the deceased to their family for burial, the pathologist has to ensure that every aspect of the investigation from a forensic medicine point of view is handled in the manner in which it should be and that *all* means at his or her disposal are utilised to find the answers behind the death of an individual. [Author's emphasis]

A pathologist must have an acceptable and working knowledge of many areas of forensic science and medicine including pathology, evaluation of a crime scene, anatomy, microscopy, forensic dentistry and anthropology.

It is not necessarily the case that all of these disciplines will be required during their time as a pathologist but it is certainly worth having a working knowledge of them as each crime scene - and indeed each crime - is different and can throw up many different scenarios.

Estimating time of death
Estimating the time of death is something else that the pathologist will have to do during the course of the autopsy. Additionally, he or she may be called upon at the scene of a crime whilst carrying out their external examinations to try and judge - or best guess - *when the victim died*.[134]

It must be said, however, that the time the individual took their last breath is not necessarily the time at which they died. This may sound bizarre but taking into consideration the human body can function for a period of time without oxygen - the human brain reportedly surviving several minutes without it - then it is reasonable to assume that the time of death may not always be accurate.

Time of death is categorised in three ways: the point at which the deceased's body - including vital organs - ceased to function is called the Physiological time of death.

A best guess based on available information is the Estimated time of death.

The time at which the body was discovered or physically pronounced dead by another individual is called the Legal time of death. This is the time that is shown - by law - on a death certificate. Explore Forensics informs us that it is a legal requirement for the time of death to be shown on a death certificate.[135]

How to estimate the time of death
One method is to measure body temperature. The normal equation for this is:

$$37.5°C - 1.5°C \text{ per hour}$$

This formula equates to the body temperature (37.5°C), which loses 1.5°C per hour until the temperature of the body is that of the environment around it, known as the ambient temperature. This ambient temperature - depending on how low it is - may take minutes or hours to be reached and is a good indicator as to how long a body has been in situ.

The most common way of taking the temperature of the deceased is to use a rectal thermometer or to take a temperature reading from the liver, which can achieve a more realistic core body temperature.

---

[134] This was apparently never done in the Tony Martin case. You may like to ask why.
[135] When I applied for a copy of the Barras death certificate in 2015, no time of death was shown.

Rigor Mortis also acts as a good measuring stick for estimating the time of death. This natural process occurs in all of us when we die and is the natural contracting and relaxation of the body's muscles caused by changes in the body's chemical balances.

Clearly it is imperative that when coming upon a body, a pathologist takes the temperature as soon as possible in order to try to ascertain the time of death. But there was no indication that Dr Skinner, said to have come upon the body of Barras, had taken the temperature of the body in order to ascertain the time of death. This is, of course, a fundamental flaw in the case.

Ordinarily Barras would have had a temperature of around 37.5°C at 10pm, when police records lead us to believe was the time that he was shot. If we say that he died within a minute or two – the prosecution claim which I do not support – then his body would lose 1.5°C per hour each hour until his body reached the same temperature as his surroundings. Thus, by 11pm, the body would have been approximately 36°C and by midnight 34.5°C. By 2am – when the police claim the helicopter went up over Bleak House - the body of Barras would have been around 31.5°C or 88.7° Fahrenheit. This would have been picked up by heat-seeking equipment without a doubt.

Meteorological evidence

Evidence obtained from data published by the Met Office[136] showed that the average temperature on that day in that area was approximately 13°C, which equates to 55.4°F. The shooting was alleged to have occurred at approximately 10pm and, it was further alleged, the body was found at around 2:30pm the next day – some 16½ hours later. Thus we can scientifically estimate that the body would have lost approximately 24 degrees and would have been around 14° when discovered (using all the available data we have).

It was obviously critical to take the temperature of the body as soon as possible after it was found. This could have been achieved rectally, which gives a reasonably accurate reading. That the taking of Barras' temperature was not (allegedly) achieved seems particularly at odds with a professional handling of

---

[136] In a statement dated 22 September 1999, attributed to Michael J. Walley. He had been employed by the Met Office since 1962, and a forecaster for fifteen years. His forecasting experience included the provision of forecasts and warnings for aviation, principally military. In addition, he spent a period of five years giving instruction on aviation meteorology to members of HM Forces and to those of other governments. Most recently (at the time of the statement) he was Senior Meteorological Officer with the RAF on Ascension Island, South Atlantic, and held the same position with the Army in the Western Isles of Scotland. In his current post at the time of the statement, within the Meteorological Office Commercial Services Department his main duty was to prepare reports and certified statements on the weather in connection with legal matters, both civil and criminal, as an "expert on the weather".

this case and leads me to conclude that the witness statement attributed to pathologist Dr Michael Heath had been fabricated or altered.

Rate of decay

The rate of decay within the human body after death is normally split into two distinct categories: autolysis and putrefaction. The former is a process of self-digestion where the body's enzymes contained within cells begin to go into a post-death meltdown. The process can be speeded up by extreme heat or alternatively slowed down by extreme cold.

Bacteria that escape from the body's intestinal tract after the deceased has died are released into the body and begin the process of literally melting the body down. This is known as putrefaction.

Putrefaction follows a predetermined timetable in nature and after the first 36 hours the neck, the abdomen, the shoulders and the head begin to turn a discoloured green. This is then followed by bloating – an accumulation of gas that is produced by bacteria toiling away within the deceased. This bloating is most visible around the face where the eyes and the tongue protrude as the gas inside pushes them forward.

As the body continues to putrefy, the skin blisters, hair falls out and the fingernails of the deceased begin to sink back into the fingers. These skin blisters are also filled with large amounts of liquid just as in a blister you might get from running or walking too far.

The body's skin tone then becomes what is known as 'marbled'; an intricate pattern of blood vessels in the face, abdomen, chest and other extremities becomes visible. This is the result of the body's red blood vessels breaking down, which in turn release haemoglobin.

As the process reaches its conclusion, the body will become almost black-green and the fluids – known as purge fluid – will drain from the corpse. This happens normally from the mouth and nose but also occurs from other orifices.

It is important to note that the internal organs of the deceased will begin to decay in a particular order starting with the intestines, which as well as holding bacteria also hold various levels of acidic fluid which – when unable to circulate – begin to eat through their surrounding tissues. As the intestinal organs decay, so too do the liver, kidneys, lungs and brain. The contents of the stomach may also slow down the rate of decay if there is undigested food in and around that area.

The last organs to give way to decay are the prostate and/or the uterus. This may sound all very unpleasant but it is a natural calendar of events for the body to go through and one which the pathologist and SOCO will find useful in their quest to determine the time of death.

Explore Forensics inform us that Rigor Mortis and Lividity are two natural occurrences within the human body after death that can be used as a means of determining - or at least estimating – the time of death.

Rigor Mortis

Rigor Mortis is the stiffening of the body after death because of a loss of Adenosine Triphosphate (ATP) from the body's muscles. ATP is the substance that allows energy to flow to the muscles and help them work and without this the muscles become stiff and inflexible.

Rigor Mortis begins throughout the body at the same time but the body's smaller muscles - such as those in the face, neck, arms and shoulders - are affected first and then the subsequent muscles throughout the rest of the body; those which are larger in size, are affected later.

Rigor normally appears within the body around two hours after the deceased has passed away with the facial and upper neck and shoulder muscles first to visibly suffer from its effects.

Once the contracting of all the body's muscles has taken place this state of Rigor - technically referred to as the Rigid Stage - normally lasts anything from eight to twelve hours after which time the body is completely stiff; this fixed state lasts for up to another eighteen hours. The process of rigor mortis actually reverses and the body returns to a flaccid state; the muscles losing their tightness in the reverse of how they gained it: i.e., those larger muscles that contracted last will lose their stiffness first and return to their pre-rigor condition.

We should consider that the process of rigor mortis begins around two hours after death, takes up to 12 hours for full rigor to be achieved and then stays in full rigor for up to 18 hours thereafter. In all, the entire process lasts for a maximum of 32 hours.

In terms of minimum times, we have 2 hours, plus 8 plus 18 – a total of 28 hours. For the purposes of this narrative, we'll look at the *maximum length of time - 32 hours* – that the body is in the full process of rigor mortis before becoming flaccid again. *It is of vital significance for this entire case.*

Rigor mortis is a good means of indicating time of death and Lividity is also useful for this purpose.

Lividity

Lividity is the process through which the body's blood supply will stop moving after the heart has stopped pumping it around the inside of the deceased. What normally happens at this point is that the blood supply - or at least any blood that remains within the corpse depending on the nature of their death - will settle in direct response to gravity. For example, an individual found lying on their stomach would be found with all the blood from their back heading towards the ground. Lividity, also referred to as Livor Mortis or Post-Mortem Hypostasis, also displays itself as a dark purple discolouration of the body.

It is worth noting that lividity begins to work through the deceased within thirty minutes of their heart stopping and can last up to twelve hours. Only up to the first six hours of death can lividity be altered by moving the body. After the six hour mark lividity is fixed as blood vessels begin to break down within the body. Rigor mortis and lividity are some of the key factors that are used when estimating the time of death.

Contents of the stomach

In most autopsies the contents of the stomach are an important piece of evidence, which can sometimes prove to be the difference between accidental death and foul play.

Perhaps you will have seen television and film autopsies played out where the pathologist will empty the contents of the deceased's stomach and will analyse them with a view to establishing what they ate and when they ate it; this is actually a very useful tool in the pathologist's arsenal.

The process through which food is absorbed into the body can take anything from twenty two hours to two days to complete and within that time food is broken down and reduced to a liquid pulp from which essential proteins are extracted.

Given that this process can take such a long time, the contents of the stomach - and in particular their condition at the time of autopsy - can help to estimate the time of death. As a generally accepted rule, stomach contents are analysed for trace elements of poisons or other toxins that might not normally be found in the deceased's system. This is useful if there is a suspicion of drug abuse or poisoning.

Not all pathologists use the stomach contents as a means of proving anything; this is perhaps most common in a case where the victim's death has been accidental and has been witnessed by many. Obviously in such a scenario there is nothing to be gained by examining the contents of the stomach but more often than not in investigations where cause of death is in doubt the contents of the stomach may offer up clues and insights that would normally go unnoticed.

Insects as an indicator of time of death

Another important factor in estimating the time of death of the deceased can sometimes be their surroundings, which includes what creatures are present in those surroundings. Many insects and flies are synonymous with the decaying of a corpse and from the point of view of a pathologist – accompanied by a forensic scientist – are blatant indicators in the how, why and when a corpse came to meet its end.

A forensic entomologist is best qualified to help with the categorisation and identification of these insects and flies.

It is worth noting also that a corpse – if left exposed outdoors after death – can become predatory food for animals such as foxes, wild dogs and the like, but the most likely means of aiding in the decomposition of a corpse are the myriad insects and flies which appear within 24 hours of the individual's demise.

The locale and temperatures surrounding the corpse are also indicative of the insects and flies to be found feeding and nesting within the body after death.

Blowflies are a prime example and often lay their eggs in the moist areas of the human body, usually within the first hour following death. The mouth, nose, groin, armpits, and eyes (if they are open) are all common anatomical locations in which the blowfly's eggs are laid and will normally hatch within 24 hours.

Blowfly larvae reach half an inch in length and continue to feed on the corpse for up to 12 days, in which time they grow and continue to moult until they eventually transform into the blowfly and begin repeating the cycle over again.

If a corpse is found outdoors and is only exhibiting the signs of having had eggs deposited upon it, *it is taken as a given by the entomologist that the body has been left out in the open for less than 24 hours.*[137] The appearance of maggots but no pupae means that the body has been outdoors for less than 10 days.

During this time, it is worth noting that, given the ambient temperature around the corpse and the fact that this temperature will rise and fall, rigor mortis and lividity will already have been and gone from the body. Also worth bearing in mind is the fact that blowflies do not lay eggs at night.

The entomologist will collect up live insects and flies, as well as those that have expired and also their empty pupae cases. He or she will then use them to estimate the life cycle and also how long they have been able to use the deceased body as a breeding ground for their activities. This is an important part of the forensic process.

Entrance and exit wounds

Entrance and exit wounds are more often than not the result of an individual being shot by an assailant with some kind of firearm. Of course entrance and exit wounds can be made if an individual is stabbed with a large sharp knife or spike but as already mentioned more often than not the wounds are created by a bullet entering the body and leaving through another area of the body.

The entrance wound is normally smaller and quite symmetrical in comparison to the exit wound, which can sometimes be ragged with skin, tissue, muscle and bone damage. Entrance wounds are often ringed with the residue of gunpowder and cordite - the two substances contained within a bullet.

Exit wounds are usually larger than the entrance wound because, as the round moves through the body of the victim, it slows down and explodes within the tissue and surrounding muscle. This slowing down of the projectile means that as it reaches the end of its trajectory it has to force harder to push through. This results in the exit wound normally looking larger and considerably more destructive than the entrance wound.

Exit wounds will often bleed profusely as they are larger but entrance wounds

---

[137] Hang on to this scientific fact – it gains great significance as the police narrative begins to unfold.

can sometimes look only like small holes - unless the weapon is fired at close proximity to the victim.

As with all instances of a firearms offence that results in an injury, measurements and photographs are taken to aid in the identification of the weapon used. Powder residue samples are taken and where possible - *if the victim dies as a result of their gunshot wound - the round is removed for ballistic analysis from the corpse at the autopsy stage.*[138]

We should remember that we are not dealing with bullets in this case, but shotgun pellets. Or so we were told.

The process of an autopsy
So, what actually happens in an autopsy? An autopsy is performed when there are suspicious circumstances surrounding someone's death; or when no signs of natural causes can be located. An autopsy takes the form of six stages: the Y-incision, the removal of the organs, an examination of the stomach contents (where deemed to be necessary), the collection of samples, an examination of the head and brain, and the report containing the conclusions based on the findings from the body itself.[139]

The Y-incision
The Y-incision is the procedure used by the pathologist to open up the breastplate of the deceased and gain access to the body's major organs; heart, lungs, liver, stomach, spleen etc. This incision is so called because it resembles the shape of the letter Y and is cut from either shoulder to the lower end of the sternum and then downwards in a straight line over the abdomen to the pubis.

After the Y-incision has been made all of the organs are removed and weighed. This is done because certain types of illness can cause a reduction or increase in the weight of organs such as the heart and/or the lungs. Most times when removed, these organs are removed in one unit but sometimes - depending on trauma to the body - are removed in a specific sequence. Blood samples are taken, samples for DNA testing (as and when necessary but not necessary in all autopsies), and toxicological tests are carried out on the heart for signs of poisoning if no physical injuries have manifested themselves.

After this the abdomen is examined and tissue samples taken for analysis and sometimes the contents of the stomach are examined. This is vitally important if

---

[138] Hang on to this fact, too, because it is of tremendous significance. In all of the legal documentation provided to me by Tony Martin (who had had it provided to him by his solicitors), *there was no record of any ballistic analysis* of any bullet or cartridge in this case. Isn't that odd?

[139] Contrary to the rule of law, not one of the *three* autopsy reports was ever entered into evidence in Tony Martin's trial. The prosecution relied entirely upon a *witness statement* from the first pathologist, Dr Michael Heath.

determining time of death is a major factor. Samples of bile from the gall bladder, ocular (eye) fluid, liver tissue and urine are taken for toxicology testing as some poisons may not show in one part of the body but will show in others.

Once these procedures have been completed the pathologist will then turn his or her attention to the head area. The first thing they will do is look for signs of head injury, which should have been visible during both external examinations. Sometimes, however, head trauma cannot be visible simply by sight alone. The pathologist makes a triangular incision across the top of the scalp to reveal the brain and first of all examines it inside the head. Then once this has been completed satisfactorily the brain is removed for a more thorough inspection and also for tissue samples to be taken.

After all of these procedures have been carried out the organs are then placed back into the body and the body is carefully sewn up again.

It is then the pathologist's job to report his or her findings to the police,[140] who will then be charged with the task of what to do next. It is important to note that although these procedures are carried out more often than not in the case of natural death; if carried out as the result of a violent death or murder then the body is not released to the family for burial until all investigations have been completed and inquests carried out.

Thus, having given you a brief glimpse into the world of a pathologist, let's pause to reflect on the injuries sustained by Fred Barras and the condition of his body when eventually 'found', because this is fundamental to the entire case.

Discovery of the body of Barras

There are a number of different scenarios why the body may not have been discovered for so long (if we subscribe to the 'official' version of events). Some are unpalatable, others are more reasonable to our sensitivities. But we must explore as many scenarios as possible in the interest of Justice and to try to establish the Truth for Tony Martin's sake (who still wishes to clear his name, as is his right) and for the sake of Fred Barras and his family.

Firstly, let us imagine – as the prosecution was keen to force on an unsuspecting public and jury - that the injuries Barras sustained killed him within two minutes. It seems that he managed to climb out of a window and walk or stagger five metres away from the house. Let us imagine that he collapsed and then died within seconds or minutes. If he was dead, his body would have retained a lot of heat, given the time of year – 20 August. Having retained a lot of its heat (though obviously gradually cooling down), the body must surely have shown up on the thermal imaging equipment on board the helicopter, which went up – according to the official police account - around 3½

---

[140] Note the accepted and proper protocol – that the pathologist will examine the body *prior to contact with the police* and then report his or her findings to the police. We are told that this did not happen in this case.

hours after the shooting. (At this point, we will not enter into an analysis of why it allegedly took so long for a helicopter to be deployed because our focus must be on Mr Barras.)

Although we saw in the statements of PCs Gotts and Cant, for example, the operation appears to have been grossly under-staffed and under-resourced from the start, we must still consider the possibility that those officers who were in attendance were not professionally deployed. From the chronology that I pieced together from reading the witness statements of the officers involved, it appears that the majority of officers were deployed inside and outside Foreman's Cottage (the Leets' bungalow) whereas, of course, they would have been better deployed at Bleak House searching for Barras. It was already known to the police that other injured parties were unaccounted for (according to PC Gotts' statement).

We must ask why the police apparently did not commence a more thorough search of the immediate grounds surrounding Bleak House. The Leets apparently allowed the police to use their house as a base and a number of them were said to have been ensconced in this temporary incident room or in their cars outside. Records show that two cars were in the driveway leading to the house and, if we subscribe to Supt Hale's witness statement [entry **285**] in which he described Bleak House as being silent and in darkness, we are led to assume that officers *had* visited the house and walked all the way around its perimeter in order to ascertain that were no lights on or anybody making any kind of noise inside.

Now, if they had indeed walked around the perimeter of the house, one has to wonder why they failed to spot Barras allegedly lying less than five metres away from the rear exit window. He might, of course, already have been dead and therefore would not have been able to call out. But what if he was not actually dead at this point but been *unable* to call out? We also need to consider the fact that although Barras was allegedly found in the bushes to the rear of the house, we were also told that his legs were sticking out and he was wearing a pair of white trainers. Surely, if someone had walked around the outside of the house to ascertain whether or not it was in darkness, they could not have missed seeing the body.

Thus we are forced to conclude that either the officers made only an extremely cursory walk of the perimeter, or that they did not walk around the house at all but merely claimed it was in darkness by looking only at the front of the house – Barras was, of course, allegedly found at the rear. But where is the evidence that he died where he was found? He could have been found anywhere on Tony Martin's farm and been thrown into bushes by the police in an attempt to delay 'discovery' of the body and to make it appear as though he had exited the rear window.

We are told that a police helicopter went up and that it contained thermal-imaging equipment and a powerful searchlight. Had Superintendent Hale deployed the personnel at his disposal more appropriately and efficiently and had officers searching the grounds rather than sitting in their cars or inside Foreman's Bungalow, Barras might have been found a lot sooner. But you might now ask, "What difference would it have made if he was already dead?" and I'll return to this issue in forthcoming paragraphs.

And, post-Hillsborough, we must now consider yet another possible scenario that night, as unpalatable as it may be.

Let us assume that the heat-seeking equipment actually *did* spot the body of Barras lying on the ground (and it certainly should have done had the body actually been there). It is possible that a police officer – probably of senior rank - saw the injuries sustained by the young man and a decision was taken to allow the boy to die and fit Tony Martin up for murder. As bizarre as that might sound, let us first examine the rationale behind that statement before dismissing it in its entirety if, indeed, we do dismiss it.

Tony Martin had long been a thorn in the side of the police. Fred Barras was a traveller and already had a string of convictions. To the police, both were expendable – let Barras die and fit Tony Martin up for murder. Two problems solved with one neat finish and then the constabulary basking in the glory of solving a murder whilst grabbing a public relations bonus – championing the defence of the travelling community throughout the trial against an eccentric loner who had long been a pain in the constabulary's arse.

Now, if you are minded to dismiss this as paranoid nonsense, then I refer you to the Hillsborough Independent Panel website and to my 10 Prisons, 12 Weeks website. [Author's note: currently removed by the authorities. I have one banned book, had three websites removed and numerous gagging orders imposed. Lambeth Council – where I reported child abuse, racism and bullying – tried to obtain a permanent gagging order against me at great public expense in 2013. That application failed, but the Council did succeed in having me imprisoned at HMP Pentonville for alleged contempt of court by not removing all traces of the banned book from the internet – as if it were possible for any one individual to police the entire internet!]

Some people have great difficulty in accepting that the police and the courts are anything other than honest and upright at all times. These people have a deep need to cling to such beliefs because they simply do not want to think that the authorities can be so corrupt or amoral. So think Hillsborough, where senior police officers tore up witness statements made by lower-ranking constables and *fraudulently created* other statements which reflected well on them and covered up their operational deficiencies. As PC Gotts had stated:

"It was clear more resources were needed to achieve any of the earlier options considered in safety so a request was made to arrange for further support. As this support would take a considerable amount of time to assemble it was decided to also request air support with specialist equipment."

Records show that this assessment was allegedly made at 0:34am, around an hour-and-a-half after it was said that PS Davidson first arrived on the scene. It must have been clear to any right-minded copper – of any rank – that the operation (if we are to believe the official records) was greatly under-resourced, both in terms of personnel and equipment. But why did it take so long for this assessment to have been made?

It appears to me that this was either deliberately under-resourced because the police were well aware that it involved Tony Martin, or that it was under-resourced because Norfolk Constabulary was genuinely under-resourced, which was – ironically – something that Tony Martin had been saying for years. "There's never anybody there when you call them," he – and other farmers - often used to say.[141] And in this operation, involving himself, he was right. It appears from the available evidence that it was hugely under-resourced and that personnel available to the operation that night were incorrectly deployed.

I have little doubt that the police would not agree with this assessment and that they would no doubt say that they could not approach the house because they were fearful that a gunman might fire on unarmed police officers. Whilst that would be a valid point to make under certain circumstances, it does not apply in this case for the following reasons: firstly, they claimed they had established that Tony Martin's car was not there (so it was unlikely that he was in the house) and secondly, the police themselves claimed that the house was silent and in darkness. So, here's the thing – they could not state this unless (a) they had actually checked or (b) they were lying. Now, you can't ascertain this information unless you get close to the house itself, because the house is in a clearing amongst a clump of trees.

The point is, you could not possibly say that the house was silent and in darkness unless you had gotten right up close to it. So let's assume they had gotten right up close. If that were the case, why did they not come across Fred Barras, wearing white trainers?

Or did officers actually find him and leave him there to die?

Many of the pieces of this particular jigsaw simply do not fit together. Was Fred Barras even at the farm at this time? Whilst that might sound like a ridiculous question at this point in the government propagandist narrative, you might like to consider it in any event. Nothing in this case was as we were told it had been. As George Orwell had written: "Early in life I had noticed that no event is ever correctly reported in a newspaper."

---

[141] See the entry for 10 January 1999 and the Sheridans' murder and the views of the locals about the police.

And what of the burglars' car allegedly being stopped at Balderton just minutes after they had set off for Bleak House?

Is it possible that, if it happened at all, this was no routine stop but that it was part of the planned surveillance of these men because the police already knew that they were driving to Emneth to burgle Tony Martin's house? It was, after all, common knowledge in Newark that these men were out to burgle a house and if the average man in the street knew this, it is likely that the police, with their substantial network of informants, did too.

In the next chapter, we will return to the police operation following the discovery of the body of Fred Barras (at least the time of the discovery according to the official records). It is inconceivable that his body was not discovered for 16½ hours after the shooting. And it is even more inconceivable that the police – through DCI Martin Wright – were later to claim that they couldn't find the body because Tony's "vicious, snarling dogs" – yes, the very same dogs that burglar Christopher Webster had admitted patting on the head during the May burglary – had prevented them from finding the body. Only a fool would believe such nonsense and the government found that it had 60 million fools ready to digest any information about this case as was fed to them.

Following the
'discovery' of the body

Part 9: following the 'discovery' of the body

Sat
21 AUG
4 pm
UNUSED
148

Queen Elizabeth hospital
According to official records,[142] *PC 677 Richard Brian Walker, of Terrington St John and PC 9034 Caroline Jayne Reid of King's Lynn were on duty in plain clothes when they attended a private room off Leverington Ward at the Queen Elizabeth Hospital. PC Reid "arrested Fearon on suspicion of burglary on 20 August 1999 at Bleak House."*

She is reported as having cautioned him, to which he is said to have made no reply. The statement added that she also informed Fearon that "a man had been arrested on suspicion of shooting you."

Fearon allegedly asked for the name of the person, but Reid's statement recorded that she replied she was unable to tell him.

At 4:12pm, the statement shows that Fearon is alleged to have said, "We only went in so we didn't get bit."

Reid allegedly didn't respond and Fearon "appeared to go to sleep. He was very sleepy and had a drip running into his right arm, *hence he was not able to sign this unsolicited comment*." [Author's emphasis – note the lack of proper police and legal protocol. You are reminded of the unsolicited comments allegedly made in the Robbie Auger case and those allegedly made by Tony Martin in this case.]

The statement showed that at 6:30pm, PC Emma Cross and PC Sloan attended the hospital and took custody of Fearon. "PC Cross signed my pocket notebook to this effect."

We do not know at what time PC Reid made this statement, nor the location in which it was made (although we are forced to assume it was the hospital – but this would ordinarily have been recorded and it wasn't). It was not signed and not witnessed. Additionally, I could find no witness statements from PCs Cross and Sloan to corroborate anything that PC Reid had claimed. Nor could I find any reference to Cross and Sloan in the HOLMES database.

Is this of concern to you?

---

[142] Statement attributed to PC Reid dated 21 August 1999.

Sat	
21 AUG	
4.50 pm	
witness 105	
149	

Bleak House

*In a statement made on 26 October 1999 (see entry **344**) – some two months after the shooting - DS John Henry Eglen's statement informs us that he arrived at Bleak House at 4:50pm on the Saturday – some twenty hours or so after Tony fired his gun. Eglen, who was said to have been working alone, stated that he "cleared a common pathway amongst the rubble".* **He had therefore unilaterally and unlawfully interfered with the alleged crime scene.**

CORRUPTION ALERT   *Serious omissions in police evidence*

In HOLMES, DS Eglen is shown as having made six statements in all – but only five were entered as evidence into court. The 'missing' statement was actually his first one, dated 28 September 1999 in which it was recorded that Eglen "at 10:50 on Sunday 22-08-99 at Bleak House seized from main living room hold-all bags and contents and handed them to DC Peters."

Now, given that the statement made on 28 September was his *first* statement of six, wouldn't you think he'd have mentioned in that *first* statement that he'd been at Bleak House on the Saturday 21st August? He doesn't mention being at Bleak House and covering up the body of Barras on the Saturday until 26 October – a month later.

Perhaps even more bizarrely, DS Eglen stated in his first statement that he'd seized the holdalls and silver and yet on 16 November 1999, he makes another statement (his fifth of the six that we know of) to say that he'd only just made exhibits of the bin liners allegedly found in the holdalls almost two months earlier. There is more than a strong suspicion that all of these statements have been carefully crafted to suit the false police narrative, not reality.

Sat
21 AUG
6.20 pm
witness 83
150

Redmoor House, Wisbech St Mary

According to official records, DC 503 William John Durrant,[143] normally based at Swaffham, went to the home of Hilary Martin, Tony's mother, in Wisbech St Mary with DC 7 Bowell.

The detective took possession from the downstairs kitchen/ dining area of a single barrel pump action shotgun and a note from Hilary Martin regarding her son leaving the gun there.

After DC Bowell had taken a statement from Hilary Martin, the two detectives left and headed to the armoury at King's Lynn police station. [See entry 152].

Throughout my research, I could find no statement from DC Bowell.

Sat
21 AUG
6.25 pm
UNUSED
151

Redmoor House, Wisbech St Mary

Official records show that the 91-year-old[144] Hilary Mary Martin (born 11 March 1908) made the following unused statement to DC 7 Bowell at her home address of Redmoor in Wisbech St Mary:

"I have a son Anthony who was born 16 December 1944. He now lives at Bleak House, Smeeth Road, Emneth Hungate. He has lived there for about the last 20 years on his own. The house and contents were left to him by his aunt, Gladys Garner, on her death. She had not had any children; she was his godmother and they were very close.

My son has always been very highly strung and had a tendency to worry about things.

Throughout the years he has lived in Bleak House he has had many thefts from the house, outbuildings and land. I can recall just after his aunt died in 1986 or 87 he caught someone who had stolen items from his home. The person had a bag of silver and Anthony chased him and he threw the bag away.

Just before he died (I can't recall when that was) his uncle, Arthur Garner, was hit over the head by an intruder. Anthony has been so worried about someone breaking into his house.

Earlier this year someone stole items from Anthony's house. He was very upset because they took a lot of items that were his aunt's.

Since that event he has talked more and more about his worries and fears.

---

[143] In a statement dated 21 August 1999. It was not signed, no person to whom the statement was made was recorded, no location, no time. I doubt the full credibility of this statement.

[144] Tony has insisted to me that his mother was born in 1918, not 1908 as recorded on the police statement. I have not researched his ancestry.

On Friday 20 August I saw Anthony in the late afternoon. I cooked him a meal - he would very often call in for a chat and a visit. He seemed well. He was concerned the bad weather was delaying work on the farm. He did not mention thefts or anything during the visit. I would say he arrived about 4pm and left about 6pm. He was driving his own car, a beige estate.[145] I don't know the make.

The next time I saw or spoke to him was later that same evening, about 10:30pm. I was getting ready for bed and he came in with a shotgun. He said, "I'm just dropping this off for your safe-keeping."

I did not think anything of it as he has brought things round for me to look after in the past and a long time ago he brought a gun for me to look after. It did not seem unusual.

Anthony seemed normal; he was not upset or distressed. He did not stay very long at all. He was wearing grey trousers and a navy blue faded long sleeved jumper. He stood the gun in the kitchen dining area and left. I left the gun where he placed it. My other son David Robin Martin, known as Robin, visited me today (21 August 99) and I showed it to him and we have both touched it.[146]

Robin told me Anthony had been involved in an incident with a gun and we reported the fact we had the gun at the premises to the police.

At 6:20pm today DC Durrant took possession of the gun Anthony brought to my home."

From my perspective, this statement accords with virtually everything Tony has ever told me about the night of the shooting, particularly in relation to the fact he left his mother's house around 6pm and the car journey to his home would be around 15-20 minutes. Tony has consistently told me that he was anxious to return home before it got too dark.

Sat 21 AUG 7.55 pm witness 83 152

armoury, King's Lynn police station
According to official records, DC Durrant handed the shotgun to PC White, an authorised firearms officer, and he was present in the armoury at King's Lynn when the constable declared the gun safe.

At 8pm, PC White handed the gun back to the detective, who placed it in a cellophane bag and then a brown paper bag which was sealed.

Critically, in my view, DC Durrant failed to record the number of the seal in his statement, which would be normal police protocol. Placing such a vital piece of evidence in a cellophane

---

[145] Whilst his mother described Tony's car as a "beige" estate, he actually drove a silver car, as we have seen.
[146] Technically, the fact that Hilary Martin and Robin Martin touched the gun and had their fingerprints on it, surely rendered the gun inadmissible as evidence.

bag and a brown paper bag and not recording any seal number could lead the reasonable person to believe that the shotgun could have been used wrongly by the police. Surely, at least there is room for reasonable doubt. I will return to this issue again.

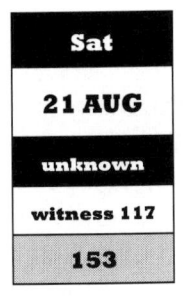

Sat 21 AUG — unknown — witness 117 — **153**

unknown location
According to official records, Wisbech PC 1369 Kevin Robson made the following statement: "At 5:50am on Saturday 21/8/99 I attended the Marmion House Hotel, Lynn Road, Wisbech. At 7:05am that same day, I conveyed a silver Nissan Bluebird registration C460APW to Wisbech police station where I booked the key into vehicle property 95/99."

On its face, this matters little, though it was entered as evidence into court. As a defence barrister I would have cross-examined PC Robson with regard to the security of Tony's car between the time of his arrest and it being taken to the police station. Anything could have been planted in or removed from that car in the hour-and-a-quarter following his arrest. I'm not saying anything was planted or removed, but an item or items could have been.
[See also **303**].

Sat 21 AUG — 10 pm — UNUSED — **154**

King's Lynn police station
Our focus now shifts to 10pm later this day and to King's Lynn police station, where Darren Bark – commonly referred to as "the getaway driver" – is being interviewed by DC 422 Trevor Robert Buxton.

You will recall that official records show that Bark was first interviewed at Terrington St John police station in the early hours of Saturday morning within a few hours of the shooting incident. Then there was the three-minute interview. Here's what Bark now had to say (I've redacted certain names to protect their identities since they have no bearing on this story):

"I live with [landlord and landlady]. I am a lodger at their house but treat them as I would treat my mum and dad, both of whom are now dead. I have lived there for around five years but have known [landlord] longer than that.

I have a girlfriend called Dawn Jepson who lives at [address].

I am currently unemployed but I have in the past been employed as a butcher, a roofer and a builder. I will do any work that I can get to earn a living.

About two months ago (I cannot remember exactly when), I was working with Billy Price and Robert Carlisle from Newark, doing what I call knocking and tree work. We would go out and knock on people's doors asking for tree felling work or similar. We travelled in Robert Carlisle's transit van, colour red which is a 'P', or an 'R' registration. He is a rich kid with plenty of money. We travelled down to the Wisbech area which is the area where Billy was brought up. He is a traveller and knows the place like the back of his hand.

Whilst there, he pointed out a road leading to where he said were a couple of derelict houses. I have no idea where they are but I could drive there from the main A47 road at Wisbech. I did not see the houses but Billy said they were derelict and in the middle of some woods. All there was there were four or five rottweiler dogs and a miserable old farmer who wouldn't give you the time of day.

Billy said that they were full of antiques and that he had set up a burglary there where antiques were stolen. He had sent Chris Webster and Owen Hirrel down there a short while before that and they had burgled one of the houses and got away with antique furniture. He also said that they[147] were arrested on the way back in Sutton Bridge[148] whilst driving a transit van full of the stolen antiques, but were released without charge because they (the police) were unable to find out where the furniture was from or if it had been stolen or not. [Author's note: We will read more about those arrests in a forthcoming chapter because it is of some significance to our story.]

Bark added: "Webby and Owen Hirrel went back to Newark and sold the furniture for five thousand pounds.[149]

Shortly after Billy had told me this, I stopped working with him and Robert and started working with Webby. We were still knocking but this time buying furniture and antiques. We did this mainly in the Yorkshire, Nottingham and Derbyshire areas.[150]

---

[147] 'They' suggests that both Webster *and Hirrel* had been arrested, but there was no mention of this in the HOLMES database.

[148] Sutton Bridge is in Lincolnshire. It would be on the burglars' route back to Newark in a northerly direction from Wisbech. However, you will later read that the police were to claim that the transit van was stopped at Sutton Business Park in Ely (Cambridgeshire), in a southerly direction from Wisbech – hardly the route the burglars would take as they made their way back home. All of which suggests that the statements made by the Cambridgeshire police officers at Ely had been entirely fabricated. Or, if the burglars had, in fact, been heading south to swiftly dispose of the stolen property, then either Bark is lying or the police have doctored his statement.

[149] Approximately worth £8,000 in 2019 with an average inflation rate of 2.8% p.a.

[150] Bark confirms what many of the farmers (including, of course, Tony Martin) already knew: that there were various 'hit squads' of burglars who would travel across county boundaries, commit burglaries and other crimes, and swiftly return to their own 'patch'.

Whilst I was doing this work Webby was telling me about a burglary at the derelict house with the rottweilers. He told me that there were two old blind dogs inside that would not hurt a fly and the other three were running about outside. He described the house as being absolutely loaded with antique furniture, but that it appeared that nobody had lived there for years. We never visited there but I knew that the house Webby was talking about was the same one as Billy Price had pointed out.

I stopped working with Webby because he went on the run after doing a burglary in Newark so I stopped work for around three weeks.

After that, I was approached by an old mate of mine called Brendon Fearon. He asked me if I knew where he could earn some quick money. This was just over a week ago on the Wednesday. He was working as a doorman for Lightning Jacks Club in Newark and he only earned £30 per night.

I told Brendon about the two derelict houses where the rottweilers were and it was potentially a good burglary target if he were not scared of the dogs.

From that day Brendon pestered me to take him there but I kept refusing to go and said that I am terrified of dogs. He kept on and on asking me to take him and I felt under pressure to do so. I am frightened of his family and feared that they may harm me if I did not do what they wanted. I refused to go anywhere near the dogs but eventually agreed to take Brendon and a mate of his to the houses on the understanding that I had nothing to do with whatever they did when they got there and that it was their intention to have a look around and 'suss out' the job to return and burgle the houses later.

Around 8:30pm[151] on Friday 20 August 1999 I left home in my white Ford Granada car, which I bought from Joe Price, the brother of Billy. I went to pick up Brendon from his mum and dad's house and Brendon told me to stop outside the Devon Road shops to pick up his mate.

I have no idea who the mate was and Brendon never mentioned his name.[152] When I picked him up, Brendon sat in the front passenger seat and his mate got in the back behind him. He was only about 17 to 20 years old and was drinking strong lager from cans. He talked about what cars he had taken and police chases and the like and after a few minutes Brendon turned round and told him to shut up. He never said another word. I cannot remember what he was wearing, but he was about six feet tall, skinny with a fresh face and clean shaven. I cannot remember much about him as he sat in the back so I did not actually see him face to face. I think he was smoking.

The increasing ownership of vehicles since the 1960s had contributed to this "ever-rising crime wave", as many farmers were to describe it.

[151] This is some 20 minutes later than PC Knight stated in his report.

[152] Do we believe that in the entire journey from Newark to Emneth Hungate that Fred Barras' name was never mentioned (if Barras was ever in the same car)?

After only a few minutes we were in Balderton near Newark when I was stopped by a marked police traffic car and the officer gave me a ticket for my number plate which is written in italics instead of straight lettering.[153]

The officer knew who I was and also knew Brendon, but he did not ask who the lad in the back was.

I continued the journey and arrived at the end of the road which I recognised as the one where Billy had pointed out the two houses, about half past nine or a little afterwards.

From there, with the end of that road on my left I continued forwards around a sharp left hand bend[154] to a crossroads where I turned left and along there a couple of hundred yards to a gateway with some farm buildings set back off the road on the right. I turned the car round in the gateway and dropped off Brendon and his mate and as they left Brendon said I was to be back at the gateway in about half an hour.

It was dark so I just dropped them off and drove away to the bottom of the road from where I had just come and turned left at the junction. There is a bungalow on that junction on the left.[155]

I continued to a village called Outwell and up to a main road where I turned around and stopped in a gateway on the right hand side of the road. I waited there for about twenty-five minutes. It was fine outside and I just sat there watching the clock in my car.

About twenty past ten I decided to return to the original gateway to pick up Brendon and the boy. When I reached the junction with the bungalow at it, I turned right and noticed an ambulance in the garden of the bungalow and a small police car on the roadside. I drove past and back to the gateway where I was supposed to pick up Brendon and I turned off my headlights before turning around in the gateway.

My immediate thought was that someone at the house was pregnant or ill or something and needed rushing to hospital.

---

[153] This is at odds with PC Knight's statement in which he said he stopped the vehicle because of a defective tyre. And note that, according to Bark's timescale, if he left home at 8:30pm and went to pick up Fearon and then Barras before driving to Balderton (all of which would have taken at least 20 minutes), then they could not have been stopped at 8:10pm as PC Knight claimed. Furthermore, if they left Newark around 8:50pm, they would not have arrived in Emneth much before 10:20pm – by which time Tony Martin was on his way to his mother's house in Friday Bridge and he could not have shot them according to the evidence.

[154] In my view this is an example of 'police register' the specialised language employed by police officers in their witness statements and reports. I have listened to tapes of Bark being interviewed and these are not specifically his words.

[155] This is Foreman's Cottage, the home of Paul and Jacqueline Leet.

I sat and waited for about ten minutes or so but Brendon and the boy did not show. I got out and topped up my petrol tank from a spare can I had in the boot. I saw the ambulance leave and I saw another police vehicle arrive at the house followed by a third.

I then started to think that something had happened to Brendon[156] so I drove straight up to the police car and stopped in front of it.

I panicked and told the police officers a false story that I was looking for Joe Price who had broken down in his van. This was a lie and I only said it to protect myself and mates. I was told after about thirty minutes that there had been a shooting incident.[157]

I never went to the derelict houses; in fact, I never went further than the end of the track that leads to where Billy told me they were.

I had no idea that Brendon or his mate had been shot and I am shocked to hear that they have.

This is a true account of what happened on the evening of Friday 20 August 1999.

I will go to Court and give evidence about these matters if I am required to do so."

As we now know, Bark was never called to Court by either the prosecution or Tony's defence counsel.

However, some doubt was cast upon the notion that Bark was the getaway driver when the police interviewed his girlfriend [see entry **189**]. It is just another twist in this incredible story.

On 13th July 2019, I visited Newark again, and a neighbour of Dawn Jepson and her father informed me that she was dealing drugs ("mostly heroin") from the house and that it was "common knowledge that Chris Webster was the driver in the August shooting."

---

[156] Note that the statement did not mention Barras at this point – a peculiar omission.

[157] The claim here is that Bark did not know about the shooting until 11:30pm (half an hour after Jacqui Leet was said to have called the police) because he had driven to the neighbouring village of Outwell. This raises (at the very least) four very important questions: (i) was Bark lying? (ii) did the police alter the transcript of his police interview? (iii) was he even the driver? or (iv) any or all of the above.

SMEETH ROAD

Sunday 22 August 1999

Part 10: Sunday 22 August 1999

Sun 22 AUG 1999 155

King's Lynn police station
According to the witness statement of senior interviewing officer DS Peter Newton dated 31 August 1999, "no interviews took place with the suspect because he was instructing his solicitor, which made him tired." Apparently a doctor stated that Tony "needed to get some immediate rest."

However, there is some doubt as to whether Tony Martin was first interviewed on the Saturday after he had fired his gun or the Sunday. I will provide you with evidence of this doubt in due course.

Other events were taking place outside of cell 4 that were, in my opinion, shaping towards the persecution of Tony Martin though you, of course, will come to your own conclusions.

Sun 22 AUG 9.30 am UNUSED 156

King's Lynn police station
Records show that the 58-year-old Terrence Owen Howard, who described himself as "a personal friend of Tony's for over 30 years having hit it off after we first met in the Three Horseshoes pub in Roydon through a relation of his", made the following statement to DC 503 William Durrant:

"I normally see him about once a week. He calls in to see me at home. I would describe him as a loner, very intelligent, rather eccentric but overall a smashing bloke and someone who I would trust.

I know that Tony farms about 300 acres out at Emneth where he lives. He also has land out at March. I know he does most of the work himself.

I am aware that several years ago there was an incident on his farm and the police subsequently took away Tony's firearms. I had no idea he had any left.

Although he had a lot of valuable property in his house, Tony never spent any money on himself or on the general repair of his house which, quite frankly, is in a state.

Apart from a relationship with a woman many years ago, I've never known Tony to have a girlfriend. He is friendly with a woman called Helen [Lilley] who runs the Marmion House Hotel in Wisbech.

I have known from conversations with Tony that he has had numerous thefts and burglaries at his farm over the years and obviously this has been annoying to him as it would to anyone.

Overall Tony is not a man with a violent disposition – in fact, he would not allow anyone to shoot game or vermin on his farm and did not shoot anything himself on the farm.

I last saw Tony about a week and a half ago at my house when he came and had lunch and he appeared perfectly normal. There was nothing in his behaviour to make me think anything was wrong."

That all seems pretty positive to me, though Mr Howard was to make a second statement in due course. [See entry **282**]

Sun 22 AUG 10 am 157

Downham Market police station
According to police records, the day began with a 10am briefing session at Downham Market police station.
Nothing wrong with that, of course, except that one of those present was said to have been pathologist Dr Heath who, according to official records, had not yet seen the body of Barras.

CORRUPTION ALERT   *Pathologist in meeting with senior police officers prior to seeing the body*

You'll recall that it's the job of a pathologist to remain impartial and objective and allow the body to inform him or her about how death might have occurred. The official record shows that those present at the conference were: DSupt Grant, DCI Wright, DS Eglen, Principal SOCO Rowlands, SOCOs DC Aldous, Laura Bishop, Theresa Bradley and Barry Wells, together with forensic scientists Brian Arnold and Andrew Palmer.

With Dr Heath sitting amongst the investigating team prior to seeing the body and conducting an autopsy, how impartial and objective do you imagine he remained?

Now, a strange thing occurred in the witness statement attributed to Dr Heath.[158] He listed all of those present at the briefing session and he listed all of those present at Bleak House following the meeting. He listed DS Eglen as being at the meeting, but not at Bleak House. A mere oversight? Perhaps.

Heath's attendance at the police station causes me great concern. You have

---

[158] According to official records, this statement was made on 2nd September 1999. It was one of a number of statements made by Dr Michael Heath in the run up to trial.

probably seen films and tv dramas in which the pathologist turns up at the scene of the crime and examines the dead body and gives the police his (or her) early diagnosis of the cause and time of death. It is such common practice that we almost take it for granted. But I caution against taking *anything* for granted in this case because it is not what you and I were told it was. Let's examine the facts as far as we can be certain of them from the available records: Barras was found (we are told) at 2:32pm on Saturday 21 August – some 16½ hours after the time Tony Martin was said by the police to have fired his gun.

We have a witness statement purporting to be from Dr Skinner which said that he was called out to pronounce the body dead.

And we are told that the pathologist was in a conference at the police station in Downham Market at 10am on Sunday 22 August – some 36 hours or so after Tony was said to have fired his shotgun – and *he still hasn't seen the body*. Does that sit right with you? The role of a pathologist (as we saw earlier) is to advise and inform the police with regard to how he or she believes death occurred *based on the evidence that the body itself provides* and not based on any theory the police provide to the pathologist first.

So, if we have some concern about all of this, could the true chronology be that Dr Heath *didn't* first come across the body as late as 11am on Sunday 22 August? Could he have seen the body on the Saturday (as we might reasonably expect) and then performed the autopsy later that same day?

Let's examine the first witness statement attributed to Dr Heath (dated 2 September 1999):

"At 11:10am [on Sunday 22 August 1999] I attended Bleak House where I was shown the body of an adult male lying on his front with the left side closer to the ground than the right.

The right hand was to the right of the body and flexed at 90 degrees at the elbow. There was a rubber glove on the right hand."

And that is the only information we have in Dr Heath's statement about the body of Barras at the scene of death. There's nothing about the temperature of the body and nothing about an estimated time of death. Does that concern you?

Sun	
22 AUG	
10.50 am	
UNUSED	
158	

Bleak House

In a statement attributed to DS Eglen,[159] the SOCO placed himself at Bleak House.

At 10:50am he stated that he was "assisted by other officers in an examination of the premises."

He failed to name these other officers.

Let's not forget that, according to official records, it was DS Eglen who conducted a "brief examination" of the house on the previous day and cleared a "common pathway" amongst the rubble. [See entry **344** for DS Eglen's main statement.]

Sun	
22 AUG	
unknown	
UNUSED	
159	

unknown location

According to official records, Jean Thompson, a 52-year-old near neighbour of Tony's made a statement to an unknown police officer, at an unknown location and at an unknown time.

Mrs Thompson's house was situated around 60 yards on the Outwell side of the Hungate Road, around half a mile from Bleak House. The surrounding area is generally flat.

"Sometime between 9pm and 10pm on Friday 20 August I was in my lounge with my husband John – our daughter Ruth had already gone to bed.

I cannot be any more precise with regards to the time but I recall that we had been watching Des O'Connor on ITV for a short while before switching it off before the programme had ended. I recall my daughter had gone to bed at 9pm.

As we sat chatting in the lounge, I heard a loud bang which caused me to jump. The noise was loud enough to startle me. I thought it may have been a car backfiring. I glanced out of my lounge window but saw nothing. I remember it was dark outside. I should say the bang came from the Moyse's Bank direction. I can confirm the noise was a single bang."

Mrs Thompson believed that she heard only one shot – this could have been because two shots fired in quick succession could sound like a single shot, but it may well be that there *was* only one shot fired near to her house.

Had I been Tony's defence counsel, I would have wanted Mrs Thompson on the stand to tell the jury about the timing of the gunshot and to ask her whether her statement had been altered in any way.

---

[159] According to official records, this statement was made on 26 October 1999. It was one of six statements made by DS Eglen in the run up to trial.

Sun
22 AUG
unknown
witness 33
160

unknown location

According to official records, Peter Chapman, a 65-year-old near neighbour of Tony's made a statement to police – (the name of the officer was not recorded and nor was the time) – which adds to our knowledge of this case.

Peter and his wife Jean lived in a semi-detached cottage situated around 60-100 yards on the Outwell side of the Hungate Road.

He said that "around 10pm on 20 August" he was in the lounge with his wife, Jean, watching television which was turned down low.

He added that they heard "two *loud* bangs from outside which sounded like fireworks. I would say the bangs were simultaneous with no real delay between each noise. I didn't look outside or investigate the noises."

Clearly this statement is saying that the shooting took place at around 10pm, that there were *two loud shots* and that he didn't venture outside to establish what the bangs were.

And there is no mention of any police helicopter.

Do we accept the veracity of this statement? We have no idea where it was made, or at what time, or to whom.

It appears somewhat contrived to me – I suggest that it was written or altered by the police and not by Mr Chapman at all.

However, if the shots had been fired at 10pm, this could not have been Tony. He was, by that time, away from the scene and on his way to his mother's to drop off the shotgun. So, if it wasn't Tony, who was the real killer?

On the same day, Jean Chapman, 67,[160] allegedly made a statement which mirrored that of her husband's in every respect except one – the name of DC 7 Bowell was added, suggesting that she made the statement to that officer. However, neither the time the statement was allegedly made nor the location where it was made were recorded.

Both of the statements made by the Chapmans were entered as evidence at trial whereas their neighbours, the Thompsons, were not.

Sun
22 AUG
midday
witness 39
161

Foreman's Bungalow, Hungate Corner, Emneth

According to official records, Jacqueline Leet, 48, had made the 999 call just before 11pm following Fearon apparently appearing on their front lawn. She was recorded as having been interviewed by DC Peters at midday. Here's the statement attributed to her:

"Many of our neighbours, like my husband, work for the farmer Deptford. It is a very rural area. One of our neighbours is a

---

[160] Witness number 34.

farmer called Tony Martin, who farms land opposite our house. He is not a family friend. I do not know him very well - only really by sight. I have rarely spoken to him and it is rare for him to visit us.

At about 10pm on Friday 20 August 1999 I was in the bathroom at our bungalow when I heard the sound of a car pull into our driveway. My initial thought was that it was our son. As I listened I heard what I recognised to be the voice of Tony Martin who was talking to my husband Paul.

I would say that Mr Martin's tone seemed quite normal; I could not hear the contents of the conversation which lasted, I would say, for a couple of minutes. Then I heard a vehicle leave our driveway. I did not see what car Mr Martin was driving - the car he normally drives is an old grey estate car.

I left the bathroom and walked into the kitchen. I met Paul there; he was just walking into the kitchen from our driveway. I presumed he had watched Mr Martin off the premises. Because of the time, I said to Paul: "What's he (meaning Martin) want this time of night?"

Paul's reply - which I can clearly remember - was "He's just caught three men[161] who had broken into his house. He'd took a shot at them;[162] they had dropped their rucksacks and ran."

Paul told me that he had advised Mr Martin to phone the police. I wondered if we should do anything about what Mr Martin had told us. Paul and I discussed what to do, but as Mr Martin is a bit eccentric we thought he might be making it up and so we dismissed the idea of doing anything ourselves and basically forgot about it, despite the fact that it was a very unusual occurrence.[163]

About half an hour after Mr Martin had left I was vacuuming the lounge, Paul was getting ready for bed. As I walked into the kitchen, I saw through the window the head of a man above the hedge just outside our property.

The man started walking into our driveway. I could hear that the man was shouting but I couldn't hear what he was actually saying. The man was a stranger to me. I had never seen him before. I could see the man clearly as he was illuminated in the light from our outside lights.

The sight of the man frightened me and I connected him with what Mr Martin had told Paul earlier. I ran to the bathroom and said to Paul: "There's a man outside shouting." Paul told me to ring the police, so I went to the phone which is in the bedroom, and dialled 999. As I went into the bedroom Paul went into the kitchen. I could hear the man shout to Paul something to the effect that

---

[161] Notice the mention of "three men". We do not have to believe it.

[162] Notice that Mrs Leet reported that Tony had told her husband that only one shot had been fired. Her statement may have been altered, or her husband may have inaccurately reported what Tony had said. It may well have been that only one shot *was* fired.

[163] We ought to consider that there was a possibility that the Leets *did* call the police after Tony left them and that it was as a result of that call that the police put up the (first) helicopter around 10:30pm.

he had hurt his leg. Then I clearly heard him say: "I think I have been shot." By this time I had got through to the operator on the phone. I could hear Paul talking to the man and I relayed what was being said to the operator; Paul was talking to the man trying to get information.

Then I heard Paul say: "I've got to go out to him." Paul went out to the man in the front garden; I transferred to our living room phone so that I could see what was going on and to make sure Paul was alright. By now I was certain in my own mind that this was one of the men who Mr Martin had spoken about. Paul went to our garage and got out an old blanket. I was still on the phone while all this was going on. In fact I stayed on the phone until the police arrived. The man was very poorly and lying on our front lawn covered in our blanket. The man did not seem to know where he was and he did not know who had shot him[164] and he did not explain why he had been shot. By the time the police arrived the man was in serious shock. *He never at any time suggested that anyone else was with him.* [Author's emphasis]. I would describe the man who had been shot as a slightly built man with a tanned complexion. The man refused to tell the ambulance driver who he was."

What this adds to our knowledge

What do we make of Mrs Leet's alleged comment that: "Paul and I discussed what to do, but as Mr Martin is a bit eccentric we thought he might be making it up and so we dismissed the idea of doing anything ourselves and basically forgot about it, despite the fact that it was a very unusual occurrence"?

Given that it was "a very unusual occurrence", wouldn't the neighbourly thing to have done would be to invite Tony Martin in, perhaps make a cup of tea and call the police if only just to be on the safe side?

And what do we make of her comment that: "*He never at any time suggested that anyone else was with him*"? You see, to me that doesn't make any sense, and it doesn't make sense because it was allegedly Mrs Leet herself who called the police just before 11pm and mentioned that Tony had allegedly said he thought that there were three intruders in his house, and she also repeated that her husband Paul had said this to her. So, what does she have to gain by saying "*He never at any time suggested that anyone else was with him*"?

I don't think she *did* say that or, if she did, that it was of her own volition. It appears that it's been added to try to exonerate the police from 'not finding' Barras. What do you think?

---

[164] Clearly if he had been shot inside the house by Tony, he'd have known who shot him – if not by name, then the 'homeowner' or the 'farmer'.

| Sun 22 AUG 12.40 pm 162 | **St John's Fen End post office**
According to the CAD report, a decision was made that, due to the enormous press activity in the incident, undertakers Bowers from Methwold would meet DC Aldous at the post office and be taken to Bleak House. The CAD report failed to record the name of the person making that decision or the names of the undertaker's staff. |
|---|---|
| Sun 22 AUG 1.09 pm 163 | **Bleak House**
According to official records,[165] PC 214 Simon Stephenson (describing himself as a trained dedicated exhibits officer) attended Bleak House where he met DC 8 Aldous. He was shown the body of Fred Barras apparently still lying at the rear of the premises – 23 hours after having being 'discovered'. |
| Sun 22 AUG 1.16 pm UNUSED 164 | **Bleak House**
According to the following statement allegedly made on the same day, Downham Market-based PC 1221 Richard Bodley, who was on uniform duties in the Smeeth Road and Marshland St James area, arrived on the scene.
See the note following this statement, which was not entered as evidence into court: |

"My tour began at 7am and I accepted the responsibility of the incident log from PC Hooper.[166]

At 1:16pm, I accepted a handwritten letter from Mrs Elizabeth Johnson[167] addressed to Mr Martin. I seized this letter as Exhibit RJB/1."

And now we have another problem with the management of this case because we have two very different exhibits listed as RJB/1: this letter from Elizabeth Johnson and, in a sleight-of-hand, a "rough draft of the surveyed area around Bleak House."

---

[165] In a statement attributed to the constable dated 30 September 1999.

[166] The constable has not stated whether this was PC 935 Patricia Hooper or PC 816 Stuart Hooper or any other PC Hooper.

[167] We will meet Mrs Johnson again in future entries.

Sun
22 AUG
2.10 pm
165

Bleak House

According to official records, at 2:10pm members of staff from Bowers[168] Funeral Directors in Methwold attended the scene. They recovered the body of Barras and conveyed it to the Queen Elizabeth Hospital mortuary. Records show [169] that PC 214 Simon James Stephenson escorted the body to the mortuary, arriving at 2:35pm.

At 2:50pm the constable *formally identified* the body to pathologist Dr Michael Heath, who was said to have begun a post-mortem examination during which the constable acted as exhibits officer. [Author's note: it is imperative – in the light of subsequent entries – that we take note that the body of Fred Barras was *formally identified* in the mortuary to the pathologist.]

The same record shows that DCI Wright, DCI Christopher Grant, Principal SOCO David Rowlands, SOCO Laura Bishop, SOCO Theresa Bradley and mortician Pat Phoenix were also present.[170]

During the course of the post-mortem examination PC Stephenson claimed to have received two rubber gloves amongst a number of other exhibits. It would appear that the teenager had gone equipped to commit burglary. Bizarrely, there was no mention that these gloves were heavily blood-stained which they surely ought to have been, given his injuries. And, apparently, Fearon was unaware that his pal had any gloves with him that night.

Sun
22 AUG
2.30 pm
166

King's Lynn police station

According to official records, DC 8 Richard George Aldous requested that the Council dog warden be informed that his services were no longer required as the third dog had now been "caught by officers."

---

[168] In a statement by PC Stephenson dated 30 September 1999, this is recorded as "Bowes", not "Bowers". The latter spelling is correct and it is spelt the same as witness Roy Bowers (a friend of Darren Bark's) [See also entry **230**].

[169] See the previous footnote regarding the constable's statement.

[170] I could find no witness statements from any of those alleged to have been present apart from SOCO Laura Bishop. The HOLMES database had DCI Grant listed as 'Detective Superintendent' but there was no record of his making any statement with regard to his alleged attendance at this autopsy. There was no mention at all of mortician Pat Phoenix in the database, or of any statement made by DCI Wright. And nothing from "principal SOCO Dave Rowlands" about his alleged attendance at this autopsy.

CORRUPTION ALERT — *Police falsely claimed the farmer's dogs "delayed search for Barras"*

*In a newspaper article dated 21 April 2000 [see entry **386**], DCI Martin Wright claimed that Barras had not been found earlier because Tony's dogs had been running wild. If that were true, how had Barras been found 24 hours before the third dog had been rounded up? It was a lie, and with full access to all the material I have provided to you here, DCI Wright must have known it to be a lie.*

Sun 22 AUG 2.32 pm — 167

Bleak House
According to official records, the press were overheard by the police to say that they had found out the name and address of Fred Barras's mother and that they would be visiting her.

Sun 22 AUG 2.50 pm — witness 69 — 168

mortuary, Queen Elizabeth Hospital, King's Lynn
Dr Heath's statement[171] placed him in the mortuary at the Queen Elizabeth hospital at 2:50pm. According to the statement, there were a number of other people present: DSupt Christopher Grant, DCI Martin Wright, Principal SOCO David Rowlands, SOCOs Laura Bishop and Theresa Bradley, PC 214 Simon Stephenson (Exhibits and Identification Officer), Pat Phoenix (Senior Mortuary Anatomical Technician), and radiographers Cherie Stanfield and Leslie Hill, both of whom were recorded as arriving at 4:05pm.

CORRUPTION ALERT — *X-rays taken of Barras not used at trial*

The purpose of the radiographers, of course, was to take x-rays of the body. Which is pretty much bog standard stuff. Except for one thing – these x-rays were never referred to at trial and they ought to have been as I'll explain in a forthcoming chapter.

---

[171] Dated 2 September 1999.

Why do you imagine that pathologist Dr Heath failed to mention these in his post-mortem report? Why take x-rays if you're not going to refer to them? Even if the x-rays were of little probative value, you'd surely mention that fact in your report.

Leslie Hill's statement[172] informs us that he produced four x-rays in all: two of the right leg and two of the chest of the deceased. He added that at all times he was accompanied by senior radiographer Cherie Stanfield.

Stanfield's statement[173] (not signed, no location, not witnessed, no name of the police officer to whom it was made was recorded on it) appeared to confirm that 4 x-rays were taken and developed immediately and then taken to the mortuary by Leslie Hill, who handed them to SOCO Laura Bishop.

We must be clear: pathologist Dr Michael Heath had ordered these x-rays to be taken (which would, of course, be standard procedure). Thus far, all seems to be in accordance with normal protocol.

However, there is a problem. The (alleged four) x-rays taken of Fred Barras by Leslie Hill were, quite properly, given exhibit numbers of LH/1 – LH/4. But, on turning to Mr Hill's witness statement, he claimed: "Around 3:35pm[174] on Sunday 22nd August 1999. I attended the mortuary at the Queen Elizabeth Hospital. I then saw a Dr M Heath who was conducting a postmortem examination of the body of an *unidentified male person*." The emphasis is mine: how can Barras be an *unidentified* male when he has been identified to the pathologist by PC Stephenson?

Leslie Hill then added: "Under Dr Heath's direction I took a number of x-rays of this body." What does "a number" mean – two, five, ten, fifty? He should have been specific. Further into his statement he lists only four x-rays: two of the chest and two of the leg. But, realistically, taking only two x-rays of the chest wound was hardly enough. You'd need an x-ray from the front, another from the back and both sides of the body. The minimum number of x-rays of the chest alone ought to have been four. According to this statement (if it has not been altered) only two were taken of the chest.

But now the lid on the can of worms is removed entirely when we refer to the statement of SOCO Laura Bishop. In her statement dated as late as 11 October 1999 [see entry **328**], SOCO Bishop stated that she had taken photographs of the body (as it was her job to do so) and she then created a photograph album which she exhibited as LXB/1. She added that she had taken the four x-rays to Ian Munday at police HQ in Norwich to have them photographed. In *his* statement (dated 8 September 1999), he said that he made photographic copies of the x-rays and included them in exhibit LXB/1. So Leslie Hill's exhibits (the four x-rays labelled LH/1 – LH/4) have now disappeared and become LXB/1. But it doesn't

---

[172] Dated 27 August 1999, a week after the shooting.

[173] Dated 27 August 1999, a week after the shooting.

[174] This is half-an-hour prior to the time Dr Heath placed him in the mortuary.

stop there because when we look at the official Exhibit List which was handed into court at the trial, exhibit LXB/1 was recorded not as the four x-rays but merely as photographs of Fred Barras.

Yet the corruption did not end there. The HOLMES database listed Munday as having made *two* statements – the one already mentioned and a *second* statement on 23 November 1999 which claimed that he had received *six* x-rays on 10 November and that he had made "photographic copies". It was not recorded who these x-rays were of.

Furthermore, although the HOLMES database had recorded that Munday made *two* witness statements, the official list of statements entered into court, shows that he only made a one-page statement dated 23 November 1999 and there was no mention whatsoever of the statement of 8 September.

> **CORRUPTION ALERT**
>
> *How could Barras have been 'unidentified' when he had been 'identified' to the pathologist by the identification officer?*

But, as we have read, radiographer Leslie Hill stated that his x-rays had been of an "unidentified male" – were they even x-rays of Barras? See also entry 305 because PC Stephenson wrote in a statement attributed to him that "at 2:50pm on 22 August 1999, I formally identified the body to pathologist Dr Heath. He then began a post mortem examination of the body during which I acted as exhibits officer."

This raises yet another issue – if PC Stephenson was only acting as Exhibits Officer, who was the real Exhibits Officer in this case?

Furthermore, x-rays of Fearon were entered into court as exhibit number 5 (JCG/1) and photos of Fearon's injuries were entered as exhibit number 6 (IM/1) despite the fact that SOCO Laura Bishop (LXB) had taken the photographs. According to the statement attributed to her dated 11 October 1999, she said that "Photographs of the injuries [to Fearon] are incorporated in the photograph album exhibit LXB/1." Recorded properly, the photographs of Fearon's injuries ought to have been a separate exhibit, not "incorporated" into another exhibit.

If you are now confused, you might like to consider this: that the legal engineers were pulling rabbits out of the hat and re-labelling them to suit their own perverted narrative. Had this case been run in accordance with the rule of law, there would have been a clear paper trail of all of the exhibits clearly numbered and labelled and not the trail of confusion that was improperly created against an innocent, law-abiding farmer.

We now have a unique opportunity in which to look at the findings in Dr Heath's report on the body of Fred Barras and compare them with what we learnt in previous entries about a scientific examination of a dead body – in other words, we'll see if Dr Heath maintained his professional integrity when examining the corpse.

Rigor mortis
Now our attention is immediately caught and the narrative becomes increasingly more complex because the autopsy report states that: "Rigor mortis was complete and intense throughout all muscle groups."

On the face of it, that sounds somewhat normal. We've read how rigor mortis sets in after death when the body stiffens. But, as we have seen in a previous chapter, what few people realise is that, after rigor has set in, it eventually leaves the body within a set timeframe and the body becomes flaccid once more.

And it's this specific timeframe which is of particular significance here. At this point, you're about to become something of a pathologist yourself…

Rigor Mortis, as we have seen, acts as a good measuring stick for estimating the time of death. The process normally begins roughly two hours after death and can last for anything from twenty to thirty hours. Rigor leaves the body after these time frames have elapsed. As we have learnt, official records show that the body of Fred Barras was subjected to an autopsy at almost 3pm on the Sunday following what we were told was the Friday night shooting at around 10pm – some 41 hours later.

Thus, from what we have already learnt about the process of rigor mortis, the muscles ought to have been relaxed again as rigor left the body. The fact that rigor was still prevalent throughout the body suggests that Barras could not have died within two minutes of being shot as the British public and the jury were told. I invite further discourse from any pathologists reading this. Any comments or corrections would be made in a subsequent edition.

Clearly, one of the primary functions of any pathologist is to establish the time of death. Again, this was not done by Dr Heath. Or so we are led to believe, since there was no mention of such a time in his report, or that of Dr Skinner's who, we were told, first examined the body on the Saturday afternoon following the shooting. Or so we were told.

It's vitally important that we pause and consider for a moment what we've just read. The pathologist has the ultimate say in what happens to the body and thus we are forced to conclude that Dr Heath gave instructions for it to remain in situ outside Bleak House (if the official records are true). Given that a pathologist would normally want to get the body into the mortuary as quickly as possible in order to conduct an autopsy, isn't it somewhat odd that the body apparently remained in situ for so long? I don't believe the narrative that the public was asked to swallow.

Clearly it is imperative when coming upon a body, that a pathologist takes the temperature as soon as possible in order to try to ascertain the time of death.

As we know, there appears to be no record of this having been done by either Dr Skinner or Dr Heath. Tony's defence counsel failed to pick up on this point at trial. Is it not room for reasonable doubt?

I think we also need to pay attention to the facts about putrefaction: that it follows a predetermined timetable in nature and after the first 36 hours the neck, the abdomen, the shoulders and the head begin to turn a discoloured green. If we accept that Barras was shot at 10pm and died within two minutes on that Friday night, then 36 hours after that brings us to 10am on Sunday morning, by which time we might expect that much of the body would have turned a discoloured green. However, Dr Heath refers only to "slight green staining of the right iliac fossa" (the hip area), and so it appears that this was only the very start of the body's process of turning green. Again, this leads us to believe that Barras did not die at a few minutes after 10pm as was disseminated in the press and at trial or that the autopsy was not conducted on the Sunday afternoon.

Furthermore, after this period of 36 hours, the eyes and the tongue start to bloat and, again, there is no mention of this in Dr Heath's report – which again leads us to believe that this had not occurred. Which, in turn, leads us to believe that he did not die immediately, but sometime after and, had he been attended to, he need not have died at all. Indeed, Dr Heath states: "the tongue showed no sign of bruising."

Dr Heath's report does not say that any of the internal organs had gone into a state of decay – in fact, he states the very opposite: "the diaphragm was intact; the heart was normal size; the small and large intestines were healthy; the stomach mucosa was healthy." Given that the intestines are the first to break down in a corpse, the fact that Dr Heath states that they were healthy in Barras suggests that his body had only the very first signs of decay – and remember that it had apparently been left in situ for some 40 hours or so *in August* – which leads us to conclude that (a) he simply could not have died around 10pm but some considerable time thereafter, (b) or that the autopsy was not conducted on the Sunday afternoon but some time on the Saturday, or (c) both.

The stomach – or gastric – mucosa that Dr Heath refers to is the lining of the stomach. Dr Heath states that this was healthy which further suggests that decay had not yet set in. The stomach, as we know, is full of acids, and these eat their way through the lining after death in a natural process. However, this had not occurred, which lends even greater credibility to the view that Fred Barras could not have died at 10pm but much later if the autopsy had genuinely been on the Sunday afternoon.

Dr Heath makes no mention of any state of decay in the vital organs or of the estimated time of death. Now, why would an experienced pathologist such as he not include such vital data in his report?

In most autopsies the contents of the stomach are an important piece of evidence, which can sometimes prove to be the difference between accidental death and foul play. There is no part of Dr Heath's report which includes an examination of the stomach contents, although he said he had removed them in his statement.

Given that the cause of death was associated with – but not necessarily due to – a gunshot wound, this is probably why Dr Heath chose not to conduct a further examination into the contents of Barras's stomach. However, if he were determined to establish a time of death – so crucial to this case – then he ought to have examined the contents.

Insects as an indicator of time of death

It is evident that the collection of blowflies or their eggs is all part of a pathologist's job and Dr Heath stated that he collected "numerous fly eggs over the right lower eyelid, the lower attachment of the left ear, and the left side of the sweatshirt." Now, it is taken as a given by an entomologist that a body has been left out in the open for less than 24 hours if there are few eggs on it. Dr Heath had said that there were "numerous eggs" on two body parts (eyelid and earlobe) and a sweat shirt. But what does the word 'numerous' mean in this context: a hundred eggs, a thousand, or a hundred thousand? We were told that the body had been outside for some 40 hours and so I do not believe that Barras died many hours before the autopsy or been left outside for so long because otherwise his body would have had far more eggs on it in far more places.

In any event, it seems that the eggs removed from the face for preservation were never tested with regard to establishing their age and therefore a likely time of death. We should remember that a pathologist's primary concern is to establish the manner and the time of death.

Entrance and exit wounds

With continued reference to Dr Heath's witness statement, we learn that the main gunshot wounds were of the following pattern: "Gunshot entry wound over the left side of the back of the chest. The hole measured 4 x 5.5 cm with pellet abrasions extending to 7 x 9.5 cm. The gunshot wound passed upwards and inwards at 45 degrees and caused damage to the left side of the neck. A 9 x 10 cm gunshot groove through the outside of the right thigh."

It would seem that Barras sustained two injuries, one to his left lung and one to his right thigh. With the main injury to the left lung, the police ballistic evidence suggested that an object entered the body at an angle of approximately 45 degrees and passed upwards and inwards. This angle leads one to surmise that Barras had sustained the wound whilst crouching on the floor, perhaps after being shot in the leg first. At least this is what the police wanted the general public to believe.

Sun **22 AUG** 3.22 pm – 5.25pm UNUSED **169**	**Queen Elizabeth Hospital, King's Lynn** *According to official records, Brendon Fearon was interviewed in his hospital bed by DS 3254 Mark Taylor and DC 422 Trevor Buxton. Fearon's solicitors, David Payne and Rosemary Holland, were also recorded as having been present.* *The record shows that Fearon was offered exactly the same deal as Bark had been offered the previous day (see entry **146**).*

This interview highlighted an interesting comment from Fearon when he was asked by DS Taylor: "Driving to the cottage, were you not stopped in Mr Bark's Granada by the police?" to which Fearon is alleged to have replied: "No, but I was stopped by the police on Friday who said something about his number plates and let him go."

This causes a problem: the police narrative had been that Fearon and Barras had been shot on the *Friday* but the impression given here is that it must have been the early hours on the *Saturday* morning.

Fearon gave a description of the farmer: "He was short and about 70. He had a bit of a beard and looked bent over. I only saw him for a second. I think he was wearing a brown checked top. He looked mucky looking brown all over."

That doesn't sound like a description of Tony at all.

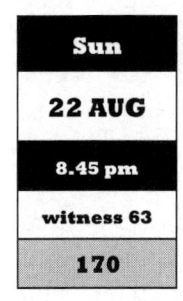

Sun **22 AUG** 8.45 pm witness 63 **170**	**chapel of rest, Queen Elizabeth Hospital** *Official records show that two hours after the first autopsy had been completed by Dr Heath, DC 603 Andrew David Lovick[175] of Norwich CID was on duty at 8:45pm when he visited the chapel of rest at the hospital to show the body to Mrs Ellen Barras and Mr Fred Barras, senior.*

DCL: Mrs Barras, is this your son, Frederick Barras?
MRS B: Yes.
MR B: Yes, it is.

Parents had lost their young son. Tears were in their eyes and a whole series of thoughts about the future of their teenaged offspring had been cruelly curtailed.

---

[175] On 10 February 2011, it was reported in the *Eastern Daily Press* that Detective Sergeant Lovick had been thanked by the Prince of Wales at Clarence House for his work as a Family Liaison Officer.

The 16-year-old Frederick Jackson Barras was lying in the Chapel of Rest, but who was *really* responsible for him being there?

And, against all normal protocol, why were Fred's parents not asked to identify the body of their son until hours *after* the autopsy? Do we believe the official police chronology?

Sun 22 AUG 11 pm UNUSED 171

unknown location

Official records show that PC *588 Brian Sidney Lilly[176] made a statement which was not used as evidence in the trial.*

The CAD *report had Lilly partnered with Cathleen Gore-Rowe (see entry below) yet this fact was not recorded in the statement attributed to him:*

"With reference to the Computer Aided Despatch message showing involvement at Emneth regarding the shooting incident, I never attended either the scene or area in relation to the matter between its occurrence and the submission of this statement at 11pm on 22 August 1999."

Sun 22 AUG unknown UNUSED 172

unknown location

I found an Unused statement allegedly from the 40-year-old PC *9102 Cathleen Gore-Rowe within all of the legal papers from Tony's case. We do not know to whom the statement was made, nor the time or location:* "On Friday 20 August 1999 I was on uniformed mobile patrol accompanied by PC 588 Lilley.

At no time of my tour of duty did I attend the incident at Emneth, Wisbech as stated on the Computer Aided Dispatch (CAD) message."

---

[176] In this statement, 'Lilly' is spelled this way. In his partner's statement (Cathleen Gore-Rowe) and in the HOLMES database it is spelled 'Lilley'. I have not investigated the correct spelling but continue to use the spelling from the database. Tony has told me that the constable is, to his knowledge, no relation to Helen Lilley of the Marmion House Hotel.

Sun	
22 AUG	
11.30 pm	
UNUSED	
173	

unknown location

Official records show that a statement dated 22 August 1999 (but which need not have been made on that date) was made by PC Graham Allan Bavin, *though we do not know to whom he made it or where it was allegedly made.*

"At about 1:43am on Saturday 21 August," Bavin claimed to have been deployed as the duty driver for Inspector Chilvers when he attended Hungate Road in Emneth.

"Upon arrival Inspector Chilvers spoke to other officers at the scene and I was deployed with armed officers to the junction of Lady Drove and Hungate Road for the purpose of control entry to the scene by checking of persons and vehicles wishing to pass the area. *About* 6:30am the same day we returned to King's Lynn." [Author's emphases.]

> **What this adds to our knowledge**
>
> Firstly, isn't it odd that PC Bavin doesn't mention the helicopter that was allegedly flying over Bleak House at this time, according to the police?

Secondly, why deploy Bavin at the junction of Lady Drove and Hungate Road (a good mile and a half from Bleak House) and not have him searching the house and grounds for Barras?

Thirdly, who gave the order to Bavin to return to King's Lynn instead of searching the house and grounds once it had become light?

According to the CAD report, the car Bavin was driving had the call sign AN01 and it was dispatched at 1:51am, arriving *one second later*. The collar number associated with that entry was 4699, presumably Chilvers' number since Bavin was 1025. The report added that car AN01 was cleared to leave the scene at 6:08am. Bavin's collar number did not appear in the CAD report anywhere, yet he claimed to have been deployed with PCs Girton and White. If that was true, why was there no record of his deployment?

Sun	
22 AUG	
unknown	
UNUSED	
174	

unknown location

Official records show that a statement dated 22 August 1999 (but which need not have been made on that date) was made by PS 3093 Richard Davidson, *stationed at Downham Market, in which he claimed to have been on duty in uniform in a marked police vehicle on general supervisory duties in Tilney St Lawrence. At 10:57pm on Friday 20 August 1999, he received a radio message of a person outside Foreman's Bungalow, Hungate Corner with gunshot wounds.*

"Driving via Terrington St John, *I collected PC 543 Mann and together we made our way to the scene*[177] via the villages of Tilney, St John's Fen End and Marshland St James, arriving at Hungate Corner at 11:06pm. I saw an ambulance parked in the front drive of Foreman's Cottage and an ambulance crew treating an injured male person who was writhing around on the grass front lawn and screaming in agony.

I could see the kitchen light of the house was on and the two occupants watching from the kitchen window which overlooked the front lawn. I instructed PC Mann to assist the ambulance crew and try to ascertain what the injured male could tell us about his sustained injuries. I entered Foreman's Cottage and ascertained the occupants to be Mr Paul and Mrs Jacqueline Leet. I ascertained from them that a Tony Martin, a local farmer, had attended their home (Foreman's Cottage) earlier in the evening *alleging that 3 persons had attempted to break into his house and he had fired a gun at them.*[178]

The Leets stated they were afraid, and had advised him to return home and contact the police.[179] A short while later, the injured male had turned up in their front garden screaming and pleading for help.

Whilst they were recounting this initial information to me the ambulance left the house to convey the injured male to the Queen Elizabeth Hospital.

Joined by PC 543 Mann in the house, I instigated a scene log to be kept, established landline communications, tried to ascertain further and fuller details of Tony Martin and briefed further officers arriving as to what had allegedly occurred and organised their deployment to protect the Leets and their own colleagues. I remained at Hungate Corner until 7:08am on Saturday 21 August whereupon I was relieved by PC 1267 George. The scene log forms the basis of what occurred throughout this period of time."

---

[177] Author's emphasis. This is critical information for reasons which will become clear in later entries.

[178] Author's emphasis. From a very early stage and on their own admission, the police had been informed that (at least) three intruders had been at Bleak House. All subsequent claims that they did not know of a third person are inaccurate and designed to misinform the public, as was the notion of there having been burglars at all.

[179] If they were that afraid, why didn't the Leets call the police? Or, in fact, did they and has that 999 call been hidden from public knowledge? [See my Freedom of Information Act request, entry **384**.]

> **CORRUPTION ALERT**   *Police witness statements do not match official police reports*

Three days later, PC George's statement corroborated the time of this alleged handover. However, the CAD report showed that Davidson left the scene at 6:08am and that PC George didn't arrive until 7:08am, an hour later.

We should consider that the HOLMES database shows that PS Davidson made three statements, dated 22 August (above), 2 November in connection with his being the custody sergeant when Bark had been taken into custody on 18 September, and a third (undated) one in connection with his organizing a police search team at Bleak House in the driveway and garden areas on 10 September.

Yet it was only this first statement which found its way into court.

Ongoing 'investigation'

Part 11: Ongoing 'investigation'

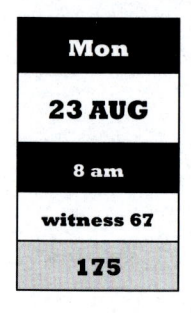

Mon
23 AUG
8 am
witness 67
175

police headquarters, Martineau Lane, Norwich
If the official records are to be believed, SOCO Laura Bishop, stationed at the scene of crimes office in Bethel Street, Norwich, started her shift at 8am and took four x-rays of the body of Fred Barras to police headquarters in Martineau Lane, Norwich, where she handed them to the head of the photographic department, Ian Munday, for him to photograph. It was recorded that she received these back from him at 12:15pm the same day.

As innocuous as that simple act might seem, it is actually an incredibly important piece of the jigsaw and leads, as I later argue, to Tony's innocence.

Mon
23 AUG
10.30 am
UNUSED
176

home address of Neil Fearon
According to official records, 32-year-old Neil Fearon made a statement to a DC 564 Maskell who was not listed in the HOLMES database as having taken any part in the case whatsoever.

Neil Fearon told police that he had two brothers called Gary and Brendon who were alive and two other brothers who had died. He added that he had a sister called Michelle and that he had lived at the parental home until he was about 20 years old.

"My brother Brendon was close to my brother Leon. When I was younger I moved in different social circles to Brendon. I can remember Brendon got into a bit of trouble with the law in his late teens. He started off with petty thefts and it has escalated since. I would describe him as being a rogue but not as being violent. When my brother Leon died, seven years ago, I became closer to Brendon. I would never say he was a drug abuser.

Recently I would say that Brendon's 'best mate' was Roy Bowers. They have not seen as much of each other in the last month or so since Roy has been with a new woman.

In the last year and a half I would say that Brendon has been keeping himself out of trouble. He has been living at our parents' house.

Brendon has been working as a doorman at the local clubs. He keeps himself fit by weight training, jogging and going to the gym. Brendon has always lived in Newark. I would not describe Brendon as a heavy drinker. Brendon frequently socializes but he doesn't drink too much. He'll often drink water or soft drinks.

Brendon has a girlfriend called Kerry. They have three children together. They are a couple who love each other but have an on/off, love/hate relationship. They have been together for about 15 years or so. Brendon is a good, caring, loving father.

I know that Brendon has mood swings - these usually occur when he is bored, because of lack of work or when he has been arguing with Kerry.

I know that in the last couple of weeks that Brendon has been hanging around with a bloke called Darren Bark. I know this because my parents have discussed it with me. I do not know much about Darren, but I have heard that he is bad news. I know Brendon met him whilst he was in prison.

On Friday 20 August 1999, I saw Darren Bark about 7:15pm on Smith Street in Newark. He was driving a big white car, which I think was a Granada. He was the only occupant I could see in the vehicle. This was the last time I saw Darren Bark.

I can remember a boy called Fred Barras from about 5 years ago.[180] My first recollection of him was that he would occasionally tag along with my brother Brendon. I've known him to be at my parents' house before. Since that time, Fred has not really socialized with my brother. I have seen Fred occasionally over the last five years. I have known that he has been into thieving but he has always been polite and friendly. He is the sort of person who would talk to anyone. Fred lives with his mother and his sisters. He has always been the sort of lad who was wandering around on the Hawtonville Estate in Newark.

On Saturday 21 August 1999 at about 2:40am[181] I heard the phone ringing. I was then made aware that my brother had been shot and was in hospital. I then told my brother Gary, and then went to my parents.

We then sorted ourselves out, had some breakfast and went to the hospital. Gary drove and my mother, Glenis, my sister, Michelle and Kerry also came.

We arrived at the hospital about 9am on Saturday morning. I went in to see him first. I was on my own with him for a couple of minutes before Gary joined me. Brendon's voice was slightly slurred, he appeared slightly sedated and was clearly in pain.

I asked him what happened and his first reply was "He kept shooting." He then said, "He shot me in one leg. I said to the man: 'You've shot me - please no more."

Brendon then went on to say that the man shot him in the other leg. Brendon said that he thought he heard Fred Barras shout words similar to "I've been shot mister, please don't shoot again."

Brendon said that the man kept shooting. I asked Brendon about the man. Brendon said that he was a 'nutcase' and that he was wearing a 'combat jacket'.

---

[180] Fred would have been about 11 years of age.
[181] This is more than an hour after Mrs Fearon – the boys' mother – had said she had been called. Perhaps one of the statements has a typing error in it.

I asked Brendon about the type of gun, but Brendon did not know. Brendon insisted that the man kept shooting. He said that when he was shooting, the male kept saying "Yeah".

Brendon did not say what he was doing in Norfolk. He mentioned something about "going for a piss" and something about there being dogs. Then he showed me his wounds, talked about his operation and the pain he was in. I asked him about Fred; Brendon had assumed that Fred had got home.

Brendon stated that after he had been shot he went off to get help. He stated he couldn't walk because of his injuries and had to drag himself before collapsing. He stated he got to a man's lawn, stood up and shouted and then collapsed. Brendon was adamant that he had asked the man to stop shooting and that the man had kept shooting, throughout our conversation. I spoke with Brendon for a 'good' fifteen minutes.

I was surprised to hear that Brendon had been with Fred Barras. *I was concerned for Fred's safety so I asked the hospital to check the other hospitals.* [Author's emphasis.] They did not find Fred. We all left the hospital just before 11am and when I got back to Newark, I made some enquiries to see if I could find out what had happened to Fred. I tried his relatives and they stated that they were also worried. I then telephoned Norfolk Police and told them of my concerns as to the safety of Fred Barras."

What this adds to our knowledge	Neil Fearon described his brother as being a "good, caring and loving father". This could have been a brother creating a fantasy version of his burglar sibling, but Fearon's common law wife said the same: "Brendon is a caring person and a very good father, who enjoys spending time with his children." [182] Indeed, there was some suggestion that he committed thefts in order to provide for his children since there was a high degree of unemployment in the area.

Now, if he was a good, caring and loving father, is it likely that he wouldn't have reported that Barras had been shot to the authorities? The Fearons had known Fred (who had babysat for them) since he was of primary school age and I can't imagine that Brendon wouldn't have told anyone that Fred was badly injured.

It's interesting to note that Bark was known as "bad news" in the Newark area, though his landlord and landlady spoke well of him.

Interestingly, Neil Fearon had placed Bark in a white Granada in Smith Street at around 7:15pm. Had this statement been altered to include this detail?

---

[182] Kerry Smith in a statement to police made at 2:50pm on 24 August 1999 to DC 564 Maskell. However, there was no record of a DC Maskell in the HOLMES database.

Crucially, Neil Fearon informed us that he was concerned for Fred's safety – something which seemed to have escaped the police and it would appear that he was pro-active and asked the hospital staff to call other hospitals in the area.

Fearon's family arrived at the hospital at 9am and Neil went in to see his brother first. Thus, between 9:10am and 11am Neil Fearon had informed the hospital about his concerns for the safety of Fred Barras. Can we assume that someone at the hospital informed the police? And, if they did, why didn't the police find Barras earlier than the time they claimed they found him?

Neil Fearon added that he and his family left King's Lynn at 11am and, assuming a 90-minute journey, he would have called Norfolk police at somewhere between 12:30 and 1pm. Again, why didn't the police allegedly find the body of Barras until 2:42pm?

Mon
23 AUG
10.40 am
UNUSED
177

King's Lynn police station
Tony was interviewed for a second time.[183] *But this time, things had changed - an additional charge of the murder of Frederick Jackson Barras was now added to that of the "attempted murder" of Brendon Fearon. But things had changed in other ways, too. Tony now had legal representation – Paul Croker from Kenneth Bush Solicitors in King's Lynn.*

I contacted Mr Croker in January 2015, but he refused to meet with me or discuss the case or his role in it in any way.

'Appropriate adult'
Just for good measure, the police introduced another pawn into the game – this being John Ravnkilde, an "Appropriate Adult." The role of an appropriate adult in such circumstances is usually when a suspect is perhaps mentally impaired or has insufficient understanding of what has occurred either through their age or their lack of intelligence. The police in this instance claimed that Mr Ravnkilde, a Dane, was present "to see fair play." Given that Tony Martin was not mentally incompetent and given that he was not a 'vulnerable adult' (although at this present moment in time he was extremely emotionally vulnerable), it is difficult to comprehend why Mr Ravnkilde should have been present at all.

Official records show that the interview commenced at 10:40am and was conducted by DS Peter Newton and DC Stuart Peters. After the usual preliminaries, solicitor Paul Croker confirmed that he had explained the role of the appropriate adult to his client. In an excellent move, Croker then added:

---

[183] For the avoidance of doubt, ALL of Tony's witness statements were listed in HOLMES as having been entered into court at trial (as they ought to have been), but the official list of witness statements shows that they weren't.

"Before the officers put any questions to my client, again for the benefit of the tape, I understand that DC Peters will be able to confirm in due course that when my client was interviewed on Saturday[184] about an offence of wounding at that stage,[185] that my client repeatedly told the officers that the events on Friday evening which the officers questioned him about … he repeatedly used the word 'nightmare'?"

DS Newton responded with: "That's correct."

Now this had been a useful opening by Croker because he had got the senior interviewing officer to confirm that Tony had described the break-in as a 'nightmare' and this led to his feelings of being in fear of his life and that, in turn, can give rise to the defence of self-defence and an acquittal.

Croker also got the officers to agree that his client had told them that he did not wish to engage in conversation with them in his first interview. Newton confirmed that that was indeed Tony's position.

So, that was a good start, but – in my opinion and I am not a solicitor or a barrister (although I studied Law at the University of Greenwich in 2010) – his role started to deteriorate from this point onwards because he informed the police that his client had prepared some notes which he would wish to refer to during the course of the interview. Croker asked the officers to show a degree of forbearance with Tony as he went through his notes in trying to explain what happened, together with some of the background leading up to the shooting.

I have serious concerns with this approach. In my opinion, Croker should not have allowed this to happen knowing his client's propensity to ramble on and potentially incriminate himself. Perhaps this was one reason why Mr Croker did not wish to meet with me.

DC Peters confirmed that Tony was initially arrested for the attempted murder of Fearon[186] and then for the murder of Barras. Note that there were just the two charges at this stage – though other charges were to follow, conjured out of thin air by the legal engineers and magicians working at the CPS at the behest of the Home Office and, I suggest, government ministers.

Stream of consciousness

After a pause of three minutes in which Tony spoke with his solicitor, he then gave the officers his account of that night. But it was not an account along the lines of "I did this, then I did that, and then this happened and then that

---

[184] There is some doubt as to whether Tony was interviewed on the Saturday or the Sunday. The doubt about the day will be explained in due course.

[185] Author's note: it wasn't an offence of wounding – records show that he was interviewed on suspicion of the attempted murder of Brendon Fearon. However, when I spoke with Tony about this, he was adamant that he was actually arrested on suspicion of wounding but interviewed – as we have seen – on suspicion of attempted murder.

[186] See previous footnote.

happened" – no, it was a long, rambling affair, a stream of consciousness, an outpouring of emotional baggage which had lain dormant in him for years, a confessional, a mourning for the loss of a "decent" way of life, a lost England, a diatribe against the police, against thieves, against perverts.

It was an opportunity for Tony to be heard and it was some kind of relief for him to be in a crowded room and have an audience who would listen to his every word without interruption, like the family discourse he had never really had. But he had chosen the wrong people to pour out his soul to. In the previous 'interview' – if we can call it that – he had told the police that if he said too much they would be likely to twist it, but his solicitor did not rein him in and the transcript shows page after page of the farmer's emotional troubles being released into the interview room which was completely the wrong place because much of what he said in innocence was to be twisted and bandied about a courtroom and splashed all over the newspapers and on television and in pouring out his soul, he unwittingly contributed to his own downfall in the media. He had given the police much ammunition with which to attack him. This, for me, is part of the tragedy of the Tony Martin story.

Previous burglaries in 1999
Tony began with the story of the burglaries in January and May 1999, of how he had curtailed his freedom of movement at night, not going out as much because of his fear of further burglaries. He described where he lived as a "fearful place" and that he thought that by parking his car where it could be seen, he'd put off prospective burglars at night.

Tears for his father
Tony then mentioned the old Rover car his father used to drive, parked outside the garage and rusting away. Then he broke down in tears at the memory of his late father and he told those present that there were still many artefacts belonging to his father in that car – his old army knife, half-used tins of ointment and other mementoes once belonging to the late Walter Martin.

It was touching when reading the transcript, but I could not help thinking that it was in the wrong place – this ought to have been heard in a counselling room or, better still, a family living room, not in a police station interview room.

I believe it is his emotional issues which have contributed to much sadness in his life. These have hardly been dealt with and he carries them around like a second layer of skin. It is my belief that he had never properly grieved for his father or his aunt Gladys and suddenly – when under pressure and faced with this interview in the police station – he allowed his grief to show. It forced its way out – it had found an outlet. And, once that grief surfaced and was partially vented, other repressed emotions came to the surface as you will read.

The orchard incident

Tony then spoke about the incident with Aldin in the orchard and how he felt he had ended up a loser when his guns had been taken away.

He said that he'd had many threats over the years on his own property, minding his own business. He stopped reporting them to the police because he felt that he was not being taken seriously.[187]

On occasions, he said, he did contact the police because he felt that the information he had to give was reasonable enough for them to do something, but they'd always declined and told him to see his MP (who'd also do nothing).

Only one light

Tony then mentioned that there was only one light on in his house, that being a low wattage one in his bedroom. He said that he left it on day and night. Hang on to this tiny detail, because it will have some significance in due course.

DC Peters asked Tony whether he had a torch with him when he ventured out of his bedroom and onto the landing. The farmer said that he didn't have one – at least a working one.

Then Tony described how he went back into his bedroom to get the gun and load it with an unknown number of cartridges. He said that he'd never used the gun before, that he felt terrified at the unknown number of intruders in his house and that, because he couldn't bear the uncertainty, he left the comparative safety of his bedroom to venture to the stairs.

The tapes were then changed and the interview resumed five minutes later. Tony had been allowed to ramble. This had been deliberate on the part of the police because they had wanted to provide him with a platform to open up and implicate himself in the murder of Fred Barras.

It's at this point that I cast serious doubt on Paul Croker's representation of his client. It's clear to all who meet him and engage in conversation with him, that Tony has a rambling nature and in my view Croker ought to have reined his client in somewhat. It should also be noted that there had not been any intervention whatsoever from the Appropriate Adult.

Tony explained that he only decided to use the gun because he was sure that people were coming up the stairs.

DC Peters asked Tony if could remember how many times he fired the gun, but Tony said he couldn't. The policeman offered: "Until it was empty?" and Tony, without thinking, replied: "Until it was empty."

Notice the ease with which Tony had adopted the suggestion that he kept firing "until the gun was empty." This can have several meanings, of course. The implication is that he loaded the shotgun with the maximum number of cartridges – five – and that he kept firing until all five cartridges had been used.

---

[187] This view – that of no longer reporting crimes to the police – was (and continues to be) a common feeling throughout the Fens. Tony was far from alone in this view.

But he is not sure how many cartridges he actually put in the gun and all neighbours except one spoke of hearing two gunshots. So, if it is correct that he did fire off only two rounds, this has much less of an impact than someone "firing until the gun was empty." Yet it was precisely this type of linguistic gameplay that was to become a feature of the trial.

DS Newton tried to get Tony, rambling again, to focus on the shooting. The farmer then described what he did immediately after the shooting, which we've read about in a previous chapter.

DS Newton then asked Tony if he was aware of having shot anybody and Tony replied:

> No, 'cause all I know ... there was at least one person I can only put it that way, there must have been at least one person with a torch but how many people there were and how many torches there were, I don't know."

Legal definition of murder

Let's now pause for a moment and turn our attention to the legal definition of murder. The CPS website offers this definition:

"subject to three exceptions [author's note: none of which apply in this case], the crime of murder is committed, where a person: of sound mind and discretion (i.e. sane); unlawfully kills (i.e. not self-defence or other justified killing); any reasonable creature (human being); in being (born alive and breathing through its own lungs); under the Queen's Peace (not at war or under martial law); with intent to kill or cause grievous bodily harm (GBH)."

The farmer had told police that he discharged his shotgun not at people but below the level of a torch shone in his face. We should recall that he fired at Aldin's tyres in the orchard in 1994 (witnessed by Tony's cousin), so there is a record of his not wishing to inflict injury but merely to deter intruders or trespassers. We have to ask ourselves the simple question: "Based on all of the evidence before us, can we be sure beyond all reasonable doubt that the farmer *intended* to kill or cause grievous bodily harm when he pulled the trigger?" I believe that we already have considerable doubt against a charge of murder and attempted murder, but let's see how the interview progressed:

DSN: So, you're saying you fired at the torch?
AM: No, I fired below the torch.
DSN: In the direction of the torch but below that?
AM: Below.

Tony was asked what he did with the gun – the officers already knew this, of course, because his mother had called the police about it. His reply appears to have been somewhat strange:

> Well I didn't know what to do. What do I do with this gun? I'm going to have to give myself up and I wanted a little bit of time left for a little bit of freedom to get me into a state of rationality and everything and I hid it in a toilet."

DS Newton then asked Tony an excellent question: "You say that you had to give yourself up – why? For what? What did you think you had done other than discharge your shotgun?"

And we ought to pay particular attention to Newton's words: "What did you think you had done other than discharge your shotgun?" because, in my view – based on all the available evidence – that is *all that Tony had done*. He hadn't hit anybody at all and I believe that Newton knew this. Tony had been a patsy – he'd played his part in the murder of Barras by firing his shotgun but he didn't kill Barras. According to the police's own evidence, there were no shotgun pellets around the doorway to the breakfast room and, since Tony had been firing from the stairs, how on earth did it happen that no pellets were embedded in the wooden door frame?

DS Newton then asked him why he hid the gun in the toilet at his mother's house, to which Tony replied: "I didn't hide it. I just put it in there and I left it. It wasn't any good to me."

Tears for his mother
Tony then got on to the subject of his thrombosis and he asked the police not to mention it to his mother who was unaware and because "she will not be here much longer."

He then began to cry again. Tears for his late father and tears for his elderly mother. It is evident that he was in considerable emotional pain and I don't believe he had great clarity of thinking at this stage, so we have to show caution around some of what he says.

And then we come to what I believe is another tragic element of this Bleak House shooting, something which the general public never got to hear about:

> My mother, for several years, has tentatively hinted that she would like to come and live with me. I always replied with excuses. The real reason actually is that I have felt, and was sure, she wouldn't be safe when I was not about."

Notice here how Tony spoke of his fears for his mother's safety should she live with him. Doesn't every son (or daughter) have the basic human right to have their parents live with them if they want them to?

Tony's fear for his mother's safety – a very real, primeval fear for one's personal safety and those you care about – was shared by many families living in the Fens and other rural parts of the UK. And why should they move from what are often beautiful parts of the country and where they are earning an honest living? Tony's point was that our taxes are meant to provide for a positive police presence – an honest and professional organisation – but that throughout the 1980s and 1990s, the numbers of police were decreasing, a lack of professionalism was becoming an increasing problem and corruption was rife. He was not alone in those views. In a later chapter I explore this same point about a lack of professionalism in the police made by Lord Stevens, a former Commissioner of the Metropolitan Police in London.

Unchartered territory
And then the interview went even further into unchartered territory when Tony mentioned his retired local beat officer, Rodney Gooderson:

> I've been in contact with the police for many, many years. Rodney Gooderson came to see me and said to me, 'All you want to do is mind your own business and do your own thing.' I found that most reassuring and it gave me great comfort. He had a difficult name for me to handle."

Tony asked his solicitor if there was any point in mentioning this, and Croker replied, "If you feel it's relevant, Mr Martin," before the tape came to an end.

Defence of self-defence
Within a couple of minutes of tape four of five starting, Tony came out with a crucial statement:

> I found, reading back earlier, that I hadn't made it clear to you about my horrendous experience at this break-in and with the gun on the staircase. I want to make it clear that when I fired my gun I genuinely thought my life was in danger and with the torch pointed at me, I really didn't know what was coming behind that."

The farmer's state of mind would surely force a juror to conclude that this was a case of self-defence. But do you agree? Could Tony Martin have been lying? Was this an elaborate charade to protect himself from the charge of murder? We are duty bound to consider all possibilities.

And then, in a single heartbeat, the whole tone and manner of the interview changed and it became something of a confessional again. The interview room was completely the wrong place for what was about to be said. I am morally and legally bound to include it here for reasons which will become obvious to you as you read it:

> "Many things have been said about me that are not true. Rodney Gooderson has got the same name as a man who was a friend of our family. His name was Rodney Townley [author's note: now deceased.] His father was the vicar at Upwell and his brother was married to my mother's sister and he used to stay with us.
>
> We had a little cottage over at March and suddenly as I got older he used to try and molest me and that's had a great effect upon my life and some people say that people play on that, but I've had the experience and it's something like many things, it doesn't leave you. It's a scar and this is why, one of the reasons why, I live on my own.
>
> I find it very difficult to live with other people and it's rather a shame but I've taken some lovely girls out in my time, which seems rather contradictory and I've upset a lot of girls because at the end of the day I always felt however much we went out together that ... yes, it made me very self-conscious when I was a youngster and I really thought people thought I was queer. I had people say they thought I was queer but somebody said to me the other day that in those days queer meant odd, not what people are called it today.
>
> I do spend an awful lot of time with people but I don't have a relationship anymore because I've tried it several times. There was a married woman came along several years ago, got children and whether she just wanted a little bit outside the marriage or whether she was unhappy in her marriage and wanted another man, but hadn't notified me that, and unfortunately I'd had a few drinks and when I've had a few drinks I am a very nice man, and all your inhibitions go and all your problems ... but when it comes back the next morning, in the cold light of day ... horrible, it's horrible and I've had to struggle with my emotions the best I can."

I question Paul Croker in allowing his client to ramble on in this way. It is common knowledge that the police took this information and used it against him, despite their function being to keep the peace and investigate crime, not to create false narratives or engage in defamation and disinformation. As previously stated, I did write to Mr Croker on two occasions asking to meet with him, but he declined my first hand-delivered invitation and did not reply to the posted second. (He may not have received it.)

Secondly, the police never asked Tony to make a formal complaint about his allegations of child sexual abuse in respect of Rodney Townley or Glebe House School. I believe that this is a major failing by Norfolk Constabulary and a dereliction of their duty.

the 1967 murder of Robbie Auger revisited

The interview then turned to the murder of Robbie Auger, whom we have previously read about. Tony mentioned this at this critical time because it had played on his mind for decades. He lived in daily fear of his life and that fear was shared by many others in the area. DC Peters asked how Tony felt once he knew there were intruders in his house:

> " That the nightmare was upon me - it was just like being in a horror movie."

Then DC Peters asked Tony where he got the cartridges from. Tony replied from a carrier bag on his chest of drawers near the bedroom door.

Tony said that he had never used that gun before and that he was frightened because when he came to use it, he suddenly realised that he had not previously used it and didn't know how it worked or even whether it worked.

Tony's position on the stairs

The detectives asked the farmer how far down the stairs he went and whether he got to the bottom of the stairs. Tony said that he descended the stairs only as far as he dared go to give him a view of the doorway into the breakfast room.

In their last few questions on tape four, the police were attempting to focus their attention on Tony Martin's position on the stairs, the position of the Welsh dresser in relation to the stairs and how much of the breakfast room you could actually see from any point on the stairs. This became a central point of the trial – the position of Tony Martin on the stairs when he fired his gun.

Tape number 5 was placed into the recorder and the interview continued at 2:52pm. Let's listen in:

DSN: You were down the stairs; I think you were very, very frightened and those people were in your house and you fired your gun. You do not know how many times but until it was empty. Your first shot was towards where the torch was and possibly lower than the torch. Is that absolutely correct?

AM: Correct.

Notice that the fallacy that Tony kept firing until the gun was empty is repeated here – but we know that the gun still contained at least one cartridge after it had been fired because one was found on the floor of his car after he had checked that it was not loaded prior to leaving it at his mother's house. This is why it is so important to correct such mistakes as early as possible, before they become unchallenged 'fact'.

DC Peters asked: "Did you at any time warn or shout to anybody that you were there?" and Tony replied that he didn't and that neither did the intruders say anything to him. Clearly Tony wouldn't want to give his position away – he was, in effect, under siege because the intruders had apparently smashed their way through a double-glazed window at the front of his house and who, in time of war, would give his position away? Tony did not know whether they were armed in any way.

DC Peters then asked: "Were all shots fired from the same position, in other words half-way up the stairs?" and Tony said that he believed so, "though everything was so fast and it was a nightmare." It seems to me that Peters' question was a fishing expedition – he wanted to know what Tony would say because he (Peters) knows that the angles do not work.

The issue of intent (mens rea)

The detective constable then asked: "What was your actual intention when you went down with the gun?" and this is of vital importance because it goes to the heart of the case, the *mens rea* or intent:

> My intention was, I was in fear of my life or being very badly maimed or beaten up or anything. Unfortunately this last couple of years I had this thrombosis so you had to be careful about knocking yourself when you are working. All those things crossed through my mind: I'm getting older and I don't want to get into trouble and fights and things like that. It seemed to me that the gun was the safest way for me and I don't know why that torch just kept on peering at me for so long."

Tony, describing what he did after he fired his gun, told the officers that he drove around the back of his house. He then asked a question, the significance of which he could not possibly have known: "Have you been in the garden?"

DSN: Are we talking about around the back of the house?
AM: Have you seen the wheel marks, in the grass?
DSN: Yes.
DCP: Have we seen the wheel marks?
DSN: Yeah, no, I know about the wheel marks ...
AM: Right, well...
DSN: We were concerned it could be a different car but thank you for confirming that you drove round.
AM: Yeah, as far as I could see there was dew on the ground and wherever I went I couldn't see where, where anybody had been walking...

And it wasn't until November 2018 that I spoke with Tony about the significance of his comments when I asked him why there were no footprints in the heavy dew on the grass at the rear of the house *if the intruders had fled the house via the rear window*. He looked at me without speaking, the slow dawn of realisation breaking out upon his face.

Paul Croker, it would seem, did not realise the significance of his client's words and he certainly didn't speak at this point.

Swiftly, the police changed the subject, DS Newton asking if Tony realised that he'd actually hit anybody:

> I can only tell you there was nobody in that room when I went down again; nobody followed me up the stairs and I heard no noise at all and when I went downstairs there was nobody in that house."

DS Newton then claimed that the police were not sure just how many people were in the house that night. But let's look at this realistically – if Fearon and Barras had really been in Bleak House and had they really been shot by Tony, how did they come to be shot without crying out and how did they come to escape without leaving a trail of blood and how did it happen that the contents of the room were not peppered with shot? After all, at trial, the prosecution was to claim that Tony walked down the stairs and fired from the doorway into the room "shooting them like rats in a trap". Had that been true at all, from the distance Tony would have been at, almost everything in that room in front of him would have been peppered with shot and it wasn't. This was one reason why (a) the Police claimed that Bleak House was an exhibit (thereby preventing Tony's friends and neighbours from seeing the house and asking too many questions and (b) seizing the entire contents of that room and removing it to Downham Market so that nobody would notice the absence of shotgun pellets and blood. As I said, Tony Martin was fitted up by Norfolk Police and Bleak House was nothing more, at this stage, than a Hollywood film set.

Then DS Newton informed Tony that Barras was found dead just fifteen feet from the exit window. Note that Newton didn't actually say that Barras died there (although, of course, that was the implication).

DC Peters asked Tony: "Why didn't you phone the police by the way?"

> Good question. I suppose it's because whatever happened at the time, I hadn't got a gun licence and I don't know, I was stood there so ... I'm afraid I was put in this position and unfortunately I haven't got a gun licence."

DC Peters replied: "When you say that the only reason you didn't contact the police was because you hadn't got a gun licence, realistically Mr Martin, Tony, that is the least of your problems isn't it?"

Midway through this interview, there was the following exchange:

AM: I was looking for where these people had gone. I was hoping that I might see a car with lights somewhere I mean I don't, you, you or somebody told me *yesterday* there was a man with a car...
DSN: Did ...
AM: Is that right?
DSN: Did you ever ...?
DCP: Sorry, we didn't speak to you yesterday...
DSN: No, it was the top of the day before yesterday...

Note here how Tony introduced the notion that the first interview had been on the Sunday, not the Saturday as the police claimed. But note how DC Peters was swift to challenge the farmer and then also note how the detective sergeant added to the confusion by saying that the first interview had been at "the top of the day before yesterday." Since when was 2pm "the top of the day"?

[When I asked Tony for clarity on which day he was first interviewed, he was unable to recall.] A little further into the interview and we have this exchange:

DCP: You're explaining how you were searching round your house in your car and about the marks that you left on Friday. Did you find anybody?
AM: No, I never saw anybody at all.

So the nonsense that the public was asked to believe was firstly that Fearon and Barras were ever at the house and, if that lie was believed, then the public was asked to believe that Barras, who allegedly died within two minutes of being shot, had managed to hang on to life with a huge hole in his chest which was pumping out blood until his mate had pulled a window out of its opening, climb out of the window and stagger five yards before collapsing into some bushes. All within two minutes. Allegedly.

And as for Fearon ... he'd had half of his left knee blown away and yet he somehow managed not to cry out, then he managed to climb on to a wooden box to lift a heavy window out, then he managed to crawl some 400 yards to the Leets' bungalow. All within less than an hour. Allegedly.

The State attempted to label Tony as eccentric and a loner, then that he had a distorted view of gypsies and travellers, then that he had a propensity to use firearms at every conceivable opportunity, then that he was mentally ill, then that he was a fantasist when speaking about child abuse by Rodney Townley and at Glebe House School, and then that he was a fantasist about the inordinate number of thefts and burglaries that he had suffered. The State's corrupt officials knew no boundaries when it came to stopping this most dangerous critic of police ineptitude and corruption – a Teller of the Truth.

Sadly, as at Hillsborough, the broad mass of the people bought into Die Große Lüge. Just as Hitler had written, they had been easily corrupted in the deeper strata of their emotional nature and caught up in the argument of self-defence, a person's right to defend one's self and one's possessions. The little details (in which the Big Lie could be exposed, as I have managed in this book) didn't really concern the public – they were arguing about the bigger issue of a person's rights and not asking too many questions about the finer details. But it is in these finer details that the Big Lie is exposed.

On tape four of the second interview, there was a fascinating revelation:

AM: Are you still searching the premises?

DCP: Yeah, I think we are still.

AM: Well, I suggest you go and look in the garage roof.

DCP: What's there?

AM: In there is a sawn-off shotgun.

DCP: In the garage roof?

AM: In the garage, where the solid fuel boiler is, above it is a hole which allows smoke to escape when you open the door...

DCP: Whose is that?

AM: That gun? I don't know, it's something I found after my house was broken into in May this year and I found it on my lawn near the apple store and what it's about, whether somebody's just dumped it or whether it was to do with my house being broken into, I don't know.

This is a quite remarkable interchange. It's interesting that Tony was honest enough to tell the police where they'd find a sawn-off shotgun. It's even more interesting that – according to official records at least – that the gun wasn't tested for DNA or ownership. If it was dropped by one of the burglars in May, perhaps some DNA might have led the police to another member of the gang in that burglary.

Bizarrely, Tony wasn't charged for illegal possession of that gun. Wouldn't you have thought that it would have been mentioned at trial and a great deal made of it? Of course you would have – but the police didn't want that gun anywhere near the trial and nor did they want the public learning too much about the May burglary, those involved in it or any firearms they may have had.

Inevitably the interview got round to the following:

DCP: While you're talking about this, can you tell us where you got this gun

	from? [Author's note: the gun Tony fired on the stairs.]
AM:	This gun relates back to Arthur Garner. This gun was a surprise. I found it in my car with a message ... with a, with a small note and it's apparently somebody who had admired Arthur Garner, or was a friend many years ago and it was just a brief letter. I can't remember exactly what the words were, but they knew of my ... of what was happening down the Hungate and the problems I'd been having and they just mentioned they're ... that they knew my problem and they thought that ... they basically said they didn't need the gun and they thought I might need it.

That apparently cleared up the issue of how Tony came to be in possession of the single-barrel Winchester shotgun. But was it really left by a "friend"? Could it have been left by someone determined to create a situation in which he felt forced to fire it? Or did Tony Martin acquire it illegally?

The interview then turned to the issue of the holdall that Tony said he'd seen in the breakfast room after the intruders had left the premises:

DCP:	This is a Rogue sports bag, colour black and multi-coloured.
AM:	No, I didn't see that.
DCP:	What? That?
AM:	No, I didn't see that.
DCP:	Purple? Purple bag?
AM:	No, I didn't see that either.

Thus two of the bags that the police claimed to have found in Bleak House had not been seen by Tony. Towards the beginning of interview tape five, we find the following fishing expedition from the police:

DCP:	Did the intruders ... or how many, how many people do you think there were?
AM:	Well I'd got in my mind, I don't know why, whether it was to do with the mumbling, like a crowd, I got the feeling there was more than two people in that room.
DCP:	More than two?
DSN:	That was your impression?
AM:	That was my impression.

Why does this matter? Because I believe that Tony was right – that there were more than two and I also believe that neither Fearon nor Barras was amongst them. And it's possible that the intruders weren't burglars but police officers – part of a tactical operations team. I will provide more evidence to substantiate this view as the story unfolds.

DSN: At what stage did you realise that somebody had been hit, somebody had been shot?

AM: I never realised, never assumed anybody had been shot. I assumed that there wasn't anybody in the house. The time I went up the stairs and I came down again ...

DSN: This is after the shooting?

AM: Yeah.

DSN: There was nobody around?

AM: I went up the stairs, nobody followed me up the stairs ...

DSN: Did nobody scream or shout for help?

AM: Nothing.

DSN: Did somebody, did you hear somebody shout for their mother, their mum?

AM: No. Not a thing.

DSN: You didn't hear anything at all, and no shouts, no moans, no ...

AM: The only thing I heard was the blast of the gun ...

DSN: Because it would echo around, I appreciate that, but I have to ask you, cos you didn't, you heard not even a shout?

AM: No.

DSN: Did you realise you'd hit anybody at all? Did you think you'd hit somebody?

DCP: If you're firing at a torch or just below a torch level, you would perhaps...

AM: I can only tell you there was nobody in that room when I went down again. Nobody followed me up the stairs and I heard no noise at all and when I went downstairs there was nobody in that house.

So, how does it happen that (allegedly) two men get seriously injured with a shotgun inside a house and the person firing the gun doesn't hear anyone cry out, and that when he looks into that room minutes afterwards, nobody is there?

Tony told the police that at some stage during the early part of the day he met a man called David Cooper who was supposed to be cutting corn but that it had been too wet. In December 2018, Tony told me that he'd put him to work clearing out some sheds. And he added that Cooper worked at Fred Deptford's yard (along with Paul Leet) and that, somewhat ominously, "I think he knew too much about me and my movements."

As the interview entered its final stages, DC Peters misinformed Tony about Jacqueline Leet's witness statement:

DCP: Right okay. I think we've hammered this business about the shooting long and hard enough, erm, when we first interviewed you on that first day[188] before you had Mr Croker representing you, we, er, *we read from a statement by Mrs Leet which is her account of what you said to her husband*, when you went round there and she said that she could remember Paul's reply clearly. She said, "What did Mr Martin want?" and his reply to her was "He's just caught three men who had broken into his house. He took a shot at them, they had dropped their rucksacks and ran. Can you, can you just confirm that I'm not ...

PC: That's hearsay what you're asking my client there ...

DCP: I can appreciate that ...

PC: ... and therefore my advice to you, Mr Martin, is that that is likely to be inadmissible and that's not something that you should make any comment on. Therefore I'd advise you to decline to answer the officer's question.

AM: Alright.

DSN: I mean, obviously the same thing will be said by Mr Leet which would not be hearsay. At the end of the day, I don't think that's going to be the major of our worries.

DS Newton seems rather too confident that Paul Leet will say exactly what his wife allegedly said. Unless, of course, he is right to be confident because he knows that both statements had been fabricated...

But as tape five draws to a conclusion, DC Peters described to Tony how Fearon made his escape, and it makes for very interesting reading:

DCP: The other one that was injured, the one that went to hospital, made his way round, as he describes it, to the gravel drive because he knew that when he reached gravel he'd have a fair idea of where he was cos he was disorientated and in pain ...

AM: So you're telling me that he was actually down my front driveway?

DCP: He's saying you know, a gravel driveway ...

---

[188] Notice that DC Peters avoids stating on which day the first interview took place.

And why is this significant and so helpful to Tony? It's quite simple really. It drives a coach and horses in the statement attributed to Fearon in that he exited the rear window and went down the garden at the rear of the property and on his epic journey through an orchard and a cornfield on his way to the Leets.

And, as if that doesn't help Tony enough, then this bit might – because if Fearon had really gone down the pea gravel driveway then *Tony would have seen him as he drove down the driveway, round to the rear garden, and back down the track to the Smeeth Road on his way to the Leets* and, of course, he didn't see anybody. So, if Fearon went down that gravel driveway after being shot, then it would have been at a different time from that which the police claimed which means, of course, that Tony didn't shoot him.

So, on the police's own evidence and comments to Tony under caution, the farmer could not have been guilty of murder.

As the interview reached its conclusion, detective Peters asked the following:

DCP: What I'm trying to, what I'm trying to ask is, is did you take aim and, and look down the barrel with your eyes?

AM: No, no.

It's clear, then, that if Tony didn't look down the barrel and take aim, he could hardly be said to have deliberately intended to hit anybody – making it a nonsense that he ever stood trial for murder. And it gets even better for Tony:

DCP: Okay, were you firing from the waist?

AM: Yes.

So, what we're really being asked to imagine is that Tony was on the stairs and that he fired not down the barrel at a specific target, but randomly fired from the hip and *deliberately aimed to kill or cause serious injury*. It simply doesn't add up. The firing from the hip suggests nothing more than a warning shot.

DS Newton then asked: "All I want to say really is how do you now feel, for the fact that there's a young lad that is dead and another man that is injured as a result of you shooting them?" Notice how the senior detective, who knew more than he was letting on, had introduced a form of emotional blackmail in order to make the farmer feel guilty for the death Barras. Tony, buying into the propaganda, replied:

> 66 Well, I actually bitterly regret it but I also ... I find I was in a very regrettable position. I don't know if that's the right way to put it, but that was the position I was in ... sorry."

And, in my view, that piece of neuro-linguistic programming had been successful – Newton had successfully implanted in Tony's mind two entirely separate events: (i) that Tony had fired his gun at an unknown number of intruders and (ii) (that at least two of) those intruders had been burglars Fearon and Barras. Tony, emotional and vulnerable after the most frightening experience of his life in which he felt that his life was under threat, readily bought into the lie: five decades of feeling guilty for the sexual abuse perpetrated *against him* meant that he readily acquiesced with the fictitious narrative created by corrupt officers as a cover for the murder of Barras by *someone other than Tony*.

Alleged lack of remorse

Throughout the trial, the press were later to make great capital out of the fact that the farmer had shown no remorse. As we can see from this part of the transcript, Tony Martin did, in fact, bitterly regret the death of Fred Barras, and of course he had no way of knowing that he had not been responsible.

Summary

Those are extracts from the transcripts of the interviews in respect of a murder trial. Are you satisfied that they were professional in all the circumstances? Are you satisfied that they were fair? Are you satisfied to learn that an "appropriate adult" was present? Are you satisfied that Paul Croker performed his function to defend Tony thoroughly and robustly? Do you believe that Tony Martin told the truth at all times, or do you think that some of his responses were somewhat evasive? Do you believe that the police asked all the questions necessary to investigate a murder or do you think they fell substantially short of what we might have expected of public servants?

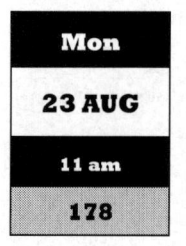

Mon
23 AUG
11 am
178

Leverington Ward, Queen Elizabeth Hospital

After having been operated on, records show that Brendon Fearon was being interviewed by DC Buxton at 11am on 23 August 1999 – two and a half days after he had been shot - while Tony was being interviewed in King's Lynn by DS Newton and DC Peters.

This was not Fearon's first statement to the police – according to PC Clare Smith, he had given an initial account to her on 21 August.

He had, we were told, been shot on 20 August and had undergone extensive surgery to his knee and genital area which would later require plastic surgery. This statement to the police was somewhat lengthy and began with a description of his early life, working history and family circumstances. You can now read a synopsis of his statement.

Fearon told the police that he used to work as a 'knocker'[189] but that he had recently been helping out a friend by doing a bit of security work as a doorman at the Lightning Jacks club in Newark, where he claimed to be earning £30[190] a night.

He said that on Thursday 19 August 1999, he met up with Darren Bark, someone whom he had first met in HMP Ranby in 1989. Bark had a car and so Fearon asked him to take him to the dentist. On the way back Fearon asked Bark if he would drive him down to Wisbech. Fearon claimed that he did not tell Bark why he wanted to go but he knew that Bark was aware that he knew a chap in Wisbech called Jo-Jo who had a tip, a re-cycling centre: "There are loads of lads in Newark who have worked for him." Bark, who gave Fearon his mobile number, agreed to drive him but wanted petrol money.

Fearon rang Bark the next day and asked him to pick him up that evening, which Bark, driving a white Granada, did at about 7:20pm[191] on Friday 20 August. Before they had left Fearon's house, he had put a black holdall containing four or five other bags in the boot. Fearon told Bark they had to pick up another lad, Fred Barras, at Eton Avenue. Fearon had known him since he was 10 or 11 and the teenager often hung around the Devon Road shops.

They set off: Bark driving, Fearon in the front passenger seat. Barras was drinking strong lager and Fearon was worried that the youngster would not be in a fit state to do the job. He was talking a lot and Fearon had to tell him to shut up. Fearon saw him drink two cans of strong lager but Barras said he'd had four.

After only a few minutes they were stopped by a policeman at Balderton. The officer recognised Bark and Fearon but did not say anything to Barras. Bark received a ticket for a 'dodgy number plate' and the known burglars were allowed to proceed on their way. [Author's note: there is no mention in the officer's witness statement of his searching the car. If I'm a policeman and I've stopped a car and I recognise burglars leaving town on a Friday evening, I'm sorry, but I'm going to search that car. In *The Sun* dated 28 April 2000, a spokesman for Nottinghamshire Police said, "In a case of a routine stop, officers would have the powers to inspect the vehicle but not to search it. That would amount to a full stop-and-search which police can only carry out if they have good grounds for suspecting a crime is about to be committed."]

Fearon claimed that after a while he told Bark what they were intending to do: that is, burgle Bleak House for 'smalls.' He claimed he told Bark that he need have no part in it and all he had to do was drop them off. Fearon added that he told Bark he would ring his mobile if they needed him but that he had

---

[189] A 'knocker' is someone who goes from house to house in a targeted area asking people if they have any antiques to sell. Clearly this activity can be misused by burglars to 'case the joint'.
[190] Allowing for inflation this would be equivalent to approximately £50 in 2018.
[191] Compare with Bark's statement (entry **154**) in which he stated they left at 8:30pm.

no need to wait for them.

Fearon said they went straight to the house and Bark dropped them off on the Smeeth Road where it meets the end of the farm track. Before that, they did a drive around and found a place where Bark said he would wait for them. Fearon allegedly had said he need not worry, but Bark insisted he would wait for half an hour or so in case they could not get in or something. Fearon said he told Bark that they would hitch a lift home if he was not there.[192]

The place they chose for Bark to wait was a left turn off the road opposite Deptford's farmyard on the right [author's note: this would appear to be Moyse's Bank]. A couple of hundred yards along that road was a gateway on the right.

Fearon said that he took the large bag out of the boot containing the other bags and held on to them. He said that he had a small torch around his neck on a piece of string and a pair of black woollen gloves in his pocket. Fearon claimed that it was very dark and added that he did not have any tools with him.[193]

He claimed that although it was dark, they could clearly see the outline of the house. He described a barn to the left of the house with some tractors and farm machinery around it. He said that he'd seen the house before when he was in the area about eight weeks previously, driving past on the road when he was "down near Wisbech having a look around and a few beers at the time."[194]

Fearon then went on to relate a story about them trying to evade a dog (singular) and so they broke into the house to get away from it. He was adamant that he could not see any more than one dog.

Once they'd completely smashed a window to the front of the house, Fearon said that he went in first and Barras threw the bags in to him. Barras apparently had trouble getting through the window as the ivy caught in his face and arms.

Once inside, Fearon shone the torch around to see where they were. He described it as being "like an old shed."

They walked through the only exit Fearon could see which was a doorway with a door hanging off or leaning up against it. As he walked through there, he looked to his right and saw a big heavy church door with metal bars on it. He described it as looking welded up or something. Right beside the big door was a set of stairs which were either sanded down or white pine [author's note: this description is incredibly accurate in every detail. It's actually rather *too accurate* for someone who only had a small torch hanging round his neck in a pitch-black house.]

Fearon claimed that Barras had no torch – evidently they were not the most

---

[192] Does that even sound credible if you're carrying four or five bags full of 'smalls' with a considerable combined weight?

[193] If this is true, how did Barras allegedly acquire the large, wooden-handled chisel?

[194] This building is not actually Bleak House, which could not be seen from the road. It was a cottage about 75 yards up the farm track from the Smeeth Road. Bleak House is at least another 100 yards from the cottage.

professional of burglars - and that the torch he had was throwing light out in all directions as it swung around.

The older man said that he tripped over some rubbish and when he picked himself up he noticed an old dresser and some drawers in the room. Barras allegedly followed closely behind his mate, as without Fearon's torch he could not see.

At this point in the statement attributed to him, Fearon claimed that he no longer had any intention of committing burglary but that they simply wanted to get away from the dogs (plural.) He said that they started walking around to see if they could see a light or a window when suddenly he heard Fred shout: "It's got me!" or "He's got me!"

Fearon claimed to have heard a loud bang, but that he didn't know what the bang was and he wasn't sure whether he heard Barras shout first or the bang first. Fearon suggested that it might even have been that the bang and the shouting were at the same time. He added they had only been inside the house about two minutes, but it "seemed like ages."

It is claimed that Fearon said that he panicked; the torch was spinning on its string around his neck and he heard noise.

He said that he "could see in the flickering torchlight Fred's arms waving around frantically." Fearon added that he was on the opposite side of the room from where he had entered through the doorway and he was frantically pushing and pulling at the wall trying to find a door or window. He found a window then heard another loud bang and his left leg went numb. "I spun round and saw someone standing on the stairs pointing what I thought was a torch at me. At the same time I heard another bang and felt pain in my right leg."

Two issues we need to keep in mind as we read on – that from this description there were three gunshots, although it's not entirely clear from the statement. The second – and critical issue – is that Fearon placed the shooter on the stairs at the time the gun was fired. Whether two shots or three shots, the crucial factor is that the shooter – *according to Fearon* – was on the stairs for all the shots. But more of this later, because Fearon's presence in the house at all is in serious doubt, as we have seen. We also need to consider that you cannot see the stairs from the windows in that room.

In the statement attributed to him, Fearon claimed that Barras was screaming out, "He's got me, I'm sorry, please don't! Mum!" and that "there was a lot of confusion."

The statement then included a passage to the effect that Fearon had been shown a copy of a plan of the breakfast room where it was alleged that they sustained their injuries (exhibit JE5) and he allegedly placed three marks on it where he was standing (Point A), where Barras was (Point B), and where the shooter was (Point C). Look at the precision with which Fearon described the position of the shooter:

"He was more than halfway up the stairs when I saw him. I estimate about three stairs higher than half way up the staircase."

Now, by anybody's standards, that is an incredibly precise description. Far too precise if you ask me for someone who possessed only a small torch and who was standing in complete darkness but for the torch.

Fearon claimed to have escaped out of the window, his legs hurting and becoming numb. He "assumed Fred was following me out of the window but I never saw him again so I cannot be sure." If this is true, we have to ask why he didn't make sure where his young accomplice was.

The statement added that Fearon then said that he may have heard three or four more shots after he exited the house but that "they could have been from all the ringing in my ears."

Having staggered his way through part of the orchard, Fearon's statement claimed that he emerged into a cornfield and spotted a light in the distance - this would be the bungalow on the corner of Moyse's Bank and the Smeeth Road, Foreman's Cottage, the home of Paul and Jacqueline Leet – and he said it was his clear intention to get to the building and seek medical aid for the injuries to himself *and Barras*. [Author's emphasis].

He said that it seemed like hours before he managed to pull himself along on the low branches through the orchard and into the cornfield where he saw the police helicopter whilst laying on his back, recovering from his exertions. This would have been around 10:30pm but only if we believe the truthfulness of the statement, which I do not.

He described arriving at Foreman's Cottage and seeing Paul and Jacqueline Leet, who called the emergency services just before 11pm, or so we were told.

The statement described how he became very cold (one of the signs of shock, of course) and he lost his temper with Paul Leet, calling him a "little prick" for not covering him up. Very soon after that, he collapsed to the ground again. (In Paul Leet's statement, he claimed that he *did* cover Fearon up with a blanket.)

Fearon added that he remembered an ambulance arriving and the crew looking after him. According to Fearon, someone else got in the ambulance, but he did not know who it was. (From PC Mann's statement, it was him who got into the ambulance to ask questions of Fearon.) When they got moving Fearon recalled saying to the crew, "There's somebody else been shot."

The reply he heard was, "You're in shock."

He remembered being given an injection and something falling onto him from above his head in the ambulance.

That was, we were told, Fearon's statement made to the police under caution in hospital.

In my view, it had been contrived. It contrasts spectacularly with his earlier comments to doctors that he and Barras had been shot in the open after walking some 20 or 30 yards up a track. Are you more inclined to believe his first statement made almost on the spur of the moment and without much thought, or do you prefer the second statement which, being so precise and full of small details, must surely be true? I ask you to recall Die Große Lüge (the Big Lie): "in the big lie there is always a certain force of credibility" (the descriptions).

Mon
23 AUG
11.55 am
witness 29
179

police headquarters, Martineau Lane, Norwich

The 35-year-old communications officer Carol Woods, whose position involved receiving both emergency and normal calls made by members of the public which went through to the central control room in Norwich, is alleged to have made the following statement about the time Tony called the police after the burglary in May:

"On Wednesday 12 May 1999 I started a night shift duty at headquarters. This started at 11pm and finished at 7am on the morning of 13 May 1999. Shortly before midnight on the 12th,[195] I took a call from a member of the public. As is normal practice I immediately opened a text on my call-taking system. As the member of the public gives the information I then write this down on the computer. Once all the information has been received I then dispatch the message to the appropriate area control room for allocation.

This call was from a Mr Martin of Bleak House, who stated that his house had been broken into and antiques stolen. Mr Martin stated that if the offenders came back he would "blow their heads off, if you know what I mean."

I have been shown a copy of this Computer Aided Dispatch (CAD) text by DC Cross and can confirm that it was me who took the message. I can confirm this because my operator number is on the message in the top left hand corner. This is PF052. Also on the message is my pay number which is 098269. I can produce a copy of this Computer Aided Dispatch (no. NC-19990512-679) as exhibit CJW/1 to be used in evidence. I handed this to DC Cross at 12:25pm on 23 August 1999. I cannot personally remember this call as I take 30-40 of these calls per shift."

Thus, to be clear, the statement attributed to Carol Woods claimed that Tony Martin had said to her in May that if any burglars came back to his house he would "blow their heads off."

We should then pay regard to her final comment: "I cannot personally remember this call as I take 30-40 of these calls per shift."

---

[195] For the sake of accuracy, this call was made on 12 May 1999, the day of the second of three burglaries Tony suffered in eight months that year. In a police interview, it was claimed by the police that this burglary had taken place on 13 May 1999.

Whilst apportioning no blame on her whatsoever, Carol Woods might take between 30 and 40 calls per 8-hour shift (between 4 or 5 an hour, or one every 12-15 minutes) but surely not everyone who calls the police threatens to blow someone's head off. Isn't that kind of call or threat relatively unusual so that you *would* actually remember it?

We should note the chronology too. The call Tony made to report the burglary was made on 12 May 1999 and it's now 23 August and she's been asked to make a statement about having received that call from Tony – not just *any* call reporting the burglary, but one in which it was alleged he'd blow the heads off any burglar daring to return.

Now, given that Carol Woods was unable to remember that call from the farmer, one would logically turn to the voice recording – all calls to the Constabulary were (and are) recorded.

So, if the communications officer herself was unable to remember such a threatening telephone call, all the investigating officers would have to do would be to obtain a copy of the tape recorded call [see also entry **260**].

Mon
23 AUG
unknown
UNUSED
180

home address of Glenis Fearon
According to official records, 55-year-old Glenis Fearon, mother of Brendon, made what for her must have been an extremely difficult statement to PC 1018 Caine.

In the event, the prosecution decided not to use her evidence at trial or call her as a witness. Tony's barrister had the option of calling her, but chose not to:

"Since Brendon's late teens he has been in and out of trouble with the police and has been to prison on a number of occasions. In the main his convictions have been for burglary but he has always admitted what he has done when caught. It is true to say that, to his detriment on occasions, he will never 'shop' his mates and so has been left to face the consequences when others have played a larger part. We have told him in the past that he should look out for himself and that so-called mates were taking advantage of Brendon but he always remains loyal to them.

It is my opinion that Brendon is easily led by others and that, in the main, this is why he has got into so much trouble.

Brendon is also partially deaf and this slightly affects his speech.

Brendon has lived with us for about the past 18 months and to the best of my knowledge has not been in any trouble for this period. We both made it clear to Brendon that if he got into any more trouble we wouldn't let him live with us anymore.

Brendon was given 120 hours' Community Service when he was last at court and he has been going 2 or 3 times a week in order to work it off.

In the last week or so he has not gone out much because a friend called Darren kept coming round for him. He was in a white car and they would go out together in it. Darren did not come in but waited outside in the car. We were both concerned that Brendon was getting into trouble with Darren but he denied this. He said that Darren had some antiques in a hidden warehouse and that he had had them for years. He was going to sell them and they were cleaning them up. He also said that they would go to auctions buying and selling antiques. I do not know Darren's surname or where he lives and prior to the last week or so had not seen him before.

Brendon knew Freddie Barras well as he has known him since he was a young lad. When Freddie was little he used to come around to the house but he has not done this for years.

On Friday 20 August 1999, Brendon took his children out during the day and returned home about 5pm. He had a snack with his brother Joe and a friend of Joe's.

They then went to collect some slabs from an ex-colleague of Joe's and got back around 6pm for tea. Our son Neil also helped them. We had tea and I knew Brendon was waiting for Darren. I do not know what they were going to do. Darren came around at, I think, about 8pm. Brendon asked if Darren could bring some stuff to our house to clean it up but I refused this. […]

I was woken at 1:30am on Saturday 21 August 1999 by the phone. My husband Joe answered it and said that Brendon had been shot in an incident and was at the hospital in King's Lynn. Joe was so shocked he passed out after a minor epileptic fit.

We made arrangements and all went to see Brendon. Myself, Gary, Neil, Michelle and Kerry (Brendon's girlfriend) went, and we arrived about 8:45am.

I saw Brendon in hospital and he had gunshot wounds to the top of his legs and groin. He had been to theatre and was on morphine and a drip. I was very shocked by all of this and we had to take turns to see him.

Brendon said that the man was mad and kept shooting. He had shot him in one leg and then in the other. He then shot again. He also said that Fred was shot. By this I knew he meant Freddie Barras. I don't know whether this was inside or outside of a building. […] *He also said that Darren must have heard the shots.*[196]

He kept repeating that Freddie had been shot[197] and that the man had been mad and wouldn't let them go. […] We left and I got home about 12:15pm."

---

[196] Author's emphasis. If parked where they had agreed – in Moyse's Bank – of course any driver ought to have heard the gunshots.

[197] Author's emphasis. I will discuss this point in greater detail within this chapter.

> **What this adds to our knowledge**
>
> Had you been Tony's barrister, wouldn't you have wanted to call Mrs Fearon to court to inform a jury about her son's partial deafness?

Wouldn't you have wanted her to tell a jury that her son wouldn't shop his mates and not tell on Bark or whoever was the getaway driver? The prosecution, of course, attempted to claim that Fearon's propensity not to 'shop' his mates proved that he didn't tell anyone about Barras having been shot.

If her statement has not been altered in any way, wouldn't you have wanted the prospective burglar's mother to tell a jury that in the week prior to the shooting Bark had been seeing her son on a daily basis which adds to the view that it was Bark who planned the burglary and not Fearon?

Wouldn't you have wanted her to tell a jury about a warehouse full of hidden antiques (assuming it was true)? It's highly likely given the large number of burglaries and thefts throughout the region and it does rather suggest that Bark was someone slightly higher up the food chain than previously believed. Did the police know of this warehouse? Were they "taking back-handers" from the criminal fraternity to turn a blind eye? Or was the 'warehouse' actually Bleak House? I have also been told by locals that Tony was often followed home after having purchased antiques at auctions.

And wouldn't you – had you been Tony's barrister – have wanted to have questioned Mrs Fearon about her comments that "I don't know whether Brendon was shot inside or outside of a building"? According to the police, there was no doubt that her son had been shot *inside* Bleak House.

Given that the Fearons had known young Freddie Barras since he was a little boy, and given that Fred had babysat for Brendon, is it feasible that he would *not* have told anybody that the boy had also been shot? I don't believe so.

If this statement has not been doctored by the police, Mrs Fearon seems to suggest that her son left the house around 8pm which would appear to fit the timescale of Bark's car allegedly being stopped around 8:10pm.

According to the statement, by 8:45am on the Saturday following the shooting, the Fearon family were at the Queen Elizabeth Hospital in King's Lynn and Mrs Fearon stated that Brendon had told her that Fred had also been shot. "He kept repeating that Freddie had been shot." Is this a mother lying for her son, to protect him from others? Or is it the truth? I favour the latter.

If we assume that Fearon's mother was telling the truth, then we have to ask why no-one at the hospital told the police. (At least, that's the official version).

But, if you had been Tony's barrister, wouldn't you have wanted Mrs Fearon to tell a jury that her son had told her "Darren must have heard the shots"? Any incorruptible barrister would have called Mrs Fearon to court to tell the jury what her son had said, and then called Bark to court to give his account.

From reading her statement, Mrs Fearon came across to me as a hard-working, caring and supportive mother who did her best for her children and set down rules, making it clear to Brendon that she wouldn't have any of the antiques in her house (probably believing them to have been stolen) and "we both made it clear to Brendon that if he got into any more trouble we wouldn't let him live with us anymore." I believe that parents up and down the country (and members of the jury) would have readily identified with her.

And the denouement – by 12:15pm, the Fearon family were apparently back in Newark. Allegedly, the body of Fred Barras had still not been found.

> **Mon**
> **23 AUG**
> **unknown**
> **UNUSED**
> **181**

unknown location
According to official records, 54-year-old communications officer Pauline Webster, who'd been in the job for 2 years, made a statement in which she described her role as receiving both emergency and normal calls made by members of the public which went through to the force central control room, situated at Headquarters in Norwich:

"On Friday 20 August 1999 I was on duty carrying out a 4pm - 2am shift. At 10:53pm this day I took a phone call (999) from a member of the public called Mrs Leet. She stated that someone was outside her house, saying he had been shot. I immediately started to take details of the call and enter them into the constabulary's Computer Aided Dispatch system. I have printed a copy of this text from our computer system (Zenith Data Systems) at 12:50pm on the 23/8/99 and can produce this as exhibit PW/1 to be used in evidence. I handed this printout to DC Cross at 12:55pm the same day. This text can confirm that I took the message due to the fact my operator number is in the top left hand corner of the first page. This is PF086. Also on the text is my pay number, which is 228506."

> **What this adds to our knowledge**

If it has not been tampered with or falsely created, it certainly seems to confirm that a call was made by Jacqui Leet just before 11pm on the night of 20 August 1999. What it doesn't tell us is whether there were other 999 calls made that night about the shooting and I'll return to this important point later.

CORRUPTION ALERT
CPS withhold critical evidence from the jury

This computer-aided dispatch report is allegedly what set the entire case in action – the 999 call from Jacqueline Leet. Yet it was never entered into court by the prosecution because it contained a good deal of incriminating evidence against the police.

Had Tony's barrister been incorruptible, he'd have made sure that this document was entered into court and he'd have made sure that Pauline Webster was called as a witness. He did neither.

Mon
23 AUG
2.15 pm
witness 67
182

Downham Market police station
According to official records, SOCO Laura Bishop drove from police HQ in Norwich to Downham Market police station where she handed the Exhibits Officer, PC 214 Stephenson, "4 original x-rays taken of Fred Barras at the first autopsy."

Clearly these x-rays mattered and we'll return to them on several occasions later in this story.

Mon
23 AUG
5.12 pm
UNUSED
183

Downham Market police station
According to official records, DC Lovick took a statement from John Dolan, the eldest uncle of Fred Barras on his mother's side.

We should bear in mind that the statement contained a note that Mr Dolan was unable to read and write.

We should also bear in mind that it was not used at trial, no doubt because it caused the prosecution considerable problems:

"On Friday 20 August 1999 at about a quarter past to half past eight in the evening I was driving my wife and children in my privately owned blue Sierra along Eton Road, Newark when I saw my nephew Fred walking out of the garden to his old house at St. Mary's Gardens. He was with about four or five younger lads who I didn't know. Fred wasn't carrying anything and I could see that he smiled at us. I waved to him and Fred waved back. As I drove on I watched Fred in my rear view mirror and saw him waving to us as we drove out of view. I can't recall the last time I had seen Fred before this - probably about 6 or 7 weeks ago. I was in the area in order to visit my family who live here. I can't recall what Fred was wearing at this time."

The 46-year-old John Dolan said that he'd seen Fred on foot with a group of young males in Eton Road, Newark around 8:15 – 8:30pm on Friday 20 August 1999 which, if true, means that Fred couldn't have been in Bark's car allegedly stopped at 8:10pm in Balderton and couldn't have been at Bleak House at the time stated (or at all). If this is correct, how did Barras come to be shot, why was he shot, and how did his dead body come to be "found" outside Bleak House?

The HOLMES database recorded the fact that Mr Dolan's statement was not used as evidence in court. Presumably this would have been because it drove a coach and horses through the police narrative being created at that time. We should also consider that Tony's barrister knew of the existence of this statement and yet failed to call Mr Dolan as a witness. His attendance at court would have provided reasonable doubt in the case against Tony.

To be clear of the significance of this statement, and the reason for it not being used as evidence in court: the police had evidence - within three days of Tony firing his gun - that called into question the whereabouts of Fred Barras on that fateful day.

Now, realistically, why wouldn't Tony's barrister have called Mr Dolan as a witness?

Do you still believe that Tony Martin shot Fred Barras?

Mon
23 AUG
8.45 pm
witness 67
184

operating theatre, Queen Elizabeth Hospital
More than 12 hours after her shift started, SOCO Laura Bishop was apparently in an operating theatre at the QE Hospital, accompanied by DC Buxton.

Her role was to take photographs of the injuries to the legs of Brendon Fearon and to collect some lead shot from the injury to the right leg.

According to the statement attributed to her, after having taken the photographs, Bishop created an album, which she exhibited as LXB/1 and the lead shot samples were exhibit LXB/2. At 5:30pm the following day, it is claimed that she handed exhibit LXB/2 to principal SOCO Dave Rowlands at Downham Market police station. We have no idea what he did with the shot because it apparently wasn't mentioned in the only statement he made [see entry **365**].

Mon
23 AUG
unknown
UNUSED
185

unknown location

The statement below is attributed to the 21-year-old Kim Ellen Bygrave, employed as a clerk/typist in the central control room of Norfolk Constabulary headquarters, Martineau Lane, Norwich.

We do not know to whom she made the statement, where she made it or at what time. I suspect that it has been altered/ amended in some way. It is of great significance:

"Part of my responsibilities is the production of copy tapes from the master tapes of emergency calls received via the 999 system by our control room.

In response to a request by DCI Wright from King's Lynn police station, I produce the master tape of incident report, ref NC19990820-816 received on Friday 20 August 1999 commencing at 10:51pm, as my exhibit KEB/1. I have retained this tape. On Monday 23 August I produced a copy tape of that incident between the hours of 10:15pm[198] and 11:05pm as my exhibit KEB/1(A).

On Monday 23 August I forwarded my exhibit KEB/1(A) to PC 677 Walker at 12:24pm."

CORRUPTION ALERT   *Critical evidence goes 'missing'*

This short statement raises a number of issues about police and judicial corruption:

- *Every criminal case will usually include a* CAD *report outlining the deployment of officers to the scene of a crime and the 'facts' as they are reported.*

- *Kim Bygrave's statement was **not entered as evidence at trial**.*
- *Neither the master tape nor the copy tape was ever used as evidence at trial.*
- PC 677 *Walker is listed as having made a statement about his having taken possession of the copy tape of the* CAD *report. This is listed in* HOLMES *at line* S43. **However, his statement was not entered as evidence at trial.**
- *I could find no reference to exhibit* KEB/1(A) *anywhere in* HOLMES.
- DCI *Wright made no statement about this important piece of evidence.*

---

[198] This appears to be a typing error and it's likely that it should read 10:51pm since that's the time she referred to earlier.

- *In an appalling and corrupt sleight-of-hand, this CAD report was substituted at trial for CAD NC19990512-679 - **that was the report for the May burglary.***

- *Entering the wrong CAD report into the trial renders the entire trial improper and unlawful.*

- *The trial being improper and unlawful means that Tony Martin is innocent of all charges and needs to have his convictions quashed with immediate effect.*

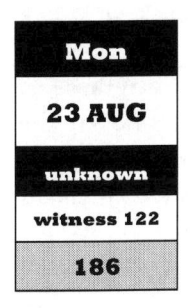

Mon
23 AUG
unknown
witness 122
186

unknown location
The following is a statement attributed to Norfolk Constabulary audio tape librarian Pippa Gooderson,[199] whose role involved the secure storage of both the master and working tapes for all police audio tape interviews within the King's Lynn division. Placed throughout police stations within the division were secure tape storage boxes. At King's Lynn, the box was situated in the custody area.

"After interviews, officers immediately place the master tape into this box via a small letter box type hole in its lid. They retain the working copy from which they will produce a summary of the interview. The working copy is then returned to me at a later date to be stored until the conclusion of the case.

The master tape is stored for a minimum of 3 years but if a person is convicted, for the duration of their sentence/imprisonment.

I normally empty the boxes held at King's Lynn every Monday, Wednesday and Friday or more regularly if they become full during the missed days.

On Monday 23 August 1999, I collected the master tape box from the King's Lynn custody area. I emptied the box, which as previously mentioned, is locked and secure, and upon request of PC 376 Matthews, selected 3 master tapes from it. These tapes were as follows:

1) 2 x tapes referring to Darren Bark master tape reference number D(a)2054/99 exhibits SJP/8 and TRB/1.

2) 1 x tape referring to AE Martin master tape reference number D(a)2057/99 exhibit SJP/5.

This was done at 8:28am. At 8:32am that same day I handed these tapes to PC 376 Matthews in the CID office at King's Lynn.

At 8:10am on Tuesday 24 August 1999, again on request of PC 376 Matthews, I removed 4 master tapes from the custody storage box at King's

---

[199] HOLMES book line S41.

Lynn. These tapes related to AE Martin master tape reference number D(a)2057/99 tapes 2-5 inclusive.

At 8:15am that same day I handed these tapes to PC Matthews."

In short, this is a run-of-the-mill procedural statement whereby the prosecution can line up a witness for the jury and the media simply to make it look as though everything about the investigation was above board and carried out with diligence and all due process. In reality, of course, it added nothing to the question about who killed Barras. With all due respect to Pippa Gooderson, this type of evidence is relatively meaningless and it certainly added nothing to the case.

However, Pippa Gooderson made *two further statements* – neither of which was entered into evidence at trial.

On 23 September 1999 – she made a second statement [see entry **279**] in which, according to the HOLMES database, she stated that on the same day she removed the master tape of the Fearon interview from the tape store and handed it to PC 376 Matthews, the exhibits officer. However, his own statement shows that he *wasn't* the exhibits officer in the *R v Tony Martin* case but was rather the exhibits officer in the *R v Fearon & Bark* case. Another sleight-of-hand in which crucial evidence in the Tony Martin case went "missing".

Her *third* statement was made on 25 October 1999 to the effect that three days earlier she had removed the master tape of the Bark interview from the tape storage box and later handed it to PC 376 Matthews.

Realistically, why on earth didn't Tony's barrister draw the Court's attention to all this skulduggery? Had YOU been defending Tony, wouldn't YOU have wanted the judge and jury to learn about these sleights-of-hand?

Mon
23 AUG
unknown
witness 71
187

unknown location

The following is a statement attributed to PC 960 Andrew Plumb, a police officer in the Cambridgeshire Constabulary who was assigned to the Air Support Unit at RAF Wyton.

It was said that, at 5:30pm on Friday 20 August 1999 he was on duty when he placed blank video tape no 2458 in the aircraft's video recorder.

"At 1:45am on 21 August I attended Emneth Hungate where I took a video of the area of a farm premises, this being in relation to a firearms incident being controlled by Norfolk Police. I produce this video as exhibit AP1.

On return to the Air Support Unit, I made a working copy of this evidential tape which I also produce as exhibit AP2. I then sealed the master video with seal no 4375 and placed it in the master tape store."

| CORRUPTION ALERT | ***Significant lack of crucial detail in statement of helicopter pilot*** |

This short statement raises a number of interesting questions which we need to deal with.

Notice that PC Plumb didn't state which aircraft he loaded the tape into. Lots of different types of aircraft fly in and out of RAF Wyton.

Notice that he didn't state which farm he videoed. We might assume that it was Bleak House but making assumptions in any criminal trial – let alone a murder trial – is never wise.

Notice that he didn't state what he did or didn't see. Notice that he didn't state at what time he arrived back at RAF Wyton (if he did).

Notice that he didn't state that he used the searchlight.

Or heat-seeking equipment.

Notice that the time of 1:45am conflicts with the time of the helicopter flight recorded by several police officers.

Does this catalogue of omissions and contradictions alarm you? It certainly does me. I don't have any faith in the validity of this statement whatsoever and go so far as to say that it was fraudulent – falsely created. It wasn't signed. We have no idea to whom the statement was made, where it was made, or at what time it was made. It wasn't witnessed. Does all of this concern you?

| Tue 24 AUG 1 pm witness 38 188 | **Foreman's Bungalow, Hungate Corner, Emneth**
Paul and Jacqueline Leet – Tony's nearest neighbours – had lived in the Deptford's tied cottage for the past 18 years.
According to official records, Brendon Fearon, having been shot, made his way across a lawn, through an orchard and across a cornfield towards a light – the home of the Leets - about a quarter of a mile away. |

According to the police records, DC Peters took a statement from Paul Leet on Tuesday 24 August. It would be wise, I suggest, to note that DC Peters was involved in taking statements from several key witnesses.

Given that the Leets apparently had their home requisitioned as a base for the police on the night of the shooting, we would do well to consider why it took the police so long to take a statement from Paul Leet – surely he would have been available over the weekend. So I urge caution for this – and other – reasons. Let's see what Mr Leet is recorded as having told the police:

"I work as a foreman for FW Deptford Farms at Emneth Hungate. It is a rural area and because of the length of time we have lived there I know most of the people in the area around my home. One of my near neighbours is a man I know as Tony Martin. Tony lives in a house which is down a track by Titkill Bridge - the house is called 'Bleak House'. I have never been inside Tony's home.

I have known Tony for at least 15 years; I often see him to speak to and thus have come to know him quite well.

I would describe Tony as an eccentric whose behaviour does not conform to what I would consider normal.[200] Tony farms land around his home; one of his fields adjoins Moyse's Bank opposite our home.

At about 8:45pm on Friday 20 August 1999, Jacqueline and I returned to our home from Wisbech where we had been late night shopping. Our outside lights were on as were lights in the house. Our curtains were open so I guess we could be seen from outside.

Sometime, say about an hour after we had got home,[201] I saw through the kitchen window Tony Martin's car, which I would describe as a silvery grey estate car, pull into my drive.

I went out of the house into the drive. Tony got out of the car and walked towards me; he was wearing a short sleeved shirt and trousers. I cannot recall his footwear. Tony said to me: "You're never going to believe this. I've just come home from visiting my mother and caught three blokes in my house. I took a shot at them; they dropped their rucksacks and ran. I don't know whether or not I hit them." I said: "Well, you've got to phone the police, Tony."

With that and without any further conversation, Tony got back into his car, reversed out of the drive and drove off towards his house. That was the last time I saw Tony.

When I got back in the house my wife asked me what Tony wanted and I told her what he had said. We discussed whether or not we should phone the police ourselves and tell them what Tony had said. *I think we decided against it because Tony is so eccentric and it could have been something and nothing.*[202]

A short while after this my wife called me and told me that there was a man making funny noises in our driveway. I came into the kitchen and saw the man clearly through the kitchen window. I would describe the man as slimmish with dark skin. I think he had a kind of goatee beard - he was wearing tracksuit

---

[200] Note the lack of any examples of such "abnormal behaviour".

[201] Notwithstanding the approximate timings, this would mean that Tony called on the Leets around 9:45pm. Given that Tony himself has told us that he spent some time after the shooting in his bedroom and then driving round his farm, this would bring the time of his firing his gun forward to anywhere between 9:00pm and 9:30pm.

[202] Author's emphasis. Does this sound like a realistic decision you'd make if your neighbour called round and said he'd fired his shotgun at burglars? Did Paul Leet say this, or has his statement been altered by senior police officers?

bottoms and a black jacket; he had training shoes on his feet. I did not know the man and I have never seen him before.

The man was illuminated in the light from our outside lights. He was moaning and bending over holding the backs of his legs. I opened the fanlight window in the kitchen and said, "What's the matter?"

The man said, "I've hurt my legs."

I said, "How have you hurt your legs?"

He said, "I think I've been shot,"[203] and with that he turned around facing back towards the road and I could see a great big hole in his left leg. On seeing that, I connected the man with the earlier account which Tony Martin had given to me.

By this time Jacqueline was on the phone to the emergency services and was relaying what I was telling her to the person on the other end of the phone.

I was instructed not to go outside, but despite this I went outside because I could see that the man was in distress. He asked me for water and he seemed to know that I had a tap at the front of the house.

I went out into the driveway and by that time the man was helping himself to water from my tap. He turned the tap off and started to walk back up the driveway to the road. I said to him, "Don't go, the ambulance will be here in a minute." When I said that, he collapsed on the lawn.

He told me he was cold and I went and got a blanket from the garage and laid it over him. The man just kept saying he was cold. I asked the man, "Where have you come from?"

I asked him this several times but I got no reply to my questions. I did not ask him any other questions; he did not tell me who he was or what he had been doing.

The ambulance arrived within a few minutes of me covering him with the blanket. The ambulance men asked the man for his name - he did not reply to them in my presence. Shortly after this the police arrived and I went back into the house. I saw the man being put into the ambulance and that was the last I saw of him.

The police used my home as a base and I was pleased to help them. It was clear that they were looking for other men and at one stage a helicopter came and flew over the area - I could see the searchlights from the helicopter.[204]

I stayed in my house the rest of the evening and I gave a brief account of my movements to a police woman, as did Jacqueline.

At no time did the man who came into my driveway mention to me or to anyone while in my presence the existence of any associates in the area.[205]

---

[203] Does that sound realistic to you – that Fearon would say "*I think* I've been shot"?
[204] Author's emphasis. Note that Mr Leet did not mention a time at which the helicopter arrived or for how long it stayed.

The following morning[206] I saw a white Ford Granada registration number F98LHJ parked up against the hedge by the side of my house. I have never seen this car before and I do not know who it belongs to. The police, I noted, moved the vehicle later that day."

What this adds to our knowledge	This statement – if completely genuine - raises a number of important questions. Firstly, Leet is keen to label his neighbour as 'eccentric'. This is a police tactic against a target – to defame him, vilify him and create a negative image against him to the public at large.

Secondly, Leet informed the police (if we trust the veracity of it) that he and his wife arrived home at "about 8:45pm". The first thing we need to consider is the time at which Paul Leet says Tony turned up at his bungalow – "an hour or so after we returned home". Given that he says he returned home around 8:45pm, that would, of course, time Tony's visit at around 9:45pm. Given PC Knight's timing of when he stopped the burglar's car (8:10pm), Tony could not have shot Fearon and Barras around 9:20pm because they hadn't yet reached the farm.

After firing his gun at an unknown number of intruders, Tony went back upstairs, then went to his car to get a torch before returning inside and finding a holdall in the breakfast room, and given that he spent time driving round the immediate area, then he had to lock the house up and let the dogs out and drive to the Leets, all of that could not have been possible had they been shot *after* 9:45pm. Something's seriously wrong with the timings – the *earliest* the prospective burglars could have arrived at Bleak House would have been the very same time as Tony called on the Leets for a second time.

Thirdly, Leet was said to have told the police that Tony had told him he had shot at "three blokes". When I spoke with Tony about this, he said he didn't think he had mentioned any number because he simply wasn't certain – all he had done was hear voices – plural - and he couldn't be certain about the number of intruders he had in his house that night.

---

[205] Author's emphasis. I question the veracity of this statement because Mr Leet had already said that Tony had called round and mentioned "three men" – so this sentence is completely redundant and has been included, I suggest, simply to exonerate the police and himself.

[206] Mr Leet claimed that he had only seen the "white Ford Granada" the following morning. Yet police witness statements had placed it right outside his house at 11:30pm. Given that he claimed he didn't go to bed until after 2am, how is it possible that he failed to notice this car right outside his bungalow that night?

So, we need to ask ourselves these important questions: (1) is Paul Leet lying? (2) If he is, why would he lie? (3) Is he trying desperately to sell the idea that Tony had shot the intruders? (4) Has his statement been altered in any way? (5) Why didn't *he* call the police?

Fourthly, what do we make of this paragraph: "*We discussed whether or not we should phone the police ourselves and tell them what Tony had said. I think we decided against it because Tony is so eccentric and it could have been something and nothing*"?

Is that a normal response to such a strange scenario – how often does a neighbour turn up on your doorstep to tell you he's had intruders and resorted to firing his shotgun?

I would have been inclined to have invited my neighbour in and suggest that we call the police *there and then* – not avoid the issue as if it's the strange musings of an 'eccentric' neighbour. So, do we believe that this is a genuine statement or, could it have been altered in any way?

Fifthly, Leet is keen to promote the notion that he got a blanket to cover Fearon up with – we will return to the issue of this blanket in due course.

Six, according to Leet, Fearon told him he *thought* he had been shot – surely Fearon *knew*?

Seven – Leet claimed that the police were looking out for others.

Eight – Leet added that he had seen a helicopter but doesn't put a time on it but added that he "stayed in [his] house the rest of the evening."

Nine – Leet is keen to say that at no time did Fearon mention the existence of any associates. However, doesn't that contradict what he himself said about Tony Martin saying there were three intruders and the fact that he (Leet) said that the police were "looking out for others"?

Paul Leet's statement was relatively short considering the fact that he was Tony's nearest neighbour, that Fearon had turned up seriously injured on his doorstep and given that his home had allegedly been used as a base by the police.

But Leet was not finished – he would make two further statements (that we know of) and those statements caused further important questions to be asked.

Tue
24 AUG
1.15 pm
UNUSED
189

home address of Dawn Jepson

Official records show that Bark's 26-year-old girlfriend, Dawn Jepson, made a statement to DC Adcock which is listed in HOLMES at line S26 but it was not entered as evidence in court and nor was she called as a witness by Tony's barrister at the forthcoming trial. She was unemployed and had known Bark for at least 3 years and got to know him through him being friends with her former boyfriend.

"I have been having a relationship with Darren for about 6 weeks but I suppose it started somewhat earlier when Darren, who was in prison, began writing to me.

At the time Darren began writing to me I was serving a term of imprisonment in a Staffordshire prison. When he got released I began ringing him up and finally when I got released we started seeing each other properly.

I am aware of Darren's record but as far as knowing Darren's history intimately I really don't know because I haven't been seeing him for that long. From my point of view I find Darren a very caring person [who] would do anything for anybody. He does however come across as a bit of a joker and seems to enjoy winding me and others up. Darren to my knowledge has never smoked and he is very anti-drugs. He likes to drink occasionally and to play pool and fruit machines down his local pub, The Broadway, on the estate.

I do get on very well with Darren and not only is there a physical relationship but we are the best of friends. I do not put him under any time constraints or pressure and our relationship is quite relaxed. I sometimes go over and stay the night with Darren and sometimes he comes to mine. Darren is a terrible time keeper and I have got used to him turning up later when he says he wouldn't be long. Darren is unemployed and is quite hard up. He has worked with a friend, Edward, who lives on the estate helping with lopping trees and facia board replacements.

I do not, as stated, put him under pressure by asking him what he's doing all the time and he doesn't really volunteer too much to me either.

However when I do ask him what he's been doing he will tell me. I have made it plain to him that if he is up to no good then I would leave him.

On Thursday 19 August 1999 Darren got his giro cheque and I believe we stayed at mine most of the day. Later we got a couple of videos out, had a Chinese and Darren stayed at mine for the night.

On Friday 20 August 1999 we got up around 11am. Within an hour or so Darren went out in his white Ford Granada; he didn't say where he was going.

I went shopping in town and got back in the afternoon sometime. Darren got back to my address around 6pm. I made tea and we decided to watch one of the videos we had got the day before.

At about 9:10pm I was in the kitchen when Darren's mobile telephone went and he answered it.[207] It was a short conversation and I do not know what was said. Darren came into the kitchen and said that it was Brendon on the phone. I have known Brendon for years as he lives in Newark and quite close to where I live. I know him to say hello to. I do not know his history or who his friends are. Brendon had rung my house a couple of times during that week to speak to

---

[207] In his statement dated 21 August 1999 [see entry **116**], Darren Bark claimed that he thought the call had been to Dawn Jepson's home telephone number.

Darren. As far as I knew I did not know that Darren was associating with Brendon as I see Darren as being a bit of a loner with not many close friends.

In relation to the phone call on 20/8/99 at 9:10pm, Darren said he was giving a lift to Brendon to go and have a look at a job. I told him I didn't want him to do anything like that and he gave me the impression that Brendon just wanted to look at this job. He never told me where it was or anything else other than he was to drive only. I did get the impression that they weren't actually going to do a burglary just to "case the job" with a view to Brendon doing it later.

As far as I was concerned I had no problem with Darren driving Brendon in that way but I didn't want him to do the job. He left in his car within 30 minutes and said "I'll be back later."

I went to bed about 11pm and watched TV until about 2am when my dad went to bed. At that time I wrote a note for Darren to use the side door and stuck it on the front door.

About 4:50am I was woken by the police knocking on the door. I was asked questions about Darren, where he was and who he was with. They were only there for a few minutes.

I rang Darren's landlady, Christine Evans, to find out whether the police contacted her about Darren. Then about 6am, Neil Fearon came to my house asking where Darren was and [telling me] that his brother Brendon had been shot. I was completely shocked and had no idea of what was occurring; I had no idea where Darren was.

About 9am Darren rang me at home; he said he was locked up in King's Lynn on suspicion of attempted burglary. He said that Brendon had been shot and that he didn't know about the other lad.

This was the first time he had mentioned a third person. Darren said that he didn't know his name.

I asked him what had happened. He said that he was sat in the car away from the buildings when the armed police turned up. He said they took a witness statement off him for a couple of hours and then arrested him. He said he didn't know why he'd been arrested as he hadn't gone anywhere near the buildings. He said he hadn't been interviewed and he was waiting for a solicitor.[208] I asked him if he had anything to do with it - he said no that he just drove and sat in the car. He mentioned that he knew the address/buildings and that there were big dogs there. I know that Darren is petrified of dogs. He said he didn't understand everything that was going on. He finished by saying that he would ring me later.

I then fell asleep and Christine Evans rang me about 12 o'clock for any update on Darren's situation. During the afternoon I saw Christine at the

---

[208] There is clearly some confusion here: did Bark make a statement without a solicitor present – if so, was it under caution? Or has her statement been altered to include this detail because, almost immediately afterwards in something of a contradiction, she says that Bark hadn't been interviewed and was waiting for a solicitor to attend.

Broadway pub and had a couple of drinks. I still wasn't really sure what had gone on.

Around 7pm that day Darren rang me again and asked that somebody pick him up as he was being released and get some clothes for him. He asked me if I knew that the third lad was dead. I said that I did know because during the afternoon I had rung the CID in Norfolk and they had told me.[209]

As a result of another phone call from him a short time later I left home about 9:45pm to collect Darren.

In the car on the way home we spoke briefly about what had gone on. He said he didn't really believe what had gone on and found it all difficult to understand. He never went into detail and kept saying that he only drove and sat in the car. He again said Brendon had been shot and that he didn't know the other lad and that he was a mate of Brendon's. We got back about 1:30am.

Darren and I have obviously spoken about it since and he has maintained the same account, the fact that he drove to King's Lynn,[210] he dropped them off and he stayed in the car. He had no intention of doing the burglary because of me and that he didn't want to lose me. He also had no intention of doing the burglary because he is scared of the dogs.

I do not know of a Fred Barras. I have never heard the name and to my knowledge nor does Darren."

> **What this adds to our knowledge**
>
> This statement is possibly something of a game changer. In my view, once you scrape away at the veneer of lies that the police and prosecution put forward as a true narrative, you will more often than not usually arrive at the truth. It is always easy to dismiss something as rubbish once you disagree with a certain part of it. When I first read this statement, I dismissed it as rubbish but kept returning to it because something wasn't right. Two things jumped out at me: the role of Bark as getaway driver and the timings.

---

[209] This seems incongruous – that she had called the police on the Saturday afternoon (no precise time given) and had been told that Barras was dead. This is important on at least two issues: (i) that it's difficult to believe that the police would tell a random member of the public that Barras was dead when the press had not been fully informed, and (ii) it is clear that the police knew the identity of the body on that Saturday afternoon, which means it could not have been 'unidentified' as medical staff were later to claim on the Sunday afternoon.

[210] Surely this should have been Wisbech.

In discussing this statement, we have to bear in mind that Dawn Jepson had had several opportunities to discuss the matters in question with Bark prior to making her statement and thus they could have simply agreed a certain narrative to ensure that Bark wasn't held too accountable for anything. However, that said, we really do need to unpick what she's told the police because it could possibly change everything we thought we knew so far.

Dawn Jepson's account of her movements on 20 August are possibly critical. Of course she could have been lying, of course her statement could have been altered by the police, but for our purposes right now, let's assume it's accurate and run with her narrative and chronology.

She claimed that Bark returned to her address around 6pm on the night of the shooting. She added that she "made tea and we decided to watch one of the videos we had got the day before."

If we assume that the meal preparation and eating took around 30 minutes, that would make it 6:30pm. The average video lasts for about 90 minutes, bringing the time up to 8pm or thereabouts.

Neil Fearon had said he saw Bark in his car around 7:15pm driving along Smith Street. It could be that his estimate of the time is inaccurate or has been altered. It is possible that Jepson's timings are a little out and that she and Bark did all the things she said and then he left to go on the job. However, she added: "At about 9:10pm I was in the kitchen when Darren's mobile went."

She added that Bark answered it, that it was a short conversation and that he was going to pick up Brendon Fearon. Now, was he driving to Emneth to pick up his mate, or was he just driving up the road to pick up Fearon and Barras and take them to do the job at Emneth?

If it was the former – that he was driving to Emneth to pick up Fearon (and any others) – then he *couldn't* have been the "getaway driver" on the Bleak House job. So who was?

If it was the latter – that he picked up his mates from down the road in Newark to take them to do the job – then Tony Martin *couldn't have shot Fearon and Barras* when he pulled the trigger because (a) he had left his house around 9:30pm and (b) the alleged burglars hadn't yet arrived at the scene.

Something's not right here and still the plot thickens. Jepson added: "About 4:50am I was woken by the police knocking on the door. I was asked questions about Darren, where he was and who he was with."

This doesn't make sense at all and it doesn't make sense because *Bark was allegedly already in police custody and had been in custody since 11:34pm.* Here we are – according to this statement – expected to believe that the police called on Jepson *six hours* after they'd taken Bark into custody to ask the whereabouts of Bark. Consider the statement of DC Peters made on 22 August:

"At 1:50am on Saturday 21 August 1999 I went to Hungate Corner and saw and spoke to a man I now know to be Darren Henry Bark, who was sitting in a white Ford Granada, index F98LHJ, which he identified as his vehicle.

I took Bark to Terrington St John police station and took a statement. At 4:54am that same morning I arrested Bark on suspicion of burglary and cautioned him. He made no reply."

If we believe the veracity of this statement, then clearly the police had had Bark in custody since before 2am – around four hours after the alleged time of the shooting. So why would police turn up at 4:50am on the doorstep of Bark's girlfriend asking where he was? They supposedly already knew. She could, of course, have been lying but I don't think she was and the main reason I don't think she was is because the prosecution didn't call her as a witness. She would have had too much to say that would have turned the police narrative on its head.

But why on earth didn't Tony's barrister call her as a witness?

Tue	
24 AUG	
1.40 pm	
witness 103	
190	

search of Bleak House
Police records show that there was a search on this day, led by POLSA Inspector Nigel Ralph Gant.

In a statement,[211] SOCO Barry Wells (normally stationed at Norwich) said he attended at 1:40pm and assisted in a search of the grounds in the vicinity of the rear windows and path of Bleak House.

[See also entry **313***]*

At 2:20pm, whilst searching the rear garden of the property, PC 9022 Alison Harvey, normally stationed at Woodcock Road in Norwich, was said to have located a blood-stained fern stem, lying on top of the ground cover.

At 2:30pm, whilst continuing in the fingertip search of the rear garden, she was said to have found a large wooden-handled chisel. This was supposedly hidden in the undergrowth and ivy a few metres from the rear void window.

At 4:25pm the search was concluded. But were these searches of Bleak

---

[211] As far as I am aware from an exhaustive search of the legal paperwork Tony put at my disposal, SOCO Barry Wells made three statements to the police: (i) dated 4 October 1999, (ii) dated 6 November 1999, and (iii) dated 16 November 1999. You might question the veracity of these statements given that the dates are – relatively speaking – far removed from the date of Mr Wells' involvement in the case. I do not necessarily apportion direct blame to Mr Wells. Furthermore, although all three statements were said to have been entered into court, I have been unable to locate statements (ii) and (iii).

House merely 'style over content'? The legal issue – if Tony Martin *had* shot them - was whether he had shot in self-defence, whether the use of force was reasonable and whether, when shooting, he *intended* to commit murder or cause serious injury. These finds added nothing in real terms. Furthermore, by now we have some evidence to show that Fearon and Barras were not shot in the house at all and that they were *not* shot by Tony Martin.

But let's pause a moment and consider what we've just read: that PC Harvey was said to have located a blood-stained fern stem just outside of the rear window. This raises a number of issues – firstly that the results of a forensic test on the fern came back as "Unknown DNA". Secondly, we are being asked to believe that Fred Barras used the chisel to break into the front of the house and held on to it as he progressed through Bleak House. He then allegedly held on to it as he allegedly put items of silver into the holdalls. And then he held on to it once he was shot in the chest and "frantically waved his arms about" (according to Fearon's statement) and he also held on to it as he climbed out of the window and as he staggered along the pathway before – allegedly – collapsing into some bushes. It seems to me that the chisel had been planted. There is growing evidence to suggest that it was part of a carefully stage-managed crime scene in which a low-ranking copper would undertake some amazing detective work and find the chisel used in the execution of a burglary. At least that's what you were meant to believe.

Inspector Gant's statement (dated as late as 17 September 1999) suggested that there was no search of Bleak House on Monday 23 August which is possibly why I have been unable to locate any documentation for that day. But why would the police waste a whole day of searching and the possible contamination of evidence? I struggle to believe that this would happen. Had I been a senior officer in charge of this case, I'd want as many personnel in Bleak House and its environs as soon as possible after the shooting. There appears to have been a more than lackadaisical approach to this entire operation from the moment the 999 call was made.

It has to be remembered that whilst all of these searches of the house and grounds are taking place, Tony Martin is being interviewed and going into 'emotional meltdown', other people are providing witness statements and senior police officers are, I suggest, creating a narrative that they can sell to the public and to the CPS. If you think that the last sentence is somewhat too far-fetched, or paranoid, let's look at the next search and what occurred there.

Tue	**Queen Elizabeth Hospital, King's Lynn**
24 AUG	*It is alleged that on this day, Brendon Fearon made his second statement to the police (to DC 422 Buxton) which was unused and in which he added that when he was going through the orchard "after escaping from the house," he lay on his back for a rest at one point. The torch around his neck was "tangled up and annoying me, so I took it off and dumped it." Allegedly.*
2.40 pm	
UNUSED	
191	

"I also removed my gloves at some point after getting out of the house but I have no idea where it was. I threw them down. It may be near to where I was stung by nettles. It was before I got into the cornfield."

Nothing remarkable about that you might imagine. But there's an important element he's left out of this statement – the helicopter. He claimed to have seen it, you may recall, whilst lying on his back in the cornfield. He mentioned lying on his back again in this statement, he mentioned the cornfield, but he didn't mention the helicopter.

And for good reason – he told me in a phone call that he'd been told by the police to "*never mention the helicopter again.*"

Now, if true, why would the police say that to him?

And, additionally, why was this statement not used in court?

Tue	**home address of Barry Cooper**
24 AUG	*Barry Cooper, aged 63, ran a haulage firm on the Walsoken Road (also known as the Wilkins Road) and was Tony's closest neighbour, apart from the Leets.*
6.20 pm	*His house was a little over a quarter of a mile from Bleak House. According to official records, he made the following unused statement to DC 7 Bowell:*
UNUSED	
192	

"On the evening of Wednesday 12 May 1999,[212] I saw two men walking along the Smeeth Road towards Marshland St James. My attention was drawn to them because they kept walking backwards and forwards two or three times. I did not see where they went or what they were doing. I would state the time I first saw them was 8pm.

I would say the time was about 8:30pm when I went with my son Anthony in my truck to look at a vehicle I thought they had with them.

---

[212] This was the night of the second burglary that Tony had suffered that year.

I pulled out of Walsoken Road, turned right towards Hungate Corner and about 100-125 yards along the road on my offside I saw a vehicle parked. I don't know if it was a Montego or Maestro parked unattended. I don't know exactly where the men were at this time. The car was facing Marshland St James.

I turned round on the Hungate Corner and drove straight back to my house. The car had moved further along the road about 100 yards, now about 25 yards from the junction with Walsoken Road, very close to the Titkill Bridge and the entrance to Tony Martin's lane.[213]

The same two men whom I'd seen walking past my house were now sitting in the car. I can still not be sure of the type of vehicle but I saw the number as G843TES. It was slate blue coloured.

I can't describe the two men at all other than they were both male, white.

I did not see the men walking about anymore and then at 9:30pm I went out and looked for the vehicle but it had gone.

I wrote down the number of the car in my diary with a description as best I could give at the time. Two males: one 5'4" to 5'5", dark hair and slim build.

I now produce a copy of the page from my diary (BAC/1) and will make the original available if needed."

Mr Cooper was to make a second statement to the police on 21 September [see entry **272**]. In certain ways it was markedly different and I do not impugn him for this.

Now, having been given the index number of the car, wouldn't you have thought that arrests would have been made following that May burglary?

Tue
24 AUG
unknown
UNUSED
193

unknown location
Below is a statement attributed to PC 338 Paul Derek Cant, an authorised firearms officer normally based at Bessemer Road traffic office in Norwich. It is of major significance and wasn't used at court. A feature of this case is that on almost every statement made by the public, information regarding the time and location of the interview is recorded together with the name of the interviewing officer, but on almost every statement made by a police officer (of varying rank) this information is not available. We have to ask why.

It calls into question the veracity of these statements – and this one is no different. We should also consider what happened at Hillsborough – that around 200 statements made by lower-ranking police officers which criticised their

---

[213] By this, Mr Cooper meant the farm track leading first to the cottages by the side of the track and then on to Bleak House, sitting at right angles to, and some 100 yards or so, from the track.

superiors were altered, torn up, or completely re-written. That in itself is bad enough, of course, but what then occurred was nothing less than fraud and the perversion of the course of justice because they then fraudulently copied the signatures of the officers who had made the original and critical statements.

By anyone's reckoning, the following police statement is something of a game-changer on a number of levels. Firstly, because of its content and secondly because of the fact that we do not know where the statement was taken, to whom it was made or at what time it was made.

Cant claimed that at 9:35pm on 20 August 1999 he was on duty in an armed response vehicle (ARV) with PC 485 Gotts when they were sent to King's Lynn for a suspected firearms incident. He does not say what this was about. It's possible that it was as a result of Tony firing his gun at Bleak House (and not hitting anybody). The description of "King's Lynn" could have been designed to mislead – to put the casual reader "off the scent" – because there are several villages miles from King's Lynn which include that town's name in their postal address.

Whilst "engaged on the King's Lynn incident", Cant claimed that they heard a radio message at 10:56pm concerning a firearms incident at Emneth "where it was believed a male had been shot".

Now we must pay particular attention to what Cant described next: that on arrival, they saw an armed response vehicle from King's Lynn crewed by PC 400 Girton and PC 852 White, a King's Lynn-based traffic vehicle crewed by PC 155 Beer and 364 Cole, and "several Kings Lynn divisional mobiles were also in attendance".

Now, that's a lot of police officers in the area and yet no-one was apparently searching for Barras. But Cant's statement becomes all the more incredible as we read on: "There is no street lighting in this location and the area was in total darkness. I could view the copse through a night viewing device but could not see any buildings in the copse nor signs of movement."

PC Cant added that the Cambridgeshire police helicopter arrived at 1:05am. This time is of great significance to this story and, in my view, to Tony Martin's innocence:

"I took up communications with the helicopter which was circling the property for approximately 20 minutes. Throughout that time the helicopter radio operator informed me that there were no vehicles in the location nor was there any movement or heat source except for two dogs."[214]

Let's unpick this for a moment: Firstly, the statement alleged that the helicopter had been circling for 20 minutes. We need to hold on to this information.

---

[214] Compare even this scant level of detail with that provided by the crew of the helicopter – see the entry dated 23 August 1999.

Secondly, it was claimed that there were no cars in the area but there were – right outside Bleak House is a double garage (with a tall chimney – surely a helicopter would have seen *that*) and outside that garage, rusting away, was a Rover car belonging to Tony's late father. How did the helicopter miss *that*? And how did the helicopter crew ascertain that there were no vehicles at Bleak House if they claimed they couldn't even find the house?

Thirdly, there was no movement but for two dogs? The land around Bleak House teems with wild life: rabbits, hares, foxes, badgers, pheasants and deer and just before he left the property after firing his gun, Tony's last action was to release all *three* dogs from the cottages adjoining the farm track. Can we believe that the helicopter could see no other movement?

Fourthly, what do we make of the claim that there was no heat source except for two dogs? Can we believe that the body of Barras was not picked up by the thermal imaging equipment? After all, I suggest that he was still alive but even if I am wrong and he had recently died, this was August and his body would have retained almost all of its heat as we have previously seen.

"We also had difficulties in identifying the exact location of the farmhouse itself. *The helicopter could not locate a building where I was directing.*[215] My information was coming from local residents who were adamant as to the point in the copse where the house was."

Presumably these "residents" would have been Paul and Jacqueline Leet, since the police were using their bungalow as a temporary headquarters and they both knew of the precise location of Bleak House of course.

Despite the fact that the house was surrounded by vegetation, *any* helicopter would have picked out a roof top and a chimney stack and a second chimney stack which was part of the double garage near to the house which was itself situated in a clearing amongst the trees. Furthermore, in due course, you'll read about a local making a statement to the effect that the helicopter was *flying low* over Bleak House. But see also entry **95**, in which the helicopter asked the central control room to instruct officers in cars on the scene to put their blue lights on.

Do you buy into Cant's story? Be careful if you are about to say "Yes" because of what the PC states next:

"The situation was re-discussed and it was decided that the two ARVs, a dog handler and CI Curtis would approach the buildings along the entrance track whilst phoning the property to attempt to make contact with the occupant either by phone or visually. Whilst doing this the helicopter remained above us to monitor the surrounding area.

---

[215] Author's emphasis.

On our approach to the buildings there was no reply to the telephone calls and even on the scene we could not identify the farmhouse from the track. It was decided to withdraw to our original position to re-assess the situation as it was felt this forward position was still too vulnerable."

So, we now have evidence from a constable that the police couldn't even find the house. Further shades, I suggest, of Hillsborough. How could the helicopter with its powerful searchlight not find the house and yet the public was being asked to believe that two amateur burglars with only one small torch between them managed to find it in the countryside darkness?

And as for the forward position being "too vulnerable" - it had already been established that Tony's car was not on the farm (though his late father's was). PCs Cant and Gotts allegedly took up a position at the Hungate corner but what use was that? The statement says that they left the area at 4:10am.

So, night vision goggles, a helicopter, a searchlight, thermal imaging equipment, a police dog, blue lights and they still couldn't find Fred Barras laying, the police claimed, within five yards of the house? Significant questions have to be asked.

Now I'm going to throw another spanner in the works of this futile, inadequate and, I argue, corrupt operation.

Every statement recorded the 'fact' that the house was in darkness. Not so. Tony Martin left a light on in his bedroom *day and night*. He never turned it off. And he told me that, being some 3-400 yards from his nearest neighbour, he had no need for curtains. And the police failed to see this light? Come on. Believe that if you will. If you do believe it, then it can only mean that they didn't go near to the house and they certainly didn't walk around the curtilage.

Supt Hale claimed in his statement that at 2:45am he was briefed that the house was silent and in darkness and that Tony's car was not on the property.

Or so his statement says. Like so many other police statements, there is no record of the time the statement was made, no record of to whom it was made and no record of where it was made.

I'll ask you again: do you still think Tony Martin received a fair trial or is there already sufficient evidence to show that the case against him was fabricated, or to use Tony's phrase "legally engineered"?

Tue 24 AUG — unknown — UNUSED — witness 37 — 194

unknown location

According to the official list of witnesses in the trial, eel fisherman John Spalton was listed as number 37. According to that same official list, he made a statement to the police on 24 August 1999. I have been unable to locate that statement.

We are therefore forced to ask why the HOLMES database didn't list it and why the only statement attributed to Mr Spalton was allegedly made on 7 September 1999 – some two weeks later. Given that Mr Spalton claimed to have dialled 999 after knocking Fearon over, you'd think that he'd be one of the very first people the police would want to interview since he was on the scene within minutes of the shooting.

Given that this is yet another example of 'missing' statements or falsified statements, we are surely driven to conclude that police corruption played a major part in Tony Martin's conviction.

Tue 24 AUG 1999 — 195

home address of Ethelwyn Higman, BA

Also on 24 August 1999, the following letter to Neil Jacutine (a friend of Tony's), was sent by 83-year-old Ethelwyn Mary Higman, BA in response to an article in the Times:

"I read that you will be organising a petition on behalf of Mr Martin. Please will you add my name to it. He has stood up for all of us for our rights ever since Magna Carta to protect our person and property. He doesn't know me but as a soldier's daughter and an ex-fencer, I hope I would have the guts and ability to take similar action if my modest dwelling were attacked. My best wishes to you and to Mr Martin."

Wed 25 AUG — unknown — UNUSED — 196

unknown location

The following – unused - statement is attributed to trained negotiator CI Richard Curtis. We do not know to whom he made the statement, at what time or in which location.

It is an example, I argue, of complete police corruption, fraud, perverting the course of justice and misconduct in public office (to name but a few offences perpetrated by the police in this case):

"On Friday 20 August 1999, I was on duty at King's Lynn police station when, at around 11:30pm,[216] I received information concerning a shooting incident at Emneth.[217]

At 12:10am the next day, I left King's Lynn police station, with PC Cant and PC Gotts, who were crewing an armed response vehicle, and went to Hungate Corner, Emneth, where we met with other officers, including PS Davidson, and two other ARV officers, PC White and PC Girton.

We discussed what action should be taken about the shooting incident, having been briefed by PS Davidson.

I was aware that a police helicopter with thermal imaging equipment was on its way, and as a result, we waited for its arrival before making any move towards a house believed to be occupied by the suspect, Tony Martin.

It was also possible that there may have been an injured person somewhere in the area who may have been shot by the suspect.[218]

The helicopter arrived *about* 1am, and I watched it circle Mr Martin's farm on several occasions, and received information from them that the only heat sources that they could see were animals.

As a result of this information, I went with PCs Cant and Gotts, with the second ARV following, and also PC Claxton, the dog handler, to the track leading to Mr Martin's house.

I made 3 or 4 attempts to contact him by phone, using a mobile phone, but each time there was no reply, and after about 7 or 8 rings, the fax machine 'cut in'.

As a result of this, we withdrew to the road where the ARVs remained, and I arranged for further local enquiries to be made to try and locate Mr Martin.

Shortly after 6am that morning, I was on duty in the road outside Wisbech police station, when I saw Wisbech police officers bring into the station a man I now know to be Mr Martin. They had walked with him from a nearby hotel."

I do not trust the validity of this statement at all. I don't believe that CI Curtis didn't hear about the shooting incident until 11:30pm – that's half an hour after Jacqui Leet's 999 call (if the time of her call has been correctly recorded).

If it is true, why did it take him 40 minutes to leave the police station in King's Lynn to be driven to Emneth?

---

[216] Note the lack of an accurate time – he should have been able to note the precise time at which he became aware of the incident.

[217] Notice how the Chief Inspector – who admitted to having been on duty that night – didn't mention the shooting incident alleged to have been in the King's Lynn area at 9:30pm. As probably the most senior officer on duty in the station that night, we would expect him to have been informed of it.

[218] Author's emphasis – it is clear that senior officers had always been aware of the possibility of other injured parties.

Why does he not record in his statement the time at which he arrived at Emneth?

He claims the police waited for the arrival of the helicopter before making any move towards Bleak House. This seems somewhat contrived to me – as if the police are desperate to create documents which somehow show that they never went to Bleak House to look for Barras.

What do you make of the notion that the thermal imaging equipment could only find animals and not Barras? Do you believe it?

And note that Mr Curtis claimed they only reached as far as the track leading to Bleak House and not the house or its immediate surroundings at all.

I completely challenge the veracity of this statement and I'll explain why as we move through the story. But we need to consider this major point – this statement was given to Tony's defence counsel and he therefore had an opportunity to do two things: (i) introduce it as evidence and (ii) call CI Curtis to the stand. He did neither. This one incident – amongst many others – proves that Tony Martin did not receive a fair trial and that the police and the entire judicial system were set against him to ensure a 'guilty' verdict when it knew him not to be guilty at all.

And let's not forget that in his statement, CI Curtis didn't account for 5 hours between 1am and 6am.

Wed 25 AUG 1999 — 197

north Wales

A letter signed simply P. Hughes of North Wales expressed the sentiments of thousands of people in wishing Neil Jacutine every success with his petition and campaign in support of Tony Martin and added "you can add my name to the list":

"The person who was killed could quite easily have done that to Mr Martin and I can guarantee he would have been given a few hours' community service if he had. One only has to frequently read the newspaper to see the <u>criminal</u> is protected in most instances and the law needs changing."

The emphasis was the letter-writer's. The notion that the criminal was protected more than the victim was a recurrent theme in many letters.

The following letter from a Mrs Sheila Barker, also dated 25 August 1999, was just one of a large number from the elderly throughout the country:

"This is just a letter to back up your effort to start a petition on behalf of Mr Martin. I am 85 and find that no matter what the young do, whether it be stealing, holding up bank clerks etc, excuses are made for them; and maybe now there is a chance, for while saying Fred Barras should not have died, he was totally in the wrong and maybe if he had succeeded in the burglary Mr Martin would have had a stroke or heart attack after so much trauma and also died."

The notion that he might suffer a stroke once intruders had broken into his house was, as we have seen in a previous entry, uppermost in Tony's mind. And Mrs Barker echoed what many others had written – that Tony Martin might have been the one to have been killed had he not protected himself.

Ms Higman had written that Tony had "stood up for all of us for our rights" and it is little wonder, therefore, that the nation took him to their hearts. But there is considerable evidence to suggest that the nation was mistaken in its view that Tony had actually killed or wounded anybody...

Wed 25 AUG 11.30 am UNUSED witness 38 198

Foreman's Bungalow, Hungate Corner

Paul Leet – according to official records – made a second statement to DC Peters the day after his first. Rather than clarifying anything from his previous statement, it actually added to the confusion and raised some important questions including, but not limited to, "Why was this statement not used in court when two others made by Paul Leet were?" and "Why were only two of the three statements attributed to his wife, Jacqueline, used in court?":

"Further to my previous statement dated 24/8/99, I have this day handed to DC Peters a black plastic bag containing the blanket which I used to cover up the injured man who came to my house on Friday 20 August 1999. In between covering the man up with the blanket and handing it to the police I lent the blanket to my friend Les Walker of Leverington who was doing some decorating. I refer to and exhibit the blanket as PL/1 and to the plastic bag I put it into as PL/2."

Isn't this an odd statement on a number of levels?

One - why didn't Leet mention this piece of evidence in his first statement?

Two – why wasn't this alleged blanket seized as evidence on the Friday night while the police used his home as their base?

Three – who on earth lends out a blood-stained blanket to a friend to do some decorating? Or had Leet washed the blanket *prior to* lending it out: in other words, he'd interfered with evidence.

Four – was this blanket even Paul Leet's or did it belong to someone else?

Five – did it contain Barras's DNA or even another (unnamed) associate?

This statement wasn't entered as evidence into court – why? We are not completely done with Mr Leet because he was to make yet another statement...

| Wed |
| 25 AUG |
| 2.50 pm |
| witness 102 |
| 199 |

Bleak House

Official records show that SOCO Ian Bradshaw attended Bleak House at the request of DS Eglen for the purpose of swabbing a staircase area for possible firearms gunshot residue.

The farmer, who had admitted to firing his gun, told police <u>four days previously</u> that he'd fired from the stairs.

Only now is the staircase going to be swabbed. Where's the sense in that? Where's the justice? Police have been in the house, going up and down the stairs and even with the best will in the world, they would have been interfering with the crime scene simply by brushing up against the wall or holding on to the banister rail as they moved around the property. Not necessarily deliberately, but inadvertently. And SOCO Bradshaw is now only just being called in? Are you happy with that? Did you even know that? Do we even believe it?

According to the statement attributed to him, Bradshaw arrived at the scene at 2:50pm and spoke to DS Eglen at 3pm. It was said that he commenced his examination of the staircase at 3:15pm and used a total of three swabs - one each for the banister handrail, banister newel post, and wall adjacent to the staircase. It is said that he sealed the swabs in an exhibit bag and completed the examination at 3:30pm.

I don't know about you, but I am concerned about these swabs being taken five days after the shooting – how accurate can they be?

I have an issue with the length of time that Bradshaw spent on swabbing the area – only fifteen minutes. Does that seem thorough and meticulous to you? It seems to me more like a cursory, routine, going-through-the-motions scenario rather than a thorough and professional examination of the crime scene, albeit one undertaken five days after the shooting. We must never lose sight of the fact that a man has been charged with murder and a possible life sentence could result. If it were *you* in Tony Martin's position, would *you* be happy with this brief examination of the crime scene? But what of you as a taxpayer – do you think you received value for money from this public servant? Or is a fifteen-minute examination of the scene more than enough time to ascertain whether or not there was gunshot residue on the staircase? But the issue of possible gunshot residue doesn't rest here. You'll read much more about it in later chapters.

According to official records, there appears to have been no search of Bleak House or its environs on Thursday 26 August.

Wed
25 AUG
3 pm
witness 55
200

Queen Elizabeth Hospital, King's Lynn

Whilst the staircase at Bleak House was allegedly being tested for gunshot residue according to official records, DC Buxton was said to have gone to the Radiology Department at QE Hospital and spoken with Mr Jonathan Gore, who handed the detective copies of the x-rays taken of the gunshot wounds to Fearon.

Wed
25 AUG
unknown
witness 79
201

unknown location

According to official records, PC George, stationed at King's Lynn, made the following statement:

"On Saturday 21 August I was on duty in full uniform when at 7:08am I attended the location at Bleak House and took over the seal duty and the log from PC 543 Mann and Sergeant Davidson. I remained there in situ until 8am when I was relieved by PC 78 Thexton.

At no point did I enter inside the outer seal zone as I had no reason to."

What this adds to our knowledge

Despite being short, this is an important statement for reasons which I'll explain.

Firstly, PC George is listed as witness 79, and in HOLMES he is listed at line S54, yet it did not include his statement as being listed as evidence. I suggest that this statement has been created to distance PC George from Bleak House. Notice that in this statement, PC George did not mention the name of the partner he was crewed with, PC Cook. That's an odd omission, don't you think?

And the location was not noted on the statement, nor was the time it was allegedly made and nor was the name of the person taking the statement recorded. You will have noted by now that several of the statements attributed to police officers were not processed in accordance with normal police protocols.

This statement needs to be read in conjunction with that attributed to PC Cook [entry **224**] because the two statements contradict one another. Cook, you see, claimed that he was nowhere near Bleak House. That's odd, don't you think?

Thur

26 AUG

unknown

witness 52

202

Queen Elizabeth Hospital, King's Lynn

According to official records, Shivkat Jagannathan, was at the QE Hospital on 24 August when he took a sample of blood from Fearon. HOLMES (line 58) recorded that he handed the sample to DC Buxton.

It also recorded that the statement was entered as evidence into court, but I have been unable to find the statement attributed to him. When I cross-referenced the HOLMES entry with the separate document entitled "*Index to Statements – Chronological Order*", Shivkat Jagannathan's statement was not listed.

What this adds to our knowledge

I suggest that it is yet a further indication that the entire police investigation against Tony Martin was deeply flawed on a number of levels from the very beginning, that due process was not followed and that the farmer did not receive a fair trial.

Thur

26 AUG

unknown

UNUSED

203

unknown location

According to official records, 27-year-old King's Lynn-based PC 9078 Carmel Ann Fitzpatrick made a statement to someone whose name was not recorded. It was not entered as evidence. [See entry **123**]

Constable Fitzpatrick is shown in HOLMES at line S52 as having made a statement claiming that she was on duty in King's Lynn at 07:15 on 21 August and that she never attended Bleak House.

CORRUPTION ALERT   *Another PC claims not to have been at Bleak House*

This is another statement by a police officer who declared that she wasn't at Bleak House. It's another statement which failed to record the location, the time or to whom it was made. According to the official Norfolk Constabulary Computer Aided Dispatch (CAD) report, constable 9078 Fitzpatrick is listed as having arrived at Bleak House at 7:14am and having departed at 8:03am.

Therefore, if we assume that the CAD report is accurate (and we are not obliged to), then constable Fitzpatrick's statement is clearly bogus. We are forced to ask what she had been doing for the three-quarters of an hour she was recorded as having been at Bleak House.

Alternatively, the CAD report is either inaccurate or has been falsely created. Either way, Tony Martin was fitted up.

Thur
26 AUG
unknown
witness 55
204

unknown location

According to official records, DC 422 Buxton - normally based at King's Lynn - made five statements in all and yet the one made on this date was the only one which was entered into evidence at trial.

On Monday 23 August and Tuesday 24 August 1999, he claimed to have spent time at the QE Hospital with Brendon Fearon who was detained in a private room off Leverington Ward with shotgun injuries to his legs:

"Over those two days I obtained a lengthy statement from him during which I showed him a photocopy of a sketch plan JE/5. Fearon marked the plan to identify his position in relation to the shooting. He handed me that marked copy as his exhibit BF/1. I retained the exhibit BF/1 until 6:30pm on Thursday[219] 25 August 1999 when I handed it to exhibits officer PC 376 Matthews. Whilst I was with Fearon on Monday 23 August 1999 at 8:45pm I was present in an operating theatre when Mr Chakrabarti examined wounds to Fearon's legs and removed lead shot from them. SOCO Laura Bishop was also present and took photographs of the injuries."

What this adds to our knowledge

Brendon Fearon marked the plan of the breakfast room with the positions in which he believed he and Barras had been standing when they were shot. He was clear in his mind where they had been and he was consistent on this issue. Yet in previous statements, Fearon claimed that he and Barras had been shot after walking 20-30 yards up a track. In which case, they were never inside the house.

DC Buxton's other statements are 26 August & 14, 23 & 24 September.

---

[219] This should be Wednesday, not Thursday.

Thur
26 AUG
unknown
UNUSED
witness 55
205

unknown location

The statement below was DC Buxton's second statement of five. It was not entered as evidence into court.

"At 3pm on Wednesday 25 August 1999, I went to the radiology department at Queen Elizabeth Hospital where I spoke to Mr Jonathan Gore who handed me copy x-rays as his exhibit JCG/1. I retained this exhibit until 8:20am on Thursday 26 August 1999 when I handed it to PC 376 Matthews."

What this adds to our knowledge

Put simply, this statement was never entered into court because of police and prosecutorial corruption – it is as stark as that. These particular x-rays had supposedly been of Fearon, but earlier ones had been taken of Barras showing that he hadn't died *within two minutes of being shot* as the prosecution claimed. Had Fearon's x-rays been entered as evidence and discussed, the jury would surely have wanted to learn about the x-rays taken of Barras.

Thur
26 AUG
1999
206

Wimbledon, London

Yvonne Antrobus, of Wimbledon, London, wrote:

"Dear Mr Jacutine,
I am so glad that you are planning a petition in support of Tony Martin. How can anyone say a shotgun is not 'reasonable force' when a man is faced on his own by three marauders? It is very sad that a young man had to die, but people who live in isolated situations must be allowed to protect themselves."

And she made an excellent point, of course, with regard to the term 'reasonable force'. One home-owner. An unknown number of intruders. Pitch black. Isolated farmhouse. Seen in these terms – factual terms – it is difficult to argue against the notion that Tony Martin used 'reasonable force' when defending his life and his property. But according to Fearon's, Bark's, Dawn Jepson's and John Dolan's statements, Tony Martin couldn't have shot them – the timing is wrong.

John Read, of Wyck Farm in Burrough Green, Suffolk wrote:

"There is massive support for Mr Martin. He should not be punished for an action he was provoked into taking. I will support any action taken for the charges against him to be dropped", while David Read, of Hall Farm, Carlton near Newmarket wrote:

"Jack Straw should get out of Whitehall and talk to the people. He would not be left in any doubt of the strength of support for the action Mr Martin took.

What a sad state of affairs that he should be facing a charge of murder when all he was doing was protecting himself. If the government faced up to facts and gave more support to honest people living in the rural areas then we would not have to resort to defending ourselves.

Mr Martin has brought to the fore the problems facing people living in the country. He should be given every possible support, i.e. financial, moral, and protection if needed in the coming months.

Mr Martin has been the victim of crime for long enough and I hope common sense will prevail and all charges against him will be dropped."

Many letters included the hope that all charges would be dropped against Tony but, of course, the politicians – whilst claiming that they never become involved in 'on-going legal cases' - were clearly meddling in this case, perhaps through the umbrella of the Privy Council. Tony Martin had, as David Read so eloquently expressed in his letter, "brought to the fore the problems facing people living in the country." Tony was, as he says, "a catalyst for the silent majority."
Ian Wylie, of Park Cottage, Carlton wrote:

"I feel I must express my support for Mr Tony Martin who was the victim of several robberies recently. Mr Martin has been a very private person, living quietly and going about his business. It seems quite reasonable that he should want to defend his property and belongings from unwelcome visitors. When faced by THREE men, one can only imagine the fear the poor man felt, and I can fully understand his reaction.

The victims of crime MUST be given more support and for this reason I will support any action taken on his behalf."

The emphases were those of the letter-writer. When reading through several hundred letters and cards, I was struck by the decency of the authors: men and women, young and old. Their sentiments were based on calm reasoning and the notion of 'good and evil' and right and wrong and on the Common Law that has supposedly existed in this country for at least 800 years since Magna Carta. It seems strange to me that Ian Wylie in Newmarket could understand the fear that Tony Martin was put under, but that the trial judge, the prosecution and the jury (not to mention Tony's defence counsel) could not. But Mr Wylie was working from a notion of empathy and justice and common decency – those in government, the police and the legal profession were working to a different agenda, one in which the maverick and outspoken farmer would have to be punished so that the "common masses don't themselves take up arms."

Thur
26 AUG
1999
witness 52
207

unknown address

According to official records, the HOLMES database recorded (at line 58) that a Dr Shivkat Jagannathan took a sample of blood from Brendon Fearon at the QE hospital on 24 August 1999. It further recorded that he handed the sample to DC Buxton, but the date this handover was supposed to have taken place was not recorded.

Furthermore, in a statement attributed to DC Buxton dated 26 August 1999, [see also entry **205**] it stated: "At 12:30pm on Tuesday 24 August 1999 I was present when Mr SJ Nathan,[220] police surgeon, obtained a blood sample from Brendon Fearon, with Fearon's consent. I took possession of the blood sample and produce it as my exhibit TRB/5. I placed it in the secure freezer at King's Lynn custody office until 6:30pm on Thursday 26 August 1999 when I handed it to PC 376 Matthews."

CORRUPTION ALERT   *Worrying discrepancies in police witness statements, official list of witnesses and the official HOLMES database*

*The action of DC Buxton taking possession of this blood sample was not recorded in HOLMES on this date, but there was a note (at line S6i) that "with reference exhibit TRB/5 (blood sample) Dr Nathan is also known as Dr Shivka**nt** Jagannathan." (Note the extra 'n' in the name).*

Yet I could find no statement from Dr Jagannathan at all in the papers delivered to Tony by his lawyers.

*Additionally, the statement attributed to DC Buxton about the blood sample was dated in HOLMES as being made on 18 November 1999 and I could find no statement attributed to him on that date, despite the official list of witnesses showing that a statement on that date was listed as having been entered into evidence at trial. Yet there was also a statement (allegedly about the blood sample) listed as being from Shivka**nt** Jagannathan.*

Fri
27 AUG
1999
208

unknown location

The following letter from PW Watson to David Barnard, a local counsellor from Upwell (now retired), is indicative of the kind of letter Tony – and his legal team – received in their hundreds within the first few days after Tony fired his gun:

---

[220] This would appear to be Shivkat Jagannathan.

"Will you please convey to Mr Tony Martin our sympathy and support. We all know that such things as this tragedy are brought about by the lack of adequate policing all over the country. Instead of fewer police personnel and police stations, we need more. We need more policemen on motorcycles or bicycles, instead of them sitting two in a car at roundabouts etc waiting to catch motorists.

I am sure there are thousands of people all over the country who feel for Mr Martin, and who do not see why the thieves and thugs should be free to rob us of our treasures as and when they want, with very little chance of being caught.

If any newspaper or person should raise a petition in support of Mr Martin, my wife and I will most certainly sign it.

I hope you will excuse me writing to you, but I saw your name in the *Daily Mail*. In it, you were quoted, I think, as deploring the lack of police officers in the rural areas. It is not only in the rural areas that we suffer from lack of police protection – our police station is not manned at night, and any calls for help are directed to another town, which is not conducive to a swift response!

So, Mr Barnard, if you could be so kind as to tell Mr Martin of our support for him, we will be much obliged."

What is most notable is not only the high degree of support that the Great British Public had for Tony Martin, but that they corroborated everything he had been saying for years about the police.

On 17 July 2016 I was kindly invited to the home of Mr Barnard's mother and they gave me another box of letters and cards from well-wishers across the country and even beyond these shores.

Mr Barnard had regularly been in the media in support of the farmer and he helped empty Bleak House of its furniture with businessman Malcolm Starr,[221] the men putting Tony's belongings into storage.

A no-nonsense, forthright man, Mr Barnard told me that he felt all along – and he had a number of people who were in agreement – that Tony was "set up"; that he was being made a scapegoat by the authorities because he dared to speak out about the cuts in police that I have written about in previous chapters. This was, Mr Barnard suggested, "politically motivated. Many people around these parts sided with Tony. They knew the problems. In fact, I presented a list of 47 crimes in Upwell alone (thefts from sheds, burnt out vehicles and the like) that the police didn't want to know about. They took the view that you could claim

---

[221] Mr Starr, usually described in the media as a well-connected millionaire Wisbech businessman, often speaks with the media in relation to Tony but not always with Tony's knowledge and consent. However, when I wrote to Mr Starr asking to interview him for this book and put to him many questions about his 'help' for Tony, I did not receive a reply despite the fact that I drove to his house and posted the letter in his post-box. Tony told me that Mr Starr had claimed that he had not received the letter.

off the insurance. This, of course, annoyed a lot of people and they, like Tony, wondered why on earth they were paying a large proportion of their taxes on the police for a service they weren't really receiving."

Fri 27 AUG 1999 UNUSED 209

unknown location
Official records show that on this date PC 322 Philip Clarke made a statement in which he said that he had been telephoned at home at 2am on 21 August 1999 and told to report to King's Lynn police station for "a briefing". He added that he and PC 1088 Gray made their way to Emneth and, once there, they relieved PCs Girton and White. They took up a position about 150 yards to the Marshland St James side of the track leading to Tony's house.

The statement claimed that they were in that position from 4am until 6am – which raises questions. How long was the "briefing" at the police station? If he had been called at 2am and it took him two hours to get to Emneth, why?

But now I have a real issue with the way in which this statement concluded: "Not at any time did we drive into the driveway of Bleak House." Now, why would he have needed to have said that (if he did make that statement)?

It's yet another statement attributed to police officers in which they extricated themselves from ever being at Bleak House. However, the CAD report recorded that Clarke and White left for Bleak House at 3:27am and arrived at 4:33am. The report added that the constables left the scene at 6:08am.

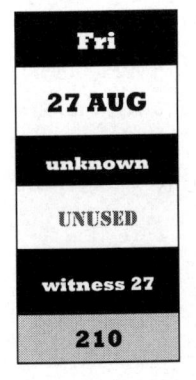

Fri 27 AUG unknown UNUSED witness 27 210

unknown location
Official records show that PC 1189 James Owen Wells serving at Terrington St John police station made the following unused statement:

"Around the period of late June early July, (I can't be more specific as it seemed to have no evidential value at the time, so was not recorded), I spoke to a male I know as Mr Tony Martin of Bleak House. I was on duty in full uniform at the police station, when Mr Martin attended in his vehicle to apparently speak to an officer.

I met him outside the police station and asked how I could help. He replied: "I would like to speak to an officer, please." I said that I was an officer and again offered to help him.

He then replied: "No, I don't deal with uniform. I want to speak to CID."

I told him that there were none on duty and again requested that if he had anything to say I could pass the message on.

With this he then informed me that he had been burgled several weeks previously and that CID had attended. He could not, however, remember the name of the officer.

I asked Mr Martin if he knew the crime number, which he didn't, and because the Terrington St John police station has no computers, I could not look this up.

I asked for a description of the CID officer that attended and Mr Martin said that he had come and taken fingerprints. At this point I realised that scenes of crime had been down to the address which normally would follow after crime details had been obtained.

I then informed Mr Martin that I would make enquiries to find out who had attended and could pass a message on but he refused this and requested that the officer concerned should contact him as soon as possible.

Mr Martin did seem angered that there were no CID on duty[222] at Terrington that day and treated me like I was incompetent.

After Mr Martin had left the police station, I telephoned King's Lynn Scenes of Crime Department and spoke to Rick Aldous who said he had originally attended and that Jim Welham had been allocated as OIC.[223]

I then contacted Jim Welham and informed him of Mr Martin's request to see an officer with some information he wished to tell us about.

From that day onwards I had no more dealings with Mr Martin.

These are my original notes on this matter."

PC Wells was listed as prosecution witness number 27 yet his statement had not been officially entered into evidence according to HOLMES – does this bizarre anomaly concern you?

PC Wells apparently didn't make any notes when a member of the public arrived at the station to inform him that he'd like to speak with a detective about a burglary that had taken place at his house a month previously. I have great difficulty in understanding why you *wouldn't* make a note of that encounter. Surely it's completely relevant to take notes about a burglary.

---

[222] It is my view – and therefore entirely personal – that if this country had *more* people like Tony Martin who demanded better services for the taxes we pay, that we'd have better public transport, a better national health service, more teachers and nurses, a better level of firefighting capability and so on and so forth. The reason we do not have better public services is simply because successive governments have brainwashed the electorate into the notion of "keep calm and carry on". Most people put up with inadequate services, local authorities rife with corruption and paedophiles in every branch of government and so it becomes a self-fulfilling prophecy.

[223] Officer In Charge (of the case).

The officer (who didn't take notes) apparently recorded that he felt that Tony had thought of him as incompetent and I must say from his statement that I am in Tony's camp on this one, too. Had I been the officer, I'd have invited Tony into the station (why didn't Wells?) and called through to King's Lynn *with Tony there* to assuage any concerns a decent member of the public had about the efficiency of the police *service* which ordinary members of the public have now been brainwashed into calling a police *force*. Emotional intelligence in the police isn't a strong point I've found after many encounters with officers of all ranks.

And what of Norfolk Constabulary having no CID officers on duty and no computers in a station? Tony demanded better and because he demanded better, he became a target of the police. [See also trial day one – 12 April 2000]

Fri 27 AUG 11.05 am 211	**Bleak House** *Records show that a search began at 11:05am under POLSA Inspector Gant and team leader PS 3065 Ian Fletcher.* *At 2:20pm, it is said, SOCO DC Aldous took photographs of two areas of disturbance in nettles in a ditch adjoining an orchard beside Bleak House.*

At 2:43pm, PC 280 Michael John Coley[224] was, according to his statement, in an orchard working alongside an employee of Norfolk County Services ground maintenance who was cutting down the vegetation along a ditch at the side of the orchard when a small black torch was uncovered. It was apparently Fearon's.

At 2:45pm, PC 566 Roland Smith[225] found a blue Adidas baseball cap beside a ditch in the orchard. Again, it was apparently Fearon's.

At 2:56pm PC 774 David John Craske[226] was searching the orchard to the rear of the house when he found a woollen glove lying in the grass under the

---

[224] According to official records, the 48-year-old PC Coley made a statement on this day but it was not recorded at what time it was made, to whom it was made or where it was made. This statement was listed in HOLMES at line S59, and was also listed in the *Index to Statements* document. PC Coley was listed as witness number 58.

[225] According to official records, PC 566 Roland Smith made a statement on this day but it was not recorded at what time it was made, to whom it was made or where it was made. This statement was listed in HOLMES at line S39, and was also listed in the *Index to Statements* document. PC Smith was also listed as witness number 100.

[226] According to official records, PC Craske made a statement on this day but it was not recorded at what time it was made, to whom it was made or where it was made. This statement was listed in HOLMES at line S38, and was also listed in the *Index to Statements* document. PC Craske was listed as witness number 99 in the *Witness List*. On 14 September 1999, a statement attributed to him was made but not entered as evidence. [See also entry **257**].

branches of an apple tree. This glove (apparently Fearon's) was partly inside out.

Was this a genuine search adding to the question "Did Tony Martin commit murder?" or an example of Norfolk Constabulary's style over content?

Were these statements even genuine?

I can find no evidence of any police searches during the period 28 August to 1st September, presumably because of the Bank Holiday. However, what we do know is that there was still a police presence at Bleak House and in the immediate area and several witnesses said that the entire house and gardens were lit up at night for 'several months on end.'

No such luxury of illumination was afforded to Fred Barras on the night of 20 August. Apart from the helicopter which went up around 10:30pm or 1:05am or 1:45am depending upon whom you believe.

Fri
27 AUG
11.35 am
witness 6
212

business address of Alan Giles
According to official records, 49-year-old Alan Michael Giles, a farm business consultant employed by Carter Jonas Estate Managements made a statement at his business address to DC 564 Maskell. I was unable to find any reference whatsoever to this detective in the HOLMES database:

"I am an associate with the firm, and head of the National Farm Management Department. I joined the firm in 1996, and before that I was a director of a farm management consultancy, which I had been involved with since 1988.

During 1994 I met a male person called Tony Martin. Tony had phoned my company and I went to meet him at his farm. My first impression of Tony was that he was a "working farmer" due to his appearance. Tony appeared to be educated with a broad range of interests.

Our first meeting was to discuss the arable side of Tony's farm. Tony wanted to increase his production to maximise his profitability. Over the last five years I have consulted with Tony perhaps fifty times, (usually about ten times a year). Most of our correspondence is by telephone, fax or written reports. I have met with Tony on about 12 occasions, and this would usually be on his farm. I have never seen the inside of Tony's house. I have seen the outer shell on one occasion from the front garden.

I always found Tony to be a genuine, enthusiastic person. He always seemed pleased to see me. I formed the impression he was an interesting person and quite friendly. I would describe his only quirk, as that he would always try to engage me in wide-ranging conversation. Our relationship was purely of a business type. Whenever I visited Tony, I knew he would want to keep talking and I would consciously keep an eye on my watch.

The last time I spoke with him was in June of this year, by telephone. I think I last saw him in March of this year. On both occasions he was his usual self.

I think it was either 1998 or 1997 - it was around post-harvest time - which is August or September when I spoke with Tony in front of his grain store. I cannot remember the exact conversation, but Tony mentioned he had been having problems with members of the travelling fraternity. Tony mentioned that they had tried to break in. He was not specific as to what building he was talking about. I cannot recall what property he was talking about. I am sure if he would have mentioned antiques I would remember it. I remember Tony mentioning that there had been a threat that someone would come back and kill his dogs. Tony had two doberman and one rottweiler dog.

I have never known Tony to carry a gun. Although most farms do have guns, I have never known Tony to mention guns. Most farmers would have guns to control vermin."

It seems that Mr Giles was able to present an extremely positive account of Tony, describing him as friendly, genuine and enthusiastic. The business executive also confirmed that Tony had mentioned having problems with the travelling community and that he'd been burgled. However, according to Mr Giles, he'd never mentioned guns. This clearly undermined the prosecution's claims that Tony would tell everybody that he hated gypsies and travellers and wanted to shoot them all.

And I think it's significant that Mr Giles mentioned that almost all the farmers he knew possessed guns to control vermin on their farms. Through the media, the police and the CPS portrayed Tony as unusual because he had ready access to guns: being a farmer, it was completely natural for him to possess guns. And we should not forget that at all times Tony had obtained licences for his guns and the only reason he didn't have a licence in August 1999 was because of a technicality and the obdurate and unlawful manoeuvres taken by the police.

Fri
27 AUG
2 - 2.45 pm
UNUSED
witness 67
213

second post-mortem, Queen Elizabeth Hospital
According to a statement attributed to SOCO Laura Bishop, she attended the mortuary at the QE Hospital to assist with the second post-mortem of Fred Barras.

Her role involved taking photographs of the deceased as requested by Dr Dick Shepherd – the second pathologist in the case. From the negatives developed, Bishop created a second album which she called exhibit LXB/3.

I draw your attention to the length of this autopsy – forty-five minutes. And I also draw your attention to the fact that in this statement attributed to Bishop, she made no mention of the number of photographs that she had taken whereas, in an earlier statement, she carefully logged the number of x-rays.

I can find no records to verify this next point, but it appears that a second autopsy was called for by Tony's defence team. This would be a fairly reasonable request because, despite the prosecution claim that Barras died from a simple gunshot wound to the chest and that he died within two minutes of being shot, only an idiot would take that information on board without wanting to conduct your own post-mortem.

This *second* autopsy becomes an integral part of our overall narrative and it proves that Tony Martin did not receive a fair trial and that the Great British Public was well and truly misled by corrupt agents of State. But we'll get to that all in good time.

And we should take great heed of the fact that this statement was not entered into evidence at trial and yet Bishop's first statement had been. The reason for this, of course, was that the prosecution did not want any mention of there ever having been a second autopsy. The jury – and the British public – were completely deceived by the CPS, who knew that this second autopsy had taken place (as did Tony's defence counsel).

Fri
27 AUG
2.43 pm
witness 58
214

unknown location
The 44-year-old PC 480 Michael John Coley was on duty as a member of the police search team and working in an orchard at the farm. The POLSA was Inspector Gant and the team leader was Sergeant Fletcher.

The team was tasked with searching Bleak House Farm, and "at about 11:05am" the search commenced:

"On Friday 27 August 1999 I was working alongside an employee of Norfolk County Services ground maintenance who was cutting down the vegetation along a ditch at the side of the orchard. I saw a small black torch uncovered. I stopped the man from cutting and saw that the torch was a Philips make. This I produce as exhibit MJC/1. The torch I pointed out to DC Aldous, who then took control of it."

According to records, that one-page statement was entered into court. However, we need to see entry **348**.

Tue
31 AUG
unknown
UNUSED
215

unknown location

Records show that DS *3132 Thomas Neill, normally stationed at East Dereham, made a statement in connection with his having interviewed Darren Bark between 9:39pm and 9:42pm.*

The detective sergeant offered Bark a deal which had been worked out with the CPS. *[See also entry* **146**].

Tue
31 AUG
3.40 pm
UNUSED
216

home address of Dawn Gosling

According to official records, Emneth resident Dawn Gosling, 53, made a statement to DC *Adcock in which she said that at about 8:30pm on 14 July 1999, she and her husband saw a dark coloured car (index A218BAB) travelling along the footpath they were using. She added that she and her husband were suspicious of this vehicle and when they got home they called the police about their sighting.*

She added that it was so unusual to see a car on the footpath that her suspicions were aroused, especially after the local paper the *Fenland Citizen* had asked for any suspicious sightings to be reported to the police "due to the number of burglaries and thefts in the area." [Author's emphasis].

Records show that on the same day, her husband – 44-year-old Edwin Gosling – made a separate statement at the same time to PC 1018 Caine which replicated what she had said.

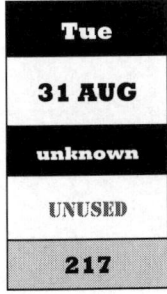

Tue
31 AUG
unknown
UNUSED
217

Home Farm, Wisbech St Mary

The letter written by Keith Bass of Home Farm, Wisbech St Mary, was indicative of local support for the farmer being described as "an eccentric bachelor" and having his reputation shot down in flames at every conceivable opportunity. This letter was not read out at his trial and nor was the author of it called to the trial by Tony's defence team.

"In the 25 years or so that I and my family have known Tony Martin we have found him to be the most loyal and reliable person you could wish to meet. He is a sound and respected member of the public and an asset to the farming community, of which I am a member.

I find that the crisis he is presently experiencing is completely out of character for this man, knowing him as well as I do."

Tue
31 AUG
unknown
UNUSED
218

unknown location

The unused statement below is attributed to PC 364 David Andrew Cole and was dated 11 days after Tony had fired his shotgun.

About 11:24pm on Friday 20 August 1999 he claimed to have been on duty in uniform together with PC 155 Beer when they attended a reported shooting incident.

On arrival PC Cole saw that PS Davidson and other officers were present at the premises.[227]

"Within a few moments of arriving I saw a white Ford Granada car approaching along Moyse's Bank towards the Smeeth Road. As the vehicle got closer I saw the registration mark was F98LHJ. Because the road was narrow the Granada was unable to pass us and it came to a stop. I spoke to the driver with PC Beer and found him to be a person I now know as Darren Henry Bark of Newark.

Bark stated he was in the Wisbech area looking for friends who had called him at home stating they had broken down.

Bark stated one of the persons was a traveller named Joe Price from Newark, and another unknown male. Full details were obtained from Bark and relayed to PC 543 Mann who maintained an incident log.

I carried out computer checks on Bark and his vehicle by radio.

I remained at the scene until about 2:20am when I visited St John's Fen End where I made enquiries with Mr Edward Martin as to the possible whereabouts of his cousin Mr Tony Martin. The enquiries were negative. This again was relayed to the incident log. At 4:30am I resumed from the scene to go off duty."

It seems that within a few moments of arriving at Foreman's Cottage, PC Cole saw Bark. Had he been there all night, or had he just arrived from Newark following a call which said, "Me and Brendon are in trouble"? Notice that PC Cole didn't mention the result of his computer check on Bark.

Wed
1 SEP
10.40 am
witness 39
219

Foreman's Bungalow, Hungate Corner

According to the official records, Jacqueline Leet made a second statement to the police, to DC 503 Durrant. It's incredibly short:

"Further to my previous statement I wish to state the following: I first saw the injured man walking along Moyse's Bank in the direction of Smeeth Road. I saw his head above my hedge and he then came fully into view in my driveway when he made eye contact with me and came into my drive."

---

[227] Note that PC Cole didn't record which premises he claimed to have attended.

Now, why would she have needed to have make this brief statement? I believe it was so as to deceive. Fearon was knocked over by John Spalton. The eel fisherman claimed he had seen Fearon in Moyse's Bank, but evidence shows that it was the Smeeth Road. Why does this matter? Because the police were creating a narrative that Fearon had crawled through a corn field on his way to the Leets' bungalow – thus erasing the fact that he had been knocked down by Spalton, which was never mentioned at trial.

Wed
1 SEP
1 pm
UNUSED
220

unknown location
Official records show that 37-year-old PC 471 Paul Menarry[228] of Cambridgeshire Constabulary made a statement to DC Peters in which he said that at 12:30pm on Thursday 13 May 1999 he was on uniform patrol in the Sutton area of Ely when he was called to assist colleague PC 4 David Bishop who had stopped, and was checking, a white transit van index number E576JBF on Sutton Business Park.

We should be clear that this statement was never used in evidence at the trial and that the constable was not called as a prosecution witness. However, had I been Tony's defence counsel, I would have called the constable as a witness for reasons which I think will become obvious as you read on.

PC Menarry claimed to have arrived two minutes after receiving the call to find PC Bishop talking to a Christopher Webster in the police car. Apparently Webster had told the constable that he was in the area looking for his brother.

PC Menarry claimed that he searched Webster's van and in the back of it he saw a large, old chest of drawers which took up most of the back of the van which was "filthy dirty and covered in dust." The constable checked the drawers in the chest and found them all to be empty except for some sort of lining paper. Some of the drawers had been pulled out of the chest and placed on top of it.

PC Menarry then claimed that he checked the front of the van and saw a pewter tankard and some chinaware which included plates and what he thought was a tureen "all in the style of Royal Doulton, or something similar." [Author's note: how would he know? Did he have an interest in antiques himself?) Menarry described these items as being just as dusty and filthy as the furniture he'd seen. He asked Webster where the furniture and china had come from, and Webster told him that he had a contact on the Milton dump, just outside Cambridge, and had got them from there. Because of the condition of the items, Menarry thought this explanation "seemed quite reasonable." Would you have arrived at that conclusion?

While searching the vehicle, PC Menarry found what appeared to be a

---

[228] Spelt in the HOLMES database as 'Mennary'.

controlled drug on a spoon. Webster identified the substance as 'speed.' Menarry said that because of this, his attention was then more focused on the misuse of a controlled drug rather than on the furniture. Would you have made that decision?

Webster was said to have been arrested by PC Bishop and apparently taken to Ely police station. I do not think you will quite believe what happens next. It's straight out of the Keystone Cops series of police farces.

With Webster locked up in a cell, Menarry made enquiries into his identity with Newark police. His enquiries revealed that Webster was known to them and was believed to have been involved in a very recent aggravated burglary in another force area where a farmer had been hit by one of the intruders with a wheel brace. "From memory I believe I was told that there was a blue transit van involved in the burglary which was in some way connected to Webster." Now, this raises a whole host of questions.

Firstly, what had caused PC Bishop to stop the van and then call for backup? Having arrested Webster for a controlled drug, why did PC Menarry then not consider the idea that people who use drugs often steal in order to pay for their habit? With Webster in custody, why did Menarry not visit the Milton dump where Webster had claimed he had picked up all the property from (and surely the constable would have known that this type of furniture would not normally be disposed of on a council tip in any event)?

PC Menarry is recorded as having made his unused statement to DC 356 Peters on 1st September 1999, twelve days after the shooting incident.

Records show that PC Bishop, also said to be stationed at Ely, didn't make his statement until 5th February 2000 (why so long after Menarry's?) He said that he received information at 12:20 that caused him to stop the white van, though he did not say what that information was. He added that whilst in the police station car park, he and Menarry conducted a "thorough search" of the transit van and discovered "a lot of antique furniture which appeared very dirty."

Bishop said that he and Menarry then interviewed Webster in relation to the drug offence but not, it seems, in relation to the furniture, despite Menarry having been told that Webster was thought to have been involved in an aggravated burglary. Would this not have alerted you to the possibility that the furniture and china had not, after all, been removed from the Milton dump, but actually stolen? I find it incomprehensible that the focus would have been entirely on the drug offence and not on the possible burglary involving the furniture in the white van and then to try to find links between that burglary and the one in which a wheel brace had been used against a farmer. It is this lackadaisical (or corrupt) approach that so infuriated Tony Martin: "Time and time again I used to complain to the police that they weren't actually doing anything after I reported thefts and burglaries and what have you," and it would seem that he was not wrong in this case.

What's even worse is that Webster is said to have collected his van – still full of the stolen possessions from Bleak House – and, released on bail, *drove it out of the police station car park to his home and then later sold the antiques.*

Does this raise your suspicions that some police officers were actually involved in the burglaries at Bleak House on some level? You see, when I investigated this a little further, I could find no reference at all to a statement made by PC Bishop in the HOLMES database. I found a reference to PC Menarry's statement (and the fact that it was unused) but not to Bishop's.

And why would you not want to enter this statement into court as evidence of the burglaries that had occurred at Bleak House? It appears as though "deals had been done" to ensure that Webster was not called to trial. So we have the *extremely unusual occurrence* of alleged drivers Webster and Bark not being called to court despite allegedly being heavily involved in burglaries at Bleak House. How does that happen? Who was protecting them? Just how far were Webster and Bark connected and what did the young Barras know that he wasn't meant to know?

We should note that Menarry's statement was recorded as having been made to DC Peters and we would be well advised to consider Peters' role in this entire case and the number of key people that he was recorded as having interviewed and the significant exhibits which he had supposedly handled.

It was Peters who claimed to have dealt with the HORT/1 form allegedly issued by a PC Knight after stopping "the burglars" en route from Newark to Emneth.

It was Peters who took control of the holdalls and silver items and who was said to have transported them from Bleak House to King's Lynn police station.

It was Peters who failed to enter into court the blanket allegedly used by Paul Leet to cover Brendon Fearon.

It was Peters who allegedly interviewed Bark at Terrington St John police station on 21 August and yet who failed to enter that statement into court.

It was Peters who allegedly drove down to Exeter to collect Bark, who was said to have gone on the run after the August shooting.

It was Peters who interviewed Fearon as late as 18 September on suspicion of conspiring to burgle Bleak House.

It was Peters who failed to enter into court a dozen witness statements from farmers and neighbours praising Tony Martin.

It was Peters who failed to ensure that a red address book said to have belonged to Bark was not entered as evidence into court.

It was Peters who interviewed Barras's best friend, Stephen Buckland.

And it was Peters who was the common denominator in interviewing all of these key people.

Wed
1 SEP
unknown
UNUSED
221

unknown location

Records show that on this date, PC 155 Mark Beer, a serving traffic officer stationed at King's Lynn, made the following unused statement (to whom we do not know).

At approximately 10:52pm, he was on uniform patrol in company with PC 364 Cole on Friday 20 August 1999, when as a result of a radio call, they attended Moyse's Bank, Hungate Road, Emneth following a report of a person having been shot.

"At 11:24pm on arrival at that location I saw the lights of a vehicle approaching us along a lane which runs from Moyse's Bank to join Smeeth Road at Hungate Corner. We caused the vehicle to stop and found it was a white Ford Granada motor car, index F98LHJ.

The driver I now know to be Darren Henry Bark from Newark. Bark stated that at about 10pm that evening whilst at his home address a call was received from a male who he knew as Joe Price, who had stated that he and a mate had broken down near to Wisbech. He then gave me a description of the male known as Price which I recorded. He stated he was possibly with a male called Fearon and again provided a description.

A supervisor was already present at our location and I was informed by PS Davidson that a male had been conveyed to hospital with gunshot wounds.

I informed him of Bark's story and was advised to remain with Bark until a CID officer attended.

I then remained at that location with Mr Bark with other officers.

I also assisted in a vehicle check along Smeeth Road when it was ascertained we were looking for a vehicle believed to be owned by a Tony Martin which was not resident at his home address.

At 4:41am, I was relieved from the area and returned to King's Lynn p.s.."

This statement appears to agree with that of Darren Bark's. But more of this in subsequent entries Then we learnt that the two-man crew were deployed checking vehicles along the Smeeth Road and that, at 4:41am they returned to King's Lynn police station.

Now, with other injured parties still allegedly being sought, who gave the order to deploy two men on vehicle duty instead of searching for Barras?

Who gave the order to return to King's Lynn as dawn was breaking which would have aided a search of the house and gardens?

And why do you imagine PC Beer (if we believe that his statement is genuine) made no mention of the helicopter flying over Bleak House? Since it was a major part of the police operation that night, don't you think it would have been mentioned in his statement?

However, if he and PC Cole arrived at 11:24pm, they would have missed it if, as locals said, it had been flying above Bleak House around 10:30pm.

If it had been flying overhead somewhere between 1 and 2am, then surely he would have seen it and mentioned it in his statement.

Thur
2 SEP
10.50am - 3.45pm
UNUSED
222

search of Bleak House
Official records show that there was a formal briefing at Downham Market police station at 9am and police officers from other stations also attended. At 10:50am, a POLSA search team, led by PS 3125 Michael Mizen, carried out a Section 18 search authority under PACE.[229]

The legislation states that: "a constable may enter and search any premises occupied or controlled by a person who is under arrest for an indictable offence, if he has reasonable grounds for suspecting that there is on the premises evidence, other than items subject to legal privilege, that relates to that offence."

This power can be misused by the police (and often is – see entry **487**, the police unlawfully seizing my initial manuscript of this book), but let's assume that Norfolk Constabulary are abiding by the rules and searching Bleak House and its grounds in the belief that they can obtain further evidence in this case. But we then have to ask, "Evidence for whom?" Are they trying to find anything against the farmer, are they trying to find incriminating evidence against themselves that they can cover up, or are they genuinely trying to solve a murder? I'll let you decide.

In a statement attributed to her, PC 9059 Nichola[230] Louise Marshall seized an Eley empty case and thirteen Eley live cartridges and one Gamebore cartridge in the hallway. Presumably all these were missed by the previous week-long search in August.

In a statement attributed to him, PC 297 Stephen Jobson found an Eley Grand Prix empty case in the hallway, together with three live cartridges.

Not only did the week-long search fail to discover the 14 cartridges found by PC Marshall, but it also failed to find a further three live cartridges and two empty cases.

The two empty cases were found in the hallway.

The very same hallway at the side of the stairs.

The stairs from which Tony Martin said he fired his gun.

---

[229] The Police and Criminal Evidence Act (PACE) 1984. It is a piece of legislation which is often misused by the police to conduct illegal searches. They will, of course, deny this.
[230] Spelt this way (as opposed to Nicola) in both her statement dated 24 September and the HOLMES database.

Yet this information never reached the jury. We cannot overlook the catastrophic failings by Tony Martin's own defence team to ensure that the jury heard this evidence.

I spoke to Tony about the various house searches and he told me that after he came out of prison, he was being escorted by acting DI Matthew Sharman and they had gone to the George public house in Stamford:

> **"** I realised that Sharman thought I had a jaundiced attitude against the police. I soon worked out that he wasn't working for me – which is why we have a police service – but that he was working only for himself and the police."

Thur 2 SEP
10.50am - 3.45pm
witness 96
223

unknown location

Records show that on this date, Police Sergeant 3125 Michael Mizen, stationed at Bessemer Road, Norwich made the following statement:

"I am a Police Search Advisor. As the result of information received at 10:50am on Thursday 2nd September 1999 I attended at Bleak House where I organised and conducted a search operation. During the course of the search, I took possession of a large number of assorted coins and a few banknotes. These were placed in a sealed bag and handed to DS Eglen. *The value of the money found is not known.*

The search was completed at 3:45pm the same day. This statement was made as my original notes at 6:15pm on 2 September 1999."

The emphasis is mine. Note that this search was said to have been conducted *two weeks* after the shooting. Just how valuable was it?

Thur 2 SEP
unknown
UNUSED
224

unknown location

Records show that on this date, 35-year-old PC 1255 Graham Clive Cook, stationed in King's Lynn, made the following unused statement – but it was not recorded to whom it was made.

On Friday 20 August 1999 he was on duty and crewed with PC 1267 William George. They were on mobile patrol in the King's Lynn and Cook claimed: "At no time during that duty did we attend at the incident in Emneth."

"On Sunday 22 August 1999 I attended the Queen Elizabeth Hospital where I spoke to Brendon Fearon. I then completed police bail form C36 and read this in full to Fearon. Fearon was bailed to return to King's Lynn police station on **Saturday 18 September 1999 at 5pm.**"

The emphasis is mine. Why would you make a statement to show where you *weren't* rather than where you *were*? PC Cook doesn't mention anything about the Saturday. His colleague, PC George, had said on 25 August "On Saturday 21 August I was on duty in full uniform when at 7:08am I attended the location at Bleak Farm and took over the seal duty and the log. I remained there in situ until 8am. At no point did I enter inside the outer seal zone as I had no reason to."

So that's another constable distancing himself from having been there on the Friday evening and from having entered the outer seal zone.

CORRUPTION ALERT — *Worrying discrepancies in police witness statements*

On turning to the CAD report, constables Cook and George are recorded as having been dispatched together in the same vehicle to Bleak House at 6:30am, arriving at 7:08am. The report shows that the constables were cleared to leave the scene at 7:09am. Now, who (if anyone) gave the order to send them away within a minute of their arriving and why weren't they deployed to search for Barras? PC George, as we have read, claimed that he left the scene at 8am. Do these considerable discrepancies in the official timings cause you concern?

Thur 2 SEP — unknown — witness 26 — 225

unknown location
Records show that on this date, PC 801 Jonathan Alan Chapman, stationed at Terrington police station, made a statement – but it was not recorded to whom it was made, where it was made or at what time it was made:

"I cannot remember the date, but sometime during the month of May 1999, I spoke to a Mr Tony Martin on the telephone.[231]

---

[231] For the avoidance of doubt, we have a police officer telephoning a member of the public about a burglary and he *doesn't* record any information whatsoever about that call? How does that actually happen?

I had telephoned him in relation to a burglary that he had suffered recently. My intention was to arrange a convenient time to allow me to obtain relevant crime details and pass these to the CID department.

Whilst on the phone to Mr Martin he refused to let me go to his address, claiming I would be of no use to him as I was a uniformed officer. He explained that he would only speak with CID officers as they knew what was happening around the area. I attempted to explain that in the initial stages regarding the crime details I could do just as much as a CID officer.

Mr Martin was not forthcoming and still refused to let me go to his address. I explained to Mr Martin that I would attempt to sort something out with CID to meet his requirements. Before the conversation concluded I can remember Mr Martin explaining that a cigarette butt had been left at the crime scene which could possibly have been left by the offenders.[232]

I subsequently contacted DS Taylor[233] at the King's Lynn CID Department regarding this matter. Unfortunately he did not have the resources to send anybody out to Mr Martin's home address. Finally it was arranged for DC Aldous of the Scene of Crime Department to visit Mr Martin and also obtain details. As far as I was concerned, the matter was now out of my hands and any subsequent inquiries or work would be conducted by the CID department.

Regarding Mr Martin's attitude on the telephone, I would say that he was stubborn and in my view had the opinion that me visiting his house was useless and no help; however, he was not rude at any time."[234]

What this adds to our knowledge	Firstly, are you at all concerned that a serving police officer cannot be more specific than "at some time during the month of May" when he was making this statement (allegedly) in the following September? Where were his notes from that call? Surely he had them easily available – after all it was only three months prior to the statement being made.

---

[232] Since Tony doesn't smoke and since he no longer allowed anybody inside his house, the most likely source of that cigarette butt was a burglar.

[233] From information I have researched, this would appear to have been DS 3254 Mark David Taylor who on 22 August 1999 was said to have interviewed Brendon Fearon at the QE Hospital between 15:22 and 17:25 with DC Buxton. According to official records, DS Taylor did not make a statement to police about his involvement in the case at all (why might that be?) and nor was he listed as a prosecution witness.

[234] With reference to an article headed "Investigation after three police cars crash in training exercise" in the *Eastern Daily Press* dated 17 May 2019 (p.2), it would appear that constable Chapman had progressed to the rank of Inspector.

Secondly, note, too, that PC Chapman stated that the CID department was under-resourced – this was precisely what Tony had been complaining about for years. Isn't it ironic that the man who continually complained about the lack of police resources can't have his burglary investigated because of the lack of police resources?

To give PC Chapman some credit, at least he noted that Tony wasn't rude whilst being assertive. I've found in the time that I've known him, his assertiveness can be misinterpreted as either being arrogant or rude whereas, in my view, it's simply him being assertive.

This statement was entered as evidence in the forthcoming trial but the prosecution 'spin' put on it was that Tony hated the police. He didn't (and doesn't). We have had many conversations about this issue and he is always consistent in his view that he doesn't hate the police per se, but he despises the cutbacks, the lack of professionalism, the corruption, the way they will distort the truth to gain a (wrongful) conviction and the continual erosion of community relations and civil liberties.

Thur
2 SEP
unknown
witness 88
226

unknown location
According to official records, on Thursday 2 September 1999, PC 754 Matthew Michael Wright was on duty at Watton police station when he attended Downham Market at 8am for a formal briefing at 9am.

He was a member of the search team and at 10:50am attended at Bleak House. Whilst undertaking the search at 12:10pm, he found a shotgun cartridge in 'room one'.

"I handed the item to PS Mizen,[235] who sealed the item in a sealed bag. At 2:15pm, whilst searching 'his bedroom', I found a shotgun cartridge, again handing it to Sergeant Mizen who sealed the item in a sealed bag.

These are my original notes written at 6:15pm on 2nd September 1999."

Thur
2 SEP
unknown
witness 87
227

unknown location
According to official records, PC 946 Gillian Whitfield Murray was on duty in her capacity as a trained search officer along with other officers at Bleak House when, at 11:25am whilst searching an area of the hallway on the ground floor, she found 3 live shotgun cartridges of 'Eley Classic' make in a black plastic case. She handed the cartridges to PS 3125 Mizen as exhibit GWM/1. She claimed to have made her statement as original notes at 6:15pm on 2nd September 1999.

---

[235] Also variously spelt as 'Missen'.

What this adds to our knowledge

Three live cartridges were found in the hallway of Bleak House a fortnight after the shooting. Why had these not been found sooner? And we ought to ask ourselves, so what if they found three live cartridges inside the house? What does it prove? I suggest that it adds nothing to the case.

Thur
2 SEP
unknown
witness 86
228

unknown location
According to official records, PC 517 Christopher L. Jackson, normally stationed at Diss police station, stated that at 10:50am on Thursday 2nd September 1999, he went to Bleak House as part of a trained search team under POLSA PS Mizen and commenced a crime search of the premises.

"At 11:25am that same day whilst searching room 1, I found a .22 cartridge (item marked CLJ/1) which I handed to Sgt Mizen. In the same room at 11:30am I found a pistol cartridge (item marked CLJ/2) which I also handed to PS Mizen.

At 2:20pm that same day whilst searching 'His Bedroom', I found 2 x .22 rounds and 1 x .38 round (item marked CLJ/3). I also handed this ammunition to PS Mizen, who placed all the above items in sealed exhibit bags which I later signed. PS Mizen also recorded the finds on Search Forms C114."

What this adds to our knowledge

In my view, it demonstrates that Norfolk police were determined not to seek truth and justice, but to paint Tony in as bad a light as possible. I ask again: so what if he had ammunition dotted about his house? How would that prove he murdered Fred Barras? This statement was entered as evidence into court.

Thur
2 SEP
unknown
UNUSED
229

unknown location

According to official records, DC 352 Gary Corbett, a Technical Support Officer in the Norfolk Constabulary, made the following unused statement, but we do not know where it was made, at what time it was made or to whom it was made:

"At 9:30am on Friday 27 August 1999, I received from PC 837 Cracknell sealed bag no. A245090, containing an Orange Motorola mobile phone, exhibit SJP/3. I removed the Sim card number, which I placed in an Orga Kartensysteme, producing a printed record, timed 9:39am."

The phone was said to have belonged to Darren Bark and was one of two alleged to have been found by DS Peters in his car immediately after his arrest. Following an examination of the first mobile phone, DC Corbett then examined the second and it seems that it belonged to a chap named Roy Bowers [see entry below]. The record shows that at 10:45am, the officer completed his examination of the phones and handed them back in a sealed evidence bag to PC Cracknell. Yet no seal numbers were recorded in the statement.

Thur
2 SEP
unknown
UNUSED
230

unnamed Norwich police station

According to official records, Roy Bowers, 39, made a statement to police, but neither the time nor the name of the officer taking the statement were recorded. It's highly likely that this interview was as a direct result of the examinations of the mobile phones that morning:

"On Monday 16 August 1999, I met a friend of mine, Brendon Fearon, in town. He asked me if he could borrow my mobile phone for a few days and I could have it back over the following weekend. I didn't ask him what he wanted it for because he's a mate and I trust him. He did say he was going away with his kids.

The phone is a Motorola GSM 1800 and is an Orange Just Talk 'pay as you go' phone. The number of the phone is _____. I have several phone numbers in the memory of the phone. I have known Brendon since I moved to Newark in 1985 and I also know all his family. They also know me well. I was not aware that he was going to Norfolk on Friday 20 August 1999.

I know the name Fred as a young lad who would pop into the Zoo Pub in town and play pool on occasions. I know him by sight but can't recall ever having a conversation with him.

I have been asked about the name Darren Bark. I do not know Darren Bark, although I have seen him a couple of times, again in pubs."

Bowers' phone being found in Bark's car could lead us to suggest that it was left there in case of emergencies and that Fearon and Barras had their own mobiles with them when they approached the house.

Another possible scenario was that Fearon – allegedly having borrowed it from Bowers – simply left it behind in the car because he was focused on the burglary.

We should also consider the possibility that it was planted in Bark's car by the police after they had taken it from Fearon at the Leets' house.

We might consider that Mr Bowers was present at the Bleak House job and that he called the emergency services. And, we ought to ask whether Bowers *did* know Bark and that this statement has been created to distance the former from the We also ought to ask a very difficult question: did Fred Barras have a mobile phone on him and did *he* call the emergency services at any time? When I made a Freedom of Information Act request for a list of all 999 calls made that night in relation to the shooting, this request was turned down without lawful reason. Isn't that highly suspicious? If the police had nothing to hide, wouldn't they simply have provided the list?

Thur
2 SEP
unknown
witness 85
231

unknown location
According to official records, 26-year-old PC 9022 Alison May Harvey, stationed at the Woodcock Road police station, Norwich made a statement in which she said that on Thursday 2 September 1999 at 10:50am she assisted in a crime search in her capacity as a search trained officer at Bleak House, along with colleagues including PS Mizen as POLSA.

"At 11:05am, in room 1, I located on the floor amongst the rubbish a fax from Norfolk Constabulary reference the shotgun certificate. I seized this as exhibit AMH/3 and placed it in an exhibit bag and handed to PS Mizen.

Later the same day we began to search 'his bedroom' on the first floor. At 1:57pm I located newspaper cuttings which I produce as exhibit AMH/4. These were handed to PS Mizen."

Public money was spent on getting a statement to the effect that she had found a fax in the breakfast room pertaining to Tony's shotgun certificate and a few newspaper cuttings from his bedroom floor. Neither had anything to do with whether Tony Martin had committed murder or actually shot anybody. I cite this statement as just another example of a waste of public funds and adding to my view that PC Harvey's 'evidence' was just part of a substantial body of 'evidence' entered into court which was, in reality, meaningless and irrelevant.

Thur
2 SEP
10 am
232

Coroner's Court, King's Lynn

Coroner Bill Knowles was unable to release the body to the family. It was stated that the youngster had died as the result of a gunshot wound. At least that was the official version.

It was reported in the media that the inquest heard that Dr Heath had carried out a post-mortem the day after the body was found.

Bill Knowles said, "On that evidence I would normally be able to release the body. But as a result of a telephone call I have just received, there's some checks the defence want to make on the body."

Fred Barras's grandmother, Mary Dolan, said the family were very upset that there would be further delays to the funeral: "We want to be able to get on with our grieving. Fred's mum has had the psychiatrist and doctor every day. She's very upset and cries all the time. He was the only boy and had five sisters and so he was very special."

Fri
3 SEP
unknown
witness 78
233

unknown location

According to official records, the 53-year-old PC 543 Richard William Mann, stationed at Terrington St John, was on uniform patrol in company with PS 3093 Davidson at 11:06pm on Friday 20 August 1999 when, as the result of a radio message, they attended Foreman's Cottage. Upon arrival Mann claimed to have seen an ambulance backed into the drive with the crew attending to a male person lying on the lawn:

"Whilst PS Davidson went into the house, I remained outside with the ambulance crew and the injured person, who was being treated for what I considered to be fairly serious leg wounds. The ambulance crew told me that these were consistent with shotgun injuries.

The man appeared to be in considerable pain and a state of shock. Once he had been loaded into the ambulance and his condition stabilized, I was able to talk to him. Because of his condition this was difficult but I was able to establish that his name was Brendon Fearon and he came from Nottingham. I asked him what had happened and he said: 'Went down land somewhere and man shot me *twice*.'[236] Asked if he was alone when shot, he didn't answer but this may have been because medication was taking effect. Because of his deteriorating condition the ambulance crew insisted that he had to go to hospital immediately.

I remained at the house and on instruction from PS Davidson opened and maintained the Scene Log and manned the telephone communication. I left the scene at 7:20am the following day."

---

[236] Author's emphasis.

Firstly, PC Mann didn't mention the helicopter – yet another officer failing to mention this aspect of the police operation. Secondly, he said that Fearon told him he had been shot *twice* – possible further evidence that there had only been two shots. Thirdly, PC Mann said that Fearon didn't reply to the question of whether there was anyone else injured, yet other officers had claimed that Fearon had specifically said there wasn't anyone else who had been shot with him. This point is clearly of great significance and you'd think that Tony's barrister would have made great capital out of this. He didn't, and we'll learn why he didn't as the story This is yet another statement in which Fearon was said to have told the witness that he had been shot on "some land" and not inside a house.

> **CORRUPTION ALERT** *Police witness statements seriously contradict one another*

But there are other, even more significant, problems with this statement by PC Mann. The statement claimed that Mann and Sergeant Davidson had travelled together. However, the official Norfolk Constabulary CAD report recorded under the heading of 'Resource Activity' (showing where specific police officers have been deployed to) the fact that within three minutes of Jacqueline Leet's 999 call, PC Mann was dispatched to Emneth. According to this report, he arrived 35 minutes later, at 11:31pm.

The same report shows that PS Davidson was dispatched in a separate vehicle at 10:57pm, arriving at 11:06pm – in other words, some 25 minutes prior to constable Mann arriving. According to the CAD report, Davidson was the first police officer to arrive at Foreman's Cottage.

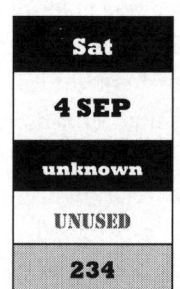

Sat
4 SEP
unknown
UNUSED
234

unknown location

According to official records, Swaffham PC 17 Duncan Maxwell made the following statement which was not used at trial:

"About 4:30am on Saturday 21 August 1999, I attended Emneth Hungate in my capacity as a firearms officer. I manned a checkpoint at this location until 6am on the same day and / had no further involvement in the investigation, returning directly to King's Lynn police station arriving at about 6:30am."

The emphasis is mine. Here is yet another statement – purporting to be bona fide – in which a constable apparently goes on record claiming he had little or no involvement in the investigation.

Does that concern you? It concerns me because PC Maxwell failed to say that he was teamed up with PC 70 Andrew Coller.

Are you concerned that this statement wasn't made until more than two weeks after the shooting? And are you concerned that the statement attributed to PC Coller was dated five days after Maxwell's – 9 September 1999? [See also entry **248**].

Sun
5 SEP
1.15 pm
UNUSED
235

home address of Rachael Green
According to official records, 33-year-old Rachael Green and her husband and two sons aged 8 and 5 regarded Tony as a family friend. She knew him through her father, who lived in King's Lynn. Her statement to DCI Barker had ominous overtones for Tony:

"A few weeks ago, I became aware that Tony had been charged with murder and believing that his family was not supporting him, I subsequently made an offer to his solicitors that my address could be proffered as a 'bail address' if Tony were released from custody. Having discussed this idea at length with my husband, I now wish to withdraw this offer and would not allow Mr Martin to reside at my house if he were bailed. My reasons for this are:

1. I would fear for the safety of my children.

2. I am concerned that my address would not remain secret. This is primarily due to my father's knowledge and relationship with Mr Martin and the continued media interest in the case.

3. The unprofessional manner of his new legal representatives, 'M&S' from Ashby-de-la-Zouche, whom I have tried to contact on numerous occasions to withdraw my offer, which they have never discussed in detail with me.

4. I fear for the safety of Mr Martin and feel that my house is not appropriate to guarantee his safety and secret whereabouts. I withdraw my initial offer and will not allow my home to be used as a bail address for Mr Martin."

I cannot say with any degree of certainty that he did not exist, but I could find no statement or report attached to a DCI Barker in all of the legal papers that I examined, including the HOLMES database.

Mrs Green's emotionally-intelligent comments that Tony's solicitors were "unprofessional" grabs our attention, because if you're up on a murder trial you certainly want the best legal team around you that you can get.

Mrs Green's statement was found in the Unused Material file – it was never entered as evidence into court. Now, if you had been Tony's defence counsel in a murder trial, wouldn't *you* have called Mrs Green to give evidence?

Sun
5 SEP
2.40 - 3.50 pm
witness 67
236

third autopsy, Queen Elizabeth Hospital
In a 70-minute procedure, SOCO Laura Bishop attended the Queen Elizabeth Hospital mortuary again to assist with a third autopsy where she took further photos of the deceased Barras as requested by the third pathologist, Dr Cooper.

These photos were enlarged before being put into an album as exhibit LXB/4.

CORRUPTION ALERT — *CPS withheld critical evidence regarding autopsies from the jury*

I found these bare details in a statement allegedly made by Laura Bishop dated 11 October 1999 – that's almost two months after Tony had fired his gun and more than a month after the <u>third</u> *autopsy. Do these dates concern you?*

The statement was not signed, no time was shown on it and no location where it was allegedly made. Furthermore, the name of the police officer to whom she allegedly made the statement was also not recorded. There was no witness to the statement. Do these omissions concern you?

And does it concern you that this statement – her third – was not entered into evidence and yet her first statement had been? You will recall that in her first statement she made mention of the x-rays taken of Barras, but these had not been taken into account by pathologist Dr Heath in his witness statement.

In other words, the CPS was 'cherry-picking' which evidence it would or would not put before the jury in order to secure a conviction. The jury and the Great British Public were entitled to know that there had been three separate autopsies and that the results of these autopsies showed that Barras had not died "within two minutes of being shot" – in other words, the CPS went to trial knowing full well that their prosecution was fraudulent and that they were deceiving (not simply misleading) the court. This entire trial showed an indifference to the essential conditions for the rule of law which was objectionable and deeply worrying. And the Great British Public allowed it to happen. No-one thought to question "the authorities".

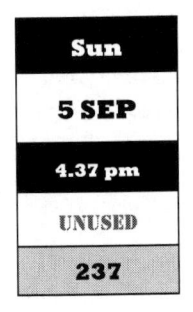

Sun
5 SEP
4.37 pm
UNUSED
237

Bleak House

It seems[237] that immediately following this relatively brief autopsy, Dr Cooper then went to Bleak House where he was involved in "an examination" of the crime scene with Graham Renshaw, the firearms expert for the defence. Tony's solicitor, Nick Makin, was also present.

I have contacted pathologists Dick Shepherd and Nigel Cooper, but neither replied to me. Now, this could be because they do not want to correspond with me, or because my emails were interfered with.

Because of the obvious corruption and probable prison sentences for high-ranking police officers and others, some people in some very high places did not want this book published.

However, the very fact that there were three post-mortems for such a simple affair tends to suggest that someone, somewhere did not believe that the cause of death was necessarily a shotgun wound to the left side of the chest as Dr Heath was keen to suggest. Or that someone was arse-covering in the event of this going completely pear-shaped.

> **"** My barrister, Scrivener, took me to Renshaw near Cambridge railway station. Scrivener did not agree with Renshaw and they argued about the ballistics side of things, Scrivener relying entirely on the Home Office evidence. My own barrister didn't want independent evidence which went against the crackpot theory he was going to run with at trial that I had walked down the stairs and shot them in the breakfast room as they were leaving the house."

Disturbingly, when I spoke with Tony about this event, he told me that he *had given his permission* to his defence team to shoot a shotgun inside the breakfast room to show the extent of shotgun spread inside that room.

Thus, to be clear, Tony's *own defence solicitor* allowed a shotgun to be fired inside *the crime scene* and prior to a murder trial in which the jury would be shown that very room.

This was the level of depravity of police and judicial corruption in the Tony Martin case. He had been set up not only by Norfolk Constabulary but also by his own defence team. They were clearly not acting alone and I suggest that this entire affair was orchestrated at government level through the Home Office.

---

[237] According to DS Eglen's statement dated 26 October 1999.

Mon
6 SEP
238

Coroner's Court, King's Lynn

At the resumed hearing, coroner Bill Knowles said: "I understand that ballistics tests and examinations have all been completed by the defence and the body is not required any further."

Fred's uncle, Tony Joynes from Newark, said it was a relief that the funeral would be able to proceed. "There'll be hundreds of family at the funeral from all over the country. We're from a close-knit travelling background."

Mon
6 SEP
unknown
witness 82
239

unknown location

According to official records, PC 979 Jennifer Elton, normally stationed at Attleborough but working out of Downham Market police station, made a statement in which she said that on Sunday 22 August 1999 she was handed the keys to Bark's white Ford Granada by PC 376 Matthews, the Exhibits Officer at 12:50pm. At 1:40pm she was present when a driver from Pimlotts Recovery placed the vehicle in a garage in the rear yard. PC Elton secured the vehicle and locked the garage.

Ostensibly, this statement and these actions were of little significance. It meant nothing – yet the prosecution lined up a succession of such statements by police officers to create overwhelming "evidence" against the defendant to provide a paper trail that Bark was the driver on the August job and that he was the owner of that vehicle.

Tue
7 SEP
unknown
witness 37
240

home address of John Spalton

According to official records, John Spalton, a 43-year-old professional commercial eel fisherman who'd been in the job for two years, and who fished areas as far as Littleport in Cambridgeshire and locally at Marshland St James, Tilney and Terrington, made the statement below to DC Cross. Spalton claimed to have been working on Askew's land which he said ran between the Smeeth Road and Moyse's Bank.

"This land is near to a farmer's land who I know to be Tony Martin. On Friday 20 August 1999, I finished work when it was dark. I cannot say what the exact time was as I don't wear a watch, but it had been dark about 2 hours.[238] On this

---

[238] This would make the time around 10:30pm – or the time Fearon appears to have been shot. However, on his son's various websites, it is claimed that Mr Spalton drove down Moyse's Bank at 1am on the Saturday morning (see entry **501** and also entry **71**).

evening I was travelling along Moyse's Bank and was about 200 yards from the junction with the Smeeth Road when I suddenly saw a person on the left hand side of the road. As I drew closer I could see this person was male. He was stationary but bent over double and looked in considerable pain. He motioned for me to stop by raising his right arm in the air. This I didn't do. As I drew closer I could see that this male was about 29 years old with dark straggly hair; he had dark coloured skin. I would say mixed-race coloured skin. He had a goatee beard and I think he was wearing a t-shirt.[239]

The thing that I noticed the most about this male was that he was wearing black tracksuit bottoms but these were covered in red. I actually thought that these were red and black tracksuit bottoms. I didn't stop to help this male because I was worried that this may have been a set up and if I'd have stopped I may have had my vehicle stolen. The vehicle I was driving on this night was a Mitsubishi L300 car colour beige,[240] index number C678FBW.

As I passed the male I carried on towards the junction. To my left I noticed there was a bungalow. The kitchen lights were on and I noticed there were two people in the kitchen.[241] I thought about stopping to let them know what I had just seen but I decided against it as I didn't want to worry them.

This bungalow was on the corner of Moyse's Bank and Hungate Corner. It wasn't until Saturday evening that I heard about the shootings at Emneth Hungate and then realised that the person I saw the previous night may have been one of the people shot by Tony Martin.[242] I phoned the police on Sunday to tell them about what I had seen.[243]

Throughout the evening of Friday 20 August 1999, during my travels around the Emneth area I never saw any other vehicles, either blue or white in colour.

I have known Tony Martin about 4 years but only to say hello to. I met him when I was working for Askews who are a fruit produce company. I used to collect fruit from Martin's farm on behalf of Askews. He was a little eccentric but I wouldn't have said he was capable of shooting anyone, although he was obsessive about being burgled. I never saw him with any firearms."

---

[239] This is a remarkably accurate description of a man who was "bent double".

[240] In a future entry, a local woman saw a beige vehicle leaving the direction of Bleak House at high speed. It may or may not have been this car.

[241] This appears to be contrary to what Jacqueline Leet was alleged to have told the police in the statement attributed to her: "About half an hour after Mr Martin had left I was vacuuming the lounge, Paul was getting ready for bed." Neither appears to have been in the kitchen at the time Mr Spalton claimed to have driven past.

[242] How is Mr Spalton in a position to say who shot Fearon?

[243] I have seen no phone records to substantiate Mr Spalton's claim that he called the police on that date. In any event, why did it take the police nearly 3 weeks to interview him?

> **CORRUPTION ALERT** *Strong suggestion that this statement has been altered*

There are a number of issues that I have with this statement. Firstly, he didn't mention anything about knocking Fearon over – why would you omit such crucial details?

Secondly, I am somewhat concerned that he saw a man bent double in pain and yet apparently didn't help him. I completely understand the issue of not wanting to be set up and have his vehicle stolen, but surely you'd then stop at the Leet's bungalow (or any other nearby residence) and point out what he'd seen. He claimed, of course, that he didn't want to bother them which seems reminiscent of the Leets not calling the police to tell them that Tony had said he'd fired his shotgun because it "might be something and nothing."

Then I struggle to believe that *anybody* would describe someone as looking "about 29". Most people would surely say that Fearon looked from 25-30, yet apparently Spalton thought that Fearon looked his precise age – 29. All this remarkably accurate description was from a man driving his van late at night who didn't even stop – according to his statement at any rate.

I noted that Spalton was purported to have said that he hadn't seen any other vehicles "either blue or white in colour". Nobody would just happen to pick those colours out of thin air – so he'd obviously been asked by the police whether he'd seen any vehicles of those colours.

When Spalton called Tony "a little eccentric" suggested to me that, again, the police had specifically asked him this – which is hardly an open-minded investigation.

As pointed out in a footnote, Mr Spalton's son, Chris, has produced a series of comics called the *Eelman Chronicles*. In one of these, Chris Spalton has drawn a moonlit night, his father driving a van and the date and time is given as "Friday 20 August 1999, 1am." Does that refer to the *Friday* morning (i.e. late Thursday night) or the *Saturday* morning (i.e. late Friday night)? One would reasonably assume that the son consulted the father about the time the eelman was driving his van, yet there is a significant departure from his statement to the police. Or had the time in his statement been altered?

There was just something about this statement which didn't ring true. According to the official court list of witnesses, Mr Spalton was sworn in as a witness on Tuesday 11 April 2000.

Tue	
7 SEP	
unknown	
UNUSED	
241	

unknown location

According to official records (HOLMES, line S162), 33-year-old DC 105 Paul Flatt of the Norfolk Constabulary Drug and Serious Crime Squad, who had been involved in the Sheridans' murder inquiry, made the unused statement below.

At 9am on Tuesday 7 September, 1999, he was on duty engaged on 'Operation Allclear'.

"I was the driver of an unmarked police vehicle whose duty it was to transport Tony Martin from HMP Norwich to a secret address. I was on duty with DC 1013 Rettie, who was the front seat passenger. As soon as Mr Martin spoke to me I immediately recognised his voice as the person 'Tony' whom I had first met on 18 March 1999 at Mr Hugh Ward's address."

What this adds to our knowledge

Tony was moved between various "safe houses" and one of these was Coleorton Hall, some 82 miles from Emneth and a few miles to the west of the M1. Coleorton Hall is a 19th-century country mansion, formerly the seat of the Beaumont baronets of Staughton Grange. Situated at Coleorton in Leicestershire, it is a Grade II listed building now converted into residential apartments. In the early 1990s the hall was rented to Fison's Pharmaceuticals. The Hall was redecorated and refurbished and in 1997 it was sold for redevelopment and converted into residential apartments.

There was no need for Tony to have been held in a safe house. It was all part of corrupt agents of State abusing their authority and trying to control him so that he wouldn't mix amongst his people and ask too many awkward questions – the old 'divide and conquer' principle. Furthermore, they didn't want him at Bleak House seeing how the police were manipulating the evidence against him.

DC Flatt had first met Tony on 18 March 1999 at Hugh Ward's house [see entry 55] during a house-to-house fingerprinting operation after the murder in Outwell of Constance and Janice Sheridan. As we have seen, these murders also played heavily on Tony's mind.

	Downham Market police station
Wed	*A statement made on this day is attributed to 50-year-old Pimlotts*
8 SEP	*Garage Services' recovery vehicle driver and mechanic, Michael*
noon	*Joplin to the effect that "at approximately 12 noon on Wednesday 8*
	September 1999, at the request of Norfolk Constabulary," he attended
witness 119	*Wisbech police station, where he collected a silver Nissan Bluebird,*
242	*registration no. C460APW (exhibit HAR/1).*

"I transported the vehicle to Downham Market police station, arriving at 12:50pm that same day, and upon direction of acting DI Sharman, unloaded it into the rear yard of the station."

In my opinion, this was yet another example of style over substance. Let's recall Hitler's words: "in the Big Lie there is always a certain force of credibility." The police never had a real case against Tony under the rule of law, and so they had to create a false narrative which included real elements such as a vehicle recovery driver confirming that he did, in fact, move the car between the police stations. When the prosecution is putting up nonsense like this, you can be pretty sure they know they don't have a bona fide case.

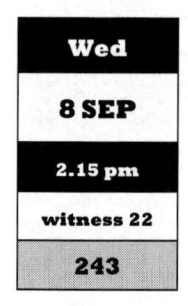

	home address of Aubrey Millard
Wed	*According to official records, DC Buxton took a statement from 83-*
8 SEP	*year-old Aubrey Alan Millard (known as 'Dick') who lived with his*
2.15 pm	*wife near Tony. He moved to Norfolk from Gloucestershire 24 years*
	previously and had lived in the same house ever since. Despite his age
witness 22	*and 'retired' status, he still farmed some land and produced soft fruits,*
243	*potatoes and hay.*

"When I first moved to Norfolk in 1975, there was a man called Garner[244] who farmed at Bleak House Farm,[245] Emneth Hungate, which is next door to my house. The houses are very isolated and rural and although Bleak House is my next door neighbour's house there is about half a mile between the two houses.

After a couple of years Mr Garner died and his nephew, Tony Martin, moved to the house and took over the farm. Since that time I have come to know Tony Martin quite well as a neighbour and friend.

Martin is not a farmer as we know it, as he is different and a little eccentric. He does not conform to the normal farming methods and over the years I have helped him out and found it necessary to 'point him in the right direction' on

---

[244] Tony's uncle, Arthur Garner, married to Gladys, who left Tony the farm in her will.
[245] It is not called Bleak House Farm but rather Cowcroft Field Farm. Bleak House is the name of the farmhouse only.

occasions. As a result of our neighbourly chats and the assistance I have given him, we have become close friends and on occasions Tony would turn up at my house around teatime so we supplied him with tea and cakes!

I walk over his land every day to get to my land, so I do not mind at all when he calls in.

I have been into his house on occasions and I have to say that it is a strange experience. He gets ideas from *Country Life* magazine and decides to 'alter' his house to look like what he has seen - unfortunately he never finishes any of his alterations.

Tony does most of his work on the farm himself until he falls behind schedule and then he has to employ friends and neighbours to help him out.

I remember several years ago Tony asked me to go with him to Spalding[246] to a firearms dealer to buy a shotgun. He asked me to go so I could use my shotgun certificate to buy it, as at the time he did not have a certificate. I knew that I should not really do it, but I went with him anyway as I knew that he had applied for a certificate. He bought the gun and then lent it to his cousin who lives at Marshland St James.[247] That is what he told me later and also that he had been granted a shotgun licence.

Two or three years ago, I remember Tony in a field of kale using a double-barrelled sawn-off shotgun. I asked what he was doing and he said he was driving away the pigeons. I looked at the gun and saw that it was dangerous. It was a side-by-side double-barrelled gun with a large gap between the stock and breach. I pointed out to Tony how dangerous it was and I never saw him with it again. I do not ever recall seeing Tony with any other gun but I did hear from someone recently that he had found a shotgun in his orchard that had been dropped by intruders. I cannot remember who told me that.

I remember Tony telling me on more than one occasion that he had been burgled and returned home to find some of his furniture stacked outside. I cannot remember when this was.

On the evening of Friday 20 August 1999 I remember hearing shots during the evening, but thought nothing of it as living where I do, it is quite common to hear gun shots - most of the farmers or landowners have shotguns and I often hear them.

I was bitten quite badly by one of Tony's rottweiler dogs two or three years ago and I had six weeks without the use of my right hand. The dog has died since and I am not sorry. I think he had at least three dogs at a time."

Dick Millard confirmed the isolation of his house and also Tony's. Clearly this added to Tony's fear of the increasing lawlessness in the area – something which the police were failing to address and some locals believed that the police were a

---

[246] In Lincolnshire.
[247] Edward Martin.

party to some of the criminality. Mr Millard informed us that Tony was a little different from many other farmers but being different, of course, isn't necessarily bad.

Mr Millard is one of a very small select band of people who were allowed inside Bleak House, and his description of Tony as a man who gleaned ideas from many magazines and other reading material is correct, as is his view that Tony rarely finished anything when it came to the refurbishment of his home.

I was surprised that Mr Millard admitted to the police that he had unlawfully purchased a shotgun on behalf of Tony, and the police were to take this information about Tony and use it against him at trial. The prosecution view was twisted to make Tony appear to be a man who would stop at nothing to obtain firearms.

Although Millard claimed to have seen Tony in a field of kale shooting at pigeons, Tony rarely shot. He disliked the idea of harming innocent creatures.

Mr Millard stated that he had heard shots on 20 August, but unfortunately did not state how many he heard, or at what time he had heard them.

The statement that I have seen attributed to Dick Millard has a paragraph missing between his having heard the shots and then the final paragraph about being bitten by one of Tony's dogs. This suggests, of course, that this statement has been altered in some way.

To be clear, the dogs were not vicious – they looked far more menacing than they actually were.

This statement was used at trial and we can see why. It came from a friend but actually caused Tony considerable problems, mainly because of the way he obtained a shotgun through Mr Millard and the bite on his hand. Even the most gentle of dogs will bite in certain circumstances and we have no idea why the dog bit Mr Millard.

It is evident that the police thought all their Christmases had come at once with this statement: they had all the ingredients with which to take their false narrative to court – an eccentric farmer, illegally obtaining firearms, and 'vicious' dogs. Soon, these innocent elements would be woven into a poisonous narrative against a man forced to defend himself in the dead of night after an unknown number of intruders had smashed their way into his remote home.

Wed
8 SEP
7 pm
244

Emneth village hall

More than 300 people crammed into Emneth village hall at a public meeting called by the parish council. In attendance were South West Norfolk MP Gillian Shephard, Superintendent Steve Thacker (divisional commander for West Norfolk) and police authority member Harry Humphrey. According to the local newspapers, all were shouted down.

Chairing the meeting was Reverend Rachel Larkinson, who asked for TV cameras to be turned off so people would not be identified. (Well, that's the 'official' reason. The real reason was that the authorities did not want the general public to see the strength of feeling against the police and in support of Tony Martin.)

One woman told the meeting: "I was burgled at the beginning of the year. I came home and found the burglar and the first thing I went for was a knife. Had I caught that burglar, I would have gone for him with it because it would have been him or me. When I dialled 999 it took the police half an hour to come. When they came I was asked seriously whether I wanted to press charges because if there were repercussions the police would not be able to support me."

Tony Martin, it seems, had been the voice of reason. The police *were* ineffective. There *were* too few of them. They *did* take a long time to respond. They *were* often unprofessional when they did respond. All the things that this "eccentric farmer" had been saying for years.

Wendy Coles, *Wisbech Standard*, reported that response times and the feeling that it was not worth reporting crime came across strongly at the meeting.

Emneth resident David Martin (no relation) told the meeting that although residents had made their homes secure, this needed to be supported by the police: "The police are not visible enough and although I accept it may be a question of resources, can we be assured they are being focused correctly?" he wisely asked. Again, Tony had consistently raised this point, too.

Gillian Shephard MP said, "People will be tempted to take the law into their own hands unless they feel they can report crime without being intimidated, that the legal system is fair and that the police have sufficient resources to make them feel safe in their own homes."

Had Tony Martin been saying anything different for the past two decades?

Wed
8 SEP
unknown
witness 51
245

unknown location

According to official records, Ian Munday, employed by the Norfolk Police Authority as a photographer based at police headquarters, Martineau Lane, Norwich made a statement in which he said that on Monday 23 August 1999 he received from Scenes of Crime Office Laura Bishop four (4) x-rays reference LH1-4. He photographed these x-rays and made photographic copies.

"I produced these copies as part of albums reference LXB/1.[248] I returned the x-rays LH1-4 to Laura Bishop at 12:15pm on 23 August 1999. In addition I wish to add that I received exhibits LH1-4 at 8am on 23 August 1999."

---

[248] The initials 'LXB' refer to SOCO Laura Bishop.

The initials 'LH' refer to Leslie Hill. It's only a short statement, but is of tremendous significance. These four x-rays were said to have been taken of the body of Fred Barras at the first autopsy and were taken on the instructions of pathologist Dr Michael Heath.

Notice, too, how in a sleight-of-hand exhibits LH1-4 have been relabelled as exhibit LXB/1.

CORRUPTION ALERT — *Crucial evidence regarding x-rays of Barras withheld from the jury*

Bizarrely, although this statement was entered as evidence into court, Dr Heath never referred to them during the course of the trial. The question then becomes "Why take any x-rays at all if you're not going to refer to them?"

There was a very good reason why Dr Heath failed to mention these x-rays but we'll have to wait a while before we learn why.

Thur 9 SEP 1999 246

St Mary Magdalene Church, Newark
A 16-year-old lad with criminal convictions he may have been, but Frederick Jackson Barras was still somebody's son and at an age when he had years ahead of him to change his ways. Of course he may not have done, but we will now never know.

The body of Barras was laid to rest in the St Mary Magdalene Church in the centre of Newark, Nottinghamshire.

Some newspapers said that at least 450 people attended the funeral, others put the figure at somewhere around 300.

I leave the last word on this painful subject to the Reverend Richard Harlow-Trigg at his funeral: "Everybody here knows that Fred should not have been where he was. Equally everybody knows that he did not deserve to die like he did."

On the same day, Tony Martin had his bail revoked and was "returned to Norwich Prison for his own safety" in yet another example of the police abusing their authority.

Thur

9 SEP

unknown

witness 84

247

unknown location

In a statement attributed to authorized firearms officer PC 852 Paul White (stationed at King's Lynn traffic department), he claimed to have been on duty in full uniform in company with PC 400 Adrian Girton at 9:33pm on Friday 20 August 1999:

"I was the observer in the King's Lynn based armed response vehicle when, acting on information via the force control room, we attended Hillington Square, King's Lynn for a suspected firearms incident. Whilst engaged on this incident, at 10:56pm I heard a radio message regarding another firearms incident in Emneth where a male was believed to have been shot. I immediately phoned the control room central inspector and liaised with him. On being released by the central control room inspector we attended Hungate Corner, Emneth arriving at 11:50pm, where some divisional and traffic officers were already on the scene.

I saw that on Moyse's Bank PC 155 Beer and PC 364 Cole had stopped a Ford Granada colour white with a male driver. PS Davidson appraised us with what he knew so far, showed us a copse of trees about three hundred metres from us stating a local farmer Mr Tony Martin had a house in the copse, a male person had been shot in the legs and taken to the QE Hospital by an ambulance.

I spoke to the driver of the Granada and said, "Is there anyone else in there?"

The male replied, "I don't know – I'm here looking for a mate who has broken down." We then had a conversation regarding the type of vehicle and who might be driving it; the male was very evasive and even when told that someone had already been shot stuck to the story about a broken down transit van.

About 0:34am on Saturday 21 August 1999 the second armed response car crewed by PC 338 Cant and PC 485 Gotts arrived on the scene with Chief Inspector Curtis.

The copse area was very dark and we viewed the area with night viewing aids. I could see no movement, light or vehicles in the copse area.

Chief Inspector Curtis and the ARV crew discussed the options available regarding locating the premises which could not be seen from our location, locating Mr Martin's vehicles, locating Mr Martin, safe approaches, protecting unarmed officers and public and our action plans. It was decided more resources were required before taking further action safely.

About 1:05am the same day, contact was made with the Cambridgeshire police helicopter which then proceeded to search the location. The helicopter reported two heat sources which moved about and were dogs and stated it was difficult to identify the exact location of the farmhouse.

The officers present re-discussed our options and it was decided the two ARVs followed by PC Claxton in the dog van would approach the buildings along the main drive whilst CI Curtis would attempt to make contact with the farmhouse via the phone, the helicopter would remain overhead to monitor the area. I was informed as we entered the track that no contact was made via the phone and I could not identify the farmhouse from the track; we withdrew from the track as this was too vulnerable a position.

Following further discussions the ARVs took up a position either side of the track to monitor vehicle movement, we positioned ourselves 150 metres King's Lynn side of the premises until relieved by the early turn ARV."

> **What this adds to our knowledge**
>
> Firstly: the officer's statement asserts that he and his crew mate arrived at Emneth "where some divisional and traffic officers were already on the scene." I am concerned about the use of the word "some" because it's not specific – he should know who was also in attendance and he should be able to name them. This lack of detail concerns me when lined up with everything else that I've pointed out so far.

Secondly, PC White was careful to point out that PS Davidson "appraised us of the situation" which would mean, of course, that the constable would have been told that the 999 call was said to have mentioned "three burglars" and also the Leets mentioned this to PS Davidson who would naturally have informed PC White. So why would the constable ask Bark if there was anyone else in there when he already knew the answer?

I am also concerned that the statement attributed to PC White claimed that he could see no movement or light coming from the copse when (a) there were dogs running around and nocturnal animals and (b) there was a light shining at the back of the house in an upstairs window (Tony's bedroom). Nor were we told the distance from which the copse was observed – the 300 or so yards from the Leets' or did they move much nearer by way of the orchard, for example?

My concern about this statement deepens at the mention of the timing of the helicopter flight and that "it was difficult to identify the exact location of the farmhouse." I have been to the farmhouse on many occasions and I argue that it would be impossible for a helicopter *not* to identify the house, garage and Rover car whilst hovering above. I've spoken with Tony on this point and the measurements of Bleak House and garage give the property a footprint of some 17 metres by 12 metres, or approximately 200 square metres which *excludes* the areas laid to lawn at the front and rear of the house. Additionally, there was an avenue of lime trees and a pea gravel drive from the farm track to the house itself and this would have been an obvious marker for any helicopter pilot. And we've already read how the helicopter asked the central control room to get the drivers of the police cars at the scene to put their blue lights on. I do not buy into the notion that the police could not find the house. It was a false narrative created to divert attention away from their own wrong-doing.

The point attributed to PC White that the ARV was deployed 150 yards to the King's Lynn side of the track also doesn't make much sense.

Given these concerns about the statement attributed to PC White, I believe that it had been fabricated or significantly altered and that there was little truth in it at all. And I offer as evidence the following proof: in the Norfolk Constabulary CAD report, it stated that PCs White and Girton were *dispatched* at 23:49 to the Hungate Corner, yet White's statement had claimed he and Girton *arrived* at that time. The CAD report showed the officers arriving at three seconds past midnight and so we are asked to believe that they drove from "the incident in King's Lynn" to the Hungate Corner in just 11 minutes. I don't believe it is possible to do that journey in that short space of time even at high speed because of the winding roads once you leave the A47.

Notice, too, that PC White didn't state at what time they were relieved, or by whom. Turning to the CAD report again, it shows that they were cleared to leave the scene at 5:19am on the Saturday morning.

Thur 9 SEP — unknown — UNUSED — 248

unknown location

We have previously read a statement attributed to PC Duncan Maxwell dated 4 September and now his colleague, PC Andrew Coller,[249] an authorised firearms officer stationed at Dereham, allegedly made the following statement:

"At approximately 4:30am on Saturday 21 August, I was on duty in full uniform in a marked police vehicle with PC 17 Maxwell. At this time we attended Hungate Corner where we liaised with Inspector Chilvers.

At the junction of Moyse's Bank and Smeeth Road a marked police dog van was parked along with a marked police ARV. Myself and PC Maxwell were deployed at this point in order to relieve the ARV. We remained at this point until approximately 6:10am when we were stood down by Inspector Chilvers.

At no time did myself or PC Maxwell enter the land or buildings of Bleak House."

---

[249] Listed in HOLMES as 'Collier'.

> **What this adds to our knowledge**
>
> Thus, according to this statement, constables Maxwell and Coller were not deployed until 4:30am. Notice that this statement refers to PC Claxton, the dog handler, but doesn't actually say how or whether he was deployed.
>
> And what do you make of Coller's claim that *"At no time did myself or PC Maxwell enter the land or buildings of Bleak House"*?

In my view, this statement has been created to provide yet another false narrative. On 6 February 2018, I conducted brief research into this constable and found that since the shooting he had been promoted to the role of Superintendent. And there is some irony to be found in this because on 8 November 2017, the *Eastern Daily Press* ran a story with the headline 'Norwich City tackles child sexual abuse with new booklet'.[250]

Referring to the Norfolk Constabulary website,[251] there was an article about the Sexual Abuse and Sexual Violence Week (5-11 February 2018) which stated that:

"Sexual abuse and violence can have devastating and long-lasting effects on the victim.

There are many myths surrounding this type of crime which often leads people to believe that perpetrators and victims are strangers, when in fact they are usually known to one another.

Therefore, it is crucial both men and women are aware of what constitutes abuse and the help that is available to them here in Norfolk.

Speaking out is the first step and services are available at the Sexual Abuse Referral Centre, which allows information to be taken confidentially and in a comfortable setting.

We understand that victims can sometimes feel too afraid to approach the police to report offences, but we hope the 'self-referral' route will encourage those to at least seek help and advice."

Those were the words of former firearms officer Andy Coller – now promoted to the rank of Superintendent and Head of Safeguarding.

The irony, of course, is that Tony had complained to the police about sexual abuse at Glebe House School and had given them the name of a family friend who sexually assaulted him *and the police did nothing.*

---

[250] http://www.edp24.co.uk/news/crime/norwich-city-tackles-child-sexual-abuse-with-new-booklet-1-5270427
[251] https://www.norfolk.police.uk/news/latest-news/02-02-2018/victims-sexual-abuse-and-violence-urged-speak-out

And when I brought the abuse of Tony to their attention in 2015, *they still did nothing.*

And let's not forget that the Chief Constable of Norfolk, Simon Bailey, was at the time of publication the police national lead in child sexual abuse. And, once I had reported the abuse of Tony to him as it was my responsibility to do, having had Tony reveal the abuse he suffered to me, *the Chief Constable did nothing.*

And when I called for a vote of 'No Confidence' in the Chief Constable to the Police and Crime Commissioner, the Constabulary's response was to have me arrested in Gaywood Library (near King's Lynn) whilst I was actually working on this book. I was unlawfully held in a police cell for 6½ hours before being released without charge or interview. As they released me, the police officers laughed at me.

In that moment, I precisely understood what Tony had told me about the time he'd walked into Downham Market police station to report a burglary and they simply laughed at him saying, "Oh no! Not you again!"

It is for this reason that I say the murder trial was a complete travesty of justice which exposed all that is rotten in the police and judicial system.

Having been at Hillsborough, I witnessed the police over almost three decades attempt to re-write history and sell The Big Lie to the British public. The Tony Martin case threatened the inept, corrupt and unprofessional police and brought out the worst in human nature from those employed in the "justice system" at every level.

And all the time the police promote those officers who are corrupt or who are prepared to 'turn a blind eye' to criminal activity perpetrated by corrupt officers, then the British public can have no expectation of a fair and just society.

According to official records, PC Coller claimed in his unsigned statement: *"At no time did myself or PC Maxwell enter the land or buildings of Bleak House."*

I do not believe that claim at all and the reason that I do not believe it is because, according to the CAD report, PCs Coller and Maxwell were never dispatched to the incident and yet were officially cleared to leave the scene at 6:08am. So, with no record of them being dispatched or arriving, these firearms officers could have been up to anything that night...

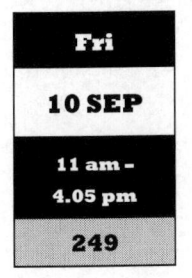

Fri
10 SEP
11 am – 4.05 pm
249

Bleak House

According to official records, a further search was conducted on Friday 10 September – some three weeks after the incident and with literally dozens of police officers and some members of the public having already traipsed through the house.

If, like me, you are wondering why all your public funds were being spent on yet another search, I suggest the following reasons: (i) the police were struggling to bring a legitimate case against Tony Martin and therefore deployed several dozen officers in scouring the house and grounds for anything – anything at all – that might implicate the farmer, (ii) the use of foot soldiers to 'tidy up' after the *real* shooting of Fearon and Barras and (iii) the public, press and PR. The more officers swarming all over the house and gardens the better. The thinking goes like this: "The press and the public will see a significant police presence for months on end. They will assume we are doing a professional job and thus we must have got a proper verdict based on 'all' the evidence we found."

The simple question to be asked is this: "If Norfolk Constabulary could muster all these resources *after* the event, why was it unable to muster the same resources (i) to investigate all the crimes against Tony Martin and other farmers in the area, and (ii) why couldn't they muster these resources when allegedly looking for Barras? I believe it's because they already knew where Barras was. Stalham-based 40-year-old PC 222 Philip Henry West:

"On Friday 10 September 1999, I was part of a Search Team that carried out a search of Bleak House. On arrival at the scene, I completed a sketch map of the house and its grounds at that location. On this sketch map was marked the zones used to conduct the search. I produce this sketch plan as exhibit PHW/1.

During the search of the grounds, I found a small metal multi-tool laying in the grass in Zone 22. I seized this item and produce the tool as exhibit PHW/2.

Both of my exhibits I handed over to acting PS 622 Terry Stevens.

This statement is my original notes, made at 5:15pm on the same date, at Downham Market police station."

If you ever wonder whether you receive value for money for every pound of your taxes spent on policing, then this entry (if all the others haven't) might yet convince you that your money was wasted on this case. Maps and diagrams had already been drawn up under Inspector Gant. Now, the wheel is being reinvented at public expense. But all this activity looks good to large sections of an unsuspecting public.

During the search of the grounds, PC West claimed to have found a small metal multi-tool laying in the grass in Zone 22. Thus the public had paid the wages of a man to draw up yet another plan of the area and to find a tool dropped by ... another policeman in a previous search. Or so we are led to believe. It's just as possible that it was dropped by a tactical operations officer involved in the raid on Bleak House and/ or the shooting of Fred Barras...

Fri
10 SEP
unknown
witness 88
250

unknown location

Official records show that police search team member PC 754 Matthew Michael Wright, normally stationed at Watton, made a statement in which he said that on Friday 10 September 1999, he had been on duty undertaking a search at Bleak House.

The search of the grounds was said to have commenced at 11am, and concluded at 4:05pm.

"At 12:35pm, whilst searching 'Zone Seven', an external garage, I found a live Eley cartridge, which I handed to acting sergeant Terry Stevens, who duly placed the item in a sealed bag, ref. no. 01456314. I produce the exhibit as MMW/3. These are my original notes, written at 5:05pm, 10 September, 1999."

Fri
10 SEP
11 am – 4.05 pm
witness 90
251

Bleak House

According to official records, the 41-year-old Thetford-based PC 556 Richard Craig Currie made the following statement:

"On Friday 10 September 1999, I was a member of a police search team, which conducted a search of the grounds at Bleak House. The search began at 11am and ended at 4:05pm.

During the search, I seized a number of items: 4 shotgun cartridges (one green, three orange) found in Zone 1; a live shotgun cartridge, colour orange; and a live shotgun cartridge, colour black found in Zone 7; and a used shotgun cartridge, colour orange, found in Zone 8.

At the completion of the search, we returned to Downham Market police station, where I completed my statement."

Fri
10 SEP
unknown
witness 40
252

unknown location

Brendon Fearon made his third statement to the police (that we know of). It was not recorded where this was made (he was out of hospital by this time and back home in Newark), nor do we know the time it was made, and nor was it witnessed.

After allegedly agreeing that a torch he had been shown was the one he had dropped in the grounds after fleeing the house, he added:

"I can also state that when Fred and I were shot and I first heard Fred shout, "It's got me!" or "He's got me!", we were standing fairly close to each other, and were the kitchen side of the dresser. I hope that this will help to identify exactly where we were.

I am certain that the man was on the stairs. I saw him and the stairs quite clearly.

When the second *and third* shots were fired, we were again quite close and on the window side of the room. Fred was on my right hand side, and I was facing into the room."

The emphases are mine. Note the clarity with which Fearon continued to describe the position of Tony Martin – on the stairs. Up until this point, he had always been consistent on this issue.

But we must now pay particular attention to the notion of a *third* shot. Previously, it was alleged that he had said that there were only *two* shots (confirmed by ambulance driver Mick Kiff in his statement made on 31 August 1999 and by paramedic Derek Sands in his statement made on the same date) whilst neighbour Jean Thompson had actually told the police as early as 22 August that she thought she heard "a single shot". Neighbours Peter and Jean Chapman had told the police (also on 22 August) that they had heard two shots simultaneously "with no real delay between each noise".

Thus, within two days of the shooting, the police had gathered sufficient evidence to show that there were probably only two shots.

But slowly, and almost imperceptibly, the notion of a third shot had been introduced by the police in order to find "evidence" supporting the injuries sustained by Fearon and Barras. This was a game of chess – not an investigation: the target of their attack was King Tony and their only objective was checkmate.

And part of the game was to produce sufficient evidence to show that Fearon was *inside* Bleak House when he told medical staff and some constables that he had been shot *outside* – thus making it impossible for Tony Martin to have shot him.

Tue
14 SEP
10 am
UNUSED
253

Bleak House

I could find no record of a search on the dates between 11 and 13 September 1999, inclusive. Police records show that a further search was conducted some 25 days after the event.

PC John Tacey was said to have been part of the team.[252] His finding (and seizing) of an empty shotgun cartridge is of tremendous significance to this case.

During a search of the hallway, it was recorded that he found a spent shotgun cartridge at 1:02pm which he handed to acting exhibits officer PC 376 Matthews. At 1:44pm, the search was concluded.

---

[252] The HOLMES book shows that PC John Tacey (no number provided) made a statement on 14 September 1999, the same day as he had taken part in the search. The statement was not entered as evidence at trial.

Another empty shotgun cartridge found in the hallway. In case you're not counting, that's two: one by PC Stephen Jobson and this one by PC Tacey. At all times, Tony Martin said that he fired from a position high up on the stairs.

However, on 24 September 1999, there was a statement attributed to PC Nichola Marshall (see also entry **222**) in which it was claimed she had found a third empty cartridge case in the hallway. This statement referred to a search on 2nd September *before* Fearon's third statement on 10 September in which he claimed there were three shots and yet was authored two weeks *after* Fearon's statement. All rather neat, don't you think?

Tue
14 SEP
10.40 am
witness 43
254

Queen Elizabeth Hospital, King's Lynn
According to official records, 41-year-old staff nurse Christine Rumble made a statement to DC Buxton.

The nurse was in full-time employment at the Queen Elizabeth Hospital, King's Lynn, working in the Accident and Emergency Department. She had been employed there for 4 years. On Friday 20 August 1999 she started work at 9pm. She was on duty until 8am on the following morning.

"About 11:45pm, a patient arrived by ambulance from Wisbech. I ascertained his name was Brendon Fearon and he had shotgun injuries to both legs.

During the initial examination I removed the patient's clothing (which had previously been cut away) and placed them in a white plastic bag. I handed this bag to the police officer[253] who was in the room at the time. *I did not notice any foreign material in or around the wounds, nor in the patient's clothing.*[254]

During the time the patient was in the care of the Accident and Emergency Department he was seen by orthopaedic and surgical doctors on call and I supervised his welfare. I spoke to the patient at one point and asked him what had happened. He said, "I was dropped off, walked up this drive to ask for directions and was shot at"[255] - or words to that effect. I asked if he was attempting to burgle the house at the time and he replied, "No."

I did not speak to him anymore, except to ask questions about his welfare in relation to his injuries.[256]

---

[253] According to a statement attributed to her, this would have been PC 9130 Clare Smith. [See entry **84**.]

[254] Author's emphasis. Compare this with Ashish Prabhudesai's statement made 12 days later: "The wound was contaminated with corn cobs." [See entry **284**.]

[255] Author's emphasis. This is another reference to Fearon having been shot *outside* of Bleak House (and thus not by Tony Martin).

[256] Author's emphasis.

I cannot remember what the patient looked like, nor can I remember what clothes he wore.

When Mr Fearon arrived, the ambulance paramedic handed him over, together with a patient report form, which I signed. This is normal procedure for all emergency patients. The form that I signed is kept with the patient's notes in the Accident & Emergency Department."

How accurate do we imagine it to be if this statement was taken almost a month after the incident? I apportion no blame on Christine Rumble – but I question the veracity of a statement made so long after the event and thus I suggest that this is not the staff nurse's bona fide statement.

Surprisingly, Christine Rumble stated that she did not notice any foreign material "in or around the wounds, nor in the patient's clothing." I question this, because in statements attributed to doctors who attended to Fearon it was claimed that they *did* see pieces of corn in the wounds and on his clothing. I do not say that the staff nurse lied or was mistaken but rather that I think her statement had been altered – perhaps to erase all mention of the helicopter because, as we have seen, Fearon claimed he fell over in the cornfield and saw it flying above Bleak House. Something's not right about an experienced staff nurse not seeing any foreign material on Fearon's wounds if it was there.

We should also consider that - apparently – she didn't ask Fearon whether there were any others injured or, if she did, then it wasn't mentioned in the statement. Does that seem realistic to you?

But what do we make of this: "I did not speak to him anymore, except to ask questions about his welfare in relation to his injuries." Is that likely, especially if you've taken the time to ask Fearon how he acquired his injuries? Don't you think the next likely question would have been to inquire whether anyone was with him and whether they had been injured too? Again, I must make it clear that I do not say the staff nurse has lied – I think her statement had been 'edited' by senior police officers.

Tue
14 SEP
10 am - 1.44 pm
witness 97
255

Bleak House

According to official records, Gorleston-on-Sea based PC 1048 Paul Bassham made a statement (in which his name was also spelled 'Basshan' and 'Bassean'). He claimed that on Tuesday 14 September 1999, he had been on duty as part of the search team, led by POLSA PS 3175 Mizen. He claimed to have been searching Bleak House in company with PC 45 Robin William Allard. The search was said to have been conducted under Section 18 of the Police and Criminal Evidence Act (PACE), 1984.

"During the search, I found and seized four items, which I list below, and handed directly to the exhibits officer, PC 376 Steve Matthews.

At 10:45am, I found a live 'Eley' cartridge, in Room 1 as per the plan. I produce this as exhibit PB/1.

At 12:00, I found a quantity of loose coins in the Utility Room, exhibit PB/2 refers.

At 1:05pm, in the kitchen, next to the sink work surface, 1 x live cartridge, which I will produce as exhibit PB/3.

Exhibit PB/4 refers to a shotgun cartridge found at 1:35pm in the kitchen."

I seriously struggle to understand why, in what was a relatively simple murder case, the police would want to seize loose coins. They weren't, for example, forensically examined for gunshot residue or blood spatter, so what other plausible purpose could there have been to seize them?

As for the live cartridges, they offer nothing to the narrative save for a greater show of "police evidence" at trial (PC 1048 Paul Bassham was witness number 97) to impress, no doubt, a gullible jury, the gullible press pack and the gullible Great British Public.

All at considerable taxpayers' expense.

Tue 14 SEP | **unknown** | **witness 98** | **256**

Bleak House

Official records show that Dereham-based trained search officer PC 988 Sandra Kaye Scarlett[257] *made the following statement to an unnamed officer in an unidentified location at an unknown time:*

"During the course of the search, at 10:25am I seized from Room 3, a black Eley Classic shotgun cartridge, which I produce as exhibit SKS/1. I immediately handed this exhibit to exhibits officer PC Matthews."

In reality, absolutely nothing. PC Scarlett was witness number 98. The police strategy was to overwhelm Tony with numbers. I can't help thinking that whenever he needed the police, he couldn't see one for miles but when they came to bury him, they turned out in their droves.

---

[257] Line S113 in HOLMES.

Tue	**unknown location**
14 SEP	*Normally based at Bessemer Road, Norwich,* PC 774 *David John Craske was an authorised search officer.*
unknown	*According to official records,* PC *Craske made a second statement. His first (see entry* **211***) was apparently entered into evidence at trial,*
UNUSED	*but not this second one.*
witness 99	PS *Mizen was said to have been acting as* POLSA.
257	

"At 10am on 14 September 1999, I commenced a search of Room Two on the ground floor of the premises.

At 10:45am, I found and seized a spent .22 short round cartridge case, which I produce as exhibit DJC/2; this was found at the carpet edge against the fireplace.

At 1:05pm, I found & seized seven packets of twenty-four explosive caps with two dummy .410 cartridges, which I produce as exhibit DJC/3; this was found under the table made of packing cases and a door.

At 1:15pm, I seized a quantity of coins, postage stamps, & one £5 note, found spread around the floor of Room Two, this I produce as exhibit DJC/4.

The search of Room Two being completed at 1:15pm.

I then commenced a search of the hallway area on the ground floor, and at 1:38pm, I found & seized a spent .410 cartridge, this was found in the corner on rubble, and I produce this as exhibit DJC/5.

All the above exhibits were handed directly to PC 376 Steve Matthews, the search concluding at 1:44pm on Tuesday 14 September 1999."

Tue	**unknown location**
14 SEP	DC *Trevor Buxton's second statement (unused):*
unknown	"At 10:40am on Tuesday 14 September 1999 I spoke to Mr Anil Chakrabarti at the QE Hospital. He handed to me 12 pages of patient
UNUSED	notes (photocopies) which are his exhibit AJC/1. I retained the exhibit
witness 55	until 9am on Thursday 16 September 1999 when I handed it to exhibit officer PC 376 Matthews."
258	

This crucial exhibit – the twelve pages of patient notes supposedly relating to Brendon Fearon – was never entered as evidence into court. DC Buxton's statement relating to his collecting the notes was not entered into court. Anil Chakrabarti's statement was not entered as evidence into court.

Furthermore, Mr Chakrabarti is alleged to have made a second statement on 14 September 1999 in which he made mention of him exhibiting these patient notes as AJC/1. There is no mention of this statement in the HOLMES database and this statement was never entered as evidence into court, despite the 36-year-old consultant stating "I can make the original notes available at court if required."

Wed 15 SEP 8.45 am witness 17 259

home address of Stewart Mayfield
Stewart[258] Mayfield had moved from the village of Tilney St Lawrence to live in Emneth some three years or so before the shooting incident. He made friends with Tony who lived about half a mile away. They had first met in about 1993 when Tony went onto land that Mayfield was farming and introduced himself. They usually discussed farming – a topic of conversation close to Tony's heart and that of most farmers.

Mayfield described how the two men grew "more friendly" and saw one another "more frequently" – sometimes 2 or 3 times a week, sometimes not for months at a time. According to Mayfield, their conversations revolved around farming, antiques, architecture and history[259] and on occasions they discussed "the criminal fraternity" and Tony's dislike for people who committed crime. Tony had apparently told his friend that he'd been burgled twice since Christmas 1998 (this would have been in January and May 1999 prior to the August incident).

Tony had also confided in Mayfield that he'd discharged a shotgun at a vehicle belonging to someone who had been thieving on his land – this was, of course, the incident in the orchard in 1994.

Mayfield added that Tony had had a bureau stolen in May and that inside the bureau were a lot of personal items – as we have seen, this loss caused Tony considerable emotional distress.

And Mayfield – somewhat crucially for the purposes of a murder trial – added the following to DC 751 Paul Cross:

"Since the second burglary, I would say Tony was quite fearful of being burgled again. To this end he told me that he had moved all his property upstairs and

---

[258] Invariably spelled as either 'Stewart' or 'Stuart' in various police documents. I have retained the spelling from HOLMES. If Mr Mayfield wishes to contact me, I will be happy to make any necessary amendments in a further edition of this book.

[259] I have had many similar conversations with Tony on all of these subjects and many others. He is extremely well-read and capable of conversing on many diverse subjects with all manner of different people – he is far from the "eccentric loner" that the police were keen to promote through the prosecution.

had put bars across the doors.[260] He mentioned nothing about doctoring the stairs.[261]

In all the time I have known Tony he never said that he had any firearms. The only time he spoke about firearms was when he told me that he'd had his shotgun licence revoked because of an incident involving a traveller on his land.

Tony's attitude towards travellers was the same as mine and just about every other person in this area in that they were a nuisance and were a law unto themselves and that the police didn't seem to do anything about their criminal exploits.

Tony never expressed an opinion about firearms, although he was well into nature and would never do anything to harm the wildlife on his land.

Tony is a man of the land – very strong and robust and is not easily intimidated. Having said that, since the burglaries I know he was fearful about going home of an evening because of what he might find or come across when he got there.

When I found out that Tony had shot an intruder at his home, I can't say I was shocked, although I didn't know he had a weapon. It was only a matter of time before something like this happened in this area."

| **What this adds to our knowledge** | This section of Mr Mayfield's statement is surely crucial to this entire story – if a farmer (or anybody else for that matter) has put iron straps across every door and window preventing entry to burglars or any other unwanted 'visitor', he can surely never be accused of "lying in wait for burglars to shoot them like rats in a trap" as the prosecution were to claim at trial. It was a nonsensical hypothesis, designed to pander to headline writers and an unwitting public whilst simultaneously casting aside any notion of truth or justice. |

---

[260] Although Mr Mayfield didn't mention it, Tony also placed bars across every window except two – the double-glazed one to the front of the property and one at the rear.

[261] It is clear from the way Mr Mayfield stated this that it had been suggested to him *by the police* that Tony Martin had "doctored" the stairs – booby-trapped them. He hadn't. The wooden stairs had rotted over time and Tony had simply placed a small aluminium ladder in the shape of the letter 'M' to provide access up and down the stairs. Besides, a booby-trap is usually something which cannot be seen and these ladders were highly visible. I also suggest that even if Tony had "doctored" his stairs, so what? It was inside his house and a danger to no-one but it shows how desperate the police were to put some form of spin on *anything* they could use against Tony. The notion of "doctoring" the stairs was, in reality, nothing more than a red herring.

Wed
15 SEP
unknown
UNUSED
260

unknown location

According to a statement attributed to him, PS 3262 Paul Watson, 35, worked as a control room supervisor at police HQ in Norwich and had been in the job "for about 2½ years." His role was to "keep an eye" on and review tapes which were used to record all traffic and radio messages, both incoming and outgoing which were routed through the control room. These included all 999 calls received from the public.

"The system used to record all these messages is a Phillips CLS 9000 call logging system. The tape recordings are retained using a 24 hour, 60 channel cassette tapes which are logged and stored in the control room's secure tape library.

After having viewed the tapes for the 12 May 1999 and 13 May 1999, I can say that the call from a member of the public which resulted in CAD number 679 of the 12/05/99 being opened by communications officer Carol Woods at terminal 11 in the control room *was not recorded on the tapes.*[262]

The only reason I can give for this is that the Phillips CLS 9000 communications logging system *was not working properly at the appropriate time.*[263]

The same officer on the same terminal received another call at 0:09am on 13 May 1999 and opened another CAD message. Again this action was not recorded. Having checked the tapes for any other calls made to the control room around about this time, I can confirm that other terminal messages *have been recorded*[264] on the Phillips system, this proving that terminal 11's connection through to the Phillips system was faulty."

So there you have it. The communications officer, Carol Woods [entry **179**], couldn't remember the call or the famous phrase "I'll blow their heads off!" and the tape which was supposed to be recording the call wasn't apparently working. Well, technical glitches happen of course, so what about the other terminals (remember that Carol Woods was sitting at terminal 11)? PS Watson informed us in his statement that all other terminals were working properly that night.

Had the police really had a tape of that famous phrase, they would have used it. If the controller couldn't remember it being said and if there isn't a tape recording of it on terminal 11 and all the other terminals were recording properly, then I believe we can safely assume it probably never existed, despite Tony admitting to saying those words. I suggest that he may have said them in general conversation to people but not specifically in that 999 call.

---

[262] Author's emphasis.
[263] Author's emphasis.
[264] Author's emphasis.

The prosecution put out the sound bite that Tony had said "I'd shoot their heads off!" and while they distributed this propaganda *they always knew that they couldn't prove the farmer had said those words in that call.*

Alternatively, we should consider that the police *did* have a recording of Tony saying those immortal words but that he also mentioned child abuse at Glebe House in the same call so they took the decision of claiming that the machine hadn't been working so as to avoid a cover up of a child abuse scandal.

CORRUPTION ALERT *Evidence of key witness withheld from the jury*

In another example of what Tony refers to as "legal engineering", this statement was not entered as evidence.

Tony's defence counsel ought to have ensured the attendance of PS Watson so a jury could decide if he had been telling the truth about the 'faulty' machine.

Wed
15 SEP
afternoon
witness 40
261

Bleak House

Having made three separate statements on 23 and 25 August and 10 September 1999, in which Fearon placed the farmer on the stairs when the shots rang out, the police took him to the house on 15 September 1999 in the company of acting DI Sharman, DCs Buxton and Cross and SOCO Bradshaw, together with his legal team of David Payne and Rosemary Holland. You will recall that it was Bradshaw who was said to have swabbed the stairs on 25 August 1999.

The police claimed that Fearon walked through the route taken on the night of the shooting incident and the 'walk' was video recorded by Bradshaw.

However, before we move on, I must point out that I could find no evidence that SOCO Bradshaw was actually there. Statements from Buxton (24 September), Cross (24 September) and Sharman (28 September) all placed Bradshaw at Bleak House and video-recording the interview with Fearon. It appears that the officers might have colluded in their statements because of the dates and also because of the fact that not one of the officers recorded the time they made their statements (or location or to whom they were made) and all simply stated that they attended "during the afternoon of 15 September". Now, realistically, what are the odds of three officers all failing to record the time they visited and all of them using exactly the same phrase if they *hadn't* colluded?

Add to the fact that I could find no statement from Bradshaw in which he placed himself at Bleak House on that day. In reality, it could have been *anybody* behind the camera.

Furthermore, statements attributed to Buxton and Cross were not entered into evidence, and not one of the police officers named here actually produced the video as an exhibit, and this video was not listed in the official Exhibits List.

Fearon was said to have been initially quite happy that his original statement was accurate and that the positions of the farmer, himself and Barras were correct as stated in his first interview. Note that it was daytime and that there were several officers of all ranks present, as well as his legal team.

CORRUPTION ALERT *New Fearon statement engineered*

Now notice the serious change of direction by Fearon, no doubt brought about by the presence of police (who want to convict Tony Martin) and Fearon's legal team (who wish to seek mitigation for their client):

"The only slight difference I wish to state is that I think that the man was probably at the foot of the stairs when I saw him and not half way up as originally stated. Having seen the knob of the banister rail and compared it to the height of one of the officers who stood on the floor next to it, I can say that I am sure that the man was standing at the foot of the stairs. From the point that I indicated I was at when I was first shot, it is possible to see the very bottom of the stairs only and not the whole staircase."

I'll remind you of Fearon's alleged first statement (23 August):

"I spun round and saw someone standing on the stairs pointing what I thought was a torch at me ... He was more than halfway up the stairs when I saw him. I estimate about three stairs higher than half way up the staircase"

and in statement three (10 September):

"I am certain that the man was on the stairs. I saw him and the stairs quite clearly."

In two separate statements some three weeks apart, he was extremely consistent in saying that the farmer was on the stairs, more than halfway up the staircase – perhaps three stairs higher.

Now, having been taken back to Bleak House in the presence of the police, he has changed his mind. It's often wise to look at the rank of people who attend any kind of event. They are like pawns on a chess board and all will have a different function to fulfil. Why send such a high-ranking officer like DI Sharman to such an ordinary event? Was it because (we were told) he'd been the most senior officer in the case from the start? Was Fearon's videoed "testimony" needed to shore up the false narrative that the police were going to run with?

Let's look at some of the salient points from the transcript of the video:

A crucial question was asked: "At what point did you see the man?" to which Fearon replied, "When I was near the window. I remember seeing a flash; I didn't know what was going on. I just saw a flash, I heard the noise and then I saw a torch."

Clearly this is nonsense on a number of levels. Firstly, if Fearon was shot 20-30 yards up a track as he first told the medical staff, he couldn't have been inside Bleak House at all.

Secondly, it was impossible to see anything in that room, let alone Tony Martin standing on the stairs some 9.7 metres away – see entry **237** for the experiment conducted by Tony's defence and (it was said) the third pathologist to establish the level of visibility into the breakfast room.

Thirdly, Fearon changed his statements regularly but not, I suggest, of his own volition. I believe he was 'encouraged' by officers from the Constabulary.

On the 28 September, the HOLMES database shows that DI Sharman made a statement about the filming. However, that statement was not entered as evidence into court...

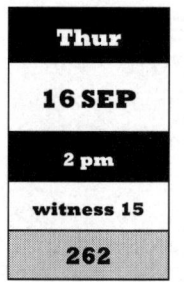

Thur
16 SEP
2 pm
witness 15
262

home address of Peter Huggins
According to official records, 51-year-old pig farmer Peter Huggins farmed 14 acres of land and also dealt in straw.

His son Christopher [Huggins] who lived at Holm Farm, St John Fen End, also helped him on the farm.

Here is the father's statement to DC 178 Noel Adcock:

"Having been aware over many years of the problems of trespass, theft and vandalism in the area, I made contact with Tony Bone who runs Farmwatch. Farmwatch is a company I suppose which gets farmers together to swap information about the movements of criminals in our area. They produce bulletins usually on a monthly basis to update members about incidents which have occurred and any suspicious person or vehicles in our area. As a result, about two years ago I joined the scheme.

To my knowledge my farm has never suffered at the hands of migrant travellers but I know of many incidents where friends of mine in the farming community have. Since joining the Farmwatch scheme I have been very impressed with it and fully support it.

In January or February 1999 I contacted Tony Bone to make arrangements for a meeting to be held in Marshland St James with a view to getting other local farmers in the scheme. The word was spread to other farmers that this meeting was to take place at Rod Herbert's engineering firm at Marshland St James.

I was assisted by Dave Golding of Crown Farm, Middle Drove with getting enough people to attend. I cannot recall the exact numbers but the meeting was held on Tuesday 23 February 1999 and upwards of 30 people were there.

As I recall there was Tony Bone and Derek Stuart who were there to explain to the farmers exactly what Farmwatch was about. They mentioned that it was a partnership in order to quell the problem of crime in the area. They explained their role in Farmwatch fully and I supported what they were saying, thinking this to be an excellent idea.

The meeting was held in the early evening and I knew most of the people there as I had personally invited them. However, I was aware that as the meeting progressed that there was one person at the meeting whom I had not personally invited. His name was Tony Martin of Bleak House. He had arrived with Stuart Mayfield, a neighbour of his.

I had no problem with Tony Martin being there as I know Tony, but I do find that he goes on a bit. By this I mean that he has made it very clear to everybody that he knows that he would stand up for his rights, that the police were a waste of time and that when the police caught any criminals they did nothing with them. Tony for many years has gone on about this almost to the point that you get bored with the same old conversation with him.

Returning to the meeting, it seemed to be progressing smoothly until Tony Martin got up from the back and started his usual subject. He went on again about the lack of police, the fact they did nothing, that people should stand up and be counted and stand up for their own rights. It didn't ruin the meeting, it was just Tony Martin going on again and most people, certainly I, thought he was off again. The meeting finished and no real conclusions were made, but it seemed to go reasonably well. When Tony spoke out you could not help but hear his point of view. This was a point of view that I had heard many times from Tony over the years. *Tony made no threats that I recall on the night of the meeting and certainly never mentioned about shooting anyone.*[265]

I would like to recall a couple of incidents involving Tony Martin. Firstly, I have known Tony since the early 1970s. I first met him I believe in March, Cambridgeshire through pig farming. Tony is known locally by most farmers who know him as 'Mad Man Martin'. This is due to his manner and his constantly going on about how the police are useless and that he would take matters into his own hands should anybody cross him.

---

[265] Author's emphasis.

The first incident was about 2 years ago. There had been the theft of a milk float from Marshland Smeeth, I believe a Ford transit. Tony Martin believed a local had stolen it. This milk float apparently turned up on Tony's orchard at Bleak House.

Instead of phoning the police, Tony decided to keep observations on it in order to catch the culprit returning to it. Apparently however, when Tony's back was turned, the milk float was moved.

Then I believe I was just leaving the local public house called England's Hope with my wife. We were driving in our blue Land Rover Discovery back towards our house when I was overtaken by a vehicle which I thought was a Granada with all its lights off. We followed this vehicle and it stopped close to the council houses just up the road. We stopped behind him and noticed that it was Tony Martin who had overtaken us. He said words to the effect: "Sorry mate, I'm chasing the bloke who's had that milk float away and it's no good having your lights on."

The last time I saw Tony was either 2-3 days before the shooting incident. I recall this because I was at Martin Works engineering in Wisbech picking up some bits and pieces. It was mid-afternoon and I saw Tony Martin there. He got on to his usual subject and I recall him saying that he was worried about burglaries and what he called the "light fingered pikies". *He said to me if he caught the bastards, he would shoot them.* I was unconcerned about this as Tony has said similar things on many, many occasions."

What this adds to our knowledge

Firstly, the statement attributed to Mr Huggins has informed us that Tony Martin did *not* disrupt the Farmwatch meeting.

Secondly, it seems that the pig farmer was unable to resist dropping little jibes about Tony into his statement and it smacked to me as if he had been encouraged by Tony Bone – the Farmwatch owner and former policeman – to 'drop in' a few negative comments such as "He said to me if he caught the bastards, he would shoot them." That was nothing but hearsay. Huggins could have been lying. Yet Huggins added that he wasn't concerned because Tony had said similar things on "many, many occasions". What does that actually mean? 'Many' to some people might be five or six, to others five or six hundred.

Thur
16 SEP
2 pm
witness 23
263

home address of Jane Betts
The 41-year-old Jane Betts worked in the Firearms Administration Department of Norfolk Constabulary in the capacity of Firearms Clerk. She had held this position which entailed the registration of firearms and shotgun certificates in the county of Norfolk for 13 years. She was also responsible for the files relating to these certificates. She made the following statement to DC Cross:

"According to records held by us a man named Anthony Martin of Bleak House, Emneth Hungate, was issued with a shotgun licence on 15/11/85. This licence was revoked on 21/12/94 (File No K39/901/94).

Martin appealed against this on 13/02/95, but this appeal was unsuccessful. The reason why it was unsuccessful was that Martin lodged an initial appeal but failed to follow this through. Had he done so, it was thought by the council's legal department that he would have been successful with the appeal.

I can produce this file (K39/901/94) as exhibit JB/1 to be used in evidence. I handed this file to DC Cross at 12:30pm on Thursday 16 September 1999."

What this adds to our knowledge
The reason that the prosecution used this evidence was firstly to follow due process and produce evidence that Tony's shotgun certificate had been revoked (on a legal technicality) and secondly to drive home the fact that Tony's possession of the shotgun used in the shooting was unlawful.

Fri
17 SEP
unknown
UNUSED
264

unknown location
On this day, PC 396 Andrew John Harrison made an unused statement in which he distanced himself from any active involvement in a search of Bleak House, despite being a team leader under the direction of the POLSA, PS Mizen:

"On Tuesday 14 September 1999 I attended with other search team members at Bleak House. I did not take an active part in searching any room, and I did not seize any property."

Fri
17 SEP
unknown
265

Wakefield, Yorkshire
It was not only individuals who were writing letters in support of Tony. Organisations of various sizes and membership numbers were also rooting for the Norfolk farmer.

For example, Philip Platts, Chairman of the Wakefield Branch of the National Farmers' Union wrote the following letter to Tony:

"I am writing in my capacity as Branch Chairman and wish to offer our support in your ensuing court case. All members present at the recently held branch meeting had great sympathy with your current plight and most felt that "there but for the Grace of God go I." It is hoped that the authorities take note of the unacceptably high crime rates in rural areas and that something is done."

Again, not only was there sympathy expressed for Tony, but also corroboration of the high crime rates in rural communities throughout the country. You might like to ask what happened to all the money that was no longer being spent on rural police stations or police officers in those communities. Prior to the closure of such rural police outposts and prior to the thinning of the ranks, public money *was* spent on such buildings and personnel. Once they had disappeared, where *did* your tax pounds go that were previously spent on that level of policing?

On 31 August 1999, the Federation of Small Businesses (Agriculture Department) issued a newsletter which contained not only support for Tony but also a remarkable (and in my view well-deserved) diatribe against government:
"Speaking for the FSB and its 140,000 members, Bob Robertson, Agricultural Spokesman (who once faced a similar risk) said today: "We wish to express our profound sympathy for Mr Tony Martin, who has lost his freedom and been forced to pay for defending his property, which should be the inalienable right of all free men. We condemn the incompetence of the present authorities and, most of all, their persistence in defending the present policy of abandoning the countryside.

As the police can't do much to help, our proposal is that grants should be made available to help country people install their own security systems. We also propose that the laws be strengthened with regards to rights to defend property."

Once again, Tony's criticisms of the lack of police in the rural communities and their ineffectiveness were being corroborated by others. As David Read had written: "Tony Martin has brought to the fore the problems facing people living in the country." This is why he became a national icon – his case was the case that any number of people might themselves have been facing had they had their home broken into whilst asleep at night and if they, too, had encountered intruders who outnumbered the owner.

Fri
17 SEP
4.20 pm
witness 38
266

Foreman's Bungalow, Hungate Corner, Emneth
Official records (which we do not have to believe, of course) show that Paul Leet made a third statement to the police at his home address, this time to DC Adcock.

Further to his statement "made between 20 August and 25 August 1999" regarding an incident involving Tony Martin of Bleak House, Emneth, he said that he would like to add the following:

"On 20 August 1999 I went shopping with my wife to Wisbech at about 7pm. I returned to my house between 8:30pm and 8:45pm. It was just getting dusk and after unpacking my wife and I had our tea. About 9:30pm-9:45pm that evening Tony Martin turned up at the bungalow in his vehicle as explained in my previous statement. I have no knowledge of Tony Martin coming to our address on any other occasion that evening. He may have come round earlier whilst we were shopping or perhaps while we were eating our tea. In either case I did not see him on any other occasion other than the incident as mentioned in my previous statement.

I did know that Tony Martin had been burgled before during May 1999 and he had on occasions said to me that he was concerned about being burgled again.

I work at FW Deptford's and the premises are virtually opposite Bleak House and Tony Martin would have a habit in the mornings to come into the yard and see what we were up to. One of these mornings about a week before the shooting incident Tony came into the yard. We struck up a conversation and somehow the subject of burglaries came up again. I remember Tony saying words to the effect that if he caught anyone trying to burgle him again he would shoot them.[266]

Tony was not a man I would want to get wrong with; he wasn't a man who showed fear and I believe Tony could lose his temper quickly. He could be intimidating towards people he didn't like and I think he himself could not be easily intimidated.[267]

Tony had an extreme dislike of the police and the system and he showed extreme dislike of gypsies or travellers - in fact he sometimes referred to them as perverts. I do not know which he disliked more: the police or the travellers.

I would describe my relationship with Tony Martin as an acquaintance; we were not over-friendly but would have no problem conversing and passing the time of day. Tony and I have never fallen out and I found him to be a very hard worker. I have known him work until 2-3 o'clock in the morning on occasions.

As far as I am aware my wife knows Tony Martin to look at but has never spoken to him."

What Paul Leet appears to have done in this statement is to have confirmed the time that he says Tony Martin called round for the second time (according to the farmer) *after having fired his shotgun* – sometime between 9:30 and 9:45pm. If this is correct, it would surely put the time of the shooting at between 8 and 9pm. This is significantly different from the time of 10pm put forward by the police.

But it also raises other important questions – if the shooting had occurred between 8 and 9pm, surely that lends greater credence to the belief that there

---

[266] Is it not remarkable that Mr Leet did not mention this in his first two statements?
[267] See previous footnote.

was a police helicopter flying over Bleak House at 10:30pm and not sometime between 1 and 2am depending on which senior police officer's statement you choose to believe. Unless there were *two* flights...

If Tony fired his shotgun around that time of night, he couldn't have hit Fearon and Barras because (i) the police claimed to have stopped the car at 8:10pm and the drive to Emneth was at least an hour and a half, (ii) Barras was said to have been seen by his uncle between 8:15 and 8:30pm still in Newark, (iii) "getaway driver" Darren Bark claimed to have still been in Newark at 9pm, (iv) Tony Martin was away from the scene and on his way to his mother's by 9:45-10pm having completed a number of tasks after having fired his gun, including having called round to the Leets' house.

Clearly Mr Leet was asked by the police in their biased questioning of possible witnesses whether he thought Tony could be easily intimidated.

Leet was keen, it seems, to promote the notion that Tony disliked the police and gypsies. What a pity that Mr Leet didn't inform the police that Tony had used travellers and gypsies on his farm from time to time to pick the apple crop. Given that Mr Leet's home and his place of work were opposite Tony's main orchard, and given that Mr Leet had lived and worked in the area for 18 years, wouldn't you have thought he might have seen gypsies and travellers working on Tony's farm in all that time? It would seem that – like most of the other prosecution witnesses – Mr Leet had "forgotten" things which would have provided a more balanced and accurate picture of Tony.

Furthermore, note the fact that this entire statement was designed to manipulate the time that Tony fired his gun to a more plausible time by when the alleged burglars could have arrived in Emneth.

Fri 17 SEP
6.30 pm
witness 39
267

Foreman's Bungalow, Hungate Corner, Emneth
According to official records, Jacqueline Leet also made a <u>third</u> statement:

"I have made a statement to the police with reference to a shooting incident which occurred at Bleak House on 20 August 1999. I would like to add the following: About 7pm on 20 August, 1999, my husband and I went shopping in Wisbech, returning about 8:45pm. As stated in my previous statement, Tony Martin arrived at our house about 9:30pm. I am unaware of Tony Martin coming round to ours on any other occasion during that evening. As far as I am aware, he only came round to ours once as per my statement.

I didn't really know Tony Martin to speak to, and cannot give a true picture of his character. I only knew him to look at and to say hello to."

Sat	
18 SEP	
2.40 pm	
witness 40	
268	

Downham Market police station

According to official records, just three days after the video "re-enactment", Fearon was interviewed yet again, this time by DC 356 Peters and DC 422 Buxton at Downham Market police station with solicitor, David Payne of Payne and Gamage, Newark, also present.

The interview, a full month after the incident, was said to have commenced at 2:40pm and concluded at 3:20pm. DC Peters told Fearon that he had been arrested on conspiracy to commit burglary.

It can't be a charge of burglary itself, because nothing was actually stolen. DC Peters explained to Fearon that the main purpose of the interview was to ask him about the arrangements that were made on 20 August in terms of getting from Newark to Emneth Hungate. So, a month later and the police are only just asking about this important aspect of the case?

Fearon claimed that he first got to hear about Bleak House in a pub in Newark. He claimed that when he broke into Bleak House on 20 August, it was the first time he had ever been there (this actually contradicted his first statement in which he'd seen the house "from the road six weeks earlier". We also have to consider how he broke into Bleak House if he had been shot on a farm track leading to the house as he told medical staff).

When DC Peters asked what arrangements the men made the day before, solicitor David Payne interjected: "There was something else you knew as well wasn't there, about a family dispute, that you told me about in the car?"

It seems that Fearon had told his solicitor that he knew of a family dispute between Tony Martin and – we can probably safely assume – his brother. But how would Fearon know about this dispute?

Was it common knowledge in Newark that the Martin brothers did not get on? Was Robin associating with these criminals? He had, as we have seen, a conviction for handling stolen goods but it doesn't necessarily follow that he would be involved in arranging for his own brother to be 'burgled' and then fitted up for murder. But neither does it discount that notion. Or did a rogue police officer or two pass on this information to the criminals, since many officers in Downham Market and Swaffham police stations had known about this feud for years, as we have previously seen?

Now, the strange thing is that this statement – allegedly made by Fearon on 18 September 1999 - was included in papers served on the defence, but it was never used at trial.

Additionally, DC Buxton was recorded as having made a statement on 28 September about this interview. It was not entered as evidence into court.

Furthermore, DC Peters was recorded as having made a statement on 20 September about this interview. It was not entered as evidence into court.

That's three statements about an important issue in the case and not one of them was entered into evidence at trial.

Wouldn't you have thought that Tony's defence counsel would have wanted to get Fearon on the stand and robustly cross-examine him about what he knew of this family dispute? Or why he suddenly changed his mind about being in Bleak House when he had said he'd been shot on a track outside of the house? Or what pressure he was under from the police to make so many different statements aligning, it would seem, not with reality but with the false narrative being served up to the nation by the Norfolk and Cambridgeshire Constabularies?

Sun
19 SEP
unknown
269

Manor Farm, Owston, Leicestershire
Richard Harvey of Manor Farm wrote the following letter to Tony:

"I hope you can take heart from the fact that I have not spoken to a single farmer or rural people recently who is not sympathetic to the position in which you find yourself. Most people could easily have been exactly where you are now and would all feel that they had done nothing wrong.

Policing of small crimes has all but ceased in the countryside. If I ring Leicestershire Police to report an 'intruder on site', I face a long wait to speak to a human being and then the invitation to leave a message on my local bobby's 'voicemail'. This may result in the visit of a perpetually new face in about 3 days hence. Please be assured that there is much feeling in your support and I shall be encouraging contributions to be made to your fighting fund, through my many business contacts."

These criticisms of the police were an exact echo of those voiced by Tony Martin, making him unpopular with them because of his honest, direct approach. Clearly Tony was not alone in holding those views.

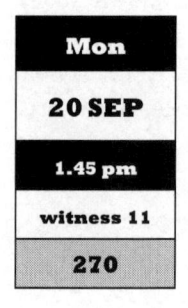

Mon
20 SEP
1.45 pm
witness 11
270

home address of Eileen Sutton
Mrs Eileen Sutton, the 64-year-old wife of Donald and a neighbour of Tony's living at the Hungate Corner, stated that she'd known him for the last ten to fifteen years but only really gotten to know him to talk to for the past six or seven years. She was recorded as having made the following statement to DC 603 Andrew David Lovick:

"He would often come to our house and have a chat or ask for advice from my husband over farming matters.

Tony has always had dogs at his house which is where we generally got to know him from. Rottweilers were his favourite choice of dogs and there was one in particular called Daniel which would wander off the farm and come over and see us. It would spend time with us as we would feed it and give the dog a lot of attention.

When this dog died, about 6 years ago, it took Tony about a week before he told us about it. He said that he had buried the dog on his land wrapped up in an expensive carpet. He was so fond of the dog that it apparently took him a long time to fill the grave in. I did offer help but Tony wouldn't accept any. He is a very private man who kept himself to himself.

I knew he had a brother who he didn't get on with and is now in Spain and his mother who I initially thought lived in the March area. Apart from that I know little of Tony - as I say he is a very private man. I never knew of any visitors to Tony or friends; in fact I would describe him as probably a recluse. I have been on Tony's land; in fact Tony has shown me round but not the house. Tony was very keen on the environment and wildlife. He never allowed any shooting on his land and as far as I'm aware didn't have a shotgun.

Tony wasn't a clean man and wouldn't have a bath from one week to the next. In fact I used to joke with him about this as sometimes he would say 'Sorry Eileen, but I do smell a bit.' I would tell him that if he could smell himself then it was time for a bath. As far as I'm aware he would have to light a wood burner to heat the water for his bath.

About a couple of months before the incident in August, Tony had a break-in at his farm where a chest of drawers was stolen from his house. A second set of drawers was apparently moved from the house to the driveway but left out in the open. Tony was really upset about this mainly because the drawers that went missing were full of memorabilia.

I remember talking to Tony about this a few days after it happened when he was convinced the people who broke into his house were 'travellers' or 'perverts' as he called them. He said a few days before this a white van (which he had the number of) came onto his land and asked if they could feed their horse on his land. Tony told them 'no' because it was 'set aside' land which doesn't allow it and told them to clear off. This they did but as far as Tony was concerned they were the same people that broke into his house. Tony did have other things go missing from his farm over a period of time like generators etc and didn't seem to get any help from the police when he reported it."

What this adds to our knowledge

In my view, Mrs Sutton has shown us a glimpse into the emotional landscape of Tony Martin and broadened our knowledge of his capacity to express his feelings. She described their chats over a cup of tea and we learned that Tony was not too proud to seek help on farming matters from her husband.

The knowledge that Tony was extremely fond of Daniel the rottweiler helps us to understand the man better as an animal lover.

Mrs Sutton also confirmed that Tony had had a number of thefts from his farm over a number of years and that he didn't get any help from the police.

Mon
20 SEP
2.25 pm
witness 3
271

home address of Roger Putterill

In a statement attributed to Roger Putterill, at the time a general assistant at the Marmion House Hotel and son-in-law of the owner Helen Lilley, he provided background information on his knowledge of the farmer to PC 1018 Huw Caine.

Putterill, 39, had known Tony for about 17 years to speak to and prior to that would often wave if they passed one another.

"I live with my wife Julie, and my 3 children, Matthew, Nathan and Liam. As I used to work on farms in the area I got to know him when he took over Bleak House. Since then he has almost become a member of the family as he would come around most days for a cup of tea and a chat. In fact I have left Tony looking after my children on occasions as I went to the shops.

I was happy doing this as he got on very well with my children despite Nathan being autistic and Liam having learning difficulties. They would get presents from Tony at Christmas.

I have never worked directly for Tony although on the odd occasion I have helped out at the farm. Although I have visited the farm in this respect I have never actually been into his house, prior to 20 August 1999. I would always drive into the driveway and sound my horn and Tony would appear. I do not know of anyone who has been into his house. I can remember an occasion last year some time, when Tony phoned to ask if I could run him to hospital. He had thrombosis and told me he didn't want an ambulance picking him up. I turned up in the driveway to find Tony sat on a wood pile with his pyjamas on. He has always lived alone to my knowledge and I am not aware of any girlfriend or relationship he has ever had.

When Tony would come around for tea we would talk mainly about farming issues and more specifically farm machinery that he had bought or was broken down, and I would offer advice. He struck me as well educated and I would describe him as careful with his money, never splashing out or being flash, but he would always pay for things up front. If ever I helped him he would insist on paying for my help. He has mentioned in passing conversation that he has been burgled in the past at Bleak House. He didn't make a big thing about this but he did also say that a grandfather clock had been taken. Apart from this he did not mention it. He would always say 'You have enough problems of your own without me giving you mine.' I think he was happy coming around here and comfortable talking to me because I never questioned him about things. If Tony wanted to tell me, he would, but I never pressured him for answers.

The last time I saw Tony was about 4pm on Thursday 19 August 1999. He popped around and had a quick cup of tea. He was talking about the start of harvesting and he seemed to be looking forward to it. He was in good spirits but didn't stay long, as he wanted to get his trailers ready, having already tried the combine harvester. He left at about 4:30pm. I was unaware that Tony had any firearms at the farm and he had never mentioned them. He has also never mentioned gypsies specifically although I do know that he used them occasionally to pick his apples.[268] He has never mentioned any problems he has had with travellers/gypsies.

I have never known Tony to raise his voice or get angry in any way. He has always been mild mannered and very rational about things. I do think that if something had been getting to Tony or praying on his mind that he would have told me. However, I did notice that over the last 3-4 months, Tony would leave mine earlier to go home. This I think is because he was worried about the house having been broken into although he never said so. I was aware that Tony was interested in antique shops and fairs and would buy odd pieces of small pottery, some of which he gave to me. I'm not aware that he had vast amounts of antiques.

I am aware of Tony visiting my mother-in-law, Helen Lilley, at Marmion House Hotel, and that in the past they had gone to agricultural shows and sales together. He would also pop in and have a cup of tea at the Hotel with whoever was there as he knew all the staff there.[269]

The only other thing of note about Tony is that he was very fond of his dogs. He has 3 rottweilers, which are large dogs but I have never seen them do anything other than bark. They lived in an outhouse at the farm."

We have to question why Putterill didn't mention finding the body at all in this

---

[268] This fact has been corroborated by other independent witnesses. It was never mentioned at trial, not even by Tony's barrister, who knew of this fact.
[269] We perhaps ought to consider whether one of these members of staff was passing on information about Tony's acquisition of antiques to the criminal fraternity or to a rogue police officer.

statement. Surely if you're a member of the public and you're helping the police round up Tony's dogs because the dogs are used to you and you come across the body, you're going to mention that in your statement. Unless, of course, the statement had been doctored in some way.

Tue
21 SEP
2.40 pm
UNUSED
272

home address of Barry Cooper
Barry Cooper, who had lived at his address for the past 28 years and was a neighbour of Tony's (albeit living a quarter of a mile away), had first made a statement on 24 August. It was not used at trial.
He now made a second (also unused) one to DC Adcock:

"I have known Tony to say 'Hello' to on the odd occasions for many years. Until about 1995 I never really had a conversation with him, but as a result of two lorries being stolen from our yard about that time, Tony came round to see us. He was, I suppose, being a bit nosey wanting to know all the details of the theft of my lorries.

I have not really spoken to him on any other specific occasion that I recall; however, I do remember an occasion (when, I don't know) that Tony was talking about burglaries and thefts and he said that he had a gun and that he thought by him having this gun that it would frighten any burglar away. I did not get the impression that he would shoot anybody. *I got the impression that he had his gun as a deterrent.*" [Author's emphasis]

I'm breaking into Barry Cooper's statement at this point to remind you that I found this statement in the 'Unused Material' file, which means, of course, that it was not used by the prosecution against Tony because it provided a bona fide reason for his having a gun which most right-minded people, I suggest, would be able to identify with, given the lawlessness of the area and lack of police response. Not being used by the prosecution, the statement (and witness) was open to the defence to use. Now, if you were Tony's barrister, wouldn't you have wanted to turn Mr Cooper's comments to your advantage and show a jury that the gun was a deterrent and not meant to be used by Tony, that it was a self-defensive measure and damned good defence to murder?

As we read on, notice how Mr Cooper has been asked specific questions about Tony – he is being led at this stage by DC Adcock who, in turn, is following orders to "ascertain Tony Martin's attitude towards gypsies and travellers". In other words, the entire investigation is not independent and impartial - it is designed to 'dish the dirt' on anything that Tony Martin felt about gypsies and travellers. Now, once an investigation is biased, we need to ask what the police had to gain by being so biased and we should consider that any trial based on such bias is fundamentally flawed and cannot possibly be fair.

"I do not think I am qualified to give any opinion on Tony's attitudes towards travellers or gypsies. I did not find him intimidating and I cannot comment on how other people saw him. I am unaware of whether he could be intimidated.

I have been a neighbour of Tony's for many years and I have never really got to know him. I keep myself and my family to myself and Tony did the same."

Tue
21 SEP
3.45 pm
UNUSED
273

home address of Christine Clarke
Official records show that 49-year-old Mrs Clarke, who lived on the Smeeth Road with her husband, Robert, and step-daughter Katie, made a statement to DC Adcock.

Like so many others which presented a completely different picture of Tony and the area, this statement was not used at trial:

"The position of my house is approximately ¼ mile away from Bleak House. I am now aware of the name of the person who lived there, Tony Martin. However I have never met him and would not recognise him.

I wish to recall an incident which occurred on 19 August 1999 [author's note: the day *before* the incident]. It was about half past nine, twenty to ten in the evening and I left my house to pick up my husband who was on late shift.

I drove along the Smeeth Road towards Emneth and towards Bleak House. As I approached where I knew to be the driveway to Bleak House I saw a man on the nearside of the road.

He was a few yards away from the driveway facing some bushes and appeared to be looking in the general direction of Bleak House. As I saw him I was immediately suspicious because it was so unusual to see someone there at that time of night. I slowed down and as I did, the male tried to make it look as if he was picking fruit from a nearby tree. This aroused even more suspicion in me.

As I approached the driveway to Bleak House I saw a motor vehicle parked in the driveway pointing down the driveway towards the house. The vehicle I can only describe as a Fiesta-size vehicle, a hatchback possibly. It didn't appear to have a boot. The colour was definitely black. I had my lights on full beam and I could see the car clearly but I am not very good in makes of cars. I did not get the registration number. As I passed it I was doing no more than 5mph. I noticed the vehicle had no lights on at the time.

Also in the vehicle with me was my step daughter, Katie (15years).

I only ever saw the one male person near to this vehicle. I would describe him as follows: male, white, 16-19yrs, 5'8" tall, light coloured, fair hair, he was wearing jeans. He was of slim build. I cannot recall anything else about him.

I picked up my husband and when we returned past Bleak House the man had gone and this was about 10:15pm.

I would not recognise this man again as I never saw his face.

The following day, 20 August 1999, I was at home with my step-daughter and Bob was at work. I recall that sometime after 7:30pm, I heard shotgun noises coming *from the orchard* close to my house. The orchard is in the direction of Emneth and Bleak House.

I can say that it came from that direction rather than any other direction because it is so open and quiet of a night time and to distinguish the direction of a noise is not difficult. I believe the time of these shots was no later than 8pm but after 7:30pm. *There were two distinctive shots about 1-2 seconds apart. They were the only shots I heard that night.*"

What this adds to our knowledge	Firstly, Mrs Clarke informed the police that the night *prior to the shooting* there was a vehicle, with its lights off, parked on the track leading to Bleak House. It had no business to be there and her suspicions were aroused by the behaviour of the male pretending to pick fruit. The description virtually fits that of Fred Barras. Was he there the night before the shooting as a lookout while others "cased the joint"? Or had the date in Mrs Clarke's statement been altered?

Now we come to the gunshots. Can we be certain that the shots she heard were those fired by Tony Martin? If her statement has not been altered in any way, then her timing puts Tony firing his gun much earlier than the police narrative.

CORRUPTION ALERT	*CPS and Tony's barrister appear to have conspired to withhold evidence from the jury*

This statement was not used as evidence in court. Not only did the prosecution decide not to use it (because it would mean they would have to call Mrs Clarke as a witness and she obviously had much information which the CPS didn't want the jury to hear), but Tony's defence barrister also didn't use this material and call her anyway – this opportunity was open to him, since the CPS didn't call her. Withholding critical evidence is a criminal offence, and yet the CPS get away with this sort of thing every day in every court in the land. And the gullible British public allows them to do so.

Wed
22 SEP
unknown
UNUSED
274

letter to Kenneth Bush solicitors, King's Lynn

Peggy Watts-Russell, a cousin of Tony's, wrote the following letter to his former solicitor Paul Croker of the Kenneth Bush law firm in King's Lynn:

"I have been given to understand that you are representing my cousin, Tony Martin. If this is correct, I wonder whether a few facts I can supply would help his cause.

Bleak House, or Cowcroft Farm, has been known to me all my life, and I know that when our uncle and aunt lived there, they were plagued by itinerant travellers. If caught stealing fruit, they were abusive and threatening, and on one occasion two young travellers were caught in a deep litter fowl house, armed with two garden hoes, attempting to kill and maim as many birds as possible.

It is many years since our uncle – Arthur Garner – was attacked and tied up, and only the fact that his wife produced a shot-gun at the window that caused them to retreat. (At a later date to attack and kill another farmer.)

At one time, while staying at Bleak House with my aunt, a lorry approached along the drive and three men who appeared to be travellers approached the house, when we released a very large doberman dog. They very quickly ran to their vehicle. Another occasion I recall when my aunt was still in residence, some very unsavoury men demanded we sell them antiques. I told them to leave immediately or I would call the police.

Tony has had his life plagued with these types of people since he has lived there. What could he do? Wait to be murdered? Law and Order seems to have been abandoned in this country and if someone breaks into my house what do I do? – unless I have firearms I am helpless – I cannot even attack them unless they make the first blow and by then it would be too late."[270]

In her *unused* letter, Mrs Watts-Russell made an intelligent and emotional (yet restrained) plea on behalf of her cousin which was soon to be echoed throughout the nation – the law favoured the criminal and not the victim of crime. The law was out of step with the man and woman in the street. Politicians were as far removed from the lives of decent, hard-working citizens as they had ever been.

---

[270] Strictly speaking, Mrs Watts-Russell was wrong on this point: a householder does not have to wait for someone to strike first. See part 13 – the defence of self-defence.

Wed
22 SEP
2.18 pm
UNUSED
275

unknown location

According to official records, the 24-year-old PC 9118 Fiona Lucy Bowles made the statement below. However, it was never used at trial and once you have read it, you may agree that serious questions needed to be asked of Tony's barrister with regard to the reasons why he failed to call this constable to court:

"On Monday 31 August 1999 I was on duty in uniform on mobile patrol with PC 190 John Coles when, at 11:15pm, I arrested a driver called Neil Hirrel at the Shell petrol station, Hillside Garage, Fakenham, as a result of information received that a car had been driven into a petrol pump. [Author's note: Coles is referred to as 'DC' in HOLMES.]

Hirrel was placed in the public order van and I drove to the police station. Throughout the journey he engaged in conversation. One subject which he talked about was the recent Emneth shootings. Hirrel stated that the male who was injured in the shootings was very close to him. I could not hear what exact relationship he was with the male.

Hirrel said that he knew what had happened. He said that he could understand and agree with the farmer if he was protecting himself yet he stated most forcibly "This is not what he did." Hirrel went on to say that "the lad" was shot once and when he was down on the ground he shot him again "in cold blood."

Hirrel stated that he would probably be refused bail, as only the night before he had been arrested for driving whilst disqualified. Hirrel said he would probably go to Norwich jail and that if the farmer was there he would "cut his throat at the first opportunity - I shall seriously fucking do him over."

I am aware that Hirrel does carry a knife on him and is very violent. He continued to speak about his connections with new age travellers in Newark."

This statement – which Tony's barrister was provided with in the Unused Material file – is a possible game-changer. If Hirrel's comments can be believed, Fred Barras was shot in the leg and went down and whilst on the ground was shot in the back in cold blood. If true, it tells us at least three things: (i) that Tony Martin could not possibly have shot him, (ii) that if Tony didn't shoot him then someone else did, and (iii) that Hirrel was either at the farm himself or he had been told about what had happened by others who were.

Let's turn to the statement – *also unused* - attributed to her colleague, PC 190 John Coles of North Walsham police, made we are told on 16 September 1999, some six days prior to PC Bowles' statement:

"During [Hirrel's] subsequent detention I was supervising him in the exercise yard when he entered into conversation about the Emneth shooting. He stated that he was a close friend of the surviving suspect [Fearon] and that he had visited him in hospital at King's Lynn prior to his transfer to Newark. He explained that he had been told by this person to speak to the Sun newspaper and give them the full story. He stated he met the Sun in a hotel in King's Lynn Market Place but due to reporting restrictions they told him they were not interested and gave him £50."

This statement is, of course, tremendously significant since it appears that Hirrel, having spoken with Fearon in the hospital, had some kind of inside knowledge which differed substantially from the official police version and that Fearon wanted the truth about the shootings to be told.

If the statement is true, then it would also appear that the *Sun* was complicit in a cover-up. Having been at Hillsborough in 1989, I know at first-hand how the Thatcher government used that newspaper as a propaganda tool to support corrupt police officers and vilify the innocent Liverpool FC fans. Naturally I have to be very careful not to allow my contempt for that "newspaper" to cloud my judgment in this matter, not only for Tony Martin's sake but also for Fred Barras's and indeed Brendon Fearon's. But, if Hirrel's comments are true, we have to question the integrity of the so-called "free press" in the UK.

Being such a possible game-changer, we have to seriously question why Tony's defence counsel didn't call Hirrel to court. Or, put another way, if *you* had been Tony's barrister, wouldn't *you* have ensured Hirrel's attendance at trial?

Wed
22 SEP
2.30 pm
witness 3
276

home address of Roger Putterill
According to official records, there is a second statement attributed to Roger Herbert Putterill dated 22 September. This causes the police considerable difficulties on a number of levels, not least in what Putterill had to say about his visiting Bleak House in an attempt to round up Tony's dogs:

"When I found out about the shooting involving Tony Martin, a very good family friend, I immediately went down to the scene at Bleak House. I found out about the shooting from Helen Lilley, who is my mother-in-law. I have been married to her daughter, Julie, for sixteen years. Helen is the owner of Marmion House Hotel, where Tony was arrested. She phoned me about 7:00am on the morning of Saturday, 21 August 1999, to tell me Tony had been arrested. I attended the scene the first time with Kevin Bunton, who is Julie's brother. He is currently living at the hotel.

Because I've known Tony for seventeen years, I've looked after his dogs, currently three rottweillers, on several occasions. The dogs' names are Bruno, Daniel and Otto. I've never known Tony have doberman dogs. I believe he has had other rottweillers prior to this, and both of them have died naturally. I thought the dogs may have been running loose.

When I got to Tony's house I was turned away by police officers at the scene. I gave them my telephone number, so they could contact me if they wanted any help with the dogs.

I returned to the scene later in the day with Paul Fordham, who is also a friend of Tony's. I don't know where Paul is living at present. Again, we were stopped by police originally but, after I explained that I could help with rounding up the dogs, they let me onto Tony's property.

Paul stayed with the vehicle we were in, which was a Peugeot 205 van, colour maroon, the registration number of which I do not know. I was accompanied onto the property by a uniformed police officer, I don't know his name, nor can I describe him.

After about one hour of being at Tony's address we'd managed to catch one of the dogs. We caught the first dog near to the grain store. The second dog was found on the shingled driveway to the front of the house, about ¾ of the way down the drive. The third dog proved more elusive to catch. It kept coming towards us, then running away. When it did this, we followed to where it had ran. This took both myself and the officer around the back of the house. The dog then ran into some undergrowth which was positioned to the right of the house as you looked at it when standing in the rear garden. Both the officer and I followed the dog into the undergrowth. We'd walked about 5-6 steps into it when the officer stopped and said, "Oh, there's a body."

I continued to walk forward until my foot kicked the feet of the body. I saw the body had white trainers on it and blue jeans. I didn't look any further up the body because the undergrowth was fairly thick, so I couldn't say what position the upper body was in, and I can't recall whether the body's toes were pointing upwards or downwards. The officer asked me to go and get one of his colleagues. This I did by walking from the undergrowth and back around the bottom left hand side of the house to where a police officer was standing with a female colleague, near to the shingled path at the front. I told them what I had seen, and was left with the female officer."

Putterill concluded his statement by saying that he had never been inside Tony's house in the 17 years he'd known the farmer, but since the shooting, he'd been inside on about four occasions – "always accompanied by police officers."

I found it remarkable that Mr Putterill made no mention of the discovery of the body in his first statement (just two days earlier) but in saying that I cast no aspersions upon his character. There may well have been very good reasons why he didn't. His statement might well have been substantially altered or even fabricated.

On Tuesday 13 January 2015,[271] I drove to the Marmion in Wisbech to meet with Mr Putterill. He presented as a "hail fellow, well met" character which is what one might expect from a man working in the hotel business – after all, you can't be rude to people and expect them to return.

I introduced myself to him and told him about the book that I was writing with Tony. He said that he thought this had "all gone away."

I find it remarkable that people should adopt such an attitude. Tony Martin's life was destroyed that night and he has been living that nightmare ever since. Neither Mr Putterill nor anyone else has the right to "hope it will all go away" just because it might suit them for it all to go away. If Justice has not been served then it can't go away. In hoping it will all go away, they are projecting their own fears and insecurities or secrets on to the case. Some will have something to hide in hoping it all goes away, others will not. Some people will merely say they have moved on – yet Tony has not. He is partly stuck in a time-warp dated 1999. He has the right to have his voice heard, hence this book.

Many things were put into the public domain about the August incident and Tony's character that were (and are) palpably untrue. All through this book I have attempted to remain detached and present only the facts as are available in the evidence. I do not sensationalise and I do not criticise (unless it is necessary to do so.) So, it is my belief that no human being has the right to tell another to "move on" if that person is not ready to move on or if that person's voice has not been heard.

Professor Phil Scraton, author of Hillsborough: The Truth, stated in the *Belfast Telegraph*: "To me you can't draw a line until there is resolution and people have a right to that resolution in their lifetime. If they die then their sons and daughters and grandsons and granddaughters have a right to resolution."[272]

Despite his pleasant manner, Mr Putterill made it clear that he would not speak with me. He was not rude and he delivered his refusal with a great deal of social aplomb learned from years of working in the hotel trade, but he was adamant, nevertheless: "What I saw and what I know about these events, I will take to my grave."

I asked him if he stood by his statements to the police. "Yes. It's all in there."

I asked if he would confirm for me if he had 'discovered' the body of Fred Barras. "Yes. I kicked his feet as I walked through the brush. I had a policeman

---

[271] Two months after this meeting, the author was unlawfully imprisoned on a bogus charge of breaches of a restraining order. He was sent to ten prisons in just twelve weeks as a means of gagging him – the reader is referred to the book *10 Prisons, 12 Weeks*, Pead, B., Melville Press, 2017, ISBN: 978-0-9574301-6-7.

[272] https://cdn-03.belfasttelegraph.co.uk/news/article34834905.ece/. Queen's University Professor Phil Scraton, who played a key role in uncovering the truth about the 1989 Hillsborough disaster, talked to Deborah McAleese about the long road to justice in an article published in the Belfast telegraph on 27 June 2016.

on my left and a policewoman on my right." In fact, in his statement he said that he went round the back of Bleak House with only one (male) uniformed constable.

He told me that he was aware that the police sent up a helicopter with heat-seeking equipment on board before he came across the body, and he confirmed that he had been inside Bleak House whilst it was still a crime scene and an exhibit in the case.

Thur
23 SEP
3.35 pm
UNUSED
277

home address of Elaine Barras, Newark
According to official records, Elaine Barras, one of Fred's sisters, gave the police a piece of lined paper on which Fred had drawn various pictures, words and symbols.

There were pictures of a shotgun, knives, a syringe and a knife, fork and spoon. The various symbols, looking somewhat Masonic, seem indecipherable but probably meant something to Fred. The words included 'dope', 'shit', 'the mad man', 'bang' and 'dead'.

The sheet of paper had the exhibit number of EB/1 but was never used in court. Furthermore, Elaine Barras had told the police that days prior to the shooting incident, her brother had told her that he was "going on a mission" – the police were later to claim that Fred was recruited "at the last minute" to go to Emneth.

It was officially recorded that the exhibit was handed over to DC Lovick and his role was particularly interesting. There was an official statement attributed to him in which he claimed he showed the body of Barras to his parents at the hospital. But – according to various witnesses – he had taken statements from Malcolm Starr, Michael Coleman and others. Yet DC Lovick apparently never made a statement to set down that he had interviewed these people.

The exhibit – with the words 'dope' and 'shit' and drawings of a syringe, gun and knives could lead the reasonable person to conclude that there never was an intended burglary at Tony Martin's farmhouse, but rather a drug deal nearby which went wrong and which the police always knew would involve firearms. That Barras was killed had to be explained away by blaming a fierce critic of the police.

Thur
23 SEP
unknown
witness 109
278

unknown location

According to official records, 43-year-old PC 837 Douglas 'Danny' Cracknell, stationed in the murder incident room at Downham Market police station, made a statement in which he said that at 9:45am on Thursday 23 September 1999, he was on duty when he received from PC 376 Matthews exhibit SJP/2,[273] exhibit reference E38/1529/99 in bag number A245099.

"The exhibit was a red address book[274] seized by DC Peters. I opened up the bag and removed the book and read the contents. I found it to contain a quantity of telephone numbers and names or initials. At 10am on 22 August 1999 I handed exhibits SJP 1, 2, 3, 4 and 11 to PC 376 Matthews, the exhibits officer."

Clearly the fact that Bark apparently had two mobile phones is of some significance for reasons which I will explain in much further detail later in this narrative. When I checked the list of numbers shown by PC Cracknell, the number for Christopher Webster was present. If these phones belonged to Bark, this would seem to confirm that Webster and Bark were known to one another.

CORRUPTION ALERT — *Police allegedly failed to check two mobile phones and failed to enter them as evidence into trial*

Surely the most amazing thing about Cracknell's statement is that he provided the numbers only from the red address book and not the two mobile phones that had also been seized along with the book.

Of great significance is the fact that neither the address book nor the mobile phones were entered into evidence at the trial.

Now, why would such a glaring oversight have taken place and why would Tony's barrister have allowed it?

---

[273] SJP/2 refers to the second exhibit entered as evidence by DC Stuart John Peters.
[274] According to the statement of DC Peters, this belonged to Darren Bark and was seized from his car by DC Peters between 5:30am and 5:40am. Note that the detective claimed to have also seized a black wallet, a Motorola mobile phone and a Motorola mobile phone in a blue cover. Note that we were told that Bark had *two* mobile phones in his possession inside the car that night.

Thur
23 SEP
unknown
witness 122
279

unknown location

According to official records, Norfolk Constabulary tape librarian, Pippa Gooderson, made a second statement in which she wished to add that at 2:40pm on Thursday 23 September 1999 upon the request of PC 376 Matthews, she removed from the audio tape store at King's Lynn the master tape of the interview D(B) 118/99 relating to Brendon Fearon (exhibit SJP/21).

"This tape was placed into the King's Lynn store during the morning of Tuesday 21 September 1999 following collection of the Downham Market police station tape storage box which this tape had been placed in by the interviewing officer(s).

At 3:50pm on 23 September 1999 I handed this tape to PC 376 Matthews."

What this adds to our knowledge

In reality, this statement offered very little. It was merely another procedural statement included to give the impression that due process had been duly followed in all aspects of this murder 'investigation'. It hadn't.

Additionally, we would do well to remember that PC Matthews was *not* the exhibits officer in the Tony Martin case, but in the *Crown v Fearon & Bark* case. Thus it would seem that the master tape exhibit in one case had been spirited away to become an exhibit in a different case.

Thur
23 SEP
unknown
UNUSED
witness 55
280

unknown location

DC Buxton made a fourth statement. This was unused. In fact, official records show that DC Buxton made 10 separate statements but only 3 of them were entered into evidence – more "legal engineering":

"At 10:30am on Friday 3 September 1999, I went to the Queen Elizabeth Hospital, where I spoke to the Casualty receptionist, who handed me the Patient Report Form (DHS/1) in respect of patient Brendon Fearon, which was held at the hospital with the patient notes. I retained this exhibit until 9:45am on Monday 6 September 1999, when I handed it to exhibits officer PC 376 Matthews."

On the face of it, it added nothing to the case – being merely procedural. However, since this statement was unused, I couldn't help wondering what was in the notes that the police didn't want revealed.

Fri 24 SEP
unknown
UNUSED
witness 55
281

unknown location

DC Buxton made a fifth statement which was also unused. The police and the CPS really were playing footloose and fancy free with the rule of law:

"During the afternoon of Wednesday 15 September 1999, I accompanied Brendon Fearon around the house and grounds at Bleak House. He explained, as he went, what he had done and where he had been on the evening of Friday 20 August 1999.

The interview was video recorded by SOCO Mr Bradshaw, and acting DI Sharman, DC Cross, Mr David Payne and Ms Rosemary Holland were present throughout. Mr Fearon and I were the only two persons who spoke during the interview, and I made notes in my rough book, which I can produce as my exhibit, if required."

What this adds to our knowledge

This entry simply confirmed Fearon having been taken back to Bleak House to discuss the position he and Barras were allegedly in when sustaining shotgun injuries. Had I been Tony's barrister, I would have wanted to call DC Buxton to examine him about that video and I would have insisted that DC Buxton bring along his rough book and produce the notes he claimed to have made. And I would have cross-examined Fearon about his claims of having been shot on the track, not inside a house.

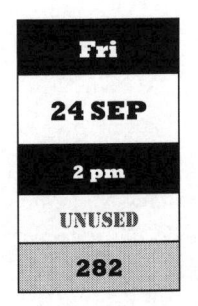

Fri 24 SEP
2 pm
UNUSED
282

home address of Terry Howard

Records show that in a second statement to DC Buxton, Terry Howard made the following comments:

"Further to my previous statement, I wish to add the following:
I am Tony Martin's best friend and he is mine. I have known him for many years and I would say that we are very close. I see him regularly and speak to him very often on the telephone.

I know that Tony has become a bit of a character over the years, but he has also suffered a lot of petty crimes on his farm. I have no idea of the details, but would say that he has probably had six burglaries from his house and garage. There have also been numerous thefts from the farm in the way of generators and tools and other such things. As a result, Tony always expressed a disappointment with the lack of action by police in the area and often told me how he feared further burglaries when he returned home. He was convinced that the thefts were all committed by travellers and he used to call them "perverts".

I know that Tony had his shotgun certificate revoked a few years ago and I know the circumstances of why it was revoked. Since then, I have never heard Tony mention anything at all about shotguns or any firearms in any way. He has never discussed the use of firearms with me. I know that he never uses a shotgun on his land, nor does he allow anyone else to shoot on his land, as he feels for the creatures and will not see them harmed.

When I stated I was Tony's best friend, I meant outside farming circles. He has numerous friends within farming circles as I know that he has his farm at heart. He is definitely eccentric and, having visited his home on numerous occasions, I think he is embarrassed by the state of it.

Tony is not easily intimidated and nothing much frightens him. He is a man of principles and he sticks to them. However, he was in fear of returning home to discover further thefts had taken place. I will go so far as to say that Tony was extremely wary about going home after dark for fear of what he may find or, more seriously, whom he may disturb. I know a lot about Tony and I will be willing to help the police in the future if any further information is required."

| **What this adds to our knowledge** | This statement, of course, was extremely helpful to Tony which was why the prosecution didn't enter it as evidence in court. Mr Howard described how Tony had suffered at least six burglaries and dozens of thefts from his farm with no assistance from the police whatsoever. In response, the police claimed Tony was "a fantasist". |

| **Fri** **24 SEP** unknown witness 75 283 | **unknown location** *According to official records, 34-year-old Inspector Paul Andrew Rush of the Central Control Room in Norwich, made a statement to the effect that on the morning of Saturday 21 August 1999, he attended Bleak House in his role as a Police Search Adviser. During the course of his activities he completed a Police Search Report, which he exhibited as PR/1.*[275] |

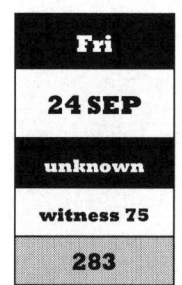

"I retained this exhibit and the following morning I forwarded it via the internal mailing system to the Operations Department at Bessemer Road, Norwich."

---

[275] This exhibit was not entered into court. In my view, it ought to have been.

> | CORRUPTION ALERT | *Significant omissions from Search Advisor's unsigned statement* |

This statement causes considerable concern on a number of levels. Firstly, it was not signed by Rush. The location, the time and the person to whom the statement was made were not recorded on it.

Then we ought to consider why the person leading the search on the day the body of Barras was allegedly found had not noted anything more than the fact that he (allegedly) produced a report of the search. According to the CAD report, it was Rush himself who telephoned the Control Room to inform his superiors that Barras had been found and that acting DI Sharman should be informed.

He did not state at what time he arrived at Bleak House (if he did), nor the time at which he left.

And there was no mention of DI Sharman being with him, which Sharman was later to claim [see entry 307].

Clearly these are worrying concerns and go to show that there was more than an overwhelming suggestion of police corruption throughout this case.

| Sun |
| 26 SEP |
| unknown |
| witness 48 |
| 284 |

Queen Elizabeth Hospital

According to official records, 30-year-old Ashish Prabhudesai made a statement but we do not know the time or to whom it was made. However, it was allegedly witnessed by Julie Berry, a receptionist at the hospital. I haven't reproduced the statement in its entirety because it contains a lot of medical information which is not strictly relevant, but I have retained the 'flavour' of the statement:

"I am Ashish Prabhudesai, Senior House Officer in Orthopaedics, with the following qualifications: MBBS, MS General Surgery, FRCS. I currently practice from the Queen Elizabeth Hospital, King's Lynn, Norfolk.

On 21 August 1999, at approximately 0:05am, I received a phone call from Mr Mandal, Staff Grade in Orthopaedics on-call, about a 29-year-old male who was brought in by ambulance after sustaining gunshot injuries to both his thighs. I attended the call promptly and saw Mr Brendon Fearon (the male mentioned above) in resuscitation room 1 of the Accident and Emergency Department.

I found out that the patient had sustained gunshot injuries at a farm in Norfolk, *where he was hit from approximately twenty yards about two hours before.*[276] Exact details of the event were not available then.

The patient told me that he had no significant history of medical illnesses. He said he was not on any medications and had no known allergies. On examination I found that he was conscious and oriented. I noticed that he was in a lot of pain.

On examining both his groins and thighs, I found that he had multiple pellets embedded in the skin and subcutaneous tissues. There was a circular swelling (approximately 5 cm x 5 cm) in his right groin.

His left thigh had a deep laceration, 20 cm x 20 cm, with underlying muscles exposed. His left knee had full range of movement and was not swollen. There were multiple pellets embedded in skin and subcutaneous tissues. *The wound was contaminated with corn cobs.*[277] These injuries are consistent with Mr Mandal's description.

X-rays of both thighs revealed multiple pellets embedded, but no fractures. One pellet lay at the base of the penis, while another lay anterior to the right hip joint.

The patient was resuscitated in the Accident and Emergency Department. He received Tetanus toxoid, along with intravenous Cefuroxime 1gm and Metranidazole 500mg. His wounds were cleaned and dressed with dressings soaked in Povidone Iodine. Thereafter he was prepared ready to go to the operating theatre.

The patient was in the operating theatre at approximately 1:45am on 21 August 1999. I assisted Mr Anil Chakrabarti, Consultant on-call, and Mr Mandal. The patient was re-examined under anaesthesia. [...]

On the left thigh there was a 10 cm x 10 cm wound in the distal part of the thigh, with underlying muscle exposed and *grossly contaminated with shot pellets and vegetable matter.*[278] On the right thigh there were multiple areas of shot entry. At the base of the penis there was a pellet palpable subcutaneously.

All wounds were irrigated with copious amounts of hydrogen peroxide and normal saline. Devitalised tissues were excised till free bleeding was obtained from the tissues. All wounds were explored and several lead shots were removed. The shot at the base of the penis was removed with the help of a stab incision.

All wounds were left open and dressed with Jelonet, gauze and crepe. In the post-operative period, the patient received intravenous antibiotics, and his legs were kept elevated.

---

[276] Mr Prabhudesai does not record who provided him with this information.

[277] See Christine Rumble's statement in entry **254**. Her statement completely contradicts this point (but was never brought up at trial by Tony's barrister).

[278] This again undermines the statement attributed to nurse Rumble.

This description is consistent with the account given by Mr Mandal."[279]

What this adds to our knowledge

Clearly there's the issue of pieces of corn and other vegetable matter in Fearon's wounds which nurse Rumble had said in her statement she didn't see. Isn't that odd?

Where did the information come from in which Ashish Prabhudesai claimed that Fearon had been hit from approximately twenty yards about two hours before? As we have seen, Fearon claimed to have walked 20-30 yards up a track before being shot.

The statement provided to Tony did not flow. It was repetitive. It had all the hallmarks of having been interfered with.

Sun
26 SEP
unknown
witness 74
285

unknown location

Official records show that Supt John Richard Hale, stationed at police HQ in Norwich, made a statement about his role in the incident. It was alleged that he first attended Bleak House at shortly after 2:45pm and undertook overall command of the officers present. Yet, despite being in overall command of the situation, his statement was a mere 1½ pages in length. This is the official statement attributed to the Superintendent:

"At 2:45am on Saturday 21 August 1999, I went to Hungate Corner where I met CI Curtis, Inspector Chilvers and PS Davidson and took command.

I received a briefing and understood that an individual had been taken to hospital with leg wounds, having alleged that he had been shot at Bleak House.[280]

I also understood that the owner/occupier of Bleak House, Anthony Edward Martin, could not be contacted, that Bleak House was silent and in darkness and that Martin's motor vehicle was apparently not at the house.[281]

As a result of subsequent inquiries, I went with Inspector Turner of Cambridgeshire Police, and CI Curtis to Wisbech police station, where I liaised with acting Supt Hobbs, Cambridgeshire Constabulary.

---

[279] This appears to me to be a strange comment to be made, since how would he know what was in Mr Mandal's statement if the statements were made independently in the interest of justice? And why would he mention it twice in the same statement?

[280] According to the statements of police officers, paramedics and Paul and Jacqueline Leet, Fearon didn't mention at what location he had been shot. This 'fact' has been included to sow a seed that Fearon was shot by Tony inside the house.

[281] Refer back to entry **105** – the police had had sight of Tony's car at the Marmion and were aware that he would be inside.

At approximately 5am the same day, I went to the Marmion House Hotel where I saw parked in the rear yard a silver Nissan Bluebird estate, reg C460APW.

Shortly after 6am on the same day, I was present at Wisbech police station when Cambridgeshire officers brought to the station an individual I now know to be Anthony Edward Martin.

I subsequently stood down the armed containment at Emneth Hungate. I handed the investigation over to Western Division officers, and a search of the scene was arranged."

And that was that – the entire statement of the commanding officer of a murder investigation. Do you think it's credible? If so, why did he not mention the helicopter having been deployed, particularly since he'd admitted liaising with high-ranking officers from Cambridgeshire?

This is the first statement I could find that even mentioned that some police officers had apparently gone to the property after all. According to Hale, he had been briefed that the house was in darkness. He failed to say who briefed him. He failed to state what checks and balances he had employed in order to satisfy himself that the quality of the information he'd been given was credible. This is, I suggest, a glaring error in what was, in my opinion, a deeply flawed, biased and corrupt investigation.

In order to ascertain that Bleak House was in darkness, one would surely have had to circumnavigate the entire property, i.e. the front, sides and rear. I remind you that the official version is that Frederick Jackson Barras was lying close by and so, if this statement is to be believed, why on earth didn't anyone find him? Put another way, do you believe this statement? Do you trust the authenticity of any of the police statements?

I don't and I'll tell you why – Tony's bedroom was at the rear of the house and during his refurbishment of the house, he had rigged up the electricity in such a way that the low-wattage light bulb was *never* off. Thus, in the darkness that is the darkness of the countryside (and believe me it is incredibly dark in that area – I've been to the house on 20 August at the same time of night as the alleged burglary and it really is extraordinarily dark with little light pollution), a light would have been shining from Tony's bedroom. *It could not have been missed.* And for this reason, I say that these statements were fabricated, that they are fanciful and that some officers lied and fraudulently created them.

Hale claimed in the final paragraph of his statement that he arranged for a search of the scene to be conducted *after* he had allegedly handed the case over to officers from Norfolk's western division.

Why hadn't he arranged – being the officer in charge – for a search to be conducted as soon as possible after he had been informed that the house was "silent and in darkness" and that Tony Martin's car was not there? Surely this suggested that there was no lone gunman holed up inside the house ready to take pot-shots at the police. Surely this suggests that it would have been completely safe for the police to have conducted a search as early as 2:45am.

I'll remind you again of the statement by PC Cant made on 24 August 1999: "There is no street lighting in this location and the area was in total darkness. I could view the copse through a night viewing device but could not see any buildings in the copse nor signs of movement."

And, of course, the police narrative at that stage was that they couldn't even find the house. Someone, it appears, had slipped up in fabricating the evidence against the farmer because Hale claimed he had been told the house was "silent and in darkness" and in order to ascertain that it was silent you'd surely have to get pretty close.

So, the issue remains that the police either did go to the house much earlier than they told the public, or that they didn't go to the house that early, in which case Hale has lied. The police cannot have it both ways.

CORRUPTION ALERT — *Strong evidence of falsified statement of police superintendent*

I draw your attention once more to the fact that Hale made no mention of the helicopter – isn't that an appalling 'oversight' for the commander of the police operation to have made? And yet Hale's statement was entered into evidence and read to the jury to peddle the lies and false narrative concocted by the police.

And in what is a sad indictment on the complete rottenness and corruption of the court system in England & Wales, Tony's barrister failed to call Hale as a witness and robustly cross-examine him with regard to the truthfulness of his statement. You see the only reason that Hale's statement had been read out and Hale not required to put in a personal appearance at court was because Tony's defence counsel would have agreed the statement with the prosecution prior to the commencement of the trial – knowing that he would pass over on the opportunity to ask questions of the "commanding officer".

In the Norfolk Constabulary's own CAD report, I could find no confirmation that Supt Hale had attended Bleak House at any time.

Sun
26 SEP
3.15 pm – 3.30pm
witness 102
286

unknown location

There is a statement attributed to SOCO Ian Bradshaw on this date, but it was not recorded where he made it, or to whom it was made, or at what time it was made. Apparently on Wednesday 25 August 1999, at the request of DS Eglen, he attended Bleak House for the purpose of swabbing a staircase area for possible firearms and gunshot residue. [See also entry **199**].

"I arrived at the scene at 2:50pm and spoke to DS Eglen at 3pm. I commenced my examination of the staircase at 3:15pm and used a total of three swabs - one each for the banister handrail, banister newel post, and wall adjacent to staircase.

I sealed the swabs in an exhibit bag numbered 380793 as IB/1 and the remainder of the examination kit in a bag numbered C143424 as exhibit IB/2. I completed the examination at 3:30pm and left the scene at 3:54pm. I later placed both exhibits in the secure Scenes of Crime exhibit store at King's Lynn police station bearing the reference BRW/233/99-D."

On its face, a seemingly innocuous statement, but it was to have great significance in the months to come. Are you at all concerned that Bradshaw didn't make this statement until a full month after he had allegedly swabbed the stairs? How long does it take to write a 146-word statement after all?

Sun
26 SEP
unknown
witness 53
287

unknown location

There is a second statement attributed to 29-year-old PC 9130 Clare Alexandra Smith in which she stated "Further to my last statement, of 21 August 1999, I would like to add that at 3:00am on that date, I handed Exhibits CAS1 to CAS10 to DS Newton at King's Lynn police station." The statement did not contain the usual details of to whom it was made, at what location or at what time. It was not witnessed.

Sun
26 SEP
unknown
UNUSED
witness 53
288

unknown location

There is a third statement attributed to PC 9130 Clare Smith which was recorded as having been made immediately following her second statement.

   Again, the statement did not contain the usual details of to whom it was made, at what location or at what time. Nor was it witnessed.

   Of the three statements attributed to this constable, this was the only one not used at trial:

"Further to my last statement I would like to add, that on 21 August 1999, I made notes on a piece of paper, concerning names of people involved in the treatment of Brendon Fearon, whilst at the Queen Elizabeth Hospital, King's Lynn. I also made additional notes on the paper.

I can exhibit this piece of paper as CAS/11. On the same day at approximately 2:15am, I received from PC 1282 Miller a piece of paper, which were his original notes of the conversation with Brendon Fearon. I took possession of the paper, and passed it along with my exhibit CAS/11 to PS[282] Newton, at King's Lynn police station at 4:30am."

Clearly this statement and her previous ones raise a number of issues, not only with regard to police officers using random pieces of paper when they have pocket notebooks provided, but also because of the fact that the constable claimed to have prepared a list of all the people involved in treating Brendon Fearon and yet this list never got entered into evidence.

And did you notice that she claimed to have given *her* piece of paper an exhibit number, but not the piece of paper allegedly handed to her by PC Miller? Clearly, the Miller piece of paper never found its way as an exhibit into court.

Even more worryingly, PC Smith exhibited Fearon's clothes as CAS 1-10 and yet only exhibits CAS/1, CAS/2, CAS 5-7 were entered into evidence at trial.

So that we are sure, the items *not entered into court* were: a pair of blue socks, CAS/3 and CAS/4, a pair of Nike trainers, left shoe as exhibit CAS/8 and right shoe CAS/9. The plastic carrier bag into which Fearon's clothes were said to have been placed by the hospital staff was exhibit CAS/10.

The trainers would have, I believe, told a different story from the police narrative that Fearon had gone across a lawn, through an orchard and across a muddy cornfield (there had been an inordinate amount of rain that August) on his way to the Leets'. Any half-decent analysis of the soil and plant seeds or matter on the trainers would have shown, I believe, that Fearon did not undertake that epic journey that night and that they were relatively clean. Which is the most likely reason why they were not entered as evidence into court. But, again, we are forced to ask "Why didn't Tony's barrister ensure that they were shown to the jury?"

---

[282] I think this should be DS Newton.

Mon	
27 SEP	
unknown	
witness 102	
289	

Harborne, Birmingham

Amongst the plethora of legal papers that Tony put at my disposal were literally hundreds of letters from members of the public.

The following one was sent by Mark Curren to Nick Makin, Tony's new solicitor from M&S Solicitors in Leicestershire. On the advice of neighbour Richard Portham and Malcolm Starr, Tony dispensed with the services of Paul Croker and Kenneth Bush solicitors.[283]

"Thank you for taking the time to speak to me at the end of last week. Please do pass my good wishes on to your client.

As I said, if there is anything I can do to help, then I'm quite happy to volunteer such time as you are able to use an extra pair of hands. I'm a veteran of quite a few murder cases during several years of private practice in Leicester. I have been a manager at the CCRC for the last eighteen months and I'm not too proud to muck in with a bit of filing and typing if that's what's needed! Give me a call at your absolute convenience."

As far as I have been able to ascertain, Mr Curren did not receive a phone call from M&S Solicitors.

Mon	
27 SEP	
2.30 pm	
witness 19	
290	

Bethel Street police station, Norwich

Tony Bone's accomplice at the Farmwatch meeting was Derek Stuart. Bone verbally gave the presentation whilst Stuart "listened and took notes as necessary".

Seven months after the meeting, a statement was produced in which the following observations were made by Mr Stuart:

"During [Tony Bone's] presentation he was frequently interrupted by a male who was sat at the back of the room on the left as I looked at the room. This person's comments were obstructive to the meeting. He kept saying that what we were proposing was a waste of time and that people had to look out for themselves. As we have a number of years' experience in the security of farms and our practices, I dismissed this male as someone to take no notice of,

---

[283] Tony has told me on more than one occasion that when he first met Makin, the solicitor told him that it was "vitally important to get inside the house to preserve evidence" and that Croker had told the farmer that the police "won't let us into the house." If what Croker had claimed was true, the normal procedure would simply have been to seek a court order forcing the police to allow entry to Tony's defence team. We also have to ask why the police wouldn't allow entry to Bleak House – what had they to hide?

although this was difficult as for the main part, this male spoilt the presentation. I have never seen this male before and at the time of the meeting, did not know who he was.

Following the shooting incident and on speaking to another local farmer, I have realised that the male described above as disrupting our meeting is Tony Martin. Although gypsies/travellers were discussed at length during the evening, *I cannot remember Martin specifically mentioning them or making any comments regarding the use of firearms.*[284]

As a result of this meeting, I can say that it is apparent to me that the farmers[285] living in Fenland/West Norfolk, have a real fear of crime which they feel the police struggle to address. They believe the majority of the crimes are carried out by gypsies/travellers."

Mon
27 SEP
6.45 pm
witness 31
291

home address of Darren Cooper

According to official records, 32-year-old Darren James Cooper, landlord of the Cardinal's Hat pub in Newark, made a statement to DC Buxton. This statement is listed in HOLMES on line S148.

What did he add to our knowledge of the case? Firstly, he informed us that he knew of Bark "because he is now the owner of a white Ford Granada that I used to own. It is F98LHJ, and I owned it for about a year up until the middle of July, 1999, when I sold it to Joe Price for £230 when it had failed the MOT test.

Joe Price was a regular at the Cardinal's Hat, and is a bit of a dealer in scrap and cars. He told me afterwards that he had sold the car on to Bark. I asked him who it was so I could fill in the new owner details before sending the registration document off to Swansea.

Joe did not know Bark's address, so I left the document with him to give to Bark so he could fill it in himself. Bark had bought the white Ford Granada from him."

---

[284] Clearly this is of great importance. See entry **352**.
[285] Note the use of the plural word "farmers" – Tony Martin's long-held (and accurate) views that farmers and locals "have a real fear of crime which they feel the police struggle to address. They believe the majority of the crimes are carried out by gypsies/travellers" was clearly held by many in the region. Yet the Police and the CPS tried to portray Tony as a lone voice with widely-differing views from "the norm". He wasn't a lone voice – the only difference between him and others was that he had the courage to speak out against corruption and ineptitude within the police and, as a result, found himself targeted by the very organisation meant to ensure one's safety and keep the peace.

The official Norfolk Constabulary CAD report had the car registered to Darren Cooper since 20 February 1999 and that it was still registered to him at the time of the August incident, not Bark or Price. Had the car really been sold to Price? Had it really been sold on to Bark at the time of this incident? If it really was the "getaway car", could Cooper or Price have been driving the Granada that night?

The pub landlord added the following which is of some interest to us: "I've heard about the shooting incident at Emneth, and can state that I did not know Fred Barras and have not heard of any connection between him and Bark.

I do know Brendon Fearon, as he was an occasional visitor to the Cardinal's Hat. I have never seen Fearon and Bark together.

Whilst working behind the bar at the Cardinal's Hat I heard all sorts of talk from various people. A pub regular told me that Bark had burgled the house twice before and had been warned off going for a third time."

Clearly this is of some significance because if the rumours were true, Bark had been to Bleak House on two previous occasions. If he had been "warned off" going a third time, this would suggest that there were others higher up the food chain doing the warning. But just who was doing the warning and why?

Again, if you had been Tony's barrister, wouldn't you have wanted to explore all you could about the rumours?

And what do we make of the fact that Mr Cooper's step-daughter, Lisa Dobbin, was going out with Fred Barras? Even though she supposedly kept her meetings with Fred a secret, can we be sure that her mother, two sisters and brother or no pub regular informed the landlord that his daughter was seeing Fred? In her statement dated 27 September 1999 (recorded as having been taken at 8pm at her home address – though the name of the officer taking the statement wasn't recorded), Lisa Dobbin said: "My mum found out that I was seeing Fred and banned me from going out with him." Yet apparently Mr Cooper did not know about Fred Barras.

Mon 27 SEP
unknown
witness 76
292

unknown location
According to official records,[286] police inspector Alan Henry Menrig James stationed in the Operations Department at Bessemer Road, Norwich made the following statement:

"I can state that in relation to a police search at Emneth sometime after 21 August 1999, I received documents relating to this search from the police search advisor Inspector Rush. These documents (ref PR/1) I placed in the relevant office file."

---

[286] HOLMES, line S157.

What this adds to our knowledge

Surely the inspector could have been more precise than simply stating: "Sometime after 21 August..." and he should have listed all the documents to which he referred. [See also 20 April 2000]. Exhibit PR/1 was, in fact, a police Search Report said to have been written by Inspector Paul Rush. The search was in relation to 21 August 1999 – the day after Tony fired his shotgun. [See entry **281**].

CORRUPTION ALERT — *Search report not entered into court*

According to the official list of exhibits entered at trial, this very important search report had not been entered. It contained the 'discovery' of the body and no doubt the time the body was found and the circumstances of its 'discovery'.

Mon 27 SEP — **5.55 pm** — UNUSED — witness 76 — **293**

home address of David Fitzjohn

David Fitzjohn, 55, a self-employed painter and decorator, used to work at Woods' Garage at West Walton where Tony took his cars. He stated to PC Caine that he had known Tony for about 15 years. In the last five years or so Fitzjohn had gone to Tony's orchards to pick apples and plums. Tony would never take money for these, but Fitzjohn's mother would make him chutney and jam in return. Fitzjohn saw him about twice a year and he described the farmer as "a normal, pleasant chap." Fitzjohn also confirmed that Tony had on occasions used travellers to help pick the apples at harvest time.

What this adds to our knowledge

This statement provides a fascinating insight – that Tony would not accept money for the fruit that Fitzjohn took because he would receive chutney and jam in return. This is the image of the rural idyll that the farmer longed for - when neighbours would help one another out and when money need not change hands because "one good turn deserves another."

> Yes, I certainly did employ travellers to help pick my apple crop. I did not employ them often, but I did use them after I had my thrombosis because I was in a lot of pain from it. I agreed a price and we shared the money that the crop earned. By 'shared' I mean that I went 50-50 with them. This seemed to be the fairest way of doing business. They needed my land, my trees and my crop, and I needed their labour."

Again, this appears to be indicative of Tony's real mind-set. To my knowledge, he has never hated travellers or gypsies per se – his anger was directed towards people who stole or who committed other crimes or who threatened and offered violence. His dislike was for those who threatened his concept of a rural idyll.

Mon
27 SEP
7.20 pm
UNUSED
294

home address of Margaret Hodgson
A small-holder in Outwell and someone who went on to become a local parish councillor, Margaret Hodgson was motivated to call the police about what she had seen on the night of the shooting:

"On Friday 20 August 1999, after 10pm, as my husband was at home, I heard the unusual noise of a helicopter flying overhead. As this was so unusual, I went out onto my driveway and noticed it flying near to Emneth and Marshland St James. I noticed a very powerful searchlight, which again got me wondering what was happening. As this was happening, I was aware of two sets of headlights travelling along Robbs Lane towards my house and the Wisbech Road. Although the Wisbech Road is busy, Robbs Lane is very quiet. My suspicions about these two cars were roused because of the helicopter.

I watched the vehicles approach the junction of Robbs Lane with the Wisbech Road. I moved along my driveway and noticed that both vehicles were turning onto the Wisbech Road in my direction and towards Downham Market.

As the first vehicle passed me, the headlights of the second vehicle illuminated the registration number of the first car. I recall the registration number as E557DJF. I did not write this number down, but I am absolutely certain that the number is correct. I noticed that the colour of the car was blue. I recall that the second car was beige in colour. I cannot give any other details of the make of vehicles, other than they were saloons rather than estates or vans. The second vehicle I recall the numbers of the index number as 337. Again, I am certain that the numbers were in the registration number.

The visibility that night was good, the sky was clear and it was a starlit night. I am unable to say how many occupants were in each vehicle."

> **CORRUPTION ALERT** — *Civilian witness contradicts police over times of helicopter flights*

I found this statement in the Unused Material file. Why would the police or prosecution not want to use it?

Quite clearly, Mrs Hodgson mentioned the helicopter flying above Bleak House around 10:30pm and this militated against the times given by senior police officers. So, who to believe?

We need to again seriously question the integrity of Tony's counsel at trial. Any incorruptible barrister would have called Mrs Hodgson as a witness because her testimony seriously challenged the timings being promoted by the police.

And we ought to consider the possibility that there were two helicopter flights that night – one around 10:30pm (sent up as the result of Tony firing his gun inside the house) and another around 1am (following the shooting of Barras and Fearon on farmland).

Mon 27 SEP — unknown — UNUSED — 295

unknown address

PC 1282 Jonathan Miller allegedly made a second statement on this date. Like the one he was said to have made on 23 August 1999, neither was entered as evidence into court. Both should have been in the interests of justice:

"I was on uniform duty on Saturday 21st August 1999 in the company of PC 9130 Smith. At 00:50 hrs I attended the Accident and Emergency resuscitation unit at King's Lynn Queen Elizabeth Hospital and made written notes on a piece of paper. The notes were taken from the answers given by Brendon Fearon, the male being treated by medical staff at that time.

I can exhibit these written notes as JM/1."

Tue 28 SEP — unknown — witness 60 — 296

unknown location

According to official records, Norwich-based PS 3065 Ian Fletcher, a fully trained search officer having attended Home Office approved courses, was the search team leader on Thursday 2 September 1999 with PS Mizen as POLSA. Fletcher stated that "During a search of the farmhouse, officers seized various items from the house. These were handed to PS Mizen, who maintained a full log of the search."

| CORRUPTION ALERT | *Jury misled as CPS again 'cherry-pick' evidence entered into court* |

PS Fletcher apparently made two statements – the second one being on 28 October 1999. From HOLMES, *we learn that the second statement apparently referred to his being part of a search team on 21 August. However, I have been unable to find that statement. Intriguingly, the first statement was not entered into court as evidence, whilst the second one was.*

Notice, too, that PS *Fletcher referred to the seizure of "various items" and a "log of the search". Ordinarily, these would have been listed and exhibited. But this was no ordinary case...*

Tue
28 SEP
unknown
witness 105
297

unknown location

Norwich-based DS *Eglen – whom we first met the day after Tony fired his shotgun and who gained entry into Bleak House via the exit window (thus disturbing the alleged scene of the crime) - made six statements in total[287] that I could find and on 28 September 1999, whilst the truth was emerging about the Farmwatch meeting, he mentioned that he found the holdalls allegedly taken to the farmhouse by Fearon and Barras and the silver inside the breakfast room and that the house was in a state of disrepair:*

"At 10:50am on Sunday 22 August 1999[288] I attended Bleak House, where I assisted other officers[289] in a scenes of crime examination of the premises.

The house was in very poor repair, overgrown outside, with rubbish and rubble in all rooms of the ground floor.

---

[287] Lines 150, 150a, 150b, 150c, 150d and 150e. The statement made on 6.10.99 consisted of 16 pages. That made on 24.11.99 consisted of one page, that on 28.9.99 (two pages), that on 21.10.99 (one page) and that on 5.11.99 (two pages).

[288] Notice that this is DS Eglen's *first* statement of six and yet he didn't make any mention whatsoever of having attended Bleak House on Saturday 21 August 1999. Surely, in your first statement, you'd want to start at the beginning of your work on the inquiry and mention the very first time you arrived at Bleak House and commenced your investigation? This first statement was not used as evidence and I found it in the Unused Material file.

[289] Notice that he doesn't mention the names of the "other officers" who were allegedly in attendance on this day. This is either slipshod work or deliberately vague so as not to be held accountable.

To one side of the main living room was a Welsh dresser and between it and a ladder in the centre of the room I saw three holdall bags which I seized.

Exhibit JE/2[290] was a Rogue sports bag, colour black. I searched the bag and took from it exhibit JE/2A, a silver jug, and exhibit JE/2B, a silver pot.

Exhibit JE/3 was a Borderline holdall, colour purple, it contained two other black holdalls and two bin liners.

Exhibit JE/4 was a Canton holdall, colour black. I searched the bag and took from it exhibit JE/4A, a silver jug.

I packaged all the items and at 3:08pm I handed exhibits JE/2, JE/2A, JE/2B, JE/3, JE/4 and JE/4A to DC 356 Peters."

DS Eglen he makes no mention of having previously attended the farmhouse. This becomes significant in later entries.

Secondly, it appears that some of the holdalls had items of "smalls" inside them – silver mustard pots and the like. The narrative being created is that Fearon and Barras placed these items in the bags they allegedly brought with them from Newark. In all the time I have known Tony, I have never seen him with any kind of bag and he has told me (as he had told the police) that the bags were not his and he had never seen them before.

Tue 28 SEP 2 pm witness 14 298

unnamed Norwich police station

The record shows that Tony Bone - a former firearms officer - made a statement in which he described himself as a director of Farmwatch, a company which was formed and owned by him and which collated intelligence about which valuables were on which farms and which farms were not part of the scheme, gave crime prevention advice and assistance to the farmers who were members of the scheme.

Bone stated that in January 1999 he was contacted by member Peter Huggins, a farmer of Marshland St James [see entry **262**], to the effect that there was a need for additional members in his area. Huggins specifically mentioned problems that farmers were having with the travelling community. Bone agreed with him that there was a need for additional members (he would, he's hoping to make money) and a meeting was arranged for 23 February.

It began around 7:30pm. Bone's intention was to inform those present at the meeting how Farmwatch worked. There were around 30 people present, the room was full and there were people standing at the back and sides of the room.

Bone gave a brief history of the forming of Farmwatch and then gave advice as to good practice and how the scheme could help between the farmers and the

---

[290] Notice that, in his first statement, he has commenced numbering the exhibits from 2, rather than, as we might expect, from 1, of which he makes no mention.

police in enforcing the service they got and reducing crime in the general area.

Bone claimed that in the course of this meeting *every* time [author's emphasis] he made a constructive point about how crime could be prevented or police action gained, one of the farmers who was sitting in the rear of the hall "took it upon himself to comment in a derogatory manner." Bone claimed that Peter Huggins told him after the meeting that this was Tony Martin. Apparently Bone and Huggins "had a discussion that he was a bit eccentric."

Bone – a former firearms officer who had colleague Derek Stuart making notes – claimed that he could not recall any specific comments but that Tony Martin was basically saying that it was a waste of time working with the police and with Farmwatch. Bone claimed that the farmer also said that "out there, you're on your own and you were the law and that you should stand up for your rights."

Bone added that he recalled "desperately trying to get these farmers on board to the scheme" (he would, it's his business – and note his use of the word 'desperately') but that he was "*constantly being interrupted by this one farmer.*"[291]

Bone added that he had had experience of speaking to large numbers of people and could normally handle the situation adequately. The Farmwatch director stated that the difficulty he had was that he had no idea of Tony Martin's 'gripe'. Bone described Tony as "very anti-establishment",[292] and that Tony referred to the loss of his shotguns. Bone claimed that Tony Martin specifically mentioned the problems he had with travellers and that if you involved the police, the travellers were likely to "burn your property down." [Author's note: Tony Martin, supported by the evidence of other farmers who were there that night, told me that he never said this at all, but a farmer sitting at the front of the hall had said it. Did you notice, by the way, how, for someone who claimed that "specific comments were difficult to recall", Bone had apparently recalled a significant number of comments after all?][293]

Bone claimed that as a result of Tony's "vociferous interruption" Farmwatch lost a large number of members wanting to join the scheme. [Author's note: so Bone would have a 'gripe' against Tony Martin because the farmer has allegedly

---

[291] As we have seen by way of the independent witness statements of other attendees at that meeting (which were suppressed and not entered into court as evidence), this comment by Bone is demonstrably untrue.

[292] Tony's view is "What right-minded individual would want to side with the Establishment when it is inherently corrupt and riddled with paedophiles?"

[293] At the top of each page on a witness statement is the following warning: "This statement, consisting of X pages each signed by me, is true to the best of my knowledge and belief and I make it knowing that, if it is tendered in evidence, I shall be liable to prosecution if I have wilfully stated in it anything which I know to be false or do not believe to be true." Bone, a former firearms officer, would obviously have been familiar with this warning.

lost him income – how much would you trust this witness statement based on this fact alone?]

Bone claimed – but provided no evidence - that after the meeting he notified the superintendent in community relations at police HQ, Norwich of his "concerns about the policing in that area", whatever that means. Bone stated that King's Lynn Division was "made aware of the situation in that area" yet failed to state precisely what "the situation in that area" was.

Tony Bone wanted farmers to join his scheme (and pay him money) and he would collate the information they gave to him and pass it on to the police. Tony Martin – and others – felt that this was an unnecessary step in the reporting of crime.

If a farmer experienced crime, he or she – as taxpayers - ought to be able to pick up the phone and get through to the police directly, not go through a 'middleman'. Some farmers felt that this was a dangerous precedent to set: those farmers who were members of Farmwatch might actually meet with the police and have their reports of crimes investigated, whilst those who were not members of Farmwatch might never get to meet the police and might never get their reports of crimes investigated. These farmers felt that it was, in effect, policing by private payment. I find it difficult to disagree with that point of view. It's also possible that Farmwatch was nothing more than a 'filtering system' for the police.

Some farmers thought that by collating information about what valuables certain farmers possessed and what security precautions they employed, Farmwatch was putting itself in a position of intelligence gathering not unlike that of burglars.

The comment Bone made – under penalty of perjury in his witness statement - about Tony Martin saying that if you involved the police, the travellers were likely to 'burn your property down' needed, in my opinion, further research. In all the time I worked with Tony, I'd never heard such a comment from him, or any comment whatsoever about burning any kind of property.

Tony told me that he had not said this at all, but that another farmer – sitting towards the front of the canteen – had said it. Again, I could not possibly just take his word for it, so I set about speaking with Richard Askew and some farmers who were there that night to try to establish the truth. What they told me astonished me. [Author's note: for the record Herbert, Askew, Melton, Cammack, and Judd all declined to give a statement to the police about the meeting and "the attitude of Martin" following the shooting in August.]

All of those I interviewed told me the same thing – that Tony Martin had never said any such thing about travellers being likely to burn down your property but that another farmer had said it.

And one man who attended that meeting told me – off the record – that the comment was actually posed by another farmer as a question to Bone in the form of "What do we do if travellers threaten to burn down our homes if we report them to the police?", to which Bone was alleged to have replied, "Then you tell them you'll burn down their caravans."

This man told me that he was so appalled at this statement from a former police officer that he immediately distanced himself from Farmwatch that night.

We have to accept that these comments were made to me "off the record" on the basis that I would not identify the man in this book and therefore he might not be telling the truth. However, he had no reason to lie and, in fact, he gave me the distinct impression that he knew that lies had been told at the trial and that he wanted to correct a wrong. He had nothing to gain from lying.

Note that Bone did not say anywhere in his statement that Tony Martin said the words: "I'd shoot the bastards!" at the meeting and it is logical to assume that either he, or his accomplice, would have remembered such a phrase being uttered. In fact, the opposite is true – Bone could not recall anything specific that Tony Martin said or was supposed to have said. We will return to this point – an extremely important point – later.

On pages 11 to 13 of HOLMES, entries A185 to A230 (some 45 lines of inquiry) inform us that the police had decided to take a statement from 45 different people "re the attitude of Martin towards gypsies and travellers". Given that a murder inquiry – in fact, any police inquiry – ought to be driven by a need to establish the truth, it is difficult to imagine why 45 statements were taken from people on the basis that they were trying to establish "the attitude of Tony Martin". This is an extremely worrying document, since it provides a unique insight into the narrow inquiry that was taking place: let's try to establish that Tony Martin was 'a loner, an eccentric and that he had a poor attitude towards gypsies and travellers.' Given these parameters, most of the farmers in Norfolk – indeed, most of the farmers in England – would be guilty of murder if they ever shot at an intruder in their homes.

Was Tony Martin being 'fitted up' by the police because he was a constant thorn in their side and because he reflected back to them their inadequacies and unprofessionalism as perceived by him and many others?

Was he being 'fitted up' by the police because he kept telling everyone about child abuse at Glebe House which the police didn't want to investigate because some of them might have been involved in the abuse?[294]

Or was Tony Martin being 'fitted up' by the police because his brother was in league with some rogue officers who might help Robin acquire Tony's land "via the back door"?

Were some members of the Norfolk constabulary in league with, and taking 'back-handers' from, the burglars and thieves stealing from Bleak House and the farm and other houses and farms in the area? Many locals were of the opinion that it was "highly suspicious" that the police never caught anybody or gained any convictions. We ought to consider all of this in the interest of justice.

---

[294] The author refers the reader to his book *Blueprint for Abuse*, Melville Press, 2017.

Perhaps in order to answer these questions, we need to examine the Unused Evidence book provided to Tony Martin's initial legal team. It is in this book that one can often find 'golden nuggets' of information that provide us with the 'bigger picture.' It is 'Unused' material for a reason and not by happenstance.

Bone's statement to the police was included in the Used Material book – in other words, it was entered at trial. Indeed, Bone's testimony was such that he spoke negatively about Tony Martin, who had, it should be remembered, allegedly cost Bone some money by turning some farmers off the Farmwatch scheme. Not the most reliable of witnesses one might assume, but a witness that Scrivener, Tony's barrister, failed to robustly cross-examine on his client's behalf.

CORRUPTION ALERT *Tony's barrister failed to robustly challenge police witness Bone*

It would have been easy to discredit Bone on the basis that he was angry that he had lost prospective members that night which had ultimately cost him money. So a jury could have heard that Bone might have been motivated by money when defaming Tony Martin. It would also have been easy to challenge Bone's fanciful claim that the farmer had been disruptive in the meeting by calling witnesses to the contrary. A little thought and preparation, and Bone's testimony could have been reduced to nought. Yet Tony's counsel never took that opportunity on behalf of his client. Why?

Wed
29 SEP
12.45 pm
witness 4
299

Hungate House, Hungate Corner, Emneth

Official records show that DC Cross took a statement from Mark[295] Riddington, the 35-year-old grandson of farmer Fred Deptford. Riddington said that Tony would often talk about crime in the area but had never mentioned gypsies or travellers to him and nor had he mentioned guns or firearms to him, although he knew "via the grapevine" that Tony had had his shotgun licence revoked. "It was common knowledge amongst the men in the area and within the farming community":

"Tony did speak to me about being broken into but, again, he didn't go into specifics. He would always put down the police when talking about crime, saying they were useless and never caught anyone. I felt Tony took the break-ins and

---

[295] Listed on the official list of witnesses as 'Martin' Riddington.

thefts personally. When he spoke like this, I informed him that we had been broken into 12 times in a period of 18 months.

Because of Tony's repeated break-ins to his property, I got the impression that he was intimidated by the fact that he was broken into so many times."

Riddington's statement adds to our knowledge because it highlighted the scale of the crime wave that was enveloping Emneth and the surrounding villages and, as Tony would often say:

> The police were in denial – they failed to record most of the crimes so as to massage their figures. They rarely, if ever, caught anybody."

This view, as we have seen, was shared by many farmers and locals in the area and also on a national basis, too. And, if they hardly ever caught anyone, the reasonable person might be driven to conclude that the police were in some way colluding with the criminals.

If you regard that comment about police corruption as fanciful, consider this:

"In a panoramic overview of police corruption, Phil Scraton examines the recent acknowledgement of embedded police corruption over Hillsborough, in the investigation of the murder of Stephen Lawrence and the infiltration and instigation of sexual relations with animal rights activists and others. The myth of policing by consent shatters when set against 'institutional differential policing', the manufacturing of evidence, entrapment and surveillance. *And, as Scraton shows, police corruption cannot be seen as a peripheral activity undertaken by the occasional officer, but rather needs to be understood as something related to the broader institution and activity of policing. Further, as Joanna Gilmore and Waqas Tufail go on to show, the mechanisms charged with 'policing the police' (most specifically the IPCC) not only fail to hold them to account, but can embed corruption further.*"[296] [Author's emphasis]

I believe that the level of police corruption in the Tony Martin case was on an industrial scale and that corruption within the police is not limited to a few "bad apples" but is culturally endemic and that the more you are prepared to be corrupt, the higher up the ladder you will rise. Like Gilmore and Tufail, I agree that the IPCC is as equally corrupt as the police it fails to properly investigate.

---

[296] Article entitled *How the Neoliberal Project Embeds Corruption in Britain*, by Jon Burnett, 1 July 2015, including a book review of *How Corrupt Is Britain?*, edited by David Whyte, Pluto Books, 2015. http://www.irr.org.uk/news/how-the-neoliberal-project-embeds-corruption-in-britain/.

Wed	
29 SEP	
1 pm	
witness 12	
300	

business address of David Patrick

According to official records, a statement was made by 53-year-old blacksmith David Patrick to DC Lovick which considerably adds to our knowledge of Tony. Patrick was the owner of Martin Works Agricultural Engineers in Wisbech. This was a general blacksmiths firm which mostly did repairs for the farming community. He had been in Wisbech for the past 35 years or so:

"In the past 5–6 years I have got to know a customer called Tony Martin. He would call in regularly at my works on probably a weekly basis if not for business then for a chat and coffee. He would always be on his own and I have never seen him with anybody else.

I have been to Bleak House to do work for Tony more than a dozen times or so – the last of which was a couple of weeks before the incident in August, where I fixed part of his combine harvester.

I remember this day because Tony wanted to show me round his garden. He had planted a lot of trees and shrubs and 'palms' around his garden which he had collected from all over the country. He had even planted a redwood tree in a pile of earth by one of the outbuildings.

Tony had told me about a lot of 'thieving' that had gone on at his farm which bothered him a lot. He would hide a lot of things amongst the trees and shrubs in his garden, including one of his tractors and a lawn mower. On one occasion he had hidden a 50-ton jack around the farm and forgot where he had hidden it for a while. He apparently eventually found it amongst some oil cans which were stacked by the side of one of his barns.

Tony also told me that he had collected 'Teddy' bears. Again he had got these from all over the country for one of his friend's kids. I never saw this collection however, or where he was meant to have taken it.

Tony has told me about the thieving from his farm, mainly tools etc. He told me about a grandfather clock which he had stolen and also a chest of drawers. He wasn't so much upset about the drawers but mainly about what was inside it. It was apparently family photographs and the such and this really upset him. He was not a happy chap. He did manage to get some of these photos back but I don't know how or when.

Tony has told me about a couple of incidents on his farm over the last year or so. The first was when he chased some people off his land who were in a white transit van.[297]

The other was when he chased some people who were stealing apples from his orchard.[298] Tony told me he had actually shot at these people, hitting their van and then reported them to Downham Market police.[299]

---

[297] A "white transit van" features regularly in this story. See entries for 1 September 1999 and 4 October 1999.

It was because of this incident that I always assumed that he had a shotgun but never had cause to ask him.

The time I was at his farm fixing his combine harvester (sometime this summer) Tony told me he had found a sawn-off shotgun all rusted up in his garden. He never showed it to me or said what he had done with it and I never thought more of it.

There was also an incident at Tony's where he had had a go at some travellers who had put their horses near his land. I know this because while Tony was visiting me at my work one of these horse-owners came in and Tony had a go at him complaining about the horses. Tony seemed more concerned that the horses would get insecticides in them and so hurt them.

I would say that Tony was a very law-abiding man. He would always make sure he had his car taxed on time and on one occasion drove into someone's parked car. Apparently he spent a lot of time knocking on doors to find the owner and when he eventually did, offered to pay for the damage. He could easily have driven off and left it.

Tony was physically a very strong man and not frightened of anyone. He was very strong-willed and not at all intimidated. Although very unclean, he is a very well-educated man and this comes across when you speak to him or hear him talking to others.

Tony had a strange word for describing thieves. He would call them 'perverts' which I couldn't understand.[300] He was concerned with having things stolen as *he had ordered some iron bars and bolts to do some sort of security to the inside of his house.* This work he did himself. This job I did on 24 May this year. I can state this because of the invoice for this work, number 11362. I produce this as my exhibit DJP/1. (The other invoice concerning the work done on his combine I will find and hand to the police.)"

---

[298] This refers to the 'shooting in the orchard' incident on Sunday 23 October 1994.

[299] Mr Patrick is mistaken (or his statement had been altered) – Tony didn't shoot at anybody at all: he fired into the ground. Additionally, he did not shoot at 'people' plural, but shot into the ground when Mark Aldin, singular, threatened the lives of his dogs. [See entry dated 23 October 1994.]

[300] In the five years that I have known Tony, he has often used the word 'perverts' to describe the paedophile teachers he was abused by, or thieves or other criminals. The word can, of course, be used when referring to those individuals who are corrupt. Common usage has meant that the word 'perverts' is associated with sexual offenders, but in its wider context, it can be used to describe – and this is how Tony often uses the word –*anyone* who perverts or distorts the natural order of things or the course of justice, as in *perverting the course of justice*.

> **What this adds to our knowledge**
>
> I suggest that Patrick's statement provides us with greater knowledge of the mind-set of Tony Martin, and also provides (I argue) a robust defence to the charges he faced.

Patrick had known Tony for around 5 or 6 years and been to the farm and worked with the farmer on fixing machinery or, as he later said, to make bars and bolts for *internal security*. I'll return to this point shortly.

Patrick also pointed out Tony's love of plants and trees. I have seen this myself when he has given me tours of his land. He knows many of the Latin names of the plants and he has told me that he has a deep passion for the giant redwood and sequoia trees and it is an ambition of his to visit California (he has never been) to see the vast forests of such trees.

Clearly Patrick confirmed that Tony had been the victim of several thefts, something the police were later to deny in their attempts to make Tony out to be a liar.

And then we learnt from Patrick that Tony collected 'teddy bears' from all over the country as presents for a friend's child. I am confident, from having worked extremely closely with the man that his motives for doing this were entirely honourable, but he has told me that if his case was brought nowadays, he'd be labelled a paedophile or accused of grooming the child. In my view, Tony can be innocently naïve – he means well without always seeing how his kindnesses can be misinterpreted by those with a hidden agenda. I was also with him when he visited Wisbech Sunday Market just prior to Christmas 2017 and he bought a beautiful merry-go-round and a large cuddly toy for children of friends. I mentioned that if certain people were keeping him under surveillance, they'd probably make a great deal out of a [then] 73-year-old man buying such presents when he had no children or grandchildren. "If they're that stupid, let them make something of it if they want!" was his response and I couldn't help but laugh and think he's got it right – he doesn't waste his life worrying about what others think of him.

The "white transit van" was mentioned by several people in the village in their statements to the police – Emneth had been targeted by criminals from near and far, especially from Newark and the Nottingham area. Tony was alive to new vehicles or strangers being seen in the area and I wish I had such a community-spirited neighbour. However, some in the village thought themselves mature by laughing at him or calling him names like 'Mad Martin' or 'Lord of the Manor' or 'busybody'.

In all the time I've known Tony, his love of nature shines through, so I was not at all surprised to read that he didn't want horses on his land, not to be mean to travellers but rather to look out for the welfare of the animals, since he used insecticides on his crops which would, of course, have been harmful to the horses. It's so easy for small-minded people to criticise when they are not in possession of all the facts.

Now we return to David Patrick informing the police that he had prepared coach bolts and iron straps for Tony which the farmer fitted to the windows and doors himself.

However the police would spin the truth in this case, it is difficult to imagine a negative angle to a man who was so desperate about the high number of thefts and burglaries on his farm that he felt compelled to fix iron straps across the doors and windows *to keep burglars out* – surely an example of self-defence. "Little did I know it at the time," Tony told me, "but I was creating a prison for myself."

We will return to this issue when I come to discuss the trial.

Wed 29 SEP 4.20 pm defendant 301

secret location
Tony, the defendant in a murder trial, now made a statement to the police about the invasion of his property so that Fearon and Bark could be prosecuted for conspiracy to burgle (it can't be burglary itself because nothing was actually stolen on the night):

> On the evening of 20 August 1999, I was asleep in bed in my house at Bleak House. Sometime after nightfall, I heard what sounded like intruders breaking into my property. Upon going downstairs I disturbed the intruders. An incident occurred which I will not expand upon in this statement.
> I went back upstairs and when I came back down again the intruders had fled. Upon getting a torch I found bags on the floor which did not belong to me. In one of the bags I saw a sugar caster and another piece of silverware belonging to me.
> Nobody had permission to enter my house."

What this adds to our knowledge
Very simply, this statement was necessary to prosecute Bark and Fearon for their part in the alleged burglary, which is why Tony was not required to expand on the precise events of his firing his shotgun.

Wed 29 SEP 7 pm UNUSED 302

home address of David Golding

David Golding, 61, had lived and farmed in the area for over 30 years. He told DC Peters that since he and his wife had lived at their current address they had been the victims of crime on several occasions, having had equipment, roof tiles and diesel stolen.

Mr Golding confirmed that Tony Martin had not disrupted the Farmwatch meeting.

Farmer Golding added that he did not find anything that was said by Tony to be upsetting or distressing. He stated that Tony Martin did not say much more than many others at the meeting and "in fact some of what he said made a great deal of sense." He said that he was of the opinion that Tony did not seem to have much time for the police and that he and the people who were running the meeting did not exactly 'hit it off.'

After about two or three days after giving the matter some thought, farmer Golding joined the Farmwatch scheme.

Other farmers supported Tony Martin's version of events that night rather than that of Tony Bone's. In making a statement to DC Peters (who had interviewed Tony Martin in the days immediately after the shooting), Michael Doubleday,[301] then aged 49, said that, as far as he could recollect, Tony did not speak for long. He did not find what Tony said offensive: "in fact, it seemed at the time to make good sense." He also got the impression that many of those present were in agreement with Tony's remarks. Doubleday also formed the impression that Tony Martin and Bone did not see eye to eye: "I can recall Mr Bone said to Mr Martin that he didn't want either him or his type in Farmwatch, but I cannot recall that he gave any reasons as to why not."

It had been suggested to Doubleday by the police that Tony had tried to take over the meeting but he refuted that suggestion claiming that Tony had no more to say than many others. Doubleday added, "I would not say that Mr Martin's behaviour at the meeting was disruptive to the meeting, and I must confess to feeling some sympathy for what he had to say."

Perhaps the most enlightening comment made by Doubleday was that Bone had said to Tony Martin, "We do not want your sort in Farmwatch." Whilst Bone was entitled to have any member he wished in his scheme, it was a strange comment to make and appears to have been extremely defensive. Did Tony Martin touch a raw nerve with a former armed police officer who was touting for more business and who was apparently not willing to learn from others or take on board alternative views from his own? I leave you to judge.

---

[301] In an unused statement attributed to him dated 29 September 1999 and made at his home address at 1pm to DC Peters.

Philip Didwell[302] lived on the family farm with his wife Jean and two children (one of whom lived away), and he, like Doubleday, told police that in his opinion Tony had not been out of step with anything he said in the meeting.

CORRUPTION ALERT *Tony's barrister and CPS omit more evidence favourable to the farmer*

None of these positive statements made their way into the courtroom and yet Mr Bone's did. It's possible that a skilled barrister could have made out a good case to implicate former firearms officer Mr Bone in the shooting at Bleak House because Tony Martin seriously threatened his Farmwatch business.

Wed 29 SEP 11.51 am witness 118 303

unknown location

According to a statement (no location, no witness, no time) Paul Wade, stationed at Swaffham, was the duty Inspector at 11:51am when he authorised officers under Section 18 of the PACE Act 1984, to search a Nissan Bluebird motor vehicle Reg No. C460APW for articles connected with an offence of murder or attempt, articles such as firearms or cartridges which may have been used in a shooting incident.

The statement recorded that he completed a search form in respect of this authority which was entered onto the custody record of Tony Martin. (Custody No 2057-99 which he produced in evidence reference PAW/1).

The statement did not record whether anything was found in Tony's car. However, it raises some questions. If we refer back to the entry dated 9th September 1999, DC Adcock claimed that he and PC Caine found a live cartridge in Tony's car. Why would it need to be searched again, almost three weeks later and six weeks after Tony had fired his shotgun?

---

[302] In an unused statement attributed to him dated 2 November 1999 and made at his home address to PC Caine. (No time recorded).

Thur
30 SEP
unknown
304

letter sent to Bleak House

Some of the letters that Tony received were of a somewhat prosaic nature – reports on soil samples taken from his land and even an estimate: "To supply and fit steel plate to the outside of all windows and doors. To fit flat steel bars to inside of all windows and doors and secure with coach bolts."

The estimate to completely seal off Bleak House was in the sum of £3,300 (excluding VAT), but the cost to Tony Martin of sealing off his inheritance was incalculable.

Thur
30 SEP
unknown
305

unknown location

HOLMES lists at line S167 a statement attributed to PC 214 Simon James Stephenson, a trained dedicated exhibits officer[303] usually stationed at King's Lynn. There are also statements attributed to him listed at lines S167a and S167b which I will discuss after we have read his first one:

"At 4pm on Saturday 21 August 1999, I began duties as *assistant*[304] exhibits officer regarding an enquiry into the death of a male person who I now know to be Frederick Jackson Barras at Bleak House.

At 1:09pm on Sunday 22 August 1999, I attended Bleak House where I saw DC 8 Aldous[305] and I was shown the body of a deceased male lying at the rear.

At 2:10pm that day members of staff from Bowes[306] Funeral Directors, Methwold attended the scene. They recovered the body from the scene, conveying it to the Queen Elizabeth Hospital mortuary at King's Lynn. I escorted the body to the mortuary, arriving at 2:35pm that day.

At 2:50pm that day I formally identified the body to pathologist Dr Michael Heath. He then began a post-mortem examination of the body during which I acted as exhibits officer.

Also present were DCI Wright, DCI Grant,[307] Principal SOCO Rowlands, SOCO Bishop, SOCO Bradley and Pat Phoenix, mortician. During the course of the post-mortem examination I received the following exhibits, amongst a

---

[303] Note that he does not specifically state that he was the Exhibits Officer in this case.

[304] If PC Stephenson was the *assistant* exhibits officer who was the *official* exhibits officer?

[305] Notice that he does not mention seeing SOCO Bradley present. Cross-reference this with entries **305** (SOCO Bradley, who doesn't mention being present) and **344** (DS Eglen, who mentions her as being present). A mere bureaucratic oversight or a further example of police corruption?

[306] This should be Bowers.

[307] It is possible that Stephenson meant Detective Superintendent (not DCI) Christopher Grant who is listed in HOLMES at line 231.

number of other exhibits:[308] MJH/18, Rubber glove, right hand, and MJH/19, Rubber glove, left hand. At 6:45pm that day, the post-mortem examination was concluded.

I retained all the exhibits seized, including MJH/18, and MJH/19, in my possession. At 9pm that evening I went to the Scenes of Crime office in King's Lynn police station where I opened drying cabinet number 1. I placed a number of exhibits into the cabinet, including exhibits MJH/18, and MJH/19. At 9:40pm I resealed the drying cabinet, and turned it on.

At 2:10pm on Thursday 26 August 1999, I returned to the Scenes of Crime office, where I reopened drying cabinet number 1, removing the exhibits within. These included exhibits MJH/18, and MJH/19, which I then rebagged. At 3:30pm that day I placed exhibits MJH/18 and MJH/19 into the secure Major Incident Property Store at King's Lynn police station."

Stephenson took care to mention all those in attendance at the mortuary, a list which included SOCO Bradley but he didn't place her at Bleak House on the Saturday afternoon when others did place her there. This leads me to conclude that since she didn't place herself there that afternoon, she wasn't there and that those who did place her there had an ulterior motive. DS Eglen placed her there and I'll discuss this in greater detail in due course. [See also entries dated 28 September, 21 & 26 October, 5, 16 & 24 November].

CORRUPTION ALERT *No chain of custody regarding Barras's clothes*

It's evident that if PC Stephenson had seized the gloves allegedly worn by Barras, he'd also have seized the clothes that were removed from the body and placed them in the drier, too. However, I suggest that these clothes have mysteriously disappeared from his statement because they reveal far too much about how the teenager was killed and might well have shown that Tony Martin did not kill him.

---

[308] Had this case been run in accordance with the rule of law, all of these "other exhibits" ought to have been listed individually and given exhibit numbers. This routine procedure was not complied with and thus the entire trial was corrupted.

Thur
30 SEP
unknown
witness 108
306

unknown location

Records show that Thetford-based DC 178 Noel Andrew Adcock made a statement on this date, but we do not know where it was made, to whom it was made, or at what time it was made. Adcock had been engaged in the investigation of a shooting at Bleak House since 20 August 1999 and during the investigation it had been necessary for him to travel by car from Downham Market to Newark.

"Bearing in mind that Emneth Hungate is 2 miles away from Outwell which would have been on my route to Newark and Balderton is a short distance away from Newark, I am able to estimate my travelling time by car between Balderton and Emneth Hungate between 1hr 30mins and 2hrs. I would further state that these times vary this much due to traffic conditions and weather etc."

| CORRUPTION ALERT | *Evidence 'shuffled' between official documents to ensure its 'disappearance'* |

This statement was listed in HOLMES as not having been used in evidence, yet it WAS listed in the official list of witness statements used in court.

Yet the statement dated 15 November was listed in HOLMES as not being used as evidence, but it WAS listed in the list of witness statements entered into court.

Fri
1 OCT
unknown
witness 120
307

unknown location

Records show that on this date, acting DI Matthew Sharman made a statement in which he claimed that during the late evening[309] of Friday 20 August 1999, he was called on duty after a reported shooting incident at Emneth Hungate. On arrival at King's Lynn police station at 11:15pm, he took charge of the investigation, and remained in charge until relieved by DCI Wright at 8pm on Saturday 21 August:

"At 11:30am on 21 August, I went to the scene at Bleak House along with Inspector Rush and his police search team. Together we made an assessment of the area. We drove to the front of Bleak House. *Neither of us entered the house, and I took no part in the subsequent searches.*[310]

At 1:15pm the same day, I returned to King's Lynn police station."

---

[309] Note the lack of a precise time. This is probably because it is a lie. The Constabulary's own CAD report shows that Sharman was informed at 11:16pm, not earlier.

[310] Author's emphasis.

> **CORRUPTION ALERT** — *Bizarre and unrealistic claims made by officer in charge of case*

So, the very man who was recorded as having taken charge of the operation on the night of the shooting and who was still in charge until 8pm on the Saturday evening (after the body of Barras had allegedly been found at 2:32pm) and who had taken Fearon back to the house where the burglar was coerced into changing his mind about where Tony Martin was standing, now made an incredibly short statement about his role in the entire 'investigation'.

Notice that acting DI Sharman stated that, *some 12 hours after having been put in charge of the case*, he drove to the *front* of Bleak House and left. No mention of his getting out of his vehicle, no mention of others leaving the car, no mention of anyone going round to the *rear* of the house where the young Barras was said to have been lying. But omitting these possibilities from his statement does not mean that he did not take these actions.

Acting DI Sharman claimed he took no part in a search of Bleak House, but we cannot be sure because why wouldn't he get out of his car to assess the situation? How can you accurately assess the situation unless you get out of your vehicle? What, then, was he doing in the two hours that he was allegedly at the scene? What is clear is that he was recorded as having been in charge (which does not mean that he *was* in charge because he may have been the "fall guy" for an unnamed superior officer for whom Sharman was covering up.)

Are you convinced when the officer purporting to be in charge of a murder incident claims that he didn't enter the house in which the murder allegedly took place or walk all the way around the outside of the house? In other words, do you believe him when he says he didn't get out of his car? This was never brought up by Tony's barrister at trial, of course.

According to HOLMES, Sharman made a total of six separate statements, not all of them entered into court. The sequence went unused, used, used, unused, used, unused. Such is the integrity of the British legal system.

Fri
1 OCT
unknown
witness 104
308

unknown location

In a statement attributed to SOCO Theresa Bradley, it claimed that on Tuesday 24 August 1999 she had been present during a search of the area at the rear of Bleak House. At 2:40pm, as a result of the search, she was given possession of a large wooden-handled chisel, exhibit reference AMH/2, which she packaged and labelled.

At 7:40pm the same day, at King's Lynn police station, she handed exhibit AMH/2 to PC 376 Matthews.

| **What this adds to our knowledge** | Firstly, the chisel was said to have been that used by Fred Barras. We have no definite proof because he was alleged to have been wearing rubber gloves and thus there were no fingerprints. But, as I have previously pointed out, how did he manage to keep hold of that chisel after allegedly having been shot inside Bleak House and, clutching his chest, climbing out of a window to make his escape? It's simply not credible. |

SOCO Bradley played a much greater part in the murder inquiry than this brief statement would indicate – so that immediately causes me concern. She made no mention of having (allegedly) been at Bleak House on 21 August to assist DS Eglen in erecting a tent over the body of Barras. She made no mention of attending Downham Market police station at 10am on the Sunday following the shooting to be present at a conference. Nor did she mention then going to the QE Hospital that same day to be present at the post-mortem on Fred Barras.

Thirdly, I'm concerned that this brief statement was allegedly made some six weeks after the alleged finding of the chisel. Why would it take so long to make such a simple statement?

Fourthly, I'm concerned that SOCO Bradley failed to mention precisely where this chisel was found – "at the rear of Bleak House" is far, far too vague, particularly for a police statement. Nor has she provided the serial number on the evidence bag.

Thus, are we forced to conclude that this statement was entirely fabricated or at the very least edited? SOCO Bradley was prosecution witness number 104. Yet her evidence had little probative value – it didn't add to the questions "Did Fred Barras even reach Bleak House?" or "Did Tony Martin even shoot him?"

Furthermore, what adds to my concern is that HOLMES listed SOCO Bradley as having made *three* statements: a second (consisting of two pages) on 11 October 1999 in which it was alleged that on 25 and 26 August she had made a video of Bleak House including outbuildings and the surrounding area.

On 8 November 1999, she was alleged to have made a *third* statement (consisting of two pages) which was listed as "SOCO who attends Bleak House. Produces various exhibits from the scene."

> **CORRUPTION ALERT** — *'Missing' statements from Scene of Crime Officer*
>
> *I have been unable to locate statements two and three. Does that concern you as much as it concerns me? Even if all three statements attributed to SOCO Bradley are genuine, why would she omit (allegedly) assisting DS Eglen erect a protective tent over the body of Barras? Why would she omit attending a conference to discuss the murder? Why would she fail to mention being present at the first autopsy?*

As we have seen, in his statement dated 30 September 1999 [see entry **305**], PC Simon Stephenson had also placed Theresa Bradley at the first autopsy. Yet Theresa Bradley herself didn't make a statement to show that she was there unless, of course, she mentioned this in her second or third statements which I have been unable to locate.

However, the HOLMES book recorded that she didn't have any involvement in the investigation until 24 August 1999.

Fri
1 OCT
1.15 pm
UNUSED
309

home address of John Balls

Records show that the 43-year-old local postman John Charles Balls made a statement to DC Adcock which was never used as evidence in support of Tony. Postman Balls had been working in that role for 14 years and delivered letters etc on the morning round in the area of St John's Fen End and Marshland Smeeth. His last delivery each morning, around 11:30am, was to Peddar Meadow House, Fen Road, Marshland Smeeth.

"This road is known locally as Moyse's Bank. Travelling from this last delivery towards Hungate Corner, I am aware of a property to my right. I did not know at the time but have since found out that the property is Bleak House. I do not know the owner and I have never delivered post there.

When I have finished my round each day, I travel down Moyse's Bank towards Hungate Corner. Then I turn right onto Smeeth Road and then left onto Wilkins Road, also known as the Walsoken Road.

As I drive along the Smeeth, having finished my round, I am aware of the orchard which runs along the front of the property belonging to Bleak House. I recall this orchard because, last year, I remember the apples were not picked and allowed to fall from the tree and rot. Beyond the orchard are farm buildings; to the Moyse's Bank side of these is woodland and shrubs. Working closer to Moyse's Bank is an area of grassland.

About 11:30am on Friday 20 August 1999, I recall driving onto the Smeeth Road and seeing two vehicles parked in the orchard to Bleak House, near to the trees. Both vehicles were unattended and both were facing in the direction of Moyse's Bank. The first vehicle was a dark blue saloon similar to a Sierra. Parked behind this was a white, flat-backed truck with drop sides.[311] I can give no further description of these vehicles. I did not see anyone in the orchard. I do not ever recall seeing any vehicles in the orchard before.

I then went on holiday and, upon my return, I heard of the shooting incident and reported this matter to the police guarding the house."

What this adds to our knowledge

This statement was found in the Unused Material file. It is of significance to us, of course, because when Postman Balls saw these vehicles, it was the day Tony fired his gun. The "dark blue Sierra" is also of importance, as it was referred to by various people including Margaret Hodgson on 27 September and Rosemary Cousins on 4th October.

We are also forced to consider why Tony's solicitor, Nick Makin, or barrister, Anthony Scrivener, failed in their duty to their client by not calling Mr Balls to trial or investigating the owner of the dark blue Sierra.

As we have seen (entries **63** & **183**), Fred's uncle, John Dolan, admitted to owning a blue Sierra.

Fri
1 OCT
2 pm
UNUSED
310

Downham Market police station

*According to official records, the Terrington St John-based 37-year-old constable Lindsey John Wakefield (whom we first met in 1994 – see entry **43**) had recently been engaged on seal duties at Bleak House. He claimed that during the course of these duties he lost possession of a stainless steel, multi-tool implement. On Friday 1st October 1999, at Downham Market police station, he spoke to PC 376 Matthews, who showed him a stainless steel, multi-tool (exhibit PHW/2) that he recognised as his and he took possession of it.*

---

[311] When I spoke with Tony about these vehicles on Sunday 2nd December 2018, he had no recollection of them or understanding of how they came to be on his land and was surprised to learn that they had been.

> **What this adds to our knowledge**
>
> On its face, it's the simple recording of a police constable confirming that a stainless steel multi-tool implement which he had lost during a search of the grounds of Bleak House had been found and that he had been re-united with that tool.

But nothing in this case was straightforward or simple. We need to ask a few questions. Notice that the constable didn't say on which day he allegedly lost the tool. Why was he unable to say?

Why did the public pay one constable to lose a tool and another to find it and yet another to return it to its owner?

But then we might want to ask if it was his tool in any event. As unpalatable as it might be, we ought to at least consider – if only to dispose of the question – whether it belonged to a police officer who might – heaven forbid – have shot Barras. It might sound fanciful, it might not, but as Sherlock Holmes would have said, "Rule nothing out".

I have spoken with Tony on the issue of the relationship between the police and the criminal fraternity and in particular the travelling community. His view – which I share – is that certain police officers have an extremely close relationship with some criminals and are, in fact, involved in criminal activity with them: overlooking crimes, turning a blind eye and sharing the proceeds.

I have little doubt that some members of the public would decry that previous paragraph and that the police would describe it as 'fanciful' - that's a favourite word of all branches of government to describe truth-tellers and investigative authors and journalists. Few members of the public have any inkling of how the police are abusing – I use the word advisedly – the Protection from Harassment Act 1997 (which was designed with the sole intent of protecting people, mainly women, from *being stalked*.) Nowadays the police issue – like confetti – Police Information Notices (also known as Harassment Warning Notices) to anyone who challenges the police, their local authority, large corporations and so on. We live in an age whereby those in power constantly abuse that power to rule and subjugate the masses and expect not to be held accountable, such is their hubris.

In my book *Blueprint for Abuse*, I included a chapter entitled *The Trial of the Scotland Yard Detectives, 1877* [see entry **15**]. As we have seen, it recounted the famous trial of very senior Scotland Yard detectives who had been working closely with criminals and fraudsters and had received more than £5,000 from the conmen over a 5-year period. That equates to approximately £530,000 in 2018.[312] That sum of money was obtained from just *one* conman and the Scotland Yard detectives had been working with several such conmen throughout their careers.

---

[312] The *North Otago Times* (New Zealand) Volume XXVI, Issue 1702, 3 October 1877, p.2.

At his trial, one of the conmen told the jury that the police had been involved in taking and distributing pornography at a time when photography was in its infancy.

One senior detective was – predictably – allowed to retire and even those who did serve prison sentences to appease an angry public were given paltry sentences and released early.

Such was the level of organised corruption that Scotland Yard had to employ an entirely new workforce of detectives and made hollow promises to the public that they could now have confidence in the police.

Thus, I argue, if senior Scotland Yard officers are involved in corruption (and some are), it's highly likely that your lowly constable is also on the take. Occasionally – just to placate a gullible public – a police officer will be "investigated" and offered as a sacrificial lamb and sent to prison. The thinking goes along the lines of "If the public see us put one or two officers in prison, they'll think we're straight and rooting out corruption." It's a fallacy. You're being deliberately misled.

So, the tool that PC Wakefield allegedly dropped in a search of Bleak House – was it dropped by him during a search, by him because he was at the farm on the night of the shooting, or by a tactical operations officer who 'eliminated' Barras?

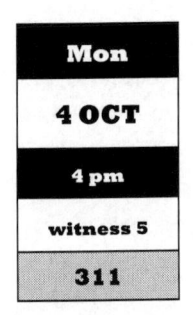

Mon
4 OCT
4 pm
witness 5
311

home address of Gillian Samuels
Gillian Mary Samuels lived in the village of Emneth with her husband David, who frequently worked away.

They had lived at their address since April, 1994 and Mrs Samuels busied herself running the house, which involved the keeping of four large dogs and twenty chickens. I'll let Gillian tell you what she'd heard about the farmer:

"Soon after moving in, were told by our immediate neighbours about the man that lived in the adjoining farm. I am referring to Tony Martin of Bleak House Farm. I did not know the name of the farm until the recent incident in August, when someone was shot, but I can see the farm buildings, due south from the front of our house. I also didn't know Tony's Christian name until then, as he has always been referred to as "Mad Harry." We were warned not to upset him, as he was a bit strange, and not to have anything to do with him if you could help it. I didn't pursue this, but accepted this advice. In fact, I would go so far as to say that the lady at No. 4, Anne, was and still is frightened of Tony Martin. I have not been given any reasons for this, but it is the impression I get from them."

'Mad Harry' and 'Mad Martin' were just some of the names Tony was referred to by various villagers. It is also evident that some villagers feared him. How much of this fear was real or imagined I cannot tell.

"Within a year of moving in we were made aware that Martin carried a gun in his car with him. This came from my neighbour at No. 2, Arthur Webb, and came up in general conversation, I can't recall exactly when. Certainly since then I have heard gunshots from over at the farm and surrounding fields. These were clearly not from an organised shoot, as it was only one gun and the occasional shot. This we would hear all year round, on and off, and I can certainly remember hearing gunshots during the beginning of this summer from over at Bleak House. I have not, however, seen Tony Martin with a gun.

The first time I spoke to Martin was in the summer of 1994, when I confronted him about his dogs. It was a summer's night and we were in the back garden having a barbecue when, I think, two rottweilers turned up in our front garden. Initially there was nobody with them, but they were causing problems with my dogs. Martin turned up a while later in his car. On this occasion I only spoke briefly to him, telling him to keep them under control. He said he'd been looking for them, but he didn't appear to know where they had been. They ran off and he drove off after them. The reason I told him to keep them under control is that they are large and imposing dogs, and can be very dangerous. Martin never apologised or explained why they were roaming about. He was very scruffy and dirty, and has always been like this whenever I have met him.

Shortly after this occasion I again spoke to Martin about the dogs being loose. Again, this was at my house and this deteriorated into an argument. He said the reason for him having the dogs was because he had been burgled. I sympathised with him, but told him they shouldn't be at our house without any control. He also said that it wasn't his fault, but people kept letting them out. During this, he remained in his car and I couldn't make him see any reason. He struck me as an articulate, well-educated man and, although he was never aggressive or violent, he made me feel intimidated by the way he spoke to me. I have had a number of "run-ins" with Martin about the dogs, but not for about four years. I have also had to speak to him about his driving, as he would race down the road outside our house. This road becomes a grass track and leads to his farm eventually, but is very bumpy and narrow. I have found parts of his cars along this track, where they have fallen off due to the way he drove and the condition of his cars."

Clearly Mrs Samuels had some angst against Tony and perhaps justifiably so. Now, I would not wish to disparage Mrs Samuels in any way (in fact I liked the way she stood up to Tony and told him what she thought – he'd have appreciated that, too) but she did say that she heard from "Arthur Webb at number 2 that Tony carried a gun in his car." We'll see in the following entry if Mr Webb mentioned it in his statement.

Mrs Samuels was witness number 5. Her function was to show that Tony's dogs were "vicious". The false narrative is building: a remote derelict farmhouse, an eccentric farmer driving around with unlicensed guns in his car and vicious dogs who'd attack anyone who dared venture onto their owner's land.

Mon
4 OCT
4 pm
witness 9
312

home address of Arthur Webb

Official records show that 77-year-old Arthur Webb had lived near Tony with his wife, Pamela Jane, for 21 years and, until he retired in around 1985, he had worked for Mr Fisher as a farm worker. He made the following statement to DC Adcock:

"Mr Fisher farms and lives at Thorney (near Peterborough) and also has 250 acres of land which adjoins his neighbour, Tony Martin, who lives a few hundred yards away from our cottage, and all the years I have known him I have never known his postal address. I live in a line of four cottages, and my particular cottage is still owned by Mr Fisher. This cottage has a track which is regularly used by tractor traffic and runs from Rustons Road to Tony Martin's house.

When I first came to this address, I knew Mr Garner, who lived in the property that Tony owns now. I believe his aunt left him the house with another brother to run. I think Tony and his brother fell out and Tony, I think, began farming there on his own about 15 years ago.

I have had many conversations with Tony Martin in the past, the last being about eighteen months ago in King's Lynn, when I saw him shopping.

Prior to this I spoke to him on quite a regular basis. I recall cycling down to his on many occasions and passing the time of day. I found Tony rough and ready, and I did like him as a person. I found him to be generous and caring. He used to give me fruit and always came over to me as a very nice person. He appeared to be a loner and, possibly, lonely. Tony had three rottweilers and he thought the world of his dogs. He used to treat them like his children. I recall that he would feed his dogs as well as he fed himself. I remember him saying that he used to buy cream cakes for himself and his dogs each week. I know he cooked all kinds of food, including sausages, for his dogs.

Tony would always stop and talk whenever he passed by on the track. I haven't seen him much to talk to in the last eighteen months as I no longer get about as much as I did. I found Tony to be articulate and could hold a conversation on many subjects. He also appeared very well educated.

I was told by the paperman that Tony had been broken into, but I was personally unaware of this until I was told. Tony never mentioned about his recent burglaries, as I never really saw him.

Tony never seemed to be short of money, and he used to show me some of his machinery he had bought in sales. I find it difficult to find anything derogatory to say about Tony Martin, and I have heard rumours about him in the village. I did not find him eccentric.

I knew he had shotguns as he has said to me that he shot the odd pheasant, but this was several years ago. I was unaware that he had his guns taken away from him. Last summer we had a problem with travellers' horses being tied up on the track, the horses having been left to fend for themselves. I was aware that Tony would not, under any circumstances, allow these travellers' horses on his land. If they did get on his land, he would go barmy. I know Tony had no time for the travelling fraternity."

What this adds to our knowledge	Mr Webb was witness number 9 and his function was not to show what a good man he thought Tony was but simply to build on the false narrative that Tony hated travellers – this was a racist card that the police could play. They could be seen as the heroes for "getting justice" for the dead boy in particular and travellers in general. Mr Webb made no mention of Tony keeping a gun in his car as Mrs Samuels had suggested in her statement.

Mon 4 OCT unknown witness 103 313	**Bleak House** *According to official records, Norwich-based SOCO Barry Wells made a statement on 4 October about his role in a search of Bleak House some two months earlier. He claimed that on Tuesday 24 August 1999, together with other officers, he assisted in a search of the grounds in the vicinity of the rear windows and path of Bleak House. He claimed that "This area was very heavily overgrown."*

"As the result of what I was told by PC 9022 Harvey, I took photographs of flagged areas 25 & 26 and from the negatives developed photographs were produced and are contained in albums exhibit reference BJW30."

Mon 4 OCT unknown witness 1 314	**unknown location** *According to official records, Anthony Cooper, a partner of a haulage business based in Emneth Hungate at Walsoken Road, had a yard about 100 yards from the junction with Smeeth Road, almost opposite the entrance track leading to Bleak House.* *He made a statement to PC Caine, but we do not know where it was made, or at what time:*

"I have known the owner of this farm, Tony Martin, for about ten years, but only occasionally to talk to as and when I met him. This would be roughly ten to twelve times a year. He appeared to be well-educated and articulate, and could talk on all sorts of subjects. He could also speak on all levels, e.g. he would swear when talking to me but, if my mum appeared, he would become a gentleman.

He had strong opinions on certain things. He believed that the police were only keen on stopping and prosecuting motorists, and didn't do anything to help or solve people's crimes. He also had no faith in the courts and, I think, believed in ancient values that, if you got caught stealing, you had your hand cut off. Tony had been the victim of crime and he told me that the people responsible were travellers, and were wasters and a drain on society. *He went on to say that how they were dealt with in the war by Hitler was right, and that today they are not punished.*[313] He had said that he had been stopped whilst driving and I think these were for no lights and no tax, etc.

He appeared to work hard on his farm and, I believe, almost ran it on his own. He was always very scruffily dressed, and often wore hats, recently a beret. He had three rottweilers, which he thought the world of. They lived in an outhouse/ cottage near the house. He said that he had a doberman dog killed by someone in the yard, and that this upset him greatly. He implied he knew who had done this and that, if he'd caught them, he would have done the same to them. He replaced the doberman with two other rottweilers and, in recent years, they have always been at the farm. If he went out, they stayed. I think that Tony worried about his dogs when he was away, and also the farm but, when he was at home, I do not think he was intimidated or worried.

About four weeks prior to the shooting at Bleak House, I saw that a forked truck had fallen on its side in the orchard to the front of Bleak House. I went down towards the house to make sure all was alright. Tony met me at the buildings and, initially, was hostile or confrontational. This is always how he was until he realised who you were. This gave me the impression that he didn't welcome visitors. Once he knew it was me his attitude changed, and he then welcomed the help that I gave him. I was there for about three hours, and he was very chatty. It was almost as though he talked to you as a one-way conversation.

He showed me around the gardens and, on one occasion, I saw the house. I commented on the trees growing very close to the house. Tony said he had planted them to protect it, but I have since found out that they were in pots and just took root. This is not unusual for Tony to elaborate on a story, and I was never sure whether he was actually telling the facts or exaggerating.

He also said that he had been burgled, and I got the impression that this was recently. He did not mention that he had informed the police, but he said that someone had found some of his personal effects at Walpole. Because these had

---

[313] Author's emphasis.

been left outside, they had been ruined and, as they were family heirlooms, and irreplaceable, this had really upset him. He didn't seem concerned about the monetary loss. He also said that he had had things stolen off an old tractor, but this was on a different occasion. The only thing he specifically mentioned he had had stolen from the house was a chest of drawers.

I have never seen Tony with a shotgun, and I didn't know that he had one, although I have heard guns over towards his house. He has never mentioned guns to me."

| **What this adds to our knowledge** | Why would the Prosecution enter this as evidence? Put simply, the comment about Hitler was "food and drink" to the perverse narrative that the CPS were creating. It's a headline-grabbing name and a false narrative can be constructed which reads along the lines that Tony was a far-right nutter with guns who'd willingly shoot anyone who got in his way. This was all done to provide a 'motive' for the shooting, to show that Tony had intent to kill when he fired his gun. |

home address of Roger Western

Mon 4 OCT 11.40 am UNUSED 315

Official records show the 60-year-old Roger Western, who had lived in the Emneth area since January 1981 and had suffered at least two break-ins at his home, made a statement to DC Lovick which read as follows:

"Generally you can't leave anything lying about at your home in this area because, if you do, it would be stolen. Tools and lawn mowers are usually the favourite to go missing. As a habit I do not leave anything outside, as I'm sure it would be stolen if I did.

The last break-in at my home was about 3 weeks before the shooting. I do not know Tony Martin or, to my knowledge, ever met him. I reported my break-in to the police at the time and it's being dealt with at Downham Market.

About 6 months before this, around February/March 1999, a white Ford transit van pulled onto my land with three males inside. I have been in the antiques trade for a lot of years and I'm used to 'knockers', but I didn't feel happy with these people at all. The van drove onto my land which I was able to see from the house. I immediately went outside to see what they wanted. None of the occupants got out the van yet the driver asked me if I would sell the table in one of my outhouses. I told them "No." This immediately made me suspicious as they must have had a look around before to know the table was there, as it isn't fully visible from the drive area.

The men in the van said they were dealers from Newark, but I doubted their motives. They looked more like tinkers to me rather than antiques dealers.

None of the occupants got out the van but as I went over to them to speak, I had a brief look. I would describe the driver as aged in his late 40s, about 5' 10" tall, lean build. He had beady eyes and a long face. He looked as if he had only shaved yesterday and had generally shabby clothing. The driver was the only one who spoke to me, but didn't have an accent as I recall.

Sat in the middle was a young lad, which immediately made me think "Why aren't you at school?" He would be around 12-13 years old, with a baby, round face and dark brown, collar length hair. This lad looked quite similar to the photograph of the boy who had been shot dead at Emneth. He was a bit shorter than the other two in the van, who were sat either side of him.

The only thing I recall about the third male (who was sat in the passenger seat) was that he was in his late 20s, swarthy/tanned complexion, with noticeably thick, dark hair. I haven't seen any of them before, nor since.

The only thing I can remember about the van was that it was a Ford transit, possibly a 'D' or 'F' registration, not the sort of van I would expect a successful antiques dealer to be driving about in.

I told these men I didn't want their business and saw them from my property.

About a week after my recent break-in, another white transit van drove on my land with a male driver and a lady and baby sat in the front. This was a different van and driver as previously described and was generally asking for work which I didn't have. I again reported this to the police."

What this adds to our knowledge	Firstly, Mr Western had completely corroborated what Tony Martin had been saying – and doing – for years: that there were a large number of thefts and break-ins in the area which the public reported to the police. Mr Western didn't say that he had had no positive response from the police but Tony and others were angry that no-one was ever found and prosecuted.

Secondly, Mr Western confirmed that the occupants of the first van were from Newark and his descriptions appear to fit Fearon (in the passenger seat) and Fred Barras, albeit he has described Barras as looking only 12 or 13 years of age whereas, of course, we know he was 16 (with a 'baby face'). It's quite easy to be wrong about the age of people and Mr Western said he thought the photos he'd seen of Fred Barras fitted the boy he'd seen in the van.

The driver (late 40s/ lean build) doesn't quite match that of Darren Bark, but it doesn't mean it wasn't him – it could be that Mr Western's description is somewhat inaccurate because, after all, none of the occupants got out of the van. Or perhaps it was Christopher Webster.

Mr Western then told DC Lovick that a week or so after the break-in at his home, another white transit came on to his land which he reported to the police.

Tony Martin had repeatedly contacted the police to inform them of these unwelcome visits to his land and in the area generally. Can you believe that some of Tony's neighbours thought he was a nosey, busy-body and yet, in reality, he was ever-watchful and performing a civic duty by remaining alert to any danger in the area. I know which type of neighbour I'd prefer.

Mon 4 OCT 1.35 pm UNUSED 316

home address of Michael Coleman
Records show that on this date, Michael Coleman - a friend and business partner of Malcolm Starr's - made a statement to DC Lovick in which he said that on 20 August 1999, he went to the White Lion Hotel in Wisbech "at around 8pm."

He claimed that as he walked in he noticed three males, who he immediately thought were travellers, sitting in the lounge area:

"My main concern with these was the age of one of them. He only looked around 16 years old. He was very nervous and acting oddly. He kept getting up and walking out to the lobby and then returning again. I've seen the photograph of the boy who was shot at Emneth and he certainly had the same sort of description. The other two with him were sat down, and the only thing I can say about them is that the eldest was around 40-45 years, white, heavy build, wearing a lightish coloured, check shirt. The second was around 27-28, again white, with fair hair and a distinctive "boxer's nose". By that I mean it looked as if it had been broken.

I asked the barman what these three were doing in the pub, and he told me that they had said they worked at Smedley's [a food processing plant in Wisbech]. I doubted this, however, and as part-owner of the hotel, instructed him not to serve them again. I left the hotel at around 8:20pm and, as I understand from the barman, these three left shortly after that."

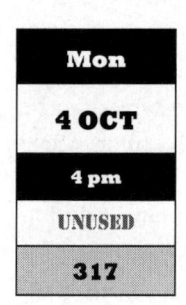

Mon 4 OCT 4 pm UNUSED 317

home address of Rosemary Cousins
Records show that the 47-year-old Rosemary Anne Cousins, who had lived in Emneth for the past 20 years, made a statement to DC Peters which was not entered as evidence into court:

"At about 5:30pm on Sunday 20 June 1999, I was in my house, in the bedroom drying my hair, when I saw what I would describe as a battered, blue Sierra car. As I watched from the bedroom window, the vehicle drove up the driveway to the back of the house. It stopped on the gravel facing our garages, which were open, and contained equipment and vehicles. After what seemed like a long while, the vehicle turned around and then drove back down the drive and out into the Hungate Road. As it drove out I noted down the registration number on an old envelope. The number I took down was E949FNP. I have handed this piece of paper, which I exhibit and refer to as RAC/1, to DC Peters.

About 5 minutes later the same vehicle returned. It drove straight up the driveway and parked near the back door. The passenger got out of the car and walked up to the back door. As soon as he did this, I popped my head out of the upstairs window and asked him what he wanted. He looked up at me and seemed surprised to see me. When he looked up at me, he smiled at me. I can remember his exact words: "We are totally lost; can you tell me where the Gaultree Inn is?" I pointed up towards the village of Emneth. He seemed to want more detail and remained standing by the door.

I was quite concerned for my safety, because I couldn't remember whether I had locked the door. It was my feeling that the men were up to no good. After giving the man some directions, he got back in the car, turned and drove off.

I can describe the man who got out of the car. He was in his early twenties, about 5' 10" tall and he had fair hair and was clean shaven. The driver appeared to be a big man."

Rosemary Cousins was a neighbour of Tony's and she got the impression that the two men were "up to no good" – Tony had been saying for years that such men were regularly appearing in the area and stealing and committing burglary and other crimes. Mrs Cousins also described a tall man with fair hair – this sounds like the same man in the White Lion as described by Michael Coleman. He described the fair-haired man as in his late 20s while she thought early 20s.

Mrs Cousins noted down the number plate and hand it to the police. As far as we can ascertain, they didn't investigate the owner.

Notice how Mrs Cousins apparently failed to mention the night of 20th August 1999 in her statement. I have approached her on three separate occasions to provide her with a right of reply – she has failed to contact me.

Mon
4 OCT
7.15 pm
witness 20
318

home address of Andrew Stokes

According to official records, 48-year-old fruit grower Andrew John Stokes made a statement to DC Buxton at his home address where he lived with his wife, Janet, and his son, Ben, aged fifteen. He had a daughter, Caroline, who was away at university.

Mr Stokes had lived and worked in the Marshland area of Norfolk all of his life.

"Up until about eight years ago, I lived at Marshland St James and farmed land in that area. As a result, I came to know a man called Tony Martin, who farms land at Bleak House and was a neighbouring farmer. By that, I mean he farmed land within about a mile of mine.

I would say Tony Martin is eccentric, although I never really got to know him well. He visited me once asking if I could spray his orchards and, apart from that, he was just a passing acquaintance. The only conversations I have ever had with him were brief and about fruit-growing. I have never spoken to him about travellers, and I have no knowledge of him using or owning firearms. I know he felt quite strongly about the poor state of farming in general.

Earlier this year, I was invited to attend a 'Farmwatch' meeting at Herbert Engineering, with several other farmers. The idea was to form a Farmwatch group in the area. Tony was at the meeting, and *he interrupted the meeting to have his say*. He was vociferous, loud and persistent in his objections to the whole 'Farmwatch' idea. I formed the impression that Tony was of the opinion that 'Farmwatch' was organised by the police and, therefore, I felt he was anti-police. He was not shouting as such, but just behaving in his normal, loud, outspoken way, which is how he always came across to me. He continued to go on about how he had been a victim of crime repeatedly, and eventually the meeting broke up. I personally did not agree to join the Farmwatch scheme at that time, *as I felt that I was somewhat detached from most of the people there*.

I have no idea as to whether Mr Martin was easily intimidated, and he never gave the impression that he was scared to go home."

What this adds to our knowledge	All the emphases above are the author's. Clearly, Mr Stokes did not have a lot of good to say about Tony, but the worrying factor here is that he was wrong to say that Tony interrupted the Farmwatch meeting. We have learnt from other statements that he didn't.

I believe you also have to question the character of a man who labels someone 'eccentric' and yet – on his own admission – never got to know him well. This suggests that he is himself quick to rush to judgment of another human being.

We should also consider that whenever the police come a-knocking asking if you're prepared to make a statement, some people are quick to jump on the bandwagon, have their "5 minutes of fame" and be seen to assist the police (sometimes so that the police don't come a-knocking again in case they see too much or ask too many questions).

It is clear from his statement that Mr Stokes was primed by the police before telling his story. In my view, a skilled barrister at the top of his profession would have slaughtered Mr Stokes in court, but Tony's defence counsel let him down badly.

Mr Stokes was prosecution witness number 20. His function was simply to jump on the prosecutorial bandwagon and claim that Tony was an 'eccentric' (as if that's a crime) and that he 'interrupted' the Farmwatch meeting.

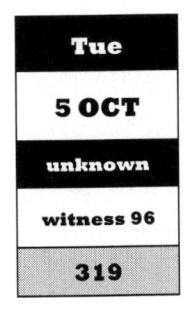

Tue 5 OCT
unknown
witness 96
319

unknown location
According to official records, there was a <u>third</u> statement attributed to PS Mizen:

"As the result of a search operation, conducted by me in my role as a Police Search Adviser, at Bleak House on 2 September, 1999, I produced a police Search Report (item MRM/3). It was posted by me via the internal mailing system to DCI Wright at Downham Market police station."

We must surely ask the question why this statement was not made until 5 October if it referred to a search more than a month earlier.

Tue 5 OCT
unknown
UNUSED
320

secret address, Newark
The anonymous letter below to Neil Jacutine offered support and at the same time some sympathy for the deceased Fred Barras and his family:

"We feel we must let you know there is majority support for you in and around Newark. Having lost a son in an accident, I do feel sorry for the parents, but no sympathy for the people who rob others. It is widely known around here when these people left to go and rob, also that they have been before to the same location. These people are of the gypsy/traveller community and therefore myself and friends are not willing to give names and addresses.

If donations are required for legal help, we will send monies to it. Best wishes to you all. PS: Check out the background of these people."

Mr Jacutine said: "Tony has got the complete backing of most people in the area. I am completely behind him and am going to start a petition and poster campaign for him." True to his word, a sign saying, 'Tony Martin – Good Bloke' appeared on the A47 near Emneth.

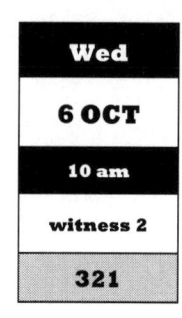

Wed	**home address of Fred Deptford**
6 OCT	
10 am	
witness 2	
321	

Fred Deptford owned and ran the farm enterprise known as Deptford & Son Ltd and he lived in Hungate House, about a quarter of a mile from Tony's. He had lived in the house for 54 years.

In a statement to DC Buxton, the 84-year-old Deptford said several things which assisted Tony Martin's case. The reason this was entered into court at trial was to give the impression that the trial was fair to the defendant.

He had known Tony Martin since he was about 8 years old (the age at which he went to boarding school) and Deptford knew all of the family, especially the Garners. He said that Tony could be a nuisance because he'd often walk over to the yard and stop his men from working by engaging in conversations on all manner of subjects.

Deptford added that he'd never had a conversation with Tony about gypsies or ownership of guns. "I do know, however, that he used to employ gypsies to pick his apples in his orchards, but he never allowed them to camp on his land. I can recall a number of gypsies in his orchards up until about 10 years ago."

This clearly adds to our knowledge that Tony had employed gypsies and travellers on his farm.[314]

Deptford confirmed that Tony was rarely at Bleak House and added that his workmen had told him that Tony was "scared to go home to Bleak House due to gypsies" and he knew that Tony had had problems previously with them, though he wasn't aware of what the problems actually were, nor did he know about any burglaries at Bleak House. However, he added that "there are many thefts and burglaries in the area. In my time at Hungate House, we suffered countless thefts and burglaries from the farm, but only one burglary from the house."

This clearly confirmed what Tony had been saying for years. And what the police had been in denial about – also for years.

Wed	**home address of Chris Baker**
6 OCT	
11.55 am	
witness 56	
322	

The 37-year-old Chris Baker, a video producer from Norwich and the proprietor of 'Treasured Videos' which he operated from his home address, made a statement to DS Eglen which was not witnessed.

Mr Baker described his main work as copying and editing video tapes. In addition, he undertook some filming on location.

He was instructed by Norfolk Constabulary to video Bleak House.

---

[314] Compare this with the nonsense contained in the statement attributed to PC Jim Welham. [See entry **57**].

"At 10:07am on Tuesday 28 September 1999, I visited Bleak House, in company with an assistant, Mr John Allen.

I met DS John Eglen at the premises and, as a result of what he told me, I made a video film of the house and surrounding area. I worked until 5:52pm that day, and returned at 10:32am on Wednesday 29 September, again in company with Mr Allen. I completed filming and left the scene at 4:52pm on Wednesday 29 September.

In making the film I used a Sony DV Cam tape for the unedited source material. I retained that tape for editing.

During the course of my work I made rough working notes. I kept them all and at 1:55pm on Wednesday 6 October 1999, at my home address, I made copies of them all. I produce the copies of my working notes as exhibit reference CB/7. I will retain the originals of those notes until I am informed by the Norfolk Police that I can dispose of them.

At 11:45am on Wednesday 6 October 1999, DS Eglen visited my home address. Together we packaged and sealed the exhibits in my possession. At 2:05pm that day, I handed him the exhibits."

Wed 6 OCT 2.30 pm witness 57 323

home address of John Allen
According to official records, 39-year-old John Allen, a video producer, made a statement to DS Eglen which was not witnessed.

He confirmed the dates and times that Chris Baker had said they were at Bleak House.

Wed 6 OCT unknown witness 95 324

unknown location
According to official records (line S143a in HOLMES), PC 9059 Nichola Louise Marshall made a statement on this day in which she claimed that on 21 August 1999 she had been part of a police search team at Bleak House. The HOLMES database (line S143) added that on 21 August 1999 she had also guarded the scene after the body of Barras had been found.

I have been unable to find this second statement and it wasn't included in the documents handed to Tony from his legal team.

> **CORRUPTION ALERT** *'Missing' evidence and improper chronology of statements*

According to the HOLMES *database,* PC *Marshall made a statement on 24 September 1999 about her involvement in a search of Bleak House on 2nd September and her alleged seizure of exhibits. However, on 6 October, she allegedly made a statement referring to a search on 21 August 1999 and her 'guarding' the body of Barras. These entries in* HOLMES *are out of sequence and leave me to conclude that they have been fabricated.* [See also entry **125** which placed her at Bleak House on 21 August 1999].

Thur
7 OCT
3.30 pm
UNUSED
325

home address of Stephen Buckland, Newark
According to the official police files, a statement was made to DC *Peters by 18-year-old Stephen Buckland, a good friend of Fred Barras'. They had been next-door neighbours for 5 years.*

This was an interesting statement because it adds to our knowledge and yet at the same time raises some serious questions. Buckland said that Fred was "big mates with Brendon Fearon"[315] but that neither he nor, to his knowledge, did Barras know Darren Bark. The teenager added that on the day of the shooting he rode his bike to the Eton Road shops where he met a number of his mates including Fred. Buckland said that Fearon rode up on a bike and wanted a private word with Fred which lasted for about 5 minutes before Fred re-joined his mates.

According to this statement, these events occurred around 7pm which suggests that either Fearon and Barras met up with Bark earlier than had been suggested by the prosecution or that the times have been altered.

However, this entry should be read in conjunction with that of John Dolan (entry **183**) who placed Fred Barras in the area at between 8:15 and 8:30pm.

---

[315] This is further evidence, I suggest, that Fearon would have mentioned the existence of Barras to the police and ambulance crew and that the youngster was severely injured too.

Sat
9 OCT
5 pm
witness 7
326

home address of Janet Portham

According to official records, the 45-year-old Janet Lorraine Portham made a statement to DC Peters in which she said that she had moved near to Tony with her husband Richard and two sons in the Christmas of 1995. She first met Tony in the spring of 1996 and, since that first meeting, Tony had become a family friend and a frequent visitor. He and Richard would "have long and involved discussions on all manner of subjects."[316]

"I knew Tony lived on his own; in fact, he never came to our home with anyone else. He often would turn up at meal times and would share with us whatever I had prepared to eat.[317]

The last time I saw Tony was on Friday 20 August 1999, at around 1:45pm. Tony stayed and had lunch with myself and the children.[318] He seemed in good spirits. I cannot now remember the contents of any conversation we had, but it was just what I would describe as general 'chit-chat'. Tony was wearing a navy blue, polo-neck jumper and navy coloured trousers and, I guess, he would have had his boots on. That was the last time I saw him. He arrived and left our home, as usual, in his car, which is a bronze coloured estate.

I never went inside Tony's house, and I never went and looked inside but, from the conversations I had with Tony about Bleak House, and from what I could see of it from the grounds, I imagined it to be quite run-down. Tony told me that part of the staircase had fallen down. I got the impression from Tony that it was his intention to do the house up and restore it to its former glory. I hoped he would restore it because it was, to my mind, in a beautiful location.

I would describe Tony as eccentric and kind.

I have been asked about Tony's fear of crime. Tony never discussed with me his fear of crime and, in fact, I did not know about the burglary that he had had in May of this year until shortly before the shooting incident. This came about as a result of him clearing up some papers that the burglars had scattered about.

I didn't know that Tony had a shotgun. I never saw him with a gun, and he never talked to me about guns. I never heard him shooting, and I know that he was against hunting wild animals. He wouldn't even kill the rats on his land.

Tony had a dislike for certain individuals within the local travelling fraternity. I don't think he mentioned names to me, and I don't think it would have meant

---

[316] This flew in the face of the prosecution's claim that Tony Martin was a 'loner' (as if that were a crime).

[317] Tony's timing would have been no accident.

[318] On 30 December 2018, Richard Portham told me that there were four other adults present at that meal. Apparently, the meal was interrupted on three occasions when Tony heard his dogs barking loudly which indicated the presence of intruders. Tony went on to his land on all three occasions before returning to the Porthams'.

anything to me if he had, since I only know a few people in the area.

Tony and I never discussed what he may or may not have done in the event of him being burgled again. We never talked about things like that. Tony appeared quite Victorian in his attitude toward me and thus the subject matter in our discussion was what I have already described as 'chit-chat'."

What this adds to our knowledge	It completely shows another side of Tony – kind, somewhat Victorian in his attitude towards women and that he wouldn't even kill the rats on his farm. This contradicts the prosecution claims that Tony was a loner, a killer and a psychopath, incapable of showing emotion and with a murderous intent towards all gypsies and travellers.

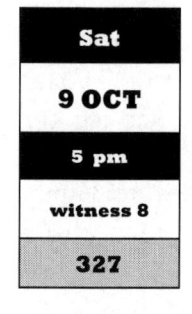

Sat 9 OCT 5 pm witness 8 327	**home address of Richard Portham** *On the same visit, records show that DC Peters also took a statement from Janet's husband, 51-year-old Richard James Roland Portham. Shortly after moving to their home, Richard Portham had been working at the bottom of their land when he first met Tony Martin, who had been walking his dogs on the opposite side of the dyke. Richard later introduced him to his family and from that time onwards Tony became a frequent visitor to the Porthams' home.*

"He usually drove to our home in his car, and was always on his own. Tony liked to talk and we would have discussions on all manner of subjects. Tony liked a good argument, and either he or I would take a contrary view just for the purpose of discussion.

I have never been inside Tony's house, but I have seen it from the outside when we have been in the grounds. Tony used to allow my family and I to go fruit-picking in the grounds, and to look at new plants he had put in his garden. I would describe Bleak House as very overgrown, but individual.

The last time I saw or spoke to Tony prior to the shooting was on Sunday 15 August 1999. As usual, Tony turned up unannounced and stayed for about three quarters of an hour. I cannot remember what we talked about on that day, and I would say that Tony was his normal self.

I have been asked if Tony had a fear of being a victim of crime. *My answer to that would be that he had no more fear of crime than myself or my wife, or many of our neighbours.*[319]

I knew that Tony had been burgled in May of this year, and that he was upset because, besides stealing a valuable piece of furniture, the thieves had also

---

[319] Author's emphasis.

damaged and discarded several items of great sentimental value. I remember that Tony asked me not to tell Janet about the burglary[320] in case it upset or worried her and, in fact, I don't think Janet got to hear about the burglary until shortly before the shooting incident. I knew also that Tony had been the victim of other thefts from his premises over the period that I knew him.

I have been asked if I know anything about Tony's use or access to firearms prior to the shooting. I can truthfully say that I did not know that Tony had a shotgun or any other kind of firearm. I never saw him with a gun and I never heard him shooting. *In fact, he seemed positively against shooting or killing wildlife of any kind.*[321] I say this because I once asked Tony for permission to shoot on his land (I have held a shotgun certificate for over thirty years) and he refused to allow me to do so.

I knew that Tony had been involved in some sort of incident years ago which resulted in him either surrendering his certificate or having his shotgun certificate taken away from him.[322] Tony told me this, he did not go into any great detail and I did not pursue the subject.

I have been asked about Tony's view of the travelling fraternity. *I don't think that Tony liked the travellers, but he was quite tolerant towards them.*[323] I know he allowed them to graze their horses on the drove adjacent to his land.[324] There were certain characters in the local travelling fraternity that he was very wary of.[325]

I have been asked if Tony told me what he might do if he was burgled again. I cannot recall having a conversation with him about this subject.

I would describe Tony as an independent, eccentric character."

---

[320] This is an example, I believe, of Tony Martin's consideration for the feelings of others – sometimes to his own detriment.

[321] Author's emphasis.

[322] This was the shooting incident in the orchard. [See entry **43**]

[323] Author's emphasis. This contradicted, of course, the prosecution's claim that Tony had a pathological hatred of all gypsies and travellers. As we have previously seen, Tony sometimes employed travellers to pick the apple crop. [See entry **321**].

[324] In fact, Tony didn't allow travellers (or anyone else) to graze horses on his land because he was concerned about the use of pesticides harming the animals. [See also Tony Martin's account (entry **67**); David Patrick's account (entry **300**) and Arthur Webb's account (entry **312**).

[325] Many other farmers and villagers were also wary of the travelling fraternity, whom the former group blamed the latter for the crime wave sweeping across West Norfolk and East Cambridgeshire. [See also statements of Stewart Mayfield (entry **259**), David Schooling (entry **332**) and John Turner (entry **349**) amongst others].

> **What this adds to our knowledge**
>
> Clearly Richard Portham and Tony Martin got along well and were sufficiently comfortable enough with one another to regularly play "devil's advocate" during their many discussions.
>
> Furthermore, Mr Portham confirmed that not only had Tony been burgled on previous occasions, but had also suffered a large number of thefts.

Additionally, Mr Portham mentioned that Tony had told him about the shooting in the orchard in 1994. This did not surprise me because Tony had nothing to hide and, in my view (and Tony's) his licence was revoked unfairly.

Mon
11 OCT
unknown
witness 67
328

unknown location
Scenes of Crime Officer, Laura Bishop, of Bethel Street police station in Norwich, apparently made a statement to police on this date, but the usual details of to whom it was made, where it was made and at what time it was made are missing. She claimed that on Sunday 22 August 1999, between 2:45pm and 7pm, she had attended the mortuary at the Queen Elizabeth Hospital, King's Lynn, to assist with the first post-mortem of Frederick Jackson Barras.

"My role involved taking photographs of the deceased, as requested by Dr Mike Heath, pathologist. From the negatives developed, I caused an album of photographs, in enlarged form, to be produced, and these are referred to as exhibit LXB/1. I also took possession of exhibits LH/1, LH/2, LH/3 and LH/4, a series of x-rays taken at the post-mortem by radiographer Leslie Hill.

On Monday 23 August 1999, at 8am, I took exhibits LH/1 - LH/4 to HQ photographic, where I saw Ian Munday, head of the photographic department, and handed them to him to photograph. I received these same exhibits back from him at 12:15pm on the same day.

At 2:15pm on the same day, I handed the same four exhibits to PC 214 Stephenson at Downham Market police station.

At 8:45pm on the same day, I attended the operating theatre, Queen Elizabeth Hospital with DC Trevor Buxton in order to photograph the injuries to the legs of Brendon Fearon and to collect some lead shot from the injury to the right leg. Photographs of these injuries are incorporated in the photograph album exhibit LXB/1. The lead shot I recovered is referred to as exhibit LXB/2.

On Tuesday 24 August at 5:30pm, I handed exhibit LXB/2 to Mr Dave Rowlands (Principal SOCO) at Downham Market police station.

Second post-mortem

On Friday 27 August 1999, between 2pm and 2:35pm, I again attended the mortuary at Queen Elizabeth Hospital to assist with the 2nd post-mortem of Frederick Jackson Barras. My role involved taking photographs of the deceased, as requested by Dr Dick Shepherd, pathologist. From the negatives developed, I caused an album of photographs, in enlarged form, to be produced, and these are referred to as exhibit LXB/3.

Third post-mortem

On Sunday 5 September, between 2:40pm and 3:50pm, I again attended the mortuary at Queen Elizabeth Hospital to assist with the 3rd post-mortem of Frederick Jackson Barras. My role involved taking photographs of the deceased, as requested by Dr Cooper, pathologist. These have now been produced in enlarged form as an album, and are referred to as exhibit LXB/4."

> **What this adds to our knowledge**
>
> It is important for us to recognise the industrial scale of the legal engineering that took place in this case. Laura Bishop's first statement was used as evidence in court but she was not called – thus Tony's defence counsel, who should have insisted on her presence, could not cross-examine her about the x-rays taken of Barras which showed that he didn't die of a "gunshot wound to the chest".

> **CORRUPTION ALERT**
>
> *Evidence of two further autopsies on Barras hidden from jury & public*

SOCO Bishop is recorded as having made a second statement to the police on 17 November 1999 in which she referred to the photographs taken of Barras during the second autopsy. Presumably she also made an additional statement in which she mentioned the photographs she'd taken in the third autopsy. There is no record in HOLMES of such a third statement ever having been made. The statement dated 17 November was never entered into court as evidence and nor was it placed in the Unused Material file. In other words, it was air-brushed out of history to make it appear to the court that there had only been one autopsy so as to call only one of the three pathologists (Dr Heath) and so as to run with the false reason for the death of Barras.

Tony Martin has often said to me he wished he had changed his barrister prior to trial – the truth is that it didn't matter who he had defending him because the guilty verdict was clearly planned prior to the trial commencing. And several members of the legal profession were complicit in the blatant miscarriage of justice.

Wed
13 OCT
unknown
witness 70
329

unknown location

Prosecution witness number 70, John Alfred Slaughter, apparently made a statement on this date but to whom it was made, where it was made and at what time it was made we do not know because these usual details were not recorded. Mr Slaughter held an honours degree in chemistry. He was employed at the Metropolitan Police Forensic Science Laboratory from 1974 until March 1996, when it became the Metropolitan Laboratory of the Forensic Science Service.

"Here, since April 1996, I have continued this occupation. From 1981 I have worked in the toxicology section. I specialise in the examination of blood and urine for drugs (including alcohol) and other chemicals (poisons) and in the interpretation of these results in general terms.

Circumstances of Case
From the information supplied, I understand that:-

(1) On 20 August 1999, at approximately 11pm, Mr Brendon Fearon was found with a shotgun injury to his leg in the Emneth Hungate area of Norfolk, and taken to hospital. It was suspected that Mr Fearon had been shot while burgling the home address of Mr Anthony Martin.[326] Mr Martin was later arrested.

(2) On the morning[327] of 21 August, the body of Mr Frederick Barras was found in the grounds of Mr Martin's home address, having sustained shotgun wounds. The body was left in situ until 22 August.[328]

(3) Later on 22 August, Dr Michael Heath performed a post-mortem examination on Mr Barras and took a blood sample (items MJH/37 and 38), a

---

[326] There was absolutely no evidence of this. The police – his paymasters - had supplied this 'fact' to Mr Slaughter.
[327] It is interesting to note that Mr Slaughter has said that the body of Fred Barras was discovered on the *morning* of 21 August 1999. As we have seen, other documents state that the body was discovered at 2:32pm. Clearly this is conflicting information.
[328] Mr Slaughter confirmed that the body was left in situ until 22 August. Under normal circumstances this would not happen and, if true, we are forced to ask why it did happen.

sample of urine (item MJH/35) and a sample of vitreous humour (item MJH/42). Dr Heath said that Mr Barras died within minutes of being shot.[329]

(4) It is believed that Mr Barras and Mr Fearon[330] set off by car at approximately 8pm to the venue. Mr Barras drank a quantity of lager, but it is not believed he smoked any cannabis or cannabis resin on the journey. It is believed that Mr Barras had previously used amphetamine by injection.[331]

Purpose of examination

To determine whether or not Mr Barras was intoxicated through alcohol, or under the influence of certain commonly abused or certain prescribed drugs at the time of his death.

Nature of examination

Preserved blood sample (MJH/37) - Frederick Barras
Urine sample (MJH/35) - Frederick Barras

These samples were examined for alcohol, methylenedioxyinethylamphetainine (MDMA, one of a group of compounds commonly known as ecstasy), amphetamine, two common benzodiazepine drugs (diazepam and temazepam) methadone and compounds expected in the body after use of heroin, cannabis or cannabis resin and cocaine.

This examination was performed under laboratory reference F99/5005.

Comments

My comments regarding the use and effects of drugs are taken from reading the medical and scientific literature:

1. **With respect to alcohol - blood sample**

1.1 The alcohol level determined represents that present at the time of death, which I understand was very shortly after Mr Barras was shot.

---

[329] Notice how Mr Slaughter did not refer to the *three* post mortems which had all taken place prior to this statement. Now, we are forced to consider that perhaps Mr Slaughter was corrupt and deliberately and knowingly left out this important piece of evidence, that this information was not supplied to him by corrupt officers deliberately and knowingly withholding this evidence, or that his statement has been altered by corrupt police officers. Whichever way, the stench of corruption hangs heavy in the air.

[330] Again, notice that there is no mention of Darren Bark or any other alleged driver. [See comments in previous footnote, since they are also applicable here.]

[331] Mr Slaughter has not provided a source to show how he came by this alleged information.

1.2 Blood alcohol levels around 80 milligrams per 100 millilitres are not associated with signs of drunkenness in normal persons, although the ability to perform complex tasks, like driving, may be impaired.

Urine sample

1.3 A urine alcohol level of 107 milligrams per 100 millilitres is approximately equivalent to a blood alcohol level of 80 milligrams per 100 millilitres. This is in very good agreement with the blood sample.

Vitreous Humour sample[332]

1.4 A vitreous humour-alcohol level of 86 milligrams per 100 millilitres is approximately equivalent to a blood alcohol level of 73 milligrams per 100 millilitres. This is in good agreement with the blood sample.

2. With respect to cannabis and cannabis resin

2.1 Detection of the metabolite of THC shows that Mr Barras had used cannabis or cannabis resin prior to the incident. From the scientific tests alone I cannot say when he used cannabis or cannabis resin, nor whether he was under the influence of either of these drugs at that time.

2.2 Both cannabis and cannabis resin are normally used by mixing the drug, typically 50 to 200 milligrams, with tobacco and rolling it into a cigarette,

---

[332] This entry could be said to have deliberately deceived the public. Vitreous humour (VH) is the fluid-like gel found at the back of the eye which is composed of approximately 98-99% of water with trace amounts of minerals. After death, the VH resists putrefaction longer than any other bodily fluid. The potassium concentration in the VH rises so predictably within the hours, days and weeks after death that vitreous potassium levels are frequently used to estimate the time since death.

Postmortem Interval (PMI) is the time elapsed between death of a person and the time of autopsy. Determination of PMI is essential in many criminal forensic investigations and certainly in this one.

Vitreous humour is the most investigated body fluid for estimation of PMI from chemical changes taking place in its constituent electrolytes after death.

Since 1962, vitreous potassium has been the most extensively studied parameter for the estimation of the time of death (but sadly not in this case).

In 1972, two forensic scientists from the Department of Forensic Medicine and Toxicology in the University of Athens, wrote a ground-breaking paper entitled *Estimation of the time of death by potassium levels in the vitreous humour* which was published on 1st April 1972 in the *Forensic Science journal,* pages 55-60. A résumé of the paper is that scientists G. Adjutantis and A. Coutselinis had developed "a method for estimating the time after death within the first 12 hours. Potassium is determined in samples of VH drawn separately from each eye at a known interval of hours. The values are plotted against the post-mortem interval in hours. The results are accurate to within 1.1 hours.

This could possibly explain why the body of Barras was allegedly not "found" for several hours; why it was left in situ for more than 40 hours (if we are to believe the timings provided by the police); why (if true) only a GP and not a pathologist was called to the scene and why there is some debate with regard to the actual time and date of the autopsy – all of which provides credible and compelling evidence of police corruption in this case.

According to the official court list of witnesses, Mr Slaughter did not swear an oath but made an affirmation before the jury on Tuesday, 11 April 2000.

commonly called a spliff, reefer or joint, which is then smoked. They both contain tetrahydrocannabinol (THC) as the active ingredient.

2.3 Effects of cannabis or cannabis resin include dreamlike euphoria, feelings of relaxation and loss of co-ordination and concentration. Effects begin almost immediately after the start of smoking, reaching a peak after approximately twenty minutes and continue for one to two hours, possibly four hours, depending on factors such as the amount smoked, the amount of smoke inhaled and the quality of the cannabis or cannabis resin. If Mr Barras did not smoke cannabis on his journey to the venue, it is unlikely that he was under the influence of that drug at the time of the incident. Cannabis/cannabis resin can increase the intoxicating effects of alcohol.

2.4 In regular, heavy users of cannabis or cannabis resin, the body breakdown product of THC may be detected in a blood sample several days after last usage, and therefore after any effects have worn off.

3. **With respect to Amphetamine**

3.1 A positive result for amphetamine shows that Mr Barras had previously used this drug prior to the incident. From the scientific tests alone, I cannot say when he used amphetamine; however, the absence of this drug from his blood sample means that he was not under the influence of amphetamine at the time of his death.

3.2 Amphetamine (trade name Dexedrine) is prescribed for narcolepsy (falling asleep at inappropriate times) in divided doses of between 10 and 60 milligrams per day, but is also subject to abuse. Illicit amphetamine occurs as powders or tablets and, occasionally, as capsules. It is usually taken by mouth in doses of 20 to 30 milligrams. It may also be taken by injection, in which case, there may be repeated dosage of this amount or more over a short period.

3.3 Amphetamine gives rise to stimulant effects such as excitement, increased wakefulness, physical activity and self-confidence. These affects start after approximately twenty minutes (if the drug is taken on an empty stomach) or almost immediately if taken by injection into a vein. In addition, if amphetamine is injected, there may be an initial rush, or 'high'. Effects last for four to six hours after oral or intravenous use.

3.4 After this period, after effects such as drowsiness and agitation occur. These can last for twelve hours, or longer after heavy usage, and may not be fully alleviated until the subject has slept. Although the subject may feel tired, he may be too agitated to sleep properly.

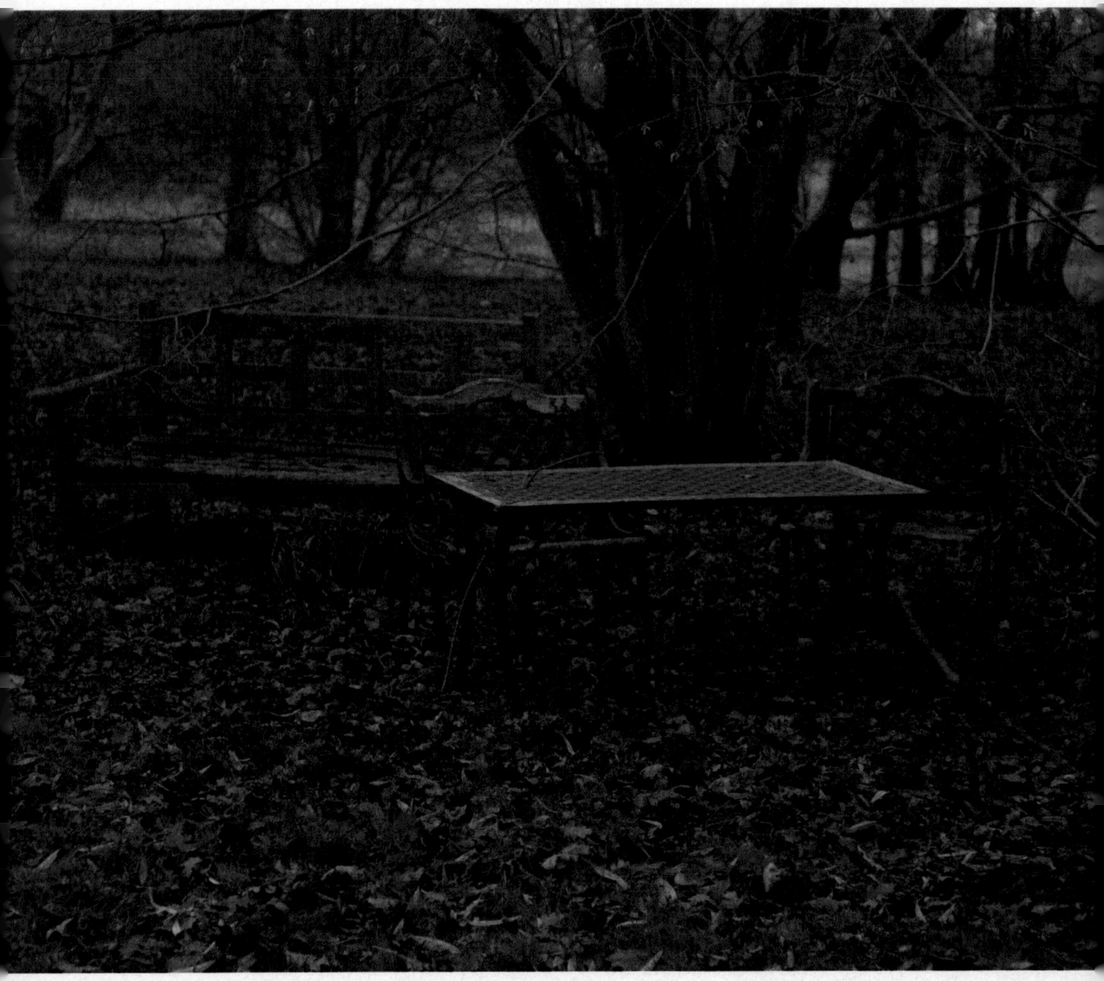

4. **With respect to other drugs of abuse**

4.1 Following use of normal abuse amounts, cocaine, heroin, methadone, MDMA or compounds arising from their use, may be detected in a blood sample for approximately 12 to 24 hours and in a urine sample for approximately 2 days.

4.2 Following therapeutic dosage, diazepam and temazepam are detectable in a blood or urine sample for two days or more.

4.3 The negative results of screening tests show that Mr Barras was not under the influence of any of these drugs at the time of his death.

Conclusions

1. At the time of his death, Mr Barras had a level of alcohol in his bloodstream below that associated with drunkenness in normal persons.

2. Mr Barras had used cannabis or cannabis resin prior to his death; however, I am unable to say when, nor whether he was under the influence of cannabis/cannabis resin at that time.

3. Mr Barras had used amphetamine prior to his death; I am unable to say when. He wouldn't have been under the influence of amphetamine at that time.

4. Mr Barras was not under the influence of diazepam, temazepam, methadone, heroin, cocaine or MDMA at the time of his death.

What this adds to our knowledge	Given Mr Slaughter's conclusions, it would appear that neither drugs nor alcohol contributed to Fred Barras's death and that he was not intoxicated or under the influence of drugs at the time of the incident.

The extreme brevity of this witness statement concerns me. It was not a professional forensic scientific analytical report (as we might reasonably expect), but a witness statement.

Due to its location in the body, which is relatively inaccessible and protected from trauma by the orbital bone and the eye itself, and its composition, VH is generally not susceptible to extensive post-mortem microbial contamination.

Synovial fluid – scientific advancements

The sciencedirect.com website states that "attempts to employ the rate of rise of VH potassium concentration in order to estimate the time of death have largely been abandoned because of the inherent uncertainty of this method. However, the use of synovial fluid, as an alternative to VH, for potassium measurement for time of death estimation has been advocated.

Synovial fluid is a viscous fluid found in the cavities of synovial joints. With its egg white-like consistency, the principal role of synovial fluid is to reduce friction in the joints.

In a study entitled *Postmortem analysis of synovial fluid and vitreous humour for determination of death interval: A Comparative Study*", the authors[333] determined that the level of potassium in synovial fluid and vitreous humour can afford the most accurate method of determining the interval between death and post-mortem.

Thus we have to question why a detailed forensic analysis of the vitreous humour and synovial fluid in Barras was not entered into court and why Tony's barrister did not insist upon it being introduced as evidence in the interest of justice.

Thur
14 OCT
10.45 am
UNUSED
330

Misten Tyre Traders, Downham Market
According to official records, 39-year-old Stephen Archer, manager of Misten Tyre Traders of Downham Market who'd worked there for 11 years, made a statement to DC Cross in which he said that Tony started to buy their products - mainly tyres for his farm tractors - from June 1997.

Mr Archer said that he spoke to Tony about 3 or 4 times per year:

"The last time I spoke to him was on 6 August 1999. This was face to face. The conversation was about tyres and farming in general. In all the times I spoke to Tony he never mentioned crime, travellers or shotguns. I couldn't pass comment on whether he was easily intimidated at all. I would class him as eccentric in the way he dressed and spoke. I personally have not been to Tony's home address but members of my staff may have.

Just to clarify, the computer the business has is only 2 years old and as such only stores information from that time. So Tony could well have been with us longer than 2 years.

I have total sympathy with Tony Martin's situation at present and I hope he is found not guilty of the offences which he was charged with."

---

[333] NK Tumram, RV Bardale & AP Dongre of the Department of Forensic Medicine, Nagpur, India published their findings in *Forensic Science International*, Volume 204, Issues 1-3, 30 January 2011, pp 186-190.

What this adds to our knowledge

Notice how Mr Archer said that he couldn't pass comment on whether Tony could be intimidated or not which means that he would have been asked that question by the police – do you think that was a loaded question or a fair one in the circumstances?

And we cannot ignore his final comment in which he said he had "total sympathy" with Tony – this was a feeling shared by the vast majority of the Great British Public, too. Thankfully.

Thur
14 OCT
1.10 pm
witness 110
331

Eley Hawk cartridge manufacturers
According to official records, PC 837 Douglas 'Danny' Cracknell (who would later join Tony Bone in the Farmwatch business), visited the premises of Eley Hawk cartridge manufacturers to take a statement from 50-year-old production manager Graham Arthur Morris, who had been involved in the production of Eley cartridges since 1974. In his role in the management team, had "seen each and every type of shotgun cartridge produced by the factory."

"At 1:06pm on Thursday 14 October, I was shown a quantity of cartridges in exhibit bags and asked to age the cartridges by production date. I can say the following:

Exhibit JE/19, a box containing Eley Classic cartridges, and JE/18, also containing Eley Classic cartridges, would have been produced by Eley in November, 1990.

Exhibit PB/1, an Eley cartridge, was pre-1971.

Exhibit IWN/2, shotgun cartridges, pre-1971, and rimfire .22 were produced pre-1965.

Exhibit NLN/2, 13 Eley cartridges, were produced before 1989. Exhibit MMW3, Eley cartridges, were made between 1981 and 1988.

Exhibit PB/4, shotgun cartridge, was produced between 1971 and 1979. Exhibit RCC/5, shotgun cartridge, was produced between 1981 and 1988.

I can age the cartridges by the materials used in their manufacture. There were no items in the exhibits produced nearer than 1990. It is not possible to state which outlet may have sold the items, or to whom we supplied them.

I handed the exhibits back to PC Cracknell at 1:40pm."

> **What this adds to our knowledge**
>
> What did Graham Morris add to our knowledge? Without being at all disrespectful to Mr Morris, precisely nothing. All of the cartridges seized by the police were manufactured prior to 1990 and thus all – or none – of them *could* have been used in the shooting in 1999.

In my view, Mr Morris was nothing more than an unnecessary expense – and I do not say that to be in any way rude to him. His bit-part role in this drama was not his fault. Vastly experienced he may have been, but his testimony added absolutely nothing to the case. The casual bystander might well be thinking from afar "What an excellent job the police have done – they even went to all the trouble to get a cartridge manufacturer to provide a statement". And it's a complete red herring, a distraction designed to muddy the waters and cloud the real issue: where was the evidence that, when Tony Martin pulled the trigger, he hit anybody? There is a good deal of evidence to show that he *didn't* hit anybody, much less Fearon and Barras.

Thur
14 OCT
unknown
UNUSED
332

unknown location
The 62-year-old David 'Chick' Schooling had known Tony and his family for many years.

Schooling had worked for Tony's uncle, Jimmy Martin, as a gang master picking potatoes and had been in the fruit and vegetable trade all his life.

This statement was unused:

"In our conversations Tony and I have talked about crime and the local criminals. I have suffered many times with crime, and Tony told me that he had also been burgled. He didn't mention specific occasions, but he did say that he had some pictures/ photos stolen once which were recovered at West Walton.

I knew that Tony's attitude to the travellers was that they were a fucking nuisance. They were also a waste of time. He was worried because someone knew about his house, where it was and what was there. He had had break-ins.

I did not know whether Tony had a gun or not. He never mentioned firearms and I never saw him with one.

The last time I saw Tony was the Thursday before the shooting and there was nothing unusual in his demeanour. He has always been a mild-mannered man, and I've never seen him lose his temper."

> **What this adds to our knowledge**

Mr Schooling confirmed that Tony had had a number of break-ins, that he was particularly worried about being burgled again and that he was generally a mild-mannered man.

Additionally, of course, Mr Schooling had confirmed that there was a lot of crime in the area and that he had also suffered as a result of crime. The police, of course, would not want this to be publicised.

Given that Mr Schooling's comments about Tony were somewhat complimentary, was this the reason that the statement wasn't used as evidence in Court?

Fri | 15 OCT | unknown | UNUSED | 333

home address of Graham Barwell

Another farmer, the 52-year-old Graham Barwell, told DC 603 Andrew David Lovick in his statement that nothing Tony had said at the Farmwatch meeting was out of the ordinary.

He added that he personally didn't join the scheme, not because of anything Tony had said but because he was thinking of selling the farm, having lived and worked in the area for 30 years.

Mon | 18 OCT | unknown | UNUSED | 334

unknown location

Official records show that the 55-year-old Kenneth Williams (not to be confused with the Chief Constable of Norfolk or the Carry On film star with the same name) made a statement to PC 1018 Huw Caine. About a year before the shooting incident, Mr Williams had seen a JCB digger standing in a field on Tony's farm. He was interested in buying such a vehicle and, as it looked as though it wasn't needed, he went down to the farm to see if the owner wanted to sell it.

"I went five or six times down to the farm, but could never find anyone there. As there were what sounded like large dogs barking, I didn't get out of my vehicle.

I eventually found and spoke to a man I now know to be Tony Martin. Tony was scruffily dressed, with dirty, old clothes on. This seemed odd as he was well spoken and, from what he said, I thought he was well-educated. He was pleasant enough to talk to, and I remember had a good sense of humour. He wasn't especially interested in talking about the digger, but did seem keen to talk about a host of other things. He was very opinionated, with strong views, and he spoke about politics, education and the youth of today, but I cannot specifically remember what he said. However, I do remember him telling me of problems he had had with 'dids' stealing his apples. Tony referred to these people as 'dids', and I knew he meant travellers or gypsies.

He said that he had a verbal confrontation with them, but they would not leave his land, so he told them he was going in to get his gun. He told me that, as he returned, the 'dids' or 'pikies' were driving off in their van, and so he had shot at the van. He then told me that, as a result of this, he had his licence revoked and his guns confiscated. Tony also told me that he had been burgled, but I cannot remember whether he said once or twice.

During these conversations I was just trying to get the subject back to the digger, as I wasn't particularly interested in Tony's views, having never met the man before. Tony then told me that, when he was young, he had been abused by his uncle. He didn't go on to say how this was, and I didn't want him to. This surprised me as this is a very personal thing to tell a stranger. I remember thinking that this could account for, or was a reason for his eccentric or extreme views about things.

I was there talking to Tony for about one and a half hours, and I didn't buy the digger as it was too much money. I have not spoken to Tony since this, although I have seen him a few times on his tractor."

What this adds to our knowledge

It provides further evidence that Tony had told people (and the police, who didn't investigate) that he had been abused as a child by Rodney Townley, who was extremely well-connected through his clergyman father as we have previously seen.

It's also possible that this statement had been 'doctored' by senior police officers because, in the hundreds of hours that I have spent in conversation with him, I have never known Tony mention his abuse by Rodney Townley without also mentioning the sexual abuse at Glebe House School. In Tony's head, the two go together like thunder and lightning. It's possible that the abuse at Glebe House was edited out of the original statement.

Mon
18 OCT
unknown
UNUSED
335

unknown location
Official records show that the 40-year-old Elizabeth Mary Gollop, who lived near Tony with her husband Clive and their two sons, made a statement to PC Caine.

At about 8:45pm on Friday 20 August 1999, she was at home. Her husband Clive was watching a film on television and she and their two sons went upstairs to bed. After a short time she was in bed "and dozed off quickly."

"I remember it being hot, and the bedroom window was open. The next thing I remember was hearing two loud bangs. I believe I was half asleep but I clearly heard them. There was a short pause of a few seconds and then a third bang. I did not pay much attention to these bangs, but went off to sleep.

I was up and out of the house by 7:30am on Saturday 21 August 1999 and, although I saw a marked police car on Moyse's Bank,[334] I drove off up Hungate Road without making any connection between the noises and the police.

I subsequently heard about a shooting incident at Bleak House Farm later that day, and then realised that the bangs I had heard were a shotgun being fired. I am happy that this was the noise, as my husband used to have a shotgun and I heard that being shot.

My bedroom window overlooks the bungalows next to Moyse's Bank, and next to this is Bleak House farmland. I can clearly see the orchards at the front of the house, although I cannot see the house. The bangs came from this general direction, although I cannot be any more specific.

I do not know Tony Martin and I have not heard any other shots from the direction of Bleak House. I have lived at this address for about 7 years."

What this adds to our knowledge

Finally, some two months after the shooting, the police get round to taking a statement from one of Tony's nearest neighbours. Mrs Gollop thought that she had heard three shots – two relatively quickly and then a pause and then a third shot. This may well have been the reality and it would certainly seem to fit the prosecution's speculative theory of Tony firing off three shots. That being the case, why do we imagine the prosecution didn't enter this as evidence or call Mrs Gollop as a witness?

Could it have been because she said she was in bed around 9-9:15pm and soon after heard the shots – suggesting that the accepted time of the shooting was not right but that when Tony fired his gun, it had been a good deal earlier and the alleged burglars hadn't even arrived at the farm, since – according to the police's evidence – the alleged burglars didn't leave Newark until 8:15pm at the earliest (though there is evidence to suggest much later).

Was her statement not used because Mrs Gollop had confirmed Tony Martin's timescale inasmuch that he'd called round at the Leets' for a second time around 9:30pm having already fired his gun? If you think that last question to have been fanciful, I offer you the words of Professor Phil Scraton speaking about the alteration of witness statements at Hillsborough:

---

[334] Mrs Gollop made no mention of having seen a white Ford Granada car outside the Leets' bungalow (if it actually had been there).

"Over the years I had witnessed corruption of evidence but I had never seen anything like this, it was shocking. Attached to the statements was a letter from one of the largest firms of solicitors in the UK, Hammond Suddards, from a senior partner, Peter Metcalf, to the head of management services of the South Yorkshire Police, Donald Denton. That letter stated that any statements without annotations made on them have not been subject to review and alteration. That was shocking, I had never seen anything like that. It amounted, in my view, to a corruption of evidence."

Thus you had a senior partner in one of the UK's leading law firms colluding with corrupt senior police officers to create false statements against the dead Liverpool fans – all at taxpayers' expense.

What chance did Tony Martin have against such establishment figures which included equally corrupt senior police officers and a barrister who was formerly head of the Bar Standards Council who seriously failed his client whilst drawing his enormous fees from the public purse?

Wed
20 OCT
5.15 am
UNUSED
336

Bampfylde Road, Torquay, Devon
According to official records, Darren Bark was arrested "whilst on the run" in the West Country.

A statement attributed to PC 3340 Charles Goodman of the Devon and Cornwall Constabulary stationed in Torquay claimed that he was on duty in a marked police car with PC 3451 Burnett[335] when they received a message at 3:30am that a man in a white Montego estate car was stealing garden chairs.

Apparently, Bark had given the name of Darren Smith to the officers and claimed that he was "just walking around". The statement read that Bark ran off but was caught by PC Goodman within about 50 yards.

After opening Bark's car, the police claimed to have found two white metal garden chairs and Bark, arrested on suspicion of theft, apparently replied, "I've never been in trouble before. I make a lousy thief."

We are told that he was then taken to Newton Abbott police station.

This appears to show that Bark apparently went on the run soon after the shooting because he feared reprisals from the travelling community because of the death of Barras.

In a statement made to PC 1018 Caine on 3 November by Brendon Fearon's father, Joe, (who are not travellers) he said that he had heard rumours in Newark that Bark had set up the burglary at Bleak House.

---

[335] There is no record of PC Burnett ever having made a statement to corroborate PC Goodman's account.

It's also possible, of course, that Bark was never actually "on the run" but that he was taken to the West country to get him out of the way whilst the police were creating their false narrative in which he would be described as the "getaway driver" but never brought to court to give evidence or be cross-examined.

Wed
20 OCT
7.50 am
UNUSED
337

Newton Abbott police station, Devon

Official records show that at approximately 6:55am, Bark was arrested by PC Goodman "for failure to answer bail in respect of a burglary at Norfolk". Bark was cautioned and apparently made no reply. We do not know to whom this statement was made – it wasn't recorded on the statement. Nor was this statement entered as evidence into court.

Clearly Tony's defence counsel ought to have called this officer as a witness to inform the jury about his arrest of Bark and the reasons why. Of course, had Scrivener called this constable, he'd have been obligated to have also called Bark.

CORRUPTION ALERT *Alleged 'getaway driver' not called to court*

The issue of not calling Bark as a witness to trial encapsulates the deep level of corruption in this case. Any intelligent member of the public would have called the alleged "getaway driver" to court to have him questioned.

Wed
20 OCT
4.20 pm
witness 43
338

Queen Elizabeth Hospital

Official records show that a full two months after the incident, the 41-year-old staff nurse Christine Rumble made a second statement.

This time we do have a location (the hospital) and a time (4:20pm) and a date and the officer taking the statement was recorded as DS Peter Newton, the senior officer when Tony was interviewed back in August.

In this statement, Ms Rumble claimed that "whilst I was in the x-ray department, Brendon Fearon said to me 'The farmer shot me because he thought I was stealing from him.' I asked him if he was stealing and he replied, 'No'. I later passed this information on to PC 9130 Clare Smith."

Now, what I find strange about this is that Christine Rumble had already made a statement on 14 *September* 1999 – some five weeks earlier – in which she said that Fearon arrived about 11:45pm (not 11:35pm as others had said) and that he had told her that he had been dropped off, "walked up a drive to ask for directions and was shot at" (or words to that effect). She stated that she asked him if he was attempting to burgle the house at the time and he replied, "No."

This statement recorded that it was made at the hospital at 10:40am to DC 422 Trevor Buxton.

Now, why would the police need that second statement since it contained nothing new from the first statement? Had it been interfered with in some way – details added or removed? I leave you to judge.

Thur
21 OCT
5.59 - 6.17 pm
witness 121
339

King's Lynn police station

According to an unsigned statement by DC Peters, he "assisted" in conveying Darren Bark from Exeter police station to King's Lynn. In this statement, Peters failed to note the name of the person he was allegedly assisting.

(In a statement dated 22 October 1999, DC Buxton stated that he had accompanied Peters on that journey.)

Peters' statement records that he interviewed Bark along with DC Buxton. Bark was said to have been legally represented by solicitor John Kendall.

At 8:03pm, Buxton formally charged Bark with conspiracy to commit burglary at Bleak House. Bark apparently made no reply to the caution.

CORRUPTION ALERT   *Alleged 'getaway driver' not called to court*

The interview was shown as having taken place in the HOLMES database:

- at line S2c, the entry states that Bark was "interviewed for burglary by DC Peters/ DC Buxton" on 21 October 1999 – this statement and interview was not entered into evidence at trial

---

- at line S6h, the entry reads "on 21/10/99 DC Buxton conveyed Bark from Exeter Police Station to KL Pol Stn. Later interviewed Bark on tape with DC Peters" - this tape was not entered into evidence at trial
- at line S14i, the entry reads "DC Peters on 21-10-99 conveyed Bark from Exeter PolStn to KL PolStn. Later interviewed Bark between 17:59-

18:17 on 21-10-99" - this statement was not entered into evidence at trial

- *according to Buxton, the tape was given exhibit number TRB/6 and his written transcript of the interview was exhibit TRB/7. However, in her statement dated 25 October 1999, Pippa Gooderson said that there were two interview tapes, exhibits TRB/6 and TRB/8 (not 7)*

It is clear from the above that this interview was of paramount importance and that Bark had said things in it that the police didn't want the public to know. Norfolk Constabulary were aided and abetted by corrupt officials within the CPS who ought to have insisted that the tapes were produced, and additionally assisted by corrupt members of the legal profession. In my view, only a fool would believe that all this wasn't being orchestrated by the Home Office.

Thur 21 OCT
unknown
witness 36
340

unknown location

According to HOLMES (line S215), a statement was taken from John Bruce Everett, described as 'a near-neighbour' of Tony's, to the effect that he heard two loud bangs "at about 10pm" from the direction of Bleak House on 20 August 1999.

However, I have been unable to find this statement. From the brief comments attributed to Mr Everett, this would seem to confirm the notion that only two shots were fired that night.

The official list of witnesses at trial shows that Mr Everett's statement was read out (presumably by prosecutor Horwood-Smart) on Monday 10 April 2000, the first day of the murder trial. But how do we know what was in that statement and whether Mr Everett had signed it, or whether his signature had been witnessed? Or whether the whole thing had been fabricated to add 'substance' to the prosecution's wafer-thin case against the farmer?

CORRUPTION ALERT *Disparity over timing of gunshots*

If we accept that Mr Everett did make a statement to the effect that he had heard gunshots at around 10pm, this blasts the case against Tony right out of the water. The Leets, you will recall, had said that Tony had called round to their bungalow around 9:30pm, **having already fired his gun***. Clearly Tony could not have hit Fearon or Barras. By 10pm he was on his way to his mother's house.*

Thur **21 OCT** unknown UNUSED 341	**unknown location** *According to official records, DS Eglen made a second (unused) statement on this date. He claimed that at 1:15pm on Friday 27 August 1999 he found a black woollen glove in orchards adjacent to Bleak House. He pointed out the glove to PS Fletcher.[336] At 5:25pm the same day he seized, packaged and sealed the glove as exhibit reference JE36. At 8:10pm the same day, at King's Lynn police station, he handed the exhibit reference JE36 to PC Matthews."[337]*

The statement is dated two months <u>after</u> the shooting incident. Why would it take so long to make such a simple statement?

Please note that there is no mention whatsoever of his having attended Bleak House on any other dates.

We should consider that Barras apparently was wearing rubber gloves, whilst Fearon was wearing woollen gloves.

We should also consider that the window allegedly removed by Fearon in the breakfast room was never tested for fibres so that we could have a match with the gloves.

Furthermore, PC Craske was said to have found the glove on the same day, also in the orchard. He exhibited it as DJC/1. It never made its way into the trial as evidence.

Fri **22 OCT** unknown witness 112 342	**unknown location** *According to HOLMES (line S210), a statement was taken from Amanda Dawn Kirkham, a forensic scientist from Hinchingbrooke Park, Huntingdon. However, I have been unable to find such a statement and am thus unable to report on what it might have said.* *According to the official exhibit list, a "forensic examination record" attributed to Ms Kirkham was entered into evidence as exhibit 167. I have been unable to find this evidence.*

However, this seemingly innocuous statement causes the police a great deal of harm. The HOLMES database at line S210 lists the *statement* as having been entered as evidence into court, but at line S142d (under Matthew Sharman), it states the following: "on 02-10-99 received by internal mail a statement and other papers from Amanda Kirkham. Also included exhibit AMK/1."

---

[336] PS Fletcher was recorded as having been the team leader in the search that day.
[337] PC Matthews was recorded as having been the principal Exhibits Officer.

> **CORRUPTION ALERT** *Manipulation of evidence*
>
> *So, the problem for the police is this: how could Sharman have received a statement from Amanda Kirkham in the internal post on 2nd October if she didn't make the statement until 20 days later? And why is there no detail about what exhibit A<u>MK</u>/1 actually contained? The exhibit was listed in the official record as A<u>DK</u>/1.*

Mon
25 OCT
unknown
UNUSED
343

unknown location
Records show that a 30-year-old near-neighbour of Tony, Tracey Drindra Smith, who lived at Joyce Nurseries, Smeeth Road, Marshland St James with her boyfriend Peter Penfold, made a statement to DC Adcock. The entrance to their house, via the Smeeth Road, was controlled by a large, wooden, electronic gate, which also had a video surveillance camera situated on the gate itself.

"I want to refer to Saturday 24 July 1999, about 4pm. I recall I was driving home in one of our cars, either the Audi or the Peugeot, having been to Wisbech. I recall driving down the Wilkins Road (also known as Walsoken Road) from the Wisbech direction towards Chequers Corner, Emneth Hungate. At this 'T'-junction I turned left onto the Smeeth Road towards the village centre of Marshland St James. My boyfriend, Peter, was in the front passenger seat.

Our house is situated about 300-400 yards along this road, on the right, and, as we got closer, I noticed a vehicle parked in our driveway. This vehicle had reversed up to the gate, with its front facing the Smeeth Road. The position of this vehicle on our drive was unusual and made us suspicious. I recognised that this vehicle was a Ford Mondeo, colour blue.

I indicated to turn right into our driveway shortly before the entrance to the drive. I turned into the drive with the front of my vehicle close to the electric gate. As I pulled up and stopped, the Mondeo sped off onto the Smeeth Road towards Marshland St James. I recall that, as I turned into our property, the Mondeo driver started his engine then drove off as we stopped.

I would describe the driver, believed male, as of Asian appearance. I can only guess their age as being between twenty years and forty years. This person had black hair, which was pulled back, and the back was in what appeared to be a bun. The reason I am unsure of the gender of this person is because of the hairstyle and, in any case, I do not believe I would recognise them again. There was also a passenger in the Mondeo, who was sitting in the front passenger seat. I recall the window being wound down, and his arm was leaning lengthways out of this window in a relaxed position.

I would describe him as follows: male, I believe of Asian origin again. He was under twenty years of age. His hair was short and dark, with no particular style.

I notified the police of this incident because of the shooting incident at Bleak House in August. I saw the face of the young lad, Fred Barras, who had been shot, and I recognised the face. I believe that the passenger was very similar in appearance to that of Fred Barras, although I am not certain.

As the Mondeo sped off, Peter read out the registration number to me. When we got into our house, Peter wrote the number down in his diary. The registration number is R801BNG.

I do not know, or have ever spoken to my neighbour, Tony Martin."

Tracey Smith gave a description of the driver as being like Fearon (who says he does not have a driving licence though he can drive) and she said that the passenger was probably Fred Barras. We should note that she made this statement to DC Adcock on 25 October – after the incident and the national media coverage – so that's how she would know his name.

However, we have to consider that she simply made a connection to Barras because of all the coverage that his death had attracted. In any event, even if it was not Fearon and Barras in the car, the occupants certainly acted suspiciously according to her full statement and it does at least show that at this time there was a lot of suspicious activity in the Emneth and Marshland St James areas, which is something Tony Martin was forever reporting to the police who, in turn, were continually in denial. I can't help thinking that it's a pity that the Emneth and Marshland residents didn't form their own 'Neighbourhood Watch' scheme and have Tony on its committee, making representations for greater security in the area.

Tracey Smith's 31-year-old fiancé, Peter Penfold, made a statement to PC Caine, which was essentially the same as his partner's though he thought the driver may have been female because of the hair style. Neither of their statements was used as evidence in the trial – perhaps because everything they said supported Tony's account of the increasing lawlessness of the area. Mr Penfold had this to add to our knowledge:

"Around March or April 1999, I attended an agricultural sale at a farm near to King's Lynn on the A47. I went with a friend, Tim Huggins. Whilst I was there I was introduced to one or two people who live locally. One of these is a man I now know to be Tony Martin. He was introduced as my neighbour. I remember he was wearing a black beret and a black top. I spoke to him for about two minutes only. I remember him saying that it was a good idea to put up security gates at my premises. He stated that he had been burgled recently. He suspected that this had been travellers. At this time I was in the process of having large, electronically-operated, wooden gates put up at the entrance to my drive. Tony had clearly seen these going up. The reason for these gates is that we have had unknown vehicles drive into the property in suspicious circumstances. I cannot remember any other specific topics of conversation with Tony, but I remember him seeming intelligent and well-educated."

Clearly the police have not used this as evidence because it supported Tony on a number of levels. Firstly, Mr Penfold described the farmer as "intelligent and well-educated". They met, he said, at an auction – so much for the eccentric loner label that corrupt State officials saw fit to label Tony with.

And then Mr Penfold said that – within two minutes of first meeting him – Tony had mentioned the electronic gates they had been installing at the nursery. This is how Tony is – you do not get the usual pleasantries which he describes to me as "false", but rather he goes 'straight for the jugular' and simply says whatever is on his mind. A lot of people find this disarming, but I like it because you always know where you stand with the man.

Peter Penfold confirmed that Tony had told him he'd been burgled earlier in the year and, given the date these two men met, it can only have been the January burglary, not the one in May.

And finally, Mr Penfold informed us that the reason he felt compelled to install the electronic gating system was because of the large number of "unknown vehicles driving into the property in suspicious circumstances".

This corroborated exactly what Tony had been saying for some years and the police failed to address the problem at all.

Tue
26 OCT
unknown
witness 105
344

unknown location
According to official records, this is DS Eglen's third statement. It causes me great concern on a number of levels which I'll discuss afterwards:

"Saturday, 21 August 1999

At 4:50pm,[338] I attended Bleak House,[339] where I met DC Aldous and Mrs Bradley,[340] fellow scenes of crime officers. The

---

[338] Note the time: in his statement dated 1st October 1999, acting DI Sharman stated that he had arrived at 11:30am. Despite claiming that he didn't enter the house or even get out of his car, it is certainly possible that he was lying and that he did enter the house and plant three cartridges in the breakfast room to be "found" by DS Eglen. Any incorruptible barrister would have picked up on this point and made it known to a jury – because it is room for reasonable doubt.

house was secure except for a ground floor window at the front which appeared to be a forced point of entry and a ground floor window at the rear where a box window had apparently fallen or been pushed *into*[341] the house. As a result of what I saw and what I was told I decided to enter the house via the rear window at 7:55pm the same day.

Having entered the house I went to a front door which I found secured by two Yale style locks. I unlocked the door and *established a common approach path into the main room.*

I then made a brief examination of rooms on the ground floor. I saw an area of shot damage below the opening where the rear window had fallen in and what appeared to be flesh and blood associated with it.

I saw three fired cartridge cases on the floor opposite the shot damage and other unfired cartridges amongst rubbish on the floor.

In company with DC Aldous and Mrs Bradley I then erected sheeting to protect the rear window and placed a protective tent over the body of a male, I now know to be Frederick Barras, in the rear garden.

At 8:40pm the same day I left the scene in charge of uniform officers.

Sunday, 22 August 1999

At 10:50am, I reattended Bleak House. In company with DC Aldous, Mrs Bradley and forensic scientists Brian Arnold and Andrew Palmer[342], I started an examination of the scene.

At 2:25pm I began a video film of the front of the house and ground floors. I completed that video between then and Saturday, 28 August (exhibit JE/1).

In a statement dated 28 September 1999, I have dealt with the production of exhibits reference JE/2, JE/2A, JE/2B, JE/3, JE/4 and JE/4A.

I began a schematic plan of the main room at Bleak House (exhibit JE/5). I showed the location of exhibits seized on that plan. I completed it during subsequent days and handed it to PC Matthews at 3:30pm on Tuesday 31 August 1999.

At 3:20pm that day I was present when Andrew Palmer and Brian Arnold made an examination inside the house. I flagged and arrowed exhibits indicated by them for collection.

At 6:38pm the same day I left the scene in charge of uniform officers.

---

[339] DS Eglen is not listed in the CAD report.

[340] You will recall that in none of her three statements did SOCO Bradley place herself at Bleak House on this day. Neither Aldous nor Bradley were listed in the CAD report.

[341] If it had been *pushed into* the house, it can't have been *pulled into* the house.

[342] There is no reference to Andrew Palmer anywhere in the HOLMES database, other than DS Eglen's statement. This means, of course, that there is no statement from Palmer and no forensic report as we might reasonably expect.

Monday, 23 August 1999

At 11:26am, I returned to Bleak House with DC Aldous.

At 3:10pm I began to collect, package and seal exhibits:

JE/6. Fired cartridge case. Floor of main room at flag 7.

JE/7. Fired cartridge case. Floor of main room at flag 8.

JE/8. Fired cartridge case. Floor of main room at flag 9.

JE/9. Cartridge wadding. Floor of main room at flag 10.

JE/10. Cartridge wadding. Floor of main room at flag 11.

JE/11. Piece of red and blue fabric. Close to wall amongst rubble. On floor of main room at flag 12.

JE/12. Piece of red fabric. Close to wall amongst brick rubble. Floor of main room at flag 13.

JE/13. Body tissue. On upper face of wooden plank by rear facing door. Floor of main room at flag 14.

JE/14. Piece of denim cloth. Close to rear door. Floor of main room at flag 15.

JE/15. Fired cartridge case. Close to wall. Floor of main room at flag 16.

At 5:35pm the same day I recovered a sawn off shotgun from the loft of a double garage adjacent to the house.[343] The gun (exhibit JE/16) was in the roof space, where ceiling boarding had fallen, in front of a large boiler.

At 6:30pm the same day PC 896 Kelvin John Steward attended the scene and I handed him the sawn off shotgun reference JE/16.

At 7:43pm the same day I left the scene in charge of uniform officers.

At 8:05pm the same day, at King's Lynn police station, I handed the exhibits reference JE/6 to JE/15 inclusive to PC Matthews.[344]

Tuesday, 24 August 1999

At 11:40am, I returned to Bleak House. I searched the hallway from the main room door past the stairs and into a sitting room opening off the hall. I included the doorway opening.

I began a schematic plan of the area on which I showed the location of exhibits seized. I completed the plan over subsequent days and handed it to PC Matthews at 3:30pm on Tuesday 31 August 1999 (exhibit JE/17).[345]

In the hallway I seized the following exhibits which I packaged and sealed:

---

[343] This find had nothing to do with excellent detective work – Tony Martin had told the police it was there when interviewed for the first time.

[344] According to his own statement (dated 1st October 1999), PC 376 Matthews was "employed as exhibit officer on the case of *R. v Fearon & Bark.*" In that role, he should not have been handling the exhibits in the case of *R. v Anthony Edward Martin*. It would appear from the police's own evidence that they were running two cases simultaneously and transferring (or 'losing') exhibits between each case.

[345] This plan was not entered into court as evidence, despite it being of some significance if it really was the scene of a crime.

JE/18. Box containing Ely Classic cartridges and spilled cartridges around it. Total 36 cartridges. In hall, at doorway, flag 23.

JE/19. Box containing one Ely Classic cartridge and thirteen loose cartridges around it. Total 14 cartridges. Floor of hall at flag 24.

I closely examined brickwork around the hole in the wall between the hall and main room. *I saw no evidence of shot marking. I also closely examined surfaces in line of sight from the stairs into the main room.*[346] Other than marks on the rear facing wall and door I found no shot marking.

At 1:35pm the same day I took possession of the box window (exhibit JE/20) from centre floor of the main room. I took possession of two areas of blood or body tissue from the upper face of the box window. Exhibits JE/21 and JE/22.

At 5pm the same day PC Matthews visited the scene. I handed the box window to him at the scene cordon. I searched the area of floor below the box window.[347] I seized, packaged and sealed a single unfired cartridge (exhibit JE/24). Also from the main room I took possession of exhibits:

JE/23. A single unfired cartridge. Floor of main room at flag 27.

JE/25. Fax machine complete. On stool in main room at flag 29.

At 6:37pm the same day I left the scene in charge of uniform officers.

At 7pm the same day, at King's Lynn police station, I handed the following exhibits to PC Matthews: JE/18, JE/19, JE/21, JE/22, JE/23, JE/24 and JE/25.

Wednesday, 25 August 1999[348]

At 12:17pm I returned to Bleak House, where I took possession of the following exhibits: JE/26. Ely Classic cartridge. Floor of main room below box window JE/20. JE/27. Ely Classic cartridge. Floor of point of entry room at flag 32.

I also added film of the first floor landing, passage, bathroom and bedroom to the video, exhibit reference JE1.

At 6:25pm the same day I left the scene in charge of uniform officers.

At 8:12pm the same day, at King's Lynn police station, I handed the

---

[346] DS Eglen claimed that he found no shot marking in the line of sight from the stairs into the main room. So, no pellets were embedded in the woodwork around the doorframe and yet we were expected to believe that Tony fired through the doorway and hit two alleged burglars. Had he fired through the doorway, pellets would have spread out and become embedded in the architrave. Notice that DS Eglen *failed* to state whether he found any pellets embedded in the floorboards in the hallway, Tony having fired his gun in a *downwards trajectory* from the staircase.

[347] In December 2018, Tony carefully examined the box window, which he had held in storage on his farm ever since it had been returned to him by the police. *He saw no evidence of blood spatter or indentations caused by shotgun pellets.*

[348] Notice that there was no mention of SOCO Bradshaw's alleged swabbing of the stairs, yet according to Bradshaw's statement (if it is to be believed) he claimed that it was Eglen who had called him in to swab the stairs.

packaged and sealed exhibits reference JE/26 and JE/27 to PC Matthews.

Thursday, 26 August 1999

At 10:34am, I reattended Bleak House. At 11:25am I commenced a check of the electricity supply to the house. There was what appeared to be an old and unserviceable mains supply with a consumer unit in the hallway. The unit did not function. On the floor in the hall I saw a two-gang cable reel. Each socket had a three way adaptor unit with three leads plugged into the adaptors. The feed into the cable reel came into the hall through a vent above the main doors. I refer to the three leads leaving the cable reel as 'A', 'B' and 'C'.

Line 'A' ran to a further two-gang cable reel in the centre ground floor room. One two-way adaptor was plugged into the cable reel but there was no appliance in the room to make use of that extension.

Line 'B' ran to a two-gang cable reel in the main room. Nothing was plugged into it. I had removed the only appliance in the room when I had seized the fax machine (exhibit JE/25). The fax machine had been plugged into the extension.

Line 'C' ran to a two-gang cable reel in the used bedroom. One plug was inserted in that cable reel and the line ran to a two gang extension block in the same room. Both sockets in the block were used. One fed a bedside television. The other line ran to a further two-gang cable reel from which a lead led to a table lamp on an upended radio on a bedside chest of drawers.

Having established the extent of wiring from the cable reel in the hall, I followed the feed to the reel from the vent above the hall doors across lawns at the front of the house to a further two-gang reel which continued to a barn beside the track serving the house and farmland.

Inside the barn the cable was plugged into a socket hanging on conduit from the wall. An isolator switch served the conduit and socket. I turned the isolator and socket switches in the barn on and checked appliances in the house. *The table lamp in the bedroom was on but dim and flickering.*[349] The television was not on but came on when a remote control was operated.

In the hallway a table lamp was suspended from the ceiling by its shade. A lead from that lamp reached the two-gang reel on the hall floor. When it was plugged in the lamp worked.

At 12:23pm the same day I was present while forensic scientists Brian Arnold and Graham Renshaw carried out an examination of the scene, in particular an

---

[349] Author's emphasis. This is an extremely important point because the police claimed that they had been to the house and found it "in complete darkness". Since this light was permanently on, and there were no curtains at the window, and since Tony had not shut off the electricity when he left the premises that night, it would not have been possible for the house to be "in complete darkness".

area of shot patterning on and around the inside of the rear facing door of the main room.[350]

At 2:05pm I added video film of the remaining first floor rooms to the video tape, (exhibit JE/1). I then removed lead shot from the rear door of the main room as indicated by Brian Arnold. I produce the following exhibits:

JE/28. Lead shot. Door in main room above bottom hinge.
JE/29. Lead shot. Door in main room above loft.
JE/30. Lead shot. Door in main room above loft.
JE/31. Lead shot. Door in main room wedged under both.
JE/32. Lead shot. Door in main room at end of hinge.

I also took possession of a piece of denim fabric on a bag in the corner of the main room at flag 34 (exhibit JE/33).

At 6:20pm the same day I left the scene in charge of uniform officers.

At 7:40pm the same day, at King's Lynn police station, I handed the packaged and sealed exhibits, reference JE/28 to JE/33 inclusive, to PC Matthews.

Friday, 27 August 1999

At 11:25am, I returned to Bleak House. At 11:50am that day, in company with DC Aldous, I made further checks concerning the electricity supply.

When DC Aldous turned the supply on in the barn the lamp in the bedroom flickered on. I then pushed the plug feeding it firmly into its socket. *The light then became steady but remained dim. I took possession of that lamp*[351] (exhibit reference JE/34). Table lamp with 15 watt Electrolux low energy bulb. Beside bed in bedroom. I also took possession of exhibit JE/35. Table lamp with low energy, 11 watt, neonlite bulb. Suspended from a cable across the hall ceiling.

At 1:15pm the same day I walked the area at the rear of the house in company with DC Aldous. As a result of what I saw I crossed an adjacent field, with DC Aldous, and entered an orchard.

In grass at the edge of the orchard I found a black woollen glove. I marked its position and informed PS Fletcher.

At 5:25pm the same day I seized, packaged and sealed the glove,[352] I produce exhibit JE/36 from flag 37. At 6:57pm the same day I left the scene in charge of uniform officers.

At 8:10pm the same day, at King's Lynn police station, I handed exhibits JE/34, JE/35 and JE/36 to PC Matthews.

---

[350] We would do well to question the integrity of that examination (if it actually took place), since it was 6 days after Tony fired his gun. The crime scene could easily have been interfered with and, in fact, I argue that the breakfast room was nothing more than a Hollywood film set – stage managed to the last detail.

[351] Author's emphasis. Note the reference to the lighted lamp.

[352] Notice that DS Eglen failed to provide the seal number as normal protocol would require him to do so in a statement.

Saturday, 28 August 1999

At 10:33am I returned to Bleak House and completed video, exhibit JE/1.

At 1:45pm I took glass from a rear facing window in the main room. The window had three broken panes.[353] I produce the following exhibits:

JE/37. Debris outside rear window.[354]

JE/38. Debris inside rear window.

JE/39. Glass removed from rear window.[355]

JE/40. Glass removed from rear window.

JE/41. Glass removed from rear window.

I packaged and sealed[356] each exhibit as I seized it.

At 4:24pm the same day I left the scene in charge of uniform officers.

At 5:30pm the same day, at King's Lynn police station, I handed exhibits reference JE/1, JE/37, JE/38, JE/39, JE/40 and JE/41 to PC Matthews.

Wednesday, 1 September 1999

At 10:53am I returned to Bleak House. I examined and now describe the staircase in the hall. The stairs comprise a wooden flight, originally of fifteen steps including the landing. The stairway is approximately 970 millimetres wide. The three bottom steps are removed and the two top steps, which turned through 90 degrees to meet the landing, are also removed. On the wall side, the case has slipped on its mountings and is 70 millimetres below its original position at the bottom. At the top the case had slipped to 270 millimetres below its original position. The bottom of the staircase is accessed by climbing onto an aluminium folding ladder at the foot of the stairs.

At 3pm the same day I made a video film showing DC Aldous[357] as he descended the stairs and crossed the hallway taking a photograph at each pause. (exhibit JE/42).

At 5:51pm the same day I left the scene in charge of uniform officers.

At 7pm the same day, at King's Lynn police station, I handed the video (exhibit JE/42) to PC Matthews.

---

[353] Tony informed me (when he examined the window in December 2018) that there was only one pane of glass missing.

[354] If Fearon pulled the window into the breakfast room, how did "debris" make its way outside the house?

[355] DS Eglen failed to state whether he found this glass inside or outside of the house.

[356] See previous footnote.

[357] I have been unable to find a statement from DC Aldous which places him in Bleak House assisting DS Eglen on this day. Not only is there no statement, but there is also no entry in the HOLMES database which supports the claim that Aldous was present on this day.

Thursday, 2 September 1999

At 9:45am, at Downham Market police station, I received the following exhibits from PC Matthews: items reference JE/2A, JE/2B, JE/3, JE/4A and TRB/3.[358]

At 10:25am the same day I handed the following exhibits to Mr Leroy Thompson: JE/2A, JE/2B and JE/4A.

At 11:30am, at Bleak House, I handed exhibit TRB/3 to PC 229 Eves.

At 1:45pm the same day, in company with DC Aldous,[359] I removed the rear facing door of the main room inside Bleak House. I produce exhibits:

JE/43, bottom bar.
JE/44 bar next above bottom.
JE/45 bar next below top.
JE/46 top bar.
JE/47 door.

During that afternoon, while still at Bleak House, I received exhibit TRB/3 from PC Eves and exhibits JE/2A, JE/2B and JE/4A from Leroy Thompson.

At 4:25pm the same day I received the following exhibits from PS Mizen, all were sealed in tamper evident bags:

AMH/3. Fax form Norfolk Constabulary.
CLJ/1. 22 Cartridge
CLJ/2. Pistol Cartridge
MMW/1. Ely Classic Cartridge
SJ/1. Ely Grand Prix Empty Case
SJ/2. Three times Ely Classic Cartridges
GMW/1. Three times Ely Classic Cartridges.
NLM/1. Ely Shotgun Case and Razor
SJ/3. Shotgun Case.
NLM/2. Thirteen times Ely Cartridges and One Times Gamebore Cartridges.
AMH/4. Newspaper Cuttings.
MMW/2. Shotgun Case, Fourteen.
CLJ/3. Two times .22 rounds, One times .38 round.
IWN/1. Newspaper cuttings and map.
MRM/1. Assorted Coins, value unknown.

At 5:15pm the same day I secured all the exhibits in my possession in the locked Scenes of Crimes Major Incident Vehicle.

---

[358] Exhibit TRB/3 was Tony's car keys. These were returned to PC 376 Matthews at 11:10am on Monday 23 August 1999, by PC 979 Jennifer Elton. It would seem, then, that DS Eglen had borrowed the keys. TRB referred to DC Buxton.

[359] I have been unable to find a statement from DC Aldous in which he places himself there.

Friday, 3 September, 1999

At 10:20am, I returned to Bleak House where I met PC Stephenson. At 10:35am I handed him the following exhibits: JE/43, JE/44, JE/45, JE/46, JE/47, TRB/3, JE/3, JE/3A, AMH/3, CLJ/1, CLJ/2, MMW/1, SJ/1, SJ/2, GWM/1, MLM/1, SJ/3, MLM/2, AMH/14, MMW/2, CLJ/3, IWN/1 and MRM/1.

Sunday, 5 September 1999

At 4:27pm, I was present at Bleak House when the following carried out an examination:[360] Dr P. Nigel Cooper, Mr G Renshaw, Mr P Harper, Mr N Makin, Mr S Makin and Mr A Whitcher.[361] Prior to leaving the scene at 8:30pm, I took possession of a window restraining bar associated with the forced window at the front of the house.

Monday, 6 September 1999

At 4:25pm, I handed the exhibit JE/48 together with exhibits reference JE/2A, JE/2B and JE/4A to PC Matthews, at King's Lynn police station.

Thursday, 9 September 1999

At 4:50pm, I received photograph albums, exhibits reference RA/1 and BJW/30 from PC Bush. I secured them in the strong room at Downham Market p.s.

Tuesday, 28 September 1999

At 10:07am, I returned to Bleak House where I met Mr Chris Baker. I briefed him regarding a video film to be made of the house and surrounds.

At 11:05am I took possession of a piece of broken bathroom furniture from below and outside the forced entry window at the front of the house. I produce exhibit reference JE/49.

At 1:15pm the same day I left the scene in charge of uniform officers.

At 3pm the same day, at Downham Market police station, I received a copy video, exhibit reference JE/42A from PC Matthews.

At 3:50pm I handed him exhibit reference JE/49.

Friday, 1 October 1999

At 11:50am, I went to Bluebell Cottage, No. 4, Kerrison Road, Norwich.

---

[360] This yet another example of police corruption – Eglen knew very well the nature of "the examination" and he had deliberately withheld it from his statement. In other words, he was deliberately perverting the course of justice. The examination was crucial to the case and we will come to it in a later entry.

[361] As far as I have been able to ascertain, not one of these people alleged to have been present at Bleak House (a crime scene) made a statement, contrary to normal protocol. Not one of the people named here is mentioned in the HOLMES database.

At 1:55pm I handed Mr Chris Baker a strip of photographic proofs marked ALD/227/99, 99/4800, 4603. I explained to him the order in which they were to appear in an edited video film.

Monday, 4 October 1999
At 11:35am, at the police station, Bethel Street, Norwich, I received the following exhibits from PC Matthews: TAB/1, video cassette. JE/1 video cassette and JE/42 video cassette.

At 1:30pm the same day I went to Bluebell Cottage, No. 4 Kerrison Road, Norwich where I saw Mr Chris Baker.

At 2:20pm I handed him exhibits TAB/1, JE/1 and JE/42. I was present while Mr Baker began to edit a compilation of the video tapes, exhibits TAB/1 and JE1.

Tuesday, 5 October 1999
At 2:05pm, I returned to Bluebell Cottage, where I met Mr Baker. I assisted him in editing the video tape, exhibit JE/42 to include the correct sequence of photographs from the strip of proofs marked ALD/227/99, 99/4800, 4603.

Wednesday, 6 October 1999
At 11:45am, I returned to Bluebell Cottage. I checked the content of video films he had made and packaged them.

At 2:05pm I received from him, exhibits:

CB/1. DVCAM tape. Original Camera Tape. Bleak House and photographs marked 99/4800. ALD/227/99. 4603.

CB/2. DVCAM tape. Edited Master, Bleak House.

CB/2A VHS tape. Copy of CB2.

CB/2B VHS tape. Copy of CB2.

CB/2C VHS tape. Copy of CB2.

CB/2D VHS tape. Copy of CB2.

CB/3 DVD Edit Master. Combined video & stills of stairs and hall, Bleak House.

CB/3A Copy of Master CB3. Stairs and Hall, Bleak House.

CB/3B Copy of Master CB3. Stairs and Hall, Bleak House.

CB/3C Copy of Master CB3. Stairs and Hall, Bleak House.

CB/3D Copy of Master CB3. Stairs and Hall, Bleak House.

CB/4 DVCAM tape. Combined JE/1 and TAB/1, Bleak House.

CB/4A Copy of Master, CB/4, Bleak House. CB/4B Copy of Master, CB/4, Bleak House. CB/4C Copy of Master, CB/4, Bleak House. CB/4D Copy of Master, CB/4, Bleak House.

CB/5 Time coded copy Red, JE/43 1/9/99.

CB/6 Time coded copy Green, Bleak House Photos.

CB/7 Copy of working notes.

In addition I received the video tapes, exhibits TAB/1, JE/1 and JE/42.

Thursday, 7 October 1999

At 12:30pm, I attended the police station at Downham Market where I met DCI Wright. I opened packages containing video films, exhibits CB/2A, CB/3A and CB/4A for viewing.

At 2pm the same day I received video tape, exhibit reference IB/3A, from PC Matthews.

At 3:20pm the same day I handed the following to PC Matthews: IB/3A, CB/2A, CB/3A, CB/4A, JE/42A, unsealed. TAB/1, JE/1, JE/42, CB/1, CB/2, CB/2B, CB/2C, CB/2D, CB/3, CB/3B, CB/3C, CB/3D, CB/4, CB/4B, CB/4C, CB/4D, CB/5, CB/6 & CB/7."

> **What this adds to our knowledge**
>
> On the face of it, that seems like a very thorough and professional statement but, upon closer analysis, it is anything but. For example, DS Eglen used the phrase "I left the scene in charge of uniform officers" on no less than 9 occasions without once ever providing the names of any officers who were allegedly left at the scene of the crime.

But there are other worrying factors contained throughout this statement and perhaps we should be concerned about the date it was allegedly written: 26 October 1999 – some *two months* after the shooting and his alleged visits to Bleak House. The statement consisted of 17 typed pages and yet he'd previously made a statement on 21 October in which none of this information was contained in its two pages.

Right from the start of this statement I began to be concerned that a SOCO who claimed to have 20 years' experience in the job informed us that he chose to enter Bleak House *via the alleged rear exit window* (where a lot of evidence ought to be if we subscribe to the police narrative) and yet he apparently had keys to the front door. Straightaway, that single statement alone should cause alarm bells to ring because what self-respecting detective would contemplate that?

But we should also consider that Fearon and Barras were never in the house on this night.

What about this: "I established a common approach path into the main room" – isn't that interfering with a crime scene? He was allegedly the only officer present and so there were no checks and balances to his behaviour. In order to establish a "common approach path" through the rubble and objects strewn over the floors, wouldn't you have to disturb the scene? And if it was strictly necessary to do this, wouldn't you have wanted a second person there to video record the event for a jury to scrutinise and to ensure fair play?

Thus, on the first page of 17, this 20-years-in-the-job SOCO had entered a crime scene via the very same window by which the intruders were alleged to have escaped the building (when he had the keys to the front door) and he unilaterally disturbed the alleged crime scene inside Bleak House. Had you been

Tony's barrister, wouldn't you have made a great deal out of this blatant disregard for normal police protocol?

DS Eglen claimed that "in company with DC Aldous and Mrs Bradley I erected sheeting to protect the rear window and placed a protective tent over the body of a male."

Now, in order to establish the veracity of Eglen's claims, we need to cross-reference the statements made by Aldous and Bradley. Taking DC Aldous first, HOLMES listed him as having made *four* statements dated 22 September,[362] then strangely 21 September,[363] and two on 4 November 1999.[364] For the purposes of this present discussion point, we can discount the statement made on 21 September because it referred only to the burglary in May.

However, in the statement dated 22 September, he made no mention of having attended Bleak House with DS Eglen on 21 August. Is this of concern?

CORRUPTION ALERT — *'Missing' police statements and lack of cross-referencing*

I have been unable to locate the third and fourth statements attributed to him – does that concern you? The HOLMES entry for the third statement (consisting of 10 pages) reads: "main statement of SOCO including producing exhibits from Bleak House", and so it would follow that perhaps he made reference to being at Bleak House with DS Eglen on 21 August in this statement. But why was it not included in the hundreds of statements provided to the defence team?

The HOLMES entry for the fourth statement read "states exhibit JE/33 was moved by himself on 25-08-99 whilst photographing shoemarks", so it's unlikely that that statement made any reference to 21 August 1999. (I haven't seen that statement because it wasn't included in the Used Material bundle.)

Before I continue to analyse DS Eglen's statement, are you at all concerned by the issues I've raised so far?

The SOCO then stated that he re-attended Bleak House at 10:50am on Sunday 22 August but made no mention of having attended Downham Market police station at 10am for a conference about the murder inquiry. Perhaps he didn't attend that conference, but others (including pathologist Dr Heath) have placed him there. Was Eglen's omission a mere oversight or a deliberate act to distance himself from that conference and if so, why?

---

[362] Line S128.
[363] Line S128a.
[364] Lines S128b and S128c.

Eglen then claimed that in company with SOCOs Aldous and Bradley and forensic scientists Arnold and Palmer, he "started an examination of the scene". Hadn't he done that the day before (according to his own statement)?

Are we concerned that Eglen claimed that "[a]lso on Sunday 22 August 1999, I began a schematic plan of the main room at Bleak House. I showed the location of exhibits seized on that plan." (The main room referred to was what Tony called the breakfast room.) If he had "prepared a common pathway" the previous day, how can we be sure that the exhibits on his plan the next day were in their original position at the time of the shooting? I argue that we can't and certainly not when a man's liberty is at stake in a murder trial. Eglen admitted that he completed the plan "over subsequent days" and how can we be sure that nobody moved anything in those "subsequent days"?

We should pay close regard to exhibits JE/6- JE/10. The first three were spent cartridge casings and the last two were wadding. Wadding is a piece of material (more usually plastic these days) which holds all of the shotgun pellets in place inside the casing prior to the cartridge being fired. Once fired, the cartridge is projected forwards, the wadding comes out and the pellets scatter. Three empty casings, only two pieces of wadding. Does that concern you?

Then Eglen referred to finding a sawn-off shotgun in the roof of the garage adjacent to Bleak House. Tony had told the police that it was there – it wasn't some masterful piece of detective work: "At 6:30pm the same day [22 August] PC Steward attended the scene and I handed him the sawn off shotgun (JE/16)."

I have been unable to locate PC Steward's statement, even though it was listed in HOLMES (line S225) and even though the constable was listed as witness number 106. Does any of this concern you?

We now come to the electricity supply at Bleak House. In the course of refurbishing his house, Tony dispensed with most of the electrical sockets in the house and took a direct supply from the main barn. This provided a supply for his fax machine in the breakfast room, a light in the hall as he entered his house and a light in his bedroom with a separate socket for the television and/or radio.

Crucially, DS Eglen informed us that when he flicked the switch in the barn all of the electrical outlets in the house came on, including the light in Tony's bedroom. Why is this crucial? Because Tony had told me that he had wired it up in such a way that *the light was never off*. And if the light was never off, any police officers going to the house would have seen it in the heart of darkness and any police helicopter certainly would have seen it, too.

Are we concerned that on two occasions at least, DS Eglen, with his car loaded with exhibits from Bleak House took more than an hour (sometimes almost two hours) to make the 20-30 minute journey from the farm to King's Lynn police station? Could exhibits have been interfered with in that time?

And then we come to the staircase. DS Eglen claimed that on 1 September 1999 he measured it and his measurements were carefully and correctly noted.

Clearly there was a major shift of that staircase from the time it had originally been installed and thus it was quite natural for Tony to have utilised some aluminium ladders in order to navigate the stairs, some of which had not only slipped below their original position, but also rotted.

Still on the issue of the stairs, DS Eglen's statement failed to make any mention whatsoever of an examination of the stairs for gunshot residue. Given Tony's claims that he had fired from the stairs, surely the first priority would have been to have swabbed the stairs for gunshot residue. Instead, we have a 20-years-in-the-job SOCO unilaterally walking up and down the stairs to make videos of the upstairs rooms *and interfering with crucial evidence*. And not for the first time. He had interfered with evidence by entering Bleak House via the rear exit window. He had interfered with evidence by "clearing a common pathway" and now he had interfered with evidence by traipsing up and down the stairs *prior to them having been swabbed*. You do not have to be a legal genius to know that this case could – and should – have been thrown out on these issues alone. Any kosher barrister would have brought all this to the judge's attention and called into question the entire police procedural failings. Any judge operating on his oath of office would have thrown the case out.

Isn't it strange that in such a detailed witness statement, DS Eglen has omitted the visit by SOCO Bradshaw [entry **286**] and his alleged swabbing of the stairs for gunshot residue? Particularly when, according to Bradshaw's statement, he had been called in by Eglen himself.

DS Eglen claimed that on 2 September he handed exhibits to a "Mr Leroy Thompson". I could find no witness statement from such a person in the HOLMES book. He was not listed as a prosecution witness. Did he even exist? If we haven't got a single shred of evidence to corroborate Eglen's claims, then we should challenge his statement.

Similarly, Eglen claimed he handed evidence to "PC 229 Eves" but he (or she) was not listed in HOLMES and was not listed as a witness.

Eglen then recorded that "[o]n Sunday 5 September 1999 I was present when the following carried out an examination: Dr P. Nigel Cooper, Mr G Renshaw, Mr P Harper, Mr N Makin, Mr S Makin and Mr A Whitcher."

As we have seen, Dr Cooper was the third pathologist in the case. Renshaw was a ballistics expert instructed by the defence. I have no idea who Mr Harper was or what his role was in being there.

Mr N Makin referred to Tony's then solicitor, Nick Makin and presumably S. Makin is a relative. I do not know who Mr Ashley Whitcher is or his role.

This was the day that Renshaw allegedly stood on the stairs (there was no statement from him and no mention of him in HOLMES) and Nick Makin went to stand in the breakfast room *with a white shirt on*. The lighting conditions were the same as on 20 August and although the man in the white shirt stood just a few feet away from the stairs, *he could not be seen by Renshaw on the stairs*. Clearly this experiment was of crucial significance for Tony's case. If you cannot see someone standing just a few feet away in the darkness, it stretches credulity to think that the farmer took aim and fired at intruders with the intention of causing them harm or killing them. And it stretches credulity too far to think that in the extreme darkness, Tony Martin fired from the hip and through a doorway at a narrow angle and actually hit anybody.

Are you confident – as a passive bystander two decades later – that DS Eglen's account was completely truthful or do you believe that it was engineered long after the dates and events to which he referred in it to suit the prosecution case against the farmer?

We now come to the issue of three spent cartridges allegedly found by the fireplace in the breakfast room. These are of great significance. Tony Martin fired from the stairs at an acute angle and yet we were asked to believe that these spent cartridges shot across the hallway, through the doorway at an acute angle, round the corner and finally came to rest on the right hand side of the breakfast room. Scientifically, it can't happen. It only 'happened' because the police set a scene. Put simply, the empty casings were clearly planted.

DS Eglen was said to have made his witness statement on 26 October 1999 – more than two months after the shooting and his allegedly finding the fired cartridge shells near the doorway. But, since he has made this statement so long after the event, it could be argued that he has created a statement to fit the prosecution's spurious allegations and not reality. And, of course, this was never put to him at trial by the disingenuous Scrivener.

[Author's note: DS Eglen made three statements in total that I could find: on 28 September 1999, he mentioned that he found the holdalls and the silver inside and that the house was in a state of disrepair. In his second statement, made on 21 October 1999, he said he found a woollen glove in an orchard near to Bleak House. Then on 26 October 1999, he made a 17-page signed statement[365] listing his visits to the house and grounds and the items he'd seized. Are you concerned about this chronology?]

Tue 26 OCT 11 am UNUSED 345

Downham Market police station

Gillian Butters worked as a station clerk at Downham Market. In the 15 years she'd been in the job, she recalled receiving a number of phone calls and personal visits to the police station by Tony. She could not be specific as to the times and dates of his visits and phone calls, nor could she recall the content of the calls except to say that they were to do with thefts or damage on his property or suspicious persons or vehicles on his land or in the adjacent area.

---

[365] Of the dozens of statements made by police officers in the case, this was the only signed one.

"In most cases I recorded Mr Martin's visits in the appropriate way on message form A89. He was always very pleasant and polite; he was never a problem to me."

Wed 27 OCT midday UNUSED 346

home address of John Allen

Records show that the divorced 40-year-old John Allen who lived alone and was Area Sales Manager for Omex Agriculture Ltd, Bardney Airfield, Tupholme, Lincoln made a statement to DC *Buxton.*

Mr Allen had known Tony for about five or six years although he only saw him about once a year, during the spring, which was the time that he would sell nitrogen-based fertilisers to the farmer.

"Tony Martin is a very well-educated and well-read man, who is always very keen to talk about a whole range of subjects and would continue to talk for hours if given the chance.

He is no different than most other farmers, with fairly strong views about farm thefts and lack of police cover in the area. However, he tends to be more outspoken than most farmers, or rather more vociferous.

I have, on occasions, had lengthy conversations with Tony and I have formed the opinion that he has a fear of crime, brought about by the isolated location of his farm and the repetitive way in which he has suffered thefts of all sorts. I am unable to remember any specific crimes that he has suffered, as I have numerous customers who have been victims, and I tend to switch off to individual cases.

I do recall that he has mentioned being a victim and he has also mentioned how he dislikes the travelling fraternity, *but no more so than many other farmers that I know. I think there is a general dislike for travellers throughout the farming community.* [Author's emphasis]

I have never seen him with a shotgun or firearm of any description and I have never discussed the subject with him.

On one occasion I was frightened to get out of my car when I arrived at his farm because of a large dog, so I drove down to view the land adjacent to the house. When I returned I was confronted by Tony with his hands on his hips in the middle of the track, ready to confront me. He apparently did not recognise me until I got closer to him. He is that sort of person. He does not miss a thing that goes on around his property. He protects his property very well.

In view of the amount of crime that occurs in the area, I am not surprised that a farmer has resorted to taking the law into his own hands, like Tony is alleged to have done. [Author's emphasis]

I have never been inside his house and have no desire to do so. It looks like a derelict, haunted house and the burglars who went in there must have been very brave or very determined. I thought at one time that he did not live there but just used it as a farm base whilst living at a hotel in Wisbech.

I always got on very well with Tony. He is an absolute gentleman, has strong views on most subjects and is able to discuss all these topics with deep sincerity.

I have never found him to be threatening or violent and in no way do I find him offensive. He is very similar to an awful lot of other customers of mine but is, perhaps, a little better educated to the extent that I feel he should not be a farmer but something that needs a higher academic input."

CORRUPTION ALERT *CPS withhold statement from the jury*

You will not be surprised to learn that Mr Allen's statement, which was so supportive of Tony, was found in the Unused Material file. Yet another example of the "legal engineering" as Tony would say.

Mon 1 NOV 3.45 pm UNUSED 347

home address of Ron Overland
Official records show that 67-year-old retired farmer Ron Overland made a statement which was never used at trial. For 24 years, until 11 October 1999 when he retired, he farmed in the area around Outwell Road and Middle Drove, Marshland St James. Because of the years he had spent working in the area, he came to know most of the local people and many of the farmers who worked land in the area.

"I, like many of the farmers, suffered from the same problems of theft, damage and trespass. I would say that this problem has become particularly bad over the past five years. I would say that I, like many farmers, have become frustrated by what I see as a lack of action by the police in order to prevent or detect these crimes. I do not blame the individual policemen, but more the system they work under, which seems to prevent them from being effective in doing their job.

I first got to know the farmer called Tony Martin of Emneth about eight years ago when I worked for him on his farm, straw-chopping. I did this work for him up until about two years ago, when Tony got the machinery to do the job himself. My son-in-law, Graham Hill, also forked for Tony.

I would describe Tony as one of the straightest, most honest men I know.[366] He always paid his debts promptly and was very fair and proper in his dealings with people. I can give a couple of examples which illustrates this:

---

[366] Author's emphasis.

Once, after I had done some work for Tony, he offered to show me the plans of his farm in order to prove how much acreage I had worked, since I didn't have a clue how much to charge him.

On another occasion he let Graham pick apples in his orchard. When Graham had picked the apples Tony asked him if he had got all he wanted, and Graham replied, "Yes." Then Tony told Graham not to go into his orchard again without his express permission. That was just how Tony was.

Since I stopped working for Tony he has still kept in touch, and he would often call around to speak to me if he was driving by.

I never went into Bleak House while working at Tony's. The ground around it was very overgrown, and the house itself was difficult to see in the summertime. I got the impression that Tony didn't stay at the farm all the time. He had a lady friend in Wisbech, and I think he sometimes stayed over there.

Nearly every time I saw Tony he had had something stolen. I remember him saying, "What do you think now? They've taken my batteries off of my tractor, and my propane bottles."

I remember the last time I had a conversation with Tony was last harvest (1998), when he came around to mine. We stood talking in my shed. Tony said, "What have I got to do? I don't interfere with anybody. I keep myself to myself, but all I get are thieves. How much can one take?" He went on to say that the police did nothing to help, and that he would have to do something himself to protect his property. By that I thought he meant to put an electric fence up, or dig a pit, something like that.

Tony seemed distraught. I think he had had as much as ever anyone could take. He seemed frustrated. I remember him saying, "I can't get any satisfaction from the police."

The last time I saw Tony was at the "Farmwatch" meeting in February this year. I know what he said didn't go down that well with the organisers, *but I would say that most of the farmers agreed with Tony's views and opinions. I feel that what Tony said was the truth.*[367] What I can remember about what he said was: "This 'Farmwatch' - what benefit is it? We report it to you, you report it to the police so, by the time anyone gets around to doing anything, the stuff they stole is gone." These are possibly not Tony's exact words, but it is more or less what he said, *and I felt most of the people at the meeting agreed with him.*[368]

Like many of us, Tony felt that there are too few police in the area, with too much to do, and therefore they can't do the job as it should be done.[369]

I never saw Tony with a gun in his hand, or a gun in his car, and I cannot remember him speaking about guns.

---

[367] Author's emphasis.
[368] Author's emphasis.
[369] Author's emphasis.

I don't think Tony blamed travellers exclusively for all the crime on his property. I remember him saying once, "I think that they're bloody 'dids' most of the time, but I don't think that they are all 'dids'." I don't think Tony had a grievance against any specific group of people. He once said: "I don't care what someone does up the road, so long as they don't interfere with me." Tony just wanted justice for all that had been done to him.

Tony is a hardworking, well-educated man. He had very definite opinions about all manner of subjects but he would listen to an alternative point of view, even if he didn't agree. I did not socialise with Tony, and most of our conversations revolved around farming and its problems. I just think that Tony took so much, probably more than most, and just got into a state about it.

But you have to imagine if you try to do some work and you can't get started because your machinery has been tampered with, or the property you need to do the work has been stolen, then I think that anyone would get in a state.

Tony could be quite jovial. I can never remember him getting dressed up; he always seemed to wear the same sort of clothes. His appearance, and what he looked like to others, never seemed to bother him.

I know that it is wrong to shoot someone, but I have to think about what would happen if we did not defend ourselves, especially when we live in such isolated areas as many of us do."

CORRUPTION ALERT   *Tony's barrister failed his client in not calling yet another witness to trial*

It is not difficult to imagine why the prosecution and the police didn't put that statement forward to trial. I have great concern around why Tony's barrister failed to call Mr Overland as a witness. This one witness alone would have shot down most of the prosecution's false narrative and so it is reprehensible that defence counsel failed to call the retired farmer.

You will have seen by now the "legal engineering" that is employed in a trial: the evidence is collated, those statements in favour of our theory (however spurious) we'll use, but those that shoot our claim down in pieces we'll conveniently shuffle out of the pack and put them in the "Unused Material" file or 'lose' them altogether. Theoretically the unused material is there to be used by the Defence (but only if it actually gets all of this material handed over to it and it more often than not does not get it), but if you have a corrupt barrister and a bent judge then that important material will not be used and the consequence of that is the defendant is often found guilty when he or she is actually innocent. This is why I am calling for, and Tony is calling for, changes in the justice system which is heavily weighted *against* the defendant. We are no better off in the 21st century than we were in the 12th century. The law will *not* protect you if the corrupt agents of state decide that they want to get you and they certainly wanted to get Tony.

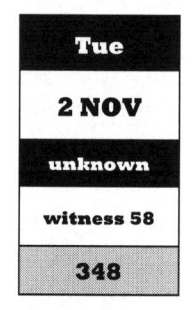

Tue
2 NOV
unknown
witness 58
348

unknown location
According to official records, (HOLMES S59A), PC Michael Coley, 44, made a statement in which he said that at 14:33 on 21 August 1999 he was part of a police search team at Bleak House.

There is an additional comment in HOLMES to the effect that he "found a male body near the house" but this information was not contained in any statement that he made which was officially part of the evidence.

In a sleight-of-hand, the initial comment that PC Coley had been part of a search team had been entered into court. The additional comment had not. In any event, why would it have taken him two and half months to make such a simple statement about allegedly finding the body? And why didn't he include it in his *first statement* dated 27 August 1999 whilst it was, allegedly, still fresh in his mind?

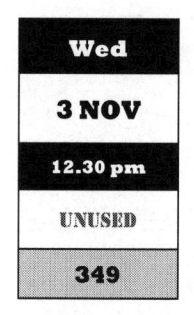

Wed
3 NOV
12.30 pm
UNUSED
349

home address of John Turner
Turning to the Unused Material again, we come across a statement from a farmer who knew Tony well and who was referred to in a statement attributed to David Golding made on 29 September 1999. The 51-year-old John Michael Turner allegedly told DC Peters that between 1980 and August 1999 he farmed 170 acres of land around the Fir Tree Farm in Marshland St James. He retired due to the financial climate within the farming industry, and also because his wife had become increasingly reluctant to live in such an isolated area "<u>which seemed to become more lawless as the years went by</u>."

[Author's emphasis] While farming in the Marshland area he claimed that he, like many of his farmer friends, had been the victim of thefts, vandalism, damage and wilful trespass, the latter being hare coursers.

Turner added that in all his dealings with the police about these problems, he had never once been informed of a successful outcome - someone being caught and prosecuted. It was Turner's belief that most of the crime committed in the area was by the "so-called travelling fraternity who live in the area."

Interestingly, Turner said that it was his view that the biggest problem he found in reporting crime to the police was in communication. He gave an example by saying that on most occasions when he rang the police, he was put through to someone in Norwich, or even further afield if on a mobile phone. This created difficulties in describing to them the location where the crime or problem was occurring, said Turner.

The Marshland St James man first met Tony Martin about ten years previously. He described Tony as "a very articulate sort of person; he seemed well-educated and well-informed on all manner of subjects. Tony Martin always dressed in the same sort of clothes and never seemed to worry too much about his personal appearance."

Mr Turner said of the Farmwatch meeting that it was his impression that Tony said what most of the rest of the farmers thought, which was basically that the police were a waste of time and that it was time that farmers got together and sorted problems out themselves. Turner said that what Tony had to say didn't go down too well with the organisers.

Turner was a member of Farmwatch prior to attending the meeting and his view was that Farmwatch was a good scheme and he encouraged farmer friend David Golding to join the scheme after the meeting.

Turner could not recall ever having had a conversation with Tony on the subject of his attitude towards travellers, but he believed that his attitude towards them was the same as most law-abiding people in the area, that is to say, all the farmers found them a nuisance and a hindrance and, on some occasions, quite menacing and threatening.

This statement appears to be at odds with former armed response officer Tony Bone's statement. Turner did not mention that Tony Martin interrupted the meeting and in fact he clarified that Tony said what the rest of the farmers were thinking. But Turner's statement was also useful because it corroborated what Tony had been saying for years: that crime was increasing as the constabulary cut back on police stations and personnel in rural communities. Furthermore, Turner explained that in his view the majority of crime was committed by travellers and that the police had never provided him with a positive outcome - a conviction - for all the crimes that he had reported. An echo of Tony Martin and dozens of other farmers in the area.

| **CORRUPTION ALERT** | *Tony's barrister and CPS withhold further key evidence from the jury* |

Several similar statements from farmers who attended the Farmwatch meeting corroborated that Tony Martin had not been disruptive at all. In fact, every statement commented on Tony Martin as being articulate, well-educated and well-informed, a man who was prepared to stand up for himself and for what he believed in. Some of the farmers admired Tony Martin for the stand he took; others despised him because of their own inadequacies.

We perhaps ought to consider why Tony's barrister failed to call to trial all the farmers who supported Tony.

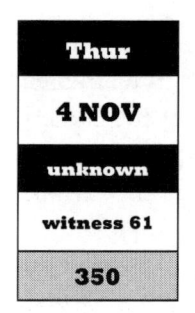

Thur
4 NOV
unknown
witness 61
350

unknown location

According to official records, Dr John Skinner made a statement on this day. The only witness statement the author has been able to locate said to have been made by Dr Skinner failed to mention either an estimated time of death or the temperature of the body.

I am driven to conclude that Dr Skinner did not write this particular witness statement on the basis that I do not believe that he would have omitted such crucial details.

And why would it take almost two-and-a-half months for such a statement to be written?

I am also interested in why Dr Skinner was allegedly called to attend the body. Swaffham to Wisbech is approximately 20 miles. Was there no doctor nearer to Emneth in Wisbech, Downham Market or King's Lynn who could have been called to the scene? [See also 21 August 1999].

And why didn't the doctor (if he really attended) secure the removal of the body to the mortuary as soon as possible after he was said to have seen it and pronounced it dead?

Fri	**home address of Philip Martin**
5 NOV	*The 50-year-old Philip Martin (no relation) who farmed 107 acres made a statement to DC Peters in which he said that he had no wish to make any observations about Tony Martin other than that he had encountered him for the first time at the Farmwatch meeting and that he had "the greatest sympathy for him since, as a fellow farmer, I know only too well the problems we have with thieves and vandals who roam the countryside."*
3 pm	
UNUSED	
351	

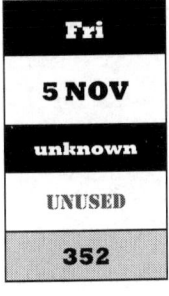

Fri	**home address of David Gathercole**
5 NOV	*The 55-year-old David Edward Gathercole, who described himself as a farmer, was recorded as having made the statement below to PC 1018 Caine. However, we do not know where it was made or at what time is was made. Listed in HOLMES at line S222, this statement was recorded as not having been entered into evidence at trial and yet it gained national significance through the police's manipulation of the media:*
unknown	
UNUSED	
352	

"I have always found Tony to be a chatty and well educated man, and sociable, willing to talk about all sorts of subjects. Although Tony Bone held the meeting, it was an open discussion and a number of farmers voiced their opinions and observations."

Clearly Tony Martin did not take over the meeting as Bone had said in his statement. But now we come to an interesting comment made by Gathercole: "At one point, I remember that problems with travellers were being discussed. I cannot remember who brought up the topic, but Tony Martin said to Tony Bone, 'Do you know how to stop them?' No-one else was talking at the time, so it was quiet in the room. He then said, 'Shoot the bastards!'"

And so it seems that Tony Martin *did* possess a murderous intent towards travellers after all. But we need to read on: "*Although I think a number of us were possibly thinking along these lines*, no one else said anything like this. I cannot remember anything else specific that was said at the meeting, but this quote stayed in my mind." [Author's emphasis.]

It seems, therefore, that a number of other farmers were thinking what Tony Martin allegedly voiced – he was not, it seems, alone in his thought processes. We have to ask why only Gathercole appears to have remembered this somewhat noteworthy quote, since no-one else there that night mentioned it – not even Bone himself or his note-taker, Derek Stuart. Don't you think Mr Stuart would have recorded that comment in his notebook had it actually been said?

CORRUPTION ALERT *Prosecution witness Gathercole appears to have committed perjury*

*Now we come to a more sinister issue – Mr Gathercole (a parish councillor at the time of publication) was not listed as a witness in the official published list of witnesses and yet other official records show that he appeared at court on Tuesday 11 April 2000 and that he was sworn in. [See also entry **610**]*

In any event, Mr Gathercole appears to have lied in his statement to the police because he must have known that Tony Martin had said no such thing about shooting travellers at the Farmwatch meeting.

Sat 6 NOV — unknown — witness 103 — **353**

unknown location

According to the HOLMES *database,* SOCO *Barry Wells made a statement which said that on 24 August 1999 he attended Wisbech police station and took photos of two cars: C460APW (Tony Martin's) and F98LHJ (allegedly Darren Bark's).*

The statement added that he also took photos of Bleak House and its outbuildings.

There are two problems with this alleged evidence – I could not find the statement or the photographs despite several trawls through all the legal papers.

The second problem I have with this information is that SOCO Wells had already made a statement about his involvement in a search of Bleak House on 24 August 1999 [see relevant entry] so why did he simply not include taking photos of the house and outbuildings and the cars in that statement? Why wait so long to mention it?

Then there is actually a *third* problem because on 16 November 1999 SOCO Wells apparently made a third statement which was not in the files provided to Tony. [See also entries for **313** and **363**.]

Mon 8 NOV — unknown — UNUSED — **354**

home address of Robert Gosling

Records show that Robert Gosling made a statement to DC *Adcock. At this time, Gosling – who lived with his wife Suzanne and two children near to Tony - was renovating his house and the family was living in a mobile home in the rear garden. Mr Gosling told the detective that he heard the sound of a shotgun about 9pm. He wasn't sure whether it was Thursday 19th or Friday 20th:*

"I recall I was disturbed by this while watching television. The only way I can be more precise is to say that it was the same evening as the helicopter was flying overhead very low."

> **CORRUPTION ALERT** *CPS and Tony's barrister withhold evidence*

Clearly this is of great significance. The only way that Mr Gosling could remember the date on which he heard the gunshot was that it was the same evening as the helicopter was flying low. Note that Mr Gosling said it was flying very low over Bleak House (and yet the police claimed they couldn't find the house.)

Let's pause for a moment of reflection and consider the times put forward by the police, an alleged burglar and members of the public:

Name	Time	Date of Statement
Brendon Fearon	around 10:30pm	23 August 1999
PC Gotts	"after 0:34am"	23 August 1999
Paul Leet	"evening"	24 August 1999
PC 338 Cant	1:05am	24 August 1999
Inspector Chilvers	1:43am	1 September 1999
Chief Inspector Curtis	"about 1am"	2 September 1999
PC 400 Girton	1:05am	2 September 1999
PC 852 White	"about 1:05am"	9 September 1999
Margaret Hodgson	"sometime after 10pm"	27 September 1999
Robert Gosling	"evening"	8 November 1999

It seems clear that there is a great deal of confusion over the time of the helicopter flight. Local people appeared to place a flight on the Friday evening, whilst the police officers claimed it was in the early hours of Saturday morning. Were there *two separate* helicopter flights and *two separate* shootings?

Margaret Hodgson's statement put the time also at around 10:30pm (as did Fearon's) but the police and CPS simply airbrushed her statement out and failed to enter it as evidence at the trial, though Tony's barrister was provided with a copy and yet failed to call her as a witness.

Now, why would he act in such an underhand way towards his own client? The reason, I'm afraid to say, is that he wasn't working on Tony's behalf at all. Lawyers assert that their first "duty" is to the court, not to their client and I suggest that Scrivener had been told by the Home Office to go through the motions and help ensure a guilty verdict. Those in authority really did want to teach Tony a lesson – he was potentially dangerous on at least three levels: his brave and vociferous criticism of the police, his refusal to stay silent about child abuse at Glebe House and the fact that he had land and was financially secure. This made him a significant 'person of interest' to the police.

Paul Leet's statement didn't pin the helicopter flight to any specific time, although he did say that he saw it the same *evening* as the shooting, which suggests that it was the Friday and not the Saturday.

And Brendon Fearon told me that in all subsequent interviews he had with the police after his first, they told him to "never mention the helicopter flight again". Now, realistically, why would they say that?

On 20 May 2016 I initiated a Freedom of Information (FOI) Act request to Norfolk Police. The Constabulary refused to comply with a lawful request for information about the helicopter flight and the Constabulary even tried to use the FOI legislation to get out of their moral, legal and ethical obligations by claiming that because Tony sought this information and because – as his official biographer at his request - I sought other information I regarded as necessary in the interest of justice, the Constabulary tried to extricate itself from its own wrong-doing. Let's get real here – if there was nothing shady about this alleged flight, they'd have provided the information. It seems that, despite Hillsborough, the police have learned nothing. Little wonder, then, that the public's faith in the police is at an all-time low. Within two weeks of sending that FOI request, I was unlawfully imprisoned in HMP Norwich for 28 days and made homeless upon my release.

In respect of the helicopter, we find ourselves in a dilemma – we have Fearon who says he is certain that he saw a helicopter flying overhead while he was lying on his back in the cornfield next to the Leets' bungalow just before he made his way there. As we have seen, Fearon cannot be referring to any helicopter flight after 10:53pm, the time of the 999 call made by Mrs Leet.

So, we have Fearon and Margaret Hodgson (and others) referring to a helicopter with a searchlight circling in the air at some time between 10pm and 10:53pm and yet we also have statements (all from police officers of varying rank) which say that the helicopter flight was between 1am and 1:45am. I find this particularly strange. And I am also concerned that DC Adcock asked Mrs Hodgson on 27 September 1999 (some 5½ weeks after the shooting) whether she was able to pinpoint the exact time of the helicopter flight. He ought to have already known the answer to this question, and so it occurs to me that he has asked this question not to elicit an answer to a question he does not already know the answer to, but to find out just what Mrs Hodgson knows. In other words, what does she know that could sink the story that the police are about to promulgate throughout the media to the unsuspecting masses willing to feed on any news item about an allegedly eccentric bachelor farmer, a break-in in which shots were fired, three career criminals and the murder of a 16-year-old youth?

But all the while the Great British Public were feeding on this media frenzy and focusing on the "eccentric loner" and the unknown number of intruders (and happy that it hadn't happened to them), and becoming embroiled in a racist argument about travellers and the right to protect one's self and one's property, others involved in the story were being overlooked – the police themselves. This is a common tactic of the police: set Peter against Paul and they'll both leave us alone while they argue amongst themselves.

The police were later to claim that Tony's dogs impeded their investigation when that was clearly a ridiculous excuse. Crucially, how did that helicopter get there – in other words, who called 999 *before* Jacqueline Leet? Who ordered that helicopter up *before* the 999 call? Was Margaret Hodgson mistaken?

Or - more likely - why were there *two* helicopter flights? I suggest the first flight was called in response to Tony firing his gun inside his house around 9pm and the second flight in response to the shooting of Fearon and Barras much later after Tony had left his property...

Tue
9 NOV
3.30 pm
UNUSED
355

business address of David Goodings
Records show that David Goodings, a 60-year-old haulage contractor who had transported grain for Tony over a period of fifteen years, made a statement to DC Peters in which he said that he first heard about the news of the shooting on the radio while driving to Great Yarmouth. This statement was unused at trial.

"I feel deeply sorry for him. My opinion is that he is the type of man who wouldn't hurt a worm, but I think that all the problems he had had over the years with criminals attacking his premises had just got on top of him."

Mr Goodings then went on to explain the type of problems Tony had experienced: "On numerous visits I have made to Mr Martin's farm, he has told me of problems that he has had with thieves, most of whom he seemed to think were travellers. On one occasion, I remember, thieves had broken into his diesel tank and let the contents out, flooding the floor where he kept his grain, which ruined a lot of his grain.

On another, more recent, occasion sometime in June of this year, I recall that while one of my lorries was loading grain, Mr Martin rushed off in order to challenge the occupants of a white van that had driven onto his premises. Mr Martin gave chase, but I believe the van got away.

The last time I saw Mr Martin was on 13 July 1999.[370] He hold me his health had not been too good. I believe he also told me that he had recently had problems with break-ins to his home.

In all the time I have known Tony Martin, I have never seen him with a gun and I have never heard him talk about guns or firearms. I never went down to his house since I had no need to, and no business there, and *thus I would not like to speculate on what it was like.*"

What this adds to our knowledge

It certainly confirmed that Tony had told many people about his problems with thefts and burglaries. I don't believe that travellers would have flooded the floor of his grain store with fuel so as to ruin the crop because in most cases anyone who has broken into a barn would have done so in order to steal – not commit criminal damage. It seems to me that this was a deliberate act of sabotage.

Mr Goodings also confirmed that he, too, had seen a white van trespassing on Tony's land – thus Tony was not a lone voice: he had a witness. Furthermore, the haulage contractor confirmed that Tony's health was not good at this time – the thrombosis on his lung. These concerns about his health would clearly have added to his worries on the night intruders smashed their way in. And in all the years that Mr Goodings had known Tony, the lorry driver told police he'd never heard Tony mention guns.

Someone with a murderous intent or someone who wouldn't hurt a worm?

---

[370] Mr Goodings also told police that his invoice number 5063 confirmed the date of his last visit to Bleak House. It was noticeable to me when reviewing the legal papers, that ordinary members of the public were quite prepared to provide reference numbers of invoices and other documents in relation to the case, but that the police – in almost all of their witness statements – failed to record seal numbers on exhibits or provide a bona fide chain of custody in accordance with due protocol.

Tue
9 NOV
6.30 pm
witness 106
356

unknown location

According to the HOLMES database (line S225), PC 896 Kelvin John Steward attended Bleak House at 6:30pm on Monday 23 August.

He was apparently handed exhibit JE16, a sawn-off shotgun, by DS Eglen which was then taken to the armoury at King's Lynn police station.

This statement was not included in the papers provided to Tony.

According to the HOLMES database, PC Steward made a statement which was entered as evidence but I have been unable to find this statement and so have no idea what else was or wasn't mentioned in it or whether it even existed. The statement was not referred to in the *Index to Statements*.

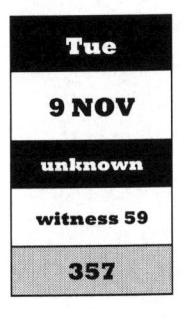

Tue
9 NOV
unknown
witness 59
357

unknown location

According to HOLMES (line 227), PC 1038 Andrew Hughes attended Bleak House on Saturday 21 August as part of a police search team. The HOLMES entry stated: "When a body was found, he performed seal duties."

CORRUPTION ALERT   *Serious flaws in legal procedure*

I have been unable to locate this statement. Why would it take nearly 3 months to make a statement? Did the statement mention the time the body was found, or by whom, or the condition of the body when found? Although listed in HOLMES as having been entered as evidence, this statement did not appear in the official list of witness statements. Yet PC Hughes was named in the official list of witnesses.

Thur
11 NOV
unknown
UNUSED
358

unknown location

According to HOLMES (line S231), Supt Christopher Grant made a statement in which he said he had: "received through the postal system forensic examination sheets marked ADK/1 and JAS/1."

That was – allegedly – the only statement made by the highest ranking officer directly involved in the case. Is that even credible?

CORRUPTION ALERT — *Serious flaws in police & legal procedure*

I have been unable to locate this statement. Why would it take almost 3 months for him to make a statement?

Looking more closely at the briefest of statements, we find that the report by John Alfred Slaughter (JAS/1) was entered as evidence into the trial as a witness statement, but the report apparently authored by Amanda Kirkham (ADK/1) was not on the official Exhibit List.

Mon
15 NOV
unknown
witness 108
359

unknown location

According to official records, DC Adcock, made a second statement in which the HOLMES entry (line S164a) stated that on 9th September 1999 (almost three weeks after the alleged incident) with PC 1018 Caine, he searched Tony's car and seized a live shotgun cartridge and two torches.

I have been unable to find this statement, but can say that it adds a good deal to our knowledge of the case because it means that if a live shotgun cartridge was found on the floor of the car and Tony had transported his shotgun in his car to his mother's, it's likely that he ejected that spare cartridge.

I asked Tony about this and he said he did eject a cartridge because he didn't want to drive around with a loaded shotgun in his car.

Furthermore, Tony couldn't have kept firing "until the gun was empty" as the Crown prosecutor was later to claim at trial.

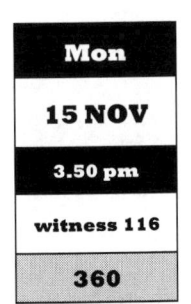

Mon	**unknown location**
15 NOV	The 51-year-old PC 816 Stuart Kevin Hooper, based at Downham Market, was engaged on uniform patrol duties in the Marshland St James area between September 1976 and 1990.
3.50 pm	
witness 116	The following statement was attributed to him:
360	"During this period I met a farmer by the name of Tony Martin on a few occasions. I cannot now recollect the purpose of my meetings with Martin, *and my paperwork and pocket books for that period have been destroyed.*"[371]

We need to be mindful of the strangeness of this alleged account because, right in the middle of a murder investigation, a local officer to Tony has claimed that he worked in the area for 14 years and met the farmer "on a few occasions". Yet he cannot now recollect anything (a favourite expression used by police in courts up and down the land) and all of the paperwork and his pocket notebooks had all allegedly been destroyed.

That sounds far too convenient for my liking and I believe this statement was created to either (i) give the impression that the paperwork has been destroyed or (ii) it actually had been destroyed. Now, why would that happen in the middle of a murder investigation?

I suspect that the police did not want evidence of Tony's many complaints to them about thefts and burglaries and nor did they want to reveal that during his complaints he would often refer to the abuse he suffered at Glebe House School and at the hands of the well-connected Rodney Townley.

Alternatively, all of the documents *might* have been destroyed, but if that were the case, why mention it at all?

Finally, the name of the person to whom this statement was allegedly made was not recorded.

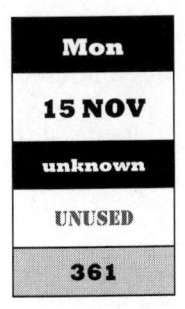

Mon	**unknown location**
15 NOV	According to official records, 51-year-old Downham Market-based PC 868 (Neil) John Thompson was engaged on uniformed patrol duties in the Marshland St James area between October 1984 and September 1997. During this period of time he met Tony Martin on a number of occasions.
unknown	
UNUSED	
361	The following is a statement attributed to the constable:

---

[371] Author's emphasis. In legal parlance, I am driven to conclude that much of that paperwork contained Tony's complaints about child abuse at Glebe House School and this is why it mysteriously "disappeared".

"I cannot now recollect the purpose of my meetings with Martin, and *my paperwork and pocket books for that period have been destroyed*.[372]

I can recall visiting[373] Tony Martin with PC 78 Wakefield. According to documentation kept by PC Wakefield, I can state that this was on Sunday 23 October 1994. The reason for our visit was as the result of a call by Mr Martin to the police about the alleged theft of apples from his orchard on that day.

I can recall that Mr Martin stated that the driver of the vehicle involved in the theft of the apples had driven the vehicle aggressively and that Martin believed his dogs were in danger of being run over and, for this reason, *had fired a shotgun at the wheels of the vehicle*.[374]

On arrival at Bleak House we met Mr Martin, who appeared calm and rational. He told us that he was reporting the incident because he feared reprisals. As I recall, we searched the locality and circulated the vehicle details to surrounding [police] forces."

This statement needs to be read in conjunction with that made by PC Wakefield [see entry **366**].

Surely this statement informs us more about Tony's character. He'd felt compelled to protect his dogs from the traveller's vehicle. He'd done the right thing and called in the incident.

Do we believe that this police officer's notes had been destroyed? And if they had, why had they if PC Wakefield's notes were still intact and both officers had attended the same incident?

This somewhat innocuous incident was to be used against Tony at trial. This statement was not used and nor was the officer called as a witness. Surely if you're Tony's barrister and working in the best interest of your client, you'd call this man to court and ask him to explain to a jury why he hadn't bothered to get out of his vehicle or bothered to take a statement from the witness, Martin Hollis, Tony's cousin.

Surely you'd want to call this officer to court to tell a jury that Tony was "calm and collected".

Surely you'd want to call him to court to explain to a jury that in shooting at someone's tyres from a standing position, you'd be firing downwards. Think of the damage a skilled barrister could have done to the prosecution's spurious claims that Tony Martin was a "nutter with guns who had a psychopathic hatred

---

[372] Author's emphasis.

[373] The officer has just said that he couldn't recall any meetings and yet apparently can, after all, recall the orchard incident (even though he claimed to have destroyed all of his records.)

[374] Please note that if you are firing at the wheels of a vehicle from a standing position, you are usually firing *in a downwards trajectory*. This becomes an important point later in the case.

of gypsies and travellers." Surely you'd want to call him to court to explain to a jury how and why his pocket notebooks were "destroyed".

CORRUPTION ALERT — *Tony's barrister failed to call police officer*

But Tony's defence counsel didn't call this officer. The jury never got to hear about Tony firing in a downwards trajectory. All the jury heard was that the hard-working, decent farmer was "a nutter with guns."

Perhaps now you will understand why Tony often uses the phrase "legal engineering" to describe trials, barristers, judges and the police. In my view, he's perfectly right. I've been on the receiving end of miscarriages of justice, too, and know exactly what he means.

Tue 16 NOV 5.30 pm UNUSED 362

home address of Graham Hill
The 40-year-old Graham Hill had lived with his family in the Downham Market area all his life and he had worked as a postman in the Denver/Wimbotsham area for the past thirteen years. Ron Overland [entry 347] was Hill's father-in-law. While Overland ran the farm, Hill used to do odd jobs for him in his spare time. Hill first met Tony through Mr Overland. This statement to DS Peters was not used as evidence.

"Sometime in about September 1992, Ron undertook to do some straw chopping for Mr Martin. This was because Mr Martin did not have the machinery to do the work himself.

When I arrived on the first day, Mr Martin gave me instructions on what to do and where to cut the straw. I remember that he told me that he had dogs, and that I should not get out of the tractor where they were or "where you see me walking the dogs." Mr Martin told me that the dogs were ferocious. He also told me not to go into the grounds around his house without his permission.

During the first week I ever worked for him, I can remember that Mr Martin had a burglary at his home. Naturally, he was very upset. I seem to remember that one of his sheds or barns had been broken into and that a space heater and various tools, including some tree-lopping tools, were stolen.

Because Mr Martin didn't know me at that time, I came under suspicion, and I believe he contacted Ron to check out my credentials. It was all very embarrassing at the time but, after he had checked me out, so to speak, we got on fine.

Besides the burglary [in 1992], I can remember Mr Martin explained to me that he had employed some van dwellers the previous year (1991) to pick his apples. He said to me, "That was where I think I went wrong", which indicated to me that he suspected the van dwellers of the thefts which had occurred since their departure. Apart from this business over the thefts, almost all the other conversations I had with him were about work and farming.

As I got to know Mr Martin during the four consecutive years I did his straw chopping for him, I found him to be a very pleasant, decent, hardworking man. He would never interfere and he would let you get on with your work.

While I worked on Mr Martin's fields at Emneth, I could see his house and grounds. I have been asked to describe them. I would say that the grounds were very overgrown, with grass and nettles around the house some three feet high. Although I saw Mr Martin go down to the house on occasions, I formed the impression that he didn't always live there. I think I got that impression from the fact that I heard he had a lady friend in Wisbech who ran a hotel or pub, and that one time he told me that if I needed or wanted to get in touch with him, I could contact him at an address in Wisbech. I think he also gave me a phone number. I never needed to use it, and I have now, after this length of time, no idea as to what the address or number was.

During the first year I worked for Mr Martin, he allowed me to pick some apples from his orchard. I remember I went into the orchard from the Emneth end. As I got into the orchard, Mr Martin's dogs started to bark. I formed the impression that the dogs were loose in the grounds, and so I got out of the area as quickly as possible without picking any apples.

When I told Mr Martin about this the next day, he arranged to have his dogs locked up that evening while I picked some apples. After I had done so, he told me that I should always seek his permission before going into the grounds around the house. I mention this because it shows the type of person he was.

The last time I saw his house was in 1995, which was the last year I did the straw chopping for him. The grounds were very overgrown, with nettles and weeds right up to the house. In all the time I worked for him, I never went to the house. I had no need to and because of my concerns for the dogs.

I never saw Mr Martin with a gun, and he never talked about the subject of guns or shooting. I never heard him shooting either.

The last time I saw Mr Martin was about two years ago (1997) when I was visiting Ron Overland down at his farm. Ron and Mr Martin were having a conversation in Ron's shed. Mr Martin looked the same as ever and seemed quite jovial. We may have said "Hello", but nothing more on that occasion.

The first I heard of the shooting was about two days after the incident. It was on the television. When I saw a picture of Mr Martin I was shocked, because he looked very old and haggard."

> **What this adds to our knowledge**
>
> I believe Graham Hill's statement provides us with a fascinating insight into Tony Martin and shows elements to his character which the authorities didn't want the broad mass of the public to know about.

Tue 16 NOV — unknown — witness 103 — 363

unknown location

According to HOLMES (line S179B) SOCO Barry Wells made a third statement in which he said that he had taken inked tyre impressions of Tony's car because some tyre marks had been found near to Bleak House.

Tue 16 NOV — unknown — witness 72 — 364

unknown location

According to official records, DC 326 Bruce Christopher Appleby made a statement in which he claimed that at 12:15pm on 28 August 1999 he took photographs above Bleak House in the force helicopter.

Although listed in HOLMES (line S229) I have been unable to find it or any exhibits. DC Appleby is listed as prosecution witness number 72, though he did not appear in court or have his statement read out in court, according to the official court records.

Tue 16 NOV — unknown — witness 68 — 365

unknown location

HOLMES lists a statement (at line S234) from Principal SOCO Dave Rowlands. The HOLMES entry states: "on 24-08-99 received exhibit LXB/1 and secured item in locked cabinet. On 25-08-99 handed exhibit to PC Matthews."

Now, being the principal SOCO in the case, wouldn't you think that his statement would be rather crucial and be at least 10 pages in length or more? Not a bit of it. Worryingly, I could find no statement and nor was it listed on the official list of all witness statements. Yet he was listed as prosecution witness number 68, although court records show that he was not called to trial and nor was his *one-page* witness statement read out.

CORRUPTION ALERT — *No report from principal SOCO*

In the statement attributed to Dr Heath, the pathologist placed Rowlands at the 10am Downham Market conference on Sunday 22 August and at Bleak House at 11am. Wouldn't a statement from the principal SOCO merit a more detailed entry than a mere line about receiving and handing over an exhibit?

Wed 17 NOV — unknown — UNUSED — 366

unknown location

We now turn to a witness statement attributed to 37-year-old PC 78 Lindsey John Wakefield made on 17 November 1999 at a time and place unknown to us because it was not recorded on the statement as is usual police protocol. However, note that this statement was made some five years after the event he was to describe. It was listed in HOLMES as having been unused evidence.

Formerly stationed at Downham Market, constable Wakefield stated that he had been posted to Terrington St John in November 1993 and first met Tony Martin soon after. He said that he had only visited Tony's premises once in connection with criminal matters.

By referring to his pocket book, he stated that he visited Tony at Bleak House on Sunday 23 October 1994, at 1:20pm. The visit was made in response to a telephone call which Tony had made to the police regarding trespassers on his premises stealing apples.

Wakefield attended with PC 868 Neil John Thompson [see entry **361**]. When they arrived, Tony informed them that an incident had occurred earlier that day which had resulted in him firing a shot at an Isuzu Trooper.

Wakefield noted that Tony had claimed a vehicle had been driven furiously towards his dogs after he had challenged the driver, who he claimed had been stealing apples from his orchard. The constable noted that Tony, who "appeared quite calm and collected" was concerned about reprisals and, for that reason, had contacted the police. The farmer identified a Martin Hollis[375] as a witness.

Subsequent enquiries revealed that the driver of the Trooper was a Mark Aldin, who lived at that time on the travellers' site behind Newfield Farm, Hollycroft Road, Emneth.

---

[375] See entry for 23 October 1994.

According to his statement, PC Wakefield spoke with Aldin about the incident on Monday 24 October 1994, at which time he was reported for the attempted theft of Martin's apples. The constable also arranged for pictures to be taken of the damage caused to Aldin's vehicle.

On Saturday 29 October 1994, Tony attended Downham Market police station, where he made a statement (taking four hours to complete) regarding the incident on the previous Sunday.

The next day, Wakefield visited Bleak House, and seized four firearms, the shotgun certificate and eight shotgun cartridges.

That is the official version of the incident. Note that Martin Hollis was never interviewed - why? This was a direct echo, as far as I am concerned, of the fight with Robin in the kitchen when police failed to take statements from half of the people present.

I am also suspicious about the timing of Aldin picking the apples – acknowledging that they were in season. Was it just a simple act of a man picking apples for his children, or had he been sent to create a problem for a man whose gun licence was due to expire less than a month later?

Perhaps it is little wonder that Tony Martin felt that the police were not supporting him and that he was, ultimately, on his own. From all the available evidence, and taking an unemotional and objective stance, I find that I have considerable sympathy for his point of view, particularly after I met Mr Hollis at on 26 February 2015 [see entry **43**], three weeks before I was unlawfully imprisoned for a year in order to disrupt my work on this book.

When I spoke with Tony regarding this incident, he gave me a further piece of information which never made its way into PC Wakefield's report and it was this: that on the Monday (24 October 1994) following Tony dialling 999 to report the fact that he'd fired his shotgun at Aldin's vehicle – and not at Aldin – PC Wakefield had called on him and "suggested that I ought not to report the incident." Now, why would a serving constable suggest that to a member of the public? And why would, a day after Tony *did* report the incident, that same constable turn up to seize Tony's guns? Was that a deliberate move on the part of the police to leave the farmer vulnerable from possible reprisals? They, of course, did not know that Tony would acquire guns elsewhere with which to protect himself and who could possibly have blamed him? He'd done the right thing in calling the police and reporting that he'd discharged his shotgun at the rear of Aldin's vehicle and yet *he* was having his guns taken off him.

Mon
22 NOV
unknown
witness 113
367

unknown location

According to official records, acting Force Firearms Manager, Richard Dennison, made a statement on this date. It's listed on line S235 in HOLMES, but I have been unable to find it. It wasn't listed in the published list of witness statements and yet Mr Dennison was listed as prosecution witness number 113, although according to the official court list of witnesses, he didn't appear or have his 3-page statement read out.

Was this simply another Norfolk Constabulary oversight or another piece of legal engineering? The entry in HOLMES recorded Mr Dennison as "identifying ammunition and cartridges and the type of licence required." Given this, his sole function was to state that Tony needed a licence for the Winchester shotgun he fired on 20 August 1999 and that he didn't have one. This was not in dispute and Tony had never tried to say it was. He fully accepted that he had no licence.

But it actually had nothing to do with a murder trial. Licence or no licence, the point of law is simple: did Tony Martin have a murderous intent when he picked up that shotgun to defend his life after an unknown number of intruders smashed their way into his remote farmhouse in the dead of night? No-one in their right mind would stop to consider whether he had a licence for the gun he felt compelled to use in order to protect his own life. And nor did it answer the question of whether Fearon and Barras were ever inside the house.

The prosecution – aided and abetted by Norfolk Constabulary – were using the old tactic of smoke and mirrors because, while you're considering or debating whether Tony had a licence or not, you're not focusing on the point of law: intent to commit murder or to wound. This is why Tony repeatedly uses the phrase "legal engineering" to me and he's right to in my view. In my experience, very few trials are run in accordance with the Rule of Law.

Mon
22 NOV
unknown
UNUSED
368

unknown location

The statement below (which was not used as evidence in court) was said to have been made by 51-year-old retired police officer John Rice, who had served for 30 years in the Norfolk Constabulary - 28 years having being at Downham Market in various posts.

One of these posts was on Section Motor Patrol which involved night duty covering the Downham Section:

"Several years ago – somewhere between 7 & 10 years - I was on night duty and was maintaining a static observation near to Moyse's Bank in Emneth. It was a summer's night and about 3am when I saw a tractor and implement being driven out of Moyse's Bank and drive towards the Smeeth Road. The vehicle had no lights on. I caused it to stop and went to speak to the driver who immediately became defensive, refusing to tell me who he was and that I would be better off going after the criminals that abounded. After some time and lengthy discussion relating to the fact that the police could not catch the thieves and mainly people of the travelling fraternity and the fact that they ruled by violence, the tractor driver then told me he was Tony Martin and I followed him to his farm. Apart from checking the premises at night from then on, I have not spoken to Martin.

His fears and views of the travelling fraternity are in my view well-founded - myself having been on the end of several violent encounters from members of the travelling fraternity." [Author's emphasis].

> **What this adds to our knowledge**
>
> I found a copy of this statement in the Unused Material file which means that, since a statement had been taken and since the prosecution didn't bother to call him, defence counsel could have called this witness – having read the statement, you'll understand why they didn't want him anywhere near the court.

I found the statement to be not only helpful to Tony but also an interesting example of Tony's character and lifestyle: it highlighted how hard Tony worked and also how Tony was defensive at first before chastising Mr Rice for not catching criminals instead of bothering a farmer who just happened to be going about his lawful business at 3 in the morning. From the Tony Martin I know, that certainly sounds like him.

And then the revelation that retired police officer Rice *agreed with Tony's views that many travellers ruled by violence.*

> **CORRUPTION ALERT** *CPS and Tony's barrister withhold key evidence supporting the farmer from jury*

Now, given that a local police officer – who had worked in the area for 28 years – agreed that the travelling community ruled by violence, if you were Tony's barrister at trial, wouldn't you have wanted this man to come as a witness to the lawlessness and the violence of many of the travellers in that area?

Even a newly-qualified barrister could have made great capital out of this witness.

Retired PC Rice confirmed everything that Tony had been saying for years about crime in the area and the propensity some of the travelling community had towards violence. Doesn't this put a completely different complexion on Tony's use of a shotgun? If an unknown number of intruders smash their way into your home at night your only thought is to protect yourself: self-defence.

Consider the defence barrister who ought to have known of the existence of this witness (and how helpful he would have been to Tony's case) and yet failed to call him into court.

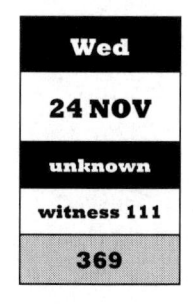

Wed
24 NOV
unknown
witness 111
369

unknown location
Prosecution witness Brian Arnold – who claimed to have specialised in the examination of firearms, ammunition and related items since 1965 – was said to have made an 8-page statement[376] dated 24 November 1999, some three months after the incident.

Arnold stated that he saw the body of Barras on 22 August and that he examined the trees and foliage around the body, (eliminating the possibility that the young man was shot where he lay.)

He claimed to have seen four empty casings in the breakfast room, one dusty and rusty. He stated that the three "fresh looking cartridge cases lay between the fireplace and the doorway to the hall and stairs." Notice that he did not say that these were (allegedly) found by DS Eglen, but merely that he saw them.

He stated that exhibit JE/6 was an Eley Maximum cartridge and that JE/7 and JE/8 were "like the cartridge cases that I have seen in two brands of Canadian ammunition. All three cases were marked as having been loaded with number six size shot." He added that he was "satisfied that, after having examined the gun and the cases, JE/6, JE/7 and JE/8 were all fired in the Winchester shotgun", which the police had had in their possession since the day after the shooting.

Arnold then mentioned the number of shots fired and the damage. He was firm in stating that "the wound to the back and the two main leg wounds were caused by *three* separate shots." [Author's emphasis]

However, he was much less certain about what damage was caused to either Fearon or Barras from any particular shot. He even suggested that there may have been *four* shots instead of two or three.

He estimated that the shot which hit Barras in the back was caused by someone standing between 10 and 14 feet away. This could have been, he noted, *the first shot from the stairs*[377] with Barras just inside the room, bending down.

---

[376] Noted on line S238 in the HOLMES book.
[377] Author's emphasis.

More mystery surrounding a simple shooting. And how can we be certain that those three spent cartridges were fired on the night of the shooting? Other spent cartridges were found throughout the house. Is this not, in itself, reasonable doubt that a skilled barrister would have seized upon to bring to the attention of a jury?

It's possible that, standing back, this statement had been fabricated by senior police officers to try to create the impression that Barras had been inside Bleak House.

I remind you at this point of Fearon's first statement: "I was shot after walking 20-30 yards up a track."

Wed
24 NOV
unknown
witness 69
370

unknown location

According to official records, pathologist Dr Heath made another statement in which he stated that he attended Downham Market police station the previous day (23 November) at 12:50pm for a conference which was also attended by several top brass, including the head of the investigation, DCI Martin Wright, and several SOCOs.

Having attended this conference – and only after having attended this conference - Dr Heath stated that "from the information obtained at the conference, it was, in my opinion, not possible to ascertain the sequence in which the shotgun injuries were inflicted to Frederick Barras and there was no pathological method by which it was possible to determine how far Frederick Barras had travelled after receiving the shotgun injuries."

This is of tremendous significance for this case which will become clear once we get to trial.

Notice the contradiction between the pathologist's statement and that of the "forensic expert" – the former could not be certain of the sequence of the injuries sustained by the alleged burglars whereas the latter was certain that the first shot had hit Barras in the back. Room for reasonable doubt in this deeply flawed police investigation?

Bizarrely, there is no mention of Dr Heath on the official court list of witnesses, yet the newspapers reported that he gave evidence on 12 April 2000 and HOLMES notes that his statements were entered as evidence into court.

~ the May 1999 burglary revisited ~

Thur
9 DEC
morning
UNUSED
371

Norwich Magistrates' Court
Tony was at court for a preliminary hearing in the murder trial when acting DI Sharman showed him a number of pieces of china. He recognised four pieces out of the six as having come from his house in the May burglary. Tony added that no-one had had a right or permission to enter his house or take any of his property:

" I think the burglary was a vicious attack on me. I am a very private person and the break-in made me feel very vulnerable. The shock of seeing the property, which is part of my history, missing from my house really affected me.

From that time I have become very security conscious and have locked away many of the pieces of furniture out of sight. I felt very strongly that having lost those items of furniture which had belonged to my predecessors was almost that I had let them down in some way.

The effect of the burglary has made me very depressed and even suicidal. I have found that since the burglary, I have been less and less able to go out during the evening for fear of being subject to another break-in."

Thur
9 DEC
unknown
UNUSED
372

King's Lynn police station
We have seen previously that Bleak House had been burgled on 12th May 1999 and that Tony had found a cigarette butt inside his house.

Following a DNA test, this butt allegedly led police to a person already known to them.

And his statement opened up such a can of worms that the police and CPS unlawfully decided not to use it:

According to official records, Christopher Webster was first interviewed on Thursday 9 December 1999 by DC 356 Stuart Peters and DC 422 Trevor Buxton at King's Lynn police station in the company of legal executive Chris Howe. Notice that, although the burglary had occurred in the May, this interview took place *after* the August shooting incident.

Webster had prepared a written statement with his legal advisor in which he admitted that he had driven a white transit van to Bleak House in May with three others. He said that he did not enter the house at any time, but that he simply drove the burglars there and helped load possessions into the van. He added that he drove the van away from Bleak House and it was then stopped the following day by police officers near Ely. He recalled that two wooden chests of drawers were stolen, along with "a writing table, plates and pots."

He said that all of the items – except those recovered from his house the previous day when he was arrested – had been sold.

Then DC Peters asked Webster how the farmhouse had been entered, which suggested that he either did not know or that he was testing Webster out. Either way, Webster said he didn't know, claiming that the possessions were all out of the house by the time he arrived and he simply drove down the gravel drive and loaded up the van. When asked how he knew how to get to Bleak House, he replied that he followed three other men in their car from Newark. [Author's note: this could be said to contradict his comment about the possessions being out of the house by the time he arrived.]

Webster told police that the chest of drawers and the bureau were approximately four feet tall. Peters commented that a blue and white tureen was also stolen along with three decorative plates and Webster admitted that they had been part of the haul that night.

He told the police that he left Bleak House in his van and followed his colleagues away from the area. They parked up near Ely and Webster got into the car with the other three men and they drove back to Newark.

The next morning, they returned to the car park near Ely and Webster collected the van before being stopped by the police.

DC Peters informed Webster that it would be helpful to the police if they could locate the property that had been stolen (of course it would, in order to save face.) Webster told Peters that he had put the silver jugs under the passenger's seat in the front of the van and that Menarry and Bishop had failed to find them when they *thoroughly* [author's emphasis] searched the van whilst Webster was in custody. Webster said he "took the jugs home and used them as ornaments."

DC Peters then said to Webster: "The question's got to be asked: 'How does a 16-year-old boy end up in a house in the middle of the Fens?'" which is a valid question. There was a long pause before he asked, "Would you be prepared to write down the names of the other guys who were on the Bleak House job?"

Webster stated that he wanted to get back to Newark so that his wife could visit him, but was told that the police could not promise him favours nor do deals for information. (This comment becomes important later on.) Peters said, "I can't make you any promises in order to induce you to tell me anything," at which point Howe, the legal executive, advised his client that he could always tell the police after the tape was switched off. (Most deals are done when the tape is turned off. They call it British Justice.)

DC Buxton asked Webster if he smoked and the detained person said that he smoked "around 100 roll-ups a day." This question was asked because it was a roll-up that had been found inside Bleak House by Tony after the burglary.

After being released by the police in Ely, Webster added: "I drove back that night. The van was parked on the Broadway Car Park and then the next morning the other three come and picked me up and I drove the van to Southsea, near Portsmouth. On the front were all the antique buyers. Halfway up on the left, as you come in from the bottom end, the sea front, is the shop. I drove around the back down an alleyway at the side and went up to the back door. I got out of the van and the dealer paid us. I got paid £300. I was the only one who had the bottle to drive the van because the other three were in the car all the time."

DC Peters then asked Webster whether a Darren Bark was one of the three in the car, but Webster said that he wasn't. [Author's note: he could, of course, have been covering up for Bark.] Peters then asked how Bark got to know about Bleak House and Webster told him that Sean Kennelly had told him: "Kennelly is the link between it all – Bark and the Gregory brothers and Owen Hirrel."

And then the interview took on a decidedly interesting tone: Peters asked if Fearon knew about all the links and the people involved and Webster replied that Fearon and "poor little Fred" knew only what Fearon had been told and that he was kept in the dark by others who were really controlling the burglary that was supposed to take place that night and previous ones. Webster was adamant, however, that *Bark was the motivator behind the proposed burglary on* 20 *August*.[378]

Buxton asked Webster if there were any dogs on the night of 12 May, and he replied that yes, he was stroking one – so much for the vicious reputation of the dogs portrayed at the murder trial in April 2000.

Finally, Webster confirmed to the police that the time of the burglary on 12 May was around 8pm and that it was "very dark." Peters stated on the record: "Your answers to us have been very helpful."

If that were really the case, why wasn't there a whole series of subsequent arrests in this matter – Webster had provided at least six significant names – and why wasn't the owner of the antique shop arrested on suspicion of receiving

---

[378] If you needed incontrovertible evidence of police and judicial corruption, it's here – Tony's defence team had this statement in their possession. Clearly, any defence acting *in Tony's interest* – would have called Bark as a witness to examine him about his alleged role in the proposed burglary. Bark was evidently being protected and it's reasonable to assume that he was being protected by the police because they were covering-up the death of Fred Barras and no doubt a number of burglaries in the Emneth area.

I know some people who *never* insure their valuables for the reason that they do not want employees of insurance companies to know what valuables were kept on the premises and those employees passing on this data to criminals. Farmwatch, of course, was a company collating such data. I do not say that it acted unlawfully in passing on such important data to criminals or corrupt police officers, but it is always possible.

stolen goods? And, if it was true that Darren Bark had been the ring-leader of the proposed burglary on 20 August 1999, why was he not called to the trial by Tony's defence counsel? I suggest that Bark knew just a little too much that the police and prosecution did not want revealed. I also suggest that it is highly debatable as to whether Bark was even the getaway driver on that fateful night.

We should perhaps also consider the notion that the shooting of Fred Barras was the result of a gangland feud because, as pub landlord Darren Cooper had told police (entry **291**), "Bark had been warned off going to Bleak House again". Perhaps the teenager knew just a little too much about the power-play between these criminals. His sister, Mary Ellen Barras, then aged 22, made a statement to the police on 23 August 1999 in which she said that Fred had occasionally worked on the local tip in Newark – and it's certainly possible that he learnt a little too much about the criminal activities of those who operated the tip and others who worked for them. Mary Ellen added that some of Fred's friends were in prison and that he was having a casual affair with a 30-year-old woman called Michelle Scrimshaw. Although he is said to have been a very friendly boy, he would also have made some enemies.

And the wise person would also consider that it's also possible that those higher up this particular food chain were in league with corrupt police officers.

Was Barras murdered by his own kind, or by police officers that night who had to eliminate him because of what he knew?

Either way, there was a cover-up of his murder by the police.

And, either way, Tony Martin wasn't the murderer. It's obvious – there is no way in the world that - had you been Tony's barrister – you wouldn't have called Webster to court to cross-examine him about what he knew of the Newark criminal fraternity and their targeting of Bleak House over several years. The failure to call Webster as a witness wasn't a mere oversight – it was a deliberate and planned move designed to ensure that he wouldn't give evidence and that Tony Martin would be found guilty of a murder he didn't commit.

Wed
15 DEC
unknown
UNUSED
373

King's Lynn police station
Incredibly, Tony was not interviewed by the police regarding the 12 May burglary until 15 December 1999 – some 7 months after the event and not until after the August incident.

It was this dilatory attitude to crime that the police displayed which so annoyed Tony.

The statement was not used at trial.

He said that on Wednesday 12 May 1999, he went to Cambridge, "returned home around 6:30pm for a flying visit and left again." When he left, he "locked the big 'church doors' which open into the hallway. The rest of the house was secure and everything was in order."[379]

When he returned home around 11:30pm, he saw "the right hand 'church door' was ajar, the locks were damaged and a chest of drawers were just outside the 'church doors' which should have been in the middle room downstairs."

He looked around the whole house and found that the following property was missing: a honey-gold coloured bureau with a hinged desk lid with short squared feet worth about £1,000; a Jacobean or Jacobean-style chest of drawers with bun feet worth anything up to £1,000; a chest of drawers which he thought was probably 19th century with bun feet and worth about £1,200; a leaf table with bulbous legs and some basic carved work on the top rail worth about £1,500 at auction; a pewter mug of one pint size; a blue willow-pattern tureen with lid about 12 inches in diameter with some gold decorative patterning around it.

As we have seen, Tony reported the burglary to the police and the following day SOCO DC 8 Richard Aldous attended the house. During his search, the officer claimed he found and removed a cigarette end in the middle room. Tony does not smoke and no-one else who had legitimate access to his house smoked. His opinion was that the cigarette end was left by a burglar.

The statement made to police by DC Aldous on 21 September 1999 claims that the officer found the cigarette butt, but Tony insists that he found it. We should also make note of the fact that DC Aldous did not make any mention of Tony having dialled 999 the previous night and allegedly saying "If they return, I'll blow their heads off." Don't you think that the constable would have mentioned this to the farmer had it been said?

Mon
10 JAN
2000
UNUSED
11.35 am
374

Lincoln police station

According to official records, Webster was interviewed for a second time (that we know of), the interview commencing at 11:35am and ending just 13 minutes later.

DCs Peters and Buxton asked the questions and Christopher Howe of Pearsons Solicitors again represented Webster.

This interview was a continuation of the previous one on 9 December 1999 [entry 372].

This statement was unused.

Peters informed Webster that a DNA profile matching his had been identified inside the house from a cigarette end and asked, "Did you at any time go into Bleak House?" to which Webster replied, "No, not at any time."

Peters asked again about the nature of the dogs and Webster confirmed that

---

[379] Tony has told me that he went to the Marmion House Hotel that evening and so there were several people who knew of his whereabouts that night.

they were friendly.

Buxton asked if Webster was under the influence of drugs at the time of the May burglary and he replied: "Yes. I was always under the influence of amphetamines. It gives you courage but does not affect your memory or judgment. In fact, it possibly sharpens them up. I remember every detail of my involvement in the burglary."

Mon
10 JAN
2000
UNUSED
375

Norwich Crown Court
Fearon and Bark appeared before Judge Mellor (case number T19990726) for the proposed burglary at Bleak House in August 1999. The prosecutor was Horwood-Smart's junior counsel, Ian James. Fearon was represented by Mr Chris Kessling and Bark's counsel was Mr A Oliver. The following is an account of the prosecution opening statement and the history of the defendants' criminal offences:

"Both these defendants appeared for plea and directions before His Honour Judge Farnworth on 8th December and both pleaded guilty to the single count against them at the first opportunity available to them. Additionally, in the case of Bark, forms have been prepared setting out a further 7 offences which he asks to be considered. Those were put to him on that occasion. There are two forms. The one with 3 offences on pre-dates the matters with which we are concerned today. The form with 4 offences on postdates these matters and indeed these offences were committed by him at a time when he had failed to answer his Part 4 bail in connection with these present matters. As we can see he had gone to the West Country where he committed these offences at a time when he was on the run. And he was arrested in Torquay, as I understand it, on 20 October [see entry **336**], since which time he has been in custody.

Turning to the matters the subject of the indictment, at some time roundabout 8 o'clock on the evening of 20 August of last year, that was a Friday, Bark set off in his motor vehicle, a white Ford Granada, on a journey from Newark in Nottinghamshire to Emneth near Wisbech. In the car with him were his co-defendant Fearon, aged 29, and in the back passenger seat a young man, Frederick Barras, aged 16.[380]

The purpose of this journey was the burglary of farm premises known as Bleak House Farm situated in Emneth. At this time those premises were occupied by their owner, one Anthony Martin. These premises had been

---

[380] Mr James – working with prosecutor Rosamund Horwood-Smart on the case against Tony Martin and therefore in full possession of all the witness statements – appears to have overlooked that the car was stopped in Balderton at 8:10pm (it is claimed) by the police en route to Emneth from Newark.

specifically targeted by the men in the car for the purpose of their activities that night.

In order to facilitate the commission of the offence of burglary they had with them a number of bags, a torch, gloves and so it seems, in the case of Barras, a wooden handled screwdriver.[381]

The journey would have taken them about 2 hours, resulting in their arrival at about ten o'clock at Emneth.[382]

Fearon and Barras left the car in the vicinity of the farmhouse and Bark, in the car, repaired to a nearby lane to await their return.[383] His role was to wait there and convey the other two, together with what spoils they might obtain, back to Newark. I should say there is no evidence that Bark ever left the vehicle.[384]

Fearon and Barras made their way on to the farm property and in the course of doing so disturbed dogs, rottweilers, which were kept at the farm by Mr Martin and effectively allowed to roam free there.

Fearon and Barras retreated from the dogs[385] and as they did so they happened upon the farmhouse which is difficult to see and locate within the farm grounds,[386] as your Honour perhaps can see if he has copies of the photographs in this case.

---

[381] Actually this 'screwdriver' was identified as a 'chisel' in police searches – see entries **190** and **308**.

[382] This is clearly false information – the police claimed the alleged burglars had been stopped at 8:10pm and they couldn't have set off before 8:15pm, thus arriving around 9:45-10:15pm. We only have to consider that Paul Leet said that Tony had called round to his bungalow at approximately 9:30pm *after* Tony had fired his shotgun. Tony had done a number of things after the shooting which would have taken, at the very least, 20 minutes, thus timing the break-in and Tony firing his gun at approximately 9:10pm. According to the prosecutor's own evidence, Fearon and Barras would not have arrived in Emneth at that time, much less been inside the house when Tony fired his shotgun.

[383] This is the first instance of Bark claiming to have been parked up at the agreed rendezvous point in Moyse's Bank.

[384] There was no evidence to prove that Bark was actually there other than a statement from him which completely contradicted his initial statement to the police. Many statements are made under duress. If he *had* been there, as the prosecution claimed, he ought to have been called to court to participate in the trial.

[385] This alleged "retreat" would have been about 100 yards – the distance between the cottages being used as kennels and Bleak House itself. On the route between the cottages and the farmhouse are numerous outbuildings and trees which could have provided shelter. This part of the narrative is entirely false. Shame on the judge for not questioning the prosecutor.

[386] A seed is being sown here that the farmhouse couldn't easily be seen and no wonder the police couldn't find it and therefore they couldn't find Barras.

JUDGE: I don't.

MR JAMES: I think it would be helpful if your Honour did, together also with a plan which should be included within the exhibits bundle and that's RJB5,[387] the plan.

JUDGE: I have RJB5D.

MR JAMES: Here is a bundle of photographs. As I say, looking at photographs 1 and 2, one can see the house is concealed by trees and the like and it is very difficult to see even when one is quite close to it.

In any event, as I say, retreating from the animals Fearon and Barras happened upon the farmhouse.

Barras effected entry on the premises, apparently by using the screwdriver he had with him using that to *prise open a window at the front of the house* [Author's emphasis]. And the point of entry, just referring your Honour to the plan, is the window which is situated looking at RJB5D, the window situated on the bottom wall, as it would be, in the centre where there is the fold in the copy I have.

This window gives into a small room. That is shown in photograph 11. And from that small room both men then moved across the hallway,[388] which is shown in photograph 13, on the photo we have moving from right to left and on the left-hand side, can't see it in the photograph, there's a doorway. But that gives into another room which is opposite there and that can be seen in photographs 18 to 21.

---

[387] This alleged exhibit has an interesting history. According to the official police records, it doesn't even exist. It's not recorded in HOLMES. However, revised plans of it are: in fact, several revised plans from RJB/5A – RJB/5G. That's an awful lot of revisions of a simple plan of the house. Revisions RJB/F and RJB/G were made as late as 17 November 1999 – some 3 months after the incident. Plenty of time in which to make an exhibit fit the false narrative being created.

Furthermore, there has been cross-contamination of evidence between the case of *R. v Anthony Edward Martin* and *R. v Brendon Fearon & Darren Henry Bark*. This cross-contamination, I argue, makes *both* trials unlawful.

[388] We should remember that Ian James is fully aware that his colleague Rosamund Horwood-Smart is going to run with the notion that Tony Martin had "lain in wait" to encounter the alleged burglars and then shot them "like rats in a trap". It was a ridiculous notion based not on fact, but on securing a sound bite for the waiting media. But consider Mr James' behaviour at Tony's murder trial – he allowed his colleague to run with the spurious notion *and said nothing when in possession of facts which he knew disproved the Crown's case.*

MR JAMES: In photographs 20 and 21 one can see a dresser, for want of a better word, the large wooden object to the left-hand side of photograph 20 and 21. And from that dresser small items of silver were removed and placed in one of the holdalls which the men had with them.

I should say that Bleak House has no electricity supply in the conventional sense and Fearon and Barras were guided by the torch they bought with them which was suspended around Fearon's neck.

JUDGE: What is an unconventional electricity supply?

MR JAMES: It has an electricity supply which is rigged up from an adjoining barn so it isn't that there is no lighting there at all but certainly not in the way that we would understand an electricity supply.

The activities of these men at the premises had disturbed the occupant, Mr Martin, who lived there alone and he occupied the bedroom upstairs. And on becoming aware of the presence of strangers, Mr Martin had armed himself with a shotgun and locating the men in the room that I have just described to your Honour and shown, Mr Martin fired the gun at them a number of times.[389]

Fearon was struck in both legs and Barras received injuries to the leg and to the back, the latter proving ultimately to be fatal. Both men at this stage sought to make their escape. Fearon was able to wrench the entire window frame out of its housing, as can be seen in photograph 18, thus creating an opening from which both of them were able to leave the house; Fearon first, with Barras following. They left behind the holdalls and the spoons on the premises. Fearon, plainly in considerable pain, eventually managed to crawl to the safety of a nearby lane, *in fact the same lane where Bark had been waiting* although he didn't make contact with Bark.[390] And Fearon thereafter made his way a short distance down the lane to a bungalow, the occupiers of which were able to notify the emergency services. Fearon, on the way, had divested himself of the torch and gloves used to facilitate in the burglary. By this time it was just before 11 o'clock in the evening.

---

[389] Notice that the prosecutor doesn't state precisely how many times Tony was alleged to have fired his gun.

[390] We do not currently have proof that this is true. It is just as possible that Fearon went to the getaway vehicle to speak with the driver (Bark or another) first and that the driver called the police.

Barras had managed to escape from the house but he was only able to crawl a matter of yards into undergrowth just close to the window where he died from his injuries.[391]

By about 11:20pm Bark, apparently aware of the continued presence of emergency services, elected to approach the bungalow which he did in the car. He did so on the pretext of looking for friends in the area. He was asked by the police to remain at the scene which he did and in due course the picture became clear, although Barras' demise was not something which was discovered until the next day.[392]

Neither Fearon[393] nor Bark, who were spoken to at the scene, initially disclosed any information about the burglary or Barras who, as I say, remained where he was, not being discovered until the next day.

Fearon's injuries were extensive. He was taken to the Queen Elizabeth Hospital in King's Lynn where he received treatment for a lacerated wound to the side and front of his left thigh measuring 5 inches by 5 inches and multiple puncture wounds over the front upper part of his right thigh. Your Honour may have noticed that he appears still to carry the vestige of that injury with him today.[394]

As your Honour will know, Mr Martin, the farmer, has himself been charged with a number of offences arising from these events including an allegation contrary to section 18 of the Offences against the Person Act in relation to Fearon and the murder of Barras.

Fearon was formally interviewed for the first time on 22 August at hospital. He was then interviewed again at the police station in the middle of September.[395]

During the course of these interviews he admitted being responsible for organizing the venture stating specifically he was the ringleader.[396]

---

[391] As I have pointed out before, the fact that the body of Barras was found in bushes just fifteen feet from the exit window does not mean that he died there.

[392] Again, note how a seed is being sown that Barras was not discovered until 2:32pm on the Saturday afternoon following the Friday night incident.

[393] As we know, Fearon claimed that he had told several people that Barras had also been injured.

[394] Brendon Fearon temporarily walked with a limp and with the aid of a walking stick.

[395] Prosecutor James ought to have known that Fearon had been interviewed on 22 August, 25 August, 10 September, 15 September, 18 September, and 3 November 1999.

He said he first came to hear of the premises about a month before the commission of the offence in a public house. He said that he'd been eavesdropping, listening to other people talking about the premises. He had overheard directions and in consequence, to quote him, "decided to take a pot shot at it" on the basis of what he'd heard. He said he believed the house to contain furniture and small antiques. He told the police he hadn't been to the house before, although at one stage there is some suggestion in the course of his interview that something akin to a recce had taken place but that hadn't involved going right up to the premises themselves.

He said that he had involved Bark by persuading Bark the day before to act as a driver. He said he also mentioned the journey to Barras on the day of the enterprise at about 6 o'clock that evening. Accordingly Bark had collected him at about 6 o'clock from his mother's house. They picked up Barras at about 7:30pm from outside some shops in Newark and then they had all gone off together.

He said he believed the property to be empty and to have been unoccupied for many years. No doubt in an effort to exonerate Bark he said that the plan was that Bark drop him off, go back to Newark and pick them up – I'm sorry that Bark would drop them off, go back to Newark and then they effectively would contact him later and he, Bark, would then come back. He said that the agreement as far as he was concerned, that's to say Fearon, was that he and Barras would sleep at the premises.

He said he and Barras would have shared the proceeds, with Bark only being given a drink for his trouble. He said that he'd bought the torch and bags.

Bark's account in interview was somewhat different. Bark told the police that sometime previously he'd been told of the house by an associate of his. He had been told that two other men had burgled the premises which were occupied by a farmer who had rottweiler dogs.

He said that he, Bark, had mentioned this to Fearon who had asked him to drive there so that he, Fearon, could steal from the premises. He said that because Fearon had pestered him so much he agreed to drive Fearon but that his role was simply to drop Fearon off and collect him again, not least of all because he, Bark, was frightened of dogs and they knew there were dogs on

---

[396] Prosecutor James would have been in possession of the Webster interview in which he said that Bark had been the ringleader.

the premises.

He said on the evening in question he had been unaware that a third man was to be involved.[397] He had not known anything about that until shortly before they picked Barras up. He described the journey and dropping the other two off and then subsequently being afraid when he became aware of the presence of the emergency services at the burglary. He said he hadn't left the car and confirmed that he expected a drink from Fearon for his role. Those are the brief facts of the case.

I wonder if I could just turn to the antecedents[398] now. Brendon Fearon is 29 years of age. He lives in Newark. Really that's all that's known about his background.[399]

His first adult conviction was in 1986 and since then he's appeared quite regularly before the courts, more often than not for offences of dishonesty and he has in the past lost his liberty as a result of his activities.

He's got burglary related convictions in March 1991 when he got community service. October 1991 when he was given a suspended sentence of imprisonment. February - sorry, July - 1994 when he was imprisoned for 12 months for dwelling house burglary. And again, over the page, non-dwelling burglary, 3 months concurrent. I think that as far as burglary is concerned that's the picture, although as your Honour will see he has more recently appeared before the courts for other offences including dishonesty. I don't think the court will be assisted by the details of any particular...[400]

JUDGE: No.

MR JAMES: Darren Bark is 33. He lives in Newark. He has adult convictions going back to 1985. First burglary related matter in 1986, community service for 3 non-dwelling burglaries. Then in September 1993, imprisoned for offences including non-dwelling burglary. Two years' imprisonment in March 1994 for dwelling house burglary with a matter considered. In December 1995, attempted burglary, deferred sentence resulting in community

---

[397] This is at variance with Christopher Webster's statement to the police that Bark was the ring-leader, not Fearon.

[398] In this context, previous offences.

[399] This is a ridiculous claim by prosecutor James. He was in possession of Fearon's first statement in which he gave (as we have seen) a detailed account of his family and working life and some previous criminal offences.

[400] Clearly there were details about that conviction for dishonesty which neither the judge nor the prosecutor wanted spoken about in open court.

service. In May 1996, Nottingham Crown Court, two non-dwelling house burglaries, another matter of dishonesty, a total of 12 months' imprisonment. In May 1998, dwelling house burglary and non-dwelling house burglary. That was the subject of appeal giving a total, we have worked it out, we believe to be 30 months in all after the appeal was resolved. In any event on the basis of information which I have had provided to me, and I think this is agreed with Mr Oliver, he is liable to recall for up to 380 days in connection with those matters.

The only other matter which I think out of fairness I ought to mention, there is, as I have said, Mr Martin is himself the subject of a prosecution. Fearon has made a statement in connection with that and as far as the Crown are concerned been cooperative in relation to that and we are expecting to call him as a witness in relation to that.[401]

Wed 26 JAN 2000 376

Defence statement

On 26 January 2000, Tony Martin signed a defence statement prepared by solicitor Nick Makin of M&S Solicitors, and his counsel, Anthony Scrivener, which was supposed to obtain an acquittal against charges of murder and attempted murder.

You might like to speculate at this point how many pages in length you think the defence statement would be against such serious charges. Ten pages? Twenty? Thirty? Fifty? More? Remember, a man's liberty and reputation are at stake here.

Below, I reproduce the entire statement so that you can judge for yourself whether you think it was the best defence statement that Tony's lawyers could have produced on behalf of their client:

> ❝ The nature of the accused's defence is that I did not engage in any unlawful activity on the night of 20 August 1999. Any use of force on my part was in self-defence at a time when my house was under attack from burglars.
>
> I take issue with the prosecution in that it is alleged that my use of force was unlawful. I take issue because I accept the fact that Frederick Jackson Barras and Brendon Fearon were in my house on the evening

---

[401] Notice that prosecutor James doesn't say that Bark will also be called as a witness. Or that the Judge didn't interject and ask why Bark wasn't going to be called to the murder trial.

of 20 August 1999. They did not have my permission to be there. They broke into my house as burglars whilst I was asleep in bed.

Upon going downstairs to investigate, a torch was shone in my face while the house was otherwise in complete darkness. I accept that I fired my gun. I did so because I believed that my life was in danger."

In signing that defence statement, Tony was, in effect, signing his own prison warrant and buying into the false narrative created by the police. Clearly, this half-page statement defending such serious charges was inadequate. Now, why would your own lawyers ask you to sign such a woefully inadequate document unless they were actually working against you? There is an argument – and I have no doubt that his lawyers would have used it – that says that the less information you provide to the prosecution the better because you can "ambush" them at trial. But that is not relevant here and besides, "ambushing" the other party is no longer tolerated in court, despite what you may have seen on television or in films.

There is another argument which says that the case against Tony Martin was extremely simple and that this brief statement was adequate, yet this doesn't hold water, because the case became unnecessarily over-complicated by the police and the prosecution, both of whom came up with various scenarios which were designed to show the farmer as a murdering gypsy-hating loner.

At the time of Tony's trial, the defence case statement was governed by the Criminal Procedure and Investigations Act 1996, which required that the statement must be in writing and must contain certain prescribed information:

(i)   the nature of the accused's defence;

(ii) the matters of fact on which the accused takes issue with the prosecution and why he does so;

(iii) the facts on which he intends to rely; and

(iv) any points of law (including those as to admissibility of evidence or abuse of process) which the accused wishes to make; and

(v)   any authority on which he intends to rely.

A complete denial of the prosecution's case or the evidence of their witnesses without any reasoning on the defendant's side would be insufficient."[402]

Clearly, according to the Act, the statement Tony Martin was asked to sign by his solicitors was little more than a mere denial of the case against him and was therefore woefully inadequate in terms of the Criminal Procedure and Investigations Act 1996.

---

[402] <www.inbrief.co.uk>

But there was a more sinister aspect to Tony's defence statement – it had been written in such a way as to make him (and 60 million others) believe that he had been burgled and not only that, but been burgled by Fearon and Barras. He did not *know* that he had been burgled. He did not *know* that Fearon and Barras were in his house. There is substantial evidence to show that they weren't. All that he 'knew' was all that the police had created to explain the murder of Barras. It was nothing more than a piece of ingenious fiction and the highly vulnerable farmer bought into it lock, stock and barrel. Him and 60 million others.

> **CORRUPTION ALERT** — *Improper & inadequate defence statement*
>
> So, we must ask ourselves, how did such a poor defence statement get entered into court in such a high profile murder trial?
>
> Tony told me how Makin visited him soon after his arrest and persuaded him to sack Paul Croker: "Croker said to me 'If you sack me and go with him, you'll lose your case' and so it turned out."

It's interesting how Tony regards himself as a very good judge of character and yet he leaves himself extremely vulnerable to a certain type of person like Makin. The reality is that whoever Tony had had representing him, he would always have been found guilty because the stench of corruption left its evil mark on every possible aspect of this case.

In the event, Makin was eventually reported to the Office for the Supervision of Solicitors for what Tony felt was a mishandling of his case, including fundamental errors of police and judicial procedure. Yet there is more than a strong suggestion that Makin was set up as a fraudster because he was going to report collusion between Tony's barrister, the Prosecution's barrister and the judge. Against such a triumvirate, Makin would have stood no chance of claiming his innocence in the financial management of the case.

Fri 28 JAN 9.45 am — UNUSED — 377

HMP Lincoln

Christopher Webster, who lived in Newark with his wife and four children, was on remand at HMP Lincoln having been charged with numerous offences at various locations in the Midlands and East Anglia.

*Webster's third statement [see also **372** and **374**] was recorded as having been made at Lincoln Prison by DC Peters and DC Buxton.*

Lincoln Prison is 20 miles or about 40 minutes from Newark. Had any strings been pulled so that his wife and children could visit?

Webster had volunteered to give information to the police about the background to the proposed burglary when Barras and Fearon were shot. He added that he had been told that he *could not be prosecuted* in relation to anything which he mentioned in this statement.

Webster stated that he first heard about Bleak House from the Gregory brothers about three or four years ago. It was generally mentioned in a pub and the Gregory brothers were bragging about who they had given information to to burgle the house. Webster claimed that he did not know specific details at that time, but he did know that it was a derelict house containing antique furniture and 'smalls'.

The Gregory brothers (Mark, Wayne and Brother) knew about it through their connections in Wisbech, where they operated the tip. At that stage Webster knew that numerous people from Newark had visited the house and burgled it, but he said he was not interested in that side. He remembered even then that the talk about the place was that there were a number of dogs there, and that the farmer was described as a "fucking nutter."

Webster claimed that he thought no more about it but knew that Darren Bark and Pimmy Bills were often going to Wisbech and the surrounding area to do burglaries. He said that they specifically travelled there to do jobs, but he could not say when or how many they did. Webster described them as being antiques burglars who would regularly dispose of their stolen goods through Wayne and Ronnie Savage at Newark.

Around April 1999, Webster said that he was doing a bit of antique knocking in the Wisbech area with Sean Kennelly, Brother Gregory and Owen Hirrel when the subject of Bleak House came up again. He said that he was nothing but their driver since he had no knowledge of antiques. The other three decided to do a burglary at Bleak House and Webster agreed to be their driver.

The day after the burglary, Webster returned to Newark from Cambridgeshire[403], driving Sean Kennelly's van full of stolen furniture from Bleak House. He drove straight to the Broadway Pub in Newark, where he knew the other lads would be. He walked in and Kennelly, Brother Gregory, Hirrel and Joe Price were already there. Webster said they were surprised to see him and made it quite clear that they were pleased to see him too.

Webster told police he could not recall exactly who said what followed, but they all knew about it. They said, "It's a good job you were caught by the police rather than the farmer. If he had caught you, he would have shot you. He's fucking mad."

---

[403] This is at variance with his first statement in which he said, "I parked the van up near Ely and got into the car with the other three men and we drove back to Newark."

Webster said that he felt that they knew all that *before* the job was done and none were prepared to do what he had been through as they were all frightened of the farmer and his dogs. Webster used the sentence: "They set me up and knew that I was putting my life at risk."

It was discussed that night in the Broadway about going back again to do a further burglary there but, when he realised that his supposed mates had set him up, he refused because he was angry with them.

A few weeks later Webster was approached by Darren Bark, who asked if he would go down to the Wisbech area with him to do some antique knocking. Bark wanted Webster to show him where Bleak House was.[404]

Webster agreed to go and they went in Bark's blue Renault Traffic van.[405] Bark knew all about the farmer at Bleak House, and that he was "dangerous." Bark told Webster about it and that he intended setting up another job there. He was very keen to find the farm, but Webster claimed that he pretended he could not find it as he wanted nothing more to do with it. Webster described how they "half-heartedly did a bit of knocking" before returning to Newark.

Webster said that Bark was desperate to find the place, and he later paid Mark Gregory £100 to show him the location. They went there in two vehicles, with Nathan Bastable, and set up two more burglaries whilst in the area. They went in Bark's blue Renault Traffic van and a red transit belonging to Gregory. All these people were well aware of the dangers involved in the burglaries at Bleak House, Webster said, both "from the mad farmer and his dogs." Webster was not certain exactly when this was, but it was "about July, 1999".

Webster is alleged to have added[406] that he had no doubt whatsoever that when Bark, Fearon and Barras attempted to burgle Bleak House and the latter two were shot, that Bark knew exactly what was likely to happen and that is why he did not go into the house and let Barras and Fearon do the dirty work.

Finally, Webster said that he was prepared to attend court in relation to the information he had provided to the police in this statement.[407]

Webster claimed that he had known about Bleak House having been a regular target for at least 3 or 4 years. If he had known about it for that length of time, we can be sure that his friends and accomplices did also and that, through paid informants, the police did, too.

---

[404] This is at variance with the statement of Darren Cooper (entry **291**) in which he claimed that Bark had burgled Bleak House twice previously.

[405] Apparently not a white Ford Granada.

[406] I use the word 'alleged' because there is a strong suspicion that this witness statement has been interfered with.

[407] Having stated that he was willing to attend court as a witness, it is even more reprehensible of Tony's barrister not to have ensured his attendance on his client's behalf.

We have seen the police intelligence reports authored on Tony Martin by Rodney Gooderson – it is implausible that such reports were not being gathered on Webster and some – if not all – of his associates during this 3 or 4 year period and equally implausible that the name of Bleak House did not come up in these reports. If we accept that it did, then why was this knowledge not passed on to Norfolk police? Or if it was, why did Norfolk police not do anything about it? Tony often contacted the police about thefts and burglaries (confirmed by PC Gooderson and Gillian Butters, the civilian clerk at Downham Market police station) and says that they did nothing and often accused him of having made it all up – clearly this was not the case as Webster confirmed to the police.

Webster added that "numerous people" from Newark had gone to Bleak House to rob it and word will have gotten around that it was an easy target. And someone – even just one person – would have been a paid police informant posing as a regular hanging around those pubs and told them about these numerous journeys to Emneth.

Upon his return from the police station, Webster realised that he had been "set up" by the others. Now, it's possible that if the others he named had set Webster up in May, then the same people probably set up Fearon and Barras. Webster also stated that these people knew of the dangers involved in burgling Bleak House – "the dogs and guns." Word might also have travelled around, too, that Tony Martin had shot at Aldin's vehicle in the orchard in 1994.

Webster also added that he had no doubt whatsoever that the people moving the chess pieces around the board were setting up Fearon and Barras because they knew of the likely consequences of their actions.

> **CORRUPTION ALERT** — *CPS and Tony's barrister failed to call another key witness to court*

Now, we have to ask this important question: since the police were in possession of this statement from Webster in January 2000 (some three months before the trial) why was Webster not called as either a prosecution witness to provide background information to a jury or, more helpfully, as a defence witness so that he could fully explain his knowledge of the large number of thefts and burglaries at Bleak House that the police had failed to deal with?

Webster could have told a jury that there were people higher up the food chain controlling the Fearons and the Barrases of this world and that Bleak House had been targeted over a substantial number of years as Tony Martin had claimed and the police denied.

If the burglaries at Bleak House were part of a concerted programme of crimes organised by people higher up the food chain, how far up do we go? Do we include Robin Martin, who had criminal convictions for theft, handling stolen goods and grievous bodily harm? Do we include corrupt police officers? Do we include the aunt – Elizabeth Chadfield - who lived near Webster in Leicestershire? Whilst these are mere suppositions, what we do know is that Webster appeared to have confirmed that Bleak House had been a target for many years and was known to contain antique furniture and 'smalls'.

We do know that Robin Martin had succeeded in having it recorded by the police that Tony was mentally unstable and that one day he would shoot somebody. Was the gun left in Tony's car one night (he says) left by Robin and were the numerous crimes a way to ensure that Tony Martin would one day reach the point of no return and shoot at intruders because he had simply had enough of the failures by the police to act?

Prior to my research, Tony had no clear idea of just how the thefts and burglaries at his house had all been linked and that they were probably carried out by foot soldiers acting on the orders of others. Robin Martin had an intimate knowledge of what prizes lay in Bleak House, but it does not necessarily follow that he had any part to play in any burglary there. Several others, including Helen Lilley and Roger Putterill also knew that Tony had many antiques at the house, but it doesn't necessarily follow that they were involved either.

The police knew that Bleak House was a target. Was there a corrupt officer or two who always 'turned a blind eye' and didn't investigate anything that occurred there because they were being paid by someone doing the organising? Did the police take the longer view that if Tony Martin was the victim of crime for long enough, he would one day shoot someone and they could put him away?

How would Webster know that the farmer at Bleak House was a "fucking nutter?" Where – or more importantly who – was this information coming from?

"Legal engineering"

Part 12: "legal engineering"

Throughout our time together, Tony has repeatedly used the phrase "legal engineering" about the trial and his case in its entirety. There are, I believe, at least four main areas of "legal engineering" in this case:

- the police interviews (how they were structured and what questions were asked and what were not asked);

- the police investigation (what form it took - who was interviewed, who was not, what statements were taken, and those which were not; the general nature of the investigation itself including forensic and ballistic evidence, following up on vehicle registration plates, following up on names of previous burglars at Bleak House provided by Webster);

- the trial (what form it took; which witnesses were called and which were not by both sides and why; the defence statement; what evidence was entered into court and what was not; what evidence the prosecution withheld from the jury [and public]); and

- the Appeal (which grounds it was based on and which grounds it was not and why).

There are, as you can see, a large number of ways in which a case be "engineered" starting with the initial arrest, throughout the entire trial process and on into any Appeal.

The Great British Public appears to operate on the assumption that "a jury of one's peers" gets to hear all the evidence, that the prosecution and defence enters all the available evidence and that all necessary witnesses are called by both sides. Sorry to disappoint you, but nothing could be further from the truth. I have borne witness, in the course of my life and my work, to several miscarriages of justice and I have witnessed police and judicial corruption at Hillsborough. There are also the cases of the Birmingham Six, the Guildford Four, the Cardiff Three, Stefan Kiszko, and many, many others. All innocent and known to be innocent, but all of their trials had been engineered so that they would be found guilty by a "jury of one's peers" and forced to serve unnecessary time in prison.

I have been sent to prison on five separate occasions (so far) and each time I was innocent, too. One must look below the surface veneer and try to establish the bigger picture.

All too often, the Great British Public clings desperately to the fallacy that the British justice system is "the best in the world" and that a jury trial must produce a valid verdict. Not so in so many trials.

And – to return to Tony Martin – it is clear to me that the *entire* case against him was legally engineered, and now, of course, my duty as the author of this book is to explain why I make that bold statement and then, of course, it is up to you whether – based on the new evidence I have presented – you agree or not. It is not my intention to persuade you one way or another, however. It is, instead, my intention merely to present information never before put into the public domain, ask various questions, occasionally put forward hypotheses and then it is really up to you to come to your own conclusions based on this fresh evidence. It is also my aim with this book to create a true historical document based on facts and not the false narrative which is thus far consigned to history.

What I'd like you to do as you read these next chapters is to try to put yourself in the jury box – to act as if you were a juror at the trial. If you had heard *all* of the evidence I have presented so far, do you think you would have decided that Tony Martin was guilty of murder, or even of manslaughter or even wounding with intent? After reading this section, please ask yourself whether you think that Tony got a fair trial and ask yourself whether, in fact, Frederick Jackson Barras and his family received "justice" because I say that the family was completely misled and deliberately deceived by the CPS and the police.

Norfolk Constabulary ensured that the Barras family vented their anger at the injustice of the death of young Fred solely on Tony Martin, whereas the fact remains Fred died as the direct result of the wrong-doing of certain members of the Constabulary itself.

The defence of self-defence

Part 13: the defence of self-defence

At common law, the defence of self-defence operates on three levels which allow a person to use reasonable force to:

(i) defend himself from an attack;

(ii) prevent an attack on another person;

(iii) defend his property.

We can ignore the second strand for our purposes: so we must focus on the law allowing a man to defend himself from an attack and also to defend his property.

Clearly Tony was under attack because the intruders (note that I do not say burglars) had smashed their way into his home. Also, he had to defend his property (the house) and his property (the antiques in the house.)

Section 3(1) of the Criminal Law Act 1967 provides that a person may use such force as is reasonable in the circumstances in the prevention of crime, or in effecting or assisting in the lawful arrest of offenders or suspected offenders or of persons unlawfully at large.

Both the common law and statutory defences can be raised in respect of any crime with which the defendant is charged, and if successful will result in the defendant being completely acquitted. However, if a defendant uses excessive force this indicates that he acted unreasonably in the circumstances. There will therefore be no valid defence, and the defendant will be liable for the crime.

So, the law made provision for Tony to defend himself and his property. But it set limits as to the amount of force he could use – it had to be 'reasonable'. But what is actually meant by the term 'reasonable force'?

Reasonable force
The general principle is that the law allows only reasonable force to be used in the circumstances and, what is reasonable is to be judged in the light of the circumstances as the accused believed them to be (whether reasonably or not).

In the case of *Palmer* v *The Queen* [1971], the issue of assessing whether a defendant had used only reasonable force arose and Lord Morris (one of the appeal judges) felt that a jury should be directed to look at the particular facts and circumstances of the case. He commented that a person who is being attacked should not be expected to "weigh to a nicety the exact measure of his necessary defensive action." Upon being besieged, Tony was forced to defend himself and he picked up his gun as we've read about previously. He had no time to think about whether it was the most reasonable weapon in the circumstances.

Lord Morris added that if the jury thought that in the heat of the moment the defendant did what he *honestly and instinctively thought was necessary* [author's emphasis] then that would be strong evidence that only reasonable defensive action had been taken. This was the reason the prosecution spent so long on defaming Tony by claiming he said he'd "shoot the bastards!" and other such comments and by portraying the farmer as emotionally cold and eccentric.

Lord Morris also added that a jury would be told that the defence of self-defence would only fail if the prosecution showed beyond reasonable doubt that what the accused did was not by way of self-defence. Can we honestly say that Tony did not act reasonably? Even if he *acted* reasonably, there is still the issue of whether the *amount of force* he used was reasonable, so we'll examine that now.

The issue of a mistake as to the amount of force necessary was considered by the Court of Appeal in *R* v *Scarlett* [1994]. In allowing the appeal, Lord Justice Beldam gave the following direction for juries:

> **POINT OF LAW**
>
> "They ought not to convict him unless they are satisfied that the degree of force used was plainly more than was called for by the circumstances as he believed them to be and, provided he believed the circumstances called for the degree of force used, he was not to be convicted even if his belief was unreasonable."

There are two points we need to consider: firstly, a jury could only convict if they thought the amount of force used was disproportionate and secondly, even if a defendant was wrong in his belief that the circumstances called for his use of force, he would not be guilty if he believed he was taking necessary action.

You might be wondering whether Tony ought to have retreated, but the law is clear on this issue: there is no rule of law that a person attacked is bound to run away if he can. A demonstration by the defendant that at the time he did not want to fight is no doubt the best evidence that he was acting reasonably and in good faith in self-defence; but it is no more than that.

Tony had told the police in interview that he did not want a confrontation due to his thrombosis in a lung. He had no duty in law to retreat. In a case from 1985 (*R* v *Bird*), the Court of Appeal quashed the conviction saying that it was unnecessary to show an unwillingness to fight and there were circumstances where a defendant might reasonably react immediately and without first retreating. It was up to a jury to decide on the facts of the case.

It is therefore a matter for the jury to decide as to whether the defendant acted reasonably in standing his ground to defend himself, or whether the reasonable man would have taken the opportunity to run away. There was no realistic opportunity for Tony to run away. Being on the stairs, it is obvious that he could not go down the stairs to be confronted – outnumbered as he was - by the intruders and so his only other option was to go upstairs to his bedroom but, had they followed him up, he would have been trapped inside his own home.

Nor is it absolutely necessary that the defendant be attacked first. As Lord Griffith said in *Beckford* v *R* [1988]:

> **POINT OF LAW**
>
> "A man about to be attacked does not have to wait for his assailant to strike the first blow or fire the first shot; circumstances may justify a pre-emptive strike."

I believe that Tony was fully justified in firing his gun in the belief that he was about to be attacked. But let's assume that Tony was mistaken in his belief that he was acting in self-defence – what then?

It is possible that a defendant might mistakenly believe himself to be threatened. In the case of *R* v *Williams (Gladstone)* from 1984 and appeal of *Beckford* v *R* from 1988 (a police officer accused of murdering an unarmed civilian), it would appear that such a defendant would be entitled to be judged on the facts as he honestly believed them to be, and hence would be permitted to use a degree of force that was reasonable in the context of what he perceived to be happening. In the case of *R* v *Williams,* the Court of Appeal quashed the conviction and held that the defendant's mistaken *but honest belief* that he was using reasonable force to prevent an offence being committed was sufficient to provide him with a defence.

I argue that this is applicable to Tony's case. It appears that I am not alone, for Lord Lane said that the jury should be directed first of all that the prosecution have the burden or duty of proving the unlawfulness of the defendant's actions; secondly, if the defendant may have been labouring under a mistake as to the facts, he must be judged according to his mistaken view of the facts; thirdly, that is so whether the mistake was, on an objective view, a reasonable mistake or not. Lord Lane added:

> **POINT OF LAW**
>
> "In a case of self-defence, where self-defence or the prevention of crime is concerned, if the jury came to the conclusion that the defendant believed, or may have believed, that he was being attacked or that a crime was being committed, and that force was necessary to protect himself or to prevent the crime, then the prosecution have not proved their case."

Furthermore,

> **POINT OF LAW**
>
> "If, however, the defendant's alleged belief was mistaken and if the mistake was an unreasonable one, that may be a powerful reason for coming to the conclusion that the belief was not honestly held and should be rejected."

Finally, Lord Lane added:

> **POINT OF LAW**
>
> "Even if the jury came to the conclusion that the mistake was an unreasonable one, if the defendant may genuinely have been labouring under it, he is entitled to rely upon it."

**The trial:
10—19 April 2000**

Part 14: the trial

Space does not permit me to provide a complete report of every day of the trial, so I have collated 'edited highlights' from various newspapers in the hope that the reader will at least have some flavour of what can only be described as a 'circus'. But in providing these 'edited highlights' I have ensured that nothing has been distorted or misrepresented. However, before taking you into Courtroom number one, I need to make you aware of a ruling by the judge.

CORRUPTION ALERT *Judge makes improper and unlawful ruling*

The judge ruled that the evidence in the first police interview was inadmissible and that it should not be introduced as part of the prosecution case. The ruling was wrong. It was not 'inadmissible' – it had been airbrushed out of the trial because it caused the police and the CPS a number of problems which we have previously explored.

In the light of this ruling, it was agreed that the jury should be told only the following concerning this interview: that Tony declined the offer of free legal advice and representation giving the reason, "I've had an horrendous experience."

The jury was told that Tony had been cautioned that if he did not mention when questioned something which he later relied on in court, it could harm his defence.

Furthermore, the jury was told that after initial questioning, Tony declined to answer any more questions in relation to the shooting. This is, of course, not true at all, but let's see what else the jury was told: that at the time of interview, it would have been apparent to Tony that the police had no idea that a second person had been present at the burglary[408] and that Fearon was lying about what had happened (having been shot on a track). Again, we know this is not true. The police had *always* known about the existence of Barras.

All of these machinations were a tissue of lies: let's remind ourselves of the language associated with fear that Tony had used in that first 42-minute interview: he used the word 'horrified' on seven occasions; 'horrendous' on seven occasions; 'nightmare' on seven occasions; 'terrified' five times; 'dreadful' three

---

[408] Proposed burglary. There never was a burglary and I argue that on the evidence not entered into Court, neither Fearon nor Barras was in the house on 20 August 1999, at least whilst Tony was present.

times; 'frightened' once; 'vulnerable' once; the phrase "you're on your own" once; the phrase "there's nobody to help you" once. Thus, in 42 minutes, he used 33 words or phrases associated with fear and isolation – that's almost one a minute. And a defence to murder – self-defence. Objectively, this seems to me that either Tony Martin is a brilliant actor or that he was genuinely terrified when intruders smashed their way into his house at night. I'm going with the belief that he was terrified.

So, the legal eagles having withheld vital evidence from the jury (and media), let's see how day one (Monday 10 April 2000) pans out in court.

Trial day one
Smartly dressed in a blue suit and lilac shirt with a polka-dot tie, Tony spoke only once to admit to possessing a shotgun without a certificate. (The issue of the likelihood of his winning an appeal against the revocation of his certificate – as we have previously read about - was never mentioned at trial.) He pleaded not guilty to the murder of Fred Barras, the attempted murder of Brendon Fearon, wounding Fearon with intent to cause grievous bodily harm and possessing a Winchester pump-action shotgun with intent to endanger life.

Fred Barras's sisters, who were sitting at the back of the court with their mother, Ellen, and father, Fred senior, sobbed quietly as they heard how their brother had been allegedly killed.

Tony's friends ensured that the public gallery was full to overflowing in an emotionally-charged courtroom.

As in all trials, the prosecution opens and reads out the case against the accused and as we have seen, Rosamund Horwood-Smart QC painted a wholly inaccurate picture of the shooting when the truth was available to her.

I reproduce below the case opening as presented by Horwood-Smart. Now that you have been given a wealth of evidence that has never before been put into the public domain (even though the prosecution and police were well aware of its existence as we have seen), you may recoil in horror at some of the statements made by the prosecutor *which she must have known to be false*.[409]

1. Anthony Martin, who describes himself and his way of life as "eccentric", was living at Emneth Hungate, Norfolk in August of last year. He is a 55-year-old bachelor who lives alone in an almost derelict farmhouse with a number of outbuildings and barns including a cottage which was used as a kennel for his three rottweiler dogs, (photos, BC All and BJW13/1).

At some stage he had eschewed the mains electrical system that had been installed at the house at the time he inherited it and had rigged up an extension

---

[409] It is highly improbable that Horwood-Smart was not aware of the falsehoods she was promulgating in court to an unsuspecting jury. I welcome her comments in mitigation.

lead from a barn which he used to power his telephone and fax line and a couple of low watt lights, *one of which was in his bedroom*.[410]

His security measures included removing the top and bottom three steps of his staircase, placing ladders on the roofs of his outbuildings and in nearby trees, the installation of iron bars on the inside of his doors and windows in the ground floor[411] and sleeping fully clothed with his boots on in contemplation of "something happening".[412]

2. In May of last year [1999] he had been the victim of a burglary. A chest of drawers and some china[413] and items of considerable sentimental value had been taken from him. When he reported the burglary at 12:06am on the 13 May 1999[414] he told the police operator that the burglars had left some furniture

---

[410] Author's emphasis. The light in Tony's bedroom is of considerable significance in this story.

[411] I suggest that it is incredibly difficult for any rational, right-thinking person to believe that securing all the doors and windows on the ground floor (except two, of course) was designed to be a trap for any possible burglars in the way that Horwood-Smart has suggested the removal of stairs and ladders in the trees were allegedly meant to be. She is deliberately conflating two completely different concepts - alleged booby-trapped stairs and alleged lookout posts with ladders in trees with the extreme measures of placing metal bars across all entry or exit points in the house. The false narrative is deliberate and, I argue that since she knows the real truth of this case, she is perverting the course of justice, as many prosecutors do.

[412] A bachelor, Tony had no-one to answer to with regard to the point she is trying to plant in the minds of the jurors and the public: that of Tony's personal hygiene. However, we have read in previous entries (see particularly 22 November 1999) that Tony would often farm late into the night or even into the early hours of a summer morning. There is nothing too unusual about this in the farming community – it isn't a 9-5 job. Tony would often arrive home exhausted from his efforts and simply fall asleep on top of his bed with his clothes and boots on. Who amongst us has never fallen asleep fully clothed and with footwear on after a hard day's work? Horwood-Smart's spin is both unnecessary and, I suggest, unnecessarily mendacious.

[413] She has down-played the amount of antiques stolen. Christopher Webster's statement at **372** provides a much fuller account, as does Tony Martin's statement in entry **373**.

[414] Beware, I suggest, the pseudo-scientific littering of "facts" throughout this entire case by the prosecution and the police. To a random observer, the "fact" that Tony reported the May burglary at six minutes past midnight suggests an attention to detail – that "the authorities" have been diligent and thorough in their "investigation" and that they must, therefore, be right. But she is wrong and what's more she knows she is wrong – she is in possession of the very same witness statements that I have put you in possession of. As early as 23 August [see relevant entry] Carol Woods, the police communications officer, made a statement in which she said she took the call from Tony on 12 May 1999 *and that she didn't remember it.*

outside and that they may be back and if they did return he would "blow their heads off."[415]

3. Over the years Mr Martin and his family had undoubtedly been the victims of crime, the house itself had not been broken into for 15 years or so.[416]

4. Mr Martin was well known to have strong views on policing matters and he made himself clear to the officers who attended to deal with the May burglary, Wells, Chapman and Welham.

He was vitriolic about criminals, especially gypsies, and talked of "putting gypsies in one of his fields surrounded by barbed wire and machine gunning them."[417]

He had made his views public at a Farmwatch meeting in February 1999 attended by a number of his neighbours and local farmers organised by Mr Bone. During that meeting he said that "Out there you are on your own and you are the law" and the police were a waste of time.[418] Mr Huggins, one of those present at the meeting and known to Mr Martin, saw him two or three days before the incident with which we are concerned. Mr Martin was worried about burglaries and what he called "light-fingered pikies".[419] He said that if he caught the bastards he would shoot them.[420]

---

[415] This is another lie. Horwood-Smart knew that on 15 September 1999, police sergeant Paul Watson had made a statement in which he claimed that the Phillips CLS 9000 recording equipment on the terminal used by Carol Woods [see previous footnote] was allegedly (my word, not Watson's) "faulty" and that *it hadn't recorded the call in which it was alleged Tony Martin had said the immortal words 'I'll blast their heads off!' to Carol Woods*. Furthermore, as we have seen, PS Watson stated that the Phillips recording machine was working properly on every other terminal that night.

[416] The comment that Bleak House had not been broken into "for 15 years" is diametrically opposed to what she has just said in her previous paragraph – that Tony had been burgled in the May of the same year as the August shooting. Horwood-Smart was providing false information to an unsuspecting jury. As we know, Tony had also been burgled in the January of 1999 – Horwood-Smart was in possession of these facts (as prosecutor) and yet chose to overlook the fact that Tony had had his home broken into *on three separate occasions* in 1999. The great British public was being deceived by the legal system.

[417] There is no evidence for this assertion. It is a myth.

[418] As we have seen – and Horwood-Smart was in possession of the statements we have read – Tony's views were shared by many of the farmers and locals in the area.

[419] I have spoken with many farmers in Norfolk who have said the same things (and often much worse) about some gypsies and travellers.

[420] There is, as we have seen, absolutely no evidence that Tony Martin ever said this at the Farmwatch meeting (except from David Gathercole who, if his statement is true, clearly lied) and considerable evidence (which didn't make its way into court) that Tony never mentioned anything about shooting anybody at the Farmwatch meeting. Horwood-Smart – paid handsomely out of public coffers to uphold the rule of law –

Brendon Fearon, aged 26,[421] Darren Bark[422] aged 33, and Frederick Barras aged 16, were all from Newark in Nottinghamshire and all had previous convictions.

At some stage before Friday 20 August 1999, Fearon and Bark became aware of Bleak House as a possible target for burglary. Fearon told police officers later that he first heard about the premises about a month earlier as he was eavesdropping on a conversation in his local public house. He said that he persuaded Bark to act as the driver[423] for the enterprise. Barras became involved on the day.[424] Fearon told police officers that he believed the house to be unoccupied[425] and derelict and to contain antiques. Fearon had with him a large holdall containing a number of smaller bags. He also had with him a torch, a chisel and a pair of woollen gloves and a baseball cap.

5. The three of them met in Newark that evening, 20 August 1999, and left in Bark's white Ford Granada F98LHJ to travel to Emneth. They were stopped by PC Knight in Balderton near Newark at 8:10pm[426] when Bark was issued with a notice to produce his documents. The police officer recognised Bark and Fearon and noted the presence of Barras.[427] At Emneth Hungate, Bark dropped off Fearon and Barras nearby Bleak House and arranged to pick them up in half an hour. The journey time between Balderton and Emneth is about one and a half to two hours.

6. Fearon and Barras made their way to the cottage near the road with a view to burgling it, mistaking it for Bleak House. When they tried to enter it they were

---

displayed an indifference to the essential conditions for the rule of law which is objectionable and deeply worrying.

[421] According to police records, Brendon Fearon was born on 11 April 1970. He was, therefore, not 26 but one day short of his 30th birthday when the trial began.

[422] Not called to court by either the prosecution or defence counsel. I discuss the possible reasons why later in this chapter.

[423] Horwood-Smart, as prosecutor, ought to have been in possession of the statement made by Christopher Webster who told police that it was Bark who was the ring-leader and had set the job up.

[424] Note the use of language "Barras became involved on the day" suggests he only heard about the job on that day but his sister refuted this. See also entry **277**.

[425] Horwood-Smart was in possession of statements from Fearon which changed his original version.

[426] We only have PC Knight's word for this. No other evidence was brought forward to confirm this time. I look upon it with suspicion. The HORT form was never produced in court as it should have been.

[427] Notice that she doesn't mention that PC Knight appears not to have asked what three known criminals were doing leaving town at night (if Barras was actually in that car).

confronted by dogs; it was, in fact, the building used by Mr Martin as a kennel for his rottweilers.[428]

You can see on the plan (RJB/4) and photos number 18 to 23 of (BJW/13/1). Fearon then saw a big dog in the track which was growling at them. At that stage Fearon says they gave up their burglary plans and retreated away from the dog backing off away from the cottage and unbeknown to them because it was camouflaged by trees, towards the main house. They were frightened of the dog[429] and as they retreated they came to the window that they forced open.[430]

Fearon still had his bags with him. They were in what they first thought was a shed. Then they moved into the larger room. All was in darkness except for the light from Fearon's torch. Fearon saw the dresser and remembers Fred Barras following closely behind him. He put his bag on the floor.

He heard this noise and shone his torch towards the stairs and saw a man *standing on the stairs*[431] halfway down. Then he heard Barras shout "He's got me!" as he heard a loud bang.[432]

He then made his way to a window and he heard a second shot and his left leg went numb. He then heard a third bang[433] and felt pain in his right leg. He managed to pull the whole window out of the brickwork and he heard Barras screaming "He's got me. I'm sorry, please don't – Mum!"[434]

Then he climbed out followed by Barras. Fearon did not see Barras again. Barras managed to cover a few yards to undergrowth where he died - exhibit RA/1 photos 32 - 34. The police were unaware that Barras had been at Bleak

---

[428] This scenario is a complete fabrication and Horwood-Smart – in possession of all of the same evidence I have put you in possession of – must have known this to be false.

[429] This would have been one of the very same dogs which burglar Christopher Webster had stroked whilst he was involved in the May burglary. She must have known that Webster had made a statement to police but the public was never informed.

[430] This window was not *forced* open, it was *smashed* open with such force that it woke the sleeping farmer. This is yet another example of the prosecutor's disingenuous use of language.

[431] This is a crucial element of the case – in some ways it is the single most crucial element for reasons which we'll discuss throughout the remainder of this book.

[432] According to Fearon's own mother [see entry **180**], Brendon Fearon is partially deaf. We are being expected to believe that he heard Barras shout "He's got me!" whilst another bang occurred.

[433] There has never been any definitive proof of "a third shot" – I welcome Norfolk Constabulary correcting me on this point. In fact, whenever I write to them about it, they unlawfully refuse to reply to my Freedom of Information Act requests.

[434] See my previous footnote with regard to Fearon's partial deafness.

House that night[435] until his body was discovered at 2:33pm the following day by search officers. He was wearing rubber gloves and a chisel was found nearby.

7. Fearon made his way over the fields towards Foreman's Cottage, Moyse's Bank, where Mr and Mrs Leet live. Photos 43 and 44 of exhibit RA/1. As he struggled along he dropped his torch, a glove by a ditch, another in the orchard and his baseball cap.[436] An eel catcher, Mr Spalton, saw him by Moyse's Bank, stationary and bent double in pain.[437]

8. Mr and Mrs Leet had been shopping that evening and returned home at about 8:45pm. About an hour later they had received a visit from Mr Martin. He told Mr Leet that he had found three people[438] in his house and he had shot at them. Mr Leet told him that he must phone the police. That conversation took place at about 10pm.[439]

When Mr Fearon arrived nearly an hour later he was obviously in great pain and had a serious gunshot wound to the leg. Mrs Leet dialled 999 and the ambulance men received that message at 10:55pm and arrived 4 minutes later. Fearon received some treatment on the spot and was taken to King's Lynn where he arrived at 11:35pm.

At that stage Mr Fearon was untruthful as to what had happened and those who spoke to him did not learn that Barras or anyone else had been present.[440]

---

[435] This is, of course, a complete lie. When the Leets had dialled 999 just before 11pm that night (according to official records), Jacqueline Leet told the police that Tony had been round and mentioned "three of them." This is another instance of the prosecutor providing false or inaccurate information to the court.

[436] Notice here how, in her elaborate description of the items of clothing Fearon was alleged to have dropped in making his way to the Leets' bungalow, Horwood-Smart (who was in possession of all of Fearon's statements to the police) made no mention of the burglar having allegedly fallen over in the cornfield and seeing the police helicopter flying over Bleak House *before he had reached the Leets' house where a 999 call was made.*

[437] There is no mention by Horwood-Smart of Mr Spalton knocking Fearon over and it isn't included in his statement to police allegedly made three days after the shooting.

[438] This contradicts her earlier statement about the police claiming they did not know of the existence of a third person.

[439] By her own statements, she is providing a jury with false information. If the Leets arrived home at 8:45 and Tony called round an hour later, that's 9:45, not 10pm. Notice how she plays footloose and fancy-free with time in this opening statement. It is for a reason. The public are being deceived as to the timing of the whole event and particularly the timing of the helicopter flights and of the death of Fred Barras.

[440] Another disingenuous use of language by the prosecutor. Worded this way, the entire blame for the police (allegedly) not finding Barras was laid at the feet of Fearon – he was the fall-guy and "a proven liar." However, I am not convinced that he did not tell another soul that Barras, who had babysat for his children, was also badly injured.

9. Officers remained nearby and eventually Bark arrived in his car.[441] He was arrested and taken to a nearby police station at 9:50am.[442]

10. In the meantime Mr Martin took a pump action shotgun to his mother's house and left it in her lavatory. That was the gun that had been used in the shootings in spite of Mr Martin having had his shotgun certificate revoked in 1994. There was a large quantity of ammunition around the house and in the outbuildings.

The gun was capable of carrying five cartridges. It was a 12-bore Winchester pump action model in good condition with the mechanism oiled, a weapon for which a firearm certificate is required.

Mr Martin has never held a firearm certificate.[443]

From his mother's [house], Mr Martin had gone to friends at the Marmion House Hotel, Wisbech. He was arrested there at 5:50 in the morning on the Saturday for the attempted murder of Brendon Fearon. At that stage police were unaware of the death of Fred Barras.[444]

11. Later on the Saturday in the early afternoon Mr Martin was interviewed. He had refused[445] to have a solicitor present but he had been previously certified as being fit for interview by a doctor.[446] He said he had heard people in his house[447]

---

[441] The court was being given contradictory evidence. Bark was alternatively said to have been in Moyse's Bank throughout the incident or that he arrived after the incident. The Norfolk Constabulary CAD report showed that Bark arrived at 11:34 "looking for two mates who he'd dropped off earlier."

[442] This time appears to be wrong – according to official police records he was taken to Terrington St John police station at 1:50am.

[443] Horwood-Smart would have had full access to all the paperwork I have reproduced here for you to consider and that means she would have known about the long-running saga of Tony's shotgun certificate.

[444] I do not give that sentence any credence whatsoever for reasons which will become obvious as the trial unfolds.

[445] He didn't *refuse* – he *declined* to have a solicitor. Yet another example of the use of language to portray Tony as anti-police, uncooperative, belligerent and generally a man with a murderous intent.

[446] "Being certified fit for interview" by a police doctor is not the same as actually being fit for interview. Police doctors – employed by the police – can, and do, lie to support their paymasters. Some have even been sent to jail for sexually abusing vulnerable suspects – so we should not automatically believe any police doctor. It is clear to me that Tony was fit for interview in the physical sense but far from fit emotionally – as became obvious during the subsequent interviews.

[447] Notice the misuse of language again here. Horwood-Smart is again being disingenuous because she knew that Tony didn't just say "I heard people in my house" as if they had casually walked in through the front door or something but that *they had*

and continued "It's a nightmare of your worst dreams - I don't want to talk about it."

As the officers were about to finish the interview, Mr Martin accused them of lying to him.[448] This comment became understandable immediately following the interview when the officers were told of the body in the grounds of Bleak House.

Mr Martin was then arrested on suspicion of the murder of Barras. Fearon was also arrested and remained in hospital under police guard. Later he was charged with Bark and pleaded guilty to conspiracy to burgle for which they are both now serving sentences of imprisonment.[449]

12. On 23 August, Mr Martin was further interviewed in the presence of his solicitor with appropriate breaks.[450] He explained that he had found the gun he used in the incident in his car with a note stating that he might need it. He did not remember how long ago this event had taken place or what car he had at the time. He acknowledged that he did not hold a shotgun certificate and claimed he had not fired the gun before and was unsure how many cartridges it held. He said he kept it under his bed. He stated he had gone to bed at about 9pm on the Friday evening having put two dogs in the cottage and leaving the third, Bruno, to roam the grounds.

He sleeps in his clothes and he has a small lamp in his bedroom giving him just sufficient light to read. He keeps that light on.[451] He said he was awoken by noises and at first he thought Bruno had got into the house.

Then he saw flashes of torch light downstairs from the landing. He said that then he returned to his bedroom and retrieved the gun from under the bed and loaded it until it was full.[452] He did not know how many cartridges there were.

---

smashed their way into his remote farmhouse in the dead of night and woke him from his sleep. This is an altogether different concept and she would have been aware of it.

[448] You have read the full transcript of that first police interview. I am unable to find a passage in which the farmer said to the police that they had lied to him.

[449] Notice how Horwood-Smart failed to inform the jury about why Bark wasn't called as a witness.

[450] That sentence is nothing more than an arse-covering exercise: "We've done everything properly because the defendant had a solicitor present and there were frequent breaks." However, this hadn't occurred in the oppressive first interview.

[451] I can only imagine that this short sentence was made unwittingly by the prosecutor because it actually shows various police statements to have been a lie.

[452] At no point did Tony claim that he loaded the gun until it was full. Still to this day, he maintains that he did not know how many cartridges he put into that gun. It was the police who put forward the notion – because it suited their fraudulent investigation – that the "gun was loaded until it was full" because this sounds more menacing in the media. Throughout this case, facts which were not facts at all have been presented to the jury and the British public as real when they were not. Compare that sentence with her

Then he returned to the landing, negotiated the gap at the top where the three steps were missing and went halfway down the stairs. At that point a torch was pointed at him and he took aim and fired a shot below the height of the torch.[453] *He continued to fire until the gun was empty.*[454] He stated that all the shots were fired from the same position, halfway down the stairs.

He said he was unaware what happened in the confusion but eventually went down into the room where he saw pieces of his silverware in bags on the floor. *He repeatedly said that he thought he was in danger.*[455]

There was no sign of the intruders. He did not recall whether he reloaded the gun but he took it with him to his car and drove around looking for the burglars. He recalled visiting the Leets but not the conversation that took place.

He took the gun to his mother's house and then he went to see his friend Mrs Lilley who owns the Marmion House Hotel in Wisbech where he remained until his arrest.

13. He did not warn the intruders nor give them a chance to surrender. He was going to hide upstairs and then thought to himself: "I've had enough of this" and went downstairs with the gun.

14. An examination of the scene showed that Mr Martin could not have shot from the position he described and hit Barras and Fearon.[456]

15. Detective Sergeant Eglen examined all surfaces in line of sight from the stairs into the main room and other than marks on the rear facing window wall and door he found no shot marking.[457] The shotgun cartridges would have been

---

next sentence: "He did not know how many cartridges there were." She immediately contradicts herself because she cannot prove – and she knows it – how many cartridges were in that gun when Tony ventured to the stairs with it.

[453] In normal circumstances, anyone pointing a gun in a downwards trajectory *has no intention to harm but merely to warn*. Tony had adopted the same downwards trajectory policy five years earlier in the orchard when a traveller attempted to run over his dogs.

[454] Author's emphasis. This is another disingenuous statement with no meaning. It has no meaning because nobody knows how many cartridges were placed in that shotgun. If you place just one and fire it, you have fired until the gun was empty and so on all the way up to five cartridges. It has no meaning in fact but had been stated by the prosecutor to put an image into the minds of the jurors and the unsuspecting public and, to be clear, the image the prosecution wanted to sell was that of a mentally unstable farmer who kept firing and firing – Rambo style - until the gun was empty.

[455] Who would not think he was in danger when an unknown number of intruders (possibly armed) smash their way into your house in the middle of the night?

[456] I completely subscribe to this view. He could not have shot them because – on the police's own evidence - he had left the house by the time they arrived.

[457] Isn't it remarkable that DS Eglen found no markings in any of the furniture in the breakfast room given the very nature of shotgun spread? Had Tony been standing in the

expelled from the gun a short distance forward and to the right of the firer's position according to the expert in ballistics, the witness Arnold. The position of the spent cartridges are on the plan - exhibit 43.

16. Detective Constable Aldous identified the area of gunshot pellet damage and took samples of blood and tissue. Detective Sergeant Eglen also deals with areas of blood/body tissue. There are two unrelated areas of shot damage to the room, the consequence of two of the discharges.

There is no evidence of shot or pellet damage in the area of the stairs. Swabs taken from the stairway on 25 August have no evidence of gunshot residue.[458]

The shot that hit Fearon in his left leg, a major injury, *may have caused* the secondary leg injury to Mr Barras, that was on his right leg and the shot that caused Mr Barras' major leg injury, also on his right leg, *may also have caused* secondary injuries to Mr Fearon, over on the front and outside of his right leg. The injury that killed Mr Barras was a shot to his back, that was from the rear and to the left of him as he was positioned. [Author's emphases]

Mr Arnold, a ballistic expert, was able to make certain calculations. When Mr Martin shot Barras he was between 3 and 4.1 metres away from him. When he shot Fearon in the left leg he was between 3.8 and 5.3 metres. When he shot Barras' right leg he was between 4 and 5.4 metres away. The injury to Mr Fearon's left leg was fired from a position to the left and to the rear of him. The distance between Barras and Martin when the shot was fired precludes any shot from the stairs *unless Barras was crouching in [or near] the doorway of the main room.* [Author's emphasis] He would have been outside Martin's sightline near the dresser. The distance between the door which bore the shot and the entrance to the main room is approximately 7 metres; that is just outside Mr Arnold's range of distances. Mr Martin must have been inside the room when he shot the two men, not on the staircase. *We cannot say with any certainty in which order the shots were fired.* [Author's emphasis]

It is Dr Heath, the pathologist who later performed a post-mortem on Frederick Barras, opinion *that death would have occurred within about 20 seconds to two minutes after the gunshot injury to his chest.*[459] [Author's emphasis]

It is the Crown's case that Mr Martin heard the burglars, armed himself and went downstairs. He fired at Barras and Fearon from downstairs, not in self-defence, but in accordance with his professed views that the only way to stop thieves was to shoot them.

---

doorway to the room (as the prosecution and police claimed) the furniture and other items in that room would have been covered in shotgun pellets. None of it was.

[458] Take note of this point – it will come back to haunt her in due course.

[459] The Crown prosecutor would have been in possession of the *three* separate autopsy reports on the body of Barras and that the second and third autopsies had shown evidence which contradicted Dr Heath's spurious claims, yet this evidence was deliberately withheld from the jury and the public at large.

17. In acting as he did, he was intending to kill or cause really serious injury to his victims and that is why he is charged with murder and attempted murder. To commit murder you must *intend to kill or to cause really serious injury*. To commit attempted murder *you must intend to kill*. [Author's emphasis]

If you are of the view that Mr Martin intended to cause really serious injury but did not intend to kill his victims, he would be guilty of murder in the case of Barras and of wounding with intent in the case of Fearon.

In all matters of the law you will take and follow His Lordship's directions. On matters of fact, what evidence you accept or reject are for you and you alone to decide. One matter of law we ask you to bear in mind throughout the trial is that the prosecution bring this case and it is for the prosecution to prove it to you so that you are *sure* of the defendant's guilt. Nothing less than that will do." [Author's emphasis]

I have studied that Case Opening countless times and can safely say that the only real truth in it is the final paragraph: "The prosecution bring this case and it is for the prosecution to prove it to you so that you are *sure* of the defendant's guilt. Nothing less than that will do."

Given that opening statement – loaded as it was with emotive rhetoric devoid of accuracy and truth in an attempt to influence the jury and the nation - any half-decent barrister representing Tony could have easily gained an acquittal because all he or she would have had to do was to have pointed out to a jury (assuming it wasn't 'bent' or 'nobbled') the enormous number of areas for reasonable doubt. I will discuss this in greater detail in a subsequent chapter.

Tue
11 APR
2000
10 am
378

court one, Norwich Crown Court
We now move to day two of the trial. With the prosecution having laid out its extraordinarily weak case against the accused which was full of inconsistencies, defence counsel Anthony Scrivener - Chair of the Bar Standards Council no less - then had an opportunity (and a legal and moral obligation) to put forward Tony's version of events.

He didn't.

Instead, Scrivener's approach was to inform the jury about Fearon's, Barras's and Bark's long history of criminal behaviour, including assaults on police. This was the false narrative being continually repeated so that the "broad mass of the people" would hear it so often and become brainwashed. Die Große Lüge was alive and well: "in the big lie there is always a certain force of credibility":

- Tony Martin had admitted to firing his shotgun inside his farmhouse.
- Two prospective burglars suffered shotgun injuries on his land.
- Therefore Tony Martin shot the burglars.

But on the evidence *provided by the police themselves* Tony Martin couldn't possibly have hit Fearon or Barras inside his house from his position on the staircase and because there was evidence to suggest that Barras was 70 miles away at the time Tony Martin pulled the trigger.

The *Glasgow Herald* reported the convictions thus:

"Market trader Fred Barras, was said to be on bail at the time of the incident and had appeared before courts 28 times. His criminal record included assaults on police, theft and fraud and he had served sentences in young offenders' institutions.

Mr Fearon, jailed earlier this year for three years for conspiring to burgle Mr Martin, had been convicted of wounding, burglaries, drug offences and had served a number of prison terms at the time he was shot. He had appeared before courts on 35 occasions.

A third man involved in the Bleak House burglary expedition, Mr Darren Bark, 33, also of Newark, had a similar history of crime, the jury was told. Bark, serving a 30-month sentence for conspiring to burgle Mr Martin, had been before courts on 52 occasions, being convicted of assaults, thefts and serving several prison sentences.

Details of the backgrounds emerged as a detective involved in investigating the shootings was questioned by Anthony Scrivener QC, for Martin."

Notice how Bark was not called to be cross-examined about his criminal career and role in the proposed burglary at Bleak House, whereas Fearon was.

Fearon – brought from prison - took the stand to give his version, admitted that he felt blame because he "took the little lad there to get killed."

Fearon insisted they had not set off to target an "old man's house" as suggested by the defence. Instead, he claimed, they planned to check an outbuilding for possible burglary, having heard that "nobody had lived there for 100 years". But chased by a snarling dog, they broke into what they thought was a shed.

Limping from his injuries, the pony-tailed Fearon said that he heard a sudden bang and in the muzzle flash from the shotgun saw a man standing on the stairs.

Playing the game of appearing to be representing Tony to the best of his ability, Scrivener described Fearon's account as rubbish, and suggested the Newark man had deliberately targeted the house and even gone to check it out weeks earlier. Some of Tony Martin's silverware had been found in two holdalls, which Fearon had taken to the house and left behind, though he denied stealing. "Do you have any explanation for how this silverware got into your holdall?" asked Scrivener. Fearon replied: "The farmer put them in to explain his actions." Contradictory police evidence shows that it wasn't the farmer and it wasn't Fearon or Barras who put those silver items in the holdalls - it was the intruders.

Scrivener - continuing his role as a loyal and supportive defence barrister - challenged Fearon on various inconsistencies in his story from police interviews and in evidence, saying: "Why did you tell the police an untruth?" Fearon replied: "I was just coming out of sedation (in hospital). I just wanted to put all the blame on me. I thought, 'You took the little lad there to get killed'."

But notice that Scrivener never once asked Fearon to explain what he'd told medical staff at the hospital – that he'd been shot walking 20-30 yards *up a track*. The police, in their cultural deceit, claimed that Fearon, with so many criminal convictions behind him was a liar and that he'd said he'd been shot *on a track leading to the house* as some kind of alibi to burglary. But, I argue, the real liars in this case weren't the known (and self-confessed) criminals, but the police.

Affirming an oath to tell the truth, John Slaughter, a forensic scientist with 25 years' experience, was called to the stand and said, as we have previously seen, that tests on the dead boy revealed alcohol, cannabis and amphetamine in his system, though not enough to have had an effect on the night. And we could ask, "So what?" This scientific information is mere grandstanding in a court of law – the issue is whether Tony Martin was guilty of murder and attempted murder. And whether he had even shot them at all – we now know that, according to the hidden evidence I have now brought to light, he couldn't have done.

But the prosecution had a propensity to wheel out a number of 'experts' who added little real value to the case in question and John Slaughter was one of these in my view. As we have seen, his 10-page witness statement did not record where he made the statement, nor to whom he made it or the time it was made.

The prosecution calling this witness was nothing more than mere 'filler' – his testimony served no useful purpose, but it's possible that some members of the jury will have been impressed by the prosecution's ability to produce such witnesses. All at taxpayers' expense. And all the while the jurors are listening to this 'scientific evidence', they are not asking too many questions about the handling of the operation by the police. I like to use the term 'smoke and mirrors' in relation to such events. In my view, this trial was being stage-managed at least at the level of the Home Office.

Consider the next Crown witness. The jury heard that the rural community around Emneth was beset by crime. Swearing an oath on the Bible, John Spalton, an eel-catcher returning from work on the night of the shootings when he saw Fearon bent over and bleeding at the side of Moyse's Bank, said he did not stop to help because of the "terrible" crime rate: "You don't stop unless it is somebody you know." Which is all well and good – it's only natural to want to protect yourself - but Mr Spalton claimed he didn't call the police until the following Sunday. [See also entry **240**]. And nor did Mr Spalton inform the jury that, according to Fearon, he knocked him over in the road just after he'd been shot – why would he have been encouraged to omit such an important part of his testimony?

Wed
12 APR
2000
10 am
379

court one, Norwich Crown Court
Day Three of the murder trial started with both legal teams meeting Judge Owen in his chambers. For those not too familiar with court protocol, this meant that they were meeting with him in his office behind the courtroom (you may have sometimes seen this in various films and tv dramas.) Records show that they were discussing letters that they had allegedly received from members of the public and the issues that this brought.

The transcript (if it is to be believed) shows that Scrivener suggested consigning the threatening letters to the wastepaper basket though Judge Owen mentioned that one letter issued a general – not specific – threat to one of the jurors (not named in the transcript): "All I intend to do, because there is nothing specific, is to say again to the jury, they must not talk to anybody else, and it is best not to say anything at all about the case, and the evidence, because it is always liable to misinterpretation." (Note the irony in the comment by the judge that 'the case and the evidence is always liable to misinterpretation.')

Scrivener mentioned one other issue: "Your Lordship knows the background to this, about threats being made to my client, and so on?"

The judge agreed that he was aware of this 'threat'. Scrivener added: "And we are very grateful indeed for the assistance the police are giving to us at this time. The apprehension is felt also by several of our witnesses."

Now, the judge agreed that he was aware of this information, too. He was aware, the record shows, that several defence witnesses were too scared to attend the trial because of possible repercussions. He was aware.

Notice Scrivener's reply: "Some [witnesses] are lost irretrievably, and we will not be able to call them. And we would like to try and work out a formula whereby their names, addresses, and it may be necessary in the case of perhaps two witnesses, not to identify their job openly. What we would ask Your Lord to consider is writing certain particulars, not controversial, on a piece of paper, name, address and if necessary lead into their evidence."

It would seem that this is evidence that defence witnesses had become too frightened to attend court in defence of the accused for fear of reprisals. You might like to ask why your tax pounds were not put to better use in securing the safety of the defence witnesses. Scrivener continued: "For instance, one witness who we decided we probably will not call, is a gentleman who is looking after the house at the moment. He has received threats recently, directly, face to face as I understand it."

Scrivener then made out a case – remember this is the third day into the trial itself – for not calling that particular witness who, in normal circumstances would have been called to court to give evidence in the accused's favour: "He immediately reported it to the police and got some help. We decided that, in the circumstances, we will not call him. His evidence was marginal and, I think, given a clear run we probably would have done, but I do not want to do that in his case." So, the man was only a marginal witness, after all.

The accused's QC continued: "It is the other witnesses I am more concerned about. Can I try and just write out *when we are sure which witnesses we are calling*, we will write out what we think we need, name, address, in some cases would be perfectly enough." [Author's emphasis]

Yes, you did read that correctly – on Day Three of a murder trial, we have defence counsel stating that he was still not sure which witnesses he would call in defence of his client. I hope you will be as equally horrified by this as I am. In my view, this entire case was stage-managed from the moment the police created a Hollywood film-set at Bleak House and the accompanying pantomime put on for a gullible public and I argue that Tony Martin was not treated in accordance with the rule of law from the moment he was arrested at the Marmion House Hotel.

Following this meeting in chambers, the judge then addressed the jury at the start of Day Three. He told them not to forget to bring their "wellies" with them and that they would be required to wear a hard hat once inside Bleak House. He also reminded them not to speak with anybody about the case, not because of any possible danger to themselves, but because the trial might have to be abandoned and "that is the last thing that anybody would want." Well, the last thing the Establishment – which is orchestrating this nonsense – would want.

The first thing we need to note is that on the following day, the judge and the jury were going to Bleak House and the Leets' bungalow and the general area. Day Four of a murder trial. I have no issue with the jury seeing the scene and the locality and its remoteness. I believe that they ought to have done.

What I am bringing to your attention is that by day three, defence counsel had already said that he was still not sure which witnesses he wished to call (or who will attend) and the next day was to be taken up with a journey to Emneth (from Norwich it's some 61.5 miles in distance or approximately 1½ hours away) and, in my view, the time ought to have been spent in court cross-examining all manner of people who were not called. This was surely not a fair trial.

Notice how Judge Owen had told the jury they mustn't speak with anybody or ask questions and so on. This is a gagging order in effect which is dressed up and sold to an unwitting public (and jury members) as being "in the best interests of justice." My own view is that if the jury members are asking questions, then that's a good thing because if Justice is about right and wrong and avoiding miscarriages of justice, then surely we want a system in which jurors are *encouraged* to ask questions and not just rely on the "evidence" before them because, as we know in this case and hundreds of others, the "evidence" before a jury is not always *all* of the available evidence and it may even have been fabricated (as in Hillsborough) and I say that much was fabricated in this case and much was suppressed as I have shown.

The prosecution had all their ducks lined up in a row. The trial was racing ahead. Former firearms officer Anthony 'Tony' Bone was called to the stand. *The Times*, under the headline FARMER FELT HE COULD NOT WORK WITH POLICE, (as if that were a crime) reported: "Mr Bone said that Mr Martin's input [at the Farmwatch meeting] was that he did not feel one could work with police in the area to combat crime. He said people were on their own." (As if any of this were a crime. Besides, Tony Martin was right – and thousands of people in the Fens, let alone throughout the country, were of the same opinion that the police were inept and corrupt and probably taking "backhanders" from the criminal fraternity in order to "turn a blind eye" to their wrong-doing.)

We have already seen how other farmers stated that Mr Bone misrepresented Tony Martin's words in that meeting. It is clear that the threat from travellers and gypsies was not merely in the mind of Tony Martin – it was a threat across the whole of the Fens; the feeling of fear and isolation experienced by Tony was a feeling shared by many others.

This was a great opportunity for the police and government to actually listen to the public. Whilst not their elected spokesperson, Tony Martin voiced what many others lacked the courage to express: that the police were doing precious little to combat the rising tide of crime and to protect householders in the rural community.

The police would, in my view, have done well to listen to Tony Martin and, if they had had any sense at all, they would have asked him to sit on community action groups. But egos get in the way and we have seen how various Chief Constables of Norfolk seemed to want to teach the simple farmer a lesson. A wise man listens to one's critics in the hope of learning more about one's self and actions – instead, the police were perceived as being in constant denial about what was happening under their very noses.

Once Mr Bone had left the stand – without the robust cross-examination that a man of Scrivener's experience could ordinarily have been expected to draw upon - the prosecution then called Peter Huggins, the very man who had called Tony Bone in the first place about organising a Farmwatch meeting! The trial really was becoming a love-fest (and free publicity) for Farmwatch.

The pig farmer told the court that he met Tony Martin a few days before the shooting. Huggins claimed: "He asked me whether I had seen any light-fingered pikies lately and spoke of the travelling community and the crime situation. He had the idea somebody was after him as he had already suffered from previous burglaries. He got the feeling he was being targeted."

Cross-examined by Scrivener, Huggins agreed that the remark did not mean people in the area were mass murderers. "No, it is the kind of thing I would say myself," Mr Huggins said. So, if the remark was something that Mr Huggins would say himself, what was all the fuss about and why have Huggins as a witness at all (unless, of course, the prosecution is merely rolling out one witness after another who would cast Tony Martin in a poor light.) And, as we have seen, Tony Martin's intuition that he was being targeted was not some delusional idea from a fantasist but a very real phenomenon corroborated by none other than self-confessed burglar Christopher Webster.

Having set the jury up to listen to what was, in effect, palpable nonsense, the prosecution then relied on the evidence of pathologist Dr Heath, the man who undertook the first autopsy. The false notion was reiterated that Barras had died "within two minutes of being shot and that he could not have been resuscitated" but this was not the case as we have seen.

Notice that the prosecution did not call the other two pathologists (Shepherd and Cooper). Once again, the police and the CPS were being highly selective who they brought to court in a blatant attempt to influence the jury – a jury which, apparently, was being stared at by relatives and supporters of Fred Barras. But their stares were completely misdirected.

But note, too, that Scrivener failed his client by not calling Shepherd and Cooper to the stand to be questioned about their autopsies on Barras.

Do you believe at this point that Tony Martin received a fair trial? Do you honestly believe that your taxes were spent in the interest of justice?

The prosecution turned to yet another 'expert witness': ballistics expert Brian Arnold, who showed the 12 bore, pump-action Winchester rifle used by Tony Martin to jurors and demonstrated how it worked. He said the burglars had been shot from a range of "*around* 15ft" and said "the evidence *suggested*[460] that three shots had been fired."

Questioned by Scrivener, he agreed that Tony Martin "may have fired downwards after a torch was shone at him." Notice the quality of the 'expert witness' here, and I do not seek to disparage Arnold in any way. But let's look at this logically and rationally: can Arnold tell the jury categorically how far the shooter was from Fearon and Barras when he shot? No. At best, his estimate is "around 15 feet." Can the expert witness tell the jury categorically how many shots were fired? No, but the evidence "suggested that three shots had been fired." Can the expert witness tell the jury categorically that the farmer fired

---

[460] Author's emphases.

downwards? No, but "he may have." Can the expert witness prove that Tony Martin shot the two men? No. Can he prove that they were shot *inside the house?* No, of course not.

As I've previously stated, it is not my intention to disparage Arnold or his work. I merely include this section in the interest of justice and so that jurors and those accused do not rely too much on what the court likes to call 'expert' witnesses. Of course a witness who knows more about, for example, chemistry than the average juror might reasonably be thought of by us as some kind of 'expert', but in every walk of life, 'experts' make mistakes and here we have a situation whereby Tony Martin's liberty and reputation were at stake. Sometimes we do better to rely on our own common sense.

Records show that it was not until 3:20pm on Sunday 22 August 1999 – two days after the shooting – that Brian Arnold ventured into the film-set that was Bleak House in the company of forensic scientist Andrew Palmer, DS John Eglen, pathologist Dr Michael Heath, DSupt Christopher R. Grant and DCI Martin Wright. A lot could have happened to the "crime scene" between 10pm on the Friday night and almost half-past-three on the Sunday afternoon. How can we (and the jury) be sure that nothing had been interfered with, whether by accident or design? More room for 'reasonable doubt'?

For the avoidance of doubt, I call into question the very notion that Bleak House was, in fact, the "crime scene". It was a "crime scene" only in the sense that an unknown number of intruders unlawfully smashed their way into the farmhouse but that's all. The hidden evidence shows that Tony couldn't have shot anybody, much less killed anyone...

Thur
13 APR
2000
10 am
380

court one, Norwich Crown Court & Bleak House
On day four of the trial the judge and jury were taken to Bleak House, but prior to them leaving the crown court, the jury heard details of what Tony Martin described as a "night of terror" read out.

Ordinarily, of course, the jury might have expected to have heard this account from Tony himself. But in this pantomime, anything could – and did – happen.

The jury was told about the orchard incident, minus all of the really relevant facts: Tony called the police, he didn't shoot at anybody, the driver hadn't pressed charges, Tony's cousin, Martin Hollis - a witness - wasn't interviewed.

In his police interview about the August shooting in 1999, Tony Martin said:

> ❝ I saw these lights like a car. There seemed to be a lot of light. At that stage I started to become frightened, fearful and terrified. The nightmare of it all was like being in a horror movie.

I thought someone was on the landing and I got very frightened. I felt someone was out there and I was not prepared to wait for the unknown. I couldn't wait for someone to walk into my bedroom.

I got halfway down the stairs and someone shone a light in my face. There was a flash and I fired the gun. When I fired the gun I genuinely thought my life was in danger. A light was pointed at my face and I didn't know what was behind it."

jury at Bleak House

The Times reported: "Before the jury reached Bleak House, they walked along a narrow track.[461] Scattered around the overgrown front of the house they saw evidence of abandoned farm machinery, a lavatory seat and a rusting Rover 2000 covered in moss. Inside, police officers pointed out the stairs, with *steps removed to deter intruders*. [Author's emphasis]

The ground floor rooms are strewn with rubble, cans and bottles. In his bedroom they would have seen the 15-watt bulb which, apart from a hall light, was the only electricity."

The normally measured *Independent* newspaper published what can only be described as journalistic rubbish:

"The night when Tony Martin is alleged to have shot and killed a 16-year-old burglar was the not the first time he had fired at a trespasser on his property.

Five years earlier, Mr Martin discovered a man in his orchard and set his rottweiler dogs upon him, Rosamund Horwood-Smart QC, for the prosecution, said. "Mr Martin went out with a shotgun and thought he saw the man trying to run his dogs down in his car. Mr Martin shot at and hit the rear wing of the man's vehicle."

As we have seen, this was not a true account of the orchard incident at all. And notice how Horwood-Smart failed to tell the jurors that a key witness as to the facts – Martin Hollis – was never interviewed by the police and, of course, he was not called to court by the defence. In the interest of justice, he ought to have been. Notice, too, how Horwood-Smart failed to tell the jury that barristers Simon Barham and Richard Daniel had, to a great extent, defended Tony's actions that day against an aggressive trespasser. We have yet another instance of where only some of all the available evidence was tendered against Tony Martin – as long ago as 15 September 1988 (entry **24**), the police failed to interview all those present in the kitchen of Ripes House following the altercation between Tony and his brother. The pattern was repeating itself. As Orwell wrote: "Lies will pass down into history."

---

[461] This 'track' was the pea gravel drive leading directly to Bleak House.

After the 90-minute journey from Norwich to Emneth, jurors looked at the hall and the staircase from where the farmer had said he'd fired his gun.

For health and safety reasons, jurors visited the upper floor of Bleak House two at a time. The jury entered the farmhouse in pairs and wore hard hats because the conditions and fabric inside were considered too hazardous for all twelve to go in together. They picked their way across a ground floor, where the bare floorboards were strewn with cans, books, bottles and rubble from repair work started years before but never completed.

Outside they saw where the farmer had erected a system of ladders in an oak tree and on part of a roof, allegedly so that he could keep a lookout for trespassers.

Police also pointed out the front window, where Barras and Fearon smashed their way in and the back window from which they exited.[462]

The jury saw poisonous hogweed, which at the time of the shootings was growing gutter high.[463]

Fri 14 APR 2000 10 am 381

court one, Norwich Crown Court
According to the newspapers, "Day Five of the trial continued to be conducted amid high security, with police on guard in and outside the Court." The Emneth farmer, forced to stay at a secret address, was driven to court under a blanket by police each day.

Witnesses giving evidence for the defence were to be referred to by number only.

After having visited Bleak House the previous day, the jury was back at Norwich Crown Court to witness the farmer on the verge of tears in the witness box as he spoke of previous raids on his home.

Tony Martin took the stand on the fifth day of the trial and admitted firing three shots[464] from his illegally-held, pump-action shotgun but insisted that he had acted only in self-defence.

The court heard that the farmer had been on bail and living in safe houses because of the threats to his life. That is, if we believe this police-generated narrative. They never provided any clear cut evidence to support their narrative that there was a price on the farmer's head. Having him in a 'safe house' was a way of controlling him and ensuring that he didn't go back to his home to

---

[462] Of course the police would point out these windows: they are keen to sell the notion that Fearon and Barras were inside Bleak House at the time Tony fired his shotgun.

[463] But not so high that it covered the roof and chimney so that a helicopter was (allegedly) unable to find the house.

[464] Author's note: to this day, he tells me he still does not know just how many shots he did fire. In fact, no-one can be certain.

examine the house in daylight. Tony Martin was too astute for the police to have allowed that.

Smartly dressed and articulate, the farmer said that at first he had lain on his bed rigid with fear and too frightened to move after he heard "a horrendous noise" downstairs. "I had this terrible thumping in my body and my heart was beating loudly. At first I thought it must be my imagination. Then I had to face the fact that something really was happening downstairs."

Terrified and vulnerable, he said, he had loaded his shotgun and had got halfway down the stairs when a light was shone in his face.

He said that he had fired the gun from his hip, but because the room was empty when he eventually went downstairs, he had been unaware he had hit anyone until after his arrest the following day.[465]

According to *The Times*, "Martin told the jury that he bitterly regretted what had happened but had been placed in a 'regrettable position'." The accused choked back tears when he was giving evidence about previous burglaries, including one in May last year when Windsor chairs he "had grown up in as a child" were stolen from the farmhouse.

He categorically rejected a suggestion from Horwood-Smart that he had opened fire "in anger, in retribution - you were shooting to kill or injure very badly". He told the jury he had been "terrified, petrified" when he had been wakened by the "horrendous noise" of intruders breaking in through a downstairs window.

"I had visions of people coming through the [bedroom] door," he said. "I became fearful. There was this terrific thumping. It seemed to fill the room. It was my heart beating. I thought, 'This is crazy'."

The defendant said he had not shouted a warning and had not heard any screams or any other noises from the intruders.

Alleged £60,000 bounty to kill the farmer

The court was also told that underworld hitmen had been offered a £60,000 contract to kill the farmer. A CID officer, DS Peter Newton, said that police had received intelligence, *which they could not substantiate* [author's emphasis], that the accused's life was at risk. Agreeing that he had heard of the £60,000 "reward" for killing Tony Martin, he said: "You cannot ignore these things. The threat is taken seriously. We would be criticised if we did not do so."

Asked if police had advised Martin never to go back to his farmhouse, Newton said that police had made it clear to him they could not protect him for the rest of his life.

---

[465] To this day, Tony Martin is still unaware that he hit anybody. He only has the word of corrupt police to go on, since he saw no evidence with his own eyes that he'd hit anyone. Some people will believe anything they're told by the police and other "authorities" and Tony wasn't alone – sixty million people had also been deceived.

Because of the unsubstantiated threats, the police had unsuccessfully opposed Mr Martin's bail application and he is now living in a safe house.[466]

Scrivener told the jury that the case was concerned with self-defence and the right of citizens to protect themselves: "Killing someone is not necessarily wrong if it is done in self-defence." In similar circumstances, he said, a wrong decision had led to the deaths of innocent people.

The judge said the jury must weigh up whether Martin believed it was necessary to use force, and whether the force he used was reasonable.

Scrivener said that in spite of being confronted by one of the farmer's dogs and passing a car that indicated that Mr Martin was at home, the two thieves had not been deterred: "They smashed the window and made no attempt to avoid noise. They couldn't care less because they were determined burglars who knew their way around," Scrivener said.[467]

He said that when Martin had gone to the stairs to confront the intruders they had not retreated and had shone a torch in his face. Scrivener added: "He didn't know whether they had weapons. He didn't have time to say: 'Hold it chaps, let's discuss this rationally.' He chose not to wait for the unknown."

Scrivener appealed to the jury to put themselves in the defendant's shoes: "This case is about self-defence, the right all citizens have."

On the stand, Tony Martin denied ever saying that he would machine-gun gypsies or criminals.

Alleged jury intimidation
Then a police officer went into the witness box, while the jury remained in their room outside of the courtroom.

It was suggested that some 'heavies' had been in court and "may have eyed the jury – could, if they remembered their faces - have followed all of them home." Judge Owen's response was simply to say that he would tell the jurors not to "talk to strangers and, indeed, if any stranger starts to talk to them and mentions this case in any way, they are to tell the police."

It appeared that the jury were individually and collectively under threat from possible reprisals by friends and relatives of Barras and Fearon. Please note my use of the word 'appeared'.

---

[466] I repeat my earlier point – that this was a 'safe house' only insofar as the police needed Tony far away from his home so that he wouldn't go round and inspect it. Had he gone there, he'd have seen the lack of shotgun pellets in the room he was alleged to have shot Fearon and Barras in, he'd have seen the lack of blood spatter, he'd have seen that all of his furniture had been removed, he'd have worked out all the angles from the stairs into the breakfast room and he would have realised that he couldn't have hit anybody that night. No, the police didn't want the farmer anywhere near their dressed set.

[467] Scrivener, of course, ought to have been in possession of Fearon's first statement to medics – that he'd been shot on a track.

Scrivener suggested that each juror be given a number to ring so that they could call the police. (You may have noted the irony in that this case is about a man who kept calling the police about thefts, burglaries and trespassers at his farm and the Constabulary's continued failures to respond to those calls.)

Scrivener added: "And that, in addition to the warning, *as we are getting to the end of the trial now*, it is very important this rule is not disobeyed and so on. I wonder if it might be possible tonight to organise police transport for them home?" The emphasis is mine: Scrivener said that the trial was reaching its conclusion - only a few hours of courtroom time had elapsed since he said he was not aware of which witnesses he would or would not call.

Secondly, he only now asked for security for the jurors. All of these details ought to have been planned weeks in advance of this trial – particularly once it was known that it had become such a high-profile case. I cannot imagine for one minute that the jurors were not picking up on all of this.

A get-out-of-jail-free card was played by the unnamed inspector from Great Yarmouth – we have got this 'intelligence' about a contract on Tony Martin's head "but we can't necessarily rely on it." Rather like all the police intelligence gathered on Tony Martin by Rodney Gooderson and others. And perhaps about the 'intelligence' gathered on you and me. How much is really credible, because all you have to do is piss off your neighbour and he tells the police he has seen underage boys or girls leaving your house after dark…

For those genuinely interested in their civil liberties, you are entitled to make Subject Access Requests under the General Data Protection Regulations to ask the police for every piece of information they hold on you on the Police National Computer (PNC). Do not forget to write to your local police station to ask what they have on their Local Area Network, because often it will be this lesser known computer network which holds 'intelligence' on you. You have no idea – unless you take these lawful and reasonable steps – just what has been collated about you. We each of us have our enemies, even if they are just jealous of us.

The judge asked if the jurors had been provided with a telephone number to call in the event of an emergency and the Inspector replied: "As far as I am aware our arrangements are not in place over the weekends so that would be through the normal 999 system."

When the judge asked who the jurors should ask for if they called 999, the Inspector replied: "If they were to ring 999 that would come through to our central control room staff. All of our staff across the force area are aware of what is taking place this weekend. In the meantime, what I will do My Lord, is pass a memo through to the central control room, where any such calls would be received, and let them know that this increased vigilance is required."

And the unnamed Inspector from Great Yarmouth left the court as the jury filed back in. Judge Owen then addressed the jury directly and repeated his warning not to speak to anyone about the case at all, not even relatives and that, if they were approached they should dial 999 and tell the operator they were serving on the Martin jury. The Judge added: "It is not a question of thoroughly alarming you or anything like that. In fact, there is no reason to be alarmed at all" which, of course, will have alarmed some jurors, if not all. He then sent them home and told them to be ready to start at 10 o'clock on the following Monday.

The judge claimed that if the trial were to be aborted then this all would have been a waste of public money – given that the case ought never to have come to trial in the first place, it seems double standards were at play. We can waste as much public money as we like in bringing innocent people to trial but don't you naughty boys and girls go wasting (your own – public) money! That is the game as it is *really* played, not how you *think* it's played.

Scrivener added: "My Lord, I anticipate the defence case will finish quite shortly into Monday."

Mon
17 APR
2000
10 am
382

Judge Owen's chambers, Norwich Crown Court

When Monday 17 April 2000 came round – officially Day Six of a murder trial in which a man's liberty and reputation were at stake – all parties started the day with yet another meeting in chambers.

The judge opened by telling all present that a juror had called the police on the previous Saturday to report that two men had approached his flat and were "eyeing him."

Scrivener then asked about trying to secure police protection for the jurors but the judge replied, "Oh, no, no. There is no question of that, no. Absolutely not. No, no, but I did say if they thought anybody was getting in touch with them they should let the police know."

As we all know, there are only twelve members in a jury so arranging some form of police protection would not have been too difficult or too costly and might well have reassured each member. Yet Judge Owen had completely ruled it out. Why would he do that? Would you have wanted police protection if you had been a juror at this trial?

Scrivener moved the discussion on to other matters: "My Lord, we should get the [closing] speeches in today quite easily and maybe start summing up."

Notice how quickly this trial is moving along. It must be obvious to even the least legally-minded reader that in the first week – five days – almost one whole day was spent at Emneth, and there were several discussions in chambers.

This trial was essentially a very simple case, but the real issue had been clouded in order to try to create a bigger case against the accused. But almost all of the time had been taken up with prosecution witnesses denigrating the character of the farmer. This is a sure sign that there was no real case against him. Bring in coach-loads of witnesses who will say bad things against the accused and don't have too much 'real evidence' – no need to introduce too much that could be challenged. The reporters at court are rarely legally minded – the court room was full to the brim with reporters looking for an angle. 'Eccentric', 'loner', 'gypsy-hater' were labels bandied about which had no substance – I suggest that the police (with the help of the prosecution) had created these labels in order to win a case to divert the public's attention away from their own wrong-doing.

Judge Owen then said that he would eventually want to give the jury a written out approach to the case, though it had not yet been typed out. He said the day's events would consist of closing speeches and the start of his summing up.

Again – and I make no apologies for labouring the point – notice the speed with which the judge wanted this case to proceed. The day in court itself had not yet commenced – this conversation was still in chambers. Yet, Judge Owen wanted the rest of the evidence, two closing speeches (one from either side, of course) and then he would start his summing up. Remember that usual court hours are from 10am until 1pm, an hour for lunch, and then 2-4pm, sometimes 4:30 or 5pm. Yes, this trial was racing ahead without a doubt.

At this point, the judge rose out of his chambers and he and his entourage of prosecution and defence lawyers then settled down in Courtroom One. The jury was brought in and the rest of the day consisted of "defence witness number three" giving evidence as to the good character of the accused, and then the prosecution and defence closing speeches. After all of those procedural activities had been completed, Judge Owen then began his summing-up.

The King's Lynn newspaper – the *Lynn News* – summarised the prosecution's cross-examination of the accused as follows:

"Tony Martin denied he was armed and lying in wait to catch burglars Fred Barras and Brendon Fearon "like rats in a trap."

Cross-examination of Tony Martin
During intensive cross-examination from Rosamund Horwood-Smart QC, Mr Martin maintained he woke up when he heard the burglars[468] moving about downstairs and was descending his staircase when he fired his pump-action Winchester shotgun.

But Miss Horwood-Smart put it to him that he heard the two men outside and was ready to catch the burglars when they broke in.

She asked him: "Were you already downstairs when Mr Fearon and Mr Barras moved into the main room?"

---

[468] He didn't hear 'burglars' Fearon and Barras – he heard an unknown number of intruders. This point needs to be made – the public was being given information and were wrongly believing that information to be 'fact'.

"No," answered Mr Martin.

"You were at least in the doorway, if not inside the room itself," said Miss Horwood-Smart, stating scientific evidence showed shots were fired from the doorway.[469]

AM: I have to accept that bullets don't go around corners, but I got the impression I was on the stairs.

H-S: Were you already there, waiting for them with your gun loaded?

AM: No.

H-S: And did you go behind them to shoot them when they were in that main room?

AM: No.

H-S: Like rats in a trap?

AM: No.

H-S: You shot them from downstairs, Mr Martin.

AM: I had the impression I was on the stairs when I shot the gun.

H-S: Your first shot was followed by the second, and the cartridge would have been ejected. *There was no cartridge on the staircase.*[470] You could not have fired that gun for the second time from the stairs."[471]

---

[469] No such 'scientific' evidence existed. All that existed was that ballistics expert Brian Arnold – for the prosecution – had stated that *in his view* Barras and Fearon had been shot from a distance of *about 15 feet* and because that didn't work *inside the house from the stairs into the breakfast room*, the prosecution had to invent a false narrative to show that Tony must have descended the stairs and walked into the breakfast room where he allegedly shot them.

Secondly, the "blood and tissue" allegedly found by DS Eglen had obviously been planted there. Had Fearon and Barras been standing where the police claimed, there would have been a good deal more blood spatter and many pellets embedded in the furniture in that room (furniture which was conveniently removed to Downham Market police station so that no member of the public could actually inspect it). The 'evidence' didn't match the police' narrative that *they* had falsely created.

[470] This sentence is palpable nonsense. You do not have to be a ballistics expert to know that when you fire a shotgun, the cartridge is expelled several feet in front and to the side of the gun. If someone fires a gun from the stairs, then the expelled cartridge isn't going to land *on the stairs*. Horwood-Smart QC would have known this because she had in her possession various ballistic evidence.

[471] Notice how Horwood-Smart appeared to have dropped the notion that Tony Martin fired *three* shots.

However, notice that Horwood-Smart failed to mention the empty shotgun cases found in the hallway during police searches in September 1999:

AM: Right.

H-S: You didn't fire it for the first time from the stairs.

AM: Yes I did.

H-S: You fired it from the entrance to the room. You intended to shoot them.

AM: No I didn't.

H-S: You were using the gun to blast their heads off, to kill them.

AM: No, I was protecting myself.

H-S: You weren't a frightened man, you were an angry man.

AM: No, I was a frightened man.

Later Miss Horwood-Smart accused Mr Martin of lying during his police interviews. "You hadn't been shooting in self-defence or fear at all," she said. "You were lying because you had not been in fear of your life."[472]

AM: No, I was a frightened man. I was certainly in fear.

H-S: You were shooting in anger. You were shooting in retribution. You were shooting to kill or to injure very badly.

AM: No, I wasn't.

He said immediately after the shooting he went back upstairs but decided to search his premises, taking his unloaded gun with him. He said he went downstairs and found the window pulled from the wall and holdall bags full of silver. Miss Horwood-Smart asked him if he placed the silver in the bags, as suggested by Mr Fearon earlier in the trial.

"No," said Mr Martin. "I think it is a frightful thing to say."

The *Lynn News* continued its report:

"Mr Scrivener said there was no evidence that shotgun cartridges in his home were anything other than mixed in with the general mess and had not been carefully placed.

---

[472] Horwood-Smart's comment is nonsense – she has the very first police interview dated 21 August 1999 in which Tony mentioned how fearful he had been. She has conveniently "overlooked" that oppressive interview and she was assisted by the judge who decided that the tapes of that interview would not be listened to by the jury.

Mr Martin had testified that he was on the stairs, which was corroborated by the account of prosecution witness Brendon Fearon.

Mr Scrivener said his client was confronted by experienced professional burglars making lots of noise, he was alone and he didn't know how many there were. He was dazzled by a torch being shone in his face and he fired.

"Would these men have allowed him to come down, look at them in the torchlight and trot off to the police station, or would they have tried to stop him doing that?" asked Mr Scrivener.

"They must have heard him coming down the stairs, yet they did not retreat but shone the torch in his face. What would you have done?" he asked the jury.

Mr Martin was a decent, respectable man who had not asked for his house to be invaded, said Mr Scrivener. Mr Justice Owen, who told the jury to decide on the facts not on emotions, said that if they found Mr Martin may have believed he was under threat, it was necessary to defend himself and he used reasonable force, then self-defence was a defence to all the charges faced by him.

It is a tragedy that this young boy is dead, but on the other hand it is a tragedy that Mr Martin, a man who has led a good and decent life has had his life ruined as well. To say it is a tragedy doesn't help."

Purpose of closing speeches
For those not familiar with the legal process, the closing speeches provide both the prosecution and the defence with an opportunity to address the jury for one final time before they go to the jury room to deliberate on their verdicts.

The prosecution, of course, will seek to paint the accused in as poor a light as possible but they are not allowed to introduce any new evidence at this late stage, or suggest theories that have not been heard in court thus far. Neither, for that matter, is the defence.

I refer you to barrister Matthew Scott's blog <www.barristerblog.com> and use some of his copyrighted material here to help us understand how Scrivener should have persuaded the jury that his client was innocent: "The simple objective of defence counsel is to raise *at least one* fundamental doubt about the prosecution case. If that is done, then it will be impossible to be sure of the defendant's guilt and he will be acquitted. Broadly speaking, says Scott, defence arguments fall into four categories:

First, and probably most common, are those cases where the prosecution witnesses' reliability is challenged.

Secondly, cases where the witnesses' honesty is challenged.

Thirdly, cases which depend upon undisputed expert evidence. An example might be a "baby battering" case where, relying upon evidence of broken ribs, bruises and brain damage the prosecution experts assert that a baby must have been shaken, even though no-one has seen it happening.

Finally, cases where the prosecution evidence is accepted but the prosecutor's interpretation of the evidence is disputed."

Now, it seems to me that prosecution witnesses Bone and Gathercole could easily have been shown to be unreliable. The 'expert evidence' of Dr Heath and his assertion that Barras died within two minutes of being shot and that he could not have been saved under any circumstances could have been shot down in flames by producing in court the evidence from the two other pathologists.

And the 'evidence' of the three empty casings found just inside the breakfast room could have been challenged. Thus the areas described by barrister Matthew Scott in which to seek an acquittal could all have been used to the full by Scrivener and he was intellectually capable of doing so, but he didn't assist his client as he should have done. He did not, by any stretch of the imagination, robustly defend his client as required by his profession's code of conduct.

Burden of proof

Before we leave Courtroom One today, let's look at what Scott says about the burden of proof: "The most important part of a closing defence speech is that which deals with the burden and standard of proof. You simply cannot take it for granted. And, given its importance, you should ideally deal with it near the beginning of the speech and at the end and in the middle. Don't forget that being "sure" means the same as being "sure beyond reasonable doubt."

The latter is a well-known phrase with a solemn ring to it. What is reasonable doubt? It is any doubt which is reasonable. So, what do you say to the jury about the need to be *sure* before convicting? Being sure does not mean you saying to yourself: "I think he did it", or "he probably did it", or even "I'm *almost* sure he did it." If the prosecution have made you *almost* sure then they have not proved the case to the high standard that the law requires. If there is a possibility that you could be mistaken then you are not sure, and the proper verdict is one of not guilty. Generally speaking, a good defence counsel will concentrate his or her fire on attacking the main prosecution points rather than trying to shore up their own witnesses. It is not, after all, defence counsel's job to prove a case but to show that the prosecution case is unsafe." (All the emphases above are Mr Scott's, though they could also have been mine.)

Having read this chapter, do you think that Tony Martin received a fair trial? Do you think you received value for money for your tax pounds? Do you think that Justice was served? Do you think it was fair that the prosecution arranged for a phalanx of police officers to line up to defame the farmer and the latter only have a couple of witnesses? In any trial, the judge should ensure that there is a spirit of even-handedness: balancing the scales of justice, as it were. Do you believe that this occurred here?

Prosecutor's closing speech

We now have to turn our attention to the role of the prosecutor in her closing speech. Horwood-Smart told the jury: "This was a man who was prepared to be his own police force, investigating force, jury, judge, and if necessary, executioner." Highly emotive words, particularly that of 'executioner'.

But so what if Tony Martin did take a particularly keen interest in his local community and the rising levels of crime in it? I argue that if we had more people like him with such a keen interest in what goes on around us, that all communities would actually be safer. But Miss Horwood-Smart was not finished yet:

"Mr Martin lay in wait for the burglars and shot them like rats in a trap. We say he was a man who was waiting for intruders. This was not a blind shooting."

She was still not finished with her emotive and delusional rhetoric:

"Mr Martin was a man that (sic) knew the power, force, and damage that a shotgun can inflict. He had that gun for one particular reason. He had that gun to use, if and when the occasion arose, to shoot any intruder who had the temerity to come in to his property, in to his home, on to his land. This was a man who was angry, who was shooting to kill."

And that was the sum total of Miss Horwood-Smart's closing speech. For any defence counsel worth his or her salt, it was a dream closing speech from the prosecution because all Scrivener had to do was – as barrister Matthew Scott had pointed out – cast some doubt, *any doubt*, on her closing remarks.

So, let's pause, stand back from the emotive rhetoric and lies being bandied about a court room and examine the *facts* as we know them so far:

- the oppressive first police interview was withheld from the jury
- the body of Barras was subjected to *three separate autopsies* and was withheld from the jury
- the alleged getaway driver (Bark) was not in court
- Bark claimed to have been at home at the time of the shooting
- self-confessed burglar Christopher Webster was not called to court (despite offering to be called as a witness)
- the ballistic evidence didn't match the firing from the stairs
- the gunshot wound to the chest was not consistent with a shotgun cartridge
- Neil Hirrel's statement to the police upon arrest was withheld from the jury

- Fearon's statement to medics that he was shot *outside* after walking some 20-30 yards up a track was withheld from the jury
- there were no footprints in the dew on the lawn to the rear of Bleak House, despite the police claim that Fearon and Barras had left the house via a rear window
- the police timings associated with the helicopter(s) differed wildly
- several police officers claimed not to have been at Bleak House, despite the Constabulary's own computer aided dispatch (CAD) system having placed them there
- certain police officers arrived at Hungate Corner in one car and left in another
- more than a dozen witness statements which were positive towards Tony Martin were kept from the jury
- statements from medical staff at the Queen Elizabeth Hospital differed considerably
- the body of Barras was still in rigor mortis (according to pathologist Dr Heath) when he should have been out of rigor according to (i) the alleged time of the shooting and (ii) the alleged time of the autopsy
- hundreds of witness statements were not signed according to the papers delivered to Tony Martin by his legal team
- x-rays were taken of Barras but not used at trial
- exhibits were moved between different trials
- information from the public was not followed up on
- confusion about whether the alleged burglars were ever stopped by the police
- confusion over dates and times in almost all of the witness statements, especially those of the police.

Defence counsel's closing speech
From the above, it would have been relatively simple to cast doubt on the prosecution's account – even if, like Scrivener, you hadn't called important witnesses as to fact, including, but not limited to, Darren Bark the alleged getaway driver, Martin Hollis the witness in the orchard incident and pathologists Shepherd and Cooper. Or any number of other farmers (all of whom had been interviewed by the police) who had been present at the Farmwatch meeting.

And, of course, Scrivener could have called into question the times of the helicopter flights and shown that even the police couldn't agree on a specific time. Any fresh-out-of-law-school barrister would have had a field day on this point alone. So let's see how Anthony Scrivener handled his closing speech and let's see what his focus was on.

Scrivener said that the defendant had been "a victim of crime. He didn't want burglars[473] in his house. He was put into a situation where he had to make some desperate decisions. A wrong decision on his part could lead him to suffer serious injury or even death."

He added that the farmer had suffered several burglaries and had been visited by a "number of dangerous people" over the years. And that, in essence, was the closing defence statement. I am staggered by its lack of passion, its inability to directly counter the prosecution's spurious claims and its extreme brevity.

Tony Martin has told me (just as he'd told Scrivener) that the gun initially dry-fired on an empty breech. If true, this demonstrates that – at most – he only loaded four cartridges into the magazine, that he was unfamiliar with the gun and was clearly not 'lying in wait' for the intruders and nor had he gone in 'hot pursuit' of them. Scrivener failed to robustly destroy the prosecution's claims against his client.

We should recall what barrister Matthew Scott said in his blog: that defence counsel should systematically set out to destroy the prosecution's arguments. I suggest that Scrivener failed to do this. I suggest that Scrivener let down his client and that the farmer did not have a fair trial.

Furthermore, we have the *mens rea* element of the case: did Tony Martin have the *intention* to kill or cause serious injury to *anybody* when firing his gun?

Let's pause for a moment longer and consider this dry-firing of the gun on the stairs. Not only does it exonerate the farmer from the allegations that he 'lay in wait' (because otherwise he would have loaded the gun properly), but it also added to the tension on the staircase. Consider this: the farmer advances to about three stairs down from the top of the staircase. The intruders hear him because he is trying to negotiate a difficult, old and creaky staircase whilst carrying a heavy gun and a torch (which isn't working). The intruders advance from the breakfast room towards the staircase and a light is shone in the farmer's face. The farmer pulls the trigger and nothing happens. In that moment, he is a sitting target himself, because his enemy has now seen him and his age and he has – to all intents and purposes – a gun which is not loaded. Their immediate reaction would surely be to think that this older man is bluffing. What next? Would they have picked up a brick and smashed it in his face? Would they have advanced up the stairs and beaten him up? Would they, in fact, have killed or seriously injured *him*?

---

[473] Scrivener employed the word 'burglars' – I choose to use the word 'intruders'. We ought not conflate two apparently separate incidents: *inside his home,* Tony shot at an unknown number of intruders (injuring none of them) and, according to Fearon, he and Barras intent on burglary were shot by a person or persons unknown *outside 20-30 yards up a farm track.*

So, if the gun had dry-fired as Tony claimed, he had only a split second's thought to activate the pump action mechanism before being possibly overpowered and attacked.

"Shooting round corners"

Two shotgun pellets were allegedly found (by DC Aldous) below the rear exit window and the police – desperate to conjure up a conviction against Tony – claimed that, because the rear exit window was out of his line of sight from a position on the stairs (and since guns don't fire round corners), this meant that Tony must have descended the stairs and entered the breakfast room. This was nothing but a 'red herring' designed to over-complicate a simple issue.

Since, like a diligent pathologist, we should consider all possible scenarios including the most unlikely, we ought to consider the possibility that the shotgun pellet damage to the exit window was created *after* Tony was in police custody (since the police had taken possession of the shotgun from Tony Martin's mother at Redmoor House, Friday Bridge Road, on the Saturday.) I am not saying this happened, only that we ought to consider all possibilities.

Another possibility based on science that we ought to consider is that the two pellets said to have been found below the exit window were ricochets and had found their way there after hitting the ladder or other solid objects in the room.

Or they could simply have been planted there.

Let's pause a moment and consider what objects were in the breakfast room and in the line of fire from the stairs: a cupboard, a large metal machine part, an aluminium ladder, a sack barrow, a metal lifting machine and a rolled steel joist (RSJ).

DS Eglen stated in his witness statement: "I saw an area of shot damage below the opening where the rear window had fallen in and what appeared to be flesh and blood associated with it." In the Virtual Reconstruction Ltd representation of the room, blood and tissue were marked near the exit window but there was no mention of any pellets. And, of course, if Fearon and Barras had really been inside that room and exited the house as the police claimed, how did they manage not to leave footprints in the dew as they allegedly fled? Nothing seems to "tie up" – there are too many discrepancies in the police narrative for us to consider it credible. And Scrivener failed to point out these discrepancies to the jury (or to the Great British Public).

We must also consider that according to the HOLMES database, DC Aldous made four statements in total (one of them being about the May burglary). Two statements (both dated 4 November 1999) were not in the bundle of legal papers provided to Tony and yet they were of crucial significance: one of them was referred to in HOLMES (line S128b) as the "main statement of SOCO including producing exhibits from Bleak House". This statement was not listed in the official list of witness statements, yet was marked as being 'Used' in HOLMES.

Judge's summing up

The closing speeches over, it was left to the judge to provide a summary of the case against Tony, together with a summary of the defence case. It goes without saying that a trial judge should at all times be even-handed and neutral.

There should be no improper comment by the trial judge in such a way as to make the summing up fundamentally imbalanced or to suggest a lack of impartiality on the part of the judge.

When you read the next section, I'd like you to decide whether you believe that Judge Owen was even-handed and unbiased. You now have an opportunity to judge the judge.

Judge's summing-up

Part 15: Judge's summing up

Mon
17 APR
2000
10 am
383

trial day 6 - judge's summing-up
Judge Owen's summing up to the jury was on Monday 17 and Tuesday 18 April 2000.

The transcript ran to some 28,702 words on 2,576 lines over 92 pages.

We would do well to consider the speed with which this trial was proceeding.

Before we examine the summing up, it's worthwhile for us to consider what the purpose of such an activity is. A legal definition of 'summing up' is the act of making a speech before a jury after the evidence has been heard. In summing up, the judge should, with much precision and clearness, state the issues and what the jury are required to find, either guilty or not guilty.

A judge should then state the substance of the prosecution's claims and then the defence's grounds of defence. It is his or her duty to state the law arising in the case in such terms as to leave no doubt as to his or her meaning, both for the purposes of directing the jury, and with a view of correcting any errors in the trial itself.

For more information about this important aspect of a criminal trial, visit <*www.nicmadge.co.uk/*summing_up_article.php>. Madge is a judge who often sits at the Inner London Crown Court and I have been before him myself. You'll be able to read about that case and a gross miscarriage of justice in my forthcoming book *Letters to my Grandchildren*.

The article by Madge includes some useful information about the capacity of a jury to remember all that it has heard and to decide what is truly relevant or otherwise. "For lay people, this can be extremely difficult."

There has been considerable research into the value of juries. For example, research by the Centre for Criminology at Middlesex University[474] found that more than half the jurors in their study did not fully understand what was happening in court and many were uncertain about how to ask a judge a question, or even whether they were allowed to take notes.

Jurors complained that the main issue they had with understanding legal proceedings was the use of legal jargon. (This is, of course, the point – lawyers will tell you that only they understand the legal aspects of a case and you couldn't possibly know and oh, by the way, we'll charge you - or the taxpayer (which is

---

[474] https://www.mdx.ac.uk/our-research/centres/Centre-for-Social-and-Criminological-Research. See also https://www.theguardian.com/uk/2004/jan/27/ukcrime.claredyer.

the same thing really) - a large fee for telling you what we know and what you don't know because we haven't educated you about the laws that we created, not those as agreed by the ordinary people. That is the game as it's *really* played.)

There is also the psychological impact of memory, recall and understanding on jurors. And then we have good old human bias.

The previously mentioned Matthew Scott's website has an article entitled "*Summing Up – A Précis or Chance to Show Bias?*"[475] and it's well worth a read. The barrister states that "News that research by the Ministry of Justice has shown that juries often fail to understand the judge's legal directions has focused attention on the purpose of the summing up in criminal trials." We ought to bear these comments in mind when examining the summing up by Judge Owen:

"Members of the jury, there may be many who will, in ignorance, or even for that matter in defiance of the law, say that Mr Martin shot two burglars and it serves them right. That is not the law. The law is not what you or I, and for that matter anyone else, think it should be: it is what is accepted as the law, and, please, you must accept the law from me. Why? Because it is my job to tell you what the law is. It is also my job to remind you of the main evidence and you will see from that very statement alone that means that I have to decide what the main evidence is. In other words, I shall remind you of some evidence and not of other evidence.

If you come to the conclusion that I have omitted a piece of evidence which you think is important, then of course it is important and you consider that evidence. Likewise, if I mention a piece of evidence which you think is of no importance then you ignore it and the reason is because that is your job and not mine. It is no part of my job to indicate to you in any way how you should decide, no way at all, because that is your job."

The game has started already: "It is my job to remind you of the main evidence." The average person in the street will be thinking that that seems a fair statement to make on the face of it. But there is a problem here of omission – we know that not all of the evidence was adduced at trial and the evidence that *was* adduced was not entirely reliable and we know that at least two prosecution witnesses perverted the course of justice with their testimony. However, the jury knows nothing of this. The jury listens to the judge in the mistaken belief that the judge is all powerful and all-knowing and that *all* the evidence has been entered into court and that everyone has been telling the truth. And the general public also buys into this myth – a myth propagated by governments to fool and control the masses.

---

[475] http://barristerblogger.com/published-articles-3/summing-up-a-precis-or-chance-to-show-bias/

Judge Owen told the jurors:

> "You are here to decide on the evidence which you have heard and, unlike many, *you have heard it all*."

My emphasis. I find that comment simply staggering in light of the evidence I have uncovered in writing this book. It would appear that Judge Owen wanted the jury to believe that they had heard all of the evidence, but this is simply not true. It's a lie and he knows it's a lie. He knows there's an Amazonian rainforest of evidence lying in the Unused File and a lengthy list of witnesses not called who should have been called. Make no mistake he knows. As he himself said, it's his job to know.

I have asked you to read this section as if you were a juror at the trial, and I think it'd be helpful if you maintained that perspective and keep asking yourself as you read this summing up "What do I think the impact would have been on me when hearing all these statements?"

A page or two further in, Judge Owen quite rightly imposed on each member of the jury the responsibility for being *certain* about facts. And he added that if a juror is sure, then the prosecution's case is proven.

Self-defence and the use of force

Then he came down to the very essence of what the trial was all about because he stated that self-defence was a defence to all of the charges. The judge went on to say that a person who believed he was about to be attacked may use such force as is reasonably necessary to defend himself. And Tony Martin did not have to prove that he was acting in self-defence: Judge Owen made it clear to the jury that it was for the prosecution to prove that he *wasn't* acting in self-defence.

He told the jurors that the law is that a person acts in lawful self-defence only if in all the circumstances he believes it is necessary for him to defend himself and the amount of force which he uses in doing so is reasonable.

So there are two main questions for the jurors to consider and answer: One, did the accused believe, or may he honestly have believed, that it was necessary to defend himself? Was it *unreasonable* that he fired into the darkness? Two: taking the circumstances as he believed them to be, was the amount of force which he used reasonable? And the law is that force used in self-defence is unreasonable and unlawful if it is out of proportion to the nature of the attack or if it is in excess of what is really required of the defendant to defend himself.

Owen again: "If you come to the conclusion that he believed or may have believed that he had to defend himself in this manner, and that he did no more than what he honestly and instinctively thought was necessary, then you may think that that would be strong evidence in his favour, indicating that the amount of force used was reasonable."

This passage of Judge Owen's summing up appears to be very much in Tony Martin's favour. Clearly what matters is what was going on in the farmer's mind at the time he pulled the trigger. A torch is shone in his face in total darkness - he pulls a trigger. A likely response time of less than one second. No time to think about deliberately murdering someone or maiming them. As Owen went on to say: "If the force used was unreasonable, then he cannot have been acting in lawful self-defence. It is as simple as that but nobody should suggest that the decision is necessarily simple. If the force used was or may have been reasonable then he is not guilty and it would be your task to say that."

The judge then went on to describe Tony Martin as a man of good character. Again, this all seems to support the farmer. The judge confirmed that by the age of 55, the farmer had not got any criminal convictions against his name and was not known for being at all violent or dishonest.

In respect of his honesty, we have read that several people made statements to the police (which were not used at trial) in which they vouched for his honesty over long periods of time. He had been dealing with a wide variety of country folk over two or three decades and people who encountered him never said that he was dishonest. We must, like Judge Owen – and therefore one would have hoped, the jury – give credibility to the notion that Tony Martin is at his core an honest man and therefore likely to have told the truth to the police and at trial. Several people made statements to the fact that they didn't like Tony as a person, some said that they felt he had an intimidatory nature, but no-one spoke about him being dishonest.

Unlawful bias from judge

But things then took a slight turn for the worse as Judge Owen continued to address the jury as the positive remarks were then subtly replaced by negative ones and remember that it is often the last thing you hear that you remember. In just 40 lines of his summing up, the judge used the words "lie, liar, lying and lies" in relation to Tony's account no less than 18 times. He didn't actually call Tony a liar, but suggested that he could be. What impact do you imagine would this have had on the jurors? Remember this has come *after* the short passage about Tony Martin's good character. It is often said that a person remembers a single criticism far more easily than a dozen compliments.

And then – I believe – the summing up took a completely different and, I suggest, a somewhat sinister tone when the judge mentioned the alleged contract on Tony's head and that it may have influenced how he gave his evidence: "It cannot be easy at any time to be giving evidence on a charge of murder. When the victim is a 16-year-old boy *for any normal person* it would be a horrifying experience. You have seen him and you will have to judge, so far as you can, the effect upon him." [Author's emphasis]

Linguistically, I find this an appalling piece of rhetoric – consider first the use of the phrase "for any normal person" (the implication being that Tony Martin is not a 'normal person') and then consider the sentence "You have seen him and you will have to judge the effect on him (of killing a boy)." As we have discussed before, *on the police's own evidence*, Tony Martin could not have hit anybody inside his house.

Slowly and by stealth, listen to the voice of the judge when he ought to have remained completely neutral: "You have seen his home. I hope you will not think I am being flippant when I say that when it is said that Mr Martin is an eccentric, you may think he has developed that almost to an art form. The idea for most of us, that he could live in a house like that, in that condition for years, is something which is hard to understand. And yet he did. It is not a crime. He is entitled to live as he wants as long as he does not commit any offence."

A court of law is not the appropriate forum for such comments about Tony's chosen lifestyle, but a seed had been sown again.

But notice how the judge then watered that seed and shone light upon it: "The idea for most of us, that he could live in a house like that, in that condition for years, is something which is hard to understand." Notice the use of the inclusive "us" ... in other words, jurors, Mr Martin is an eccentric but "we" are not. We are normal. We know how to live. We know how to keep our house tidy. We do not shoot at intruders. And so on.

But it got worse: "When you bear in mind that that main room had had a good deal of junk and rubbish removed from it,[476] all one can say is what on earth must it have been like when he was using it daily?"

I found this offensive – that an experienced Crown Court judge would stoop so low as to get the jury thinking about the condition of Bleak House when their job – their *only* job – was to consider whether a murder had been committed by Tony. And yet the judge had not finished denigrating the defendant: "What about the fact that he would sleep in his day clothes and his boots? Again, eccentric without any doubt, and you will have to bear in mind that that is the man whose reactions you will have to judge."

Judge Owen then devoted two entire pages of his summing up to discussing how the defendant inherited the house, how he used to work on oil rigs, how he got into farming, how he knocked walls down and how he was undoubtedly an eccentric. Again, we are forced to ask ourselves why he would remind the jury about all of this background information when the purpose of the summing up is to assist the jury in reaching a proper verdict based on the law and the evidence provided, not personal opinion.

As part of this background history, the judge went on to discuss the high number of break-ins and thefts suffered by the farmer and how there was a

---

[476] The judge has admitted in open court and on the public record that Bleak House – a crime scene – was interfered with prior to taking Tony to trial.

significant rise in the number of crimes in Emneth and the Fens. This is information which actually supported what Tony Martin had been telling the police for years: he was a rare man who complained and wanted better value for money for the taxes he had paid all his life. I believe that Tony Martin should be celebrated for demanding better policing and politicians who don't abuse the expenses system, whereas the "average Joe" complains and does nothing and because nothing changes, complains even more. Not so Tony Martin. If he felt an injustice, he marched down to the police station and demanded that his complaint be investigated. All too often the result was that he was laughed at, ignored and considered an eccentric. Not a particularly intelligent approach from the police.

Judge Owen did say, however, that because Tony lived on his own, he was "all the more vulnerable" which surely adds to our long list of reasons why he felt in fear of his life on 20 August 1999 and which surely gave him every justification for firing his gun in a downward trajectory into the darkness.

Then the judge reiterated facts about Tony having shot at a car (but failed to tell the jury that witness Martin Hollis was never interviewed by the police), then he reminded the jury of an allegation made by a PC Douglas 'Danny' Cracknell that Tony had gone to a meeting in April 1999 at Methwold Village Hall and said that he would round up all the criminals and put them in a field and machine gun them all. No notes or written statements were taken at the time. So, you might be asking – and I sincerely hope that you are – why did the judge allow such nonsensical hearsay to be used as evidence in a murder trial?

But then let's not forget Scrivener. Why did he allow this, too? He was an experienced Queen's Counsel - he became Chairman of the Bar Council in 1991 and then Head of Chambers of 2-3 Gray's Inn Square between 1992 and 2001. He took this case on at the age of 64, so his career was not in jeopardy and he could be used by the Establishment as they wished. He eventually retired from practice on 31 March 2011. Why did such an experienced barrister in criminal law not undertake some of the most basic duties in defence of his client? I suggest he was under instructions from the Home Office.

Why would Judge Owen spend so long telling the jury all this? What purpose does it serve other than being a mere time-filler in this charade of a trial? The answer was not long in coming: "What is said here, however, by the prosecution is that this was all a part of the history leading Mr Martin to shoot off at the burglars who came into his house."[477]

As we saw in previous entries about the police investigation, 45 witnesses were asked about Tony Martin's attitude towards gypsies and travellers. It is clear that the police had an agenda: to try to obtain as many statements as possible that would incriminate the defendant.

Finally, Judge Owen got to the Farmwatch meeting itself, to Tony Bone's

---

[477] The narrative is being repeated that Fearon and Barras were shot by Tony Martin.

testimony, to David Gathercole's testimony, and to the alleged "Shoot the bastards!" comment.

I believe you have to question very seriously the integrity of anyone who would lie under oath at trial, and especially at a murder trial where a man may receive a life sentence. What kind of person do you have to be to undertake such action against another human being, and against the very notion of justice, fair play and integrity? Or, put another way, what might the police have on you that forces you to commit perjury on their behalf?

The judge then recounted most of the story of the trial without once relating this to the law – which was his specific job. He merely abused his position to denigrate the character of Tony Martin and the condition of Bleak House. He closed the day with the following words: "I am afraid this is in one sense hard pounding but it is necessary to go through it." It wasn't – it was mere filler.

Although almost halfway through the judge's summing up, all of the time so far had been taken up with criticisms of the defendant's chosen lifestyle and with recounting testimonies from various police constables who failed to take notes. It is unusual for so many constables to be heard as witnesses in such an important case, but they are expendable. In the event that this trial went pear-shaped and in the light of fresh and compelling evidence that there was a miscarriage of justice (or, heaven forbid, corruption exposed), certain officers of lower rank (who might have been shown to have lied on oath) could be dismissed and the police thought of as acting honourably by clearing out a bad apple or two while the really rotten apples remained in their elevated posts.

| Tue |
| 18 APR |
| 2000 |
| 384 |

trial day 7

Court reconvened at 10am on Tuesday 18 April 2000. Judge Owen continued with his summing-up.

It was not until page 47 of 92, that he asked the all-important question: "What happened on 20 August?"

The judge went on to say that Bark had told police officers that Bleak House had been burgled before and antiques and furniture had been stolen to the value of £5,000 (it may well have been more, but he's not necessarily going to admit that to the police.) But this information was not told to the jury by Bark himself – it was told by DC Buxton.

CORRUPTION ALERT   *Crown court judge complicit in unfair trial*

Notice also what Judge Owen - in possession of all the facts - said about this remarkable fact: "As to Bark, he has not given evidence[478] and you must not speculate as to why. Apparently he is alive and we know of no reason why he didn't give evidence but it would not do to speculate on the reason for it."

I'm sorry, but if I am a juror on this trial and I've been told that Bark was the driver and that he had been to Bleak House before, I would definitely want to know why he was not called as a witness; I would want to know why Scrivener did not want to cross-examine him about the entire night, or the death of Barras, or why Bark himself did not do more to save Barras if he really was the getaway driver. I would be sending a note to the judge insisting that he was brought to court to give evidence and face up to cross-examination. But that's me. I'm not unlike Tony Martin in having much higher expectations of our police and judicial system than the average person.

I ask you to consider whether you think this has been a fair trial to this point. A policeman is giving evidence on behalf of the alleged getaway driver, a man with dozens of criminal convictions for burglary, affray, theft and actual bodily harm. Two pages of the 92 were devoted to Bark's list of previous convictions. So, I hope you're asking, what on earth is a policeman doing reading this out instead of the prosecution or defence calling Bark to court and why is the judge wasting so much time on repeating Bark's convictions?

---

[478] This is misleading. Although he didn't give evidence in court, we have seen how Bark *did* make statements to the police and even offered himself as a witness. [See entry **154**].

Had a deal been done? Help us to get Martin and you won't have to go to the trial and face the consequences of the travelling fraternity finally learning that you had set up a burglary knowing full well that guns might be used?

Barras's convictions were said to have included dishonesty, common assault, threatening behaviour and assaulting police constables.

Fearon's long list of convictions were said to have included assault, theft, burglaries, handling stolen goods and dishonesty.

I believe that Tony Martin did not receive a fair trial. I also believe that the jury was cheated because it was asked to reach a verdict without *all of the available information* or information which could so easily at the time have become available. I also believe that the Great British Public was deceived because it was fed a diet of nonsense about an eccentric farmer, three career criminals and whether the shots occurred on the staircase or not ... and yet this was not the narrative that they ought to have been learning.

Freedom of Information Act request

The media hype took the public's attention away from what was really going on: that Tony Martin was being set up as a murderer when others were really responsible for the death of Fred Barras. I made a Freedom of Information Act request to Norfolk Constabulary on 20 May 2016 which read:

"Dear Norfolk Constabulary,

1. Please provide a list of all calls made to the Emergency Services (including the Police) on 20 and 21 August 1999 regarding a possible shooting at Bleak House (more properly called Cowcroft Farm), Emneth Hungate PE14 8EW.

2. Please provide a list of all calls made to the Emergency Services (including the Police) on 20 and 21 August 1999 regarding a shooting at Bleak House.

3. Please provide a list of all calls made to the Emergency Services (including the Police) on 20 and 21 August 1999 for any reason in which Bleak House was mentioned/ or Emneth/ or Emneth Hungate or similar."

When you issue an FOI request, the recipient has 20 days in which to reply. Norfolk Constabulary refused to provide me with the information. They claimed that I was "working in a group with Mr Martin" and that we were "vexatious" in requesting this information. Realistically, why would the police withhold this information unless they know that the helicopter(s) didn't go up at the time(s) they said. Let's not forget that it would then follow that all the police statements would have been proven to be false, which is precisely what I believe them to be. Put another way, if the helicopter(s) *did* go up at the time the police claim, they'd simply provide that information and debunk my hypothesis, wouldn't they?

So, despite Judge Owen claiming that the jurors ought not unduly worry why Bark was not called as a witness, I believe that the jurors ought *very much to have considered his non-appearance* when weighing up whether Tony Martin was guilty of murder.

But we now encounter yet another problem – and remember the burden of proof necessary for a conviction: the prosecution must prove *beyond all reasonable doubt* that Tony Martin intended to kill anybody when he fired his shotgun. If there is even one tiny shred of doubt in the prosecution's account, the jury must acquit him.

Judge Owen repeated to the jury the doubt the farmer had about where he was standing on the staircase: "Quite clearly he was expressing some doubts and you will have to make up your minds as to whether it was a lie, whether he was saying, "I was on the stairs." If it was a lie, what was the point of it all? It is your decision. I have directed you on the correct approach to lies and I am not going over that again."

I am staggered at this piece of auto-suggestion. Tony Martin – truthfully, in my opinion - expressed doubts about which particular stair on the entire staircase he was on, but he did say that he had ventured down the staircase far enough to give him the vision to see enough into the doorway "and that's about as far as I went or dare go."

This has the ring of authenticity to me. Someone in his position would not be focused on counting the number of stairs he had ventured down – his focus was on self-preservation. I would have doubted his testimony had he been able to tell us precisely how many steps he had walked down.

But in a shameless piece of creative linguistics, Judge Owen then suggested to the jury that it may have been a lie because he used the word 'lie' on no less than three occasions within five lines of text. Of course, he did not say that Tony Martin had lied, but he surely sowed a seed of doubt in the jurors' minds through his deliberate choice of words.

He need not have mentioned the word lie at all and could simply have said something along the lines of: "There appears to be some doubt in the defendant's mind about his precise location on the stairs and you will have to consider whether this doubt is in his favour or not." No mention of the word lie, because anyone can be unsure about something but it doesn't mean they are telling lies.

The judge went on to say there were "probably three bangs." No-one can be sure. It was claimed by the police that there were three shots, but this supposition is mostly based on three cartridges being "found" in the breakfast room and Fearon's oft-revised testimony (which is in itself not completely clear.) I have already discussed the issues that exist about the discovery of these cartridges but for a moment we would do well to pause and reflect on the fact that the judge has declared in open court that he does not know how many gunshots there were on that night. The prosecution needed to have three because it supported their wild notion that Tony Martin had advanced down the stairs, through the hallway, into the main room and fired at the backs of the intruders as they were leaving the farmhouse.

The judge reminded the jurors that they had been to see the cornfield running alongside Moyse's Bank by the Leets' bungalow but at no point did he mention that Fearon said he had seen a helicopter flying near to Bleak House while he was allegedly lying on his back in the field.

Now, ask yourself this: the trial judge has all of Fearon's statements at his disposal – why would he fail to tell the jury about the helicopter? It is not because it is not relevant – it is because *it is relevant* that it was not mentioned.

But what of the jurors? Did no juror read Fearon's first statement (they ought to have been provided with copies in the jury bundle) and notice the comment about the helicopter and wonder why no mention of it was made at trial? Surely one of the twelve would have spotted this. Surely. Or had Fearon's statements been doctored to omit all mention of the helicopter in the jury bundle?

By page 60 of the 92 pages of summing up, you will have noticed that the judge had hardly touched upon legal issues at all – the complexities of murder and manslaughter and so on – and he still continued to simply recount the story they had already heard. To the uninitiated, this is what a trial is all about: to those in the know, this is mere filler. Not worth the paper it's written on.

On page 62, the judge went on to say that the "experts" claimed that Tony Martin could not have been on the stairs when he fired the gun to have inflicted the injuries on Barras and Fearon. How right the experts were – because Tony didn't hit Barras or Fearon. We now have evidence to cast serious doubt on the entire case against the farmer.

Judge Owen then said that the defendant had claimed that he was "frightened", "very fearful" and "still fearful" as he reached for his gun and decided to load it.

The judge added: "Mr Martin said, 'It is my belief that I got halfway down before I fired the first shot. That was the impression I had in the dark. I was quite clear where I was. I didn't know whether they might attack me,' and he described again the thrombosis which he had had and he thought there was always the possibility that he might pass out."

It seems clear from this evidence that the farmer was in fear of his life and that he had every justification to shoot in order to defend himself. He did not, it seems, shoot to kill but merely to scare. And, in firing his shotgun, the police evidence shows that he couldn't have hit anyone.

On page 70, Judge Owen referred to Tony Martin using the words 'terrified' and 'frightened' on three occasions on this page alone – another very good reason why firing a gun into the blackness and in the direction of the floor was perfectly understandable in my view. As we have seen, evidence exists to show that Barras died not because he was killed by Tony Martin, but because he was killed by a person or persons unknown.

Finally, on page 75, the judge got to the point of his summing up:

"All this is the picture of what happened *around* this incident. Of course, it is what happened *in* the incident which is important."

Following a short adjournment, Judge Owen focused on the injuries to Fred Barras and that the "cause of death was a gunshot wound to the chest and he would have been unconscious immediately he fell," citing the medical evidence from pathologist Dr Heath, but as we have seen, he failed to mention the x-rays which had shown a pneumothorax. And, as we know, this diagnosis was never introduced at trial. Judge Owen then added: "He could not have been resuscitated no matter what anybody had done."[479] Judge Owen ought to have had a copy of the three autopsy reports in the case management file. He ought to have known that the case against Tony Martin had strayed ominously from the path of Truth and Justice.

The ballistics expert on behalf of the defence was then mentioned: "Dr Renshaw said that the position of the injuries to Mr Barras's right leg, the location of the shot damage on the door, indicates that at the moment of discharge Mr Martin was aiming the gun in a downward direction."[480] [Author's note: I contacted Dr Renshaw in 2015, and again in 2016, but received no reply on either occasion. See also entry **622**]

Judge Owen continued discussing Dr Renshaw and informed the jury that he had gone to Bleak House in September (entry **237**) to see what the conditions were like around 8:30pm. "Renshaw had said that it was extremely dark in that room. He performed a test in which Makin, with a white shirt on, stood in the room and couldn't be seen from the stairs. Renshaw then tried another experiment. He stood on the stairs and got Makin to shine the torch into his face and he said he was temporarily blinded."

It is not until page 87 of the 92 pages of summing up that Judge Owen finally arrived at the task in hand: to look at each count in turn and we'll do the same.

---

[479] Notice how the trial judge was happy to reiterate the bogus scientific claim made by Dr Heath despite being in possession of facts which disproved it.
[480] Dr Renshaw's report said no such thing – he didn't name the shooter. The judge is conflating two separate facts: Tony fired his shotgun. Two men were shot. It does not – and did not – follow that Tony shot the men.

| **Count 1** | the murder of Frederick Jackson Barras |

> *Count 1 charged Tony with murdering Frederick Jackson Barras. The jurors had to ask themselves: "Am I sure that the accused deliberately and knowingly fired in the direction of Freddie Barras and killed him?"*

Judge Owen told the jury: "You may think there can be no doubt about the answer to that. He did." And in that single sentence, the accused would surely be found guilty of murder.

This is an incredible manoeuvre on the judge's part. We have already seen that Tony did not deliberately and knowingly fire at anybody because (i) he could not see when he fired, (ii) he had no intention of killing or seriously injuring anyone but in protecting himself, (iii) he shot low in the dark and (iv) the shot(s) couldn't have hit anyone inside the breakfast room.

Judge Owen said that the second part of this Count that the jurors needed to consider was whether Tony Martin, when firing, intended either to kill or to cause some really serious injury. Quite correctly, the judge explained that intent is necessary before anybody can be guilty of murder (or any other crime). However, the person who murders does not have to intend to kill. It would be sufficient to show that he intended to cause some really serious injury. If the jurors are not sure that the farmer intended either to kill or to cause some really serious injury he can't be guilty of murder. So, taking the circumstances as the accused believed them to be, the jurors had to try to ascertain what was in Tony Martin's mind when he discharged the gun.

Alternatively, if all sober and reasonable people would have realised that he was inevitably subjecting Barras[481] to at least some physical, albeit not serious, harm then the jurors must consider manslaughter.

The third part of this Count was that the prosecution had to show that the firing was unlawful and that the farmer was not acting in self-defence. So the jurors had to ask themselves, 'Am I sure that when firing he acted unlawfully in that he was not acting in self-defence?' It was for the prosecution to prove that he was not acting in self-defence. If Tony Martin honestly believed or may have honestly believed that it was necessary to defend himself then he satisfied the first part of the defence, the so called defence of self-defence.

The judge told the jurors that if the accused was or may have been acting in reasonable self-defence, then he was to be found not guilty of anything. If, however, he did not act in self-defence and he did intend either to kill or to cause really serious injury, he was guilty of murder.

---

[481] All sober and reasonable people would have questioned whether, on ALL the available evidence (not just that which was entered at trial), Barras and Fearon had even entered the house.

The indictment had Tony in a 'catch-all' situation. It had been deliberately written to ensure that he would be guilty of something, if not murder then at the very least manslaughter, which carries a maximum sentence of life imprisonment at one end of the scale but, at the other end, with a high degree of provocation, possibly not even a custodial sentence according to the CPS website.

The judge properly reminded the jurors that they must continually ask themselves, "Am I sure?" because this is the test - as we have seen, *beyond all reasonable doubt* means, quite literally, that if a juror had a single shred of doubt about the case, then he or she must acquit the defendant. What was initially required from them was a unanimous verdict with which they all agreed.

Are you confident that you understand all that you have just read? Is there any confusion in your mind? As a juror and as someone who has the power to put Tony Martin away for life, are you happy that you have all the facts at your fingertips and that you're following all the legal principles as they've just been explained by Judge Owen?

Count 2   attempted murder of Fearon

On Count 2, the attempted murder of Brendon Fearon, the judge told the jurors that they had to ask themselves: "Am I sure that the accused intended to murder, and that he had in his mind, 'I'm going to kill that man'?"

If the jurors believed the answer to that was yes, then they had to go on to consider whether, with that intention, the farmer did something more than mere preparation for committing the offence; "and if someone does intend to kill somebody and points a gun at them and fires that gun, then obviously that is something more than mere preparation and he would have to be guilty of attempted murder."

However, if the accused was or may have been acting in reasonable self-defence he would have to be found not guilty.

For those readers who are interested in learning more about the term 'mere preparation' you might like to read my book entitled *Framed!* (pages 167-170) which is the anatomy of a trial at Southwark Crown Court in 2009 in which I was illegally found guilty of the attempted incitement of a non-existent 14-year-old girl into sexual relations outside of the Rule of Law after I had exposed child abuse in Lambeth Council in 2006 and was then unlawfully and fraudulently dismissed. [Author's note: there is no record of that trial. It had been created against me so as to defame me and debunk my work in exposing child abuse.]

I suggest that the authorities found it necessary to imprison Tony Martin for a considerable period of time to ensure that he would be silenced. He had become a danger to the authorities because he was saying what others who lacked the courage to speak out wanted to say – and, as Noam Chomsky[482] wrote about dissidents, "if you're a dissident, you shouldn't be surprised to get all of this stuff done to you, it's in fact a positive sign – it means that you can't just be ignored anymore."

> **Count 3**   wounding with intent of Brendon Fearon
>
> *The judge stated quite firmly that Count 3 was an <u>alternative</u> count to Count 2 and that it was a charge again relating to the injuries suffered by Brendon Fearon. If the jurors decided that the farmer was not guilty of the attempted murder of Fearon (Count 2), then they would have to go on and consider Count 3, whether he intended to wound Fearon. If he was acting in reasonable self-defence, then he was not guilty. If, however, he did intend to cause Fearon serious injury and he was not acting in reasonable self-defence, then he was guilty as charged.*

I cannot help but wonder just what the jury members were making of all this. Considerable research has shown that the 'average' jury member has no understanding of the intricacies of the legal system (they are not meant to know – think social control) and some may not be all that well educated and able to absorb all of these legal complexities.

Count 3 being an alternative count to Count 2, the CPS were going to get Tony Martin one way or another. Self-defence being a defence to all of the counts, I suggest that this is why the prosecution spent so long (and so much public money) on defaming the accused at every possible opportunity and trying to show the Great British Public that he was an eccentric who had a worrying propensity to shoot guns, a "fact" corroborated by a small army of police constables displaying a remarkable ability to recall verbatim conversations and meetings they had had with the accused several years before in which he – allegedly – always spoke about shooting gypsies and travellers. And all of the officers either failed to take contemporaneous notes of these alleged comments by Tony, or they had "lost" their notebooks.

> **Count 4**   possession of a firearm with intent to endanger life
>
> *As we know, and Tony had never tried to deny it, he did have a firearm and ammunition in his possession, but the vital question is, did he have it in his possession "with intent to endanger life" or merely as a form of self-protection should the need ever arise?*

---

[482] *Understanding Power,* (Vintage Books, London, 2003), page 208.

Judge Owen stated that he'd discussed this Count with counsel and they were all of the opinion that if Tony did not act, or may not have acted, in reasonable self-defence, he was to be found guilty of possession with intent to endanger life. However, if he was or may have been acting in reasonable self-defence he was to be found not guilty.

Owen added: "*I'm sorry it is as complicated as it must seem to you,*[483] but I hope that gives you the approach which will help you to come to your decisions."

Notice how Judge Owen apologised to the jurors for how complicated it must have seemed to them. This was, it seems to me, unnecessarily complicated because of (i) the way the Indictment had been authored and (ii) his convoluted and unnecessarily long summing-up. (But they had to fill the court day up with something because they sure as heck didn't have any real evidence against the farmer.)

And then: "I am going to ask you now to retire to consider your verdicts. In due course I shall want you to let me know how you find. You must elect one of your number to be your foreman so that that person can, in due course answer for all of you and give the verdicts."

The jury retired to consider their verdicts at 12:30pm. They returned to the courtroom at 4:30pm and, still considering their verdicts, were sent home to return at 10:30am on 19 April 2000.

Having now read these entries concerned with the summing up, do you believe that Tony Martin received a fair trial? Do you believe that the judge instructed the jury completely fairly with no bias and that he kept only to the facts and to the law? Do you believe that Tony Martin was doomed to fail from the outset? Do you believe that he was properly represented by Scrivener and Makin? Do you believe that your taxes were spent wisely in (i) bringing this case to trial and (ii) during the trial itself?

In short, do you believe that Justice was served?

---

[483] Author's emphasis.

~ written instructions from the judge ~

Now we come to the specific instructions that the judge had printed out for the jury to consider. I've reproduced them here because I'd like you to continue to put yourself in the role of a juror and – with all that you know about the case (but the jury of course did not know as much as you know) – how do you think you would have found Tony on each count: guilty or not guilty?

COUNT 1   Am I sure:

1. the Accused deliberately and knowingly fired in the direction of Freddie Barras and killed him? and;

2. When firing he intended either to kill or to cause some really serious injury? and;

If not, the Accused cannot be guilty of murder.

BUT if all sober and reasonable people would have realised that he was inevitably subjecting Freddie Barras to at least the risk of some physical, albeit not serious, harm - consider manslaughter.

3. When firing he acted unlawfully in that:

i. he honestly believed or may have honestly believed that it was necessary to defend himself; and

ii. taking the circumstances as the Accused believed them to be, the amount of force used was reasonable.

If the Accused was or may have been acting in reasonable self-defence the Accused is not to be found guilty of anything.

If the Accused did not act in self-defence and intended either to kill or to cause really serious injury he is guilty of murder.

If he did not act in self-defence and did not have either of the above intentions but all sober and reasonable people would have realised that he was subjecting Freddie Barras to at least the risk of some physical, albeit not serious harm, he is guilty of manslaughter.

COUNT 2: Am I sure:

1. that the Accused intended to murder i.e. unlawfully to kill Brendon Fearon? and;

2. that with that intention he did something more than mere preparation for committing the offence?

If the Accused was or may have been acting in reasonable self-defence the Accused is to be found Not Guilty.

If both are proved then 'Guilty' of attempted murder.

COUNT 3:   Wounding with intent, an alternative to Count 2;
Am I sure:

1. that the Accused wounded Brendon Fearon?

2. that when doing so he intended to cause Brendon Fearon some really serious injury?

If the Accused was or may have been acting in reasonable self-defence the Accused is to be found Not Guilty.
If both 1 and 2 are proved and the Accused was not acting in reasonable self-defence the Accused was guilty as charged.
If only 1 is proved and the Accused was not acting in reasonable self-defence the Accused was guilty of unlawful wounding.

COUNT 4: Am I sure:

1. that the Accused had in his possession a firearm and ammunition - if so:

2. that at that time he intended by means thereof to endanger life.

If both 1 and 2 are proved and the Accused did not act in reasonable self-defence he is to be found 'Guilty'.

If the Accused was or may have been acting in reasonable self-defence he is to be found 'Not Guilty'.

This 'flowchart' was meant to assist the jurors – do you think that it did? The other vital point I wish to make about this is please refer back to Count 3.

Notice how it was worded: "Wounding with intent an alternative to Count 2" As we have seen previously, the prosecution were going to 'get' Tony Martin one way or another – he was either guilty of the attempted murder of Brendon Fearon or, if they couldn't get that one to stick, then he would be found guilty of 'wounding with intent'. Between a rock and a hard place. Catch 22 for the Accused.

But note the precise wording: Count 3 was *an alternative* to Count 2, not an *additional* count. This becomes incredibly important in these proceedings very shortly.

Jury verdicts

Part 16: jury verdicts

Wed
19 APR
2000
12.29 pm
385

trial day 8

We now come to the jury's verdicts. As we know, Tony Martin was facing four main counts:

Count 1 – the murder of Fred Barras

Count 2 – the attempted murder of Brendon Fearon

Count 3 – wounding with intent of Fearon

Count 4 – possession of a firearm with intent to endanger life.

He had already pleaded guilty to Count 5: the possession of the shotgun without a valid certificate in place. However, the jury never got to hear about the decade-long saga of the farmer and various chief constables of Norfolk wasting public money on attempting to revoke his certificates with no evidence in place to support their unlawful actions against him.

Mere words on the page cannot, of course, replicate the intense anticipation that existed in the courtroom at this time and, indeed, in the hearts and minds of the Great British Public throughout the land as the jury entered court at 12:29pm to deliver their verdicts:

CLERK: Would the jury foreman please stand. Would the defendant please stand.

Mr Foreman, would you answer my first question simply yes, or no. Has the jury reached any verdicts upon which you are all agreed?

FOREMAN: Yes.

CLERK: Have you reached a verdict upon which you are all agreed in respect of Count 1?

FOREMAN: No.

CLERK: Have you reached a verdict upon which you are all agreed in respect of Count 2?

FOREMAN: Yes.

CLERK: On Count 2, do you find the defendant, Anthony Martin, guilty or not guilty of attempted murder?

FOREMAN: Not guilty.

CLERK:	Not guilty?
FOREMAN:	Yes.
CLERK:	Is that the verdict of you all?
FOREMAN:	Yes.
CLERK:	Have you reached a verdict upon which you are all agreed in respect of Count 3?
FOREMAN:	Yes.
CLERK:	On Count 3, do you find the defendant, Anthony Martin, guilty or not guilty of wounding with intent?
FOREMAN:	I thought Count 3 was an alternative to Count 2.
JUDGE:	No, it is not. In fact, Count 3 is wounding with intent. I think if you are not too sure about that, the best thing is ...
FOREMAN:	Well, in that case the answer is, no, we have not reached a verdict.
JUDGE:	No, that is fine.
CLERK:	Have you reached a verdict upon which you are all agreed in respect of Count 4?
FOREMAN:	Yes.
CLERK:	On Count 4, do you find the defendant, Anthony Martin, guilty or not guilty of possessing a firearm and ammunition with intent to endanger life?
FOREMAN:	Not guilty.
CLERK:	Not guilty. Is that the verdict of you all?
FOREMAN:	It is.
CLERK:	Thank you. You may sit down. The defendant may sit.
JUDGE:	Members of the jury, the time has now come when I can accept the majority verdicts. I must tell you what that means. It is a verdict with which at least ten of you agree. I must ask you to retire again please. Consider the evidence, do your best to achieve a unanimous verdict, but if you cannot, then I will accept a majority verdict. Thank you.

The jury retires again

As the jury retired again at 12:31pm, the farmer from Emneth was off to a flying start: not guilty of the attempted murder of Fearon and not guilty of possessing a firearm with intent to endanger life.

Being not guilty of the attempted murder of Fearon would naturally lead most people to believe that it must follow that he would be found not guilty of the murder of Barras.

And the jury felt that the reason the farmer possessed a shotgun and ammunition was not to endanger human life. So far, so good. But we've been in this position before throughout this book, so stand by for either a complete shock or just another example of complete theatrical nonsense, depending on your point of view as the jury return with the rest of their verdicts at 3:26pm.

The jury returns

CLERK: My Lord, the jury have been in retirement for nine hours thirty six minutes. Would the jury foreman please stand. Would the defendant please stand. Mr Foreman, will you answer my first question simply yes, or no. On the remaining Counts on the indictment, has the Jury reached verdicts on which at least ten of you are agreed?

FOREMAN: Yes.

CLERK: On Count 1, do you find the defendant, Anthony Martin, guilty or not guilty of murder?

FOREMAN: Guilty.

CLERK: Guilty. Is that the verdict of you all, or by a majority?

FOREMAN: By a majority.

CLERK: By a majority?

FOREMAN: By a majority.

CLERK: How many agreed and how many dissented?

FOREMAN: Ten to two.

CLERK: Ten agreed and two dissented. On Count 3 have you reached a verdict upon which at least ten of you are agreed?

FOREMAN: We have.

CLERK: Do you find the defendant, Anthony Martin, guilty or not guilty of wounding with intent?

FOREMAN: Guilty.

CLERK: Guilty. Is that the verdict of you all or by a majority?

FOREMAN: By a majority.

CLERK: How many agreed and how many dissented?

FOREMAN: Ten to two.

CLERK: Ten agreed and two dissented. Thank you very much. You may sit down. The defendant may sit.

Having sat through the entire trial in which the judge kept saying that Count 3 was *an alternative* to Count 2, and on the basis of that information the jury had gone away to consider their verdicts, when the foreman of the jury came to deliver the pronouncement of the entire twelve members, the judge then stated – in open court and on the record – that Count 3 was not, after all, an alternative count to Count 2, but in effect *an additional one*.

Confusion in the jury

Clearly, there was some considerable confusion in the minds of the jurors. It appears that they believed that they thought they had to choose between two alternatives: Count 2 or Count 3.

They had already delivered their verdict on Count 2 – the farmer was 'Not Guilty' of the attempted murder of Brendon Fearon (which was just as well since he said he had been shot on the track leading to the house). It appears that they discounted any consideration of Count 3 because they had already dealt with Count 2. When asked by the Clerk of the Court whether the jury had reached a verdict on Count 3, the Foreman said that they had – and when asked what it was, the Foreman then showed confusion. It would seem that they had decided that Tony was not guilty of wounding with intent and had thus gone on to consider Count 2 – attempted murder, of which they found him not guilty. Which makes the guilty verdict of wounding with intent extremely mysterious and surely against the very notion of Justice.

Once this confusion had been made clear by the foreman – very bravely and rightly in my opinion – then I suggest that the trial judge ought to have stopped the trial there and then and it would have been up to the CPS whether they would go for a re-trial. But if we forget all the other evidence that I have shown that Tony Martin did not receive a fair trial, on this point alone he surely did not.

Had I been a juror, I would have protested. Ok, they might have removed me from the court (I wouldn't have been disruptive, just made my point) but then that would have messed up their plans because the jury would have no longer been the twelve (though the legal engineers would have found a way round that.)

I have often wondered – once I became aware of this – what impact Judge Owen's comments would have had on the jurors. Did they retire once again to the jury room in utter dejection? Did they retire with even more confusion? Did some of them 'give up' and allow themselves to be directed by the more forceful characters in the jury room?

Surely the proper remedy would have been to call a mistrial and then, as I say, it would have been up to the Crown to decide whether it would proceed with a new trial.

But Easter was upon the country (Good Friday was on 21 April 2000) and the rushed trial meant that Tony Martin could be locked away while the nation was otherwise distracted and the law courts were shut down until the new term.

These dates are not mere chance: they are part of the legal engineering. I suggest that this had been programmed far in advance by the Privy Council and the Home Office. I have no doubt they would disagree.

Let's consider the fact that the jury unanimously acquitted Tony Martin of the attempted murder of Fearon. He was also unanimously acquitted of possessing a firearm with intent to endanger life. Yet, after a period of three more hours, the jury convicted the farmer of murder by a majority of 10 to 2 and of wounding with intent, also by the same majority. These verdicts simply do not make sense. It is difficult to understand how a jury could acquit him of possessing a firearm with intent to endanger life and then find him guilty of murder and wounding with intent. I believe that the trial should have ended at the point it became clear that there was considerable confusion in the minds of the jury over counts 2 and 3.

The verdicts were not delivered simultaneously but instead hours apart, and the earlier pronouncements were delivered with all twelve in agreement whereas the later guilty verdicts were delivered with two jurors being in dissent.

I argue that these verdicts – and the manner of their delivery – were procedurally flawed. In my view, there was clearly a mistrial and there ought to have been a judicial review.

One last point I'd ask you to consider: if a jury is made up of twelve *random* people who allegedly do not know one another, how can we ever be sure that one or two (or more) members of the jury are not, in fact, police officers or Crown prosecutors or their like?

Thur 20 APR 2000 386

reaction to the verdicts
As you might imagine, the reaction to the 'Guilty' verdict was incredibly varied and often dependent on the role of the person giving his or her opinion or their political persuasion:

On 20 April 2000, *The Daily Telegraph* reported the following:

"At 6:52am on 21 August 1999, police carried out an initial search of Martin's farm. At 10am, a more comprehensive search was planned but the presence of Martin's three large dogs, apparently released by the farmer after the shootings, *kept the police at bay*.[484]

---

[484] Author's emphasis. This is nothing but nonsense. Indeed, the Norfolk Constabulary's own CAD report stated that at 12:25pm on 21 August 1999, acting DI Sharman requested a dog warden attend. Why had this simple request not been achieved hours earlier?

After Mrs Lilley's son-in-law had rounded up the animals, a search started and, at 2:40pm, 17 hours after the shooting, the body of Barras was found in the undergrowth at the rear of the house. *For the first time*,[485] the police realised they were not just dealing with the wounding of one burglar, but the fatal shooting of another.

Barras had died directly of the shotgun injuries, said a senior detective. "He would have died within minutes and it is at least reassuring for us to know that he didn't die as a result of the delays."[486]

DCI Martin Wright, who led the murder investigation, said that he derived no personal satisfaction from Martin's conviction and said the case had been "a tragedy" for all involved.

He added: "The lesson this sends to the public is that they should not take the law into their own hands. It is up to the police and criminal justice system to progress these things.[487]

The one problem with Mr Martin was that he was clearly a repeat victim of crime but we rarely heard from him."[488]

Can you believe that nonsense? "We rarely heard from him." As we have seen, Rodney Gooderson confirmed that there had been numerous complaints made by Tony to the police dating back as far as the early 1980s. Indeed, other constables mentioned how he continuously complained about the lack of police. (See also entry **345** and the witness statement of Gillian Butters.)

Three rottweilers kept the police at bay? Would this be the same dogs that burglar Christopher Webster said he'd been stroking in between loading antique furniture from Bleak House into a van in May 1999?

Tony tells me he only ever had three rottweilers, so how on earth did a burglar get to stroke them whilst, according to the police, the dogs "delayed their search." You couldn't make it up, except they were making it up every time they spoke to the press and the press duly did as it was told and published lies: "Early in life I had noticed that no event is ever correctly reported in a newspaper," wrote Orwell.

And what's this nonsense about the police learning for the first time that

---

[485] Author's emphasis. This is untrue based on the police's own evidence.

[486] Author's emphasis: this is a lie. DCI Martin Wright was speaking and, as the officer in charge of the investigation, he must have known it to be a lie. He had full access to the three autopsy reports which showed, as we have seen, that Barras did not die within two minutes of being shot and that he could have been saved.

[487] Author's emphasis – herein lies the real reason for the State's persecution of political prisoner Tony Martin: do not take the law into your own hands (however inept, inefficient, unprofessional or corrupt the police are).

[488] Author's emphasis: clearly another lie as the police statements bore out. Compare this ridiculous claim with the PC Rodney Gooderson report [see entry **18**].

there were three burglars? I remind you of Jacqueline Leet's 999 call at 10:53pm in which she mentioned three men. And the constabulary's own CAD report showed that at 11:11pm, "there may be other injured parties in the orchard".

And can you believe this nonsense: "He would have died within minutes and it is at least reassuring for us to know that he didn't die as a result of the delays"? We know – and the police knew - the reality was very different. How do they live with themselves? Much was made at trial of Tony Martin supposedly having told lies about his position on the stairs and Brendon Fearon having lied about breaking into the house to get away from dogs and Darren Bark lying to police about driving around looking for a mate who'd broken down. And yet some of the biggest liars of all were wearing uniforms and suits and wigs and gowns.

But why do we let them get away with it? Why don't we hold them far more accountable? Shades of Hillsborough.

From research, DCI Wright became a Superintendent not long after this "successful" murder investigation. Chomsky again: "those who have power are not going to reward people who question that power. The world does not reward honesty and independence, it rewards obedience and service."[489]

CORRUPTION ALERT — *Daylight police search allegedly failed to find body of Barras*

The Daily Telegraph's claim that the "police carried out an initial search" at 6:52am required further investigation and so I turned to the Norfolk Constabulary CAD report. There was an entry timed at 06:52:07 which stated that Inspector James had been contacted regarding a POLSA search, that a police sergeant and 6 officers were to take part and that Inspector James would contact acting DI Sharman "for details".

So, let's get this right – at almost 7am at least seven police officers are undertaking a search in broad daylight and not one of them finds Barras lying in bushes at the back of Bleak House with his legs sticking out with white trainers on? How on earth do you miss that? The answer, of course, is that you do not. Of course they found Barras. If you turn back to the entry dated 27 September 1999, you will see how Inspector James provided a statement which claimed that his only role in the case had been to place paperwork from POLSA Inspector Paul Rush into the office filing cabinet [see entry **283**]. Rush had failed to state in his witness statement at what time he attended Bleak House – and for good reason: to cover up, I suggest, the discovery of the still-warm body of Barras much earlier than officially claimed.

---

[489] Chomsky, op. cit. p. 212.

You will also recall how acting DI Sharman claimed that he had gone to Bleak House with Inspector Rush at 11:30am, that he had driven only to the front of the house, that he had not entered the house and that he returned to King's Lynn police station at 1:15pm. [See entry **307**].

On the same day (20 April 2000), *The Independent* reported the following:

"Yesterday Martin's mother, Hilary, 86,[490] said: "I am devastated, shocked and upset. Because of this verdict decent people will not be able to sleep at night. He was merely defending himself against people who were thieves and vagabonds.""

The Scotsman reported Tony's mother as saying:

"I am horrified at the way this country is leaning towards the criminals. What has my son done apart from defend himself? It's definitely a miscarriage of justice,"

and, rather poignantly, she added:

"I have lost my son at the end of my life. I will probably never see him again. I'm very sorry that it happened, but it was not my son's fault. My son should not have been convicted, he is not a murderer. He should not have been put in that position. Put yourself in that position, what would you have done?"

The Times carried these heart-felt comments:

"Tony was merely defending himself against evil people. If he had not acted as he did they would have kicked his head in. He was going to defend himself. And he panicked. I am shocked and devastated. My lovely young man will not be able to live caged up in prison."

Richard Portham, friend and near-neighbour, said: "He has been sent to prison for a crime committed in terror. The jury's decision will have devastating consequences for the safety of people in their own homes."

Mr Portham's point of view was echoed by many people throughout the land. He told police that Tony was "quite tolerant towards travellers."

It became public knowledge during his trial that Tony had had several "run-ins" with the police, not because he was a criminal, but because he felt they were not listening to him or to the fact that he, and dozens like him on isolated farms,

---

[490] Tony has told me on several occasions that his mother was born in 1918 and so she would have been 82 in the year 2000. Rodney Gooderson had recorded her date of birth as being in 1908, in which case she would have been 92. She died on 18 June 2011 and a plaque in Elm churchyard states her age as 93.

had been the victims of burglaries and farm thefts by itinerant groups.

> **❝** I am not against gypsies or travellers in themselves, but I am dead against people who spoil other people's lives."

Now let's see what Peter Tidey, Chief Crown Prosecutor for Norfolk said after the verdicts had been delivered:

"The law allows for reasonable force in defending yourself ... but it was clear when we reviewed the evidence in this case that Martin had gone far beyond the amount of force which the ordinary person would consider to be reasonable."

Well, he would say that wouldn't he? He's the Chief Prosecutor for Norfolk. He's hardly likely to say, "Oops, I wish we hadn't taken Tony Martin to court on reflection," is he? Reviewed the evidence? What evidence? Mr Tidey conveniently failed to mention the CPS suppressing disclosure, failing to tell the jury that Barras did not die directly from the gunshot wound, or that the entire police investigation against Tony had been biased from the start. No, no mention of that. And no mention, of course, of the helicopter(s). Or of Fearon claiming to have been shot *on the track* to Bleak House.

"Actions such as that taken by Tony Martin cannot be tolerated in a civilised society. When people break the law, it is for the law to punish them, not for individuals to take the law into their own hands, whether acting out of revenge or their own individual system of justice."

At this stage – and with all what you now know – do you need to ask what about the actions taken by corrupt State officials being tolerated in a civilised society?

Now let's look at the trial judge. He'd presided over this nonsense, so you can probably guess which side of the fence he's on:

> "It seems to me that this case does serve as a dire warning to all burglars. The law is that every citizen is entitled to use reasonable force to prevent crime. The householder in his own home may think he is being reasonable but he may not be reasonable and that can have tragic consequences."

Are you staggered by the level of arrogance shown by the police, the CPS and the trial judge – all of whom knew before they went to trial that Barras did not die directly from a gunshot wound and that, but for the police, he would not have died at all?

And we let them get away with it because we don't complain. Except Tony Martin had the guts to complain. You might be adding, "Yeah and look what they did to him!" but if enough of us complained and enough of us demanded better services, honest services, professional and incorruptible services, they'd have to be accountable. I ask you to think about it.

Barras's mother, Ellen, 45, his father, Fred, and his five sisters issued a prepared statement in which they acknowledged that he had 29 convictions:

"Please remember he was just 16 and the baby of our family. We are all devastated by his loss. As Fred's family, we cannot and do not condone his actions. We are aware that he had failings and would have expected him to be dealt with and punished in the criminal justice system. He was not given that chance. Fred was fun-loving and always happy with no mean streak. He was a devoted and loving son and brother. The outcome of this trial cannot bring him back and our loss has torn our lives apart."

I have, of course, every sympathy for the Barras family, and as I told Brendon Fearon on the phone and in writing, I am on nobody's side except Truth and Justice, but if I had to choose any side at all, it would be Fred's. He need not have died, as we have seen, and for almost 20 years since the shooting, his family have lived a lie. A direct echo of Hillsborough.

I posted a letter through Mrs Barras's door on 12 September 2016 asking her to contact me. Sadly, I didn't hear from her, but this may have been because I am constantly held under surveillance and all forms of my communications are unlawfully interfered with. Whilst I understand Mrs Barras's pain, I do hope that she will one day learn the Truth that her son need not have died, and that, whilst Tony Martin fired his gun, he did not murder him.

I have great sadness and great anger with regard to the Barras family. I'd better explain the apparent contradiction. My sadness is at the death of Fred – as we have seen, he ought not to have died. I lost a brother who died aged 21 – the unlived life, the stark termination of a life, the flame prematurely extinguished can bring unbearable pain. Oh yes, I understand the Barras family's pain.

But my anger is against Norfolk Constabulary who lied to the Barras family – who withheld evidence from them and who allowed them to believe that farmer Tony Martin was responsible for Fred's death. Losing a son and brother is one thing – but being deceived by the very agencies of State who are supposed to be there to protect you, is quite another, shameful action. I hope that the Barras family sues the Constabulary. Of course, it won't bring their Fred back, but they could have their day in court and demand a public apology. They deserve nothing less in my opinion.

After the trial and prison

Part 17: after the trial & prison

Thur 20 APR 2000 387

press reaction

The Sun headline screamed "JURY WAS TERRIFIED" and ran a story that the jury had been intimidated by gypsy friends of Fred Barras and also that Britain was in uproar over the jailed farmer. It was alleged that a woman had called the Broadland FM radio station to say that she had been one of the jurors and that they had to find the farmer guilty after being threatened.

Tony's lawyers were said to have referred the claim to the police and the CPS which, in my view, is similar to a woman being raped, reporting it to the police and being raped for a second time by the police officer.

Nick Makin emphasised that the alleged intimidation of the jury, if proved, would form only part of any appeal. Tony's defence team would also claim that in his summing-up Judge Owen misdirected the jury and failed to explain that there can be a defence in protecting property as well as oneself. Another ground was understood to be that the judge did not address the jury on a condition known as 'quasi autism' in which the farmer may have spontaneously fired the gun as a reflex action when the torch was shone in his face. Quasi autism is a term used to describe autistic-like difficulties following very severe social deprivation in the first year of life. I do not subscribe to the view that Tony suffered from this condition and nor do I believe it is a logical reason to explain why he pulled the trigger upon having a torch shone in his face by intruders who had smashed their way into his remote home at night.

There was huge reaction from all corners of Britain after the verdict. A friend of Tony's, businessman Malcolm Starr – who declined to be interviewed for this book – said, "I am absolutely devastated by this verdict and to be quite honest, I think the country is genuinely staggered."

Mary Dolan, a grandmother of Fred Barras said, "The farmer should be punished because you can't just shoot people like that, but I never wanted him to get life – I didn't want to see another life destroyed." Eminently sensible, but too late – Tony Martin's life was destroyed from the moment he felt forced to pull the trigger. However, it would seem that Mrs Dolan possessed far more emotional intelligence than those prosecuting Tony.

Fearon's father, Joe, 68, also had some sympathy for the farmer: "He was in his own place. They should not have been there and he was scared. But all he had to do was fire a warning shot and they would have run off."

Perhaps the strangest comment came from the Chief Constable of Norfolk, Kenneth Williams who shared the same name as the famous Carry On film star.

There was comedy of its own as the delusional and out-of-touch Chief Constable said, "Victims of burglary should scream for help, shout and make a lot of noise." Fat lot of good it would have done Tony Martin – the nearest house was over a quarter of a mile away.

Within a week of the trial verdict, Mr Williams was calling for "100 more officers" and he said that suggestions that the force was complacent and inept or did not care were "wounding and grossly offensive." [Author's note: I wonder what his response would have been in respect of my proof of police corruption – which the Chief Constable ought to have known about.]

According to the *Eastern Daily Press*, Mr Williams admitted that there had been a barrage of criticism and that switchboard operators had been subjected to abuse from "scores of irate callers." The Chief Constable added: "Despite allegations of incompetence over the last seven years, house burglaries have halved and crime has reduced from 66,000 to 57,000." If, as Rodney Gooderson told us, many burglaries were redefined as "criminal damage" then the figures would be massaged to fall and the reduction of some 9,000 crimes in seven years does not mean that there was less crime but rather that more people were no longer reporting crimes because they felt, like Tony Martin, that it was simply a waste of time. And history shows that it was.

The Conservative leader, William Hague, waded into the debate: "The Martin case has lit a touch paper that has led to an explosion of anger and resentment among millions of law-abiding British people who no longer feel the State is on their side." He was right – it wasn't. And still isn't.

Former Master of the Rolls, Lord Donaldson, backed calls for an overhaul of the law on self-defence, saying: "There is something seriously wrong with a law which compels a judge to pass a sentence of life imprisonment for murder regardless of all the mitigating circumstances." But there was nothing compelling Judge Owen to proceed with a corrupt trial. He had a copy of all of the evidence that I have provided you with.

Fri
21 APR
2000
388

Lynn News – "guarding ruin cost best part of £400,000"
Page 4 was devoted to the "Murder at Bleak House" under the headline "Guarding ruin cost best part of £400,000" by Tim Rose. The entire page, in my view, bore little relation to reality and was nothing more than Norfolk Constabulary propaganda, perpetuating disinformation and lie upon lie:

"Operational costs involved in the Tony Martin murder investigation have run into more than £400,000. And by far the greatest proportion of those costs have been run up by the round-the-clock protection and surveillance needed for Bleak

House, Mr Martin's home.[491]

DCI Martin Wright said that the protection was necessary because, for perhaps the first time in English legal history, the entire crime scene was preserved as an exhibit for use as evidence by the Crown Prosecution Service.

Although unable to reveal exactly what the extent of that protection was for "operational reasons", DCI Wright said it had involved police officers being based at the location 24 hours a day from 20 August 1999, the date the inquiry began, with support from surveillance equipment and on-site police accommodation.[492]

Early into the trial, the twelve members of the jury were taken on a visit to Bleak House to view for themselves the sections of the building where the shootings had taken place.[493]

In the seven months since the shooting, the cost of securing the scene has amounted to £185,536,[494] while the actual inquiry, which at its height involved 32 officers[495] of all ranks up to DCI,[496] has cost £82,000.[497]

The remainder of the £414,000[498] bill for the Tony Martin case has been racked up by a variety of things such as the cost of forensic examinations[499] and the use of vehicles.

DCI Wright said that because this case was fairly clear cut, in that no manhunt was necessary unlike for the murder of Janice and Constance Sheridan,[500] the costs of the inquiry were quite low."

---

[491] Be under no illusion – the round-the-clock presence at Bleak House by the police was not for its protection: it was to protect the police from concerned family, friends and supporters of the farmer so that they wouldn't gain entry and learn about the lack of blood spatter and gunshot pellets and see that all the furniture and other items had been removed from the breakfast room.

[492] If it had been true that the police had been at Bleak House on a 24x7 basis from 20 August 1999, why did they not find the body of Barras much sooner?

[493] That is if we ignore Fearon's claims that he and Barras had been shot outside.

[494] Approximately £290,000 in 2018.

[495] I do not accept this number – from the files that I have seen, around a dozen of this number made statements to the effect that they *hadn't* in fact been to Bleak House at all on the night of the shooting, despite official records showing they had attended.

[496] I do not accept this statement. It has been designed to mislead and throw us off the scent that higher-ranking police officers were involved in the death of Barras and its cover-up but, in the event of the case going pear-shaped, then only the DCI would be expendable. See entries **112**, **139**, **168**, **285**, all of which refer to Superintendents being involved in the case.

[497] Approximately £130,000 in 2018.

[498] Approximately £640,000 in 2018.

[499] The newspaper report failed to mention that none of these forensic reports made their way into court according to the official exhibit list.

[500] I have covered the murder of these two women in Part 4.

That was the first part of the article. I'll now pick it apart to separate the delusional police narrative from reality. I reserve my criticism of Mr Rose although, since he had taken the police propaganda fed to him by the Norfolk Constabulary as genuine facts, I do cast doubt upon his integrity for not investigating the drivel served up to him.

I could not help wondering why, with Norfolk Constabulary suddenly throwing taxpayers' money around like confetti (in a public relations exercise, not through proper policing), they hadn't actually supplied a local village bobby in Emneth Hungate because it would have been far more cost effective in the long run. If the average wage for a constable was £20,000 in 1999, it doesn't take a genius to work out how many officers could have been employed for £400,000. And Fred Barras may well have been alive today. So surely this case highlighted the issue of deployment of officers and budgetary decisions. If the constabulary could suddenly spend almost half a million pounds on creating a murder inquiry, why didn't it spend some of that money on *preventing* such incidents, wherever possible?

DCI Wright claimed that the entire house was "preserved as a crime scene" – if that were the case, why did the police allow members of the public into it? Why did DS Eglen enter the house through the alleged exit window? Why wasn't the staircase swabbed for gunshot residue *immediately after* Tony fired his shotgun?

Mr Rose's article stated that the jury had been taken to Bleak House during the trial, but, as I pointed out in the relevant entry [**380**], the jury were taken there during daylight and the breakfast room had been cleared of its furniture and other items and so it gave them a completely false impression.

We now come to the second of three articles on page 4 – this one was entitled "Gruesome discovery elevated shooting inquiry to murder investigation" – with a sub-heading entitled "Fred lay dead in the overgrown garden, but all involved stayed silent":

"Police had no knowledge that Fred Barras existed when they were called to Tony Martin's home following the shootings that Friday night.[501]

Even wounded Brendan[502] Fearon, who had heard Barras's dying words,[503] did not reveal to police that he had an accomplice, insisting instead that he was out late at night looking for work.

---

[501] I remind the reader of the CAD report which stated that "There may be other injured parties in the orchard and evidence relating to the injuries sustained by the male [Fearon]" as early as 11:11pm on 20 August 1999 and "A second male has arrived at [Foreman's Bungalow] looking for 'two mates' who he dropped off earlier" at 11:34pm on the same night. Since DCI Wright had led the murder 'investigation', he had full access to this CAD report.

The alarm was raised by neighbours of Mr Martin in Foreman's Bungalow. It was there, about half a mile away across a field from Bleak House, that Brendon Fearon had crawled after being severely wounded in both legs when he was blasted by Mr Martin's pump-action shotgun.

Police and an ambulance arrived at the bungalow shortly before 11pm, and Mr Fearon was taken under police guard to the QE Hospital in King's Lynn.

Meanwhile, police inquiries began under the control of Detective Inspector Matt Sharman, who had been the senior detective on call.

It soon emerged that Mr Martin had visited the same neighbour following the shooting, but before Mr Fearon was discovered, and had talked to the neighbour about what he had done."

I'll pause the article at this point – note the following: (i) that neighbour Paul Leet was not named, nor his wife, Jacqueline, (ii) that there was no mention that Tony had allegedly told Paul Leet about "three burglars", and (iii) that there was no mention of the police helicopter. All constabularies have their own Press Offices and journalists working for them. This is where the fabricated press reports which you read in your "independent" daily or local newspapers get their information from. Reporters, like the police, rarely investigate anymore.

We now return to the article, with the sub-heading "Burglar remained tight-lipped":

"And shortly before 5am, the third burglar, Mr Darren Bark, *returned to the scene* and was arrested." [Author's emphasis]

I pause the article again – this contradicts the police 'evidence' which claimed that Bark was at the scene throughout the night and that he was interviewed at Terrington St John police station at 4:50am. It was, therefore, impossible that he could have "returned to the scene" at 5am because he was firmly ensconced in the police station. Or so we were led to believe.

"He also, at no point, revealed to police that 16-year-old Fred Barras had been involved.

As a result of their inquiries, police tracked Mr Martin to the Marmion House Hotel in Wisbech, where he had checked himself in following the shooting. Officers attended and arrested Mr Martin at 6:09am on Saturday 21 August.

At that time Mr Martin was arrested on suspicion of the attempted murder of Brendon Fearon. "We had no knowledge that Fred Barras even existed," said DCI Wright, who was in overall charge of the entire investigation.

---

[502] Notice the spelling of Brendon Fearon's name. One would have thought that the journalist would have checked the correct spelling. When I spoke with Mr Fearon about the correct spelling of his name, he told me "Brendon with an 'o' – 'o' for orange."

[503] Mr Fearon has never claimed to have heard Fred's "dying last words" – in fact he stated that when he last saw Fred the teenager was still alive.

Mr Fearon had not told them about his accomplice, and when Mr Martin was first interviewed after his arrest, he had made no mention of Mr Barras either. Detectives believed they were simply investigating Mr Fearon's shooting.

Shortly before 7am, a call was made for a police search team to prepare to conduct a standard search of the crime scene at Bleak House, as would be done for any serious crime.

The search was delayed, however, on the discovery of Mr Martin's large rottweiler guard dogs in the gardens, and a dog warden was requested to catch them.[504]

Finally, at 2:40pm, the search of the heavily overgrown location began and, almost immediately afterwards, an officer discovered the body of Mr Barras lying outside the house.[505]

With it clear that it was now a murder investigation, DCI Martin Wright was called out.

A team of forensic experts, including up to 12 people led by a detective inspector, carried out a meticulous search of the entire scene, and the field which Brendon Fearon had crawled across, during the course of the next few weeks to gather evidence for the trial.

From day one, 32 officers were involved in the investigation, but by the end of the year that number had been reduced to half a dozen people working on the case part-time."

I'll pause again to comment on that part of the article.

It is, of course, untrue that the police did not know of the existence of Fred Barras. According his statement, PC Knight – who claimed to have stopped the car in Balderton, just outside of Newark – commented that he had seen Barras in the company of Bark and Fearon. Furthermore, Paul and Jacqueline Leet had told the police that Tony had been round and said he'd been visited by "three burglars". Despite the fact that Tony did not know how many intruders were in his house that night, the fact remains that *on their own evidence* the police had been told of the existence of three people.

Police did not "track" Tony down to the Marmion House Hotel – it was common knowledge that he spent a lot of his time there, but note how the

---

[504] As early as 23 August 1999, Tony had described his dogs to the police in interview in this way: "I think that anybody who gets to know my dogs knows that really they're useless, they're bowsee wowsers." The fact that the dogs were relatively harmless in spite of their imposing size was corroborated by others, including neighbours Eileen Sutton and Gillian Samuels and self-confessed burglar Christopher Webster. That DCI Wright is claiming that they held up the search for Barras is palpable nonsense and the officer should be ashamed of himself for lying to the public.

[505] Notice that this fabricated piece of fiction failed to say just how close to the house Fred Barras was found.

police always try to put a positive spin on any information which makes a gullible public believe that they are doing a grand job.

Notice how the police claimed that Tony Martin had failed to tell them about the existence of Barras – this was impossible since Tony wasn't aware that he had hit anybody when he fired his shotgun and that was because he hadn't.

I do not subscribe to the view that Fearon or Bark (or whoever was the driver) did not tell the police about Barras. Additionally, as we have seen, PC Gotts said in his statement: "I also was aware that it was possible the injured man was an intruder at the premises and *had accomplices with him who may also have been injured.*" So, just why wasn't Barras allegedly found until 2:32pm?

And what was this nonsense about the search being delayed because of Tony's dogs? We have already seen how Roger Putterill had been to the house with a bag of bones at around 8am and offered to round up the dogs *and was turned away by the police.*

And what of the request for a dog warden? According to his statement PC Claxton had attended at midnight and *was not deployed.* According to the statements of other officers he *was* deployed. Whom to believe?

And yet Bruno – one of Tony's dogs – had taken Roger Putterill and two police officers to the rear of the house where, as we have seen, the body of Barras was "discovered".

Notice the terminology used around the discovery of the body of Barras – "the search of the heavily overgrown location". As we know, Barras's legs were sticking out of a bush and he had been wearing white trainers. How is it possible that 32 officers allegedly missed this?

Notice how the report claimed that "up to 12 forensic experts" (all unnamed) led by an unnamed detective inspector carried out a "meticulous search of the entire scene" – and yet apparently waited 5 days before swabbing the staircase.

And notice how there was no mention of the helicopter(s) which went up following the gunshots.

I now continue with the article, headed "House and grounds sealed off":

"The house was sealed off, as was the area where the body was found and all the immediate surroundings up to about 30 metres away from the house, and it has remained under police protection since.

In the days immediately following the shooting, suggestions were made that Barras may have suffered a prolonged, agonising death as he bled from his wounds during the course of the night. These have been refuted by the police.

DCI Wright said: "The pathologist thinks that Fred Barras died directly as a result of the shotgun injuries, and that he would have died very quickly – within minutes." DCI Wright has been selective – he failed to mention which pathologist of the three who examined the body actually said this.

At the opening of an inquest into his death, it was revealed that the post-mortem showed that Mr Barras had been shot in the back."

DCI Wright must have lied here. As the chief investigating officer, it is incomprehensible that Wright did not know that there had been three separate reports from three different pathologists and yet he made mention only of the Dr Heath report because it had been deliberately authored to support the corrupt police version of events.

The previously hidden evidence which I have reproduced here leads us to conclude that Barras did suffer a long and agonising death, that his whereabouts were always known to certain police officers *and that he was allowed to die.*

The third part of the article entitled "Gun law is not the answer to rural crime", contained a photograph of the ubiquitous firearms officer, Mr Bone:

"Residents in remote rural areas should work with the police to solve the problems with crime, not adopt 'gun law'.

That is the feeling of Tony Bone, Farmwatch coordinator, who is working with South West Norfolk MP Gillian Shephard to secure £2.8 million Government cash for better rural policing.

Mr Bone said: "As far as I am concerned there are no winners in the Tony Martin case at all.

There will be people expressing the fear that an Englishman's home is no longer his castle and I would seek to reassure them that is not the case.

We should take notice of what the judge said about being able to use reasonable force in self-defence, but there is that very fine line about what is lawful.

I think the real issue is getting sufficient rural police and keeping them so public confidence can be restored.

We don't want gun law or vigilante groups because we can still work within the law.[506]

If a crime is reported and the police don't turn up then we will put a big complaint in.[507] That is the way forward – not to blast away anyone who comes to the front door.

We need to stop this tide of burglaries, and if we can work with the police to do this then that will make me very happy."

Mr Bone said the case also raised the issue of some criminals travelling vast distances to commit burglaries.

---

[506] Norfolk Constabulary had not operated within the rule of law during this entire 'investigation'.

[507] Most complaints to the police about a lack of a police investigation go themselves uninvestigated. Your taxes are not wisely spent.

"That is something we at Farmwatch are aware of and I would like to send the message to that part of the travelling community that if they wish to live within our society then they will have to change their ways."

Mrs Shephard said: "I intend to raise yet again with ministers the issue of resources for rural policing because Norfolk has lost 50 police officers since the last election and none have been replaced.

I intend to continue my fight, with the support of the Emneth and surrounding community, to get our rural needs recognised.

I am not part of the group that blames the police because I think they can only work with the resources they are given."

She said she would raise the issue in Parliament, and will also present a "huge" petition to the Home Office about rural policing.

Conservative parliamentary candidate for North West Norfolk, Henry Bellingham, has called for a change in the law so it states clearly what householders can do when confronted with criminals who have broken into their homes. He said: 'I personally feel the time has come to weight the law more in favour of the householder'."

The article continued under the sub-heading "Villains in prison":

"Prosecution witnesses Brendon Fearon and Darren Bark[508] are both currently serving jail terms for conspiring to burgle Bleak House.

The two men had admitted the charge and were jailed by Norwich Crown Court in January 2000. Mr Fearon, 29, received 3 years. Mr Bark, 33, also asked for seven other offences to be taken into consideration, including three burglaries, and was sentenced to 3½ years.

When they appeared for sentencing, Judge David Mellor heard that Mr Fearon, who received 196 pellets in his legs when Tony Martin shot him,[509] had suffered post-traumatic stress following the burglary in which fellow criminal Fred Barras was shot dead."

It would appear that Mr Bone had an issue with telling the truth. Lauded in the press as some kind of 'rural crime guru' – who just happened to own a business collating information on what prizes lay in store on which farms and in which houses – he also appeared in documentaries about the case. It would seem that he allowed his over-inflated ego to get in the way of truth and justice. Notice how he used the emotive phrase "not to blast away anyone who comes to the front door." That was a ridiculous thing to say. Bone knew that Fearon and Barras had not come to the front door and it is highly likely that he was made aware by his colleagues in uniform that Fearon had stated he had been shot 20-

---

[508] This is misinformation – Bark was never a prosecution witness. See later comments.
[509] As we have seen, the farmer didn't shoot anybody.

30 yards up a track. As Tony Martin repeatedly says to me, "The police are in a constant state of denial."

I could not help wondering just how much of the £2.8m of taxpayers' money (described in the article as 'government funding' – it isn't: it's your money and mine) found its way into the Farmwatch coffers. I haven't (yet) investigated that.

Despite Mr Bone claiming that the travelling fraternity ought to mend their ways if they wished to live amongst the rest of us, I have met a large number of people who were of the opinion that some rogue officers within the police (of all ranks) were actually aware of, and involved in, the thefts and burglaries. And it's not beyond firearms officers to misuse their weapons...

Notice how the article described Darren Bark as a 'prosecution witness'. He never went to the trial as we have seen. Technically he was a witness because he made a number of statements, but – as I have previously pointed out – he was clearly given protected status by not being called to court, either as a prosecution witness or, perhaps even more importantly, as a defence witness. There can be no doubt in the mind of any right-minded human being that Bark *ought* to have been called to court. Christopher Webster claimed that Bark's role was not that of a mere getaway driver (if that is even true), but the ring-leader and organiser of the intended burglary. According to Webster, Fearon and Barras were simply Bark's pawns.

Simon Barnes, in *The Times* of 21 April 2000 (p.5) wrote an interesting piece, saying that "the troubling thing is that Tony Martin seems to have been condemned because he is a deeply unpleasant man, rather than for his actual crime." He then called upon the legal profession to spell out just what it meant by the term 'reasonable force', adding "an invasion is not a reasonable situation."

In the same edition of the paper, highly-regarded barrister Francis Bennion wrote: "Before Parliament altered it, the common law would have acquitted Mr Martin. I quote from Blackstone: if any person attempts to break open a house in the night-time, and shall be killed in such an attempt, the slayer shall be acquitted and discharged. Blackstone added that burglary, or nocturnal housebreaking, had always been looked upon as a heinous offence: not only because of the abundant terror that it naturally carries with it, but also as it is a forcible invasion and disturbance of that right of habitation which every individual might acquire even in a state of nature. And the law of England has so particular and tender regard to the immunity of a man's house that it styles it his castle and will never suffer it to be violated with impunity. Nowadays the law's tender regard is for villains and burglars."

Mr Bennion sadly died on 28 January 2015, before I had an opportunity to interview him for this book. Described as an eccentric himself, he was a self-styled 'defender of the rule of law'. He had had more than 15 letters to *The Times* published. I have a feeling he would have loved to have gotten his teeth into the many human rights abuses suffered by Tony and me and my family.

Mrs Laurel Cooper, 71, of Rochester in Kent, summed up Tony's dilemma succinctly and somewhat pithily:

"Suppose I lived alone in rural Norfolk, where the police response time may be up to one and a half hours, and I hear several intruders in my house, probably intent on robbery with violence. What in my case would constitute 'reasonable force' in the eyes of the law? An appeal to their better natures? A rolling pin?"

Thankfully, there was a good deal of common sense from the *Sun*'s Richard Littlejohn, a former reporter on the *Wisbech Standard*. Under the headline of *Does anyone seriously believe this is justice?*, the outspoken Littlejohn wrote (page 11): "The jury probably felt they had little alternative but to find Tony Martin guilty of murder, given the way in which the evidence against him was presented. But the way they reached their verdicts on the other charges Martin faced was baffling. The prosecution and the police went out of their way to demonise Martin as a bloodthirsty eccentric."

And then he commented on what I consider to be the quintessential reason for the bringing of the case: "They had to make an example of him because what was really on trial in this case was the entire British criminal justice system." Littlejohn added that "they had to find him guilty of murder. They ticked the box marked 'no leniency'."

And then Littlejohn attacked the police in much the same way as Tony Martin had: "The law belongs as much to Tony Martin as it does to the Chief Constable of Norfolk. It is our law. We employ the police and the courts to protect us. We grant them certain powers and in exchange they are bound by a duty towards us. But when they fail to carry out their duty and that social contract breaks down, we should be entitled to defend ourselves and our property. The police and the lawyers think they own the law. That's why they painted Tony Martin as a mad vigilante.

Tony Martin is a political prisoner, a symbol of everything rotten about policing and criminal justice in modern Britain."

I could not have put it better myself.

HMP **Norwich**

Both the author and the subject of this book have been to Norwich Prison. In my case, this was because I reported child abuse in Lambeth in 2006 and was subsequently fitted up and wrongly accused of sexual misconduct (see my book *Framed!*). Thereafter the authorities took over every aspect of my life including depriving me of my career, separation from my beloved family, taking unlawful possession of my house and bringing six civil cases against me simultaneously, trying to run me out of money, withholding my teacher's pension and defaming me on the internet as a 'convicted sex offender'.

In Tony Martin's case he went to prison because his defence team had completely and fraudulently and knowingly mis-represented him at trial, because of an improper trial and because of a seriously flawed and biased police investigation. Like me, he had "upset the authorities" by calling things into question and trying to hold them to account.

I do not intend to devote much space to Tony Martin's time spent in prison because it adds little to the book's aim to expose what was a gross miscarriage of justice. However, it's necessary to glance at it as part of this historical record.

One of the very first things Tony did upon going to prison was to write to his mother. The letter was printed in full in the *Wisbech Standard* (28 April 2000) and I think it appropriate to reproduce it here:

> Dear Mother,
> I do not want you to worry – it will not do you any good. You must realise that there are terrible things happening to people every day, and all over the world.
>
> I know people are appalled out there and, in fact, the people who work in my new house (prison) are all very sad and surprised. I have never held high hopes in the eight months because to fall from there is a long drop.
>
> I did become very hopeful during the trial, especially what the judge said. But we'll never know why the jury came to the decision they have.
>
> They found me not guilty initially on some charges. They did not find me guilty unanimously, so ended up with a 10 to 2. I can't explain this as it would take too long and I may not fully understand it myself. Someone who knows may explain it to you. I feel Scrivener did his best and is a nice man,[510] but feel I should have said more in my own defence. Who knows? I am disappointed. I brought a teddy bear with me but they will not let me have it.
>
> It is a lovely time of the year and you must continue to enjoy Redmoor and realise you are most fortunate. I am a very happy man because I have found a safe house for my dogs, which I felt paramount, and did not want to let them down. I am happy they are in the best of hands.
>
> As I say, farmers are being murdered in Rhodesia, people are starving in Ethiopia, which is no different to Belsen considering we are able to feed them, especially with our over-production of food. I see a man in his early 30s, marriage has gone wrong, killed himself and his two children, so you see things are not so bad. I do feel for you as we all cannot believe what has happened. Events overtake.

---

[510] Although in many ways an astute man and generally a good judge of character, I have detected a worrying weakness in Tony's psyche – that he will see the best in well-spoken, well-dressed charlatans. He fails to see how they befriend him to take advantage of him.

I have had many letters from good people over the last eight months and know I will get another avalanche. We shall see. Letters do give great fortitude. I am sure you will meet many people who will talk about me in the future.

I do have some wonderful photographs of my dogs. I have always loved my dogs and ended up over-fond of Daniel, who has had a few problems in the kennels, but I feel he is now mending as he is in normal hands and well loved. I wonder if they miss me. Who knows? I suspect as long as they get plenty of attention they will take to anyone. I will finish now as I want to get this letter off to you as quickly as possible.

My best wishes to Aunt Rosemary and, of course, Aunt Joan my favourite aunt after Aunty Gladys. I did send a short letter and photograph to Nicky [Nicola Giddens] – I wonder if she got it.

My best wishes,

Your ever loving son, Tony."

Letters from the public

A common theme in many letters was that of ineffective and out of touch politicians, and this was echoed by Mr and Mrs Clayton, of Leeds. They wrote to Nick Makin expressing their "deep shock and total disbelief and sadness" at the verdicts.

They then expressed their view of the law: "Laws are made by people, for people: as such they must serve the needs of the people - the principal needs being protection and justice. If the law fails in these, as it appears to have done so for Mr Martin, it would seem that the current law exists only to serve its own purposes."

Their next paragraph was even more powerful:

"The law failed Mr Martin: it denied him both protection and justice. But the law-abiding people of this country give him unfailing support.

The facts and circumstances of this very tragic case must be re-examined and amendments made to the law where it is considered necessary. To ensure a law-abiding majority, the law must be seen to provide protection and justice.

Burglary of one's home is a terrifying experience, especially so if it occurs at night when one is sleeping. It casts a permanent dark shadow on a family's life. The violation is personal and violent, like rape: one never again feels secure."

And Mr and Mrs Clayton had no way of knowing just how accurate they were with their assessment. Tony has never lived at Bleak House since the shooting. I once asked him why:

> **❝** I was invaded. My sanctuary was invaded. I've had police traipsing all through it. The judge. The jury. Intruders. And I didn't invite a single bloody one of them into my home!
>
> I instinctively knew from the moment after I'd pulled the trigger that it was no longer my home."

And there were cards of all shapes and sizes. Mostly farming scenes, but some of teddy bears and some of art or a historical theme. And hundreds and hundreds of letters. Some typed. Many hand-written. Some people sent CDs (Alastair Morgan of Northampton on 27 April 2000 sent Beethoven's 6th pastoral symphony – a thoughtful gesture), others sent writing paper and envelopes.

People gave something of themselves because in their "lives of quiet desperation", in their lives of daily fear and state oppression, they'd found someone who finally stood tall against crime, against the lack of police, against the government cutbacks and who was prepared to deal with a situation as he saw it at the time.

I've saved one letter to last. Although all the other letters I've mentioned (and hundreds I sadly had no space for) were relevant and supportive, I think this one touches a note we've not really seen before:

"The verdict sent me down into a spiral of sadness from which I am trying to climb back. It's as if a huge weight has descended upon my heart, unutterably sad…"

That from a Mrs Christine Porteus from Hempstead in Norfolk. Poetic, moving and overflowing with emotional intelligence.

It is this sort of emotional connection with a woman that I believe Tony has sadly missed throughout his life. And, in my view, the tragedy is that whilst his soul yearns for such emotional connection, the years of abuse he suffered forced him to create strong defensive walls around his emotions in order to survive and protect himself at a time when his parents - who a child normally relies on for such protection – were emotionally unavailable.

Movement between prisons

After being sentenced on 19 April 2000, prisoner BH9000 was taken to HMP Norwich as a category 'B' prisoner. He was re-allocated to HMP Bullingdon on 20 June 2000 before being re-allocated again on 14 July to HMP Gartree. On 12 October 2001 he was removed to HMP Pentonville because of his Appeal and, being re-classified as a 'C' category prisoner, he was subsequently moved to HMP Highpoint on 11 March 2002. At least those are the official reasons.

I have also been in three of the five prisons (Norwich, Pentonville and Highpoint): see my book 10 *Prisons, 12 Weeks*. We had both been 'naughty boys' by rattling the cages of those public servants who were involved in wrong-doing and child abuse.

Whilst at Norwich, Tony was not allocated any work but when he moved to Bullingdon he worked on 'light assembly.'

At Gartree he did census work on a computer and at Pentonville he did more work on computers and also English.

At Highpoint he studied Maths and History. Records show that he passed courses in English and Maths. He spent much of his spare time reading the papers and listening to Radio 4, not changing his habits outside of prison.

Prison officer report

In a report authored by Colin Hakeney, describing himself as a senior prison officer at HMP Highpoint, Tony was described as "generally conforming with prison staff and causing little or no trouble to those in authority." He was said to relate well with other prisoners but was careful when sharing confidences with others. He was also said to have no problems talking to any person. His conduct in classes was said to be "good."

He refused to attend probation because "I have a farm to run" and he also refused to engage in any courses to "help the prisoner come to terms with his offending behaviour."

He said that if probation required him to attend when he ought to be working on the farm, he'd rather spend the rest of his sentence in prison and walk out of prison "free and clear." I completely respect him for that.

Alongside Hakeney's report to the Parole Board was a two-page report compiled by Dr E Giblin. Question one (of four) asked: "Are there any medical or psychiatric factors which may be relevant to consideration for early release on licence?" Dr Giblin answered "No."

On the back sheet of the photocopied report, Tony made a number of hand-written observations:

> I did not expect to get parole because I speak my mind. I speak the Truth. The Truth roots out the Untruth eventually.
>
> We are not being policed – it has been replaced with oppression.
>
> I am a catalyst for the silent majority,"

and I happen to think he's right. Which is why this case became so high profile for so long. Tony Martin represented the views of millions of ordinary working men and women in this country and they saw that, too. But where he differed from the broad mass of the people was that he was brave enough to condemn the police, to speak out against the erosion of civil liberties and to criticise the government for cutting back on funding to the police. Yes, make no mistake about it, Tony Martin raised his head above the parapet, climbed out of the trenches and strode towards the land of Truth and Justice where angels feared to tread. Sicut aquilae indeed – "They who wait upon the Lord will soar on wings like eagles; they will run and not grow weary, they will walk and not be faint."[511]

Author Frederick Forsyth was particularly scathing: "The Tony Martin case has exposed the tip of a growing iceberg of resentment over the way the contract between the law-abiding and the State has been broken. And it's not us, the people, who did the breaking."

Probation report

Those in the know are aware that the majority of reports written by probation officers aren't worth the paper they're written on, being pieces of fiction which justify unlawful incarceration, particularly of prisoners maintaining innocence.

Probation Officer Chris Dewsnap compiled a fanciful report in which he stated that he had met the prisoner on two occasions, once at HMP Gartree following his original conviction for murder and once at HMP Highpoint for the purpose of the report. Both interviews apparently lasted for 90 minutes. The paucity of emotional intelligence and the high level of arrogance displayed by Mr Dewsnap in his piece of fiction were simply quite staggering.

Dewsnap described the prisoner as "an extremely difficult man to interview. He comes across as being egotistical, relating elaborate stories about himself that appear totally irrelevant to the questions I asked. In my opinion Mr Martin demonstrates an attitude of discrimination toward sections of the community and has views about society which are out of kilter with the majority of 21st century thinking. He has strong opinions about how 'England' should be and makes frequent references to how wonderful society was in the fifties."

There is some truth somewhere in that paragraph: Tony can be extremely difficult and egotistical. He does ramble on at times. But I do not subscribe to the notion that all of his views are out of kilter with the rest of society. He does have *some* extreme views, but not everything he thinks or believes is off the register of social 'norms'.

Dewsnap added that Andrew Scott (a senior social worker in mental health) had interviewed the prisoner and informed Dewsnap that Tony did not display any symptoms which might indicate he had serious mental health problems.

Dewsnap continued: "He holds very strong views that he is perfectly justified in protecting himself and his property even in the extreme manner displayed in the commission of this offence. He clearly holds the view 'An Englishman's home is his castle' and he is entitled to take any steps necessary to secure that. If anything this view has been shared by celebrities, along with press and media sympathy."

---

[511] See part one – the Early Years.

And, I suggest, it has been shared by the vast majority of the population, certainly judging by the large volume of letters and cards that he received in support. I am forced to question what this particular probation officer would do if he were invaded at night when on his own in a remote farmhouse.

Dewsnap continued: "Mr Martin takes no responsibility for his actions. He believes the victims are entirely to blame for his behaviour; if they had not been at his property no offence would have occurred. Furthermore, he regards the policing of the area surrounding his home as wholly inadequate, despite himself and his neighbours reporting crimes on a regular basis. He clearly has no time for the police and had they been carrying out their duties in the way he believes he has a right to expect he would not have had to resort to self-defence."

I find it difficult to challenge Tony's mind-set here. I became fascinated by the case in 1999 because it struck me as odd that a law-abiding man would be treated the way he was by the 'authorities' after a crime had first been perpetrated *against* him.

As we have seen, Tony Martin expressed the views of thousands in the rural communities about not only the lack of police officers but also the unprofessionalism of those who were in employment. Look at the very words of Lord Stevens, a former Commissioner of the Met Police, in November 2012: "We have a national crisis of morale in the police which threatens to undermine the work they are doing," and "The Independent Police Complaints Commission should be scrapped," and "There should be stronger safeguards ... not only should chief constables be held to account, *but all those who work for the service should be individually responsible for the quality of their work.*"[512]

Thus it seems that Tony Martin's views on policing were not out of kilter with some of those operating within the higher echelons of society.

When writing in his report about Tony's release address, Dewsnap stated that "Mr Martin informed me he is determined to return to his home in Emneth Hungate when he is released. He states that the farm has become run down during his absence and requires a lot of attention. He talked at some length about his plans about which crops to grow and their respective profitability."

Dewsnap asked the prisoner how he would react if, on his return home, a similar situation were to occur in the future. Tony informed the probation officer that he would take any step necessary to protect himself and his property. Dewsnap expressed his concern about this given the ease with which a shotgun can be obtained within a farming community. The prisoner avoided this issue and informed Dewsnap that he had considered fitting a burglar alarm which he would adapt by fitting an air raid siren that could be heard all over the Fens!

---

[512] Author's emphasis. I give Lord Stevens' idea my ringing endorsement having witnessed at first hand demonstrable police corruption on several occasions. Many hide behind the uniform – in my view, they should be held personally accountable. Governments protect them because they need the police to do their dirty work.

The probation officer also raised the issue of the prisoner's own safety given the rumours that there was "a price on his head." Tony informed Dewsnap that he was not afraid of anyone and that he refused to be intimidated into giving up a lifestyle he enjoys. My own view is why should he be intimidated into giving up a lifestyle he enjoys and in which his soul is particularly nourished?

Dewsnap reported that the prisoner did not envisage any hostility toward him from the local community. "Indeed," writes Dewsnap, "if press reports are accurate he appears to have a great deal of support."

The report then stated that probation officer Annette Stewart commented on Tony Martin's likely response to supervision. She reported that he refused to say whether or not he understood or agreed to abide by any parole conditions until he saw them in black and white. And, in my view, only an idiot would agree to anything like this without first seeing all the conditions set out in writing. If they are not set down in print, it is all too easy for the police and the probation service to 'move the goalposts' and return him to prison due to some imaginary infraction of the conditions he hadn't got in writing.

Ms Stewart continued: "He has a large number of letters supporting his actions which have done little to change his views on the rights of the householder to protect his/her property or self by whatever means available.

"He made it clear to me that whilst he could not hold a gun licence in future there were other means of protecting himself but he would not take this any further in our discussion. I am concerned for his release because I believe the risk to Mr Martin and others is raised primarily because of his notoriety and his own attitudes and beliefs.

"In my view, the risks associated with this case will apply at whatever stage Mr Martin is released into the community. His reluctance to consider the conditions of parole does not bode well for a successful parole period."

Can you believe such nonsense? Tony had scribbled a note against this report: "Frankly, I don't understand this double-Dutch."

In his report, Dewsnap concluded that "Mr Martin does not believe he has done anything wrong and as a result has refused to undertake any offence-focused work. In my opinion Mr Martin's entrenched views make him a high risk of behaving similarly in future. Under the circumstances I feel unable to support his application for release on parole licence."

I don't know about you, but it seems to me that that report had been authored to keep the farmer in prison while the government of the day – through the channel of the Home Office – engineered a face-saving way out of the problem they had created for themselves.

Note too, that Mr Dewsnap was a low-ranking probation officer. Expendable should any shit hit the fan.

Fortunately, this story had gripped the imagination of the public. Large numbers of people felt aggrieved that a man whose home had been invaded and who felt that his life was in danger should have been found guilty of murder and imprisoned. There was a vast cross-section of people who felt annoyance at the police and the CPS and the government. From the young to the very old, from carpenters to doctors, people throughout England and the UK and even further afield began to make their feelings known.

At the time, I was a teacher and the case had gripped my imagination and I followed it closely in the media. I managed to see through the usual rubbish about his character and I began to question much of what I was reading. Even the more liberal newspapers such as *The Guardian* began to use negative descriptions of the farmer rather than reporting the facts. It occurred to me that they were doing this because there were precious few facts. Something about this entire case did not feel right to me. I felt that the farmer was being made a scapegoat. But life sometimes gets in the way of other plans and I was unable to do anything about it until 2013, when I met Tony Martin for the first time.

Others, however, did get proactively involved. Little old ladies on a small pension sent in money to a fighting fund. Some - like Neil Jacutine and David Barnard – organised campaigns. Yet others ensured that fields got ploughed and harvests brought in.

When Tony gave me his files on the case ("They're no use to me any longer so you'd better have them"), I read several hundred of the estimated 4,000 or so letters and cards that he was sent.

Within days of the incident and it gaining national prominence, letters of support from all over the country began to pour in. Almost every letter was in support of the actions that Tony Martin had taken that night. Many said that they would have done the same thing in similar circumstances. Effectively, this is the common law – the law of the people created by the will of the people, not some statute created by law lords in their ivory towers in the Palace of Westminster or barristers' chambers. Although it took some time, it was eventually this will of the people that obtained Tony Martin his freedom.

Another interesting aspect of the letters was that many of them focused on the role of the police, the under-funding by government and the lack of relevant laws to protect homeowners.

The police came under fire from almost every quarter – particularly the fact that rural police stations were closing as rapidly as the crime rate was soaring and the number of 'bobbies on the beat' was falling sharply. The way of life epitomised by Rodney Gooderson[513] had long since disappeared by 1999 (and it is a very distant memory in 2019.)

---

[513] See entry **18** and others for a more detailed account of Rodney Gooderson and the part he played in the life of Tony Martin.

Wed
26 APR
2000
389

Helston, Cornwall

In a well-written and intelligent letter received by Nick Makin's office on 26 April 2000, Tony Dean, of Helston in Cornwall, wrote that he was "very disturbed at the verdict in this case" and that he had serious misgivings about aspects of it. He wasn't the only one.

Mr Dean queried whether the jury had been subjected to a live firing of a shotgun in an enclosed space with a similar light level to that in Bleak House. Of course, the question was somewhat rhetorical – they weren't.

Mr Dean stated that he used to work in a gunsmith's and that "temporary deafness and blindness are very possible after the first shot."

The letter-writer also questioned the size of the shot used: "This is important because if the pre-meditated intention is to kill a human then small shot sizes that are normal around a farm (5 or 6) are not much use except at extremely close range. If, on the other hand, a shot size like LG is used, that will kill a human at 75 yards." This is, of course, a good point.

The final paragraph made for interesting reading: "Given the past actual experience of people in rural areas who have had their homes entered whilst they are in them, I would do exactly the same as Tony Martin did. The expectation is that the thieves will be armed and/or on drugs, you are likely at the very least to be attacked, it is possible you will be tied up and tortured,[514] and the thieves have the time to do this with total impunity in an isolated home. The worst case - and all too frequent scenario - is you will be killed."[515]

I believe that Mr Dean made some extremely important points.

Sat
3 JUN
2000
390

POW Trust to The Governor, HMP Bullingdon

Peter Sainsbury, the Trust's Chairman, sent a letter to the Governor of HMP Bullingdon. Those in authority who had first denied the farmer justice, were still pulling the strings in his case:

"We are disturbed to be advised today that quite extraordinarily our letter, dated 27 April 2000, has not been received by Anthony Martin at HMP Bullingdon - copy attached. You will appreciate that any papers that assist Anthony Martin in his Appeal are being denied to him by the Prison authorities is a very serious matter. I would appreciate a response by return in view of the seriousness of this matter and that Mr Martin's appeal is due to be heard within the next few weeks."

---

[514] As was Robbie Auger and also Tony's uncle, Arthur Garner.
[515] As Robbie Auger was killed in 1967. As Constance and Janice Sheridan were killed in 1999, just seven months prior to the August burglary and shooting.

Fri
9 JUN
2000
391

POW Trust to Tony Martin, HMP Bullingdon
The charity's legal adviser, Terence Ewing, was an extremely able and competent lawyer. He wrote to Tony soon after the farmer's imprisonment to inform him about the Appeal which the charity was pursuing on Tony's behalf and was critical of Scrivener: "he is as I understand a left winger, and for that reason I was apprehensive when I learnt that he was your QC. Frankly, I wouldn't have touched him with a barge pole."

Mon
16 JUN
2000
392

POW Trust to Tony Martin, HMP Bullingdon
Terence Ewing wrote to Tony to inform him that the former MP, Teresa Gorman, had agreed to become a Patron of the charity "as we are assisting her with certain matters. She is a very firm supporter of your case and feels that it is dreadful that you should be in prison. In fact, she wanted to raise your case in the House but, being sub-judice, it was not possible."

Fri
20 JUN
2000
393

POW Trust to Tony Martin, HMP Bullingdon
The prolific Terence Ewing wrote to Tony a 3-page letter which included the following: "You pleaded guilty to the illegal possession of a shotgun. You may like to consider that an additional ground of appeal could be raised in that your plea was not free and voluntary, but was forced on you by advice from your [previous] solicitors. I feel you were badly advised to plead guilty to that charge."

Fri
20 JUN
2000
394

POW Trust to James Saunders, solicitor, London
Peter Sainsbury wrote to Tony's new lawyers a 3-page letter which, although full of interesting achievements the charity had carried out on behalf of the farmer, it contained dark overtones:

"The Tony Martin Support Group will be liquidating the Trust set up by Makin with the agreement of Tony Martin and forming another Trust under the leadership of the chartered accountants, Wheeler & Co., of Wisbech.
Any other person except ourselves can be considered interlopers. And in such cases, hangers-on do come out of the woodwork as Tony Martin has found. I believe that Tony has dropped these people following advice from his friends."

The reason I used the term 'dark overtones' regarding this letter was because it became obvious that over a period of time, Malcolm Starr and the POW Trust, of which he was to become a patron himself, had – I suggest – skilfully and deviously manipulated Tony into thinking that *they* were the *only* people he could trust, but this was not the case. Even Tony's own mother was marginalised – those controlling the innocent farmer had managed to isolate him so that he would rely only on them and not his true friends. Whilst it is true that the POW Trust did some excellent work on Tony's behalf, it was at great cost – much of the monies sent in by thousands of well-wishers (and this ran into hundreds of thousands of pounds, if not millions) was misappropriated by individuals within the POW charity. It has been suggested to me that they *wanted* Tony to remain in prison as long as possible because they were profiting financially from his incarceration. The POW Trust had uncovered evidence pointing to Tony's innocence, but sat on it for years. Paul Cumby, Richard Portham, Roger Putterill and Helen Lilley (not to mention Terry Howard), were all soon shortly marginalised as Malcolm Starr ingratiated himself with the charity. When I met Robin Martin (Tony's brother) he told me that he had seen Starr in the street in Wisbech, parking his Bentley and asked, "Did my brother pay for that?" before spitting on the ground as Starr got out of his vehicle. It seems, from a review of the available evidence, that Terry Howard's words of wisdom to Tony had more than a ring of truth to them – Mr Starr was not particularly interested in assisting Tony or helping him clear his name, but in promoting himself and billing the charity (and thus the general public) for visiting Tony in prison.

He was described to me by a member of the POW Trust who wished to remain anonymous for fear of reprisals as "very suave... he dressed very elegantly and I guess many people were taken in by all that."

Tue 26 SEP 2000 395

Cambridge Crown Court
The BBC published a report on its website[516] that Neil Fearon, the brother of Brendon, had been jailed for five years for conning two elderly women out of nearly £40,000:

"Judge Jonathan Haworth told Neil Fearon, 33, who admitted theft, burglary and deception, that his crimes were 'despicable and outrageous'.

Cambridge Crown Court heard Fearon, of Newark, Nottinghamshire, had preyed on a 79-year-old woman in Cambridge and then targeted a 76-year-old in Chelsea, central London.

---

[516] http://news.bbc.co.uk/1/hi/uk/943397.stm

His brother, Brendon, 30, was jailed for three years earlier this year at Norwich Crown Court for conspiring to burgle Martin's home in Emneth Hungate, Norfolk.

Brendon, also of Newark, was shot in the groin and thigh by Martin during the raid in August 1999.

His accomplice, Fred Barras, 16, also of Newark, was shot dead by the 55-year-old farmer, who was jailed for life for murder at Norwich Crown Court in April.

Judge Haworth was told that both of Neil Fearon's victims lived alone and were showing signs of senility.

Julian Christopher, prosecuting, said the first woman, Jessie Ball, had met Neil Fearon when he called at her door.

After befriending her, Fearon had persuaded her to give him a series of cheques which she had believed were loans for a new business.

Between December 1997 and April 1998, Fearon had tricked her out of seven cheques with a total value of £11,480, said Mr Christopher.

Fearon had also befriended his second victim, Mary Goldring, and persuaded her to hand over cheques which he had said were loans to help him set up a furniture business, the court was told.

She had handed over three cheques with a total value of £27,650 between August 1999 and May this year, said Mr Christopher.

Fearon had also supplied her with three ferrets and arranged for her to have a ferret hutch built and delivered. For supplying the hutch, and taking away an old cooker, he had charged £1,700.

He had also persuaded her to hand over £400 for 'repairs to his car' and had stolen various small antiques on the pretence of clearing rubbish from her house.

Judge Haworth told Fearon: "You have committed what can only be described as a series of despicable offences. They are rightly described as outrageous. Each of your victims was targeted by you with great care. You ingratiated yourself with them and took ruthless advantage of them."

An accomplice who built the ferret hutch for Fearon - Jason Dawson, 28, of Barnby in the Willows, Newark - admitted theft and was jailed for nine months.

The court heard that both men had lengthy records for dishonesty and both had served previous custodial sentences."

Mon
2 OCT
2000
396

home address of Paul Cumby, Walsoken
With Tony serving a life sentence in prison, the POW Trust was working hard to appeal his convictions and obtain his release. A longstanding friend of Tony's, Paul Cumby, made a signed witness statement which it was hoped would be used by the Court of Appeal. It wasn't – though it should have been.

What Mr Cumby had to say was explosive. Tony Martin, when asked by the police in interview about where he obtained the cartridges which he had loaded into the gun before moving towards the stairs, had always said they were in a carrier bag near the bedroom door. The police claimed they couldn't find this bag and intimated, therefore, that Tony Martin had been lying.

"I have known Tony Martin for 14 years and I am a good friend of his. The day that the body of Fred Barras was found on Tony's land I became involved in this matter, and I have been involved ever since. I have enduring Power of Attorney, I am a Trustee for his estate and a Trustee for the Fund set up to assist in his defence. I have had access to Bleak House, Tony's home, since the 21st of August 1999. I have a key to all the buildings on the farm land. I have been running the farm for Tony since he was arrested and charged in August 1999.

After Tony was charged the Police set up a mobile office on Tony's land. This was manned by police officers working in shifts round the clock until after Tony's trial. Before Tony was convicted the only person to take anything out of Bleak House was Helen Lilley, Tony's friend. She had to write down a list of what she took, sign it and give it to the police. I think she took items like clothing, personal items and some antiques.

The police removed all the furniture out of the "Crime Scene" room and as far as I know they still have it.

Before the trial I was present on several occasions when people from the Defence team visited Bleak House - I remember for instance a Mr Ballinger from the Solicitors and the Barrister, Anthony Scrivener. A group of people I thought were a forensic team visited the house with Mr Ballinger under my supervision, although I'm not sure they were indeed a Forensic team. I remained outside while they were in the house.

I visited Tony while he was awaiting trial. He was not allowed to go to Bleak House. He asked me to look for a bag of cartridges in his bedroom. I imagined he meant a purpose made leather bag for holding cartridges. He said the bag of cartridges was in his bedroom on the right hand side as you go in, on the floor, underneath or by the chest of drawers. I looked for the bag but couldn't see it. The room was extremely untidy and chaotic with debris of all sort, papers etc all over the floor. I know the police also looked for the cartridges before the trial with no success.

After the trial a group of his friends went to clear Bleak House of all remaining objects of value. This group was myself, Malcolm Starr, Roger Putterill, Helen Lilley and Mrs Martin, Tony's mother. This job took more than one day. On one of the days that the group went in to clear the house I visited Tony in Bullingdon Prison. I think this was in the first week of May 2000. On this day they cleared out the bedroom, moving almost all of the furniture out and items of any value. They left behind a lot of rubbish and debris, papers, etc.

When I visited Tony he again asked me to look for the cartridges. He also told me he had a replica handgun in the bedroom and told me where to find it. He said they were both on the floor of his bedroom on the right as you go into the bedroom.

That day, in the late afternoon, after the meeting with Tony at Bullingdon Prison I went to the bedroom and again looked for the cartridges and the gun. I was still looking for a leather bag of cartridges and didn't find it. I did find the replica gun. It was on the floor in the place where the chest of drawers had been, in an old supermarket type plastic bag. I think the gun was in the first bag I picked up. There were other bags around. I had understood from Tony that the gun and the bags were in more or less the same place. I still couldn't find the cartridge bag. I must point out that I was still looking for a leather bag.

It is possible that there was a plastic bag with cartridges in somewhere in that room, although I think it is unlikely. I did not tell anyone except Tony that I had found the gun.

Sometime later Nick Makin told me he wanted to visit the house. I understood him to say that he was bringing a forensic team. I arranged to meet him at Bleak House as he requested. He arrived with two other men. One of them was what I would call coloured: he had dark skin and hair. I am sure Makin never told me either of the men was a journalist. Makin had a shotgun with him. It was a double barrelled long barrelled gun - I don't know what make. I asked to see his shotgun licence and he showed it to me. It had his name on and the number on the licence coincided with the number on the gun.

I asked him why he had the gun and he said he was going to shoot it inside the house. I asked him why - I was concerned that it would overlay any existing evidence about burn, fire-arm residue etc, He said he was going to prove Tony could have fired shots from the middle of the stairs through the doorway and into the 'Crime Scene' room.

I let him in with the two men. Makin asked me to leave because he was going to fire the gun. I heard him fire the gun - I think just one shot. I went back inside the house. Makin said, "The poor bloody fellow", meaning Tony could have fired from the stairs into the room.

I could see that the floor of the 'Crime Scene' room was scraped and cut and burnt where the shot had gone. I spray painted round the area on the floor boards and put a table over the area.

I then went outside and Makin invited me to sit in his car with him. He asked me not to mention the shot firing to anyone, and asked if I wanted to be part of the legal team. He then said he wanted to show me something he had found.

We all four of us went back into the house. Makin led us into the bedroom. He was the first in. The room was dark and he had a torch. He shone it on a bag on the floor, to the left of and behind the bedroom door. In front of us Makin split the bag open. He said "We've found the cartridges." He pointed it out with his torch, saying "There's the bag of cartridges."

He spoke to the two men and asked if they agreed they could be the same kind of cartridges.

I told him to leave the bag where it was and call the police. I gave him the number to call the police. The onsite mobile office had gone since the conviction. Two policemen came. One was I think CID and one had a camera and took photographs.

The police left and then Makin and the two other men left.

The following day I went back there. I was worried about the temporary lighting which was rigged up in the house. In the bedroom I found a plastic bucket containing yet more cartridges. I telephoned Makin who said I shouldn't tell anyone. As far as I know the bucket with the cartridges is still in the bedroom."

CORRUPTION ALERT — *Tony's solicitor interferes with alleged crime scene prior to appeal*

It is difficult to express the depth of corruption throughout this case, but this witness statement (if true) clearly shows that Nick Makin was not working in his client's best interest by contaminating what the police described as the crime scene. Tony's new defence team were seeking to quash his convictions and Makin would have known this. He would also have known that his action in firing a gun inside the house would have interfered with any evidence inside that room.

As pointed out earlier, it appears that Fearon had been shot outside and not inside a house but nonetheless, as far as the Police and the CPS were concerned, the crime scene lay inside the house. It is inconceivable that any solicitor would interfere with an alleged crime scene in this way.

Tony had given Power of Attorney to Paul Cumby but, after overtures from Malcolm Starr, the farmer revoked the POA in respect of Cumby and gave it to the Wisbech businessman.

It was, in my opinion based on all the available evidence, yet another cataclysmic decision from the farmer whose critical thinking skills – together with his propensity to be seduced by suave, well-spoken, well-dressed businessmen (a throwback to his days at Glebe House and other private boarding schools) and with his irrational belief that he is always right – make him incredibly vulnerable to be preyed upon.

Sun 12 NOV 2000 397

Redmoor House, Elm, Wisbech

Tony received the following letter from his mother:

My Dear Tony,

Another week has passed & I have not heard from you. My thoughts are always with you, what you are doing and how you are coping with the strain of such an unnatural life. The weather is getting better, more sun and drier. I think we are in for some frost.

On reflection, I have a feeling we have said too much to the press etc. There is no doubt that they are only in it for financial reward, and they have put a lot of rubbish and untrue things in the newspapers and I feel the less one says the better.

I have enclosed a lot of cuttings & I hope you find them interesting.

How terrible this flooding is. I feel for those poor people out there, and the train crash in Austria – how terrible.

Love as always,

Your loving mother.

PS – I am longing for good news. Aunts Rosemary & Joan send you their best wishes.

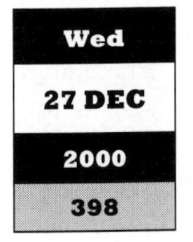

Wed 27 DEC 2000 398

Redmoor House, Elm, Wisbech

This was Tony Martin's first Christmas in prison. His mother tried to console him with the following letter:

My Dear Tony,

Another week has passed & Christmas 2000. We have had a lot of snow & ice; very pretty but not very comfortable. I keep putting food out for the birds – they are very hungry.

Once the New Year is in we hope things will start moving for you. I hope you are able to cope with prison life, at least I should think you are warm.

I have not been too well; at the moment I have a very bad attack of bronchitis which has upset my chest.

I did think there was (sic) quite a lot of good films over Christmas. I hope you were able to view.

Have enclosed some cards & cuttings.

As always, all my love, Mother.

PS –Aunts Rosemary & Joan send you their best wishes.

| Fri 24 NOV 2000 399 | **HMP Lincoln**
In November 2000, Christopher Webster, aged 41 and of Loughborough, was jailed for 2 years by judge Paul Downes for handling stolen goods from Bleak House in May 1999.
Fourteen months of the sentence was for handling, with the remainder being a recall to prison from a previous sentence and also a bail offence on 25 July when he fled Norwich Crown Court and went on the run so that he could "sort out some domestic issues". |
|---|---|

Webster had pleaded guilty to handling stolen goods but denied the charge of conspiracy to burgle Bleak House and that charge was left to lie on the file. In mitigation of handling stolen goods, his solicitor Neil Fitzgibbon said that, "He feels he may have contributed to the death of a young boy and Mr Martin's incarceration." [See also entry **372**].

| Sun 14 JAN 2001 400 | **The POW Trust, 295a Queenstown Road, Battersea, London**
Peter Sainsbury of the POW Trust wrote to Mohammed Al-Fayed, the owner of Harrods, the famous department store in London.
"I am writing to you regarding the current case of Tony Martin as I understand that you sent Mr Martin a complimentary Teddy bear for Christmas. This was a most gracious gesture on |
|---|---|

your part, and was deeply appreciated by Mr Martin.

We as an organisation and registered charity assist people with legal problems who would be otherwise denied access to justice.

We were instrumental in getting new solicitors Messrs James Saunders & Co for Mr Martin, and a new QC, Mr Michael Wolkind.

We were very concerned at the time regarding the incompetent way in which Mr Martin's former solicitor, Mr Nick Makin of M&S Solicitors, were handling Mr Martin's case and his appeal.

We felt that Mr Makin was hoping to obtain Mr Martin's farm, and these suspicions have been fully justified as it turned out.

This proved justified by the subsequent discovery that Mr Makin in fact only filed grounds of appeal in respect of the GBH charge on which Mr Martin had been convicted and sentenced to 10 years imprisonment and not the murder charge.

This has now been fully rectified by Mr Martin's new legal team, and it is hoped that his appeal will be heard sometime after Easter.

Hopefully as a result of our intervention, Mr Martin's appeal will succeed and his current convictions will be quashed altogether, or at the very least he will be granted a re-trial.

MAY 2001 401	**south London** Kenneth Fraser was arrested for the killing of his partner Miss Mary Anne Moore, 56, at their south London home in May 2001 after her body was discovered at the bottom of a flight of stairs. The pathologist, Dr Michael Heath, later gave evidence at trial that her fatal injury was not caused by a fall but through an impact with a sharp-edged surface or object. [See further entries]
Tues 8 MAY 2001 402	**the Chambers of Anthony Scrivener, QC** The barrister who had let Tony down when he was in possession of facts which proved his client innocent, sent a letter to Mrs Jushna Chowdhury at the Criminal Appeal office at the Royal Courts of Justice in the Strand, London. Tony's new legal team had sent Scrivener a bundle of documents produced for the Appeal and asked the barrister to comment:

"Where the shots were fired from
I explained the position in my letter dated 26 October 2000. There was a conflict between the expert evidence and that of Tony Martin. It would be difficult for the defence to challenge the Prosecution case on this point since the Defence expert agreed with the Prosecution.

Tony Martin was well aware of the problem. It was understandable that he may have made a mistake about this in the confusion. He was told that he must give evidence as to what he believed was the truth but that we would have to be prepared to fight the case on the basis of the expert evidence."

Breaking in to the letter at this point, it is incredible that a man of Scrivener's standing in the legal profession would not have had the intelligence to challenge the "expert evidence" or to imagine that the police planted evidence inside Bleak House.

Furthermore, Graham Renshaw did *not* "agree" with the prosecution's ballistics expert other than to say that if Tony had fired from the stairs, he could not have caused the injuries to Fearon and Barras. Tony had met with Renshaw in the presence of Scrivener (who had set up the meeting) and they had strongly disagreed. Rather than challenge the police's evidence (as any honest QC would have done), Scrivener went with the idea that Tony had lied about firing from the stairs. Back to the letter:

"For the reasons given in my first letter we believed that it would be difficult for us to explain the first shot fired from the stairs as it meant that after firing the first shot from the stairs Mr Martin had to negotiate his way down the remainder of the stairs including over the gap at the bottom where the stairs had been removed and then proceeded over the rubble on the floor to where the cartridges were found inside the room. This was a difficult scenario for the Defence because it involved Mr Martin continuing to advance towards the burglars after firing one shot and a considerable period of time passing between the firing of the shot from the stairs and the remaining shots."

Breaking in again, it is implausible to think that Scrivener did not even consider the possibility that the police evidence had been falsely created against his former client.

No homeowner in their right mind would fire off one shot on the stairs and then descend the stairs to walk towards an unknown number of intruders who may themselves have been armed with bricks or knives and rushed him. Tony's least vulnerable position in the circumstances was on the stairs and, knowing Tony as I do, there is little to no chance that he would give up that position.

"Taking the line that we did meant we did not have to suggest to Fearon that he had been 'persuaded' away from his first recollection."

This is, as we have seen, precisely what *did* happen because Fearon claimed he had been shot *outside*. Mr Scrivener had somewhat conveniently airbrushed the statement made in hospital by Fearon out of the trial, out of history. Little did he concern himself with the fact that an innocent man was in prison.

"As to the residue on the staircase wall, the advice we had from our own expert was that it was unsafe to rely on that to support the proposition of a shot being fired from the stairs. We had read the statement of Mr Blunt - the prosecution expert - and taken specific instructions from Dr Renshaw on the point."

Such was Scrivener's propensity to lie, that he failed to inform the Appeal Court that Graham Renshaw had made statements to the police but they were never used and neither was Mr Renshaw called to court. Now look out for more legal shenanigans by a man at the top of his "noble profession":

"I no longer have the 'virtual-reality' evidence but my clear recollection was that this evidence did not assist the Defence case. I did discuss with Prosecution Counsel that *it should not be used* because the base material was not in place for the opinions to be valid and eventually the evidence was not adduced in court."

I have seen this "virtual-reality" evidence. It is a piece of pseudo-scientific nonsense created to lend credibility to the false police narrative. There is a computer-generated drawing of a man on the stairs and firing through the doorway into the Breakfast Room and hitting 'Barras' in the back. *But the angle of entry is all wrong, proving that Tony Martin could not have shot him from the stairs (or at all).* No wonder this pseudo-scientific nonsense was conveniently shuffled out of the pack of "evidence" entered into court.

Leeds Crown Court
Wed 13 JUN 2001 — 403

The Yorkshire Post published a report on its website[517] that the father of Fred Barras had been jailed for 14 years for his part in an armed robbery in Yorkshire:

"The father of Fred Barras, the teenage burglar shot dead two years ago by farmer Tony Martin, has been jailed for 14 years for his part in an armed robbery in Yorkshire. Fred Barras senior, 46, was sentenced at Leeds Crown Court yesterday after a jury convicted him by an 11-1 majority of conspiracy to rob a transport depot at Normanton industrial estate, Wakefield, in May last year. Security guard Lisa Taylor was threatened with a handgun and tied up by two raiders before three lorries valued at £250,000 and loaded with £130,000 clothing intended for Next, were driven off.

Police recovered two of the stolen trailers within hours with their loads intact at a disused airfield in East Yorkshire where Barras was living in a caravan. Jailing Barras senior yesterday, Judge Peter Charlesworth told him: "You took a leading part in a very serious planned robbery in which a gun was put to the temple of the lone female security officer in the middle of the night at a depot where valuable vehicles and easily disposable and valuable clothing was kept."

The offence clearly involved pre-planning and was "executed in a professional manner." Although Miss Taylor had only minor if unpleasant physical injuries she continued to suffer from the psychological effects of her ordeal.

The judge told the jury he had made an order at the start of the case preventing the press from referring during the trial to Barras's relationship with the young burglar shot by Tony Martin in case it distracted them from the issues: "It could have had two effects, it could have made you think his son was a burglar therefore he's a bad lot, or it might have made you feel sorry for him because he lost his son in tragic circumstances, perhaps a bit of both, but it wasn't anything to do with this case, that is why I took that decision."

A second defendant, Martin Chapman, 33, formerly of Leeds Road, Outwood, Wakefield, was jailed for a total of 52 years[518] after he admitted conspiracy to handle goods stolen in the robbery, attempting to pervert the course of justice and possessing cannabis. He denied conspiracy to rob and after the jury failed to reach a verdict in his case the prosecution decided not to go for

---

[517] https://www.yorkshirepost.co.uk/news/farm-burglar-s-father-jailed-1-2418894
[518] This seems highly improbable and is likely a misprint.

a retrial and a not guilty verdict was entered.

A third man, Thomas Gaskin, 50, also of Pollington Airfield, Goole, who was found not guilty by the jury on the charge of conspiracy to rob but guilty of conspiracy to handle stolen goods will be sentenced today. His son Charles Gaskin, 19, was cleared on both charges.

Miss Taylor told the jury she was on duty alone at the depot in Normanton when she noticed a security monitor had gone blank. As she checked the wiring, she heard the handle of the door being turned and then someone knocking. She opened the door and was confronted by a man wearing dark clothing and a balaclava, who pointed a handgun at her head and ordered her to lie on the floor.

A second man entered the office and tied up Miss Taylor with plastic flex, while asking her about the site's security arrangements. "I was scared to death," she said, describing how she had not been able to continue working as a security guard because of fear since. The second man had a distinctive Irish accent which the prosecution claimed was Barras. A 17-tonne trailer unit and two 32-tonne tractor units were stolen from the site. They were loaded with clothing to be delivered to Next the following day.

Timothy Capstick, prosecuting, said Miss Taylor managed to free herself and alert police. Two of the trailers with their loads intact were found in a hanger building at Pollington airfield near Goole around 4am. The Gaskins and Barras maintained they knew nothing about them or how they got to the airfield.

Chapman was arrested by Humberside Police after abandoning the 17-tonne vehicle when he realised he was being followed in it. The clothing inside was missing and had not been recovered. He told police he had been promised £1,000 for driving it but would not name those who had recruited him.

The judge heard during the trial that Barras senior was first in trouble as a juvenile when he appeared in court for assault. He had since appeared at magistrates' courts mainly in the 1970s for offences of theft, handling, obstruction and motoring matters. He had no convictions for burglary and was last before the court in November last year for driving with excess alcohol when he was fined and disqualified.

David Sumner, for Barras, said he had to some extent lived down his past record for minor dishonesty from years ago and it was possible his return to crime might in some way be connected with events in his recent life "in relation to the tragic death of his son."

Fred Barras jnr who, although only 16, had previous convictions for assault and dishonesty, was found dead with shotgun wounds near Martin's farm[519] after the farmer said he fired at two burglars because he was in fear of his life.[520]

---

[519] Note that the article stated that Fred Barras was found "near" the farm, not on it.
[520] Note the reporting inaccuracies: at no point had Tony ever said that he had shot "*at* two burglars". He did not, as we have seen, shoot *at* anybody but *into* a darkened room.

Appeal against convictions

Part 18: Appeal against conviction

Every prisoner has the right to appeal his or her conviction and/or sentence. At least that's the theory. Such is the arrogance of the legal profession and the level of social control exerted over prisoners (innocent or guilty) that the actual process of appealing is made intolerably difficult. In a just and humane society, it wouldn't be as difficult as it is.

With Nick Makin having been dismissed by Tony soon after the trial, Malcolm Starr and Richard Portham made contact with Michael Wolkind, QC through solicitor James Saunders.

Tony put a lot of faith and trust in Malcolm Starr but it could be argued that he was let down by the Elm businessman. Described as a successful and millionaire businessman with a lot of political contacts, Starr must have performed due diligence on Makin and if he hadn't then he ought to have done. Several people whom I interviewed for this book mentioned to me that even they knew that Makin was completely not up to the job of defending Tony. No, I am afraid to say that Tony appears to have been let down very badly by some of those he was unwise to trust.

Tony had never really had any faith in Makin, who was not, as we have seen, a criminal defence lawyer. Nor had he much faith in Scrivener and, as it turned out after the QC's appearance in the BBC commissioned programme *To Kill A Burglar* (available on YouTube – but note the alarming errors in that programme), his lack of faith appears to have been completely justified.

Thus Tony was able to instruct a completely new team which, it was hoped, would be able to look at the case – and the evidence – with fresh eyes.

solicitor James Saunders
Born in 1948, James Saunders was educated at King Edward VII Grammar School in Sheffield, before studying law at Leicester University.

He became a founder member of the North Kensington Law Centre in 1970; and was admitted as a solicitor in 1972. Just two years later the go-ahead Saunders founded Saunders & Company. In 1990 he was the founder of the Westminster Drug Project, where at the time of publication he was still listed as a director.

The Tony Martin case is listed on the website as being one of Saunders' most notable cases. Saunders writes for The Justice Gap on Miscarriages of Justice and has been interviewed on Today for Radio 4.

By the time Mr Saunders came on board, he had had some 30 years' experience as a solicitor specialising in criminal defence.

The main focus of the appeal was going to be one of 'diminished responsibility'. This was a "get out of jail free" card and was a strategy clearly more motivated by politicians than the normally-savvy Saunders in order to secure Tony's eventual release to appease the broad mass of the people. We'll take a look at the law on diminished responsibility in order to see how the legal engineering was still being conducted:

the law on Diminished Responsibility

During the late 1940s and early 1950s, there were several high profile murder cases, including those of Derek Bentley and Christopher Craig, Timothy Evans, John Christie and Ruth Ellis. The imposition of the death penalty in these cases was extremely controversial and caused the public to question capital punishment. In 1956, a motion to retain the death sentence but change the law on murder was defeated in the House of Lords, as was a Death Penalty (Abolition) Bill introduced by Sydney Silverman, MP.[521] The government then introduced a further bill, which retained the death sentence but introduced degrees of murder with different sentences. This was the basis of the Homicide Act of 1957. Had Tony Martin been found guilty of the murder of Fred Barras at this time in history, it is possible that he would have been hanged.

In 1953 large crowds had demonstrated outside Wandsworth Prison in London at the execution of Derek Bentley. However, after Harold Wilson's victory in the 1964 general election, and the report of the Longford Committee, the government revisited the question of abolition and a Murder (Abolition of the Death Penalty) Bill was finally enacted in 1965.

I am indebted to <www.inbrief.co.uk> for an explanation of the law on diminished responsibility as it stood in 2000. The defence of diminished responsibility is set out in section 2 of the Homicide Act 1957 (since amended by the Coroners and Justice Act 2009) but we will not concern ourselves with that because it comes after our timeframe. When the defence is successfully pleaded it has the effect of reducing a murder conviction to manslaughter.

---

[521] Sydney Silverman (1895-1968) was a Labour politician (Nelson & Colne) and a vocal opponent of capital punishment. During the First World War he was a conscientious objector to military service and served three prison sentences. He read law at the University of Liverpool.

After qualifying as a solicitor he worked on workmen's compensation claims and landlord-tenant disputes. Silverman wrote about several miscarriages of justice in the 1940s and 1950s. He proposed a private member's bill on the abolition of the death penalty which was passed by 200 votes to 98 on a free vote in the House of Commons on 28 June 1956, but was defeated in the House of Lords.

In 1965 he successfully piloted the Murder (Abolition of the Death Penalty) Bill through Parliament, a consequence of which was that Tony Martin was not hanged in 2001.

Diminished responsibility only has the effect of reducing criminal liability rather than absolving the defendant from liability completely.

Section 2 of the Act is in four parts, and we'll look at each of the parts in turn. In plain English, part (1) states that a person who kills another will not be convicted of murder if he was suffering from an abnormal mind and that this 'abnormality of mind' impaired his judgment to such an extent that he was not responsible for his actions. The 'abnormality of mind' might arise from some form of 'arrested development' or 'mental retardation.'

Part (2) states that it is the responsibility of the lawyers defending a person charged with murder to inform the Court *at the original trial* that their client is of 'diminished responsibility.'

Part (3) states that if a person would normally be charged with murder he will not be charged with murder if he is of 'diminished responsibility' and he will, instead, be charged with manslaughter.

Part (4) deals with the issue of more than one killer, and is not relevant here.

So, what is meant by 'diminished responsibility'? Section 2 of the Homicide Act sets out the three requirements which must be established by the defendant in order to succeed with the defence of diminished responsibility:

1. there must be an abnormality of the mind;
2. this abnormality of the mind must have been caused by a recognised medical condition;
3. the abnormality of the mind must substantially impair the defendant's mental responsibility.

Abnormality of the mind

In order to establish whether a defendant is suffering from an abnormality of the mind, Tony's defence team would have needed to provide medical evidence to the court (which was not done at trial), and it would have been up to the jury to decide whether the defendant was in fact suffering from that abnormality.

The medical evidence would have to have been provided by suitably qualified professionals, but it has to be considered that the evidence is simply opinion and a jury is not bound to follow it. Ultimately it is the final decision of the jury as to whether the defence of diminished responsibility should succeed.

The test which will be required to establish an abnormality of the mind is that by which a reasonable person would regard as abnormal. This test has a very wide meaning and includes the ability to exercise will power and control.

However, in order to establish an abnormality of the mind, it is not sufficient to simply have the condition. The defendant must prove that the condition was excessive when compared to that experienced by a reasonable person.

Recognised medical condition

The second condition in order to establish the defence of diminished responsibility under the Homicide Act 1957 was that the abnormality of the mind has to be caused by an arrested or retarded development of the mind or any inherent causes or induced by disease or injury.

The courts interpreted this as meaning that the abnormality must have been caused by a source which comes from *inside* that person and not a factor which is said to be *outside* that person. Except in the case of long-term addiction, outside factors such as taking drugs and/or alcohol would not be taken into account when establishing diminished responsibility.

Impaired mental responsibility

The third aspect to establish when pleading the defence of diminished responsibility under the Homicide Act is that the abnormality must have substantially impaired the defendant's mental responsibility.

This means that the defendant must have not been fully aware of his actions due to the mental responsibility and any evidence of planning to commit the crime will demonstrate that the defendant's mental responsibility has not been impaired. Therefore, the defence of diminished responsibility will not apply to a premeditated attack, only to a murder which happens on the spur of the moment.

Diminished Responsibility is often a defence which will be stated on an appeal from a murder charge. *However, the medical condition must have been cited in the original trial for it to be later relied on as a defence in the appeal hearing.*

All of this is interesting because we have to see if it really applied to Tony. My view is that it did not apply at all for several reasons. I do not believe that he has "an abnormality of the mind." As previously stated, I find that he can be an extremely difficult man to engage with (when he wants to be) and I believe that this is because of his intense defence mechanisms when he encounters others. It's his modus operandi on his journey through life.

Nor do I subscribe to the view that he has a recognised medical condition of a mental nature. In fact, up to the age of 55 (when the shooting occurred) he had never been diagnosed with any such problems. At worst, he suffered from one or two bouts of depression, but he was never diagnosed as being clinically depressed for example.

As I've stated elsewhere, I believe his "issues of the mind" are nothing more than emotional problems which developed as a result of his not talking about them with friends or family so that he could come to understand them and deal with them. But I am not a consultant psychiatrist. And even if he was depressed about the burglary in May – which is perfectly understandable – I do not believe that this depression caused him to lose his full mental faculties and discharge his gun in the August. In fact, the prosecution said that he had lain in wait and if that were so, surely such pre-meditation is the complete opposite of a sudden impulse when "losing one's mind". No, I do not accept this at all. He knew full well what he was doing when he pulled that trigger – and it is my view that the action of pulling that trigger was, as Professor Tony Maden wrote in a report on Tony's psychiatric state: "a normal reaction to grossly abnormal circumstances."

So, there was no "abnormality of mind" mentioned at trial (being labelled 'eccentric' is not regarded as such an abnormality), no medical professional called by the defence to claim that Tony was suffering from any such abnormality, no medical history as far as his medical records would show, and thus this issue of diminished responsibility was never brought up at the original trial. Besides, hadn't the police always renewed his shotgun certificate during the on-going saga we've read about? No such "abnormality of mind" was ever mentioned in those renewals.

Which all leads us to a conundrum ... the law as it stood in 2000 at trial (and in 2001 at appeal) was such that the medical condition *must have been cited in the original trial for it to be later relied on as a defence in the appeal hearing*. And, since it had never been cited in the original trial, it ought never to have been relied upon in the appeal and the fact that it was relied upon was clearly outside of the rule of law, thus rendering the appeal verdict a nullity.

No wonder Tony uses the phrase "legal engineering." The legal machinations, the "ducking and diving" so favoured by the lawyers (whom Tony refers to as 'spivs'), was still at play in the appeal hearing.

Now we'll look at the Grounds of Appeal – the specific reasons which were advanced to the Court of Appeal to show that Tony's conviction was wrong or, in legal parlance, "unsafe". They can't bring themselves ever to admit that they can be wrong.

~ grounds of appeal ~

I have reproduced below the perfected Grounds of Appeal – which ran to some 26 pages – which Scrivener (who knew his client to have been completely innocent because he had possession of all of the evidence that I have laid out before you) put forward. Bear in mind that Scrivener had been sacked by Tony and that Wolkind was now acting for the farmer. However, in all the legal papers that Tony put me in possession of, I was unable to find Grounds of Appeal with Wolkind's name on them – only those prepared by Scrivener. In the interest of fairness, I reproduce them below:

Ground A background knowledge of crime in the area	*Emneth was in an area of high crime: numerous burglaries and thefts were perpetrated on a regular basis. The remoteness of Tony's farmhouse, the lack of a police presence and woeful response times were also drawn to the appeal court's attention.*

Ground B misdirection by the judge on the count of murder	*Scrivener argued that there was a misdirection by the judge on the count of murder. "It was not that the accused had deliberately and knowingly fired in the direction of Barras. This direction was tantamount to withdrawing the issue from the jury or alternatively it was an over strong comment bearing in mind the evidence."*

I completely agree with Scrivener's comments. In fact, he went further: "At the time the accused fired, the evidence was that it was pitch black inside the house. It was impossible to see who was there or where anyone was." As we've already seen, it was said that solicitor Makin and defence ballistics expert Renshaw conducted a test and it was confirmed that you could not see into the breakfast room from the stairs. And we ought to remind ourselves that Tony told the police during that first interview when he was unrepresented that he had seen torchlight reflected in the shoes worn by the intruders. Fearon and Barras had both been wearing trainers...

Scrivener again: "The accused fired the shots after a series of events which culminated in the beam from the torch held by Fearon[522] being shone into his

---

[522] I remind the reader at this point that Fearon said he'd been shot on a track and not inside the house. I also remind the reader that Fearon was alleged to have been wearing a torch *on his head* and not held in the hand as the intruders did. It is evident that if Fearon had been in the house and wearing the torch around his head and Tony had fired below the level of the torch, he would have hit Fearon in the face or the chest at the very least. Fearon, we know, did not sustain any injuries other than to his legs.

eyes." Tony, we would do well to recall, had told police that he thought he was firing down towards the bottom of the doorway, that he didn't intend to shoot anybody at all and that he was sure that he shot in a downwards direction.

As we've seen, ballistics experts Arnold (for the prosecution) and Renshaw (for the defence) agreed the following evidence: "It is possible that Mr Martin, on each occasion he fired the gun, *aimed in a downwards direction*."

So, now that you know this, do you feel that Owen was right in saying what he did to the jury, or was it a case of the judge telling the jury what to think?

Ground C misdirection by the judge on the count of wounding with intent	*Scrivener claimed that the judge had failed to mention the alternative verdict of section 20 of the Offences against the Person Act 1861 and failed to explain the ingredients of unlawful wounding. Nor was there any reference to this alternative in the written directions provided to the jury. Scrivener claimed that ordinary jurors with no knowledge of the law could have been confused. (The perverse verdicts showed that they were.)*

Ground D the issue of self-defence	*Scrivener claimed that the judge failed to direct the jury about the subjective element of self-defence in that the jury failed to consider all that was going on in the defendant's mind at the time of the shooting: his worries and concerns about the rising level of crime in the area and the history of burglaries and thefts from his farm. It is clear that these issues would have affected Tony's appreciation of risk and judgment in dealing with a potentially dangerous situation, yet Owen failed to inform the jury that they ought to bear these facts in mind.*

Furthermore, Scrivener claimed that the judge failed to deal adequately with this subjective element of self-defence as to whether the amount of force was reasonable. As we have seen, in the case of *R* v *Scarlett* from 1993, it was stated that provided the accused "believed the circumstances called for the degree of force used he was not to be convicted even if his belief was unreasonable."

Scrivener believed that the judge ought to have given more detailed guidance as to the nature of self-defence and that the shooting, having taken place *during* the burglary, had not been an act of revenge *after* the burglary. Nor had the judge carefully pointed out to the jurors that Tony did not fire at all until the torchlight had been shone in his eyes.[523]

The judge ought to have carefully listed the factors which reflected on Tony's mind and which made him fearful and in particular he ought to have reminded the jury that the burglars were determined to carry on with the burglary despite the farmer's presence in his house.[524]

Scrivener was also critical of the fact that the judge barely informed the jury about Tony's emotional and fearful state – much more discussion around this needed to have taken place. This lack of an explanation about Tony's horror about the break-in led the farmer to believing that his defence team had not put forward his point of view at all.

As we have previously seen, in an appeal from 1999, in *Palmer* v *The Queen*, the appeal judges said of the defendant in that case: "you cannot judge to a nicety the exact measure of the defendant's desperate action." Surely this applied to Tony's case: indeed, he often said to me that "no-one knows exactly what it was like unless they were there." Isn't that true about so many things in life?

Nor did the judge direct the jury that there was no duty to retreat and that an accused can "get in first" and he does not have to wait for the unknown. Surely this, too, applies to this case?

Nor did the judge inform the jury that Tony had a right to protect his life and his property and that, as the intruders were trespassers in his home in any event, he did not have to stand by and take no action while they remained in his premises and perhaps committed an act of violence against him.

Ground E witnesses as to attitude	*Scrivener pointed out that the judge wrongly allowed in hearsay evidence which was highly prejudicial, such as claims by the police that Tony had said he'd put gypsies in a field behind barbed wire and machine gun them. Tony's versions of such comments was never put to the jury and the judge failed to mention the dates on which it was claimed Tony had made comments about shooting people.*
Ground F the probable scenario of the shooting	*Ground F, the 'probable' scenario of the shooting, had been concocted by Scrivener without Tony's permission in order to fit the police 'evidence' of three spent cartridges being 'found' by the fireplace in the breakfast room.*

---

[523] It is interesting to note that even at appeal, Scrivener steadfastly maintained the notion that there had been a burglary at Bleak House, despite being in possession of all of the evidence I have put you in possession of.

[524] See previous footnote.

I do not subscribe to that view at all. My position is that the 'expert' evidence is not as reliable as the CPS would like us to believe. I do not believe that Tony Martin managed to descend the stairs, climb over the ladder at the foot of the stairs whilst holding a heavy shotgun and advance towards the breakfast room without having been heard. Far from being the 'agreed' scenario, I disagree with it for the aforementioned reasons.

That said, both 'ballistics experts' mentioned the concept of some of the pellets ricocheting off the injured men and into the doorframe and the wall below the exit window. The breakfast room was 7m by 4m. Thus, if Tony was standing in the room when he fired, there surely would have been much more damage to the room and to the men. Exhibit RJB/5E was compiled by PC 733 Robert Bush and was a revised scale plan of exhibit RJB/5B. It apparently showed a small area of shotgun damage below the exit window measuring approximately 18 inches in circumference, yet I could find no mention of pellets removed from this area in the Exhibits List. Only five pellets were listed as having been removed from the rear door. But those pellets could have been there for years. Or they could have been ricochets. The notion that these pellets got there and that Tony had not been able to fire "round corners" is, in my view, nothing but a red herring designed to bolster the prosecution's wild claim that the farmer had advanced down the stairs and shot at the burglars like "rats in a trap."

Are you concerned that the plan drawn up by PC Bush was not completed until 20 October 1999 – some two months after the shooting? And are you concerned that there were two subsequent revisions to that plan (F and G) which were not entered into court as evidence?

Are you concerned that when DS Eglen went into the house at 7:55pm the day after the shooting (21 August 1999), he did not mention any shotgun damage to the door at all?

Are you concerned that DS Eglen didn't make his witness statement until the 26th October 1999 – some six days *after* PC Bush revised his plan of the breakfast room?

Ground G the 'rats in a trap' suggestion by the prosecution	*Scrivener claimed on appeal – but not at trial! – that the 'rats in a trap' suggestion had not been put to Tony by the police during interview. Nor had Horwood-Smart mentioned this in her opening statement but she theatrically introduced it for the first time when cross-examining Tony.*

> **Ground H**
> inconsistency of verdicts
>
> The jury were given a correct direction as to the intent required for murder and were also correctly directed that they should consider Count 4 (possession of a shotgun with intent to endanger life) on the same basis as Counts 1 and 2 so that if they took the view that "the accused was or may have been acting in reasonable self-defence he is to be found not guilty."

As we know, the jury found Tony guilty of murder and yet not guilty of possession with intent to endanger life. The judge gave no direction to the jury as to the meaning of "endangering life" or whether there was any distinction between this term and the words "really serious injury." It is difficult to see how there could be a real distinction between these two terms on the facts of the case and therefore the verdicts were inconsistent.

> **Ground I**
> the issue of provocation
>
> Ground I was that the judge should have given a provocation direction pursuant to section 3 of the Homicide Act 1957. The provocation, said Scrivener (still maintaining the burglary narrative), consisted in burgling Tony's house when they must have known he was there and also shining the torch in his eyes. Under section 3 of the Homicide Act 1957, the law stated that:

"Where on a charge of murder there is evidence on which the jury can find that the person charged was provoked (whether by things done or by things said or by both together) to lose his self-control, the question whether the provocation was enough to make a reasonable man do as he did shall be left to be determined by the jury; and in determining that question the jury shall take into account everything both done and said according to the effect which, in their opinion, it would have on a reasonable man."

If successful, the defence of provocation would reduce a murder charge to one of manslaughter. The initial burden was on the defence to raise sufficient evidence of provocation but this had not been done at trial.

I'm pleased that it wasn't because at no point did Tony ever suggest that he lost his mind or was overcome with anger. He always said – and the evidence seems to confirm this – that he had merely fired his gun as a reaction to a light being shone in his face by intruders who had smashed their way into his house.

I can understand why this was added as a ground of appeal, but in all honesty, it appears to have been a half-hearted addition and, in any event, I don't believe there was real merit in the notion that Tony had 'lost all reason.'

> **Ground J**
> the evidence of Brendon Fearon
>
> *Although the issue of self-defence depended on what Tony believed at the time he fired his gun, the evidence of Fearon was important because he said in evidence that the silver found in the holdalls which he had taken to Bleak House had been placed there by Tony after the incident to "explain his actions."*

Clearly this was nonsense, said Scrivener, and suggested that Fearon was not beyond manufacturing evidence.[525]

Furthermore, Fearon admitted to police that he had had a "recce" of the house in daylight about a month before the burglary which showed a steely determination to burgle the house come what may. It was therefore incumbent upon the judge to warn the jury as to the credibility of Fearon as a witness of truth. The judge, said Scrivener, ought to have warned the jury to approach Fearon's evidence with care.

The judge failed to make any reference to the "recce" in his summing up.

It was clear that the "authorities" were keen to sell the idea that Fearon – with a string of criminal convictions to his name – manufactured evidence and couldn't be trusted to tell the truth. However, in my experience of life, no-one lies all the time and it seemed to me, when reviewing all of the evidence, that he may have been telling more of the truth than the authorities wanted the public to hear. Especially about having been shot on a track leading to the house...

> **Ground K**
> the first police interview
>
> *I suggest you return to the entry entitled trial day one (10 April 2000). For me, if you ever needed proof that Tony Martin did not receive a fair trial and that the Great British Public were duped by "the authorities", then it's in the very fact that Tony's first interview was not played to the jury. It should have been. He was cheated and you were cheated. Justice did not prevail.*

> **Ground L**
> threats and intimidation
>
> *Ground L dealt with all forms of threats and intimidation surrounding the trial and mentioned the alleged £60,000 bounty on Tony's head. It was obvious at court that special police precautions were being taken and after obtaining leave of the judge the fact that Tony had been threatened was adduced in evidence.*

---

[525] What a pity Scrivener didn't consider the police's willingness to manufacture evidence (or suppress it) in this case.

During the trial, the police informed the prosecution and the defence that they had information that certain persons who were said to have an interest in obtaining the £60,000 had been sitting in court and 'eyeing' the jury and that they might attempt to follow the jurors home. This information was conveyed to the judge and not to the jurors.

The judge ruled that the jurors should merely be warned not to talk about the case to anyone and that if anyone approached them they should dial 999 and say they were on the Martin jury. He turned down a request that the jurors should be taken to and from court by police vehicle.

In the event, one juror complained about being stared at by someone in the public gallery and there was also a complaint by a juror that men were outside his flat. There was also evidence that two heavily built men associated with the deceased's family were seen to point and stare at Tony and members of the jury.

However, no further warnings were given to the jury and no further steps were taken for their protection, although the jury were aware that special precautions were being taken to protect Tony.[526]

The jurors should have been afforded police protection and the possibility of the jurors' home addresses becoming known should have been avoided. The jurors could have been apprehensive as to their own safety.

The judge should have specifically asked the jurors whether they felt able to perform their duties without feeling intimidated or at all fearful. The judge should have given a specific direction to the jury that they should dismiss from their minds any thoughts that they were being intimidated or that they should in any way be fearful in bringing in a true verdict according to the evidence.

So, those were the grounds of appeal that Scrivener had prepared for the Court of Appeal.

---

[526] There were no 'special protections' being afforded to Tony. The police had him in a 'safe house' for *their* protection not his — if he had been allowed to return to Bleak House and examine the breakfast room, he'd have seen that the case against him was nonsense.

The Court of Appeal

Part 19: the court of appeal

Tue
30 OCT
2001
10 am
404

Royal Courts of Justice, Strand, London
Having sacked Scrivener, Tony Martin instructed solicitor James Saunders who in turn instructed Tony's new defence team of leading counsel Michael Wolkind, QC and junior counsel Michael Edmonds. The prosecution again comprised of Miss Rosamund Horwood-Smart, QC and Mr Ian James.

The appeal judges were the Lord Chief Justice (Lord Woolf of Barnes), Mr Justice Wright and Mr Justice Grigson.

The opening paragraph is of immediate importance:

"On 19 April 2000, Mr Anthony Edward Martin stood trial before Mr Justice Owen and a jury on an indictment containing a count of murder of Freddie Barras (count 1), a count of attempted murder of Brendon Fearon (count 2) and *an alternative to count 2* of wounding with intent (count 3). There was also a count of possessing a firearm with intent to endanger life (count 4). Finally, there was a count of possession of a firearm without a certificate (count 5) which was the only count to which Mr Martin pleaded guilty."

The emphasis is mine: clearly the Court of Appeal had confirmed that Count 3 was an *alternative* to Count 2 and not an *additional* count. We saw at trial how the jury had been confused by Judge Owen, who throughout his summing up, had described Count 3 as an alternative but when the jury was in the process of returning its verdicts for the first time, he claimed that it was not an alternative count.

The appellate judges confirmed that the jury convicted Tony Martin by a majority of 10 to 2 of murder and wounding with intent, yet acquitted him of the attempted murder of Fearon and of possession of a shotgun with intent to endanger life. The judges reminded us that he was sentenced to life imprisonment for murder, ten years' imprisonment concurrent for wounding with intent and 12 months' imprisonment concurrent in respect of his possession of the shotgun without a certificate.

The absurdity of Tony being acquitted of the attempted murder of Fearon and yet being found guilty of wounding with intent made an ass of the entire trial – if he was guilty of the wounding with intent of Fearon, why not of Barras? Yes, Barras had unfortunately died, so if Tony Martin was guilty of the murder of Barras, then surely he was also guilty of the attempted murder of Fearon.

Clearly, these verdicts were a nonsense or, to use the legal jargon so despised by Tony, 'inconsistent'. But we must note paragraph three because it provided an indication of why Tony Martin was brought to trial in the first place: "At the time the offences were committed, Mr Martin was being burgled by the two people whom he shot.[527] Because he was being burgled at the time there was considerable public sympathy for Mr Martin and media interest in his case. There were also suggestions that the law was in need of change."

The legal profession – and the government – did not much like that the case had garnered enormous public sympathy for the farmer. It seems that they had planned to teach the farmer a lesson and had completely under-estimated and arrogantly ignored the feelings of the ordinary folk of this country.

Most 'ordinary' people could see that Tony Martin had been the victim of a gross miscarriage and they were not even in possession of the facts that I have outlined so far in this book. Nor did the lawyers and the politicians welcome the idea that the law was in need of change – the endemic arrogance of the legal profession is that it always gets it right which is why appealing against any conviction is an arduous and unnecessarily complex business designed to put off all but the most tenacious.

Tony Martin was being used as a football being kicked first by the politicians and then booted back by the lawyers as Lord Woolf stated that the subject of debate was whether a defendant to a murder charge should be convicted of murder if he was acting in self-defence but used excessive force in self-defence. It had been suggested that such a defendant should be regarded as being guilty of manslaughter and not murder. He would not then have to be sentenced to life imprisonment but usually instead to a determinate sentence the length of which would be decided upon by the judge, having regard to the circumstances of the offence.

To this day, Tony Martin believes that the law on this issue needs to be clarified once and for all. I believe that few would disagree.

Coming to the facts of the case itself, the appellate judges stated (at paragraph 22) that Fearon was not cross-examined about the change in his statements about where Tony Martin was standing. The three judges stated that this lack of cross-examination was taken as the result of a considered and deliberate decision by the defence team.[528]

But then – more legal engineering here – the judges let Scrivener (one of them, after all) off the hook for potentially perverting the course of justice by claiming that he had chosen not to adhere to his client's version of events and

---

[527] There was no definitive proof of such a burglary. All Tony had known was that he had fired at an unknown number of intruders in his home. Intruders with shiny shoes or boots reflecting the torchlight and who spoke "unintelligibly".

[528] Note that the appellate judges – who ought to have been in possession of all the documents Tony put me in possession of (and more) – failed to mention Fearon's first statement in which he'd said he'd been shot 20-30 yards up a track.

instead supplanted it with his own version of events (which just happened to match the police version) ostensibly in the hope of gaining an acquittal. Were you or I to change what we know or believe to be true, we would be prosecuted for perverting the course of justice. And rightly so. But the legal profession – like the police – generally protects its own. They all eat out of the same trough and if it happens that a man like Tony Martin is wrongfully convicted and sent to prison for life, so what? They don't care. Defence barristers will get paid whether their client is found innocent or guilty. Same with the prosecutors.

At least Wolkind appeared to have had a pang of conscience because the judges stated: "This decision by Anthony Scrivener QC is heavily criticised by Mr Wolkind QC." So it should have been in my view. On this reason alone – that Scrivener played God by creating a false narrative – I believe that there was a mis-trial. Scrivener wholly misrepresented his client and went against the principles of the Bar and the notion of justice.

The judges then proceeded to discuss the forensic evidence. A good number of people that comprise the Great British Public are fooled into thinking that scientific or forensic evidence is infallible. It is not. Challenge it. ALWAYS.

In 1966 there was a terrible tragedy in Aberfan, Wales in which a slag heap of coal residue took on a life of its own and slid murderously down a mountainside towards Pantglas primary school and took the lives of 116 innocent children and 28 adults despite many previous warnings from the locals (always ignored by the Coal Board) about the instability of such slag heaps. The BBC's John Humphrys was then a junior reporter and witnessed how the government of the day tried to cover up the failings of the Coal Board until many years later when it admitted its 'mistakes'. He wrote: "If Aberfan stands for anything today, apart from unimaginable grief, it stands as a reminder of this: AUTHORITY MUST ALWAYS BE CHALLENGED." Wise words in my opinion.

The judges stated that Dr Arnold, a forensic scientist, visited Bleak House on 22 and 26 August 1999 and found three freshly-fired 12-bore shotgun cartridges which were lying between the fireplace in the breakfast room where the two men were shot and the doorway to the hall at the bottom of the stairs. [Author's note: did you spot the error from the three judges? According to official records, Arnold did not find these empty cartridges, DS Eglen did. And it was the 21st August according to Eglen's statement dated 26 October 1999.]

The judges claimed that "microscopic examination has established that all three shotgun cartridges had been fired in the Winchester shotgun" - but do you believe this 'evidence'? After all, the police had that shotgun in their possession after seizing it from Tony's mother's house within a few hours of his firing it...

It was Dr Arnold's opinion, with which Dr Renshaw, the defence ballistics expert, agreed, that at least three shots had been fired. It follows, the judges said, "from this evidence that, wherever the first shot may have been fired, Tony Martin ejected the first cartridge and fired two further shots and ejected those cartridges from a position inside the room to the right of the bottom of the stairs."

On the face of it, this looks incriminating evidence. But with a little thought and some forensic examination of our own, it might not be as damning as it first looks. Notice the precise phraseology used by the judges here: "It follows from *this* evidence..." but it might not follow from *other* evidence. We're being led down a path which I suggest we ought not to be going. Notice how the appellate judges failed to mention the spent cartridges found in the hallway.

No-one can even be certain that three shots were fired, though this number of shots had become accepted. But the fact remains – it might be wrong.

DS Eglen, on his own admission alone in Bleak House, claimed in his witness statement that he – not Arnold – found the empty cartridge cases on the Saturday afternoon (the day after the shooting and just a few hours after the alleged time of the discovery of the body of Barras). Eglen then claimed that Arnold was present on the Sunday (22 August) but made no mention of Arnold finding anything. On Monday (23 August), Eglen claimed that he collected, packaged and sealed exhibits JE6, JE7 and JE8 – the three spent cartridge cases in question. These had been lying there – apparently – since 9pm (or thereabouts) on Friday 20 August.

Are you happy, as a taxpayer, that this 'forensic evidence' is valid, that it is capable of proving 'beyond all reasonable doubt' that those cartridge cases were ejected inside that room and not from the stairs or hallway on the night of 20 August 1999 or even fired by Tony Martin at all?

CORRUPTION ALERT *Suspicions re cartridges having been planted to support false police account*

You see, SOCO Theresa Bradley was allegedly present when these empty cases were found, yet made no mention of this in her witness statement. Furthermore, 'forensic expert' Andrew Palmer was shown as being present, but made no statement at all that I could find, and DC Aldous, also said to have been present, made no mention of the sighting of these cartridge cases in two separate witness statements.

In his statement [see entry **369**], Brian Arnold – specialising in the examination of firearms, ammunition and related items since 1965 – claimed to have seen *four* empty casings in the room, one dusty and rusty. He stated that the three "fresh looking cartridge cases lay between the fireplace and the doorway to the hall and stairs." Notice that he did not say that these were found, or pointed out to him, by DS Eglen but merely that he saw them.

More mystery surrounding a simple shooting. And how can we be certain that those three spent cartridges were fired on the night of the shooting? Other spent cartridges were found throughout the house. Is this not, in itself, reasonable doubt that a skilled barrister would have seized upon to put in front of a jury?

Line of sight

And now we come to another critical part of this judgment. Dr Renshaw insisted that in consultation with the defence team he had always made it plain that, on the basis purely of the available line of sight, the first shot could have been fired from the stairs. The basis for his opinion that it had not been fired from the stairs was one of range, *based on Fearon's evidence as to where he and Barras were when the first shot was fired*. To put the matter another way, if the fatal shot was fired from the stairs, Barras would have had to have been either in the hallway or at best in the doorway to the breakfast room when he was hit. This evidence could have been elicited at the trial. The fact that it was not elicited was entirely the decision of the defence lawyers and not Tony Martin.

Notice the substantial reliance on the accuracy of Fearon's testimony made in the presence of police officers when he was taken to Bleak House a month after the shooting. And still there was no mention of Fearon having been shot "up a track". All of that had been conveniently airbrushed out of history.

The judges then discussed other forensic evidence which was said to have been available but not used at trial – that of Dr Lloyd, described as "a forensic science expert in the examination and evaluation of chemical and physical trace evidence, including firearms' discharge residue evidence."

The evidence available at trial, according to the appellate judges, was that swabs had been taken by SOCO Ian Bradshaw from the staircase wall, the banister handrail and the newel post of the stairs from positions where firearms residue might have been expected to be present if Tony's account was correct. [See entry **199**]. A single particle of primer residue was (allegedly) found in the swab from the wall which both the Crown expert (Mr Stephen Blunt) and Dr Renshaw considered to be of no evidential value. The judges stated that Dr Lloyd, who was instructed by the defence *after trial*,[529] decided to re-examine the swabs on updated and more sensitive instruments at the Forensic Science Service Metropolitan Laboratory and, at the same time, to analyse samples taken from the three relevant cartridge cases.

Five further particles were allegedly found on the banister handrail and newel post and they were found to correspond in composition to the primer particles present in cartridges JE/6 and JE/7. This evidence would support a suggestion that the source of these particles was cartridge case JE/6. While he accepted that there were other possible explanations, Dr Lloyd's view, now shared by Mr

---

[529] Author's emphasis.

Blunt, was that "the presence of five primer residue particles on the banister and banister post lends some support to the contention that a shotgun may have been fired from the stairway area."

[Author's note: notice that the judges stated that Dr Lloyd was appointed *after* the trial. According to police evidence, a statement had been taken from him *prior* to trial. It was not entered as evidence at trial and I have been unable to locate this statement. Disturbingly, I could find no mention of Dr Lloyd in the HOLMES database. As for Stephen Robert Blunt, there was a reference to him in HOLMES with a reference to a "statement of forensic scientist" but that statement was not entered into evidence at trial – why not? Mr Blunt was the Crown's own "expert witness", so why wouldn't they use the witness statement of *their own witness?*]

Swabs of the staircase had allegedly been taken but not analysed. Why not? This trial was rushed through. Why? Surely Justice is about achieving the right result, not about sending an innocent person to prison unnecessarily. Thank goodness we have done away with hanging.

The judges then turned their attention towards the summing-up of Judge Owen. Bear in mind he is one of their own: "No criticism is made of the learned judge's directions on the law of self-defence. When dealing with forensic evidence, the judge reminded the jury, in our view correctly, that the shots that had struck the wall and the door on the far side of the breakfast room from the stairs could not have been fired from the stairs as these two areas of damage were out of the line of sight.[530] He also reminded the jury of Dr Arnold's evidence about the distance that there appeared to have been from the muzzle of the gun to the point of impact on the injured people and pointed out that those measurements, *if correct*, were indicative that the shots were fired from a point "not as far away as the staircase."[531]

Notice that they made no mention of Judge Owen's management of Counts 2 and 3, his constant derogatory remarks about Tony Martin and his lifestyle,[532] and his failure to ensure the protection of the jury.

Having covered the background, the judges then focused their attention on the appeal itself. They repeated the main thrust of the appeal:

---

[530] This was correct. So if Tony had been standing on the stairs when he fired his gun, just how did those pellets get there? You are now meant to believe that Tony Martin was lying. However, an alternative point of view is that the evidence was planted. I have carried out such experiments myself and embedding shotgun pellets (size 6) into wood or plaster is a relatively easy task which can be achieved in a matter of a few minutes.

[531] Alternatively, the injuries were not sustained in the farmhouse at all but out in the open "up a track" as Fearon had told the medical staff.

[532] I remind the reader of Wallace Virgo's conviction being quashed not on the basis of any innocence, but simply because "the judge's summing up had been unduly harsh and the jury misdirected". [See entry **16**].

| **Ground 1** | *the preparation and presentation of the defence case denied Tony Martin a fair trial.* |

| **Ground 2** | *there was compelling fresh evidence to support self-defence.* |

The judges decided that it was convenient to examine both grounds together.

The essential thrust of Wolkind's argument was that in order to achieve the maximum support for Tony Martin's defence of self-defence, and to defeat the prosecution's suggestion that he was already downstairs lying in wait for the two burglars, it was crucial to establish if at all possible that Tony Martin fired the shots, or at least the first shot, from a position on the stairs. But while the farmer gave evidence to that effect, and maintained his position throughout cross-examination, Wolkind complained that Scrivener failed to challenge Fearon about his evidence as to where the farmer was when he saw him in the flashes from the gun, and in particular failed to cross-examine him upon the version he had given in his interviews and witness statements which, as we have seen, placed Tony Martin on the stairs "about three steps up from halfway" statements made *before* he revisited the farm with the police and his legal team and after much discussion changed his mind. What a pity it was that Wolkind hadn't complained about Scrivener not challenging Fearon about his statement to medical staff in which he said he'd been shot in the open.

A further complaint was that Scrivener effectively put to Dr Arnold only Dr Renshaw's first scenario, which placed the farmer just inside the breakfast room when he fired, as being the effect of the appellant's expert evidence, and did not make it clear that it was Dr Renshaw's view (as indeed it was Dr Arnold's) that it was physically possible for the first shot to have been fired into the breakfast room from a position on the stairs.

The judges stated that they had closely examined the contents of Arnold's and Renshaw's reports and the transcripts of the evidence by them at trial.[533] They came to the conclusion that "it was always plain that Dr Renshaw and Dr Arnold were agreeing that the impossibility of shots from the stairs into the breakfast room only applied to the second and third shots and not the first. That this position was clearly understood by everybody at trial seems to us to be established."

But it had not been clearly understood at trial that Fearon initially claimed he'd been shot outside. The jury failed to even consider this because that statement (and evidence supporting it) was not entered into court. Thus we can

---

[533] According to all official documents, Dr Renshaw's report was never entered at trial and nor was he listed in HOLMES.

be sure that the jury was being asked to consider a verdict when they were not in possession of ALL of the evidence.

Now read the legal twisting and turning used by the appeal judges to extricate Scrivener from his ill-conceived defence of Tony Martin: the judges stated that Scrivener was placed in an awkward position because his client had said he fired all the shots (that is, any number up to three) from the stairs. Fearon supported this account in his statements *made after his initial statement and in support of the police narrative*. However, the 'expert evidence' showed that this could not have been the case. Had Scrivener maintained his client's account – the appellate judges claim – this would have made Tony out to be a liar before the jury. So Scrivener had to 'invent' a likely scenario based on the 'expert evidence'. This flies in the face of what a barrister is supposed to do: present his or her client's account as told to them. Furthermore, what if – as in this case - the 'expert evidence' was wrong? What then? Well, there's the issue of guns not firing round corners, so the 'experts' figured that if the farmer had shot from the stairs, how could there be gunshot pellets around the alleged exit window which was not in the line of sight from the stairs? What a pity these "experts" hadn't considered the notion that the evidence didn't support Tony having fired from the stairs because *the evidence was wrong and it had been fabricated*. Aren't experts obliged to consider as many possible perspectives as they can?

Had Tony been standing in the doorway or even inside the breakfast room, there surely would have been far more pellets around the rear door and exit window and greater damage to the two alleged intruders. The measurements of the room were 7m x 4m (with the distance between the door into the room and the windows on the outside wall being 4m). Arnold had claimed that Tony had been standing in the doorway and fired off three shots, with the empty casings falling by the fireplace where DS Eglen was said to have (conveniently in my view) found them. But in another part of Arnold's evidence, he claimed that the alleged burglars had been shot from a distance of "around 5m". It wouldn't have been possible to shoot them from a distance of 5m if the depth of the room was only 4m, unless Tony had fired into the room at an angle from the doorway. In any event, it had been proven that you couldn't see into that room without a torch. Surely this all goes towards providing sufficient "reasonable doubt" and proving the farmer's innocence.

It seems to me that the trial was malevolently orchestrated against the farmer. Instead of the numerous discussions in chambers, or the trip to Emneth, or the long line of constables willing to disparage the farmer (without their pocket notebooks on hand to substantiate the hearsay they were spouting), there ought to have been much more time spent on possible scenarios based not on the presumption of guilt but on the presumption of innocence. And much, much more time spent seeking answers from the police as to why they allegedly failed to find the body of Barras until 16½ hours after he was said to have received his injuries. The police were most fortunate, it seems to me, to have escaped culpability.

The judges stated that: "It seems to us, counsel was entirely justified in seeking to gloss over the difficulties caused by his client's own evidence and to accept, as the prosecution were prepared to do, that the indications were that all three shots had been fired from the ground floor. Such an approach would eliminate the element of pursuit, and so support the defence of self-defence." [Author's note: the judges appeared to have forgotten that once Scrivener had advanced the notion that Tony fired all three shots from the ground floor, then the prosecution's retort was that he had been "lying in wait."]

The judges went on to state that it was clear that Tony was aware that the strategy which would be adopted at the trial was that, while he was under the impression he was on the stairs when the shots were fired, it was accepted that this could not have been the case. It was plain, claimed the judges, that the farmer had been fully consulted about the matter, and was aware of the difficulties presented by the forensic evidence."

> "I do not accept that I had been fully consulted about this issue. Throughout the trial I kept thinking, 'When are they going to get round to my version of events? This is all nonsense.' I was on the stairs when I fired my gun in self-defence to having been invaded and it's as simple as that. They did not have my permission to run with their version of events and they were acting outside of my specific instructions. As the trial unfolded, I began to feel that I had been ambushed by my own defence team."

But the judges' comments show that Scrivener and Makin were quite within their rights to distort Tony Martin's version of events because it was "in the farmer's best interests"! Before leaving this point, I draw your attention to solicitor advocate Julian Young[534] who has stated the following about the duty of a barrister defending an accused:

"I shall quote from the Bar Council Guide as set out in our famous 'red book' Archbold which applies to Leading Counsel, Junior Counsel and Solicitor Advocates: The following statement of principles which govern the conduct of defence counsel was made by the Chairman of the Bar following the rejection of complaints about defence counsel's conduct in the trial of *R. v McFadden*, 62 Cr.App.R. 187 at 193, CA: "It is the duty of counsel when defending an accused on a criminal charge to present to the court, *fearlessly and without regard to his personal interests*, the defence of that accused. It is not his function to determine the truth or falsity of that defence, nor should he permit his personal opinion of

---

[534] As quoted in the author's book *Framed!*, Melville Press, 2017, pp. 202-203.

that defence to influence his conduct of it. No counsel may refuse to defend because of his opinion of the character of the accused or of the crime charged. That is a cardinal rule of the Bar."

[Author's emphasis]. It is clear that the rules of the Bar Council are such that a barrister has a duty to his or her client to present *the defendant's account of what happened* irrespective of whether prosecution evidence exists which might suggest that it would be unwise to do so. Clearly the evidence could be wrong. The police have been known to create false evidence; they have been known to plant evidence and they have been known to lie when on the stand. Scrivener had no right (and breached the Bar's own rules) in substituting the farmer's version of events for his own crackpot theory which just happened to match the police 'evidence' of three shotgun cartridges being found just inside the breakfast room.

Psychiatric issues

In a magnificent piece of creative legal engineering, the appeal then became focused on 'psychiatric issues.' Initially, Makin had instructed a consultant psychiatrist, Professor Tony Maden, to examine and report on the farmer. Wolkind criticised the terms of those original instructions to Maden. Nonetheless, the professor produced a comprehensive report. He found no evidence that Tony Martin was then suffering from depression and no evidence of mental illness. His opinion was that while the farmer would be regarded by many people as eccentric and a loner he did not suffer from a personality disorder.

Maden added that Tony had described occasional periods of depression in the past, one of which may have been severe enough to warrant a psychiatric diagnosis at the time, but after such a long period with no contemporaneous accounts of the episode it was impossible to be certain. "If he was depressed then, he recovered without treatment and there was no suggestion that he was depressed at the time of the alleged offence."

The professor went on to say that not only was the farmer *not* suffering from any form of mental disorder at the time he was interviewed, but that also there was nothing to suggest that he was suffering from mental disorder at the time of the alleged offence.

The psychiatrist added that the feelings which the farmer described when he realised that there were people in the house were consistent with severe anxiety and "may be considered a normal reaction to grossly abnormal circumstances." I like that phrase – it sums up the situation perfectly as far as I'm concerned.

The professor concluded that in the absence of any form of psychiatric disorder the farmer did not have a medical defence to the charges he faced and was, therefore, fit to plead and stand trial.

So, you've read what Professor Maden stated in his report. I would have to agree with his comments. I have been extremely close to the farmer for six years and, as a qualified therapist – but not a professor of psychiatry – it appears to me that Tony Martin does not suffer from a personality disorder. He is different, unique, distinctive, knowledgeable, naïve and sometimes a complete and deliberate 'pain in the arse', but I take people as they are, not how I wish them to be. I wrote to Professor Maden in August 2016 asking for further comment but he declined to engage with me on the basis that he doesn't comment on his cases. Fair enough.

Professor Maden's opinions were then set aside in favour of those of Dr Philip Joseph, a 'distinguished psychiatrist' according to the appellate judges.[535] Up to February 2015, the non-practising barrister and consultant forensic psychiatrist Dr Joseph's expertise was reflected in his qualifications in psychiatry, psychology and the law.

Dr Joseph apparently conducted "two lengthy interviews with Mr Martin" though the dates and duration of these were not noted by the appellate judges. The psychiatrist found that Tony Martin suffered from, and was suffering from at the time of the offence, a long-standing paranoid personality disorder which *could* be classified as an abnormality of the mind arising from inherent causes within the terms of section 2 of the Homicide Act 1957. It was and remained the opinion of Dr Joseph that *if* Mr Martin intended to kill or to cause grievous bodily harm when he actually killed Barras, then his mental responsibility was substantially diminished. [Author's emphases.]

Note my emphasis on the word 'if'. It's a useful opt out for the legal engineers. *If* Tony Martin was suffering from an abnormality of the mind, then his mental responsibility was "substantially diminished." And, as they say in my neck of the woods, *if* his aunt had a pair of testicles she'd be his uncle. But what if Tony Martin didn't intend to kill – what then? And what if he didn't hit anybody at all when he fired his gun – what then?

The appellate judges would not countenance scientific and medical evidence which went to show that a miscarriage of justice had taken place at Norwich Crown Court, but they *would* accept evidence that allowed them to:

(i) keep him in prison;

(ii) manipulate the law to change the murder verdict to one of manslaughter; and

(iii) appease a public which could see that a miscarriage had taken place and needed to be thrown a morsel to comfort them while the lawyers

---

[535] The Court of Appeal judges failed to state in what ways Dr Joseph was 'distinguished' from his colleagues who had similar such qualifications.

and politicians re-wrote history and created yet another false narrative in the manner of Hillsborough.

Dr Joseph found that Tony Martin "had suffered from recurrent bouts of depression throughout his adult life and was suffering from depression at the time of the killing. This condition was a disease of the mind which exacerbated his paranoid personality disorder."

Assisting Dr Joseph was forensic and clinical psychologist Jackie Craissati, who said that Tony Martin had scored almost maximum points in a test for depressive personality traits. He had talked of an incident when he was a young boy, when a distant relative had tried to sexually assault him.[536] Ms Craissati said this had invoked great anxiety in him, to the extent that he did not want to take his clothes off, even to have a bath. [Author's note: this is simply not true. I've spoken with Tony about this and he says it's "complete rubbish." Besides, I've known him to take several baths.]

So there we have it – forget everything that Professor Maden said, because we can now say that Tony Martin was, after all, so depressed about being burgled in May that it made him fire at an unknown number of intruders in the dark after they had smashed their way into his home in the middle of the night in August.

Then the appellate judges set down in their judgment that Tony Martin had invoked great anxiety in the world of psychiatry because the prosecution responded to Dr Joseph's report by instructing Dr Mackeith to report on the farmer and by commissioning a further report from Professor Maden. (All of this at further public expense – I came across a letter which showed that Dr Joseph had been paid £1,952 for his report, a considerable sum at the turn of the century and worth a little over £3,000 in 2019).

Professor Maden maintained the opinion expressed in his first report. He told the court that when he saw the farmer while on bail awaiting trial: "his view was that he had not done anything wrong, and the vast majority of people would support him in his actions."

Dr Mackeith said it was speculative to suggest distress was indicative of a personality disorder. He said Tony Martin's unsatisfactory encounters with women as a young man were "commonplace when we are young."

Dr Mackeith found no sufficient evidence to support a diagnosis of paranoid personality disorder nor any evidence of depressive illness. He did find, however, that Mr Martin suffered from psychological problems. [Author's note: I prefer to use the term 'emotional' problems rather than 'psychological' problems because in the time that I have known him, I believe his issues arise from an inability to fully express his emotional needs (or sometimes even to identify them) and to

---

[536] Notice how the abuse at Glebe House School had been air-brushed out of her report. Tony told me he would have mentioned it to her.

discuss his emotions in a calm, rational manner.

At least since the age of 8, when he repressed his true feelings about being unhappy at being sent away to Glebe House School and in remaining silent about the sexual abuse there and that perpetrated by Rodney Townley, I believe Tony Martin learnt to repress his emotions in order to survive. It then became a habit, and so fixed in his personality that he is hardly any longer aware of his doing it and it's this default position which informs his thought processes. These in turn have led to the creation of a man with an inability on occasions to express his innermost thoughts and feelings and to trust others with them. But that's just my own view. Others, like Dr Joseph, will no doubt see him differently.]

So, we now have a situation in which Tony Martin – who once led Norfolk Constabulary a merry dance over the revocation of his shotgun licence in which they wrote to him almost begging him to fetch his guns out of the armoury – was now leading eminent 'experts' in the field of forensic psychiatry a merry dance. Who to believe?

Well, as you might expect, the appellate judges had a ready-made answer. They claimed that it was not required to choose between their respective opinions on the issue of diminished responsibility but they did find this 'medical evidence' acceptable to them.

At trial, the prosecution claimed that Tony was an 'eccentric' who had lain in wait to shoot at burglars "like rats in a trap", but now the prosecution was happy to accept the evidence of Dr Joseph as being that the farmer had diminished responsibility. They accepted this now because it enabled the Crown and the government to save face. It should never have brought this case, but now public opinion could be partially appeased. And in case you're wondering why Dr Joseph wasn't called to trial, there's another ready-made explanation: "The evidence was not available at trial. There is a reasonable explanation for it not being called, namely the negative terms of Professor Maden's report."

Apparently, it seems that Professor Maden's report – in which he stated that essentially there was nothing wrong with Tony Martin – actually harmed the farmer because it meant he didn't have diminished responsibility and so had to stand trial for murder, but now he apparently did have it. And they call these farcical sleights-of-hand 'justice.' And, I argue, you're paying for this through your taxes on a daily basis in courts throughout the land.

Dr Joseph attempted to justify his findings by claiming that "Taking into account Mr Martin's mental characteristics at the time of the killing, he would have perceived a much greater danger to his physical safety than the average person."

I do not believe that Tony Martin perceived a much greater danger than the average person. He actually stood in the presence of grave physical danger and I wonder how the appellate judges or Dr Joseph himself would have reacted in a similar situation.

All of these arguments are, of course, completely unnecessary because there has already been reasonable doubt about the entire police investigation and the trial as we have seen.

Role of 'expert' witnesses

In a case from 1975,[537] Lord Justice Lawton (a former Lord Chief Justice) spoke about the role of 'experts' in criminal trials, saying that an expert's opinion is admissible to provide the court with scientific information which is likely to be outside the experience and knowledge of a judge and jury. If on the proven facts a judge or jury can form their own conclusions without help, then the opinion of an expert is unnecessary. In such a case, said Lord Lawton, if it is given dressed up in scientific jargon, it may make judgment more difficult. The fact that an expert witness has impressive scientific qualifications does not by that fact alone make his or her opinion on matters of human nature and behaviour within the limits of normality any more helpful than does that of the jurors themselves; but there is a danger that the jurors may think it does.

This is my point entirely. Who on earth would accept the opinion of an 'expert' if that expert has just told them they have terminal cancer? Who wouldn't ask for a second opinion at the very least or challenge someone just because that other person has scientific or other qualifications?

The problem we have in the present adversarial system is that the jurors themselves may place a much greater reliance on the evidence of an 'expert' witness than they would any other witness. Similarly, there is no magic in the uniform of a police officer giving evidence at court – police officers can be wrong and they can, and do, lie when under oath.

The appellate judges confirmed (at paragraph 69) that Dr Joseph thought Tony Martin to be a truthful witness: "I believe he honestly thought that he was in an extremely perilous situation and that he needed to take immediate defensive action to counter the attack he was under." If this is the case, then that is surely a defence to murder – an honest belief that one's life was in danger. Since Dr Joseph believed this, then his report is surely redundant, as are the list of psychiatric disorders Tony Martin is said to have been victim to.

The judges allowed in fresh evidence relating to diminished responsibility on the grounds that it was admissible and relevant: "The jury did not have the opportunity of considering this issue. Although the issue was never raised at the trial this was because the evidence was not then available to Mr Martin, who is entitled to rely on the evidence for the purposes of his appeal. The conviction for murder must therefore be quashed."

Notice that the conviction had been quashed only on the grounds of alleged diminished responsibility and not because he was considered to be innocent.

---

[537] *R.* v *Turner* [1975] QB 834.

Wolkind also contended that the trial judge, having given a perfectly satisfactory direction as to the relevance of Mr Martin's good character, the judge undermined that good character because he made a remark during his summing-up debunking the reliance placed by the defence on the fact that Mr Martin was kind to children but so were Hitler and Stalin. The appellate judges stated that "There is nothing in this contention and we do not give leave in connection with the fifth ground of appeal."

The final ground of appeal with which the appellate judges had to deal was that while Judge Owen gave the jury written directions as to the offence of wounding with intent, he never provided any written direction for the jury as to the alternative offence of unlawful wounding contrary to section 20 of the Offences against the Person Act 1861. The appellate judges doubted that this was a failure, declaring it to be of no significance on the grounds that, since the jury rejected the defence of self-defence, a verdict of wounding with intent was inevitable. They rejected this ground of appeal. Somebody, it seems, really wanted to keep the farmer in prison a while longer.

Having dismissed the other grounds of appeal, the question arose as to whether the judges should order a fresh trial on the issue of diminished responsibility. They stated that they had no doubt they should not do so (no surprises there) because Section 3 of the Criminal Appeal Act 1968 allowed them to substitute a conviction of the alternative offence of guilty of manslaughter by reason of diminished responsibility. Their reasoning? "We are entitled to do this since it appears to us that 'the jury must have been satisfied of facts which proved him guilty of the other offence', namely manslaughter by reason of diminished responsibility. We therefore so find Mr Martin guilty of manslaughter."

What utter nonsense! The jury had found him guilty of murder but they based that verdict on incomplete information, police corruption, some untruthful witnesses and, in my opinion, a highly prejudiced trial judge.

Now the appellate judges were saying that if the jury found him guilty of murder, because we have now said it wasn't murder, we can now automatically substitute a different guilty verdict – manslaughter on the grounds of diminished responsibility. Yet the jury had never heard any psychiatric evidence against the farmer, so it's impossible for anyone to say that they would have found him guilty of manslaughter on the grounds of diminished responsibility. Professor Maden must have wondered what on earth was going on, since he had declared that whilst Tony Martin had some strange ways, there was otherwise nothing wrong with him.

Having found Tony guilty of manslaughter on the grounds of diminished responsibility despite the fact that this mental issue had never been raised before, they came to pass sentence. I hope you will be as horrified as I was when I first read the reasons that the appellate judges gave in sentencing Tony Martin afresh, having denied him a re-trial (in which, with all the fresh evidence I have reproduced here, he was surely bound to have been acquitted.)

Please also bear in mind when reading this next passage that the jury – who, as we have seen, were not in possession of all of the available facts of the case – were still 'apparently correct' in reaching their verdict: "It remains the position that Mr Martin used a firearm which he knew he was not entitled to have in a manner which was wholly unjustified. There can be no excuse for this, though we treat his responsibility as being reduced for the reasons explained by Dr Joseph."

We are forced to ask: Was Tony Martin's use of the gun wholly unjustified when taking into account all of the circumstances?

The appellate judges continued in what I regard as fabricated legal nonsense: "The jury were surely correct in coming to their judgment that Mr Martin was not acting reasonably in shooting one of the intruders, who happened to be 16, dead and seriously injuring the other."

And why do I say that this is nonsense? Because I take the view that he did not shoot *at* anybody and – on the police's own evidence – he couldn't have hit anybody.

Homily for the public

The appellate judges then delivered their sermon and you should all sit up and pay attention like good little boys and girls: "Any shortcomings on the part of the police could not justify Mr Martin taking the law into his own hands. We understand how frustrated Mr Martin may have been and in deciding what sentence is appropriate we take into account not only the evidence of his medical witnesses, but also the conduct to which he had been subjected. We also take into account that we must make it clear that an extremely dangerous weapon cannot be used in the manner in which it was used by Mr Martin that night."

Notice how the appellate judges did not comment on the fact that the body of Barras was allegedly not discovered until 17 hours after Tony fired his gun, that he died of a pneumothorax and not a gunshot wound, that he was subjected to three autopsies, that a dozen police officers claimed not to have attended the scene, that police on board a helicopter allegedly could not tell the difference between a human body and a dog, or even decide at what time the helicopter(s) went up and that Fearon told medical staff they'd been shot outside on a track...

Sentencing

The judges then passed sentence: for manslaughter, five years' imprisonment; for wounding with intent the sentence was reduced to three years' imprisonment; and the sentence of 12 months' imprisonment for the possession of the shotgun without a certificate remained unaltered. All the sentences were concurrent (running simultaneously rather than one after the other.) In view of the time

Tony had already spent in custody, he would be eligible for consideration for parole in about a year.

And that was that. All delivered with considerable disdain for a man who was no longer a murderer but guilty of manslaughter, who was no longer an 'executioner lying in wait' but of such diminished responsibility that he didn't know what he was doing and who would still have to remain in prison for another year and then be reliant on the Parole Board. The original miscarriage of justice was now being compounded with a second one, albeit delivered with a healthy dose of legalese to make it palatable to the gullible public.

Wolkind – on his birthday – added, "The court will understand that we continue to fight, and Mr Martin will seek elsewhere to quash his convictions." In the event, this was never pursued. Until now. With your help.

Tue 30 OCT 2001 405

press reports of the Appeal
The verdicts of the appellate judges were eagerly awaited by the broad mass of the people whose over-reliance on mere human beings dressed in robes and wigs worries me.

The Guardian[538] *actually raised some interesting points:*

"During the appeal, Martin's lawyers presented fresh evidence relating to where he was standing when he fired the shots and whether he could be said to have acted with 'reasonable force' in self-defence.

Martin's lawyers also claimed that his original defence team at the trial concentrated on legal tactics and ignored vital evidence that could have resulted in a different verdict. This morning, the judges rejected those arguments, but they accepted evidence of diminished responsibility.

A psychiatrist described Martin as having a paranoid personality disorder, probably made worse by an earlier invasion of his property by burglars.

The farmer's legal team contended that this factor was relevant not only to the question of whether he acted through diminished responsibility, but also to his plea of self-defence - because he feared a much greater danger to his physical safety than the average person. [...]

The judges refused Martin's lawyers permission to take the case to the House of Lords on a point of law concerning the admissibility, in a plea of self-defence, of psychiatric evidence on the defendant's perception of the danger he faced.

Martin's solicitor, James Saunders, said he would fight to take the case to the House of Lords in the hope of having his client's conviction quashed entirely.[539]

Mr Saunders said of Martin: "He said he was relieved that he could now see an end to his ordeal. He is relieved to be no longer branded a murderer."

---

[538] https://www.theguardian.com/uk/2001/oct/30/tonymartin.ukcrime.
[539] Author's emphasis.

But Mr Saunders added that Martin considered himself an innocent man, and wanted a chance to prove that before the House of Lords."

In the event, the case was never taken to the House of Lords (now the Supreme Court) but with your help we can achieve the quashing of his convictions.

Fri 1 MAR 2002 — 406

Lowestoft, Suffolk
Dr Michael Heath was called in to examine Jacqueline Tindsley, 55, whose body was found in her bed at home in The Hemplands, Lowestoft, Suffolk, in March 2002. Her partner, Stephen Puaca, was jailed in November that year for her murder following Dr Heath's evidence that she was asphyxiated. [See also entry 401 and others]

Sun 31 MAR 2002 — 407

Scarning, Norfolk
The body of a 22-year-old mother-of-three, Michelle Bettles, who had been working as a prostitute in order to fund her drug habit, was found in woods near Scarning off the A47 near Norwich.

The case came under the jurisdiction of the Norfolk Constabulary, which had failed to solve the murders of prostitutes Natalie Pearman in 1992 and Kellie Pratt in 2000.

The investigation was headed up by Detective Superintendent Christopher R. Grant and Detective Chief Inspector Martin Wright – the very same senior officers who headed up the Tony Martin murder 'investigation'.

Wed 10 JUL 2002 — 408

home address of Terry Howard, King's Lynn
Terry Howard (affectionately calling himself 'Badger') was a longstanding friend of Tony's (calling himself Toad) and, as you might hope any good friend would do if you 'stepped out of line', he spoke his mind to the farmer through a letter sent to prison. It raises some extremely interesting points:

"I'm sure you will agree that over the past two years or so, any recipient of a phone call from you has shown you support, sympathy, understanding, respect, encouragement and in some cases, affection.

Recently, however, your attitude and tone when calling has become so full of cant and self-importance as to prompt me to write this letter. Contrary to what you may believe, other people - including myself - have their own lives to lead.

In the last three months I have had more chest surgery and at 62, I find it very hard to take. Whilst recovering at Joanne and Andrew's at Loddon, Jo fell seriously ill and Andrew was informed that his wife stood a 25% chance of dying. During this period, I looked after the children to enable Andrew to continue to work. As a small side issue, my Rachael is being treated in Lincoln for a heart condition.

As you may now realise, my life has been busy. What I'm sure you don't realise is that in over two years you have never seen fit to enquire after my health or well-being or for that matter my daughter's health and well-being. WHY? ...

Your circle of real friends in this area is getting smaller, Tony, and I'm sure will continue to shrink so long as you treat them with such disdain. Your facile reliance more and more on a self-seeking publicist whose real agenda is to be the next Wisbech MP points to a real snow job (whitewash). Be sure my information on him is sound, Tony. I've spoken to two ex-Wisbech hoteliers and the man is KNOWN.

Finally, a few words on your letter to Lord Woolf - your crass pomposity and arrogance beggars belief in that you consider your circumstances in any way compares to the experiences of a terrified 12-year-old Dutch girl (Anne Frank) who died in a concentration camp before she reached eighteen.

So, stop pontificating from on high. Come down to earth. Start behaving like the ordinary man you are and not a celebrity. Go with the system, show some humility for once, stop believing yours is the only point of view, learn to shut up and maybe we can all have a homecoming party for you before the year is out. This is written as a friend, Tony, so I consider I have some licence to tell you what I think. Some people still care a great deal about you, so please stop ignoring them.

Yours, Badger."

I found that to be a remarkable letter. From information I received, it seems that the farmer didn't take too kindly to Terry Howard's comments, even though they were clearly for his own good.

The "self-seeking publicist" referred to here is Malcolm Starr, who took control of Tony's life, got him to sign a Power of Attorney over to him (later revoked), and who engineered many of Tony's family and friends out of Tony's life, including his mother and brother to a great extent.

It was Malcolm Starr, a property developer, who had engineered Tony's sacking of Kenneth Bush solicitors in King's Lynn and moving to M&S solicitors in Leicestershire (out of the way from Tony's family and friends). Nick Makin, as we have seen, was not a lawyer specialising in criminal law - he was, in the main, an estate agent, property developer and lawyer in civil law. That Makin was later to try to seize Tony's farm from him (citing unpaid legal bills) causes the reasonable person to "smell a rat". Mr Starr has often spoken on

Tony's behalf on radio and television and to the press *without his knowledge and consent* and often claims that Tony is "autistic". Tony has never been formally diagnosed with such a condition and thus Mr Starr is promoting lies in the media. Whilst Tony Martin displays *some* of the criteria for autism, he is by no means autistic. Besides, four eminent psychiatrists who interviewed him closely over several hours did not offer any such diagnosis of autism or refer to it in their psychiatric reports of the farmer.

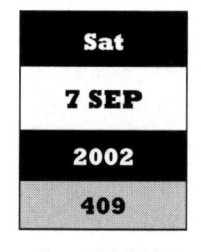

Sat 7 SEP 2002 409

letter to mother
I came across a letter to Tony's mother "and all at Redmoor" which provides us with a good indication of his mind-set whilst in prison:

> Thank you for all your letters and magazines. I don't write to be honest because there is nothing of interest, unless you wish to know the inside of a burglar's brain.
>
> Now a short political speech. I am now in no doubt we are not represented properly in Parliament. Democracy is a word. Saying all that, Henry Bellingham is about as genuine as you get. Prepared to speak up and be counted.
>
> I shall be out before August next year. I don't profess to know any more than anyone else. It's a conveyor belt: you get processed and drop off the end. There are much worse things happening to others than me.
>
> Well it follows when farming is down, industry soon follows. The laws will have to change, but will not for the girls of Soham no more than other crimes.
>
> Well you never know - The Man from Huntingdon[540] changed the establishment. Maybe the Norfolk farmer may change things. Seems far-fetched and fanciful. Truth is stranger than fiction. I feel I am the same as Tom Paine, Norfolk Quaker.
>
> The future can only change with a benign dictator or the Puritans. It is the cycle of history."

---

[540] Oliver Cromwell – a 'hero' of Tony's.

Sat 18 JAN 2003 410	**POW Trust to Tony Martin, HMP Highpoint** *Peter Sainsbury wrote a 3-page letter to the beleaguered farmer in which the charity's Chairman apologised for Tony having "to spend another period in jail."* *The charity's letter headed paper included the name of Malcolm Starr as a "company executive and social campaigner".*

Sainsbury's letter added: "It is an outrage you have not been released. In our opinion, purely political, you have been retained inside. The Police, Probation Service and the Home Office [are] all refusing to take responsibility for your release and your period on Parole. As you know, most people secure Parole on the first application in cases far worse than yours, and you have been a model prisoner ... As you appreciate, there is no route to appeal a Parole Board decision other than a Judicial Review. We can prepare such a JR from our office without cost.

We now know that Barras did not die until the following morning from the papers in the Appeal Court.

I believe this is serious argument that should be considered to take your case to the House of Lords. Please be advised that we are prepared to run your case through to Europe if need be to overturn the conviction. Terry Ewing, in our small legal department, has much experience with such cases helping ex-offenders fight their cases in Europe."

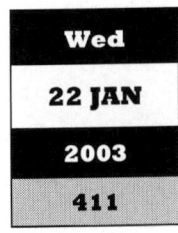

Wed 22 JAN 2003 411	**POW Trust to Tony Martin, HMP Highpoint** *Peter Sainsbury wrote the following to Tony: "The quicker you get back to the farm the better to organise its husbandry which needs much work. I visited the property some months back with the assistance of Terry Ewing and Malcolm Starr's son. You have a huge amount of work in front of you to bring the farm up to scratch, it will be difficult to live in the house in its current state. Perhaps a caravan on site will resolve the problem.*

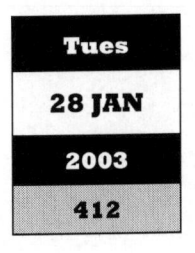

Tues 28 JAN 2003 412	**The House of Commons, Westminster** *The Rt. Hon. Gillian Shephard, MP for Southwest Norfolk, sent Tony a letter to Highpoint Prison:* "I was delighted to hear from you and to hear of your connections with my constituency and what goes on there. Henry Bellingham is in fact your MP because Bleak House is

just in North West Norfolk. The village of Emneth, on the other hand, is in <u>my</u> constituency, which is why at the start of your case I held a public meeting there.

I will immediately pass your letter to Henry, who I know has been in touch with you and will want to help in any way he can, as we all do. With every best wish..."

Fri 31 JAN 2003 — 413

POW Trust to Tony Martin, HMP Highpoint
Peter Sainsbury wrote the following to Tony: "The Daily Telegraph article was clearly a plant by the police to try to negate public opinion in case we have some success with your release. Some of the information should not have been published because you were, prior to the conviction, a 'man of good character' as they say in Court.

The reports on you produced by the probation officers were truly appalling.

Thur 6 FEB 2003 — 414

Crown Court, Canal Street, Nottingham
Before Her Honour Judge Hampton, Brendon Fearon was sentenced to 18 months in prison for supplying heroin to a fellow prisoner Interestingly, Fearon contested the allegation. He served half of the 18 months in prison and was released on licence for the remainder of his sentence.

Release from prison

Part 20: Release from prison

In this section we'll look at the days prior to Tony's release from prison, his eventual release and the eventual fallout from family, friends and the media. For a man who values his privacy, he was once again thrust into the spotlight.

| Tue 23 JUN 2003 415 | **POW Trust, 295a Queenstown Road, Battersea, London**
With Tony's release imminent, Peter Sainsbury, Chairman of the POW Trust, sent an important letter to Mrs Teresa Gorman at her home address in Orsett, Essex. Like Tony, the politician lived on a farm. I have not reproduced the entire letter here, but the most salient points. |

"As you probably know, if it was not for our charity, Tony Martin would be doing life. It was us, with [lawyer] Terry Ewing's help, that created the opportunity to appeal the original conviction without Legal Aid – for some extraordinary reason Tony Martin had been denied Legal Aid – that reduced the sentence to 5 years.

However, we failed to secure his release on Parole. Tony Martin should have been released last September. Purely Government intervention, which became clear when we organised the Judicial Review to challenge the Parole Board's decision to deny parole to Tony. The Chairman of the Board is a 'Blair crony'.

A 'secret letter' became part of the evidence and amazingly the judge refused to release the letter to the press and the public. And unbelievably, a lot of the Hearing was *in camera* (in secret). The 'secret letter' we believe is from the Home Secretary which still remains secret."

Clearly, this was no simple case of an eccentric old farmer shooting at two burglars in the night. Those practising the dark arts had made a political prisoner of the Emneth man.

| Tue 5 JUL 2003 416 | **Highpoint Prison**
A letter sent to Tony at Highpoint claimed that Makin had triple invoiced for the case: firstly, to the Legal Aid Board, secondly to the Criminal Appeal Central Fund and thirdly to Tony himself. The triple invoicing had been discovered, it seems, by James Saunders & Co who sent an 8-page letter of complaint to the Court of Appeal. |

The letter to Tony was written by Peter Sainsbury, chief executive officer of the POW Trust, a charity set up to tackle social exclusion and work with ex-offenders. The Trust had backed Tony's legal campaign against his murder conviction, which was reduced, as we have seen, to manslaughter on appeal.

In this letter, Sainsbury informed Tony that the POW Trust was working towards overturning his conviction through the Criminal Cases Review Commission.

In the same letter, Sainsbury informed Tony that he had obtained a medical report which showed that "Barras did not die immediately, but hours later – who knows how long, maybe the next morning. Certainly long enough for Fearon to take him to hospital. And if Fearon had taken him to hospital, Barras would be alive today."

But that, as we have seen, is still only half of the story...

"Why didn't the police discover the body of Barras during their searches? James Saunders agrees any normal jury would have found you innocent if all the correct information was put in front of the jury to include that Fearon, on tape in the police station, changed his evidence under police pressure. Indeed, it is quite likely that the Judge may have thrown out the case if he was aware of all the facts in the case to include that two police informers, who befriended you at the behest of the police, also gave false evidence we believe.

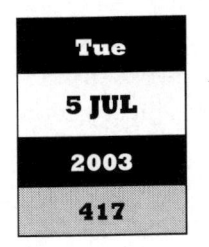

Tue 5 JUL 2003 417

Highpoint Prison

A 3-page letter sent to Tony at Highpoint from Peter Sainsbury included many interesting points. I reproduce a summary below:

- Hilary Martin's money was still being blocked as a result of Nick Makin claiming his fees
- former MP, Teresa Gorman, had offered to assist you in repairing your house
- several people had offered to provide round-the-clock security for Tony when he returned to the farm
- the Judicial Review judge said you might be dangerous to burglars if not the public at large
- you should reactivate the case between you and Makin which is currently stayed on the court's orders. I am sure with the right lawyers, you can probably secure a result with this action
- Henry Bellingham is saying your case is 'political'
- I have been in correspondence with the Deputy Governor of the prison and the Treasury Solicitor regarding the 'secret letter'."

Mon	
7 JUL	
2003	
10 am	
418	

House of Commons, Westminster, London

An early day motion (EDM) in the Westminster system, is a motion, expressed as a single sentence, tabled by Members of Parliament that formally calls for debate "on an early day". In practice, they are rarely debated in the House and their main purpose is to draw attention to particular subjects of interest.

On 7 July 2003 – just prior to the end of the parliamentary session and Tony's release - his then MP, Henry Bellingham, put forward EDM 1546 entitled BRENDON FEARON AND THE TONY MARTIN CASE:

"That this House expresses its grave concern that Brendon Fearon, one of the burglars who broke into Tony Martin's house, is now suing for civil damages in respect of the injuries that he sustained during his criminal acts, including his loss of sexual enjoyment and an ability to practise martial arts; expresses further concern that Brendon Fearon's case is now being funded by the Legal Aid Board despite the willingness of his solicitor to take the case on a no win-no fee contingency basis; urges the Government to look urgently at changing the law so that criminals who break into properties leave all their civil rights outside that property; urges the Government to reform the rules governing legal aid so that it cannot be claimed in such cases; and further urges the Government to note that 83 per cent of those surveyed by the Freedom Association believe that an intruder should have no case against a homeowner who takes direct action against them."

Fifteen MPs signed the motion, including Bellingham himself. It could be seen as a politically expedient move for the MP since the nation was up in arms against Fearon suing the farmer for the injuries he was alleged to have sustained after allegedly smashing his way into the farmer's house.

Sat	
12 JUL	
2003	
419	

office of solicitor James Saunders, Essex Street, London

A fax was sent by the POW Trust to the office of James Saunders, Tony's solicitor. The contents of this fax showed that Fred Barras did not die "within two minutes" as pathologist Dr Heath had maintained throughout the trial, and that Fred could have been saved. It was, beyond all reasonable doubt, a game-changer:

The fax comprised of a medical report with a great deal of the language employed by the medical profession. I have produced a simplified version below and précised the contents whilst maintaining the integrity of the document. The report was authored by Mr Alastair Wilson, lead clinician in the Accident and Emergency department at the Royal London Hospital in Whitechapel. Mr Wilson had been asked to look at the pathological evidence in the case and had sight of a substantial amount of evidence including all three autopsy reports and, more crucially, the x-rays:

Alastair Wilson fax: extract 1

"In his post-mortem statement on Frederick Barras, Dr Heath [541] records a shotgun entry wound over the left side of the back. The dimensions and direction of the hole are given and the wounding is noted to have extended into the neck. There is extensive bruising about the axillary muscles. On opening the chest, Dr Heath saw slight collapse of the left lung and 750 mls of blood in the left chest cavity. More extensive bruising is noted in the dissection of the right thigh. The cause of death given by Dr Heath in his statement of 22 August 1999 is 'Gunshot wound to the chest'."

The key word here is "bruising" because bruising does not normally occur after death – the suggestion, of course, is that "extensive bruising" had taken place throughout the time that Fred Barras was still alive after having been shot.

We are not, of course, surprised to read that death was due to a gunshot wound to the chest, but must we believe it? We learn more:

---

[541] Dr Michael Heath was said to have performed the first autopsy between 2:50pm and 6:45pm on Sunday 22 August 1999. It was started some 41 hours after the time put forward by the authorities as the time of the shooting – 10pm on Friday 20 August.

> **Alastair Wilson fax: extract 2**
>
> "In a further statement dated 10 March 2000[542] Dr Heath states that death would have occurred within 20 seconds to two minutes after the injury was inflicted. He does not venture a cause of death in terms of blood loss or breathing compromise, but believes death happened quickly.
>
> He would not expect that Barras was able to move a significant distance in order to place himself facing away from the window to sustain the leg injury and then exit through the window if the chest injury was inflicted first. Dr Heath does not mention any x-rays taken of Barras."

Author's emphasis: this highlights serious deficiencies in Dr Heath's report, particularly with regard to his failure to mention the x-rays allegedly taken of Barras.

> **Alastair Wilson fax: extract 3**
>
> "Dr Cooper[543] in his post-mortem report of 3rd November 1999 records the cause of death as haemorrhage due to a gunshot wound to the chest.[544]
>
> In the substance of the report Dr Cooper notes bruising to the root of the neck but does not note any large vessel damage. He was not able to assess the free blood in the chest as it had been previously removed at the first post-mortem. Dr Cooper goes on to state that the cause of death was as a result of bleeding principally from the chest wound. He states that bleeding would be heavy but it is quite possible that Mr Barras was able to function

---

[542] This statement is not listed in HOLMES and I have been unable to find a copy. Even more disturbingly, the official document '*Index to Statements*' lists one statement from Dr Heath, dated 2 September 1999. This is listed in HOLMES at line S103. A second statement is shown at line S103A with the description "additional evidence of the examination and post-mortem of 22-08-99." This alleged second statement was not entered into court and did not appear in the *Index to Statements*. For the avoidance of doubt, there is no entry in HOLMES with regard to a statement made in March 2000.

[543] The third autopsy on Barras was said to have been performed by Dr P Nigel Cooper on Sunday, 5 September, between 2:40pm and 3:50pm.

[544] This report of the third post-mortem was authored prior to the trial in April 2000. This means, of course, that the police and the prosecution and Tony's defence team *always knew* that there was the possibility that Barras did not die directly from the gunshot wound as Dr Heath claimed and upon whose evidence the entire trial was based.]

> for long enough to get from the scene to where he was found. In a rider to his first statement, Dr Cooper, in reply to Dr Heath's supplement, states that bleeding would have been heavy and into the chest cavity which would also have filled with air (pneumothorax) compromising Mr Barras' breathing."

It is apparent that Dr Cooper's report and Dr Heath's report differed in respect of cause of death. But Dr Cooper's report then mentioned the pneumothorax. This we need to note.

Alastair Wilson fax: extract 4

> "Dr Heath gives an estimate of between 20 seconds and two minutes. I believe it is possible that Mr Barras survived for up to five minutes after the chest wound was inflicted. Dr Cooper strongly disagreed with Dr Heath's belief that Barras would have been unable to move across the room to sustain a second and third injury."

Clearly these medical professionals are at odds with their diagnoses.

Alastair Wilson fax: extract 5

> "The note of Dr Heath's evidence at trial suggests that he agreed that, after being shot, Mr Barras could have negotiated the window and got to where he was found. The note also suggests that Dr Heath gave evidence that after the fall to the ground, unconsciousness and death would follow and that death was inevitable but no note of timing is recorded."

The fact that no time of death is recorded is of vital importance – as important as the fact that the time of death of those unlawfully killed at the Hillsborough Disaster was recorded to suit the needs of a police force working prodigiously to extricate itself from its own wrong-doing.

> **Alastair Wilson fax: extract 6**
>
> "Neither Dr Heath nor Dr Cooper remark on the x-rays of Mr Barras's chest performed *before*[545] post-mortem examination. These clearly show a massive tension pneumothorax. The shot, which passed obliquely upwards into the chest and root of the neck, caused bruising but there is no account of large vessel damage. The pathologists' reports do not suggest damage to any organs save the lung, *which would not of itself have been fatal.*[546] The damaged lung, in itself, was survivable, as was the hole in the chest wall."

Clearly this report is a game-changer. The x-rays – taken during the first post-mortem examination – showed a massive tension pneumothorax. Pressure was evidently building up in Barras's chest wall after the lung had been pierced. Air and blood were escaping into the chest cavity which was filling up as Barras's breathing became more rapid. A tension pneumothorax develops after air escapes into the chest cavity from a hole in the lung, and then cannot escape from the chest cavity, causing pressure to build up.

> **Alastair Wilson fax: extract 7**
>
> "At some stage, either because blood-soaked clothing plugged the hole, or because the angle of entrance and macerated tissue did the same, or possibly because Mr Barras lay down to rest, thus covering the opening, it became increasingly difficult for air to escape from the chest cavity (tension). Once the outflow of air was occluded [prevented], pressure would build up causing difficulty in breathing.
> Thereafter, with increasing respiratory effort, tension would develop. This pressure inside the chest would compress veins returning blood to the heart preventing the heart from ailing, reducing cardiac output and causing loss of consciousness. Eventually the lack of venous return of blood on top of increasing shock would mean that the heart would stop. Once tension had developed, it would take about five minutes to die."

This report provides different possible reasons why the hole in Fred Barras's chest wall might have become plugged or covered. Thereafter, with each breath he took and being unable to breathe out sufficiently, air pressure would have built up inside his chest and his heart would have stopped. The point is that during this time, he was still alive and therefore could have been saved had he received medical treatment in time.

---

[545] Author's emphasis.
[546] Author's emphasis.

> **Alastair Wilson fax: extract 8**
>
> "Dr Cooper's report dated 30 March 2000 mentions the possibility of a pneumothorax. This might indicate that he saw the x-rays, although he does not say so. Dr Heath makes no mention of a pneumothorax."

Dr Cooper's report was authored less than a fortnight *before* the trial for murder. It mentioned the possibility of a pneumothorax but this issue never arose at trial, the prosecution relying *entirely* on Dr Heath's report that stated that Barras had died within two minutes of being shot. So, to be clear, the prosecution *always knew* of the possibility of a pneumothorax and yet still took the farmer to trial for murder. The finest legal system in the world? You might like to think again.

CORRUPTION ALERT — CPS *fail to disclose autopsy report*

> I could find no mention of Dr Cooper in the HOLMES database as having been interviewed or making a statement. Additionally, this alleged witness statement from Dr Cooper was not entered into court and, of course, does not appear in the Index to Statements.

> **Alastair Wilson fax: extract 9**
>
> "As death was primarily due to a tension pneumothorax and not shock, it must be understood that death did not occur until tension began to build up inside the chest. As it is impossible to guess when this occurred, it is impossible to state the exact time of death, except to note that it would have been rather longer after the initial shot than has been estimated by the pathologists and *may have been as long as half an hour after*." [Author's emphasis]

Now, this information forces us to consider some unpalatable truths. Had Barras been found and allowed to die? If, as Fearon stated to medical staff, they had been shot *on the track* to the farmhouse, this would suggest that both men were ambushed on their way to the farmhouse and that Barras was *intentionally killed* by a person or persons unknown and therefore that the police never had any intention of "finding" him and getting him the medical attention he needed:

> **Alastair Wilson fax: extract 10**
>
> "I have often treated tension pneumothoraxes as an emergency procedure. This is done by making a hole into the chest cavity and allowing the air to escape. Had Mr Barras been taken to hospital with haste and had his pneumothorax treated, then his shock would also have been addressed. *He would have stood a fair chance of survival.*" [Author's emphasis]

"He would have stood a fair chance of survival" – this was not mentioned at trial. But who had *really* shot Fred Barras and Brendon Fearon? Had somebody stood over the teenager whilst he lay on the ground having been shot in the legs and then "in cold blood" as Neil Hirrel had told the police in evidence which was not used, intentionally shot the lad in the back?

And who on earth would concoct such a ridiculous story about a helicopter finding only dogs, or that the farmer's dogs prevented the police from finding the body, or that the getaway driver was on the scene all evening when they had evidence to the contrary, or that a blanket – covered in the blood of Fearon and Barras – was allegedly lent out by Paul Leet to a mate so that he could do some decorating?

Who would concoct a story that an ambulance could drive from Wisbech ambulance station to Tony's farm in just four minutes when it is physically impossible?

Who would concoct a story that a dog handler was taken to the scene and not deployed?

Who would concoct a story that an entire house would be a crime scene and all the furniture removed to a police station so that vital evidence of a stage-managed set would be covered up?

Yes, who would have ready access to guns? And why *did* those people never seem to arrest anybody or obtain prosecutions even after the public had provided them with names of known burglars and the registration numbers of the vehicles they drove?

And why would more than half a dozen police officers make statements in which they denied ever being at Bleak House?

Sat 12 JUL 2003 420

POW Trust, 295a Queenstown Road, Battersea, London
A letter was sent by the Trust's chairman, Peter Sainsbury, to solicitor Nick Makin:

"Mr Martin has requested us to recover the 67 pages of hand written, private, personal and confidential information that you required Mr Martin to produce for his defence during the period he was staying in your premises at Game Keeper Cottage, while he was on remand."

Clearly Mr Makin was far more heavily involved in Tony's life than merely acting as his solicitor.

Mon 14 JUL 2003 421

Queen Anne's Chambers, 28 Broadway, London, SW1H 9JS
A fax was sent from David Mackie at the office of the Treasury Solicitor to Peter Sainsbury, who had asked why the "secret letter" had not been included in Tony's dossier to the Parole Board.

"You ask 'Why was the secret letter not included in the Anthony Martin parole application submissions by the Governor from HMP Highpoint.' As is clear from the memo which we copied to you under copy of our fax of 11 July 2003, the document in question <u>was</u> included in Mr Martin's parole dossier. The reason that it was not disclosed to Mr Martin was because of its confidential nature. We regret that we are not in a position to expand further on the subject."

Mon 28 JUL 2003 422

release from prison
Officially Tony Martin was finally released from prison on 28 July 2003, but he was actually released from 'a secure location', having been taken there from HMP Highpoint. It is another prison in which we have both been forced to reside when the authorities knew us to be innocent.

It was reported in *The Guardian* and other national and provincial papers that "Mr Martin now plans to lead campaigns to protect householders who defend themselves against intruders, and to prevent burglars getting legal aid to sue for compensation if they are injured during a break-in. He is also believed to have signed an exclusive deal with a national newspaper to tell his story.

Police had set up a mobile police station outside the farmhouse following reported threats on the farmer's life. Whether he will now return to Bleak Farm, is not yet clear.

Tony's release renewed calls among his supporters, including former Conservative home office minister Ann Widdecombe, for the law to be weighted in favour of people who use a weapon in self-defence.

She told BBC Radio 4's *Today* programme: "What this case raises is a very much bigger picture, which is the whole issue of the right of somebody to defend themselves and their property. I'm saying that the presumption should be with the householder. I think where you end up with somebody dead or seriously maimed, you do have to test whether the force was reasonable, and it then becomes a matter for the courts."

"But for every Tony Martin, and this is what concerns me, there are hundreds of people every year, ordinary householders whose names don't hit the headlines, who find themselves on the wrong side of the law because they have either gone to somebody else's aid in the street and have caused injury to the assailant or they have defended themselves or their property and caused injury to the intruder. Even if it doesn't end up in court they still go through the anguish of a police investigation."

Ms Widdecombe also called for a change in the law that currently allows a wrongdoer to sue the person he was intending to wrong as that was a "complete nonsense".

Just prior to Tony's release his MP, Henry Bellingham, became a patron of the POW Trust.

Following his release, Tony was in London at the *Daily Mirror* offices. The newspaper had paid him £100,000 for his story, dubbing it "in his own words", but much of what he has said in this book was never made public in the paper. By 3rd August 2003, it was reported that Granada Television had offered him £250,000 to turn his real-life drama into a major film. He embarked upon an itinerary of public speaking engagements – which appears at odds with his professed need to be alone. Yet these are the extremes at which Tony operates. A hotel room one night or sleeping in his car the next:

> " People think I'm odd, but I've long since stopped worrying about what people think of me. I like to live out here, under the stars. It turns every night into an adventure. And the thing about living in your car is that you can just up and leave whenever you like. I can take off for Oxford at 3am if I want to. It's fantastic for a free spirit like me. People say it must get cold, but I say it's character building. We've all become too molly-coddled with electricity and radiators and every comfort. If we were all a bit more self-reliant, it might do us all some good."

Sun 10 AUG 2003 423

Sunday Express article

Within a few days of Tony's release from prison, his brother Robin was on the front pages of the Sunday Express *and pages 4 and 5 in an 'Exclusive' article penned by Michael Knapp:*

"KILLER farmer Tony Martin was yesterday branded a danger man obsessed with guns - by his own brother.

Robin Martin revealed he has moved to a 'safe' house in Cambridgeshire after fearfully telling the Sunday Express: "He'll shoot me next."

Robin's shocking allegations about his younger brother will stun a nation which has so far shown sympathy.

Martin, 59, was portrayed as a wronged man after being jailed for killing a teenage burglar. And his story has spawned a fierce debate over the rights of individuals to defend their homes and property.

But today we can reveal that his brother has accused him of being unstable - and wonders whether he will use a gun again if given the chance.

Over the years the jailed farmer has been involved in a catalogue of bizarre incidents that remain unknown even to the police.[547]

He fired a shotgun into his brother's house after he lost a game of pool. Following another row with Robin, he is said to have sat outside a pub with a shotgun on his lap.

And when the two were younger, Martin chased his brother around their garden with a carving knife.

Martin is also revealed to have spent time in a mental institution after a nervous breakdown and is accused of upsetting his desperately ill mother since his release from prison.

Speaking for the first time, Robin said: "What I can't stand is the way he's being made out to be a hero - because he isn't one.

He's fooled everyone. Only our mother and me know what he's really like. He's a complete nutter - and it's about time the public was told.

"Nobody knows what they're dealing with here. I honestly question whether he'll shoot someone else.

"I used to open up my front door thinking this could be Tony calling and he could have a shotgun. That's how I feel again now. I know he's getting old, but he could go off his head at any time."

Robin, 66, revealed he and his brother fell out 20 years ago over a plot of land left to them by an aunt. They argued over whether or not it should be sold - and eventually came to blows.

Robin said, "I went for him and he grabbed a knife. He was chasing me round the garden.

---

[547] As we have seen, these events were not unknown to the police. Indeed, it was Robin Martin himself had made the police aware of these incidents.

"There was another time when we'd had a row and he was sat in a Range Rover outside a pub with a sawn-off shotgun. I told the police, but they said there was nothing they could do. He had to kill me first.

"And he also fired off both barrels of a sawn-off shotgun into my house. Again it was some trivial row.

"On another occasion he was angry at some travellers because they were on his land. He shot out the tyres on their van. Then he reported it himself to the police and no action was taken. It's not the sort of thing you do, is it?"

Their mother Hilary, 88, who is suffering from emphysema, has still not heard from Martin. Robin said: "He's been out for days now, but he still hasn't bothered to even telephone his old mum. This is absolutely killing her. She still supports him, but not like she used to. I've seen him saying that I was the favourite and our parents didn't love him as much as me - but that's absolute rubbish. They loved us both the same."

Robin claimed that his brother was only staying part-time at Bleak House, in Emneth Hungate, Norfolk where 16-year-old Fred Barras was killed.

He added: "Tony's got a girlfriend called Helen and he often stayed with her. Very few know this, but he wasn't spending every night at Bleak House. I know for a fact he used to go back to that house every night from a different direction. He thought he was being watched, and didn't want the burglars to know his movements.[548]

"Despite what may have been said elsewhere, he was actually only burgled twice."

Speaking of the shooting, Robin said, "That night, in his vile madness, he just picked up a shotgun and kept pulling the trigger."

Robin, a four-times married grandfather, spoke of the days when his brother's erratic behaviour descended into temporary madness: "He was having trouble with his girlfriend and one day I got a call from a friend to say Tony had a World War One revolver and he was going to blow his own brains out.

I said, 'Tell him to do it outside, so he won't make so much of a mess.'

Two days later his girlfriend dumped him. She told people he climbed up a tree outside her house, got in through a window and sat in her wardrobe for two days. Later I got a call from Ely Police. They said they'd found Tony sitting by the side of the road. He'd cut all his hair off with a pair of scissors.

They took him to a mental hospital in Cambridge and I had to go and pick him up. When I got there, they'd put him in a padded cell. He was sitting in the corner like a rat.

"He had to come and live with me for a few weeks and I was a bit worried because I had two children and the bloke is clearly a bit odd. I've always thought he was a walking time bomb."

---

[548] Apparently several people knew of Tony's movements each night.

A friend of the Martin family said, "The brothers have always had a very stormy relationship because of what Robin thinks of his brother."

A spokesman for Norfolk Police said: "We are aware of one other shooting incident involving a shotgun. A lot of things said since Mr Martin's release have not been right. For instance, there's been talk of him being burgled 30 times. But there were actually only two burglaries."

In my view, the entire newspaper article was a sad indictment on the parlous state of the British press. It is evident that the campaign of defamation against Tony Martin bore no relation to a free press but to a press being compelled by agencies of State to publish black propaganda to an unsuspecting readership: I repeat Orwell – "The very concept of objective truth is fading out of the world. Lies will pass into history." In 50 or 100 years, people will look back on this case and read the papers from that period and believe all that they read (particularly the 'official' documents). Yet you and I know that what they will read will bear little or no resemblance to the Truth.

Sat 8 NOV 2003

letter to Tony Martin from Peter Sainsbury, POW Trust
Peter Sainsbury wrote to Tony on the Trust's letter-headed notepaper: "We are very disappointed that you will not be instructing us for the overturning of the manslaughter conviction which will leave you with a criminal conviction for the rest of your life."

Tony fell out with Sainsbury over the book by John McVicar which the charity was promoting. Tony felt that it did not represent the truth (it didn't) and he distanced himself both from the book and the POW Trust.

Sainsbury had wanted to take the case to the House of Lords, but the acrimony between the parties meant that this never occurred. Towards the end of his letter, Sainsbury asked Tony to donate the £100,000 the farmer received from *The Sun* to the Trust, so there may well have been a bit of emotional blackmail going on.

Sat 20 DEC 2003

Daily Express front page headline: 'SO SAD'
The newspaper published the story that Tony was living in his £300 Vauxhall Astra and that he had fallen out with his mother and several friends.
Former friend Terry Howard told the newspaper: "The fame has gone to his head. He says he's too busy to see some of us."

Diary

Part 21: diary

Tue 6 JAN 2004 426

Daily Telegraph article
The Daily Telegraph: *"Watchdog, the Charity Commission, has confirmed that it has launched an investigation into the charity that campaigned to free Tony Martin, the farmer jailed after shooting dead teenage burglar Fred Barras."*[549]

"The POW Trust, a charity set up to tackle social exclusion and work with ex-offenders, backed Mr Martin's successful legal campaign against his murder conviction, which was reduced to manslaughter on appeal.

The charity, which is understood to have had an income of between £300,000 and £400,000 last year, include former Bishop of Birmingham, the Rt Rev Hugh Montefiore among its patrons. It aims to provide legal representation and assistance, help with family visits, social welfare and employment opportunities and runs a bar-restaurant employing ex-offenders in south-west London.

The commission said it had opened an inquiry into the charity in November 2002 "because we received a complaint which involved allegations against the chief executive, Peter Sainsbury, and we also identified concerns that the charity had failed to submit up-to-date accounts." A spokeswoman added that the commission had received fresh complaints "in the past few weeks" but would not release the details.

It also said that Mr Sainsbury had been sentenced to five years in jail for his involvement in a £3m fraud case in 1990. The charity's legal consultant, Iain MacMaster, was reported to have been jailed for eight years in 1998 for laundering drug money and trafficking cannabis. At his trial the judge said that Mr MacMaster was a valuable "foot soldier" to dealers described by police as "among the world's top echelon of drugs traffickers."

---

[549] Notice the continued repetition of the same lie – that Tony killed the teenager. Goebbels - a minister in the Third Reich – had written in *Aus Churchills Lügenfabrik* (Churchill's Lie Factory) published in *Die Zeit ohne Beispiel* (The Time without Equal): "The essential English leadership secret does not depend on particular intelligence. Rather, it depends on a remarkably stupid thick-headedness. The English follow the principle that when one lies, one should lie big, and stick to it. They keep up their lies, even at the risk of looking ridiculous." I find it somewhat ironic that Tony, a victim of child abuse in an independent boarding school, developed a fascination for Churchill who covered up child abuse on an industrial scale when Home Secretary (and no doubt as Prime Minister).

Mr MacMaster said the POW Trust 'welcomed' the commission's inquiry and was cooperating with it. He said the claims concerning money laundering were "scurrilous allegations made by a disgruntled ex-trustee and director" who had been dismissed by the charity.

He added: "Like thousands of other charities, the accounts were late. I understand that the accounts have now been prepared and have been submitted."

Both Mr MacMaster and Mr Sainsbury confirmed that the details of their convictions were correct. The men said they were both planning to appeal against their convictions, but had not yet done so."

In my view Tony owes the charity a huge debt and not because of the 'successful' Appeal. We turn to the *Telegraph* again:

"Sentencing him for the fraud, which involved investors paying for non-existent industrial generators, Judge Henry Pownall told Sainsbury: "You are particularly able and it is a thousand pities that that ability was not used honestly."

Mr Sainsbury, who has also been convicted of currency offences in the Lebanon, although his sentence was later quashed, was banned at trial from operating as a director for 10 years. By 1992 he had set up the POW Trust to help the "socially excluded", including ex-offenders.

Thanks to his considerable charm, he garnered a number of patrons for the charity, including MPs Henry Bellingham and Austin Mitchell, the actress Anna Carteret, and peers including the Earl of Portsmouth. Some, if not all of them, however, were unaware of his past.

The revelations mark a low point for the charity, which achieved prominence through its tireless campaigning for Mr Martin. It placed itself at the forefront of the campaign to free the Norfolk farmer, who was jailed in 2000 for shooting two burglars at his farmhouse.

Many people sympathetic to Mr Martin sent donations to the Trust to help to fund a legal battle for his freedom. However, Mr Sainsbury and Mr Martin fell out last month over the charity's backing for a book being written about the farmer's case by John McVicar, the former armed robber turned author. The proceeds from the book were to be donated to the Trust, but today's revelations may put that deal in jeopardy."

I hate to think that the thousands of pensioners and children who contributed to the POW Trust fund had their money misappropriated by anybody, let alone an organisation fighting for Tony's release.

The book by McVicar (*A Right to Kill?*) was published, but Tony had already distanced himself from it by the time of his release:

> As far as I'm concerned, Sainsbury's a shyster. If I'd known then what I know now, I wouldn't have touched the charity with a barge pole."

Sadly, none of Tony's friends and supporters had made him aware of the report authored by Alastair Wilson which had been commissioned by the POW Trust. The farmer had, in my view, a lot to be grateful for from that organisation. And perhaps he ought to have questioned the level of support that he was getting from some of those 'friends' around him...

Wed 11 FEB 2004 427

Newark, Nottinghamshire
The Newark Advertiser *published a report on its website*[550] *that Brendon Fearon's father had passed away:*

"FEARON Joe. February 11, 2004. We are thinking of you today Dad. Never forgotten, always in our hearts. Loved always, Gary, Neil and Brendon. xxx."

In his statement dated 23 August 1999, Darren Bark's landlord, Melvyn 'Ken' Holland, described Joe Fearon as a "nurse at Newark hospital. I was there with spine problems. He struck me as a very nice man and very helpful."

---

[550] http://legacy.newarkadvertiser.co.uk/family/announcement/Joe-Fearon_NA524922

Thur 12 FEB 2004 — 428

Wisbech, Cambridgeshire

On Thursday 12 February 2004, Cambridgeshire Police said a 59-year-old man from the Wisbech area had been arrested for suspected theft of number plates. "The man was arrested sometime this afternoon," a spokeswoman said. Tony was released on police bail and no charges were brought against him:

" Soon after leaving prison, I returned to Bleak House one day to find a whole load of number plates hanging on the Titkill bridge near the Smeeth Road. Several workmen were nearby and they asked me what I was going to do. I told them that I couldn't leave them where they were, so I put them in my car.

Sometime later when I drove into Wisbech, the police turned up, saw the plates in my car, put two and two together and arrested me on suspicion of theft.

I later learned that one of the workmen had come forward and said that I hadn't stolen them, but had found them on the bridge near my farm.

The police are halfwits. I call them filing cabinets – a piece of paper goes in and a piece of paper comes out and no thought or common sense has taken place. They had no reason to arrest me and take me to the police station – they could have dealt with it in other ways."

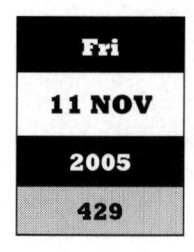

Fri 11 NOV 2005 — 429

man freed as murder conviction quashed

A man jailed for life for murdering his partner has walked free after having his conviction quashed at the Court of Appeal. Steven Puaca, now 38, from Lowestoft, was found guilty by a jury at Norwich Crown Court in November 2002 of murdering Jacqueline Tindsley at the home they shared in The Hemplands, Lowestoft, in March of that year.

But three judges, sitting at the Old Bailey in London yesterday, overturned his conviction.

Puaca, whose defence case was that his girlfriend died after taking a drug overdose and suffering a fit, was present in the dock to hear the judges announce their decision.

The key ground of appeal related to the evidence of pathologist Michael Heath, who the court heard is facing disciplinary proceedings in connection with two cases, including that of Puaca.

Dr Heath's evidence was that he believed 55-year-old Miss Tindsley died of asphyxia, but the judges heard that a number of other pathologists said there was no evidence to support that finding.

The judges quashed the conviction after hearing more than a day of legal argument and will announce their reasons at a later date.

Lord Justice Hooper said: "For reasons which will appear in the judgment that we shall hand down later, in our view there was no evidence, independent of the medical evidence, which was sufficient to make a jury, properly directed, sure that the cause of death was that advanced by Dr Heath.

"Even if we had not reached that conclusion we would in any event, in the light of the evidence which has been placed before us, taken the view that it would not be in the public interest for there to be a retrial."

Puaca's solicitor, Chris Brown of Norwich, who visited his client in the cells after the ruling while awaiting his release, said afterwards: "He is very pleased, but he is also understandably sad that he has been accused of what he was accused of and that he has carried that stigma for three-and-a-half years."

Mr Brown said that Puaca did not plan to return to the Suffolk area: "He has got options and he is going to make telephone calls to sort out what he wants. He wants to get on now with rebuilding his life."

Mr Brown said: "Our whole contention was that this was a case which should never have gone in front of a jury."

One of the grounds of appeal, he said, was over new evidence that the injury to Miss Tindsley, which the prosecution said happened at the time of death, "could have happened earlier".

But the "key limb" of the appeal related to evidence in the case from Dr Heath, whose work had included a number of high-profile cases.

A number of experts were prepared to put their names to a conclusion that the cause of death was a drugs overdose, he said, while others said the cause of death was unascertainable, but that an overdose was a possibility. But they all agreed "categorically" that there was no pathological evidence of asphyxia.

The Crown told the judges that a Home Office disciplinary tribunal hearing was expected to be held in January and pointed out to the court that "there has been no finding against Dr Heath".

Tue 29 AUG 2006 430

pathologist's fitness to practice in question

With regard to the hearing in respect of Dr Michael Heath's fitness to practice, The Guardian *reported:*

"Professor Derek Pounder, of the department of forensic medicine at Aberdeen University, said the problems exposed were symptomatic of a deeper problem. 'More than 50% of forensic pathologists work single-handedly, rather than out of an institute or university as they once did,' the professor said. 'What that means is there is no day-to-day discussion between colleagues about the cases they are involved in.

Therefore any aberrant opinion becomes uncontrolled within the system over a number of years.'

Although the attorney general has ruled out a wholesale review of cases in which Dr Heath was the pathologist, the Criminal Cases Review Commission's own review of 54 convictions for murder or manslaughter in which he gave evidence identified the nine cases which need further examination. [Author's note: shamefully, Tony's case was not one of them. In my view, and that of many others, the CCRC to this day is not fit for purpose.]

David Jessel, from the CCRC, said: "In many of the cases in which Dr Heath figures, his evidence is peripheral. But we have identified a handful in which he gives evidence of opinion which goes to the heart of the defence case. In those it is clearly sensible for us to take a fresh look at the case through the prism of what we now know about Dr Heath."

It is evident that Dr Heath's testimony in Tony's case went to the heart of the case. He was, after all, the *only* pathologist to be called to court to give evidence and it was Dr Heath who claimed that Fred Barras had died within two minutes of being shot and that he "could not have been saved", which we now know was completely untrue.

Professor Ferris, a consultant forensic pathologist in the Department of Forensic Pathology at Auckland Hospital, New Zealand and Professor Emeritus of Forensic Pathology at the University of British Columbia said, "The role of the pathologist, as I believe I have said several times, is to use his pathological findings to test the evidence or the circumstances of the instance as are presented to him. And therefore you have to keep an open mind; you cannot completely exclude a number of possibilities, and if you are going to say that such and such is the only possibility, you've got to be so sure of your findings that you should be able to convince everyone, including your colleagues."

Dr Heath, of course, had not convinced his colleagues Shepherd and Cooper. On his own admission, Dr Heath was "arrogant", he did not consider all the possibilities beyond the most obvious and he was unprofessional and lacking in medical rigour. And, I say, it cost Tony Martin 3½ years in a prison cell and an immeasurable cost to the quality of his life.

Anyone can make a mistake in his or her profession – we're all human beings and essentially fallible. But there can be no excuses for someone like Heath whom the evidence shows left a trail of lives blighted by his incompetence and lackadaisical approach to a serious profession. Other people besides Tony Martin went to prison for murder when they were innocent. And the common denominator was pathologist Dr Heath. But it would be wrong of us to think that Heath was acting alone in the corrupt case against Tony Martin.

| Fri |
| 22 SEP |
| 2006 |
| 431 |

pathologist resigns from register[551]

One of the UK's leading pathologists has resigned from the Home Office register after being severely criticised by a disciplinary hearing. The Advisory Board for Forensic Pathology upheld 20 disciplinary charges against Dr Michael Heath. It ruled that his conduct brought into question his fitness to practise.

Last month Dr Heath's evidence in the murder conviction of Steven Puaca, of Lowestoft, was criticised. Mr Puaca was later cleared by the Appeal Court.

The Advisory Board found that Dr Heath bungled post-mortem examinations on two women leading to their partners being tried for murder.

It found that in both cases Dr Heath's professional performance fell short of the standards required of forensic pathologists by the Secretary of State.

The six-week hearing in London was told that Dr Heath refused to back down on his view that the two women had been murdered despite mounting evidence to the contrary.

In one case, Mr Puaca was jailed at Norwich Crown Court in 2002 for killing Miss Jacqueline Tindsley, 55.

The second involved Kenneth Fraser, who faced an Old Bailey trial, also in 2002, for murdering Miss Mary Anne Moore, 56, but was cleared by a jury.

Charles Miskin QC, for the Home Office, told the hearing that in neither case was there any substantial evidence of unlawful killing, except Dr Heath's testimony.

The hearing, which was expected to reconvene on Monday, has now been called off.

Dr Heath had conducted hundreds of official and high-profile examinations since being appointed to his role in 1991, including into the Lynn and Megan Russell murders and the death of Stuart Lubbock in a swimming pool at Michael Barrymore's house in Essex.

The Home Office confirmed on Friday afternoon that Dr Heath handed in his resignation.

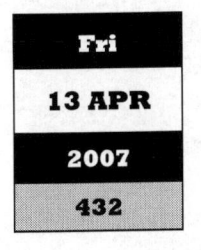

| Fri |
| 13 APR |
| 2007 |
| 432 |

Nottingham Crown Court

The Eastern Daily Press *published a report on its website*[552] *that Brendon Fearon and his brother Neil had appeared in court accused of stealing metal from a scrap merchant, Hoval Ltd, on Trent Lane, Newark, Nottinghamshire last December.*

---

[551] http://news.bbc.co.uk/1/hi/england/5372270.stm
[552] http://www.edp24.co.uk/news/bleak-house-shooting-victim-in-court-1-695924

"Both men denied a charge of theft at Nottingham Crown Court and the hearing was adjourned for trial by Judge Jonathan Teare.

Brendon Fearon, 36, of Albion Street, Newark and Neil Fearon, 40, of Vixen Close, Newark, were released on bail."

Thur 11 JUN 2009

General Medical Council hearing

We've already seen how Dr Heath was called to a disciplinary hearing in 2006 and resigned from the register of pathologists but there is far more to that story. On 11 June 2009, at a second hearing, he confessed: "It was quite apparent I had been incredibly arrogant in my approach."

"I had been doing the job for 20-odd years, had obtained a senior position and had done many, many cases. When I reflect upon things it was apparent that I was muddling up theoretical and academic argument with what I was required to do. I was not addressing the issue of my job and not listening to others. I had become my own judge and jury and that was wrong.

At no stage did I seek help. I just carried on going in an arrogant way and that was wrong. It was not in the interests of justice and I can see that now. It has taken me some time to get there."

Fri 12 JUN 2009

General Medical Council hearing

The Daily Telegraph *reported on the General Medical Council hearing in which Dr Michael Heath's fitness to continue practising medicine was being questioned.*

We have already learnt that Heath resigned from the Home Office register three years previously after he was strongly criticised by a Government disciplinary panel for his work on the deaths of Mary Anne Moore and Jacqueline Tindsley. It was reported that in 2009 he no longer worked in the field of forensic pathology yet continued to conduct post-mortems on behalf of coroners. If you've had a loved one's autopsy carried out by Heath, you might consider challenging what he found.

Dr Heath admitted his conduct in relation to the Moore and Tindsley post-mortem examinations was inappropriate, inadequate, not of a standard expected of a medical practitioner and liable to bring the profession into disrepute.

He conceded that it was unreasonable to exclude the possibility of an accidental death in the death of Miss Tindsley and he unreasonably failed to give any weight to the opinions of his experienced colleagues from the defence teams at the trial – a direct echo of the Tony Martin trial.

Dr Heath also agreed with the GMC that his post-mortem examination of Miss Moore was "so inadequate it significantly compromised the ability of the prosecution and the defence to explore matters material to the cause of death."

Yet Tony Martin's case was never re-examined. And, I argue, it was never re-examined because it had been the epitome of corruption and the Home Office needed to cover up the fact that Barras was not killed by Tony Martin.

Thur 9 MAY 2013 435

Fermoy mental health unit, Queen Elizabeth Hospital
After several further thefts from the farm including an incident with two men stealing batteries from a barn, Tony referred himself to Wisbech police on the grounds that burglars were not safe from him. He was driven in a police car to the Fermoy Centre, a mental health unit at the Queen Elizabeth hospital in King's Lynn, where he stayed for 28 days after which, clearly not mentally ill, the section was removed and he was released.

" There were weapons inside the shed so, if I had wanted to fight them off, I could have. I wished I had but, after everything I've been through in the past, I just couldn't face all that hassle again.

It isn't the first time it's happened since I've been out of prison – it's happened two or three times. I haven't changed my views about what happened in 1999 but the whole experience has made me lose faith in the system and I didn't want to be made out as the criminal again.

I put myself in the Fermoy to prevent me from doing anything stupid, for my own sanity and the safety of burglars. I can't stand burglars. I think they are a filthy lot."

Tue 16 JUL 2013 436

Royal Courts of Justice, London
Lambeth Council attempted to obtain a permanent gagging order on the author for the rest of his life. The author was accompanied to Court by Richard Fulcher, a pig farmer who claimed to have been unlawfully fitted up by Norfolk Constabulary for two counts of alleged Threats to Kill local councillors and one count of the harassment of a solicitor who sat on his claim against the local council after they illegally burnt down one of his barns, claiming it flouted planning regulations.

Thur
18 JUL
2013
437

Ivy Farm, Tilney All Saints
The author met Tony Martin in a farmhouse owned by Judith Maxey. A number of people were present and Tony Martin was surprised at the author's recall of his case and the fact that the author believed the farmer to be innocent because the newspaper propaganda was entirely focused on the farmer's supposed eccentricities and not on the facts of the case.

Thur
1 AUG
2013
438

Ramblewood Farm, Pott Row, Norfolk
The author was unlawfully arrested by armed police (including PC 400 Adrian Girton – see earlier entries) on 'suspicion of criminal damage to a car'. A fuller account of this illegal police activity can be found in the author's books Framed! and 10 Prisons 12 Weeks. When Richard Fulcher, the farmer who owned the land, made a Subject Access Request to Norfolk Constabulary in 2018 for all the information it held on him, no account of this illegal arrest was mentioned.

Wed
29 JAN
2014
439

Darby Farm, Pott Row, near King's Lynn
With witnesses present, the author was arrested by PC 1282 Jonathan Miller (see entries **84** and **288**) without being given a reason for the arrest. Eventually the author was told he had been arrested for Impersonating a Barrister and then for allegedly harassing his daughter and grandchildren by sending them letters about police and judicial corruption. The author was released on police bail with a requirement to attend the police station in King's Lynn on a twice-weekly basis.

Fri
21 FEB
2014
10.30 am
440

Darby Farm, Pott Row, near King's Lynn
Tony Martin dropped off 6 boxes of case material to the author at his lodgings, including the HOLMES "murder book", letters from the public, witness statements (used and unused) etc.

The two men shared tea and biscuits and then lunch. The farmer met the landlady at Darby Farm, who just happened to have been a huge fan of his. Around 1am the following morning, the farmer left.

Sat **1 MAR** 2014 11.23 am 441	**Darby Farm, Pott Row, near King's Lynn** *PC Karen Girton – wife of PC 400 Adrian Girton – called at Darby Farm to try to deliver court papers to the author for a bogus case of Impersonating a Barrister. The author – with witnesses present – refused to accept the papers, informed the police that it was a fraudulent case and that he wished to have no part in fraud.*
Sat **1 MAR** 2014 11.28 am 442	**Darby Farm, Pott Row, near King's Lynn** *The local postman called to say that there was a block on the author's mail – that a notice had been put up in the sorting room not to deliver mail to the author.* *This was an unlawful breach of his right to a private and family life.*
Tues **4 MAR** 2014 443	**offices of the Daily Mirror, Canary Wharf, London** *The author and Michael Bird, co-author of the banned book From Hillsborough to Lambeth, met with Tom Pettifor of the Daily Mirror. The journalist had written a number of articles – often on the front page – about child abuse within Lambeth Council. Mr Pettifor was given a copy of the book.*
Wed **5 MAR** 2014 noon - 6 pm 444	**White Lion Hotel, Wisbech** *The author met with Tony Martin and they spent six hours discussing the case and the serious issues involving police corruption that the author had thus far uncovered.* *The author showed the farmer a good deal of the paperwork which highlighted obvious flaws in the case.*
Thur **6 MAR** 2014 445	**Fermoy mental health unit, Queen Elizabeth hospital** *The author was unlawfully arrested on a bogus charge of there being a warrant out for his arrest for failing to appear in a non-existent court case of which the author had been given no prior notice.* *The author was sectioned under the mental health act by the police doctor and taken without his consent to the Fermoy Unit.*

The author slept the night and on the following morning informed the panel of doctors and nurses that he had been detained unlawfully, that he was not in need of their assistance, that he was not a danger to himself or others and that he was an investigative author who wrote about child abuse in Lambeth and was about to expose considerable police corruption in the Tony Martin murder trial.

The lead doctor apologised to the author for detaining him and stated that "it is clear you are an intelligent man and that you are not in need of our services."

Wed 12 MAR 2014 3 pm 446	**offices of solicitors Kenneth Bush, King's Lynn** *The author went to the offices of Kenneth Bush solicitors in King's Lynn in an attempt to meet with Paul Croker and to arrange an interview about his role in the case. Mr Croker's efficient secretary told me she would pass on my letter to him and that he might telephone me.* *He never did.*
Tues 18 MAR 2014 noon 447	**Bexleyheath police station, southeast London** *The author answered police bail and was promptly arrested on a bogus charge of the harassment of his daughter and grandchildren by sending them letters about police corruption. The author's daughter had never made a complaint against her father. The author was held overnight in police custody and taken to Bromley Magistrates' Court the next day, where he was released on bail but forced to attend King's Lynn police station twice a week.*
Sun 23 MAR 2014 10.15 am 448	**Darby Farm, Pott Row, near King's Lynn** *PC 9015 Powter-Robinson from Hunstanton Police called round to Darby Farm with PCSO 8692 Biggs. They claimed they had been called at 10pm the previous night by the Fermoy Unit to provide a 'welfare visit'. PC Powter-Robinson said to the author: "You look fine to me and coherent." Landlord Tim Childs asked for some supporting documentation re the visit but said each time he calls 101, Norfolk Police tell him no visits to Darby Farm have ever been made.*

The author had clearly gotten too close to exposing police wrong-doing regarding child abuse at Lambeth and also in the Tony Martin murder case.

Fri
4 APR
2014
6.45 pm
449

constituency offices of Henry Bellingham, MP

The author met with his MP, Henry Bellingham in the London Road, King's Lynn offices. The author explained to the MP that he had been forced to issue an Official Complaint under Article 3 of the European Convention on Human Rights: 'No one shall be subjected to torture or to inhuman or degrading treatment or punishment.' There is no possible excuse or justification for a breach of Article 3. When a complaint has been made, the Government has a duty of care to act.

Mr Cameron's office acknowledged the letter but otherwise failed to act as it was legally bound to do so and continued its persecution of the author and his family.

Sat
5 APR
2014
1 pm
450

police investigation centre, Saddlebow, near King's Lynn

The author was required to answer bail and was then charged with Impersonating a Barrister. He had never spoken on another person's behalf in court and had never worn a wig or a gown.

The charge was a delaying tactic and designed to prevent the author from continuing his investigations into the Tony Martin murder case.

Sat
5 APR
2014
4.20 pm
451

Darby Farm, Pott Row, near King's Lynn

The author returned to his lodgings after being charged and received a letter from the Fermoy Unit's Dr Ben Walden stating that the author had been given an "absolute discharge" from the section which had committed him to the Unit. For the record, the author replied to the doctor, stating that he had been held there illegally and that at no time had he required their services.

Thur
17 APR
2014
2 pm
452

West Norfolk magistrates' court, King's Lynn

*The author was forced to attend the local magistrates' court to be sentenced for the alleged criminal damage to a car on 1st August 2013 [see entry **438**]. The author was sentenced to two 8-week suspended prison sentences for alleged criminal damage and threatening behaviour.*

Thur **17 APR** 2014 1 pm - 6 pm 453	**Darby Farm, Pott Row, near King's Lynn** *Tony Martin met with the author and discussed his case over a Sunday roast with landlady Philippa Bensley and her partner, Tim Childs.* *The farmer explained that he had been particularly depressed of late due to the depth of corruption in his case and the fact that his version of events was never told to the jury by his corrupt barrister.*
Tues **29 APR** 2014 454	**constituency office of Simon Danczuk, MP, Rotherham** *The author drove to Rotherham to personally deliver a signed copy of the banned book from Hillsborough to Lambeth, about child abuse in Lambeth. The Rotherham MP had been particularly vociferous about child abuse in his town. The author then drove to Liverpool...*
Tues **29 APR** 2014 455	**offices of Kenny Dalglish, director Liverpool Football Club** *The author, having been unlawfully defamed on the official Liverpool FC website (being described as a "convicted sex offender") had previously written to Kenny Dalglish seeking an apology and damages – the damages to be paid to the Hillsborough families. Mr Dalglish's secretary informed the author that the former Liverpool player and manager had replied to the author but that it "had been returned unopened".*
Fri **2 MAY** 2014 456	**various locations in London** *The author spent the day in London, visiting a number of locations including the offices of solicitors Michael Mansfield and Imran Khan, and the newspaper offices of the Daily Mirror, the Daily Mail and the Independent. The author left an Information Memorandum which he had prepared at his MP's request. None of the parties contacted replied to the author.*

Wed 14 MAY 2014 457	**Norwich Crown Court** *The author had finally secured the services of a barrister in London, who stated that she was unable to travel to Norwich on this day and that the author should go into court and seek an adjournment for 2 weeks – "all routine stuff", she said. Upon asking the judge for an adjournment, the judge claimed that the author was in Contempt of Court and he was put in prison for 12 weeks.*

The author was then ghosted around the prison estate, spending time in 10 different prisons in just twelve weeks – see the book *10 Prisons, 12 Weeks*. As Noam Chomsky had stated: "if you're a dissident, you shouldn't be surprised to get all of this stuff done to you, it's in fact a positive sign – it means that you can't just be ignored anymore."

The government was clearly not ignoring the threat posed by this particular investigative author.

Tue 19 AUG 2014 458	**"the paedophile 'child expert' at the Home Office"** *The Metro, a free newspaper distributed throughout London, ran a front page story by Paul Keogh with the above headline. The article read:*

"A notorious paedophile at the centre of a forthcoming abuse inquiry toured children's homes and advised the government on the care system, it has emerged. Peter Righton visited institutions all over the country as he gathered information for a Home Office paper in child-care reforms in the 1970s.

He had earlier left a teaching job over abuse claims and was fined in 1992 after child pornography was discovered at his Worcestershire home."

Given the influence of the Home Office in all of this, what chance did author Brian Pead have when they decided to take his life apart stitch by stitch?

What chance did Tony Martin have when they decided to cover up abuse at Glebe House School and fit him up for a murder he didn't commit?

This supported Tony's view that many paedophiles present as homosexual when they are, in fact, child abusers. This applies to women as well as to men and, of course, to transgender people. Some men 'transgender' into females as a mask in order to abuse children.

Thur
4 SEP
2014
459

councillors told to keep quiet about grooming

On 4 September 2014, The Times *ran an article by Billy Kenber which stated that councillors in Rotherham were told about the abuse and rape of children in the town almost a decade previously, but were warned to keep the information "confidential" to "avoid jeopardising police investigations." (Or possibly to avoid the police or councillors themselves being held culpable for their part in abusing children - if any of them were.)*

Fri
12 SEP
2014
12.30 pm
460

Thameside Prison, southeast London

The author was released from prison, four hours after having the cell door unlocked.

His experiences formed the book 10 Prisons, 12 Weeks *which is a day-by-day diary of the unlawful treatment meted out to the author by the UK government as it sought to cover up child abuse in Lambeth and police corruption in the Tony Martin murder trial.*

Tues
16 DEC
2014
461

secret location in Slovakia

The UK government had taken down the website known as www.LambethChildAbuseandCoverUp.com and so, through a friend, the author put up the website www.LambethChildAbuse.org in Slovakia, outside of the jurisdiction of the UK government.

On this day, the new website went live.

Tues
23 DEC
2014
462

letter from MP to author

The author, being subject to an unlawful Restraining Order preventing him from contact with his beloved family or he'd be imprisoned, received a letter from MP and former barrister, Henry Bellingham, informing him that his office had sent birthday and Christmas cards to the author's daughter and grandchildren on the author's behalf.

| Thur 15 JAN 2015 463 | **email to former armed response officer Tony Bone**
Concerned at the significant discrepancies between Tony Bone's witness statement – made under penalty of perjury – and dozens of statements from farmers and others, I sent an email via the Farmwatch website to Mr Bone at farmwatchtony@me.com asking if I could meet with him to discuss the meeting at Herbert Engineering and the wildly differing versions of what occurred there. |

Three days later (no doubt after he had performed some 'due diligence'), I received a reply which consisted only of the words "No thank you". I was left wondering what he might have had to hide by refusing to speak with me.

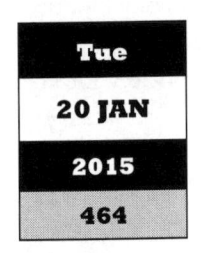

| Tue 20 JAN 2015 464 | **home address of retired PC Rodney Gooderson**
I drove to the village of Outwell in Norfolk to meet with former PC Rodney Gooderson, who had been Tony's local beat officer for a little more than two decades (1972-1993). |

Early years
"I moved to Outwell in 1972," he continued. "Initially, I didn't want to come here and fought against it, but once I was here I found that I loved the place. It takes you at least two years to become accepted around here, but they did accept me and I worked with the local community. Underpinning all of my work was that I wanted to give a fair service to the public. I wasn't a soft touch, but I worked on the principle of being firm but fair because I think this is how you get better results in the long term and good policing is a long-term affair. I walked amongst the people and was accepted by the people and my entire police career was based on people and human interactions."

Gooderson's philosophy on policing
"I never stitched anybody up throughout my career. I believed that you have to get the facts and the evidence. Without naming names, I knew of instances where people were stitched up, but I worked on the principle that if you didn't catch the criminal this time, you would next time, so why stitch anybody up?"

"I'd apprehend an out-and-out criminal every time, but with what I'd call 'first-time offenders', I'd take a long-term view – that a quiet word of advice or guidance would usually prevent any further instance of low-level unlawful activity. I wouldn't try to get instant results to tick a box or two. You can't detect or punish every crime. But some of my colleagues looked only at the law on the written page – not at the practicalities or the personalities. When you live and work in a village like Outwell, you have to adopt a sensible and pragmatic approach to policing."

Hillsborough

At this point, I mentioned Hillsborough and informed Rodney that I had attended that fateful football match and witnessed injustice and police corruption over a period of more than 25 years. I did not dwell on the subject because it was not about me, but about Tony Martin and my host. I also mentioned police corruption that I had personally encountered and written about in my book *Framed!*, a copy of which I left with him.

Gooderson on Tony Martin

"Tony is an odd man, no doubt about that," he said, "but he's not a cold-blooded killer. I can't now remember how or why we first met, but I rapidly formed the opinion that he was someone I'd need to keep an eye on. He was locally known as 'Mad Martin', owing to his appearance and chosen lifestyle. He had very strong opinions about law and order, justice, right and wrong and was firm about the protection of the public and punishment of the wrong-doer. I felt that some of his views were somewhat eccentric. I visited him often at Bleak House and a ten-minute chat could easily become an hour-and-a-half. It never crossed my mind that he was mad or in any way mentally unstable.

Reluctance to harm animals

"I am a shooting man and would sometimes go and shoot on his farmland when off duty. Tony used to grow a lot of rape and pigeons are attracted to rape, so I'd go down there (sometimes alone, sometimes with others) and shoot the pigeons, but Tony did not like to witness the killing of the pigeons and eventually banned people from shooting on his land."

"And on another occasion, when I went to Bleak House, Tony showed me a large number of mice semi-hibernating behind a wood burner in the garage. I suggested that with all the grain around, he would do well to kill them while they were all in one place, but he would have none of it – he was firmly against killing. 'You can't do that to the poor little things, can you?' he said to me."

Retirement

"After I retired, he used to visit me here in my house and remonstrate with me about injustice. It's somewhat ironic that about six weeks before the shooting, he sat exactly where you are sitting now at the breakfast bar and pleaded with me to help him – that he was having numerous thefts from the farm, that he had been burgled and that the police were doing nothing. He was convinced that he was imminently going to be the victim of a burglary. He was beginning to think that the police would not take him seriously, which seemed to upset him all the more. But I reminded him that I was no longer a serving policeman and I advised him to contact Downham Market police station."

"However, from what Tony relayed to me on that day I was convinced that something was imminent and that some surveillance or monitoring of Bleak House was deserving. If I had still been in the job, I would certainly have arranged this. I don't know if he ever took steps to pass his concerns on to the active police so I cannot comment further."

"When I retired, I left strong advice at Downham Market that they should continue to monitor the situation with regards to Tony. I could always read him. I knew when he was about to blow, but I had known him for the best part of 20 years and got to know him extremely well. Someone needed to take over where I left off, but it seems that they didn't keep an eye on him."

"I often wonder what would have happened if the police had kept an eye on Tony, or helped him more, or taken him more seriously, or secured a conviction on one of his burglaries or thefts ... I wonder if the shooting would ever have taken place."

"I knew that there was a lot of friction between the brothers. I believe it was to do with their father's will, the division of land and property. It's not uncommon in families, especially in rural communities."

"I think a major weakness in his character is that he cannot understand that he alone cannot change the world. I feel that he often acts on the spur of the moment without fully thinking through the consequences. Tony is definitely not a nutter – eccentric perhaps, but not a nutter."

"And do you believe he should have been imprisoned?"

"Yes, but not for murder."

"For what then?"

"Possession of an illegal weapon. He had to have got a custodial for that, but not for murder. I don't think Tony is capable of killing. I've given you examples of how he hated to see anything killed. Undoubtedly he felt under threat that night – who wouldn't have?"

Gooderson confirms Tony Martin reported 'many incidents'

I wanted clarification that Tony had – as he had claimed – reported various thefts and acts of trespass and burglaries over the 20 years that Rodney had known him. "Yes, he certainly did report many incidents. I would often go out to see him but wouldn't always record my visits. I only tended to record official visits but those in which I was fishing for intelligence, I wouldn't record. There weren't enough hours in the day to record every conversation I had with every member of the public. So I would simply note that I had been on 'routine patrol' rather than that I had seen Tony Martin specifically. But I did see him on many occasions about the crimes that he said had been perpetrated against him."

Thur	office of James Saunders, solicitor, London
22 JAN	*I visited James Saunders' offices in Essex Street, literally just across the road from the Royal Courts of Justice. In email exchanges with Mr Saunders, I referred him to two of my websites, www.10Prisons12Weeks.com and www.LambethChildAbuse.org.*
2015	
2 pm	
465	*[Author's note: the former site has since been re-named www.Justice4BrianPead.com]*

Now, a man with some 40 years or more experience in criminal defence is unlikely not to have clicked on the links I had embedded into all emails that I send out. I had the impression when I met him that he had conducted some research on me prior to meeting me – just as I had done on him.

After a brisk walk from Temple tube station, I arrived at the grandly-named Essex Hall. However, the ground-floor offices of Saunders and Company were anything but ostentatious. I was met by a very human receptionist. She was extremely professional and made me a cup of tea while I waited the 20 minutes or so until my appointment. She apologised for keeping me waiting, but I explained that I'm "old-school" and like to arrive early to appointments when I can. "I like old-school," she replied, "old-fashioned values. Respect. Morals."

I explained to her that I was there because I am writing a book about Tony Martin. She was of an age whereby she knew at once what the case was about.

At precisely 2pm, a door opened and James Saunders walked towards me. We shook hands and he escorted me into an office next to Reception.

I immediately repeated my assurance that I would not attribute anything to him without first giving him the opportunity to read what I had written and comment upon it before publication.

"I was keen to be involved in the case," said Saunders, "because it seemed so interesting."

Running the appeal

I was interested to learn from the 67-year-old how he had decided to run the appeal against the murder conviction.

"The appeal was forged on two main planks: the first was new scientific evidence and the second was the mental responsibility. Napoleon said that 'Time spent on reconnaissance is rarely wasted' and I agree. I read the many files involved in the case and discovered that, although a SOCO[553] had swabbed the stairs for gunshot residue and found some there, this evidence was not made available at trial. It ought to have been. It showed that Tony Martin did, indeed, fire at least one shot from the stairs – the fatal shot as it turned out – and this

---

[553] SOCO Ian Bradshaw. See entry **286** relating to his allegedly swabbing the staircase for gunshot residue on Wednesday 25 August 1999 – five days after Tony fired his shotgun and after many people had used the staircase.

corroborated exactly what my client had said all along."

"Three spent cartridges were found just inside the doorway to the room where Barras and Fearon made their escape," continued the erudite lawyer. "The SOCO took samples from the stairs and retained the cartridges and wads, but no one tested them for Firearms Discharge Residue (FDR) for the trial. The exhibits were documented and available to both sides to test, but neither did, so the important potential evidence was not heard by the jury.

When I was instructed, I ensured that these cartridges were forensically examined in terms of FDR.

I employed the services of Major Freddie Mead, a firearms expert. We built up a picture of which shots were fired from the gun and where. We were able to show that the shot which killed Barras was fired from the stairs. [Author's note: I do not concur with this view.] We also made it known that because three cartridges were found in the doorway of that room did not mean that they were necessarily fired from the place where they were found. None of this information, of course, was made available to the jury and it ought to have been."

"The *mens rea* element – the guilty mind – was rather more difficult because of things that witnesses had said about his saying he would shoot people if they broke into his house." I decided not to press this particular point further – the apparent hearsay of others (mostly serving or retired police officers) who claimed that Tony Martin was forever going round telling people that he would shoot at burglars.

Diminished responsibility

"The second plank of our appeal to the Court of Appeal was that we believed that Tony Martin had diminished responsibility when he pulled the trigger on that fateful night in 1999. Mr Makin had instructed a psychiatrist but his brief was compiled in a manner suggesting there was no psychiatric issue to find without a sufficient historical background to support a defence based on diminished responsibility (DR). DR is a partial defence to murder, though I doubt that the man on the Clapham omnibus – the average man in the street – would be familiar with the legal nuances of defences to murder."

"With DR, you have to establish a mental condition within certain parameters. It's well short of being bonkers. I therefore instructed Dr Joseph who met with my client and diagnosed that he was suffering from a paranoid condition which was exacerbated by *his history of abuse as a child*[554] and which had made him extremely fearful. The Court of Appeal took Dr Joseph to their hearts and Lord Woolf and Dr Joseph almost had a conversation during the Appeal hearing. As you know, the Court allowed the Appeal and Tony was found not guilty of murder, but rather guilty of manslaughter on the grounds of

---

[554] Note Mr Saunders' reference to the abuse Tony suffered in Glebe House School, Hunstanton. Yet nothing was done about it by Norfolk Constabulary.

diminished responsibility and eventually released." I heard in my mind Tony Martin's words: "That's bloody legal engineering! They twist the law to suit their own ends!" But of course I did not mention this to my host.

I asked Mr Saunders about the first trial and he stated that Nick Makin had not previously undertaken criminal work of this weight and in his view should not have taken the case on because it was beyond his experience. And so we are forced to ask ourselves why this man was ever instructed by Tony's family, friends and supporters in such a high profile case and we must also ask why the legal system did not establish the poor credentials of Mr Makin and why it allowed the inexperienced solicitor to proceed to trial. Of course, there can be little doubt that Mr Makin (and others) would point to the fact that the defence at trial was handled not by Makin, of course, but by Anthony Scrivener QC. But counsel's comments in the BBC video entitled *To Kill A Burglar* (available on YouTube) appear to provide incontrovertible evidence that he was not sympathetic to his client's cause and that he was merely a sop to the establishment, doing as he was told to make it appear as though he was in Tony's corner when the reality was that he covered up evidence which he knew proved his client's innocence.

Mr Saunders asked me to point out that Scrivener was a sufficiently experienced criminal practitioner capable of handling such a case and that Scrivener's competence as counsel was not an issue in the appeal. That done, I happen to challenge Scrivener's performance at trial since it appears to me from the evidence that I have provided that he failed to robustly defend the farmer or advance his client's account of the events of that night, as he was required to do, and that he deliberately withheld evidence from his own client and failed to call witnesses as to fact. Scrivener's actions were reprehensible – I would not have expected Saunders to criticise one of his own.

It seems that Tony Martin was led like a lamb to the slaughter – at trial he had as his defence team a wholly inexperienced solicitor and a barrister whose sympathies clearly lay elsewhere.

You will not be surprised to learn that in all of our meetings over a long period of time during the production of this book that the recurring theme that haunts Tony Martin is that:

> " The jury never heard my defence at all during the trial. I kept thinking, 'When are they going to get round to my defence?' but they never did. I feel cheated. Cheated by the so-called justice system and cheated by my so-called defence team."

It is clear that Nick Makin ought not to have been instructed in this case – it was far too big for him and his firm had no experience in running such cases. A man's liberty was at stake – not just his liberty but also his reputation and a sentence for life imprisonment no less. The justice system ought to have had checks and balances in place to ensure that Tony was properly represented.

But what if there were dark forces around which actually wanted Tony Martin to be found guilty – to shut him up once and for all, to 'take him down a peg or two'? To cover up the child sexual abuse in Glebe House School and by Rodney Townley? To cover up the death of Barras by a person or persons unknown?

I will return to this in future chapters, but for now, we will return to the interview with James Saunders, who unequivocally agreed that Makin was "a poor criminal lawyer."

"Not guilty"
Mr Saunders went on to say that "*I don't think my client was guilty of murder or of manslaughter.* The problem was essentially with the trial itself – it was poorly managed. A defence to murder is self-defence; that the defendant had a genuine belief that he was in fear for his life, and the force used was proportionate to the perceived threat; I think that describes this case." The emphasis was mine: I argue that this is sufficient reason for Tony's convictions to be quashed.

I have spoken with Tony about this particular legal point on numerous occasions. He never waivers in his belief that he was scared that night – and this from a man who is proud and who does not like to admit to any kind of weakness. I have tested him on several occasions, looked for a chink in his story, almost wishing – perversely – that he would trip himself up. But no, his story is consistent. I cannot subscribe, therefore, to the view that he was *not* frightened, gun or no gun.

We saw in previous entries how Tony Martin expressed that fear and the physical concerns (the blood clot on his lung) that he was also living with at that time. I have no doubt that he was frightened and that any man in that situation would also have been as equally fearful. Yet this line of defence was never fully explored at trial as it ought to have been. What was Makin thinking of? What was Scrivener doing by withholding such a crucial line of defence from the jury? Or were political sleights of hand at play in the Crown Court at Norwich? Were the police looking to make Tony Martin a scapegoat on a local level for their own inadequacies during the investigation and on a wider, national level for the gross under-funding and under-resourcing that was placing the security of citizens throughout the nation at risk?

What the jury didn't hear
I pressed Mr Saunders yet further – I wanted to know what he felt the jury did not hear. "The jury never got to hear the scientific evidence about spent

cartridges not having been forensically examined.[555] It ought to have done. The jury never got to hear that Tony Martin was fearful. It ought to have done. The jury never got to hear that the fatal shot occurred on the stairs and it ought to have done.[556] Instead, he came across as an eccentric, emotionally cold defendant." And on this point, we have to ask why Scrivener and Makin allowed Tony Martin to be put in the witness box since it was up to the Crown to establish guilt. What we might describe as 'people skills' are not Tony Martin's strong point and, viewed through a prism of intolerance, he can be seen as dysfunctional. In the past, the courts would have protected such people yet in this case his dysfunction was turned into an opportunity to denigrate him. I regard this as one of the worst aspects of the entire case: that the 'authorities' used the man's inadequacies against him in order to obtain a conviction. In my world view, that's nothing less than State bullying – perpetrated against a naïve man by people who were inadequate themselves yet holding positions of power.

Disclosure

The rules around disclosure place a duty on the Crown to provide evidence to any defendant which undermines its own case or shows the defendant's innocence. Yet it seems that the rules around disclosure were not adhered to properly in this case which directly contributed to a miscarriage of justice.

I asked Mr Saunders for his views on the justice system and how miscarriages of justice occur when the system, surely, has checks and balances to avoid them.

"Miscarriages of justice take place because the system is under-resourced."[557]

"But surely," I asked, "examining the spent cartridges was a fundamental element of this particular trial?"

"I can't disagree. The trial was a circus. The police are under-funded. Forensic science is under-funded. In recent years the funding for Legal Aid has been severely reduced. The Criminal Cases Review Commission (CCRC) has an insufficient budget to do its job properly. Police don't investigate crime any longer – they merely list it. No civilised society can justify not having a properly funded criminal justice system."

I find this a grim – yet accurate – account of the criminal justice system in Britain today, but this is not the most appropriate forum for my concerns or those of farmer Tony Martin or solicitor James Saunders.

I asked the lawyer for reasons why he thought his client became a national icon. "Lots of people live in fear of crime. Often, for relief, they watch great US

---

[555] This contradicts what the judges set down in their judgment at the Court of Appeal. They claimed that the cartridges *had* been forensically examined. [See entry **404**].
[556] I fundamentally disagree with Mr Saunders on this point.
[557] Having spent all his working life within the criminal justice system, Mr Saunders was hardly likely to have said that sometimes miscarriages of justice occur because of corrupt police officers, lawyers and judges.

heroes like Charles Bronson and Clint Eastwood shooting the bad guys and they feel relief that good triumphs over evil. In such films, they can forget their fears – albeit temporarily. So the Great British Public took Tony Martin to their hearts because what he did was an expression of what they'd like to do if faced with similar circumstances. They would like to stand tall and defend their lives and their property."

Pursuing the notion that his client had on the one hand become a national icon whilst being simultaneously vilified in the press, I asked, "Do you think Tony was misrepresented in the media?"

"The media was interested in the notion of Tony as a vigilante, doing what society didn't do – he stood tall against crime, against intruders, against the lack of police. He is a complex person and the press don't like complex people or situations – they like 'simple'."

And I could not help but agree. The media in this day and age operate in sound-bites – small pieces of easily digestible information which the public can absorb in one sitting. It does not have to be true – just easily digestible. The narrative must not be too complex. People's lives are busy; they do not want to have to think too hard. And, because of this dumbing down, Tony Martin suffered at the hands of a feral press desperate for sales and being fed disinformation by Scotland Yard. The old adage of a journalist checking his or her facts three times to ensure accuracy dispersed like shotgun pellets from a Winchester pump-action rifle.

I could not resist asking Mr Saunders what he thought of his client, giving him, of course, the option not to reply. But a reply *was* forthcoming: "Tony Martin is a proud, hard-working, law-abiding man plagued with fears. What he did that night is, in my view, understandable in any terms, but given his specific life history and his perspective on the world, it became even more understandable. He knows the truth as he sees it. He often speaks more than he listens and is quite garrulous. I had to try to represent him in court and shape what he told me about that night into a coherent argument for the Appeal."

Before leaving, I changed the topic under discussion to the helicopter search. "After seeing Fearon, I think the police felt they had to do a better search. Perhaps mistakes were made." I did not probe further.

Renewed appeal against convictions

Finally I informed Mr Saunders that Tony Martin still wants to get his conviction quashed. "The only gateway left is an application to the Criminal Cases Review Commission. There needs to be something new – new evidence – and different from the evidence available to the Court of Appeal. I wish Mr Martin every luck if he takes that route."

Banned book

Before the meeting concluded, I presented Mr Saunders with a signed copy of my book *Framed!* I did not mention his involvement in Hillsborough and nor did I tell him that I had attended that match or that my book *from Hillsborough to Lambeth* is currently illegally banned at the High Court – just a hundred yards or so away from the room we were sitting in. All of this information is available on the internet on various websites. Besides, I intuitively felt that Mr Saunders will have 'Googled' me before agreeing to meet with me. After an hour and nine minutes, we shook hands and I left Essex Hall, the receptionist thanking me and saying she was pleased that we had met. The feeling was mutual.

I found Mr Saunders measured, somewhat nervous, but thoroughly professional, articulate and knowledgeable. He thought before answering every question and I was left with the feeling that his answers were sometimes politically expedient rather than necessarily completely how he felt.

> **What this adds to our knowledge**
>
> Firstly, Mr Saunders confirmed that Tony was misrepresented at trial. His solicitor, Nick Makin, was inexperienced in criminal defence law yet *your* tax pounds went to paying him in what might reasonably be described as the trial of the decade. Do you honestly believe that your money was well spent? If you do not, then you need to complain. (All letters to me and Tony Martin via the publisher, please.)

Tony continues to claim that his defence was never really presented to the jury – and Mr Saunders corroborated this. Forensic tests had apparently not been carried out on empty cartridges and they ought to have been.

The fact that Tony Martin was in fear for his life was never properly explained to the jury at Norwich Crown Court and it needed to have been because it's a defence to his actions that night.

Disclosure of evidence had not been complied with in accordance with the Criminal Procedure Rules.

The reduction from a murder charge to one of manslaughter on the grounds of diminished responsibility appears to have been based not on law or robust psychiatry, but on political expediency. [Author's note: Mr Saunders did not say this, it's my personal view.]

The trial was described as "a circus" by Saunders.

There may have been 'mistakes' made by the police in respect of the helicopter flight(s) over Emneth Hungate and in the investigation itself.

An avenue exists in the form of the CCRC in which Tony should get his conviction quashed.

Sun 1 FEB 2015 466

home address of Margaret Hodgson

I travelled from my base at Philippa Bensley's Darby Farm in Pott Row (where Tony and I would often meet) to the Outwell home of Mrs Hodgson. I had been compelled to investigate the timing of the helicopter flight because when something doesn't sit right with me, I just have to investigate it.

I showed her a copy of the statement she had made to the police back in 1999 in the very room in which we were sitting.

"I am particularly interested in the helicopter flight, Margaret. It says here in your statement that it was just after 10pm."

"Yes, my husband, Mervyn, ran a nursery and we also leased land. At that time of year he would have just finished and got back home. Shortly after that, I heard the helicopter and went outside to get a better look because it was just such an unusual event."

"When you say, 'just after 10pm', are you able to pinpoint the exact time?"

"No, but I was definitely in my day clothes. I was still up and had not changed for bed and simply went outside to watch it circling in the area over Emneth and Marshland St James."

"Margaret, I have other statements in my possession which suggest that the helicopter was flying around anywhere between 1:05-2am. Since there are four hours between 10pm and 2am, it would be helpful if you could say whether you think the helicopter was flying closer to 10pm or 2am."

Without much consideration at all, she shot back a reply: "Closer to 10pm than 2am, definitely. I was also struck by the very powerful searchlight it was putting out and then I also saw two vehicles coming along Robbs Lane, to the side of our land as it was then. I'll tell you why I noticed this and why it struck me as odd. Robbs Lane is narrow and if you were coming along it in that direction, I'd expect the drivers to turn right towards Wisbech. But they didn't - they turned left, past our house and in the direction of Downham Market. And it was this that caused me to think that something was odd, because there is a much more direct route to Downham Market at the other end of Robbs Lane from where they'd just driven. So, you see, they need never have driven up this track at all if they were intending to go to Downham Market. It gave me the impression that the occupants of these vehicles were avoiding detection."

"How did you come to be interviewed by the police?"

"Well, how it came about was that I had been watching the local news and saw that the police were trying to trace some vehicles in the area. So, I told my husband and called the police. I then drove to Bleak House where there was still a large police presence, and told officers there that I might have some useful information for them.

About 4-5 weeks later, I had a visit from two detectives (DC Adcock being one of them) and they took the statement from me that you have got. I gave them the registration number of the first car (I had written it down on a piece of paper when I came back in after watching the helicopter) and part of the number of the other vehicle. The reason I remembered the digits '337' is that it resembled our own car registration number. I also have a good memory, especially for small details."

"I saw the spotlight from the helicopter over Emneth and all the time it was hovering, the spotlight was on."

CORRUPTION ALERT — *Police 'confusion' over helicopter flight times*

As our time together was drawing to a close, Margaret Hodgson came out with a priceless gem:

"When the two detectives came round, they asked me if I was able to pinpoint the exact time of the helicopter flight. I told them I couldn't be precise to the minute, but that it was 'sometime after 10pm'."

Now, why would the police ask such a question of a member of the public when they should already know the answer unless they wanted to find out what she knew about the time of the helicopter which might scupper their plans to create a false flight time or hide the fact that there were *two* separate flights?

Margaret took me to stand on the very spot on which she stood on 20 August 1999 (note the date – this places the helicopter flight firmly before midnight, whereas the official police version placed it on the 21 August) watching the circling helicopter with its spotlight illuminating Bleak House. "Can you see that pylon just above the trees?" she asked.

"Yes."

"That's Emneth and just off to the left there, was the helicopter. I'd say it was there for around twenty minutes."

I shook her hand and felt extremely grateful that she had given me of her time and very humble to have been in the presence of such a decent woman with a razor-sharp mind.

"You know, everyone around here felt that Tony got a raw deal. No-one saw that he had done anything wrong in trying to protect himself. Most people I spoke with about it felt that they would probably have done the same thing. We've been burgled here twice."

"Yes, I think Tony did get a raw deal and hopefully my book will show that. I also think he was castigated unfairly in the press."

And I left. I turned my car around and turned right down Robbs Lane. I understood what Margaret had meant – it is a very narrow lane, extremely meandering and you'd either have to know it was there, or you'd have to simply stumble upon it. I understood why she said that two cars travelling along it at speed at that time of night would be somewhat unusual, especially if you had wanted to travel in the direction of Downham Market because much better, wider, tarmacked roads exist in that area.

Mon
2 FEB
2015
1 pm
467

secret address
I visited the home of a retired farmer who not only knew Tony but had also attended the Farmwatch meeting. He would agree to speak with me only on the basis that I would not name him, but he wanted to "set the record straight" about this meeting and also about Tony.

After agreeing the basis on which he would talk, the farmer told me that he sat towards the back of the crowded canteen, on the right-hand side looking at the presenters.

I asked what he made of Tony Martin and of his apparent eccentricity: "Well, in some ways, Tony can be seen as eccentric, but then again, he is articulate, intelligent, hard-working and knowledgeable about many subjects.

When he first came into farming after being left the house and land, he didn't know too much about it, but he was always willing to learn. I'd say that there's a bit of everything in Tony, but he's definitely not stupid."

"Do you recall if Tony kept interrupting the meeting?"

"Not at all. Certainly not all the time I was present he didn't. He merely listened like the rest of us and took it all in."

The robust former farmer was clearly intelligent himself and what I'd describe as "worldly-wise". He understood, it seemed to me, not only the question that was being asked, but any sub-text too.

He appeared to be a fair man and one who did not like bullies. I asked him whether he knew most of the other farmers present at the meeting and, with the exception of a mere handful, he was familiar with them all.

"While you were present, did you hear Tony say 'I'd shoot the bastards!' when referring to any burglars who might invade his house?"

"Not at all. I certainly never heard him say such a thing."

So this man had scotched two myths: (i) that Tony had constantly disrupted the meeting and (ii) that he had *not* said the words, "I'd shoot the bastards!"

This clearly helped Tony's cause but, as you will have seen throughout this book, I always try to test my theories to destruction and in order to write as accurate and historic a book as possible, I have to look at all sides of Tony Martin, not just those sides of him that I, or others, like or respect.

"Around the time of the shooting," continued my host, "crime rates were rising because, I believe, more and more processes were becoming automated and fewer and fewer people were needed on the land.

This resulted in fewer people, not only on the land itself, but also in the villages as the unemployed farm workers sought work in the towns and cities.

Police stations in rural communities were closing and it got so that you hardly ever saw a policeman around these parts. Given all these factors, crime was almost bound to rise.

I know that Tony and other farmers were angry about all of this. My own farm was burgled twice not long after the shooting in August.

And, of course, the general population were becoming increasingly mobile when compared with, for example, the 1960s and this greater mobility meant that they could drive around the country, commit crimes and disappear quickly.

Also a lot of small farms were swallowed up to create very large farms with few people on them which I think added to the problems.

It wasn't just Tony who became frustrated about the rising crime rates – many of us felt the same way. Tony had the courage to speak out."

It was evident that my host had a firm grasp of the character of Tony Martin and also the wider issues affecting the farming and rural communities. "Did Tony Martin ever say in that meeting – all the time you were present – that he had had his shotgun certificate revoked?"

"No. I'm absolutely certain that he didn't say this."

This corroborated what others had told me and what my research had shown.

CORRUPTION ALERT — *Reports by public of biased questioning of witnesses by police*

I asked him whether he had been interviewed by the police about the meeting because they were putting a lot of emphasis on it. He replied that a month or so after the shooting, two detectives came to his farm wanting to speak with him about the meeting. Their first question was 'What can you tell us about Tony Martin disrupting the meeting?' and he felt that by the way they had loaded that question, they weren't on Tony's side and his view was that the role of the police was to assist the public, the taxpayers who paid for the police.

When he heard this opening question, it seemed to him that they had an agenda and that they had not come to investigate but just to collect statements that could show Tony in a bad light. The farmer said that he knew that Tony wasn't disruptive. "I told them I was not prepared to make a statement on that basis and I sent them away. Tony didn't disrupt that meeting and I didn't like the way they tried to put a spin on it."

I asked my host if he thought Tony Martin was a murderer. "No. Almost everyone around here, in England and across the world felt enormous sympathy for Tony and how he was portrayed in the media. All he did was to protect himself from intruders. Most farmers I know would have done the same in the same circumstances."

"I agree. One of the aims of this book is not only to inform the public about the truth of Bleak House and the shooting, but also to try to get Tony's conviction for manslaughter and wounding with intent quashed."

"Quite right, too. I think that's an excellent idea."

Before I left, I double-checked my notes with this most affable of men whom, I felt, was reasonable and fair, but clearly nobody's fool. He was a man who set clear boundaries for himself and others and yet could tolerate the Tony Martins of this world who choose not to conform to all the social norms that most people are conditioned into adopting.

| Wed |
| 11 FEB |
| 2015 |
| 2 pm |
| 468 |

home address of Elizabeth Johnson
On 11 February 2015, I drove to the village of Outwell, about 3½ miles from Bleak House in Emneth. The white-haired Elizabeth Johnson[558] poured me a cup of tea, showed me some photographs of her late husband, Derek, speaking at Emneth Village Hall in 1999 about Tony's arrest and the rising levels of crime in the area and we then got straight down to discussing the case and her role in it.

She claimed not to have known about the farmer prior to the incident although she used to live on Baldwin's Drove and was friendly with a neighbour, Hugh Ward, who knew Tony extremely well.

"Hugh and Tony would talk for hours on end, mostly about agriculture, farming practices, the price of wheat and things like that. It seemed to me that Hugh was something of a father figure for Tony. After Tony was arrested, Hugh became somewhat depressed and he would sit in his chair, not believing what was happening to his friend. He didn't eat for three or four days and I had this idea of starting a petition for Tony. Hugh liked this suggestion and it seemed to galvanise him.

My role in the story is that I started the petition and wrote many letters to my MP at that time, Gillian Shephard, to the Home Secretary, to Ann Widdecombe, and to the police. I felt that it was wrong that Tony was being

---
[558] See entry **164** & **468**.

punished for simply protecting himself. My husband was a former policeman and he was also outraged at what was happening and he helped me write some of the many letters that I sent out to different ministers and MPs.

Once the petition was up and running, it soon got to the stage where we had three sacks full of letters from people all around the country and cheques came pouring in in support of Tony.

However, Malcolm Starr, a businessman, came round and collected all the letters and cheques and once he had taken over, my involvement ended.

I know that Malcolm Starr emptied Bleak House of all of its furniture and put it into storage and he initially got people to undertake the farm work that needed doing. [Author's note: I hand-delivered a letter to Mr Starr's home address on 6 February 2015 asking to meet. I did not receive a reply.]

My husband and I were both retired, so we had time which we could devote to Tony's cause, but as I say, once Mr Starr came on board, my involvement ended. Besides, my husband's health was deteriorating rapidly and I then devoted my time to nursing him, of course."

This was all useful background information, but I wanted to know why she would undertake such action – after all, she had never met the farmer, so I was keen to learn about her motivation.

"Well, right from the start, I felt that the entire case was not being managed properly. Something just seemed wrong to me and I couldn't understand how a man who was faced with intruders in his home could be punished for protecting himself. Tony Martin must have been scared to death hearing voices in the dark. He had no idea how many intruders there were, whether they were armed or violent and it seemed to me that what he did was in self-defence.

"After Tony was put in prison, there was a meeting at Emneth Village Hall. The police Chief Superintendent was there, as was Gillian Shephard, the MP. My husband got up to speak and was told to sit down and be quiet, but he stood his ground and was on his feet for almost an hour. The mood in the village hall was that Tony Martin had a raw deal. Everyone around here knew that the police were under-resourced, lacked adequate finances to do their job properly and that Tony was a fierce critic of the under-funding of the police."

Then Elizabeth asked about Tony's conviction for manslaughter and what I intended to do about it. I told her that the idea of the book is to provide the Great British Public with previously hidden evidence and then to get the convictions quashed at the Criminal Cases Review Commission or at the European Court of Human Rights. "After all," I told her, "I have uncovered sufficient new evidence to show that a serious miscarriage of justice took place."

"I would really like it if Tony's conviction was quashed. He deserves that for all he had to go through. Tony deserves better. He is a decent man. He has some funny ways and sometimes he doesn't help himself with some of the things that he says, but underneath it all, he is basically an honest and decent man."

We must also consider that Mrs Johnson's role in the Tony Martin affair was somewhat less altruistic than I have thus far portrayed. Whenever there is a major case like this, the government – usually through the office of MI5 (secret service) – will infiltrate a community with a shill and that person will continually provide feedback to the intelligence services with his or her colleagues within the group or local community completely unaware that they are being spied upon and reported about. The Stephen Lawrence case is a point in question – when Doreen Lawrence accused the police of endemic racism and corruption following the racist murder of her black teenage son, action groups which she organised were infiltrated by such shills. Hillsborough, the miners' strikes – just about *every* case you can think of that threatens the establishment's ruthless and paranoid stranglehold on power will become infiltrated by double agents. Beware even old Mrs Brown happily pouring tea and supplying biscuits during meetings to achieve justice – the government's network of spies doesn't just run to those in the 'James Bond' mould but even to elderly seemingly innocent tea-ladies. And often their husbands and children have no idea of the role their wives and mothers are playing in society beyond the most obvious.

Sat
21 FEB
2015
2 pm
469

meeting at the Crown in Gayton

I met Tony at The Crown, a pub in the village of Gayton around 7 miles east of King's Lynn. We discussed many aspects of his case and he urged me to meet with a supplier of farm machinery and parts.

Tony has told me many things about his case and urged me to meet many people and it would take a lifetime to follow all of his leads.

Each time he gave me a lead, I'd have to weigh up the benefits and continually ask myself "What benefit does this person have to the overall narrative and to the overriding objective – to get Tony's conviction quashed?" But there was something about his insistence on meeting this particular man that forced me to listen and then act. I had a meeting with Rodney Gooderson on the coming Monday and also with businessman Mick Stratton, and since this storekeeper was 'in the area', I thought I'd kill three birds with one stone.

Mon	**home address of Rodney Gooderson**
23 FEB	*Rodney Gooderson invited me back so that we could go through the amendments he wished to make to the text.*
2015	*He wanted to 'get it right' and since I wanted an accurate reflection of what he'd told me about part of his life as Tony's local beat bobby, I readily agreed.*
11 am	
470	

Somewhat surprisingly, he started off by discussing my book *Framed!* which he told me he had read from cover to cover. He commented that it was obvious that I was innocent and that I had been totally truthful. "You've definitely been the victim of a stitch-up," he told me. "It's funny how you were a whistle-blower at Lambeth and now it's all coming out in the news about child abuse in Lambeth. What better way is there to cloud the issue than discrediting the whistle-blower? With regard to your conviction for incitement, I am convinced that the facts have been manipulated to label you a sex offender and further discredit you. The elements of the offence were not there. I wouldn't mind betting you're in a file marked TROUBLEMAKER at Scotland Yard."

It's always nice to have someone who was once "on the inside" corroborate that you have been the victim of an injustice and a stitch-up. I felt grateful that he had read the book and commented as he did.

As this book was nearing completion, the *Daily Mail* of 28 December 2017 ran a headline entitled: OUR VANISHING BEAT BOBBIES. More than two decades after Tony Martin had spoken out vociferously (and often spoken out alone) against drastic cuts in constables on the beat, the national newspaper was taking up the very same argument:

"Almost half the public have not seen a bobby patrolling their neighbourhood beat in the past year. This is despite the vast majority saying a uniformed presence on the streets is essential to maintaining law and order. The figures were revealed in a survey of more than 12,000 people commissioned by the independent police watchdog ... Just 7% said they regularly see police walking the streets.

The findings will raise fears in Whitehall that forces are retreating from the front line and the 'bobby on the beat' could soon be extinct. Taxpayers – who contribute more than £9 billion to police coffers every year – have repeatedly said in polls that they would like to see more officers outside of their vehicles.

Andy Fittes, of the Police Federation which represents rank-and-file officers, said: "The reality is that we have 20,000 fewer police officers in service now compared with 2010."

The *Mail* editorial urged that we "neglect old-fashioned policing at our peril." As previously stated, Tony was courageously speaking out about such cuts more than two decades ago and his former beat officer, Rodney Gooderson, had foreseen that the police were becoming increasingly remote from the public.

I suggest that the reasons for this were not entirely due to financial restrictions but more to do with social control. Separate the police from the public, and the public becomes far easier to control. We would do well to remember that policing in England & Wales is *by consent* – at least, that's the rhetoric they'd have you believe at Westminster.

Mon
23 FEB
2015
3 pm
471

business address of anonymous source

Having left Outwell, and on my way to a meeting with Mick Stratton in Wisbech, I decided to swing by the retailer of farm implements and parts. Tony's quiet insistence had spoken to my instinct and it felt right that I would need to meet this storekeeper.

As I introduced myself and mentioned the book, his defences immediately went up. He told me that he didn't really want to talk and said that under no circumstances should I use his name ("I've got a business to run") and obviously I've kept my part of the bargain.

He told me he was in attendance at the Farmwatch meeting – exactly 16 years to the day of my visit – but that he had categorically not invited Tony Martin or anyone else: "I merely informed people," was how he put it. "Peter Huggins had told me and I passed on information. I have distanced myself from Farmwatch over the years, partly because of what occurred there that night."

"How do you mean?"

"Well, one farmer asked what he should do when the travellers threatened to burn down his property and Tony Bone replied, 'Then you threaten to burn down their caravans – fight fire with fire!' I was appalled that a former policeman would say such a thing."

As we have seen, this purveyor of farming implements was not the first man to tell me that Bone had said this at the meeting. The former firearms officer had plenty to say about Tony Martin and his views on travellers at the time – but conveniently forgot to tell the public about his own incendiary comments.

Mon
23 FEB
2015
4.30 pm
472

home address of Mick Stratton

Mick Stratton is a self-made man. Worldly-wise, he does not suffer fools gladly. He first met Tony over 40 years ago, when they were both pig farmers. "I used to meet him at the pub. I can tell you that, with regard to the murder trial, he was treated disgracefully and he's definitely been the victim of a stitch up. It's a terrible injustice."

When one man has known another man for over four decades, you can be generally sure that each has a handle on how the other operates – their general character, the way they operate in business or at work, the way they conduct themselves. I allowed Mr Stratton to continue to inform me about Tony: "He's a very deep man – he's well educated and thinks a lot. But if I wanted a man alongside me in the trenches, I'd choose Tony. He's handy around the farm and can turn his hands to most things.

Tony's a nice bloke, always worked hard, kept himself to himself, doesn't squander money and he's very honest.

I hope your book helps him to get his convictions quashed and I also hope he sues the police for compensation."

And, as I prepared to leave, he added one more thing: "You know, Brian, it wouldn't surprise me to read they've found you dead in a ditch somewhere. There was definitely wrong-doing in Tony's case and the police won't like you digging it all up. Be careful. Watch your back."

His parting words were to gain significant power in the following few weeks as Tony's case and my personal story coalesced through the prism of exposing child abuse, something which "the authorities" are paranoid about covering up since many of them are involved in it.

Mon
9 MAR
2015
2.30 pm
473

Port Jackson public house, Bishop's Stortford, Essex
The author, together with Michael Bird,[559] met retired Detective Chief Inspector (DCI) Clive Driscoll, a former child protection officer in Lambeth who had been removed from an investigation into child abuse after he had named high profile people he wished to interview.

Driscoll opened the meeting in which minutes were recorded by declaring that he hoped to achieve justice for the author and his family. He added that Lambeth Council was known to be a 'corrupt borough' and that a common consensus was that 'almost everyone was on the fiddle' and that a consequence of this was that some councillors who came to learn about child abuse perpetrated by some other council officials would not expose it for fear of themselves being exposed for wrongdoing such as, for example, financial mismanagement. Driscoll added that there was a strong Catholic and Masonic presence in Lambeth and within the police.

Driscoll said: "Lambeth have been vicious to you, Brian, and it can't be just

---

[559] The author and Michael Bird met in 2005 when they worked together as counsellors in Wallington, south London. In 2012 they published *from Hillsborough to Lambeth* (corruption and cover-up of child abuse) which was unlawfully banned in February 2013 at the High Court in London. Mr Bird has attended almost all of the trials and hearings that corrupt agents of state have subjected the author to.

because of what you wrote in the book *from Hillsborough to Lambeth*." He added that he had read the book and agreed with its contents (so much for the anonymous Amazon posts that the author was a 'fantasist'), before telling the author that he was "flagged up at Scotland Yard as being a major threat" because of his research and books and that Brian Pead had been "subjected to a sustained period of persecution by the Met Police as a direct consequence of this."

Driscoll commented that it was appalling the effect that these cases were not only having on the author but also on his daughter and grandchildren and that, as a grandfather himself, he could not imagine the distress this was causing both to the author and his family members.

The author mentioned that his son-in-law owned a garage repairing vehicles for the Met Police and that the police could well have taken advantage of this business relationship to turn his family against him and feed them false information. Driscoll added that it was likely that they had been misinformed and shown false documents against the author which had led them to no longer have contact. The retired detective added that there was "undoubtedly an element of dishonesty" somewhere in all of these cases against the author.

Driscoll added that the author ought to write to his MP about numerous breaches of the Human Rights Act 1998 and that people in various agencies of State were clearly making decisions based on false police national computer records and other data.

Wed
11 MAR
2015
11.30 am
474

Canada Square, London
On 11 March 2015, Tom Pettifor, of the Daily Mirror, *a journalist who has worked closely with Clive Driscoll, put his name to a story in which it was claimed that Lambeth Council's Bulic Forsythe had been murdered because he had made it known that he was about to reveal the names of people he believed were involved in abusing children on Council premises. The salient points of the report are reproduced below in the interest of justice and the emphases are the author's:*

"A council official was murdered days after he vowed to expose 'horrible' people linked to a paedophile ring, a witness has claimed.

Detectives are investigating claims Bulic Forsythe was silenced by a children's home vice ring.

A friend of Bulic, traced by the *Mirror*, said the social services manager at Lambeth Council in south London confided in him shortly before he was murdered 22 years ago last month.

The witness claimed: "I will never forget one evening in the pub when he told me and my wife: 'There are some people in Lambeth Council who are doing really horrible, disgusting things and I am going to expose them. I won't let them get away with it.'

"I was nervous when he was telling me all of this. I could feel by the anxious, determined emotion in his voice just how serious the situation was.

"I will never forget the look on his face. He was seriously disgusted and disturbed by what he knew and was determined to see that justice was served. Several days later, he was murdered."

The witness, a former para-legal, said he contacted the police with the information at the time. He claimed: "*It was a very short conversation with no interest expressed by the police and no one ever called me back.*"

He is the second person traced by the *Mirror* who says Bulic was living in fear before his murder because of what he had allegedly discovered at Lambeth council. A former female colleague said the social services manager had become aware of claims that children were being sexually abused at the South Vale children's home.

A restricted document newly uncovered by the *Daily Mirror* shows government officials were aware in 1998 of claims the murder had been linked to a Lambeth paedophile ring and children's home pervert John Carroll.

The memo, used to brief ministers in the Blair government in August 1998, stated: "There is an unsolved murder of [an official] which some staff in Lambeth believe is linked to paedophile activity, corruption and Mr Carroll. The police do not rule this out and are re-evaluating this and other serious crimes and incidents."

Detective Clive Driscoll advised the murder investigation be reopened when he found potential links to his 1998 children's homes probe in Lambeth.

But Mr Driscoll was removed from the case and Bulic's murder file has not been touched for 15 years.

Scotland Yard finally began a cold case review 17 months ago following a *Daily Mirror* investigation. A spokesman said last month that they are still examining forensic evidence.

Kiddist Forsythe – born three months after her dad's murder – believed he may have been targeted because of what he knew and she is urging the police to fully reopen the murder investigation.

Bulic was last seen alive at 8:45pm on Wednesday 24 February 1993.

A BBC Crimewatch broadcast five months later revealed that at 10am on the Thursday three official looking men were seen by a neighbour carrying files away from his flat in Clapham, South London.

Two more men were seen in a car behind the property at 2pm. His bedroom was torched at 1am on Friday and the oven turned on.

Kiddist's mum and Bulic's widow, Dawn, 61, said: "I think someone wanted to shut him up."[560]

Bulic died at the time of an internal Lambeth council probe into alleged sexual abuse in the housing department where he had worked.

The resulting report, obtained by the *Mirror*, details allegations of rape, sexual assault and the swapping of child abuse videos and violent porn within the council. It implicated Lambeth employees as well as police and politicians.

The report, signed by chair of the panel Eithne Harris, states: "The murder of Bulic Forsythe was seen by some witnesses as a possible outcome for anyone who strayed too far in their investigation or who asked too many questions."

Published internally in December 1993, it adds: "The panel heard evidence about Bulic Forsythe while he was working in Social Services, speaking to a colleague and telling her he was going to 'spill the beans'.

"Three days later he was killed."

This is not either of the witnesses traced by the *Mirror*.

It states: "Bulic Forsythe had allegedly expressed his fear of [council employee initials] to another witness who visited him.

"He appeared very frightened to the witness. The witness at this point appeared fearful."

The report describes the atmosphere in the department as "one of intense fear". Though the panel found no 'direct link' between his death and work it said its evidence should be handed to police.

Paedophiles abused children in Lambeth's homes for decades.

A former social services manager told Mr Driscoll in 1998 that she saw a future Blair minister making evening visits to the Angell Road children's home in Brixton in the early 1980s.

The home was run by John Carroll who was jailed for ten years in 1999 for sexually abusing a string of children."

Now, I ask you, would a reasonable person imagine for one minute that child abuse in Lambeth miraculously stopped in 1998 when Driscoll was removed from his inquiries into Lambeth?

And would that same reasonable person believe that it was still not going on when Brian Pead arrived as a Head teacher at Lambeth in 2005?

And if Bulic Forsythe was murdered because he was going to expose paedophile Lambeth councillors and police officers, can you subscribe to the view that Tony Martin was fitted up for murder and jailed for life because he

---

[560] It is my contention that, apart from covering up wrong-doing in the murder of Fred Barras, the police framed Tony Martin for murder in order to shut him up about child abuse at Glebe House School that he would tell all and sundry about. What better way than to frame him for murder and attack his character so that people would not want to believe him about the child abuse in that school and label him as some sort of 'fantasist'?

wouldn't stop telling all and sundry about child abuse at Glebe House School which the Chief Constable of Norfolk (and the police's national lead on child abuse) refuses to this day to investigate?

| Tue 17 MAR 2015 475 | **Scotland Yard in dock on 14 abuse cover-ups**
The Daily Mail *ran a front-page headline with "Corruption probe over decades of VIP sex crimes": over a period of 35 years, Scotland Yard officers were said to have protected 'untouchable' figures by shutting down inquiries that reached the heart of government:* |

"The 14 alleged paedophilia cover-ups were referred to watchdogs by the Metropolitan Police Service yesterday. It threatens to be the biggest investigation into police corruption since the 1970s. Hailed as a 'momentous milestone' by one MP, the probe could lead to five former Met chiefs being interviewed. Campaigners are angry that the Met will remain in charge of the investigation."

| Thur 19 MAR 2015 476 | **unlawful imprisonment of investigative author Brian Pead**
Just over a week after meeting with retired DCI Clive Driscoll and the Daily Mirror *report about the murder of Bulic Forsythe, and a month after meeting MP Henry Bellingham - the author was unlawfully arrested on a bogus charge of five breaches of a restraining order preventing him from contacting his family by sending them Christmas and birthday cards via the MP's office (which they never received.)* |

The author was remanded into custody by the very same district judge who had unlawfully issued the restraining order on 1st November 2011.

He was later sentenced to 2 years in prison. People who commit acts of domestic or other violence have received lesser sentences. The author was constantly moved between HMP Thameside and HMP Peterborough. This pattern of constantly moving him around to prevent people from contacting him was 'legitimised' under the guise that he had a trial for alleged breaches of a restraining order in London (hence being taken to Thameside) and another trial for allegedly impersonating a barrister in Cambridge (the nearest prison being Peterborough.) To any outsider, the author's constantly being moved around the prison estate appeared to be a genuine method of dealing with a career criminal. The reality, of course, was completely different.

The authorities wanted the author out of the way while all the shit about Lambeth child abuse was making the headlines and to disrupt his work on the original book on Tony's case, in which it was known that he had uncovered considerable police corruption.

The breaches of the author's human rights – and those of his family – were being orchestrated by the Home Office. If you think that that statement is a bit 'far-fetched' then the author refers you to his book *from Hillsborough to Lambeth* (Invenire Press, 2012 and second edition 2017) with co-author Michael Bird:

"On 22 March 2010, the *Blood and Property* blog ran a further article about Brian Pead's dismissal by Lambeth Council in which it featured a telephone interview with Meg Hillier, the Hackney South and Shoreditch MP who also had a ministerial post within the Home Office. The Off Centre charity – which unlawfully dismissed Brian in June 2008 without conducting an investigation – is in Hillier's constituency. *Blood and Property* website: "When I tried to get in touch with you about Brian Pead, the initial response was that I couldn't talk to you about it without going through the Home Office press office."

Now, it had been alleged that Brian Pead had been dismissed for allegedly bullying two or three members of staff. What on earth was the Home Office doing getting involved in such a simple dismissal?

Michael Wolkind QC reprimanded

Wed 16 DEC 2015 477

The Guardian reported that Michael Wolkind, defence counsel at Tony's appeal, had been reprimanded by the lord chief justice, Lord Thomas of Cwmgiedd and reported to the Bar Standards Council, the organisation which regulates the conduct of barristers, for "patronising" and "ill-judged" behaviour during a murder trial involving a lap-dancer whose body has never been found.

The barrister, who was eventually sacked by his client, was said to have been "half-listening" to evidence during cross-examination while sending emails relating to other cases. Wolkind missed part of the trial judge's summing-up speech and his diary later showed that he had arranged a meeting in another case for the afternoon, the lord chief justice said.

Wolkind's closing speech, the judgment said, was "ill-judged, patronising and contained inappropriate attempts at humour". It was also critical of the fact that he was carrying out other work during the trial.

Wolkind's website still lists the appeal of "Norfolk farmer Tony Martin" as one of Wolkind's most notable successes. It wasn't. It was in itself another travesty of justice for reasons which I have shown.

Thur 31 DEC 2015 478

Tony Martin arrested

Two years to the day that the author made an Official Complaint under Article 3 of the European Convention on Human Rights to Government regarding its appalling breaches of his human rights (and those of his daughter and her family), Tony went and got himself arrested again, this time on suspicion of possession of an illegal firearm.

The author was being illegally held in prison at the time on a bogus charge of the harassment of his daughter and eldest grandchild when neither had ever made a complaint against him, or made a witness statement or appeared in court against him. (Tony is not the only man to have suffered a miscarriage of justice and he won't be the last.)

The author called Tony from prison and was told that he had been arrested because he had told a journalist that he "might still have access to guns," that "Britain is awash with illegally held firearms" and that the police were "in denial at the scale of illegally held guns in Britain."

Police said officers "acted on credible intelligence of illegal firearms" at a property. It would seem that the 'intelligence' they had acted upon was about as credible as that gathered almost 30 years previously from family members who refused to testify in court or speak on the record.

The *Wisbech Standard* reported that one man, who did not wish to be named, said: "I saw three armed police officers at the corner of Hungate Road. There were transit vans, forensic teams, unmarked police cars, and a helicopter overhead."

Tony was bailed without charge or conditions until late February 2016 and then Norfolk Constabulary decided to take 'No Further Action'.

The *UK Shooting News* had an interesting perspective on the arrest, suggesting that Tony had been arrested because he 'disrespected' the local police. This came from Malcolm Starr: "Unlike those from 15 years ago, who knew Tony well and knew what he was like, this new generation of officers see him as a bit of a nuisance. They think he has shown them disrespect, so it seems now they have got it in for him and they've said to themselves, we had better be showing the public that we take this matter seriously."

The police operation against Tony was said to have been pre-planned. Norfolk Constabulary refused to deny Starr's allegations that local constables wanted to teach the old man a lesson. DCI Andy Coller said: "Public safety is paramount and Norfolk Constabulary takes all reports of firearms seriously. Following the arrest a thorough search, under Section 18 of the Police and Criminal Evidence Act 1984 (PACE), was conducted and officers seized a firearm, which was believed to be an air weapon. However, following further enquiries, it was deemed not to be a viable weapon due to its condition."

This would be PC 70 Andrew John Coller[561] who, according to police records, attended Bleak House at 4:30am on 21 August 1999 with PC 17 Duncan Maxwell in an armed response vehicle, standing down at 6am.

Let's see what Tony had to say about this latest arrest (at the age of 71):

> At midday on the last day of the year, the police called me and said they'd like to meet me at the farm. I told them 'No, I know what that's all about' and so they arrested me in Wisbech. They took me to the Police Investigation Centre at Saddlebow, where they held me for seven hours in custody. I was not interviewed or charged.
>
> An inspector commented that I had no legal representation and I told him 'No, they're all spivs. I'm quite able to speak for myself.'
>
> I was released and I made sure they dropped me off at Wisbech from where they'd arrested me.
>
> This all came about because I received a call from a journalist who asked me what I thought of the old man who shot and killed his wife in a care home. I smelt a rat and when he asked me if I had any guns, I replied: 'Of course! I have a shedful of guns!' He then asked me if I minded if he called the police. I told him he could do whatever he liked. This incident shows you that the police do what they like when they like. The police look after themselves, not the man in the street."

Fri 20 MAY 2016 479

Freedom of Information Act request

With Tony's knowledge and consent, I put in a Freedom of Information Act 2000 request on behalf of Tony Martin which read as follows:

"Please provide me with a True Copy of all flight logs of any helicopters flying over Emneth on 20 and 21 August 1999. I also require details of all written communications with regard to the flight(s) in whatsoever format.

I also require a copy of all reports which describe what the searches found/ did not find.

I also require the names of all personnel on board the helicopter(s) on the dates previously mentioned."

The request was rejected on the grounds that it was 'vexatious' – a man spent 3½ years in prison and had his life ruined and they call a lawful request 'vexatious'! I hope that you, as a reader, are appalled at this obfuscation by the State along the lines of Hillsborough and I hope that you're prepared to write to your MP and complain about it. So, nearly two decades after initiating a murder trial against him when all the evidence pointed otherwise, the State is still attempting to cover-up its own wrongdoings. It has clearly learnt nothing from Hillsborough.

---

[561] See entry **248**.

Fri 27 MAY 2016
480

tickets for conference

After speaking with Tony about a conference to be held at Michael Mansfield's law chambers in London, I purchased two tickets. The conference was entitled The Last Barricade: Attacks on Non-State Experts and was to be about the need to challenge the authenticity of 'expert witnesses' and their evidence.

Since Tony's trial had been based almost entirely on the evidence of State 'expert witness' Dr Heath, I suggested to Tony that it would be worthwhile going to London, meeting Mansfield QC and asking him if he wanted to be involved in Tony's appeal.

I paid for two tickets and received notification that Tony and I had been added to the list of attendees.

Thur 31 MAY 2016 11.40 am
481

King's Lynn County Court

Tony asked me to look at the paperwork in the case against him involving Nicola Giddens, daughter of Clive,[562] whom we've previously read about. He asked me to read it through and comment. I offered to be his McKenzie Friend in court and that's a specific role – to sit alongside someone but not speak on their behalf. You are permitted to pass them notes, offer emotional support and whisper in their ear if you need to. Tony agreed and we trotted along to the court in King Street.

Tony smartened himself up for court. The Petitioner's barrister, a William Powell from Regency Chambers in Peterborough, is a former MP. He tried to engage Tony in general conversation and the farmer almost ended up telling him his life story. He told Powell things about his ownership of land that you wouldn't tell your 'enemy' and certainly not one as well connected as a former MP. This is part of Tony's naivety. I mentioned it to him afterwards – after the damage had been done – and, to be fair to him, he did accept that it probably wasn't the wisest thing to tell someone like Powell.

Long story short, Tony was asked to pay £18,730.48 or he'd lose 3½ acres of land. Losing parcels of land is not something Tony wants to do, so he wrote out a cheque there and then and the matter was settled.

A report generated about the quality of the land in question cost over £2,000 and yet was only 1½ pages in length. Tony had not even been sent a copy prior to the court hearing and so I suggested to him that he might like to challenge it, which he did and that money was knocked off the total bill. But he doesn't spot these little things which can add up to big things.

---

[562] See entries dated **17**, **21**, **25** and **26**.

As we walked out of court to find somewhere to debrief, he said he thought the judge (Pugh) was "a jolly nice chap" and that the whole hearing had gone well. It was clear to me that he would have been shafted had I not been in his corner, because he fails to see the cut and thrust in a courtroom, believing that because he wouldn't wish to cheat anybody, nobody would want to cheat him.

Wed 1 JUN 2016 — 482

email to Lorne Green, police and crime commissioner
I emailed Lorne Green, the Police and Crime Commissioner for Norfolk, calling for a vote of 'No Confidence' in Simon Bailey, the Chief Constable of Norfolk because he refused to record the child abuse I reported to him in Lambeth and to record and investigate child abuse at Glebe House in Hunstanton.

Mr Bailey is the police national lead in child abuse and head of the Operation Hydrant probe into historic abuse cases. I found his behaviour reprehensible.

Thur 2 JUN 2016 — 483

conference cancellation
The conference at Michael Mansfield's chambers was mysteriously cancelled. The given reason was 'illness.' However, seen from a different perspective, it could be read as people in high places not wanting to process the farmer's appeal. Or mine.

Sun 5 JUN 2016 — 484

arrest and imprisonment of author
The author was arrested at 9am at his place of residence in Tilney All Saints. The author was sleeping in his car at the time, having been made homeless in March 2016 upon his release from prison. Six officers in three vehicles attended the scene. A neighbour, who witnessed the arrest, said he thought it was "over the top and like a scene from a film. Clearly Brian wasn't resisting arrest or anything like that."

The author was held in a police cell overnight and taken to HMP Norwich on the Monday. No court hearing. The reason given to him was that he had to be imprisoned for 28 days because he had not informed the police where he was living – the very place where they arrested him from.

A neighbour later told the author that he saw the police search his car – which was an unlawful act in itself since they had no right to do so.

| Fri
1 JUL
2016
485 | **release from prison**
The author was released from prison on Friday the first of July. He was forced to attend probation the same day and each week afterwards, or he'd be arrested again and returned to prison. |

| Thur
11 AUG
2016
11.30 am
486 | **meeting with Sir Henry Bellingham, MP**
The author met the MP in the London Road constituency office with witnesses present.
It was the shortest of their four meetings to date (lasting just 18 minutes) and the least helpful. |

| Mon
15 AUG
2016
3 pm
487 | **unlawful arrest at Gaywood Library, King's Lynn**
The author was working on the manuscript of this book when three police officers (two in uniform) arrested him in the Library.[563] Each time the author met with his MP to report police corruption in his own cases and that of Tony Martin's or his unlawful arrest at Lambeth after reporting child abuse, he was arrested and imprisoned within a few days of the meeting. |

The author was taken to the Police Investigation Centre at Saddlebow, just outside of King's Lynn and held in a cell for five hours. He was told he had been arrested on the grounds of breaching a Restraining Order. He was not interviewed or charged and was released just after 8pm.

The real purpose of the arrest and unlawful detention? They took the author's laptop off him, his mobile phone and the manuscript of this book. Some people in very high places did not want this book to be published because it unearths so much corruption, not only by the police but also by those at all levels of the judiciary. And that's driven by the Home Office - an instrument of government - which, as we have seen, employed paedophile Peter Righton...

---

[563] See again the entry **438**.

Tue
16 AUG
2016
488

Chris Brown, Fosters Solicitors, Norwich: part one
The day after his unlawful arrest, the author went to Norwich to try to meet with Chris Brown but was told that he wasn't in the office. The receptionist was asked to tell him about Dr Heath and the Tony Martin case and that the author was trying to arrange a meeting as it was his duty to pass on the information to the solicitor in the interest of Justice.

The author called Mr Brown's office on six occasions up to 22 September and on each occasion he was either "out of the office" or "not at his desk" and he never called back. Now, given that this was one of the most famous murder trials in the UK and given Mr Brown's work on Dr Heath, it is difficult to imagine a reason for his not contacting the author, other than the author having reported child abuse in Lambeth Council which the government was content to cover up.

Sat
20 AUG
2016
489

home address of Mrs Barras, Fred's mum
I felt deeply uncomfortable being in possession of information which showed that her son need not have died, so I drove up to Newark to try to speak with Mrs Barras. I was aware of the date – the 17th anniversary of her son's death and had he lived, he would have been 33 years old – and also aware of the sensitivities around telling a woman that the death of her son had been avoidable.

I had three different addresses for her but finally managed to track her down in the late afternoon on a humid day. I knocked on the door, but she shouted out of an upstairs window that she was not well and didn't want to speak. Of course, I could not force her to meet and nor could I simply put a note through her letterbox to say that her son need not have died.

These things are always a judgment call and so I simply drove away, to return another day. I then posted my business card and a letter through the door of a relative of Brendon Fearon's since there had been no reply when I knocked.

Mon
5 SEP
2016
490

phone call with Brendon Fearon
Throughout the course of writing this book, the presence of Brendon Fearon always made itself felt to me. I tried to imagine what it must have felt like to have gone on a job to commit a crime and said to have taken a young lad with you and not have him return with you. I did not imagine for one minute that Brendon had had an easy time of it and, as we know, many people blamed him entirely for Fred's death but as we now know, he was not responsible.

At 4:20pm on 27 August 2016, I received a call from Brendon's brother, Gary, who told me he had returned that day from holiday. He said he'd pass my number to Brendon.

I left it until 3rd September and called Gary back. He told me that Brendon had given him permission to give me his number. I rang the same night, but unfortunately Brendon was just going out and asked me to call again the following day, which I did.

He told me that he wanted to put it all behind him and, short of bringing back Fred, he was trying to get on with his life which he felt had been ruined by the events. I don't believe it right for a man to carry the death of another man on his shoulders when the responsibility for Fred's death really lay elsewhere.

I told Brendon that I respected what he had told me, but asked if I could at least put some documents through his door for him to consider. He agreed that I could do that.

Then, on 5 September 2016, I received an early call from Gary. He had a driving job and was heading to the Thetford area. He could, he said, pick up the documents for Brendon on his way back home to Newark. Obviously this would save me half a day getting to Newark and back from King's Lynn, so I was grateful. I handed over the documents in a lay-by off the A47. I thanked Gary for acting as a go-between and courier. It meant a lot to me, because I had done my bit – if Brendon decided he wanted no more to do with the case, that was his choice and if he wanted to meet, well, that was his choice, too. My job – to pass on the information I had to him and, through him, to Fred's relatives – was done. Naturally I still hoped to meet Brendon but it was up to him.

Thur 22 SEP 2016 491

the CCRC: an on-going saga

On 22 September 2016 I emailed Tony's appeal against conviction to the CCRC. It was, for me, a momentous day. I am not a solicitor or a barrister but I did my best in putting together compelling grounds to show that there had been a significant miscarriage of justice.

And in case you're wondering why a millionaire won't pay for a barrister, it's simple in Tony's world: "They paid to make me guilty, so they can pay to quash the conviction." It happens to be how I see the world in this respect, too.

Thur **22 SEP** **2016** **10:57 am** **492**	**Chris Brown, Fosters Solicitors, Norwich, part two** *Whilst in the company of Michael Bird, I called Chris Brown's office again at 10:57am. His PA told me he was "not at his desk" and so I asked her to remind him that, by not returning my call about pathologist Michael Heath and the Tony Martin case, he was in effect perverting the course of justice and I was going to report him to the police and the Justice Minister if he did not return my call.*

At 11:17, I received a call from a person purporting to be Mr Brown. I carefully explained that Tony Martin wanted to appeal his convictions which were unsafe because of Dr Heath's testimony and autopsy reports and other reasons.

Mr Brown claimed that he was no longer undertaking criminal appeals. I asked him to provide me with the names of other firms in Norwich who did undertake appeals and he provided me with the names of three firms.

It was an unsatisfactory call. I do not believe that there is a solicitor in Norfolk (or England & Wales) who would not want the Tony Martin renewed appeal on their books.

After discussing the call with Michael (who had listened in on loudspeaker), we agreed that it felt as though Mr Brown had been "leaned on."

Criminal Cases Review Commission (CCRC)	*It is at this point in the chronology that we need to take a look at this organisation. Tony gave me his written authority to conduct an appeal against his convictions and, because his case never went to the House of Lords in 2001, the only avenue left open to us was, as James Saunders had told me,[564] the Criminal Cases Review Commission (CCRC).*

According to its website, "the CCRC is the public body with statutory responsibility for investigating alleged miscarriages of justice in England, Wales and Northern Ireland. It was established by Section 8 of the Criminal Appeal Act 1995 and started work on 31 March 1997. The CCRC has the power to send, or refer, a case back to an appeal court if it considers that there is a real possibility the court will quash the conviction or reduce the sentence in that case.

The CCRC's principal role is to investigate cases where people have been convicted and lost an appeal, but believe they have been wrongly convicted of a criminal offence.

In order for the Commission to be able to refer a case back to the appeal court, it will almost always need to identify some new evidence or other new issue that might provide grounds for a fresh appeal.

---

[564] See entry **419**.

The CCRC cannot perform a 're-run' of a trial just because the evidence of the defence was not accepted by the jury and the evidence of the prosecution was. They have to be able to present to the appeal court new evidence or new legal argument, not identified at the time of the trial, that might have changed the whole outcome of the trial if the jury had been given a chance to consider it.

To help the CCRC identify new evidence or legal argument, it can use its special legal powers under section 17 of the Criminal Appeal Act 1995 to obtain information from public bodies such as the police, the CPS, social services, local councils and so on. Under section 18A of the same Act, they can seek a Crown Court order to obtain material from a private individual or organisation. Their legal powers mean that they can often identify important evidence that would be impossible for others to find.

They can also interview new witnesses and re-interview the original ones. If necessary, they can arrange for new expert evidence such as psychological reports and DNA testing.

The CCRC claims to look into all cases thoroughly, independently and objectively but the legal rules that govern the work of the Commission means that they can only refer a case if they find that there is a 'real possibility' that an appeal court would quash the conviction or, in the case of an appeal against sentence, change the sentence in question."

There have been numerous articles about the significant failures of the CCRC, some saying (myself included) that, just like the "Independent" Police Complaints Commission, it is far from being independent, is at the mercy of government and not fit for purpose but space prevents me from going into further detail here. You might like to search online.

Fri 30 SEP 2016 493

Sarah Cliss, Wisbech Standard

I took possession of the first edition of this book and met with Sarah around 2pm in the Standard*'s offices in March, Cambridgeshire.*

She interviewed me for the paper and a junior reporter took a few photos. She asked a number of challenging questions and appeared fascinated to learn that Barras had not died from a gunshot wound to the chest and about the helicopter flights and other critical information proving Tony's innocence. She assured me that the article would be in the following week's paper dated 7 October 2016.

Sun 2 OCT 2016 494

gift for Tony

I drove to Bleak House, arriving around 3pm, just as Robin Hammond, an acquaintance of Tony's was leaving. I found Tony attending to a motor on a tractor. He looked up, saw me carrying a box and said, "I have to tell you, fella, I'm busy. I've got too much to do."[565]

I merely replied, "I shan't stop you. I've just come to deliver a present," putting the box on the driver's seat of his battered car.

No other words were exchanged by either party. I had so much to say to him; I wanted to show him the book, arrange for a time to meet and so on, but that conversation did not happen. When you encounter Tony in such a mood, it's as if you're in a vacuum – no emotion, no compassion, no humanity, no conversation. You encounter a cardboard cut-out of him – nothing is returned. It's a self-protection mechanism in my view.

Thur 2 OCT 2016 495

Wisbech Library

I met Jakki Racey, manager of Wisbech Library, and spoke with her about THE TRUTH – she was extremely interested and asked if I would donate a copy to the library archive so that anybody researching the case in years to come would be able to have a work to reference. I was indebted to her for her kind suggestion. I also donated a copy to the library itself.

I cannot express the gratitude I felt that the library local to Tony had a copy of the book because my aim is to get justice for the farmer.

Fri 7 OCT 2016 496

Sarah Cliss, *Wisbech Standard*

I went online and saw that the Wisbech Standard *had <u>not</u> covered the story of my lodging an Appeal with the CCRC on behalf of Tony Martin as they had promised. Obviously a bit miffed, I emailed Sarah. She replied that she had called the CCRC and they said they had not received Tony's appeal and therefore could not run with the story.*

So I drove over to Upwell, re-posted it and obtained a receipt of proof of postage to the CCRC, drove back to King's Lynn library and around 7pm emailed Sarah a copy of the receipt. I was being made out to be a liar by the CCRC and I objected to that when I knew that I had posted it (by regular mail) on 22 September.

---

[565] In my view, Tony's insistence on being busy is a device he had used for decades to prevent him from addressing the deep pain of his emotional problems.

Whilst in the library, I received a call from Satish Sekar, an investigative author (whose brother is a barrister with an office in Lambeth), who told me about a conference called *United Against Injustice* to be held in Liverpool the very next day. Sometimes in life you just don't get all the notice you'd like and so you have to make an instant judgment call – to go or not to go. I looked at the list of speakers: Paddy Hill (one of the Birmingham Six), Sheila Coleman (of the Hillsborough Justice campaign), Barbara Stone (sister of Michael Stone), Michelle Diskin-Bates (sister of Barry George), Janet Cunliffe (JENGBA – joint enterprise), Michael O'Brien (conviction quashed for murder of a Cardiff newsagent). Also speaking were David James Smith and Justin Hawkins from the CCRC.

Fri 7 OCT 2016 497	**Manor Farm Surgery, Swaffham, Norfolk** *I'd been to the surgery on two previous occasions and hand-delivered a letter for Dr Haczewski who was a colleague of the late Dr Skinner. I explained to the Receptionist why I was writing to the surgery and she recalled Tony's case and wanted to buy a copy of the book because she likes true crime books.*

I received no reply, either in writing or by phone, which I felt was extremely unusual. Since the security services (as they like to call them – they are only securing the safety of politicians, senior police officers, judges and lawyers and local authority officials involved in wrong-doing, not your safety or mine) are all over my communications like a rash, I had no option but to drive over for a third time and leave yet another request for information. I wanted a copy of Dr Skinner's report on the body of Fred Barras when he was said to have pronounced the body dead at 4:16pm on the Saturday following the shooting.

Although I am from "down south" and don't really know Norfolk all that well, I did find it odd that a doctor should be called all the way from Swaffham when doctors were available in Wisbech, Downham Market or King's Lynn – towns much closer to Tony's farm.

On Friday 7 October 2016 at 14:22, I received a 'private number' call from someone who claimed to be Dr Haczewski (but who might just as easily have been a police officer). I don't usually answer private number calls, but on this occasion I did. The male told me that Dr Skinner worked for the police "in his spare time" and any reports would be with the police, not in the surgery. He added that he had looked for the report I had requested but they could not find it in the surgery.[566] I asked whether anyone in his family would have a copy and

---

[566] It may, of course, have been held elsewhere (in storage for example) but the caller did not inform me of this, insisting that there were no copies available other than in the hands of the police.

he was politely insistent that they would not have a copy and that I should only contact the police.

Now, it is a given that Dr Skinner was a professional man. I don't know of any professional person who would write a report about pronouncing a body dead and send it to the police without keeping a copy for himself at either his place of work or his home (or both), should he need to refer to it at a later stage.

Still listed at the surgery is a Dr Joanne Skinner.

I turned again to HOLMES and to the list of every statement taken in the case. Line S219 shows that on 4 November 1999, the police took a statement from Dr John Malcolm Skinner and that this was entered into evidence at trial.

Sat 8 OCT 2016 — 498

John Foster building, John Moore University, Liverpool
A United Against Injustice conference was held on this day, commencing at 10am.

I was up at 4am determined to drive to Liverpool to meet Paddy Hill and other victims of miscarriages of justice. I have a part of Liverpool in my soul – ever since I first heard Bill Shankly speaking on the radio as an 11-year-old boy. I fell in love with the football club and my first book was called *Liverpool: A Complete Record 1892-1986*. That book took 20 years to research, as you might imagine, since it had full details of every Liverpool game since 1892. But I see now, some 30 years later, that it was just a part of my progress as a human being to reach the point at which I am at now. And, as you know from previous entries, I attended the fateful Hillsborough football match. So getting up at 4am and driving to Liverpool for a conference on injustice made perfect sense to me.

I arrived at 9:45am for the ten o'clock start. David James Smith is a Commissioner of the CCRC and he and Justin Hawkins (Head of Communication) spoke for quite some time about the role of that organisation.

Mr Hawkins stated that once an appeal had been received by the CCRC, the applicant would receive acknowledgement of their appeal "within 10 working days." Mr Smith said that most cases were dealt with "within two years" where the applicant was not in prison. After they spoke, there was a question and answer session. Smith and Hawkins were given an extremely hard time by the audience of around 150-200.

It was then my opportunity to take the microphone. I asked Mr Hawkins to repeat his assertion that all applicants would have their appeal acknowledged with 10 days from receipt by the CCRC.

He agreed that that is what he said. I then asked him why I had not received acknowledgement for lodging the Tony Martin appeal on 22 September. He told me – with the audience listening intently – that he had been the person to have taken the call from Sarah Cliss at the *Wisbech Standard* and he'd told her that the Tony Martin appeal was not listed on their database of appeals received. It could be, of course, that it was in somebody's "in-tray" (or the rubbish bin) and so I told him that I had re-sent it and obtained a receipt for it from the post office and would he now acknowledge receipt of the appeal? He agreed that the CCRC would. (One of the biggest complaints against the CCRC from members of the audience was that they often delayed appeals by claiming they had not received paperwork or documents and so on.)

I then turned my attention to the Commissioner, David James Smith. He had said that most cases were resolved "within two years" and so I informed him that I knew of a man who was still waiting to have his conviction quashed after *five years* and it was a very simple case of the man having been convicted of inciting a female into sexual activity when there never was a female. He said he'd see me at the end of the session. I had to search him out and he reluctantly gave me his card. It seemed to me as though he'd been told to avoid me. I still didn't tell him, of course, that the man was me, though I had the feeling he knew.

Sun 9 OCT 2016 · 499

the CCRC

I emailed David James Smith about Tony's Appeal and also my own case which the CCRC had sat on for 5 years. He replied saying that the CCRC is "completely independent of politicians" and he would never give in to such political pressure. He would say that, wouldn't he? He's hardly likely to speak out against the very people who employ him.

At the Conference in Liverpool on Saturday, Mr Smith came in for a hard time – the CCRC is not well received amongst people who know the way in which it *really* works, not how we're told it works. I'll nail my colours to the mast – in my view it's a very necessary organisation, but it is used as an instrument of State by the government. The CCRC is nothing more than a filter system: it buys time, rejects worthy appeals and refers back to the court of appeal incredibly few appeals. So, on 10 October, when I emailed the CCRC to enquire whether it had received the Tony Martin appeal, they agreed that they had, but they were not going to accept it because Tony had not signed it. Tony had asked me – as his McKenzie Friend – to deal with the appeal and therefore since I signed the document with my name, there was no need for him to sign it. But like I said, they buy time. The government do not want his Appeal to be famous like the original case and nor do they want me to gain any credibility for preparing it. Like I said, they like to do the bidding of their paymasters. In my view, there's a lack of integrity in that organisation. I'd love to be proven wrong.

I could, of course, have played all kinds of mind games with the CCRC and threatened them with a judicial review, but I didn't want to waste my time with that strategy, so I drove over to Wisbech on Wednesday 12 October 2016. I found him in one of his usual haunts and he was surprised to see me and, as I fixed my gaze upon him, I saw more in his eyes than I'd seen for many months. I was happy to see the life in those eyes. I asked him to sign the Appeal document and he did. So I posted it off, getting a receipt from the post office. They'll still try to wheedle their way out of it … they'll still try to deny Tony his right to have his convictions overturned and they'll still try to deny me the right to be acknowledged as the man who worked his bollocks off to ensure that justice was finally achieved. For him. For Fearon. And for Fred Barras – especially for Fred Barras. He was killed alright – but not by Tony Martin.

Wed 12 OCT 2016 500

letter from Brendon Fearon to author

The author received a letter from Brendon Fearon (dated 9 October) in response to his letter dated 5 September 2016:

"After reading your letter and statements I am happy to answer some of your queries.

Regarding the helicopter, I was on my back in the field when I saw bright lights going over me. I don't know what time this was. I was going in and out of consciousness.

I thought I saw Tony Martin on the stairs at the time of the shooting. I wasn't given any notice or verbal shouts that he was there or had a gun and only saw a flash and then Tony Martin. After going back with the police I now believe that Tony Martin was at the door.

I would like to clear something up. I am not a traveller or gypsy.

I have never heard of Tony Martin before or anyone associated with him before 20 August 1999. I knew nothing about a family feud."

Let's examine this more closely. Firstly, I do not believe that Mr Fearon composed that letter on his own. He had told me on the phone that he would consult with his solicitor before responding to me, and I believe that this letter was carefully manufactured by a solicitor (who was consulting with the police.)

However, let's not throw the baby out with the bath water: we come to the issue of the stairs again. Despite his first statement with regard to having been shot "up a track" on farmland now, in this letter, he was saying that Tony was at the door to the breakfast room inside the house.

I don't believe this at all and nor do I believe that he had not been 'advised' to write this.

It's also interesting to note that Mr Fearon said he knew nothing about a family feud. Let's remind ourselves of what his solicitor David Payne of Payne and Gamage, Newark said on 18 September 1999 [entry **268**] – just three days after the video "re-enactment" at Bleak House – "As we were driving down (from Newark to Downham Market police station), there was something else you told me about a family dispute…" Perhaps Mr Fearon and/or his solicitor had forgotten that conversation over time.

Finally, Mr Fearon wished to make it clear that he describes himself as being of "mixed race" and not a traveller or gypsy. I am happy, of course, to confirm and respect his view of his ethnicity.

Fri 21 OCT 2016 — 501

the CCRC
Despite an assurance from Justin Hawkins that he would call me upon receipt of the signed copy of the Appeal, by 21 October 2016 he had still not called. Neither did the Wisbech Standard *run with the story.*[567] *Little wonder the CCRC is held in contempt by many caught up in the criminal 'justice' system. I include myself as one of the many.*

Tue 25 OCT 2016 — 502

Sarah Cliss, *Wisbech Standard*
Despite a promise to promote the first version of this book, Sarah Cliss continued to stall. Below is a copy of the email entitled 'Tony Martin appeal' *that the author sent to her:*

"I'm incredibly disappointed that the *Standard* has not yet carried the story of Tony's appeal or, indeed, the way in which the CCRC has handled it.

There can be no doubt that the CCRC is in possession of signed Appeal forms and yet it is still attempting to deny Tony justice - that is a story in itself and I believe the *Standard* should be informing its readers of the CCRC's actions.

Do you imagine the delays could be caused by me - after all, I did expose child abuse at Lambeth Council which the parliamentarians and Scotland Yard were keen to cover up. I'll leave you to decide.

In the meantime, would you kindly call the CCRC and ask why there is such a delay and then call me to update me? (I am not always at a computer terminal.)"

---

[567] There is a misconceived notion that there is a free press in England. Try taking a story about child abuse to the 'free press' and see how it will disappear. Those stories that make the news are heavily controlled and rigidly diluted. Few names of paedophile local councillors, police officers, judges, barristers, solicitors et al actually appear, given the industrial scale of the problem in this country. Very occasionally a name or two will be made known but they are but mere morsels fed to placate (and keep under control) the broad mass of the people.

This was followed up 8 minutes later with:

"We will run the story as soon as we have confirmation from the CCRC that the appeal has been lodged and verified, I am in weekly contact with them. I understand your frustration but until the CCRC have accepted the appeal has been properly submitted I can't run a story saying the appeal has been made. As I understand it the signed forms have now gone in, but because they have been sent in by a third party the CCRC needs to verify that Tony is happy for the appeal to go ahead. Once that has been done the story will run. It is all written. The CCRC have to follow strict guidelines, as I have been told they cannot just run appeals submitted by a third party on someone's behalf, because the person involved in the case may not want to appeal.

In the case of deceased people then family members can lodge an appeal, but they must be a close relative.

I have been told the CCRC should be in a position to accept the appeal either this week or early next week, as long as Tony responds to their request for verification promptly. If they do not hear from Tony then there may well be a problem. So it may be as well to speak to Tony and encourage him to reply as soon as possible."

Clearly the CCRC were playing mind games, stalling the process of justice for Tony Martin. But however corrupt I believe that organisation to be, they can't beat the truth. As Tony wrote in prison: "The truth roots out the untruth."

Wed 26 OCT 2016 503

Sarah Cliss, Wisbech Standard

The author wrote a response to Sarah Cliss:

"What utter nonsense from the CCRC! How can Tony NOT confirm he is happy to run an appeal when he signed the paperwork? There is no problem except one being created for political reasons by the CCRC and I must add, Archant Media. Tony signed the papers. That's all there is to it Sarah and I am astonished and appalled that someone with your experience should be a puppet of the CCRC and preventing the carriage of Justice.

Tony Martin has suffered long enough.

I do not accept your response at all. I had suspected as much the moment the *Standard* failed to run the story on the date initially agreed. That the *Standard* is allowing itself to become embroiled in preventing Justice for Tony Martin is in itself anathema to Justice and shows that the paper is not independent.

As you can see, I've copied your response (and mine) to the MPs responsible for justice. Speak with John Elworthy[568] (if you haven't already) about my banned book and the cover-up of child abuse in Lambeth and my FIVE unlawful prison sentences and then say that is not linked to the actions by the CCRC. (John is, of course, aware, but he's doing nothing to expose it because he's been told not to.) Please see attached copy of Minutes of my meeting with retired Scotland Yard DCI Clive Driscoll.

This is political and not justice and you are playing your part in covering it all up. And in covering up Tony's truth, you're also vicariously accountable for covering up child abuse in Lambeth - and Archant. Look at your sister paper's article on me from 2010 - the Bexley Times (another Archant government-controlled paper) in which it claimed I had been found guilty of the incitement of a 14 year old girl. Do your research and get me the name of the girl. Then look up section 10 of the Sexual Offences Act 2003 and you'll see that person A has to incite Person B in order to be found guilty of incitement. With no Person B (and you won't find one because there wasn't one) there cannot be guilt. Lambeth Council and the Met Police brought the charges because of what I reported in Lambeth whilst working as a head teacher there (as discussed). Why do you think the Child Abuse inquiry has had three Chairs and the main counsel resigned - after Ben Emmerson slapped a gagging order on me for mentioning Tony Martin's sexual abuse in Glebe House School, Hunstanton? Another cover-up.

A woman of your undoubted experience ought to be investigating that stuff, not indulging in communications with an organisation (the CCRC) which is an instrument of government determined to cover up child abuse (despite IICSA). Anyone with even half a brain is aware that IICSA is nothing but a mere crumb offered to a gullible public. It won't go anywhere and its "report" will be a whitewash.

Shame on you for buying into the lies promulgated by the CCRC, for delaying justice for Tony Martin (and I gave you sufficient reasons and evidence to show he was fitted up by corrupt State officials as, indeed, I have been) and for playing your part in the cover up of child abuse in Lambeth. Charles Péguy wrote: "He who does not bellow the Truth when he knows the Truth makes himself the accomplice of liars and forgers."

I do not like the company you keep[569] and I make no apologies for the tone of my communication."

---

[568] At the time of publication, the Editor of the *Wisbech Standard* and *Cambs Times*.

[569] Sarah Cliss says that she is a long-term friend of Dario Grady, manager of Crewe Alexandra football club, where child abuser Barry Bennell was allowed to flourish. As long as Bennell was spotting young teenage talent (who could be sold on for cash) those who governed the club turned a blind eye to the abuse of hundreds of teenage boys within football. Bennell did not act alone, but has become the 'fall guy'. A former Crewe

Thur
27 OCT
2016
504

the CCRC
I received a letter from the CCRC which stated: "We have received the application you have made on behalf of Mr Martin. We have given the case a reference number – 01168/2016: We will now assess the case and write to you again as soon as possible to let you know what will happen next."

And still the Wisbech Standard did not run with the story of Tony's appeal.

Sun
30 OCT
2016
505

Wisbech Sunday market
I took a stall at the market for the second week running. This week I had a petition typed out and asked people to sign it. Many people were only too happy to sign it, saying he didn't receive justice.

Then a 65-year-old woman came to the stall and said she had been a carer in a home in Friday Bridge Road where Tony's Aunt Gladys had stayed. This woman said that 'Gladdie' was not the cleanest of women and that she'd hoard food in her chest of drawers – not tinned or packeted, but things like toast and roast dinners.

And then an amazing 'revelation' – she said that it was 'common knowledge' amongst the staff that Tony (who often visited) was Gladys's son, not her nephew. It was alleged that she gave birth out of wedlock before the end of the war and that the baby was given away to her married older sister to look after. The alleged father was Walter Martin.

It could also explain why Tony was sent away to boarding school – the staff believing that Gladys paid the fees. But this is mere speculation and I don't really like that sort of thing. Tony never mentioned it to me, and so I felt that I ought to bring this gossip to his attention, and not long after the bringer of the news left the stall, Tony walked past. He did not stop to speak at all. But that is Tony. I sold two copies of the book and gained several dozen signatures for the petition.

Thur
10 NOV
2016
506

letter from Brian Pead to Tony Martin
Good news – the Criminal Cases Review Commission has acknowledged your signed Appeal forms that I prepared on your behalf with your agreement. This is excellent news – copy of letter enclosed.

director, Hamilton Smith, said, "As long as scrutiny isn't happening, there'll always be paedophiles."

A version of the book TONY MARTIN: THE TRUTH is now out – you have a copy. It must be clear to you by now that you were completely stitched up by all concerned – from Sharman to Makin to Scrivener. At every step of the way, all knew you to be innocent *before* you went to trial.

The Appeal at the Royal Courts of Justice was also "legally engineered" as you describe – under the Rule of Law, the issue of diminished responsibility could not be used on Appeal if it had not been raised at trial. The law is clear on this issue – section 2 of the Homicide Act 1957 states: "The medical condition *must* have been cited in the original trial for it to be later relied on as a defence in the appeal hearing."

As you know, this issue was never raised at trial, so it was unlawful to rely on it at the Appeal. The Judges and Wolkind would have known this, of course. I have cited this unlawful action in your Appeal to the CCRC.

For a number of reasons I published the first version of the book myself. There is a second book planned because I did not – for very good strategic reasons – put all of the corruption and other detail in the first book.

I have a television company interested in your Appeal. I know the background of these people and their work in overturning/ highlighting miscarriages of justice. One of the guys is a professor of law. They also say they are interested in my role and why I chose to devote 3 years of my life to exposing the Truth in your case.

I currently rent a stall at Wisbech Sunday Market to draw attention to your injustice. I also collect signatures for a petition I aim to present to the Home Secretary (Amber Rudd) and Liz Truss (your MP and Justice Minister.)

Rodney Gooderson was pleased with the book – he's read it from cover to cover.

Ann Widdecombe[570] has asked for a copy – she was, as you'll recall, very much on your side and a person's right to defend himself. I shall send a copy to Gillian Shephard – now in the House of Lords – and invite comment from her.

Emneth Methodist Church: whilst on the Sunday market stall, a customer kindly invited me to attend the coffee mornings. I've been along three times and they always ask after you and would like to see you again. I've booked Christmas dinner. I'd like to see you there.

MANY people at the Sunday Market want Justice for you. I have been overwhelmed by their support for you. You are a very lucky man.

I would like to meet you again in the very near future to discuss:

(i) the Appeal and next steps;
(ii) a letter from you to Professor Jay, Chair of the child abuse inquiry;

---

[570] To be specific, this was the office of Ann Widdecombe and not the former MP herself.

(iii)   a letter from you to Truss re the book and Appeal;

(iv)   some very personal information given to me last Sunday about your mother.

Please call me on 07508242101 or, if that number is not working, then please call Philippa at Darby Farm (one of your biggest supporters) on [number] and she'll get a message to me. She continues to be as keen as I am to ensure that you clear your name (and eventually receive a lot of compensation!)

I am sorry that you have been so busy lately but we really do need 2-3 hours together to discuss the issues in this letter.

Liz Johnson is in hospital having major surgery. She continues to support you (and me).

As you will be aware, I have a *duty* to report the child abuse at Glebe House School, irrespective of whether you do or not. Obviously I would prefer to work with you on a letter to Professor Jay, Chair of the Inquiry, but I must make it clear that even if you choose not to sign the letter, I have a duty to report it to her and also to inform Norfolk Police. I remind you that the Chief Constable of Norfolk (Simon Bailey) is also the national lead police officer in child sexual abuse. He will have a *duty* to investigate your allegations.

When I spoke with Fearon, he confirmed that he is not a traveller but is of mixed race.

Back in 2004, you stated on Radio Cambridge that:

> "There was an awful lot of stuff that was hidden up. Evidence which is there if anyone wants to get to it. My case is a can of worms. What it's actually done is open up Pandora's Box."

I agree – too much evidence hidden and falsified and Norfolk Police are *still* doing it. However, I've reminded the CCRC that under section 17 of the Criminal Appeal Act 1995, they have the power to *force* Norfolk and Cambridge Police to disclose all 999 calls on 20 August 1999 and the helicopter flight logs. Be in no doubt that these exist or, if not, have been deliberately destroyed. Either way, it works for you.

Wolkind QC was reprimanded on 16 December 2015 – your birthday, of course – for poor behaviour during a murder trial. He was sacked by his client. You are still listed on his website as a "successful appeal" even though he knew it had been engineered.

King's Lynn County Court: as you know, I acted as your McKenzie Friend. Have you received all of the papers since the May hearing? You need them and to retain them.

Would like to meet ASAP to discuss the Appeal and other matters enclosed herein."

I drove over to Bleak House on an afternoon when it was pouring of rain. I parked up in my usual place, opposite the large barn near the cottages, and walked to the large apple store. I saw Tony's car and found him sitting inside, reading some farming newspaper. The rain ceased to fall, though the sky remained ominously dark.

"I wanted to do some work, but this bloody rain doesn't help."

And we chatted for two hours and had some very good laughs. On occasions like this, Tony is a very funny man and great company.

Wed
16 NOV
2016
507

BhatiaBest solicitors

I drove over to Nottingham to meet with Ash Bhatia, the Managing Director of BhatiaBest solicitors. This was the law firm which represented Brendon Fearon in his claim against Tony Martin for having been shot. After a national outcry that legal aid could be wasted on such frivolous cases, the claim was eventually dropped.

The receptionist informed me that Mr Bhatia was not in the building, so I asked if Matt Best was available. He wasn't. Then I asked to speak with Tim Holder who, according to the website, is a partner specialising in crime.

I waited for about 10 minutes and was met by Richard Posner, an amiable enough chap and a higher courts advocate, so he knew his way around the legal process. I showed him the book and when I mentioned that Fred Barras did not die of a gunshot wound to the chest and that he did not die "within two minutes" as the pathologist claimed, Mr Posner raised his eyebrows.

He raised them again when I mentioned that I believe that Mrs Barras has a strong claim against Norfolk Police for the death of her son. A claim that would run into millions of pounds in compensation.

I mentioned the time of the helicopter, that the thermal imaging allegedly failed to find the injured body of Fred lying near the exit window, and that the police were blocking my legitimate Freedom of Information Act requests for the flight logs. I also mentioned that Barras had died of a pneumothorax and not a gunshot wound to the chest, and that a pneumothorax takes at least 5 minutes to cause death.

Mr Posner heard all this and – having fished for as much information as I was prepared to give – then replied that his firm could not represent Tony in his appeal to the CCRC because of a conflict of interest – having represented Fearon in 2001 *against* Tony Martin, it is fair to say that there probably would have been a conflict of interest. However, there is new and compelling evidence that I have now made available and so I'm not entirely convinced that the 'conflict of interest' argument is valid, since the new evidence also aided Fearon.

Mr Posner also asked how Mrs Barras' claim against Norfolk Police would be funded and I suggested through the legal aid channel, but he felt that that route would not be possible (though didn't say why).

Then Mr Posner said that his firm didn't need the case simply to bolster its own reputation because "We're running the Brexit case," which I felt was somewhat arrogant. "We're a very big company," he offered (and I'd done my homework before driving up there) and he was correct.

Mr Posner said that he felt the biggest hurdle to overcome was that of causation: to prove that Barras died *after* the two-minutes claimed by disgraced pathologist Dr Heath. I told Mr Posner about the 70+ cases that had to be re-investigated and he asked: "Was this one of them?" and I replied that, no, it had been 'overlooked'.

The solicitor took my card, said he'd have a word with colleagues and that, if they felt there was some mileage in taking it further, he'd call me. But I had an immediate gut feeling that I'd never hear from him again. Years of experience have given me a highly-attuned sensitivity to such comments: Mr Posner's words were a polite way of ending the conversation and getting rid of me.

I was also left with the strong feeling that Mr Posner knew that something wasn't right with this at all, and that he had a sniff of corruption in his nostrils and so chose to pass on my invitation to involve BhatiaBest in this narrative for a second time.

And I was left with the feeling that Mrs Barras and Fred deserved more. Far more.

On Wednesday 30 November 2016, I emailed the above passage to Richard Posner asking him to comment on it. Unsurprisingly, I did not receive a reply.

Sun 4 DEC 2016 508

telephone call: Tony Martin to Brian Pead
I worked on the stall at Wisbech Sunday Market. Around 9:15am I went to the toilet and returned to find Tony at the stall, signing the petition to quash his convictions. My 81-year-old assistant did not recognise Tony and had asked him to sign.

I walked a hundred yards or so with Tony as he vented his spleen. He told me that he'd taken a call from Channel 4 who wanted a copy of the first interview in the police station and he said he'd now tell people to call me instead since I have all the legal papers.

Then the anger surfaced, the swearing like a trooper. I have no problem with that. In fact, I like it – it shows me he's still alive, still vibrant, still in this world, still wanting an injustice righted, still refusing to "go gentle into that good night".

"I was just defending myself! Can't anybody understand that I'm a human being who owns a house and cottages on the farm and don't sleep in either?

Can't anybody understand that I was scared when I stood on the stairs and they shone that fucking torch in my eyes?"

The pain was still there. The sense of deep injustice. You can't deal with such deep emotional pain in just a few minutes, and certainly not standing in the middle of Wisbech Sunday market. I asked to meet him later the same day, but he declined – "I just need to be left alone at the moment."

I've found that Tony goes within himself when he's feeling such deep pain – it's his personal coping mechanism. We all deal with emotion in different ways – Tony's is to retreat, to think things through, to try to rationalise and come to terms with his feelings. I stood next to him, looking him in the eye, feeling his pain (such as any other human being can empathise.) I wanted to say to him that he needed to take time out to meet with me, to talk, to discuss the issues, but you can't rush Tony, you can't impose on him. He'll do things in his own way and in his own time. I respect that, as frustrating as it is for me. It's my stuff – I own it. I want to hug him, to chat over a cup of tea or a meal, to help him come to terms with his pain, to discuss the book, the appeal and so much more. He frustrates the hell out of me at times, but I have to respect his agenda and his needs and the way he chooses to deal with his emotional pain.

We parted and I returned to the stall, to collect more signatures for the petition and sell more copies of the book. Spread the word about how the Great British Public was well and truly conned by the government of the day.

Then, at 9:43am, he called me. You have to understand how Tony's mind works. On occasions, he'll just do or say whatever is on his mind – blurt it out – get it off his chest. He can be ruthlessly blunt and he's offended many people because of it. He's never offended me, even when he once told me to "Fuck off!" when I went to Bleak House while he was working on a roof.

Then there are the times where he'll carefully skirt around an issue, discussing almost meaningless things in order to avoid the elephant in the room. You have to remain alert to his needs at any particular moment. He's quixotic, lively, rapid-thinking, whimsical, emotional. It's like riding an emotional roller-coaster and you have to hang on in order to stay with him or you'll be thrown out of the car, out of the conversation. So I listened carefully. His tone of voice and choice of words told me to remain alert. He wanted to tell me something, that's for sure. I just had to be patient. He can be hard work, but I take that as just a part of who he is. So we chatted about his position on the stairs again, we chatted about the biased judge, how the prosecutor used the ridiculous phrase "You shot them like rats in a trap!" and he vented his spleen, but I knew all this was just the lead-in to something more powerful. After I expressed the view that the book showed a deep level of corruption, he said "At least you understand, Brian, at least you speak common sense." That counts as great praise from Mr Martin, believe you me. If you ever need more from him, forget it. It's not in his DNA. That's not a criticism, just an observation.

And then came the bombshell. "I went to Newark farm machinery sales this week. I couldn't see anything I wanted, so I then went to see Barras's grave."

The minute he mentioned Newark, I imagined he'd do that. Our last few conversations have shown me that Tony Martin is finally growing, finally emerging from the dark shadow of death hanging unnecessarily over his life. I have seen the signs. They are subtle, almost imperceptible, but they are there.

"So how did you feel when you saw his grave?"

"It said 'the tragic death of Barras' and I suppose, burying the hatchet, it was tragic. You could say he shouldn't have been there and that it was tragic that he was shot or you could say that it was tragic that people took him there and that he was involved in crime at such a young age."

"And if you had to choose, how would you sum up how you felt?"

"I think you could say that it was tragic that he died."

"You didn't kill him, Tony, remember that. He died as the result of the police. Read the bloody book – it's all in there."

"I'm too busy to read it at the moment."

I knew he was fudging. I knew his busy-ness was a mask – he can't face the book at present because for so long he's had to fight an injustice and it's given him anger to face life and if that's removed, how will he feel? What will he do when his name is finally cleared, once and for all? I learnt as a trainee counsellor that you can't help someone overcome a major issue unless you replace it with something else, or there's a nihilistic emptiness to their life. I instinctively knew that he claimed he was too busy to read it because he is not presently ready to deal with the realisation that he was right all along, innocent all along.

We briefly discussed my four miscarriages of justice[571] and then the 17-minute conversation ended – his breakfast had arrived at his local Wetherspoons. That's Tony: you could have been in the most critical conversation with him but it doesn't matter. The breakfast arrives, he'll eat the breakfast. And the point of the conversation can be lost. I'd forget the breakfast and deal with the issue in the conversation, but we're all different and Tony is just how he is.

| Tue 6 DEC 2016 509 | **telephone call: Tony Martin to Brian Pead**
Tony called me at 6:33pm. He wanted to know where the record of his first police interview was. I told him I had a copy, so he said he'd give my number to Malcolm Starr (his businessman friend) and to the woman who keeps calling him from Channel Four. |

---

[571] At the time of publishing – January 2019 – this had risen to *six* miscarriages of justice as corrupt State officials sought to continue to unlawfully control my life and cover up my own miscarriages of justice and Tony's.

I suggested that Tony passes all media inquiries on to me. He agreed. Neither Malcolm Starr nor anyone from Channel 4 ever contacted me.

Fri 9 DEC 2016 510

Knights Hill Hotel, King's Lynn
I met people calling themselves Emily Turner and Dave Nath from a film production company they called Story Films TV. They wanted to read the police interviews Tony had back in August 1999 and so I made them available on my laptop. I had annotated the interviews.

The meeting lasted 4½ hours and we discussed the main elements of the case. You can tell a lot about people by the questions they ask and the questions they don't ask. Eventually, we got round to my four miscarriages of justice, but they failed to ask me a single question about them. Anyone from a film production company with a *bona fide* interest in justice would have asked me at least one question about these miscarriages, but not one question came.

I asked for Ken Loach's contact details. Loach is a director whom I much admire for his approach to film as a vehicle for social change, social justice. Turner replied: "I know him. I'll give you his details if you give us the transcripts of the interviews."

And that single sentence told me all I needed to know. I began to pack away. That's why the film/tv/music production worlds often have such a bad name. Many people involved in those industries are self-possessed, selfish, interested only in their inflated egos. She told me in asking that question that she hadn't listened to my point that I had worked prodigiously on Tony's appeal for 3 years and my main interest was not a television programme, but in obtaining justice for Tony. For the Great British Public. And for Fred Barras and his family.

Thur 15 DEC 2016 511

telephone call
I took a call from Emily Turner. She expected me to send the transcripts of the Tony Martin police interviews – note my use of the word 'expected'.

I informed her that I wanted a Memorandum of Understanding (MoU) to be in place which would include information about the programme. I reminded her of the importance of Tony's appeal. I will let nothing get in the way since I've worked so hard on it. She said she'd send an MoU by email "today."

Fri
16 DEC
2016
512

Tony's birthday
He is 72 today. I sent him a card and also called him. There was no reply to his phone, which is usual.

I never did receive the MoU from Ms Turner.

Sun
18 DEC
2016
513

Wisbech Sunday market
He turned up today as I thought he would, it being the last ever Sunday market at that venue. He asked me about Channel 4 and Emily Turner and I said that, in my opinion, they had clearly demonstrated their untrustworthiness and that he would do well to steer clear of them.

I had received no Memorandum of Understanding from them and I added that, with an Appeal in the pipeline, it would be better not to jeopardise that and lie low until such times as the Appeal is heard. My understanding was that they wanted to put out a film containing only the police interviews immediately following the shooting and my experience has taught me that if you only present a thin slice of any full narrative, you can easily distort reality. I did not want to run that risk and told him so. To his credit, he did listen, then turned and left, without saying as much as a bare "Goodbye".

Then he returned to the stall to tell me more about that night. I'd heard it all before, of course, but he needed to off-load his emotional burden. He was, officially, released from prison back in 2003 but the reality is that he is just as much in prison as he ever was, even prior to his incarceration.

As he turned away to deal with the remainder of his day, I felt enormous compassion for a man who was carrying a tremendous burden ... of the sexual abuse at Glebe House, the death of Fred Barras (not caused by him), the unwarranted police campaign against him, the media vilification. It clearly wasn't only Fred Barras who died that night...

Thur
22 DEC
2016
514

letter from CCRC to Tony Martin
Tony received a letter from the CCRC in which he was told that because he was not in custody – and therefore 'not a priority' – his case would likely "be passed to a Case Review Manager by July 2017."

I couldn't help thinking that the authorities are quick to arrest you, process you through the courts and into prison, but when you find them out and just how corrupt they've been, they like to take their time in dispensing justice and then it's through gritted teeth at the displeasure of having been found out. Just ask all the families involved in Hillsborough…

Mon 16 JAN 2017 515

letter from Tony Martin to Alastair Wilson
Tony sent the following letter to Alastair Wilson of the West Norfolk Care Commissioning Group in King's Lynn, Norfolk:

"Re: your report to the POW Charity

The author of the book TONY MARTIN: THE TRUTH, Brian Pead, has informed me that you authored a witness statement for the People's Opportunity to Work (POW) charity in which you made a number of statements which contradicted the evidence of pathologists Dr Michael Heath (and to a lesser extent Dr Richard Shepherd and Dr P. Nigel Cooper) with regard to their autopsies on the body of Frederick Jackson Barras.

As you may recall, in his witness statement Dr Heath did not refer to the x-rays that had been taken of Mr Barras by radiologists at the Queen Elizabeth Hospital upon Dr Heath's instructions.

It was, of course, imperative that he ought to have referred to these x-rays since they showed a 'massive pneumothorax tension' which means, of course, that Mr Barras could not have died "within two minutes" as Dr Heath testified at my trial for murder at Norwich Crown Court in April 2000.

Mr Pead, along with an investigative journalist Satish Sekar (whose books were instrumental in overturning the miscarriages of justice involving 'the Cardiff Three'), has shown in his book TONY MARTIN: THE TRUTH that Dr Heath eventually resigned from his post as a Home Office pathologist declaring himself to have been "unprofessional and arrogant."

You may or may not be aware that more than 70 of Dr Heath's cases were re-investigated following his resignation, including something like nine murder cases. A review of Dr Heath's cases was undertaken, I believe, by the Criminal Cases Review Commission (CCRC) although my case was not reinvestigated and in the interest of justice it ought to have been.

Author Brian Pead has worked ceaselessly on my case and in collaboration with me over a period of more than three years and has shown that the case against me ought not to have been brought as many commentators at the time believed. He provides evidence in the book of considerable police impropriety, a wholly biased police investigation, false documentation and the suppression of information which pointed to my innocence and corroborated my version of events. In October 2016 he entered my Appeal against Conviction into the CCRC who have allocated my case the number 01168/2016. My Appeal was acknowledged in a letter from the CCRC to Mr Pead dated 21 October 2016 (copied enclosed for your perusal).

I am writing to you to ask for a signed copy of your witness statement to the POW Charity and any further comments you may wish to make in respect of the medical aspects of my case. I am also seeking a meeting with you (with Brian Pead also present) in which we can discuss the finer points of your witness statement.

The CCRC has special legal powers under section 17 of the Criminal Appeal Act 1995 to obtain information in connection with criminal appeals from any third party.

I would like to think that I do not have to take that particular route but rather that we can meet to discuss the medical aspects of my case.

I understand from Brian Pead that he has written to you but that he has not received a reply. Furthermore, I am given to believe that he has telephoned you at the Council offices in Chapel Street but that his calls are not put through to you. I feel sure that you would not wish to interfere with the natural course of justice and am therefore bemused with regard to this lack of contact with Brian Pead.

I would be most grateful if you would reply to this letter in the first instance. Brian Pead's mobile number is 07508 242 101.

I am certain that you will understand the importance of this fresh evidence that Mr Pead has unearthed during his tireless reinvestigation of my case."

Mon 30 JAN 2017 516

public meeting at Guild Hall, King's Lynn

In what was nothing more than a public relations exercise by the Norfolk Constabulary to give the appearance of accountability, there was a meeting at the Guild Hall in King's Lynn. The timing of the "public event" was from 5pm to 7pm – the very time when most people are on their way home from work and need food. This is no accident. If public accountability were the real raison d'être *of such an exercise, these meetings would be held on Sundays for example.*

Under the headline "Tony Martin takes police to task over cuts in officers", it was reported in the Eastern Daily Press[572] that the Chief Constable of Norfolk, Simon Bailey, outlined the challenges facing the force's finances, saying officer numbers had fallen from 1,650 to 1,472 over the last four years.

Thankfully, the public-spirited Tony took the Chief Constable to task but it all fell on deaf ears. Tony also asked Mr Bailey how many officers it would take

---

[572] http://www.edp24.co.uk/news/crime/tony-martin-takes-norfolk-police-to-task-over-cuts-in-officers-1-4869445

to arrest a man on suspicion of drink driving and the chief constable replied, "Normally two officers."

"So why was I arrested in Tilney All Saints on suspicion of drink driving by six officers after I had only had a cup of tea with my meal in the pub?"

The disingenuous Mr Bailey trotted out the usual nonsense: "I can't comment on individual cases."

Actually, Mr Bailey *could* have commented on Tony's case but *chose not to*. This is the same Mr Bailey whom I had written to and I was then subsequently arrested, having called for a vote of No Confidence in him by refusing to investigate child abuse at Glebe House. I was later released without interview or charge. This is the same Mr Bailey who is always in the local media bleating on about the lack of manpower he has at his disposal.

The meeting was chaired by the Police and Crime Commissioner Lorne Green, a former Canadian diplomat. Mr Green refuses to reply to any of my letters, telephone calls or emails about Tony's case and child abuse in Norfolk.

Would it surprise you to learn that his office as Commissioner is in the same building as Mr Bailey's in police headquarters at Wymondham?

How you are being deceived every day of your lives. There is no police accountability – it is a myth, an illusion to quell the masses into thinking that there is such a mechanism in place. Why do you think they came down so hard on Tony, a man with the intelligence to see right through the lies promulgated by government?

Thur 2 FEB 2017 517

the CCRC

As you have read, Tony asked me to write an Appeal on his behalf and I duly did so and sent it to the CCRC. It was unsigned by Tony, but I had a signed Form of Authority from Tony. The accompanying letter was signed by me.

The CCRC were not happy with this and so I sent another copy. Finally, I asked Tony to sign the forms – which he did – and I sent them off, only to receive a telephone call doubting that the signature was genuine and intimating that I had forged it. Naturally I tape-recorded that conversation.

The upshot of this chicanery was that the CCRC called a meeting and asked Tony to be present. They wanted to ask him if the signature was his and that he was happy that an Appeal against conviction was going forward on his behalf.

The two men from the Commission called themselves John Jones and Nick Holmshaw. They explained to Tony about the role of the Commission and confirmed that they were happy that it was Tony's signature on the forms and that yes, he did want to Appeal.

Holmshaw read out the legal points and wanted to know if Tony understood all of them. He did. When it came to the point that the trial judge was biased, Tony paused, tears welling up. He regaled the point that when Helen Lilley had said that Tony was good with children, Judge Owen – as we have seen – said that they had said the same about Hitler and Stalin. Tony's tears were of frustration, the injustice, the unnecessary and unjustified vilification.

Once the legal aspects had been covered, the two men set to leave. Jones mentioned that he had been to California to see the giant sequoias and Tony asked them to sit down again and he told them he had planted more than 140 sequoias on his land.

Poor Tony. He hadn't realised that the CCRC guys had been primed to "casually mention" the sequoias to gain his confidence. Despite his obvious intelligence in some matters, he does have this worrying Achilles heel - that he leaves himself open to people who find something about him that he is interested in and they'll use that to deceive him.

Sun
5 FEB
2017
518

Waterside Press and others

Tony and I met Professor David Wilson, who describes himself as "a criminologist" from the University of Birmingham, someone calling himself Rik Hall and describing himself as a TV producer, someone calling himself David Howard, a film director, and Bryan Gibson, owner of the publishing firm Waterside Press and a former barrister in criminal law for more than 25 years.

I'd had a number of doubts about Mr Gibson prior to the meeting, but decided to proceed for Tony's sake.

It became apparent to me throughout the course of the meeting that Mr Gibson's remit was to court Tony and remove me from the scene.

It had been my understanding that the meeting was called to discuss a tv programme about Tony's case and yet no details were, in fact, discussed.

Three days after the meeting, Mr Gibson sent me an email in which he criticised me heavily and claimed that he had taken the manuscript of the book on good faith and didn't know a thing about me but after the meeting, he'd gone on the internet and found all sorts of negative things about me. Now, do you believe that a barrister of 25 years, and a publisher of 25 years, would have done no due diligence on me prior to signing a contract or meeting to discuss a proposed television programme? I'll leave you to decide.

At the bottom of his email was a single question: "Do you have Tony's contact details as I'd like to progress the programme?"

Rather gave the game away don't you think?

Mon
20 FEB
2017
519

CCRC email
I received an email from the CCRC with the news that the Appeal was going ahead and the CCRC was seeking some of the documents from Norfolk Police that they had refused to provide to us.

Tue
28 FEB
2017
520

letter to Cressida Dick, Commissioner, Scotland Yard
Having issued an Official Complaint under Article 3 of the European Convention on Human Rights as long ago as 31 December 2013, I felt I would write to the new Commissioner of the Metropolitan Police in London, in the vain hope that she would be keen to see Justice finally achieved for me and my family:

An Open Letter Re: Your Appointment and Other Matters

Firstly, may I congratulate you on your appointment as Commissioner of the Metropolitan Police Service. What a remarkable moment in history we have with the confluence of a female Prime Minister, female Lord Chancellor, female Home Secretary and a female Commissioner. Nobody, of course, commented when males held all of those roles for centuries. I hope your appointment inspires my two granddaughters, now 18 and 15.

You will have seen that, as the author of this letter, I have given it the status of an Open Letter. I believe you will understand why as you read on.

I should also point out that throughout this letter, I make reference to an article by Tom Harper in *The Sunday Times* dated 26 February 2017 (page 6) entitled 'Cool Cressida's first case: the battered Yard.'

The article painted a sorry and somewhat disturbing picture of the current state of Scotland Yard. It refers to your "icy" relationship with your predecessor, Sir Bernard Hogan-Howe, to whom I had occasion to write on at least a dozen occasions and who failed to deal with my matters in a professional manner. The baton has now been passed to you, and I am seeking your assistance in not only correcting gross miscarriages (please note the plural) of justice that I have been involved in, and also the case of Tony Martin, the Norfolk farmer who fired his shotgun when burglars smashed their way into his house in 1999. It is a case which you may well remember.

I have been the victim of FOUR miscarriages of justice. This is not only my view, but also that of Sir Henry Bellingham, my MP and a non-practising barrister. In fact, on 27 January 2017, when I met with him (with Satish Sekar, an investigative journalist also present), Sir Henry said that "All of your convictions are unsafe and unlawful and any solicitor – let alone a barrister – could see that straightaway." This is recorded in the Minutes of that meeting.

Now, the "reasonable person" as defined by the Courts, would be driven to conclude that, with an MP being able to state on the record that my convictions were "unsafe and unlawful", that it should be a simple matter for them to be quashed and my life returned to normal.

Not so. And the reason that this Kafka-esque nightmare has arisen is because of demonstrable police corruption. I have been in communication with Baroness Lawrence of Clarendon on this matter, since, as I expect you will know, she was most vociferous in the matter of police corruption in her son's murder. She managed to get a Home Affairs Select Committee to discuss the issue of police corruption.

In Mr Harper's article, he referred to a dissertation you wrote arguing that the way Margaret Thatcher used the police to crush the miners' strike had "…undermined public support by creating the impression that the police had been reduced to the status of political tools…"

Sadly, I do not have the time or space in which to give you my views of the way in which the miners were treated (although from the way I constructed that sentence you may well be able to tell where my sympathies lie) and nor do I have the space to discuss your point that the police were reduced to the status of political tools – though I must say that I do entirely agree. I think there is a worrying trend towards the Police being nothing more than an extension of Government, rather being at least one step removed. Perhaps it is a naive thought on my part to think that there should be complete independence when it is clear there is not.

Referring to your comment about public confidence in the Police being undermined, I think you are only half-correct. I believe that by far and away the biggest issue with the Police which undermines public confidence is corruption. I need only mention Hillsborough (a match which I attended) and you will instantly know that no right-minded, decent member of the public would wish its police force to lie, to apportion blame where no blame exists, to create false documents, to forge signatures and to go into a mind-set of continual and perpetual denial when the 'human thing to do' was to say, "We're sorry, we got this wrong."

I do not have the time or space to enter into all of my views about Hillsborough, though some can be found in my (banned) book *from Hillsborough to Lambeth*, co-authored with Michael Bird.

The purpose of my letter is:

(i) to draw your attention to my miscarriages of justice achieved through police corruption (and I use the term in accordance with its use by Professor Phil Scraton of the Hillsborough Independent Panel);

(ii) to seek your assistance in achieving a meeting with my beloved daughter and grandchildren;

(iii) to request a full written apology from the Metropolitan Police Service for its inhuman treatment of not only me but vicariously also my immediate family.

THE MISCARRIAGES OF JUSTICE

(i) the incitement of a female aged 14 to engage in sexual activity (s.10 Sexual Offences Act 2003) – *there never was a female and the SOA requires there to have been a 'Person B' to have been incited;*

(ii) the alleged Harassment of my daughter ▮▮▮▮▮ (née Pead)[573] by sending her a letter about police corruption in the above case, and my then 12-year-old granddaughter, ▮▮▮▮▮, by sending her a birthday card – *when neither family member had made a complaint to the Police, when neither had made a witness statement and neither appeared in Court (Bexley Magistrates') against me;*

(iii) the alleged criminal damage to a car purportedly belonging to the energy company E.ON – *when no damage was sustained and when the Board of Directors (whom I contacted) failed to provide ownership of the car and the Police failed to provide proof of damage;*

(iv) allegedly impersonating a barrister (I have acted lawfully as a McKenzie Friend for Tony Martin and others) – *when I have never spoken on another person's behalf in Court, I have never worn a wig or gown in Court and never portrayed myself as a barrister at all.*

You will easily be able to see that Sir Henry Bellingham is correct in saying that any bona fide solicitor could see straightaway that these convictions are, indeed "unsafe" and "unlawful" and they only came upon me after the age of 56 when I had reported child abuse whilst working as the Head Teacher of a pupil referral unit in Lambeth Council – which was my job to report. Thereafter, I was "unlawfully dismissed" (Sir Henry's phrase) by the Council, where I had been "set up" to quote Alex Passman of the University of Plymouth, an award-winning Employment Law Specialist who accompanied me to the first investigation meeting following my unlawful suspension (I had not been

---

[573] Due to an unlawful restraining order imposed on 1st November 2011, and further gagging orders imposed upon me since, I am unable to release this book with my daughter's name in it, or the names of her husband and children without rendering myself liable to a further unlawful term of imprisonment. I could, of course, have defied the unlawful order and released the book, but the "authorities" would only have banned it and then Tony would have suffered again. I was not prepared to let that happen.

provided with reasons for my suspension) and then this series of convictions entered my life. I had also been replaced as Head on 2 April 2007 and not interviewed until 19 April 2007 – a clear breach of Employment Law.

The article previously referred to, says that you possess "...a powerful intellect..." and so I feel certain that you will be able to see that these convictions against me have no merit whatsoever and have obviously been brought against me as a stalking horse to deflect attention away from Lambeth. As you will know, Lambeth Council is now – 10 years later - very much in the news with regard to child abuse and is being investigated by the Independent Inquiry into Child Sexual Abuse.

On 9 March 2015, I met with Clive Driscoll, a now-retired DCI from Scotland Yard, who informed me that I was "flagged up at Scotland Yard as a major threat because of my research and books" and that my family had been lied to and it was likely that they had been shown false documentation. I have, unlawfully, two Police National Computer [PNC] records. One (false) record shows that I have been convicted of rape against numerous females under the age of 13, when I have never been arrested, charged, indicted, on trial or sentenced. Indeed, Mr Driscoll commented that if the record had been true, we would not have been able to sit drinking tea together (with co-author Michael Bird present) as I would have been languishing for years in prison. I have actually been held in prison on five occasions and not once lawfully.
(Minutes of that meeting enclosed)

I could write at great length about the level of police corruption that I have encountered, but will refrain from doing so as it will get in the way of my achieving justice for me and family.

THE DIFFICULTIES FOR THE POLICE
At present my entire focus is on the second conviction – that of the alleged harassment of my daughter and granddaughter (but not my son-in-law, younger granddaughter or grandson.)

My son-in-law is a co-Director in a garage known as ▇ Garage, in ▇, southeast London.

On 23 September 2011, I had been unlawfully held in HMP Belmarsh on a charge of the witness intimidation of my then 12-year-old granddaughter, ▇, *who had never been a witness in any trial or hearing.* It would have been easy to establish the truth of that statement. However, I was held in prison for *seven weeks* and on 1st November 2011 I was forcibly taken to Bexley Magistrates' Court for the trial for Harassment. There were no witness statements and no family members in court, other than my son-in-law, who was extremely agitated and, I argue, under duress. He said in court that my daughter and grandchildren wanted nothing more to do with me on the basis that I had a conviction for alleged incitement, but there was no evidence, no trial bundle, no witness statements, no accusers against me. It follows, therefore, under the Rule of Law, that I cannot (and am not) guilty of the Harassment of my beloved family members.

The difficulty for the Police is that I am convinced that my daughter was not informed about this hearing at all - and nor was my granddaughter.

The Police have created a situation in which a man (my son-in-law) has gone behind his wife's back in order to get her father found guilty of a crime he knows the father has not committed.

When I spoke with Mr Driscoll about this, he agreed that there may well have been a financial inducement to make my son-in-law act in this way, since the garage he is a co-Director in *services vehicles for the Met Police*.

However, be that as it may, the issue is that the Magistrate, acting *ultra vires* (since he did not have the authority to act outside of the law) issued a Restraining Order *for 18 months* preventing contact with ALL members of my immediate family.

Furthermore, on March 2014, when I was forced to attend Bexleyheath police station, I was asked to make a statement saying that I wished to have no contact with my family members *in order to harass them*. You do not need a "powerful intellect" to believe that the police will have played that tape to my family without the words in italics, thus giving them the impression that I do not want contact with them. This is completely untrue.

In January 2012, I was forced to represent myself at Woolwich Crown Court on a bogus charge of a breach of a SOPO (made in error against me). The Judge (the only fair one I have met) threw out the case because she said that the police officer had lied and entered false evidence into court. It is my belief that that is, in fact, a criminal offence, but he was never reprimanded – that is not the purpose of this letter.

The difficulty for the Met Police is this: that in assisting me in becoming reunited with my family, it will become obvious to my daughter (who has no previous knowledge) that her husband went behind her back in getting her father convicted of a crime he did not commit. Whilst the *Sunday Times* article did not refer directly to your qualities of emotional intelligence and/or empathy, I am making the assumption that you must possess these because it spoke of your treatment of 'junior officers' and I know that a wise and intelligent leader pays close regard to one's colleagues, especially those in junior positions.

MY REQUEST TO YOU

I have a large claim against the Met Police for its persecution of me since I first reported child abuse in 2006. My family also has a large claim for having been denied my company for the past decade.

However, that will come in time and I sincerely hope that you are not minded to perpetuate the behaviour of "corporate denial" which I have constantly met with, particularly from your predecessor.

In the meantime, I am asking that you call a meeting with my daughter, son-in-law and grandchildren at New Scotland Yard, with Sir Henry, retired DCI Driscoll, Satish Sekar (investigative author) and Michael Mansfield QC also present with the objective being that my family is finally told the truth. Justice came (in part) to the Hillsborough families and to Doreen Lawrence, and I believe that my family and I deserve Justice too.

Prior to the Police infiltrating every aspect of my life without a RIPA warrant in place, I saw my grandchildren every week of their lives until the ages of 9, 7 and 2.

I taught my granddaughters the value in decent living and in aspiring to achieve your dreams. I took them to the cinema, to museums, to the park, to theatres, and encouraged them in rock-climbing as a physical metaphor for life. I would like my granddaughters to meet you so that they once again learn that not all police officers are corrupt, or liars, or forge witness statements or fabricate documents. Despite the Met's decade-long persecution of me, I still believe in the notion of a police service (I do not subscribe to the view that it should be a police *force*), and I still hold to the notion of the Rule of Law.

I therefore ask that you do the honourable thing and call this meeting so that I can be reunited with my family. I do not blame my son-in-law for his actions on 1st November 2011 since it was very clear to me that he was acting under duress. Only a few months later, a police constable lied and entered false evidence against me as I have shown.

ANOMALY
I do not think it will have escaped you that I mentioned earlier that a Restraining Order was issued against me contrary to the rule of law on 1st November 2011 for a period of 18 months.

I regret to inform you that the Police are still claiming that it is active. No paperwork to support their lies is ever produced. I am also presently banned from the entire London Borough of Bexley (where my family live) because the police are perpetuating the myth that I am a danger to my family and that they need protecting. The only people my family need protecting from are corrupt police officers.

HISTORY
On each previous occasion that I have written to previous Commissioners with my complaints and demonstrable evidence of corruption in my cases, I have been arrested and new further charges (all bogus) brought against me. I do hope that you are not minded to perpetuate such criminal activity.

TONY MARTIN

It may interest you to know that the Criminal Cases Review Commission has recently accepted Mr Martin's Appeal against Conviction. He confirmed to the CCRC in person that he wished me to conduct his appeal although he is fully aware that I am neither a solicitor nor a barrister. I have exhaustively researched Mr Martin's case for 3 years and found a number of worrying departures from normal police protocol in his case. I understand from the aforementioned article that your degree at Balliol was in agriculture and forest sciences and feel it would be appropriate for you to meet with Mr Martin on his land to discuss his case. (This is not to interfere with the current CCRC investigation but merely to inform you *in situ* as it were of the wrong-doing in Mr Martin's case.)

POLICE BAIL

Last week I received notification from the Met that they have placed me on police bail to attend a police station in southeast London (I live in Norfolk) in the matter of an alleged breach of the Restraining Order unlawfully issued on 1st November 2011 which Sir Henry Bellingham has agreed ought never have been issued.

I must make you aware that, because policing is by consent in this country, I have no intention of answering police bail because to answer would be for me to buy into the notion that this farcical state of affairs is lawful. I have no wish to indulge in unlawful behaviour or to perpetuate the myth that the Restraining Order is lawful. It is not.

Furthermore, on 22 February 2017, I entered into Bromley Magistrates' Court (the circuit's leading court) an Application to Revoke the Restraining Order. However, I had no need to do this since the RO is void ab initio – it was unlawfully made and therefore is automatically void. I refer you to the following ratio decidendi in Lord Greene in *Craig* v *Kanssen* [1943]:

"A person affected by a void order has the right – *ex debito justitiae* – to have the order set aside (which means that the Court does not have discretion to refuse to set aside the order or to go into the merits of the case)."

In making the Application, the very act itself served notice on the Court that the order is void and the Court has no discretion to refuse to set it aside or to go into the merits of the case. This means, of course, that I am, in fact, lawfully entitled to visit my family. However, I am prepared to wait so that they can hear the Truth from you in the first instance.

Furthermore, a void order is incurably void and all proceedings based on the invalid claim or void act are also void. Even a decision of the higher Courts (High Court, Court of Appeal and Supreme Court) will be void if the decision is founded on an invalid claim or void act, because something cannot be founded on nothing (Lord Denning in *MacFoy* v *United Africa Co. Ltd.* [1961]).

I am obliged to inform you that on 31 December 2013, I issued an Official Complaint under Article 3 of the European Convention which is still active, due to the Government's lack of appetite in dealing with the Complaint.

I look forward to your prompt and expeditious response to my letter and positive intervention in securing my reunification with my beloved family. I inform you that I continue to be persecuted by the Met and Norfolk Constabulary (who arrest me at will and then claim I have not been arrested after holding me in a police cell for over 16 hours before being released without charge) and, by extension, my family is also persecuted in continual breaches of our Article 8 Rights under the Human Rights Act 1998.

Sun
2 APR
2017
521

author arrested
The author, who had been drawing attention to his own miscarriages of justice and that of Tony Martin's, was arrested by 4 police officers for an alleged "breach of a non-molestation order". No such order has ever been made against the author (to his knowledge).

Instead of admitting their mistakes and corrupt practices, the authorities sought to bury the author under yet another bogus set of charges by claiming that he was guilty of further breaches of a restraining order.

Mon
14 APR
2017
522

'Storytime with Spalty' – the Eelman Chronicles
*Chris Spalton, the son of eel fisherman John Spalton [see entry **238**] uploaded to YouTube an 11 minute, 12 second video of his publication called The Eelman Chronicles – episode 1. He called this episode A Shot in the Dark and added "The story of my dad's involvement in the infamous Tony Martin burglar shooting incident."*

This was a remarkable video[574] for four main reasons: firstly, Chris Spalton stated that his father was travelling home around 1am – by which time Tony Martin was in the Marmion House Hotel – when he knocked over Brendon Fearon. If this time is accurate, this would render the times in the statements of hospital staff as having been interfered with and it would prove that Tony could not have shot them.

Secondly, the videographer stated that his father had telephoned the police *the same evening* – see entry **240** in which it was stated that the eelman had not called the police until *the Sunday evening*.

---

[574] At the time of publication on https://www.youtube.com/watch?v=X7R7djqew_o

Thirdly, the son stated that his father had been driving on red diesel which is illegal – did the Police have a hold over the Eelman to such an extent that they wouldn't prosecute him for driving "on red" if he assisted them at trial?

Fourthly the video stated that John Spalton had telephoned Wisbech police to inform them that he had seen "something strange" on the Smeeth Road and was told that Fearon's "red" jeans were, in fact, blood-stained. The video claimed that the eelman had been told that he was the second person that night to have called the police, after the Leets.

The video itself contained several errors of fact – but it is an inescapable fact that Fearon was knocked down by Spalton – so why didn't either of them mention this in their witness statements, particularly Spalton? What had he to hide – or was his statement doctored to fit the false narrative created by the police?

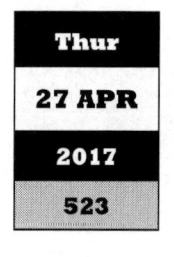

Thur 27 APR 2017 — 523

dying actress 'conned by property consultants'

It was reported that dying actress Claire Gordon (said to be Britain's answer to Brigitte Bardot) was conned by two property consultants into leaving them her entire estate in her will. The magistrates at the City of Westminster Magistrates' Court heard that Ms Gordon was "not in a fit and proper state" to sign the will which was said to have been altered to leave her money to Iain MacMaster, 69, and Morris Benhamu, 41, before she died of a brain tumour aged 74 in April 2015.

MacMaster and Benhamu were charged with conspiracy to defraud and fraud by false representation. They entered not guilty pleas and will appear at Southwark crown court in May.

Iain MacMaster was a former legal consultant for the People's Opportunity to Work (POW) charity which worked on behalf of Tony.

Fri 28 APR 2017 — 524

meeting at Knights Hill Hotel

I wrapped up a present – a book - for Tony in paper covered with a beautiful butterfly design. The book was Stiff Upper Lip *by Alex Renton and was all about boarding schools and the abuse (in all its forms) that took place there.*

He opened the present but didn't thank me. I didn't want his thanks and long ago came to terms with the notion that thanking people is not really part of Tony's emotional landscape. I do believe that inwardly he thanks them but that he's unable to express it outwardly for fear of making himself vulnerable. I regard that as a great sadness and I point the finger at Major Bailey and Rodney Townley. And his parents. Talking about one's emotions apparently did not form part of the Martin family's topic of conversation. I see the awkwardness, the wanting to thank and the fear of exposing that emotion for an even greater fear of exposing deeper emotions buried within – a veritable Pandora's box of repressed emotions that now will probably never see the light of day – never be expressed as they deserve to be expressed, as he deserves to express them.

He glanced at the words I'd written on the inside cover in ink, but then quickly started flicking through the pages. I identified that he was in touch with his feelings at seeing my words written in ink and that, because he can't handle those feelings, he distracted himself by idly flicking through the pages before resuming our conversation.

Then he became jovial – another defence mechanism. When he's in this mood, he's delightful company. At one point, I was literally crying with laughter.

Wed 17 MAY 2017 1 pm 525	**Birnberg Peirce solicitors, Camden, London** *With my friend of over 30 years' standing, David Cox, I attended the Birnberg Peirce offices and met with solicitor Sarah Robertson. I showed her a letter from the CPS dated 16 July 2011 in which they said that neither my daughter nor my granddaughter had ever made a statement against me. "This changes everything," she said. "You can't be guilty of harassment."*

Fri 26 MAY 2017 526	**Norwich literary festival** *The author heard Mexican author Lydia Cacho speak on the subject of "Speaking Truth to Power", and her book on child trafficking across the world (including the UK of course): SLAVERY INC. - The Untold Story of International Sex Trafficking, Soft Skull Publishing.*

Sun 28 MAY 2017 527	**Norwich literary festival** *Guardian journalist Ian Cobain was giving a speech about GCHQ. The author met with him after the event and provided him with an information memorandum about all of his miscarriages of justice and also fresh evidence in the Tony Martin case.*

| Tue 30 MAY 2017 528 | **Knights Hill Hotel, King's Lynn**
The author saw MP Sir Henry Bellingham on the campaign trail in the general election. He said he'd heard about my latest arrest and suggested that I contact him after the election so that we could arrange another constituency meeting. |

| Thur 8 JUN 2017 529 | **letter from CCRC**
I received a letter (copied to Tony) in which the CCRC claimed they had 'investigated' Tony's appeal and wouldn't be recommending it to the Court of Appeal. Unlawfully, they had failed to obtain the 48 pieces of evidence I had identified as being necessary in clearing Tony's name. |

| Fri 9 JUN 2017 530 | **meeting with Iain MacMaster, formerly POW Trust**
We discussed three main issues: (i) Mr MacMaster's forthcoming trial regarding alleged fraud, (ii) my own forthcoming trial regarding the alleged harassment of my daughter and grandchildren, and (iii) the letter from the CCRC which Iain agreed was "completely wrong". |

| Tue 13 JUN 2017 531 | **meeting with head teacher Stephen Elphick**
In 2015, the author had been wrongly sentenced to 24 months in prison for the alleged harassment of his daughter and grandchildren. A DC Zia committed perjury by claiming he had gone to the school which the author's granddaughters attended and collected a card that it was alleged he had sent to them there. |

The author met with Mr Elphick, the Head teacher, who stated that the police had never been to his school in relation to the author's grandchildren. Part of the author's sentence was spent in a sex offenders' prison, despite there being no sexual element to the alleged offence – such is the desperation of the Home Office to defame him and discredit his research.

Sat
17 JUN
2017
532

Grenfell Tower speech

So moved was I about the tragic fire that I went to the location. I met a Dr Hannah Caller who was speaking to the crowds about truth and justice.

When there became an opportunity for an 'open mic' session, the author seized the chance to inform the crowd about his having been at Hillsborough and the likely cover-up that would befall the victims at Grenfell and their families.

Mon
19 JUN
2017
533

meeting with Iain MacMaster

We discussed how to go about Tony's renewed appeal. The author showed Iain the letter from the CCRC in which they had stated that they were no longer regarding the author as Tony's representative in this matter.

Tue
20 JUN
2017
534

author's claims v Metropolitan Police & Shaun Pead

In November 2016, the author had been assaulted on three separate occasions by his nephew, Shaun Pead. At the time the author was attempting to put his nephew in possession of information regarding his late father's abuse in the Oval children's home, Harpenden in Hertfordshire and also a letter from Sir Henry Bellingham to Tony Martin (dated 11 May 2016) in which the MP stated that the author was "the victim of a number of miscarriages of justice".

Upon assaulting him, the author's nephew shouted, "The police have told us you're a fucking nonce!" The very same things they'd been telling Tony Martin (through some of his "friends") so that he would have nothing to do with me. Thankfully, Tony has a mind of his own.

Sun
20 AUG
2017
535

Bleak House

On the anniversary of Tony firing his gun, I went to Bleak House around 9pm so that I could see for myself the available light at that time of night and at that time of year. I parked on the track leading to the farm and it wasn't long before Tony pulled up behind me, saw that it was me recording and then reversed at speed and was gone.

| Thur 14 SEP 2017 536 | **David Greenwood, child abuse solicitor**
The author had made contact with David Greenwood some weeks previously about the abuse that Tony (and others) had endured at Glebe House School and the abuse that the author and two brothers (and thousands of others) had encountered in Harpenden. |

We had agreed to travel up together and I arrived at the farm at 8am. Within minutes, Tony showed up, but he wasn't suited and booted so I immediately knew something was wrong. He told me that something had come up at the last minute, but my belief is that Tony couldn't face it – couldn't face telling the solicitor about the abuse and re-live it again. In the event, I travelled up myself to Sheffield and met with David. He was disappointed not to have seen Tony.

| Sun 17 SEP 2017 537 | **Wisbech**
Tony signed two important letters about his appeal – one to the Home Secretary (Amber Rudd) and one to Elizabeth Truss (his MP and a former minister for justice.) We did not receive a reply to either letter. |

| Wed 27 SEP 2017 538 | **home address of author**
Four police officers called at the author's residence, claiming they had to "monitor" him in the community because he is a dangerous sex offender. He asked for their warrants cards – they were not forthcoming. He asked to see any documentation about his alleged sex offences – there was none. If you think there is a free press, you're very much mistaken. Report child abuse and see how free it isn't and how free you aren't. |

| Sat 7 OCT 2017 539 | **conference on miscarriage of justice, Liverpool**
The meeting started at 10am, but because there was an Open Day we were not in the same lecture theatre as last year. Because of severe travel delays on the roads and trains, the attendance was only about 70 compared with last year's 150 or so. |

I hand-delivered a letter to commissioner David James Smith telling him that Tony was appealing their decision. He didn't look too pleased to be handed that letter in front of an audience.

Sun 15 OCT 2017 — 540

Wisbech
I showed Tony a letter from David Greenwood at Switalskis which said that Tony's complaint against Glebe House was "in the system". Tony also gave me his authority to write to the Chief Constable of Norfolk regarding Glebe House.

Mon 16 OCT 2017 — 541

home address of Sir Henry Bellingham, MP
I went to the home address of Sir Henry Bellingham and, with a witness present taking photographs of me, I posted a freshly signed Form of Authority through the MP's door with a letter asking him to write to a large number of people including the Prime Minister, the Home Secretary, the Director of Public Prosecutions, Elizabeth Truss (Tony's MP) and others.

Mon 16 OCT 2017 — 542

author arrested
Four constables arrived on my doorstep. (Despite the Chief Constable always claiming he has insufficient numbers of police officers – he always seems to find sufficient numbers to harass Tony and me.)

I was arrested once again and once again it was for the alleged harassment of my daughter and grandchildren (whom had never made a complaint against me). But I was making waves and turning over stones in places they didn't want me to turn over.

Wed 8 NOV 2017 — 543

Tony Martin and Glebe House School
I met Tony at one of his usual haunts and I supplied him with information about some powerful figures who were connected with the school.

Mon **4 DEC** **2017** **544**	**Brian Pead on trial, Woolwich Crown Court** *The author was put on trial for the alleged harassment of his daughter and grandchildren who had never made a complaint against him. The police will wage war on those it sees as a major threat and seek to divide and conquer.* [See entry **457**]
Thur **7 DEC** **2017** **545**	**resignation of McKenzie Friend** *The author was assisted at trial by Michael Bird, the co-author of the book exposing child abuse in Lambeth entitled* from Hillsborough to Lambeth. *So appalled was he at the corruption in the trial, he felt unable to participate further and resigned.*
Fri **8 DEC** **2017** **546**	**Lambeth Council "to pay out £100m to victims of abuse"** *The London* Evening Standard *ran the story below which the author brought to Tony's attention:*

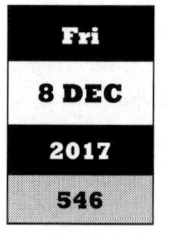

"The town hall at the heart of one of the capital's worst child abuse scandals today proposed paying out more than £100 million to survivors.

Lambeth council set out detailed plans for its redress scheme for victims of historical sexual, physical and psychological abuse at its former children's homes. It means that hundreds of people who grew up in its care at Shirley Oaks and other homes could be entitled to at least £10,000 each.[575]

Paedophiles, including staff and visitors, preyed on children on an "industrial" scale at the borough's flagship home in Croydon over three decades.

Lib Peck, leader of Lambeth, said survivors had been "very badly let down" in the past and had waited too long for redress. Many were now elderly.

"Terrible abuse occurred at Lambeth children's homes prior to their closure in the Eighties and Nineties and for many the trauma suffered by survivors lives on to this day," she said.

"As the current leader of Lambeth council I make a full and genuine apology for the abuse people suffered due to historic failings in the care system.

"We've taken the decision not to be like past administrations and instead to address the issues from a very dark period of Lambeth's history."

---

[575] This might sound like a decent sum of money, but in reality it is a pittance for a ruined life, a lost childhood, failed relationships, addictions and other life-crippling effects.

The scheme is intended to provide "swift and compassionate" redress while making sure compensation for survivors is not swallowed up by lawyers' fees. Lambeth will cover legal costs.

The borough will pay compensation to every former resident as they were all felt to be at risk, with victims of abuse receiving more.

An explosive report by the survivors' association last year uncovered widespread abuse of at least 700 children over a 30-year period at the home.

It included harrowing testimony from 40 people abused by a paedophile ring including council staff, police officers, teachers and priests.[576]

Lambeth is the first council in the country to have developed this type of scheme. Others could now follow suit. It persuaded the Government to let it borrow the money so it does not have to increase council tax to pay for it.

Raymond Stevenson, a former resident of the care home and Shirley Oaks Survivors Association spokesman, said: "This has never been about the money - it is about justice. And we don't have any faith in Lambeth council to administer the compensation fairly. It needs to be an independent team.

"Lambeth is asking people to believe in a system that has failed them repeatedly. It can't be right for the council to be overseeing the redress. Nowhere else has this happened. We don't believe in the legitimacy of the scheme."

Thur 14 DEC 2017 547

Portcullis House, Westminster

The author met with his MP, Sir Henry Bellingham, at Portcullis House in Westminster. Also in attendance were David Cox and Michael Bird, who took Minutes as reproduced below:

The main discussion points were as follows:

1) Brian Pead v Lambeth Council

Sir Henry suggested that Brian be compensated for his unlawful dismissal.

We discussed the parallels between Brian's unlawful dismissal and that of James Walker (another Head Teacher in Lambeth who was also unlawfully dismissed at the same time and involved the same Lambeth Council officers).

Sir Henry also suggested that he would ask Simon Hughes (former Bermondsey & Old Southwark MP) who commented on the James Walker case to the BBC.[577]

Sir Henry said he would write with immediate effect to the CEO of Lambeth Council in regard to Brian's claim.

It was agreed that Brian's whistleblowing while employed by Lambeth Council was 'proper' and not 'improper'.

---

[576] Author's emphasis.
[577] Source: <http://www.bbc.co.uk/news/uk-england-london-16009828>.

That Brian should never have been dismissed by Lambeth Council.

Sir Henry said he would seek a Tort law specialist to help Brian bring a case against Lambeth Council (he mentioned Leigh Day as a possibility).

2) 2009 Trial at Southwark Crown Court for alleged incitement of a non-existent 14-year-old girl

It was agreed by all parties that the original 2009 Southwark case was very simple to overturn.

Sir Henry agreed that as it was tried under the wrong law then it was grounds for either a retrial or quashing.

Sir Henry said he would write to the Criminal Cases Review Commission (CCRC) to lend weight to the quashing of the Southwark conviction.

3) Brian's existing/previous unlawful trials - 2011, 2015, 2017

- simple to quash on a point of law
- the letter from the CPS to Brian's then solicitors (BEPS) dated the 13th July 2011 stated that neither Brian's daughter nor his granddaughter had ever made a statement against him (Sir Henry was given a copy of this document)
- on Wednesday 6 December in Woolwich Crown Court (Court 5) Brian's daughter said that she had never made a statement before the current 2017 trial - thus making the 2011 trial (and 2015 trial) a 'Nullity' and any restraining order invalid and unlawful.

I hope that you agree that this is a true record of the meeting. If you wish to make any additions or amendments then please do so by reply to all parties."

Sir Henry made no amendments and the minutes stand as a true record.

Sun 17 DEC 2017 548

letter to the jury
Having resigned as the author's McKenzie Friend during the first week of the trial, Michael Bird (co-author of the banned book from Hillsborough to Lambeth) *compiled a letter to the jury which he copied to Sir Henry Bellingham, MP:*

"I am writing this testimony to you in regard to Brian Pead. As you will be aware I was Brian's McKenzie Friend for the first week of this trail – and I also want to make you aware that I have been a McKenzie Friend on two of Brian's previous court cases to which there have been many. I have been present or seen communications from many legal firms over the past 8 years and have witnessed first-hand how it is nearly impossible for Brian to get legal representation and ultimately a 'fair trial' here in the UK.

This is due to the fact that despite contacting many solicitors' firms in many cases he does not get any responses to his requests by telephone or email. Also, on countless occasions, when in front of both solicitors and barristers, not one of them have been prepared to take on his cases, which is even more surprising when you discover that he is entitled to pension credit and ultimately a 'guaranteed income' by anybody that is prepared to represent him.

On one previous occasion – at this very court house in 2012 – Brian was heading into court alongside a barrister that had agreed to represent him when he was ushered into a room (with myself present) by his defence barrister and 'advised' to change his "not guilty" plea to a "guilty" one. Brian refused and the barrister informed the judge that he would not defend Brian in that case, Brian asked the judge to adjourn so he could find someone that (sic) would defend him but the judge forced him to represent himself. Brian went on to win the case because it was proved that police officers had entered false evidence (one of which was the same arresting officer in the original trial back in 2011 from which this case relates). So by its very definition in law "beyond reasonable doubt" that if the same arresting officer had entered false paperwork against him in the trial that he won back in 2012, then this case is tainted by the fact that the same officer originally arrested him for this case. If he had entered false paperwork in that trial is there not reasonable doubt that he could have done the same in this trial?

In a trial in 2009 Brian was arrested and charged under one law and later found guilty and sentenced under a completely different law. This case is currently being looked at by Brian's MP, Sir Henry Bellingham, and I was present in a meeting with Brian, Sir Henry on Thursday 14 December 2017.

In all of the trials I have attended in regard to Brian, police have consistently entered 'unlawful' paperwork, whether it be unsigned or without reference numbers or in a way that doesn't give the full story. You may be aware of historical cases in the press including such practices happening on a large scale as in the Hillsborough trial or at present on a more subtle level as in Saturday's *Daily Mail*. I can honestly say that this practice has been a common factor and is central to why Brian has not been able to receive a fair trial in any of his previous trials.

In this particular trial you have not been privy to many of the unlawful practices that Brian has had to endure including the prosecution not serving the necessary paperwork at Stage 1 and Stage 3 disclosure. They continued this practice throughout the trial regularly handing Brian paperwork including an exhibit in which two Metropolitan Police fingerprinting experts claimed that it definitely wasn't Brian's fingerprint on the envelope. This was originally tested back in February yet was only handed to Brian during the trial and this should have been handed to Brian at Stage 1 disclosure. The judge (without you being able to witness it) reprimanded Mr Dalton for not handing this to Brian at Stage 1 and informed him that if he brought in Miss Dixey who believed that this was Brian's fingerprint despite two previous tests saying it wasn't his, then Brian would be allowed to call those two witnesses to be cross examined. Later when Brian asked the judge to add these two witnesses to the defence witness list the judge reneged on this promise and refused to allow him ANY of the witnesses that he had asked for including these two.

Brian also brought to the judge's attention the fact that this case is 'built on nothing' or a 'nullity' in law as his daughter during her statement said that she had NEVER made a statement against him in ANY previous trial (this was corroborated by a piece of paperwork given to Brian by the CPS back in 2011) which also said the same. Mr Nelson[578] – the solicitor that had been employed to ask questions of Brian's daughter on Brian's behalf – confirmed that in law if somebody's name is on a court indictment to get it that far you would need to have taken a statement from the alleged victim to be able to prove harassment. Such a case would not even be entered into court by the CPS as you MUST have a statement from the 'victim' to be able to even process the case let alone be found guilty in a court of law. You may have also been made aware that there is a simple defence (and everybody's human right) to harassment and that is section 3 (a) and (c) [of the Protection from Harassment Act 1997]:

- harassment does not apply if the course of conduct was for the purpose of preventing or detecting crime
- that in the particular circumstances the pursuit of the course of conduct was reasonable.

All of the above underlines some of what I believe to be the unlawful acts that I have witnessed in this trial and a few of Brian's previous trials. As you may or may not have heard from my previous statement, the reason that I removed myself as Brian's McKenzie Friend in this case (something I have not done in previous cases) as it was my opinion that many of Brian's basic legal and human rights were being undermined both before and during this trial.

I hereby declare that the above statement made on 17 December 2017 is true to the best of my knowledge and belief."

---

[578] Stephen Nelson of Nelson, Guest and Partners, Sidcup, Kent.

Wed 20 DEC 2017 — 549

jury verdicts returned on author

On his daughter's 43rd birthday, the author was unlawfully found guilty by a unanimous verdict of the harassment of his daughter and grandchildren even though no family member had ever made a complaint against him.

Thur 21 DEC 2017 — 550

electronic tag fitted

An electronic tag was fitted to the author's left leg as a further means of limiting his movement around the country. The person fitting the tag said that he had never before fitted one to a political prisoner.

Wed 4 JAN 2018 — 551

Wisbech

The author met with Tony in one of his favourite haunts and the farmer said, "I was told you were in prison."

More disinformation whispered in Tony's ear to try to break the author and the farmer apart to hide not only the miscarriage of justice in Tony's case but also child abuse.

Mon 8 JAN 2018 — 552

Wise Buddha, London

The author went to the offices of Wise Buddha in London to try to get Tony's case on the Chris Warburton show called 'Beyond Reasonable Doubt', on BBC Radio 5 Live. Wise Buddha produces the show.

Fri 12 JAN 2018 — 553

printer, King's Lynn

The author went to his local printer to get five new books printed and published. [See inside cover]

Mon 15 JAN 2018 — 554

St James Street, King's Lynn

The author went to the law firm of Breydons in order to get his convictions quashed.

The firm had failed to reply at the time of publication of this book (May 2019).

Fri 26 JAN 2018 — 555

Iain MacMaster phone call

The author spoke with Iain MacMaster who was busy on his case in which fraud had been alleged.

Mr MacMaster agreed that Tony Martin was being treated "abysmally" by the CCRC.

Mon 30 JAN 2018 — 556

probation, King's Lynn

Under penalty of imprisonment, the author was forced to attend Probation in King's Lynn, where a biased and inaccurate report had been manufactured against him, just as biased and inaccurate reports had been created against Tony Martin by probation officers willing to sell their soul for a promotion.

Tue 31 JAN 2018 — 557

West Norfolk magistrates' court, King's Lynn

The author hand-delivered a copy of his "Response to Probation Report" to the local Magistrates' Court.

More than a year later and he had still not received a reply.

Sun 4 FEB 2018 — 558

Wisbech

The author spent 5 hours with Tony Martin in one of his local haunts. In a recorded conversation, the two men discussed child abuse and Tony's continued desire to appeal his convictions.

| Fri 9 FEB 2018 559 | **Woolwich Crown Court, southeast London**
The author attended the hearing for Sentencing, but, just to delay him from campaigning on Tony Martin's behalf, the case was adjourned until 18 May 2018 by Judge Christopher Kinch. |

| Fri 16 FEB 2018 560 | **child abuse in football**
Channel Four's Dispatches broadcast a programme entitled 'Football's Wall of Silence'. The presenter was Deborah Davies, from the Al Jazeera Investigation Unit. One of the most interesting facts in the programme was that men don't usually reveal their abuse until the age of at least 40 – Tony first revealed it to his mother at this age. |

| Wed 21 FEB 2018 561 | **Supreme Court judgment on police failures to investigate**
In an important decision for UK human rights law which could help Tony receive compensation and justice, the Supreme Court awarded damages against the police for failure to conduct an effective investigation. The Supreme Court confirmed that the police have a positive operational duty – owed to the individual victims of certain crimes – to conduct an effective investigation under Article 3 of the European Convention on Human Rights.[579] |

| Tue 27 FEB 2018 562 | **home address of author, King's Lynn**
Two people claiming to be police officers came to the author's place of residence and forced him to attend King's Lynn police station the next day or he would be arrested. The police claimed he was a sex offender and needed to sign on the register. Obviously the author denied such nonsense and refused to sign anything, though he did attend the police station, made himself known and promptly walked back out again. |

---

[579] https://ukhumanrightsblog.com/2018/02/21/supreme-court-awards-damages-against-the-police-for-failure-to-conduct-an-effective-investigation.

Fri 16 MAR 2018 · 563

brotherly reunion, Saltburn, Cleveland

After a period of more than 50 years, the author met up with his younger brother, Alan, in Saltburn. Both boys (and their older brother, Robert) had been severely abused in the children's home in Harpenden, Hertfordshire. Alan's records from the home show that he was forced to take part in the government's Growth Study programme in which he was regularly photographed from the front, side and rear – naked. No parental permission had ever been sought or granted for the children's participation in the unlawful and unethical programme.

Sun 25 MAR 2018 · 564

Wisbech

I gave Tony copies of the newspaper cuttings regarding the murder of fruit farmer Robbie Auger in 1967.

Sat 31 MAR 2018 · 565

Skelton, Cleveland

The author and his younger brother wrote to Alan's Member of Parliament, Anna Turley, requesting her help with the severe abuse that Alan suffered in three government-controlled institutions where child abuse was permitted to flourish.

By publication, no reply had been received.

Thur 5 APR 2018 · 6.37 am · 566

Radio 5 Live

My DAB radio was tuned to 5 Live and I heard Nicky Campbell mention Tony Martin's case because a 78-year-old pensioner, Richard Osborn-Brooks, with a disabled wife had allegedly stabbed to death one of two burglars in the early hours of the morning in Hither Green, southeast London.

The BBC turned to its legal correspondent Joshua Rosenberg for his opinion on the law. Mr Rosenberg peddled the lie that Tony Martin had lain in wait.

Then Malcolm Starr was interviewed and he – quite rightly – said that he disagreed with the notion that Tony had lain in wait, but Nicky Campbell, a presenter for whom I usually have a lot of respect, failed to ask why Mr Starr disagreed. Then Malcolm Starr said that Tony had Asperger's and that this condition affected his mind and made him more fearful than your average member of the public. More nonsense: Tony has never been diagnosed with Asperger's (despite having been seen at length by several psychiatrists for the trial as we have seen) and in my view, having studied the criteria for a diagnosis for Asperger's, he does not have the condition.

I then called Radio 5 Live to hopefully be invited on to the call-in between 9 and 10am, but was told: "It's up to the producers whether they call you back or not". Clearly I wouldn't be called back. I made the point of telling the researcher whom I was speaking with that Joshua Rosenberg had peddled a prosecution lie and that he needed to be told that he was doing so and I also mentioned that Tony has never been diagnosed with Asperger's.

Not content with the appalling lack of investigative process by the BBC, I then emailed the programme and separately Joshua Rosenberg. I did not receive a reply from either – which is not to say that they didn't reply but that if they *did* respond, then I didn't receive their communications.

Sun 8 APR 2018 — 567

Wisbech
I spent 8 hours with Tony Martin. We discussed his appeal and all manner of other topics from history to nuances of language to giant sequoias. Quite some feat for an "eccentric loner with a psychopathic view of travellers" as the police were quick to label Tony.

Mon 9 APR 2018 — 568

author's letter to Stephen Nolan radio 5 live
I sent a strong letter to Stephen Nolan about the appalling way in which a police officer claimed that Tony Martin had shot Fred Barras in the back. The Richard Osborn-Brooks case had re-ignited Tony's case and the establishment was continuing to perpetuate the lies from 1999 – shades of Hillsborough. At the time of publication, I had not received a reply.

Sun 29 APR 2018 — 569

Rose and Crown, Wisbech
After several attempts, I explained again to Tony the position about the timing of the police helicopter and its importance to his case. He finally understood the issue re the helicopter.

Tony repeated that he had no intention of signing anything to do with Channel Four's proposed new programme on him.

| Fri 18 APR 2018 570 | **Woolwich Crown Court**
Sentencing having been adjourned from February, the author returned to the crown court at Woolwich before Judge Christopher Kinch. |

The judge gave me the opportunity to mitigate the three breaches of a Restraining Order (which is bogus) but I refused saying: "I have no wish to participate in corrupt proceedings by mitigating. Pass whatever sentence you wish. I have my bags packed ready for another unlawful term of imprisonment."

I received 6 months in prison for each alleged breach, making a total of 18 months. A month was taken off for the wearing of an electronic tag and the entire sentence was *suspended for 2 years* – in other words, suspended for much longer than the actual term of imprisonment.

| Thur 19 JUL 2018 571 | **Knights Hill Hotel, King's Lynn**
Just a few miles from the QE Hospital where Brendon Fearon was taken for surgery following the shooting, Tony Martin and I were involved in filming a video regarding the State persecution that I have been subjected to for 12 years following my reporting of child abuse and its cover up in Lambeth and my enduring efforts to expose child abuse suffered by Tony Martin at Glebe House School, as well as the gross miscarriage of justice perpetrated against the farmer. |

| Mon 23 JUL 2018 572 | **home address of Mrs Barras, Newark**
The author drove to Newark to inform Mrs Barras that her son need not have died and the fact that he did was not due to Tony Martin but to Norfolk police. |

Mrs Barras, who had to use a stairlift to descend the stairs, initially thought that her visitors were the police. After being reassured that we were nothing to do with such a corrupt organisation, she was informed that her son need not have died and that she has a bona fide claim against Norfolk Constabulary. The author left his contact details with Mrs Barras inviting her and her daughters to contact him to learn more about the unlawful death of Fred Barras.

Fri 27 JUL 2018 — 573

Knights Hill Hotel, King's Lynn

Just a few minutes after Michael Bird (co-author of from Hillsborough to Lambeth) *left our meeting, I received a call on my mobile from a 'private number'. It was from a woman claiming to be a police constable from Norfolk Constabulary:*

The woman claimed that she had been instructed to call the author on the grounds that he was harassing Mrs Barras and causing her alarm and distress. The author knew this to be a hoax call because no constabulary issues Police Information Notices (also called Harassment Warning Notices) in this manner, otherwise *anybody* could call anybody and claim any form of harassment. At the point the author started asking questions, the alleged police woman immediately terminated the call. Those in any form of authority do not like to be challenged or have their corrupt deeds held to account.

Fri 27 JUL 2018 — 574

café, Wisbech

At 2:46pm, whilst engaged in a meeting with Richard Fulcher, the pig farmer whom I had been assisting in 2013 and upon whose land I was arrested by four armed police [see also entry **438**] *my mobile phone was called again by a private number. I didn't answer.*

Fri 27 JUL 2018 1.30 pm — 575

café, Edinburgh

I met with Geoffrey Bacon who had re-located to Edinburgh. Mr Bacon, who had had his computer unlawfully seized by the Metropolitan Police on 31 July 2008 – ten years previously – which directly led to a miscarriage of justice, agreed to participate in the forthcoming video about the persecution of the author after he had reported child abuse in Lambeth.

Wed 1 AUG 2018 2 pm — 576

library, King's Lynn

*The author, who had defended an elderly woman in the Scrabble group following her bullying by a male library member, was unlawfully banned from **all libraries in Norfolk**. No complaints had been made (except by one member of staff) and when the author put in a Subject Access Request for all documentation relating to the ban, none was provided to him. The police were determined to slow down his progress in further researching Tony's case and the publication of this book.*

Sun
5 AUG
2018
12.04 pm
577

Rose & Crown Hotel, Wisbech
I met with Tony Martin to inform him of the threat by the police to refrain from contacting Mrs Barras or her family – which confirmed that the Norfolk Constabulary had felt threatened by my work on this entire case.

Wed
15 AUG
2018
578

King's Lynn
In a further attempt by the police to slow down the author and delay publication of this book, his State pension was not paid on the nominated date, despite the author having worked for more than 40 years and despite his having paid sufficient stamps for a full pension. (His teacher's pension is also being unlawfully withheld from him).

Fri
17 AUG
2018
579

King's Lynn
*In an example of the arrogance of some members of the legal profession and the police, the author was sent a court fine for some £1,400 for the trial regarding the alleged harassment of his daughter and grandchildren. [See also entries **544, 545, 548 & 549**].*

Thur
23 AUG
2018
580

home address of author, King's Lynn
People claiming to be police officers knocked loudly on the author's door at 7:30am. The author ignored them. They returned at 8:15am with the landlord, having forced him to drive 10 miles.

The people calling themselves police officers (but failing to show warrant cards when asked) threatened to smash the door down. I asked for sight of a warrant of entry and one was placed through a gap in the door. It was not a genuine warrant. I opened the door to the landlord and the people claiming to be police officers pushed past. One of them, calling himself DS Bond assaulted me in the presence of the landlord.

The three males claimed to be from the Public Protection Unit and claimed that I was a "registered sex offender" who needed to be monitored "for the public safety". I gave the males permission to inform the landlord of the name of the person I was supposed to have incited and no name was forthcoming. No documentation was shown.

I tape recorded the entire event.

Thur 30 AUG 2018 581

Eastern Daily Press article

The East Anglian newspaper, the Eastern Daily Press, *ran an article (page 4) entitled 'Story of Norfolk farmer who shot and killed burglar to be turned into Channel 4 drama'.*

The article, by Luke Powell, whom the author met in 2017 with regard to child abuse in football, focused mainly on the fact that the actor Steve Pemberton would play the role of Tony and not on the facts of the case.

Sadly, the article was littered with mistakes – claiming that Tony had "shot dead the young burglar Fred Barras".

The programme, scheduled to be called *The Interrogation*, was said to explore the "missing part of the famous case which sparked fierce national debate in 1999."

Executive producer Peter Beard said: "Finally we will hear exactly what Tony Martin told detectives in the confines of a police interview room just hours after he was arrested. For the first time, it's his account in his words."

The article regrettably repeated the police lies perpetrated in 1999, claiming that "Mr Martin shot Mr Barras in the back" – we have seen that this was a lie. The article made reference to the life sentence being reduced to manslaughter on appeal but failed to provide reasons and also failed to show that the appeal itself was a miscarriage of justice.

Sun 2 SEP 2018 582

Costa's, Wisbech

*The author met with Tony Martin to discuss the Channel 4 production and also mentioned the role of Christine Clarke [see entry **273**]. The farmer acknowledged that he had had no prior knowledge of her sighting of someone of similar appearance to Barras on the night before the shooting or of her informing the police.*

We discussed the EDP article and Tony stated: "It's not my bloody words! I refused to sign off a disclaimer they kept chasing after me to sign and they haven't spoken to me about my opinion on the case. They'll probably misrepresent me again!"

I asked him if he had received any financial inducements and the farmer said that he had not been paid at all.

Tue 11 SEP 2018 583

letter to Baroness Shephard, House of Lords

The author wrote to Gillian Shephard, MP at the time of the shooting to inform her about the demonstrable police corruption in Tony's case. The letter read as follows:

"I have Mr Martin's written consent and act as his Agent in the matter of his appeal against conviction. I am also the author of the forthcoming book TONY MARTIN: THE TRUTH BEHIND THE LIES[580] (Sorrel Press) and wish to put you in possession of some alarming facts about Mr Martin's murder trial.

Mr Martin and I would like to meet with you to discuss the following:

- Elizabeth Truss's continued refusal to meet with her constituent about his appeal to the Criminal Cases Review Commission ("the CCRC");
- Norfolk Constabulary's refusal to comply with lawful requests made under the Freedom of Information Act;
- the CCRC's refusal to obtain documents proving Mr Martin's innocence which it has a statutory obligation to obtain;
- the Chief Constable of Norfolk's refusal to investigate child abuse at Glebe House School in Hunstanton (where Mr Martin and others were abused);
- Mr Martin's substantial claim v. Norfolk Constabulary;
- Mrs Barras' substantial claim v. Norfolk Constabulary.

Currently, due to the intransigence of Mrs Truss and the ineptitude of the CCRC hierarchy, Mr Martin has two criminal convictions against his name which he does not deserve to have. He has told me that he wishes to clear his name prior to his death and that is, of course, the right of any human being.

Both Mr Martin and I are aware that you are no longer a serving MP but are approaching you because you were so heavily involved in the case in 1999 and beyond and because it would appear that you were deceived by senior police officers who withheld crucial evidence such as the body of Fred Barras being subjected to three separate autopsies and the fact that he did not die of a gunshot wound to the chest and nor did he die within two minutes of being shot as promulgated in the media by the police.

Furthermore, I have reinvestigated the entire case over the past 5 years and discovered false witness statements created by the police as occurred at Hillsborough. I interviewed dozens of people involved in the case and their

---

[580] The original working title of this book.

version of events differs considerably from the statements falsely created by the police.

Mr Martin and I are seeking your direct assistance to force the CCRC to obtain from Norfolk Constabulary the following items:

- the three autopsy reports;
- the helicopter flight logs;
- a list of all 999 calls made that night in relation to the Emneth shooting.

Those documents alone (as well as others I have identified) will prove *beyond all reasonable doubt* that not only was Mr Martin innocent of any crime but that he was fitted up by Norfolk Constabulary for a variety of reasons not the least of which was his refusal to stay silent about child abuse at Glebe House.

It is our intention that this Open Letter will be published in the forthcoming book and we feel that it is only right and proper to provide you with an opportunity to comment and assist.

We look forward to your cooperation in finally clearing Mr Martin's name and bringing those police officers involved in wrong-doing to justice."

Fri 14 SEP 2018 584 — author being taken to court by corrupt police

Two weeks after the notice was issued, the author received a Postal Requisition to appear at the Magistrates' Court in King's Lynn on 18 October 2018 to answer a charge of an alleged breach of a sexual offences prevention order for failing to provide the police with his address – the very address at which the police attended on 23 August.

Not being a sex offender, I clearly had not notified the police of my address because I had no obligation to. Notwithstanding that, the police had attended my property on 21st as well as the 23rd of August.

Fri
14 SEP
2018
585

author's constituency meeting with Sir Henry Bellingham, MP

*The author met with Sir Henry Bellingham, MP and former barrister to discuss the author's persecution by corrupt State officials. Also present were David Cox, a long-standing witness to the author's persecution, and Richard Fulcher, the former pig farmer on whose land the author was arrested by armed police in 2013. [See also entry **438**]. The MP agreed to go on camera and stated the following:*

"I'm Brian Pead's MP, Henry Bellingham. I've been following this case for a long time now. [4 years]

First of all, I am very concerned about the original conviction [in Southwark, 2009 for the alleged attempt at incitement of a 14-year-old girl who didn't even exist]. I don't think the conviction is safe, I think there has been a miscarriage of justice.

I also think that there are very serious grounds for looking at all the subsequent convictions because obviously everything flows from that very first conviction: if that was unsafe then it is very difficult to have any faith in any of the subsequent convictions that have taken place.

So, there is a pattern here of police and other public authorities who I think have been abusing their position and I'm prepared to help Brian in any way I can and obviously we know full well that when there is a conviction or convictions that are actually on the court register there is a mechanism for getting those convictions quashed either through appeals and once the appeal system has been exhausted then we'd be looking at getting either a re-trial or other ways of having those convictions looked at.

I think there are also additional questions here about the conduct of different authorities and the subsequent persecution of Brian which has got to stop.

I think there's another point here. We're talking about an individual who had a successful teaching career, [25 years with no complaints] who had an impeccable record and this person lodged a complaint against his then employers – Lambeth Council – took them to a Tribunal and I do believe a great deal stems from that decision to take Lambeth on. Don't forget at the time there were many different types of unsatisfactory practice going on at Lambeth and what happened after Brian took on Lambeth was this catalogue of attempts to persecute him and I think one has to view it all in an overall context.

We have someone now who has not had the opportunity to enjoy his family when he should have done; he's had his natural justice taken away, he's had his family rights removed and we have what is basically a human family tragedy when someone is deprived of their natural rights and enjoyment of their family, and so one of my further wishes in all of this is that I can get them back together again so that at least Brian – who is still a relatively young man – can enjoy his family again in a way in which one would expect."

Thur 20 SEP 2018 — 586

EDP: 'Boarding school abuse scandal'

The Eastern Daily Press *ran an article about child abuse at a boarding school in Norfolk and another in Suffolk. The author has evidence of child abuse in boarding schools spread across East Anglia. The* EDP *article explained that boys who complained of abuse were labelled liars and fantasists – just as Tony had been made out to be:*

I emailed Tom Bristow at the EDP asking if the investigations unit was going to investigate Glebe House, and pointed out that Tony Martin had been abused there. I did not receive a reply.

Fri 28 SEP 2018 — 587

author's letter to Elizabeth Truss, MP

Following my meeting with Sir Henry Bellingham, I wrote to Tony's MP in order to arrange a constituency meeting between the three of us after 18 months of failed attempts:

"I expect by now that Sir Henry Bellingham, MP and former barrister, has told you that I informed him during my constituency meeting with him on 14 September 2018, that for some inexplicable reason it has not been possible to arrange a meeting between you, Tony and myself.

Despite being neither a solicitor nor a barrister, I am Tony's chosen representative in the matter of his Appeal against his convictions. Tony's decision to choose me is largely based on my research and deep understanding of his entire case and trial for murder which will be published in November.[581] The book is entitled TONY MARTIN: THE TRUTH BEHIND THE LIES (advertising material enclosed) and Sir Henry (who was Tony's MP at the time of the trial) has very kindly written a Foreword to the book (enclosed).

There can be little doubt – because the evidence proves it – that Tony's convictions and subsequent Appeal in 2001 were miscarriages of justice and Tony and I are appealing his current convictions for Manslaughter and

---

[581] For several reasons, publication was delayed until June 2019 and the title changed.

Wounding with Intent. We are seeking a meeting with you in order to seek your full support for his appeal. It is clear that you would benefit from the concomitant publicity in achieving the quashing of Tony's convictions.

As you may know, Channel Four are broadcasting a programme based only on the first (oppressive) police interview on 21 August 1999 by DC Stuart Peters and DS Peter Newton. However, Tony has distanced himself from this programme and has signed no documentation concerning it, or been paid any monies.

Channel Four (whom I met with Tony in 2017) have reneged on an oral contract to show my book at the end of the programme. It would appear to the reasonable bystander that they are attempting to "claim all the glory" for themselves and sideline me.

Please find enclosed my copyright material outlining all of the serious issues of police corruption in Tony's case (and also judicial anomalies).

Sir Henry informed me on 14 September (as Tony himself had done previously) that you had met him in the *Hare Arms* and that the encounter had been agreeable to all concerned. I have made many attempts to bring about a meeting with you, Tony and myself and would welcome your staff providing us with three possible dates to meet. Tony and I have discussed this and are prepared to travel to *any* of your surgeries (though Downham Market is, of course, his nearest).

We believe that there are endless photo opportunities for you in this matter which can only enhance your brand as a politician. The evidence that Tony suffered two miscarriages of justices (in 1999 and 2001) is overwhelming as you will be able to read in the synopsis.

We look forward to hearing from you."

Thur 4 OCT 2018 588

letter from the Civil Aviation Authority to Tony Martin
Following the unlawful refusal by the Norfolk Constabulary to provide Tony Martin with full disclosure regarding the flight logs of the police helicopter flying over Bleak House on the night of the shooting, the author contacted the Civil Aviation Authority on Tony's behalf.

The author had written to the CAA requesting a true copy of the flight *plan* – not the flight *log* - submitted by the police to fly from RAF Wyton to Bleak House.

The CAA responded with a letter addressed to Tony in which they acknowledged receipt of the application for the release of information held by it. They provided a reference of F0003950. The letter was signed by Louie Jacombs, described as a "case correspondence officer".

Wed 17 OCT 2018 — 589

Alexandra House, Alexandra Road, Wisbech
Following the United Against Injustice conference in Liverpool on 13th October, a person calling himself Matthew Young and claiming to work for the Daily Mirror visited Wisbech to meet with the author and the farmer.

The meeting commenced at 1pm and at 4pm, Tony stood up and announced he had heard enough – the alleged journalist claimed his paper could not run with Tony's appeal because the author of this book is a "convicted sex offender" and "the editor wouldn't approve the story."

As Goebbels had written: "The English follow the principle that when one lies, one should lie big, and stick to it. They keep up their lies, even at the risk of looking ridiculous."

Sun 21 OCT 2018 — 590

the Tony Martin Action Group is formed
The author met with various people from the Wisbech area in order to formally create the Tony Martin Action Group with the specific remit to get the farmer's convictions quashed based on the new evidence presented in this book.

Sun 4 NOV 2018 — 591

Tony Martin signs fresh appeal forms
Following their meeting, Tony Martin signed fresh appeal forms and handed them to the author.

Sat 10 NOV 2018 — 592

Tony Martin signs Subject Access Request forms
The farmer signed three Subject Access Requests (SARs) for the following constabularies: Cambridgeshire, Nottinghamshire and, of course, Norfolk.

Every citizen has the right to access the information that State authorities (and private organisations and individuals) holds on them. For example, you can send off a SAR to the police, or local council, or the Home Office. Similarly, you can send off a SAR to your energy company, or local gym or garage for all of the information it holds on you. Under the new General Data Protection Regulations, an organisation or individual has 30 days in which to respond. State authorities like to flout the law and they'll often send back a letter attempting to delay the process and buy more time for themselves.

Tony was advised that it would be interesting for him to exercise his right to obtain all the data held on him by those three constabularies and he happily signed the requests.

Sun 11 NOV 2018 — 593

author arrested in Wisbech
The author was arrested by Norfolk police in Wisbech (Cambridgeshire) without being told a reason for his arrest. He was taken to the Police Investigation Centre (PIC) in Saddlebow, just outside of King's Lynn where both he and Tony Martin are frequent visitors (against their consent).

The author was finally told at the PIC that he had been arrested for not attending the West Norfolk magistrates' court in King's Lynn on 18 October to answer a charge of failing to notify the police of his address. The author had written to the court informing it that he had no need to attend because he is not a sex offender and therefore does not have to be monitored in the community. The court failed to respond to the author in writing and instead issued a warrant for his arrest. Allegedly. When the author was arrested, he asked the police for a copy of the alleged arrest warrant and they were unable to produce it.

The following day, the author was released on bail and made to sleep each night at his home address (another form of social control).

Sun 18 NOV 2018 — 594

Channel Four programme – the interrogation
The author met with some members of the Tony Martin Action Group to watch the Channel Four programme called The Interrogation. The broadcaster had condensed more than six hours of interviews with the police into a one-hour programme which bore little resemblance to reality.

There were many errors of fact in the programme, including several shots of a farmhouse which was neither Bleak House nor the cottages. Other worrying departures from reality included crucial comments made by Tony about what he saw in the breakfast room that night were edited out, that the interviews did not follow the true chronology, that the actor playing the role of Tony Martin failed to portray the sheer terror experienced by the farmer not only on the night but in the interview room and that the appropriate adult, John Ravnkilde, did not feature at all. Hardly a "true account" of events as Channel Four boastfully and inaccurately claimed.

In all the pre-programming advertising, the broadcaster claimed that it would be a programme in Tony Martin's own words. It wasn't. Here *are* Tony's own words:

> "The programme was rubbish. It didn't follow the true chronology of the interviews and large parts of what was said were edited out. Yet what I had to say was critical to the case.
>
> The programme wasn't in my words at all – that's just mis-selling the programme. It was more propaganda.
>
> The best part about the programme was the last two minutes when I was in it.[582]
>
> They kept chasing me for months trying to get me to sign a disclaimer but I wouldn't sign one. Thank God I didn't – I'd have been signing my name to rubbish!"

Sat 29 DEC 2018 — 595

Bleak House, Emneth
Tony gave permission for a weekend photoshoot at the farm in preparation for this book and his appeal. The photographs were taken by Kerry Bensley, a first-year student at the University of the Arts in Norwich.

Sun 30 DEC 2018 — 596

Bleak House, Emneth
*At the end of the second day's shoot, Tony introduced the author to Richard Portham [see entry **324**] on Portham's land, across a dyke from Tony's. The three men briefly discussed Tony's case and Mr Portham invited the author to go into detail over a pot of tea on another day [see entry **598**].*

Mon 7 JAN 2019 — 597

Norwich Crown Court
The author was forced to attend court on a bogus charge of a breach of an illegal sexual offences prevention order. Christopher Schooling – associated with the Tony Martin Action Group - sat in the public gallery.

---

[582] To the casual observer, this might be perceived as an arrogant comment. Tony did not mean it that way. He *honestly* felt that, given the appalling nonsense broadcast by Channel Four, that his part was the best part. I believe he was right to feel this way.

| Fri
11 JAN
2019
10 am –
2.30 pm
598 | **home address of Richard Portham, Emneth**
*The author arrived around 10am and discussed with Richard Portham his role in the case. He stated that he was not called to court, despite having made a statement to the police (see entry **327**).*
Later in the day, Richard's wife, Janet, returned from work and added that she, too, had made a statement to the police but had also not been called to attend the trial. |

| Sun
13 JAN
2019
3.30 pm
599 | **home address of Eileen Sutton, Emneth**
*The author – accompanied by Christopher Schooling – visited Eileen Sutton (see entry **270**). She stated that Tony's dogs were frequent visitors to her home and were extremely friendly.*
She added that she had had bricks thrown through her windows at the time because of her friendship with Tony. |

| Sun
13 JAN
2019
4.30 pm
600 | **home address of Robert Gosling, Emneth**
The author – accompanied by Christopher Schooling – visited Robert and Suzanne Gosling. Mr Gosling stated that at the time of the shooting incident, he and his wife were living in a caravan while they were building their house. He added that the statement attributed to him was not what he had said to the police. He added that he saw the police helicopter in the early hours of Saturday morning. |

| Thur
7 FEB
2019
601 | **Parson Drove post office**
The author, accompanied by Christopher Schooling, visited the Parson Drove post office in order to meet with Jayne Redman, the postmistress. She denied any knowledge of the whereabouts of John Spalton, the eel fisherman and instructed a member of her staff not to assist the author or Mr Schooling with their questions. |

Thur
7 FEB
2019
6.04pm
602

email address of Chris Spalton, son of eel fisherman, John

The author and Christopher Schooling emailed Chris Spalton, author of The Eelman Chronicles. The email read:

"I am the author of the forthcoming book *Tony Martin: The Truth Behind the Lies.* [Author's note: title has changed.]

I telephoned your office earlier today hoping to speak with you, but they said I could only contact you via email.

As you know, your father, John ("the Eelman" - I have seen The Chronicles and excellent they are, too) was involved in his own way in the Tony Martin murder case and I would like to interview him (with you also present if possible) to discuss the statements he made to the Police about the incident because I have credible evidence to show that they were unlawfully interfered with by Norfolk Constabulary (as, indeed, others were).

When I spoke with Brendon Fearon he confirmed to me that your father had accidentally collided with him [in his van].

I work with Chris Schooling, Chairman of the Tony Martin Action Group and we are Appealing Tony's convictions with Tony's full knowledge and consent. We would like to meet with you and your father as soon as possible and are, of course, prepared to travel to you.

I can be contacted on 07508 242 101 to arrange. I look forward to your response."

Fri
8 FEB
2019
603

email address of author

The author received an email response from Chris Spalton which read:
"I'm writing to confirm that neither myself or my dad are interested in revisiting this situation any further. We'll now consider the matter from our perspective closed and expect no further contact from you or any associated parties."

Fri
8 FEB
2019
3 pm
604

email address of author

The author and Chris Schooling responded to Chris Spalton:

"You appear to be ignorant of the law. We tried to assist you in stating up front that we are Appealing Mr Martin's convictions with his full knowledge and consent.

We informed you that we believe your father's statements were altered by the Police.

We informed you that we had spoken to Brendon Fearon.

The reasonable person as defined by the Courts would reasonably conclude that you and/or your father (he really does need to speak for himself and not through you) are involved in a cover-up, are in a state of denial and are perverting the course of public justice.

Now, we can do this the easy way or the hard way.

The easy way is for you and your father to meet with us as offered (he is not in any trouble - at least not at the moment) or we will go to court to obtain an Order forcing him to attend and give evidence. And how we would love the publicity!

I wouldn't bother trying to go for alleged harassment against me and Mr Schooling because you'd need to know the Law on that, too, and it shows there cannot be harassment for the purposes of preventing or detecting crime. I've copied a link for you here: https://inforrm.org/2013/06/08/case-law-hayes-v-willoughby-harassment-defence-requires-rational-belief-aileen-mccolgan/. For the avoidance of doubt, we are DETECTING police corruption in the Tony Martin case on an industrial scale and we would be PREVENTING you and your father from committing the act of perverting the course of justice.

We will provide you and your father with one FINAL opportunity in which to comply with our lawful request to meet to discuss your father's role in the Tony Martin case.

This will _not_ go away. Both you and your father will look very stupid if you do not comply with our reasonable request to meet. Furthermore, we will inform your employer that you have been reported to the Police for perverting the course of public justice.

See also https://www.mowbraywoodwards.co.uk/mowbray-life/the-source/insight/perverting-the-course-justice.

We feel we have made our position very clear - any further attempts by you and/or your father to fail to comply with a legal requirement will be severely dealt with and reported to the police and other authorities. We will also use all forms of social media to inform the public.

Do give me or Chris a call to arrange a meeting.

We are duty bound to inform you that our respective MPs and others have been provided with a copy of your email and this reply."

Sun
10 FEB
2019
605

café, Wisbech
The author met Tony in a café in Wisbech where the farmer signed two important letters: one to his MP, Elizabeth Truss and one to the QE Hospital.

Tues
12 FEB
2019
606

Parson Drove post office, Cambridgeshire

The author, accompanied by Christopher Schooling, revisited the post office at Parson Drove. Phil Redman, the husband of postmistress Jayne Redman, threatened to kill the author and Mr Schooling. Mr Redman threatened to cut their throats and he smashed his fist into the author's car window. His sons filmed the incident on their phones.

Tues
12 FEB
2019
4.03 pm
607

the Rose and Crown public house, Wisbech

The author and Christopher Schooling sent the following email to Christopher Spalton:

"You and your father really do appear to want to make this unnecessarily difficult. The Reasonable Person as defined by the Courts would wonder why - and wonder what you have to hide.

As much as your father might wish for this to "go away", I am afraid that there is a criminal appeal underway and thus his lack of contact is to be construed by the Reasonable Person as perverting the course of public justice and delaying justice for an innocent man. Given that the majority of people in this country support Mr Martin to this day, your father is playing a very dangerous game in possibly incurring the wrath of 60 million people. Perhaps your father is working on the assumption that he will be protected by the Police - always a wrong assumption to make because they would kill their own mother if they had to cover up their own wrong-doing.

Mr Schooling and I have gathered a wealth of evidence and are aware of your father's role, which is why, prior to publication of the book and prior to the Appeal (which goes in next week) your father is being given one last chance to "come clean". Otherwise, we'll add a charge of perjury to perverting the course of public justice because, as you will know, John Spalton swore on the Bible (took the Oath) on Tuesday 11th April 2000 at Norwich Crown Court).

You have until midday on 13th February 2019 to ensure that you or your father contacts us to arrange to meet to discuss your father's statement and how it differs so significantly from the real events of that night.

This is not a threat or any form of harassment. We are merely seeking justice for an innocent man and in our contact with you, we raise the defence under the Protection from Harassment Act 1997. We remind you of the following:

Section 1(3) of the PHA 1997 provides that subsection (1) does not apply to a course of conduct if the person who pursued it shows that either:

- it was pursued for the purpose of preventing or detecting crime (*section 1(3)(a)*).

- it was pursued under any enactment or rule of law or to comply with any condition or requirement imposed by any person under any enactment (*section 1(3)(b)*).
- that in the particular circumstances the pursuit of the course of conduct was reasonable (*section 1(3)(c)*).

Any bona fide court in the land would support the work undertaken by me and Mr Schooling on behalf of Mr Martin.

Mr Martin did not kill Fred Barras and your father knows it.

A failure to call me or Mr Schooling by midday tomorrow will ensure that you will be reported to the appropriate authorities, including Elizabeth Truss, Tony's MP. We will also inform Brendon Fearon and the Barras family.

Neither Mr Schooling nor myself accept responsibility for the actions of any third party once they are put in possession of the facts of your father's deliberate obstruction to justice."

Wed 13 FEB 2019 608

auction, Wisbech

The author met with Tony, who signed two extremely important letters – one to Elizabeth Truss and one to Jayne Redman (see below):

"I understand from investigative author Brian Pead that he, together with Chris Schooling, has asked you to provide contact details for the former eel fisherman John Spalton who gave evidence at my trial on 11 April 2000. I am told that you claim you do not know him, his whereabouts or any contact details for him.

Mr Pead has my authority to conduct my Appeal against conviction and you are, I believe, standing in the way of my Appeal. That is a criminal offence and I require you to provide him with the details or I shall obtain a Court Summons to ensure that you provide the details we require.

I have also been told by Mr Pead that your husband verbally assaulted them, threatened to kill them and smashed his fist on Mr Pead's car after you had been Served at your place of work by Mr Pead.

This is clearly very strange behaviour against someone who is merely requesting some very simple information as part of my Appeal against conviction.

Please call Mr Pead on 07508242101 to provide him with the true information he is requesting.

Under no circumstances should you respond to me directly."

Sun	
17 FEB	
2019	
609	

home address of Gillian Samuels

The author, accompanied by Christopher Schooling, was driving around the lanes near Tony's farm when he stopped to allow a woman on a motorised scooter to pass by. After a brief chat, the author realised that she must be Gillian Samuels [see entry **311**] *and she confirmed that she had been woken by a police helicopter in the early hours of Saturday morning.*

Tues	
19 FEB	
2019	
unlisted	
610	

home address of David Gathercole

The author met with farmer David Gathercole, with Christopher Schooling – nephew of David Schooling [see entry **332**] *also in attendance.*

Mr Gathercole confirmed that he had been called as a witness and appeared in court. He was not listed as a witness on the official list of witnesses and nor was any statement from him recorded on the official list of statements in the case.

Sat	
23 FEB	
2019	
witness 4	
611	

home address of Mark Riddington

The author, with Christopher Schooling also in attendance, met with Mark Riddington, grandson of Fred Deptford. Mr Riddington confirmed that (i) he had been phoned by Paul Leet around 1am on the Saturday morning, (ii) there was a police helicopter up at the time, and (iii) that Tony's dogs were not particularly vicious, despite them being large. [See also entry **295**]

Wed	
27 FEB	
2019	
11 am	
612	

King's Lynn police station

The author, with Christopher Schooling and Stuart and Margaret Wilkie as public witnesses also in attendance, was forced to attend the police station or he would be arrested. He was instructed to sign the sex offenders register but refused, not being one.

The Police unlawfully videoed all those present without their consent.

Fri
1 MAR
2019
6.20 am
613

author's home address
The author was arrested at his home address by six police officers. They claimed that he was arrested on suspicion of (i) the harassment of Jayne Redman, the postmistress at Parson Drove, and (ii) sending malicious communications to Chris Spalton.

The Police searched the author's property, despite being told that it contained legally privileged materials.

The author was interviewed by a DC 1893 Rachel McKenzie but not charged. He was released around 2pm.

Sat
2 MAR
2019
614

post office sorting office, Wisbech
The author and Christopher Schooling visited the sorting office in Wisbech to ask why important communications to members of Parliament and others had been intercepted and held up at the sorting office. The employee could offer no explanation.

Thur
7 MAR
2019
615

author's home address
The author's mobile phone was jammed by – presumably – MI5. This is a fairly regular occurrence and is obviously designed to keep the author incognito.

Sun
10 MAR
2019
10.30 am – 2.30 pm
616

café, Wisbech
The author met with Tony Martin and they discussed the giant redwood trees and sequoias in California. It remains an ambition of the farmer to visit these American national parks before he dies. At one point, he choked back his tears because the American government won't allow him to visit with his criminal convictions still current.

Wed
13 MAR
2019
617

letter to Brendon Fearon
Christopher Schooling sent a 4-page letter to Brendon Fearon after they had exchanged text messages. The essence of the message was as follows:

"I would like to meet you to discuss how I can make you a lot of money. I completely understand that you may feel you want nothing more to do with the case but in reality, because Tony Martin is appealing his convictions at the age of 74, this isn't simply going to go away. Furthermore, as you know, it will be the 20th anniversary this August and the newspapers will run many articles about it and no doubt approach you and Tony Martin for some quotes.

I would prefer to meet at a neutral venue in Newark such as the Asda restaurant. I will be accompanied by a colleague and suggest that you also bring a relative or friend.

The purpose of the meeting would be to see if we could work together for both of us to benefit. I estimate that you could realistically sue the Norfolk police for between 1 and 5 million pounds (£1,000,000 - £5,000,000) and I also want to sue the Cambridgeshire Police on your behalf who were working with Norfolk on the murder case.

I will have a number of questions that I'd like to ask and am happy to show you witness statements and medical evidence relating to the case which I am confident you will not have seen before. Certain statements throw a completely different light on the case and prove that you were not shot by Tony Martin, despite what the Police claimed."

Thur
14 MAR
2019
10 am – 12.20 pm
618

police station, Wisbech
Christopher Schooling was "invited" to a police interview under caution by DC Rachel McKenzie. Mr Schooling offered the detective a prepared written statement but she unlawfully refused to accept it and interrogated him about his role in the alleged harassment of Jayne Redman and Chris Spalton. Mr Schooling was represented by a Tiffany Meredith of Breydon's Solicitors in King's Lynn who did nothing to prevent the police officer from breaking the rules regarding written statements.

Mr Schooling was not charged, pending "further investigation".

Tues
9 APR
2019
619

Eastern Daily Press
The EDP ran an article entitled "All the unsolved murders need to be brought back". It was a harrowing story about the unsolved murder of Michelle Bettles, a 22-year-old prostitute from Norwich, and also two others murdered around the same time which were also unsolved.

Michelle's father, John, was calling for a re-examination of his daughter's case and the cases of fellow prostitutes Natalie Pearman and Kellie Pratt after complaining of an inadequate investigation by Norfolk Police.

Michelle's mother and father – Denise and John – complained about the "gaps in the police operation at the time", inadequate forensic evidence and no examination of important phone records.

One of Michelle's clients was the son of a retired police officer.

I remind the reader that the senior officers in the case were DSupt Christopher Grant and DCI Martin Wright.

These were, of course, the very same senior officers in the Tony Martin case...

Wed 17 APR 2019 620

London office of Elizabeth Truss, MP

Christopher Schooling, with the author present, called the London office of Elizabeth Truss, Tony's MP, requesting a meeting after almost two years of not receiving responses from her and having the author's emails to her blocked.

Fiona Walker, who styles herself "Chief of Staff", responded with an email saying that the MP was "not available to meet" (why not? – she has a duty to meet with her constituents) but that we could send written material to her on Tony's behalf which she would consider.

Tue 30 APR 2019 621

office of Nick Makin, solicitor

I went with Christopher Schooling to the office of Nick Makin, the solicitor who'd represented Tony at trial.

The solicitor was perhaps understandably reticent to discuss the case to two people who had turned up "out of the blue" but suggested that we contact him again following his return from Vietnam.

Tue
7 MAY
2019
622

home address of Dr Graham Renshaw

The author went with Christopher Schooling to the home of Graham Renshaw, the ballistics expert for the defence.

I showed the elderly Dr Renshaw some documents which the police alleged had been sent by him to a third party. The ballistics expert said that the telephone number on the documents which was purportedly his was not, in fact, his number. He added that he had no recollection of sending the documents which bore his name.

I left Dr Renshaw with a copy of the cover for this book.

Thur
9 MAY
2019
623

home address of Dr Graham Renshaw

The author went back to Cambridge with Christopher Schooling to hand over several more papers and a letter to the ballistics expert signed by Tony Martin, asking him to meet with the farmer and to answer several questions about the case which challenged the notion that there had ever been a fair trial.

Sun
4 AUG
2019
2 - 4 pm
623

the Orchard tea room, Redmoor Lane, Wisbech

The author called a public meeting at the tea room. The talk was filmed by John Elworthy, editor of the Cambs Times and the Wisbech Standard and Terry Harris <www.terry-harris.com>.

Two members of Tony Martin's family were present, as well as Richard Portham.

The author presented some of the police's own evidence to the audience who were all in agreement that Tony Martin had not receiced a fair trial. People were asked to sign the Petition which will be presented to the Home Secretary following the publication of this book.

Look for Brian Pead's next book on the Tony Martin case.

Petition

Part 24: petition

If you are convinced, having read this book, that Tony Martin's convictions for manslaughter and wounding with intent should be quashed, you are urged to contact the author at brianpead@hushmail.com with the following statement, signed and dated by you. I'll ensure that these are passed on to the Home Secretary. Just for good measure, I'll send copies to the Prime Minister and also to the Minister for Justice and as many others as necessary to achieve justice.

PETITION

Dear Home Secretary,

Having read TONY MARTIN: TARGET OF POLICE CONSPIRACY , I believe that Anthony Edward 'Tony' Martin suffered a miscarriage of justice at the Norwich Crown Court in 2000 when he was convicted of the murder of Frederick Jackson Barras and Wounding with intent of Brendon Fearon.

I also believe that he suffered a second miscarriage of justice when, at the Court of Appeal in 2001, his original conviction for murder was reduced to manslaughter on the grounds of diminished responsibility.

I am seeking your support to quash the convictions in their entirety through the CRIMINAL CASES REVIEW COMMISSION and finally clear Mr Martin's name.

I believe that the CCRC should use its special legal powers under section 17 of the Criminal Appeal Act 1995 to obtain information from Norfolk and Cambridgeshire Constabularies with regard to the number of 999 telephone calls made on 20 and 21 August 1999 regarding the shooting and also the log books of the helicopter flights over Bleak House and the farm on those dates.

I believe that the CCRC should also be forced to obtain the 48 documents that investigative author Brian Pead has identified as being necessary in the interest of justice.

Justice delayed is Justice denied.

Index

"Shoot the bastards!", 566
10 Prisons, 12 Weeks, 4, 147, 179, 209, 377, 604, 690
Aberfan disaster, 639
ACC Fraser, 192
ACC William MacIntyre, 84
Aldin, Mark, 82, 250, 251, 404, 490, 491, 513
Allen, John, 470, 471
Allen, John Alfred, 429
Archer, Stephen, 442, 443
Armin, Ann, 4
Arnold, Brian, 224, 456, 459, 460, 467, 494, 534, 541, 542, 630, 639, 640, 642, 643, 644
Article 3, ECHR, 687, 716, 746, 753, 767
Article 8, HRA, 753
Askew, Richard, 399
Auger, Audrey, 30, 34
Auger, Isabella, 38
Auger, John Robbie, 30, 31, 32, 33, 34, 35, 38, 41, 42, 64, 88, 89, 90, 255, 610, 768
autopsy, 198, 200, 204, 206, 224, 235, 237, 238, 312, 330, 331, 340, 414, 435, 534, 541, 571, 585, 663, 664, 682, 723, 775
Bacon, Geoffrey, 771
Baker, Chris, 428, 429, 463, 464
Balls, John, 414, 415
Barham, Simon, 69, 71, 82, 83, 543
Bark, Darren, 108, 109, 126, 136, 137, 138, 139, 140, 150, 167, 169, 170, 182, 194, 195, 217, 218, 220, 221, 245, 246, 265, 266, 272, 277, 283, 284, 286, 287, 288, 313, 314, 318, 325, 326, 332, 342, 379, 391, 392, 406, 423, 430, 437, 448, 449, 450, 478, 498, 499, 501, 502, 504, 506, 507, 508, 511, 512, 528, 531, 532, 536, 555, 567, 569, 586, 595, 596, 597, 599, 600, 677
Barnard, David, 305, 306, 609
Baroness Doreen Lawrence, 707, 747
Barras, Elaine, 378

Barras, Ellen, 238, 525, 589, 721, 736, 737, 770, 771, 772, 774
Barras, Fred senior, 238, 525, 621
Barrymore, Michael, 681
Barwell, Graham, 445
Bass, Keith, 313
Beckford v R [1988], 521
Benhamu, Morris, 754
Bennell, Barry, 732
Bensley, Kerry, 2, 781
Bensley, Philippa, 688, 701, 735
Berry, Julie, 159, 383
Bettles, Michelle, 789
Betts, Jane, 361
BhatiaBest solicitors, 736, 737
Bird, Michael, 4, 685, 710, 715, 723, 747, 749, 760, 761, 762, 771
Birmingham Six, 516
Birnberg Peirce solicitors, 755
Blueprint for Abuse, 15, 38, 400, 416
Blunt, Stephen, 641
Bone, Anthony, 358, 359, 360, 390, 397, 399, 401, 407, 443, 475, 477, 527, 540, 553, 565, 598, 599, 600, 691, 709
Bowers undertakers, 230, 231, 409
Bowers, Roy, 169, 244, 325, 326
Breydons solicitors, 766, 789
brianpead@hushmail.com, 793
Brown, Chris, 679, 721, 723
Bruno the rottweiler, 111
Buckland, Stephen, 430
Bunton, Kevin, 375
Butters, Gillian, 469, 513
Bygrave, Kim, 276
Cacho, Lydia, 755
CAD report, 132, 133, 136, 138, 140, 144, 147, 151, 152, 154, 155, 156, 157, 159, 161, 162, 163, 164, 167, 168, 171, 172, 174, 178, 190, 191, 192, 194, 230, 239, 240, 242, 276, 277, 302, 307, 321, 328, 343, 345, 383, 387,

392, 411, 456, 531, 584, 586, 594
Campbell, Nicky, 768
Carlisle, Robert, 194, 218
Chadfield, Elizabeth, 62, 63, 514
Chakrabarti, Anil, 143, 159, 160, 302, 352, 384
Channel 4, 737, 740, 741, 767, 769, 773
Chapman, Jean, 227
Chapman, Peter, 227, 348
Chief Constable Kenneth Williams, 591
Chief Constable Simon Bailey, 345, 719, 735, 743
Chief Inspector Finbow, 60, 61, 68, 72
Childs, Tim, 688
Chomsky, Noam, 574, 586
CI Richard Curtis, 137, 138, 140, 148, 149, 150, 151, 155, 156, 157, 158, 163, 293, 296, 297, 341, 342, 385, 479
Clarke, Christine, 371, 372
Clayton, Mr & Mrs, 603
Cliss, Sarah, 724, 725, 728, 730, 731, 732
Cobain, Ian, 755
Cokethorpe School, 25
Coleman, Michael, 424, 425
Coleman, Sheila, 726
Coleorton Hall, 335
Collins, Patrick, 33, 34, 35, 36, 37, 38, 39
Commander John O'Connor, 40
Commander Steve Thacker, 157, 192, 338
Commissioner Cressida Dick, 746
Cooper, Anthony, 420
Cooper, Barrie, 33, 36, 38
Cooper, Barry, 290, 370
Cooper, Darren, 391, 499
Cooper, David, 261
Coroner Bill Knowles, 327, 332
Coroners and Justice Act 2009, 625
Cotterell, Kevin, 92, 94, 95, 96
Cousins, Rosemary, 415, 424, 425
Cowcroft Farm, 42, 43, 336, 373, 568
Cox, David, 755, 761, 776
Craig v *Kanssen* [1943], 752

Craissati, Jackie, 648
Criminal Appeal Act 1968, 651
Criminal Appeal Act 1995, 723
Criminal Cases Review Commission, 8, 16, 661, 698, 699, 706, 723, 733, 742, 752, 762, 774
Criminal Law Act 1967, 519
Croker, Paul, 247, 248, 250, 253, 254, 257, 262, 264, 373, 390, 510, 686
Cumby, Paul, 612, 613, 614, 616
Curren, Mark, 390
Daniel, Richard, 82, 83, 543
Data Protection Act 1998, 547
DC 1013 Rettie, 335
DC 105 Paul Flatt, 93, 94, 100, 101, 335
DC 178 Noel Adcock, 283, 313, 358, 362, 370, 371, 408, 411, 414, 419, 453, 454, 478, 481, 483, 484, 701
DC 1893 Rachel McKenzie, 788, 789
DC 326 Bruce Appleby, 489
DC 352 Gary Corbett, 325
DC 356 Stuart Peters, 138, 167, 178, 179, 181, 182, 183, 184, 186, 187, 192, 227, 247, 248, 250, 255, 256, 257, 264, 279, 287, 298, 315, 316, 365, 379, 397, 407, 424, 425, 430, 431, 432, 450, 474, 477, 481, 487, 496, 497, 498, 500, 510, 778
DC 417 Ian Abel, 100, 101
DC 422 Trevor Buxton, 134, 145, 160, 194, 264, 275, 290, 300, 301, 302, 303, 313, 322, 336, 349, 352, 356, 365, 380, 381, 391, 425, 428, 434, 450, 462, 470, 477, 496, 497, 498, 500, 501, 510, 567
DC 503 William Durrant, 215, 216, 223, 314
DC 564 Maskell, 244, 246, 310
DC 603 Andrew Lovick, 238, 366, 403, 422, 424, 445
DC 7 Bowell, 215, 227, 290
DC 751 Paul Cross, 134, 269, 273, 332, 353, 361, 381, 401, 442
DC 8 Richard Aldous, 104, 105, 106, 224, 230, 231, 308, 309, 322, 409, 455, 456, 457,

460, 461, 462, 466, 467, 500, 534, 640
DC Peter Valleley, 36, 39
DCI Barker, 329
DCI Clive Driscoll, 710, 711, 712, 713, 714, 732, 749, 750, 751
DCI Martin Wright, 193, 224, 231, 232, 409, 411, 427, 465, 495, 585, 586, 593, 594, 595, 596, 597, 598, 790
DCS Bill Moody, 42
Dean, Tony, 610
Dennison, Richard, 492
Deptford, Fred, 102, 227, 266, 279, 280, 363, 401, 428
Desborough, Colin, 44, 48
Dewsnap, Christopher, 606, 607, 608
DI Matthew Sharman, 139, 178, 193, 320, 336, 356, 358, 381, 383, 411, 412, 455, 496, 586, 587, 595, 734
DI Paul Chapman, 95, 96
Didwell, Philip, 408
diminished responsibility, 8, 186, 624, 625, 626, 627, 628, 649, 650, 651, 653, 695, 696, 700, 734, 793
Diskin-Bates, Michelle, 726
Dobbin, Lisa, 392
Dolan, John, 274, 275, 415, 430
Dolan, Mary, 327, 591
Doubleday, Michael, 407, 408
Dr Ben Walden, 687
Dr Dick Shepherd, 311, 331, 435, 541, 555, 742
Dr Hannah Caller, 757
Dr Ian Haczewski, 726
Dr Joanne Skinner, 727
Dr John Skinner, 193, 225, 236, 476, 726, 727
Dr Mackeith, 648
Dr Michael Heath, 224, 225, 231, 232, 233, 234, 235, 236, 237, 238, 327, 330, 331, 340, 409, 434, 435, 437, 466, 490, 495, 534, 541, 553, 571, 598, 619, 654, 662, 663, 664, 665, 666, 667, 678, 679, 680, 681, 682, 683, 718,

721, 723, 737, 742
Dr P Nigel Cooper, 330, 331, 435, 463, 468, 541, 555, 664, 665, 666, 667, 742
Dr Philip Joseph, 647, 648, 649, 650, 652, 695
DS 3132 Thomas Neill, 140, 194, 313
DS 3135 Peter Newton, 178, 181, 182, 183, 184, 185, 186, 188, 189, 247, 248, 251, 252, 257, 263, 264, 448, 449, 545, 778
DS 3254 Mark Taylor, 238, 322
DS John Eglen, 214, 224, 226, 299, 320, 331, 388, 396, 409, 410, 413, 414, 428, 429, 452, 455, 458, 462, 463, 465, 466, 467, 468, 469, 494, 533, 534, 542, 557, 594, 632, 639, 640
DSupt Christopher Grant, 193, 224, 790
DSupt Steve Swain, 91
Early Day Motion, 662
Elphick, Stephen, 756
Elworthy, John, 732, 791
Emmerson, Ben, 732
European Convention on Human Rights, 716, 746, 767
Everett, John Bruce, 451
Ewing, Terence, 611
Farmwatch Ltd, 99, 101, 111, 358, 359, 360, 390, 396, 397, 398, 399, 400, 401, 407, 426, 427, 443, 445, 472, 475, 476, 478, 498, 527, 540, 555, 565, 598, 599, 600, 691, 703, 709
Fearon, Gary, 722
Fearon, Glenis, 245, 270
Fearon, Joe, 448, 591, 677
Fearon, Neil, 244, 246, 247, 285, 287, 612, 613, 682
Fermoy Centre, 683, 685
Ferris, Professor, 680
firearms discharge residue, 695
Fitzjohn, David, 393
FOI request, 480, 568
Fordham, Paul, 376
Foreman's Cottage, 130, 132, 136, 138, 139, 147, 151, 155, 157, 208, 209, 220, 227, 240, 241, 268, 279, 298, 314, 327, 328, 362,

364, 530
Forsyth, Frederick, 606
Forsythe, Bulic, 711, 712, 713, 714
Fountaine, Andrew, 26, 44
Framed!, 4, 147, 179, 573, 601, 645, 684, 692, 700, 708
Frank, Anne, 2
Fraser, Kenneth, 619, 681
Freedom of Information Act 2000, 83, 241, 326, 529, 568, 717, 736, 774
Fretwell, Charles, 61, 80
from Hillsborough to Lambeth, 144, 147
Fulbourn Mental Hospital, 28, 50
Fulcher, Richard, 683, 684, 771, 776
Garner, Arthur, 215, 336, 373, 419, 610
Garner, Gladys, 42, 43, 101, 215, 249, 336, 733
Gathercole, David, 391, 477, 478, 527, 553, 566, 787
Gibson, Bryan, 745
Giddens, Clive, 51, 54, 60, 67, 718
Giddens, Nicola, 718
Giles, Alan, 310, 311
Glebe House School, 15, 19, 20, 21, 52, 103, 180, 185, 254, 344, 356, 400, 446, 485, 648, 649, 689, 695, 697, 713, 714, 719, 732, 735, 741, 744, 758, 759, 770, 774, 775, 777
Golding, David, 359, 407, 474, 475
Gollop, Clive, 446
Gollop, Elizabeth, 446, 447
Gooderson, Pippa, 277, 278, 380
Goodings, David, 481, 482
Gore, Jonathan, 300, 303
Gosling, Dawn, 313
Gosling, Edwin, 313
Gosling, Robert, 293, 478, 479, 782
Gosling, Suzanne, 782
Grady, Dario, 732
Green, Lorne, 719, 744
Green, Rachael, 329
Greenwood, David, 758, 759
Guildford Four, 516

Hague, William, 592
Hakeney, Colin, 605
Harris, Terry, 791
Hart Publishing, 121
Harvey, Richard, 366
Hawkins, Justin, 726, 727, 730
Heath, Dr Michael, 571, 664
helicopter, 70, 127, 128, 129, 131, 136, 137, 138, 145, 148, 149, 150, 155, 156, 157, 158, 160, 173, 201, 207, 208, 227, 228, 240, 268, 281, 283, 290, 292, 293, 294, 296, 297, 310, 318, 328, 341, 342, 350, 364, 378, 386, 387, 394, 395, 467, 479, 480, 481, 489, 530, 555, 568, 570, 588, 595, 652, 699, 700, 701, 702, 716, 717, 724, 729, 735, 736, 769, 775, 793
Herbert, Rod, 99, 359, 399, 426, 691
Highfield Oval children's home, 15
Highfield Oval children's home, 24, 757, 758, 768
Hill, Graham, 471, 487, 489
Hill, Leslie, 232, 233, 434
Hill, Paddy, 92, 726, 727
Hillsborough Disaster, 2, 4, 35, 38, 58, 68, 102, 144, 147, 156, 159, 160, 171, 186, 209, 291, 294, 345, 377, 402, 447, 480, 516, 540, 586, 589, 648, 665, 692, 700, 707, 710, 711, 715, 717, 726, 727, 742, 747, 751, 757, 760, 762, 763, 769, 771, 774
Hirrel, Neil, 374, 668
Hirrel, Owen, 194, 218, 498, 511
HMP Belmarsh, 749
HMP Bullingdon, 604
HMP Gartree, 604, 606
HMP Highpoint, 604, 605, 606, 660, 669
HMP Lincoln, 510
HMP Norwich, 34, 37, 335, 340, 480, 601, 604, 719
HMP Pentonville, 209, 604
HMP Peterborough, 714
HMP Ranby, 265
HMP Thameside, 714
HMP Wandsworth, 625

Hodgson, Margaret, 394, 395, 415, 479, 480, 701, 702
Hodgson, Mervyn, 701
Holland, Melvyn, 677
Holland, Rosemary, 238, 356, 381
Hollis, Martin, 77, 79, 486, 490, 491, 542, 543, 555, 565
HOLMES, 13, 14, 100, 151, 277, 283, 300, 301, 309, 335, 348, 351, 391, 392, 396, 400, 409, 412, 413, 414, 451, 452, 466, 467, 468, 478, 483, 484, 489, 492, 494, 495, 727
Homicide Act 1957, 625, 627, 633, 647, 734
Horwood-Smart, Rosamund, 503, 525, 526, 527
How Stupid Are You?, 4, 709
Howard, Terry, 223, 224, 381, 382, 673
Huggins, Christopher, 358
Huggins, Peter, 358, 360, 397, 398, 454, 527, 540, 541, 709
Human Rights Act 1998, 711, 753
hypostasis, 203
IICSA, 732, 749
Information Memorandum, 688
Ings, Alison, 75
Inspector Alan James, 392, 586
Inspector David Chilvers, 137, 138, 157, 158, 171, 240, 343, 385, 479
Inspector Horn, 46, 50, 54, 55, 61, 66, 68, 72
Inspector John Meiklejohn, 41
Inspector Nigel Gant, 288, 289, 309, 346
Inspector Paul Rush, 177, 178, 382, 392, 411, 586, 587
Inspector Paul Wade, 408
Inspector Robert Turner, 163, 170
Jacutine, Neil, 295, 297, 303, 427, 609
Jagannathan, Shivkat, 301
James, Ian, 501, 503, 505, 507, 508, 637
Jepson, Dawn, 167, 170, 217, 283, 284, 287
Johnson, Elizabeth, 230, 705, 707, 735
Joplin, Michael, 336

Joynes, Tony, 332
Kendall, John, 450
Kenneth Bush solicitors, 247, 373
Khan, Imran, 688
Kiff, Michael, 132, 134, 135, 348
Kinch, Christopher, 767, 770
Kirkham, Amanda, 452
Kumar, Dhananjay, 141, 142
Kurr, William, 41
Lacey, Mel, 192
Lambeth Council, 4, 84, 144, 209, 573, 601, 683, 700, 708, 710, 711, 712, 713, 714, 715, 719, 721, 726, 730, 732, 747, 748, 749, 760, 761, 762, 770, 771, 776
Leet, Jacqueline, 111, 129, 130, 136, 220, 227, 228, 229, 241, 268, 273, 279, 280, 281, 293, 314, 328, 364, 480, 481, 530, 586, 595, 596, 682
Leet, Paul, 127, 128, 183, 268, 279, 280, 281, 282, 283, 298, 362, 363, 364, 479, 480, 502, 530, 595, 668, 787
legal engineering, 70
like rats in a trap, 354, 503, 549, 550, 554, 632, 649, 738
Lilley, Helen, 64, 66, 70, 140, 170, 175, 176, 239, 369, 375, 514, 533, 585, 672, 745
Littlejohn, Richard, 601
Liverpool
  A Complete Record 1892-1986, 727
lividity, 202, 203
Loach, Ken, 740
Lord Denning, 753
Lord Donaldson, 592
Lord Justice Hooper, 679
Lord Justice Lawton, 650
Lord Lane, 521, 522
Lord Morris, 519, 520
Lord Stevens, 253, 607
Lord Thomas of Cwmgiedd, 715
Lord Woolf, 637, 638, 695
Lubbock, Stuart, 681
M&S solicitors, 329, 390

MacFoy v *United Africa Co. Ltd.* [1961], 753
MacMaster, Iain, 675, 676, 754, 756, 766
Mad Martin, 46, 405, 417, 692
Maden, Professor Tony, 628, 646, 647, 648, 649, 651
Major Bailey, 20, 21, 23, 29, 755
Makin, Nick, 331, 390, 415, 463, 468, 508, 510, 571, 575, 591, 603, 610, 624, 629, 645, 646, 660, 695, 696, 697, 698, 700, 734
Mandal, Shantanu, 142, 143, 159, 160, 383, 384, 385
Marmion House Hotel, 66, 140, 141, 158, 170, 175, 217, 223, 239, 368, 369, 377, 386, 531, 533, 595, 596
Martin, David, 339
Martin, David Robin, 19, 42, 43, 44, 45, 46, 47, 51, 52, 53, 54, 55, 59, 60, 61, 62, 63, 64, 65, 66, 67, 68, 69, 70, 83, 102, 216, 365, 400, 491, 514, 671, 672, 673
Martin, Edward, 46, 47, 48, 51, 75, 81, 161, 314, 337
Martin, Hilary, 19, 47, 51, 54, 62, 64, 66, 108, 128, 215, 587, 672
Martin, Walter, 19, 249, 733
Masters, Patricia Ann, 49
Maxey, Judith, 684
Mayfield, Stewart, 353, 354, 359, 433
McKenzie Friend, 718, 728, 735, 748, 760, 762, 764
McVicar, John, 673, 676
Mead, Major Freddie, 695
mens rea, 121, 256, 556, 695
Meredith, Tiffany, 789
Methwold village hall, 565
Millard, Aubrey, 336, 337, 338
Moore, Mary Anne, 619, 681, 682
Morris, Graham, 443, 444
MP Amber Rudd, 734, 758
MP Anna Turley, 768
MP Austin Mitchell, 676
MP Elizabeth Truss, 734, 758, 759, 774, 777, 779

MP Gillian Shephard, 338, 339, 598, 599, 705, 706, 734, 774
MP Meg Hillier, 715
MP Simon Danczuk, 688
MP Simon Hughes, 761
MP Sir Henry Bellingham, 1, 599, 662, 670, 676, 687, 690, 714, 720, 746, 748, 752, 756, 757, 759, 761, 762, 763, 776, 777
MP Sydney Silverman, 625
Munday, Ian, 93, 94, 95, 233, 244, 339, 434
Narford Hall, 44
Nelson, Stephen, 764
Nolan, Stephen, 769
O'Brien, Michael, 726
Off Centre, Hackney, 715
Orwell, George, 543, 673
Osborn-Brooks, Richard, 768, 769
Overland, Ron, 471, 473, 487, 488
Palmer v *The Queen* [1971], 519
Palmer, Andrew, 224, 456, 467, 542, 640
Passman, Alex, 748
Patrick, David, 111, 403, 404, 405, 406, 433
Payne, David, 238, 356, 365, 381, 729
PC 1018 Huw Caine, 270, 313, 368, 393, 408, 420, 445, 446, 448, 454, 477, 484
PC 1025 Graham Bavin, 137, 138, 157, 171, 240
PC 1048 Paul Bassham, 14, 15, 350, 352
PC 1088 Mark Gray, 158, 163, 307, 565
PC 1149 Scott Hemeter, 176
PC 1189 James Wells, 307, 527
PC 1221 Richard Bodley, 230
PC 1255 Graham Cook, 300, 320, 321
PC 1267 William George, 172, 174, 241, 242, 300, 320, 321
PC 1282 Jonathan Miller, 144, 684
PC 13 John Balmforth, 62, 63, 64
PC 1369 Kevin Robson, 217
PC 155 Mark Beer, 139, 140, 147, 149, 155, 161, 163, 164, 292, 314, 318, 341
PC 17 Duncan Maxwell, 164, 328, 329, 343, 344, 345, 717

PC 190 John Coles, 374
PC 2030 Andrew Knight, 108, 109, 127, 219, 220, 282, 528, 596
PC 214 Simon Stephenson, 230, 231, 232, 274, 409, 410, 414, 434, 463
PC 222 Philip West, 346
PC 248 Russell Brett, 177, 190
PC 280 Michael Coley, 309, 312
PC 297 Stephen Jobson, 319, 349
PC 300 Hardstaff, 80, 81
PC 312 Andrew Claxton, 150, 151, 152, 190, 199, 296, 341, 344, 597
PC 320 Neil Mackley, 44, 45, 46, 47, 52, 54, 58, 59
PC 322 Philip Clarke, 158, 159, 307
PC 3340 Charles Goodman, 448, 449
PC 338 Paul Cant, 129, 147, 148, 149, 156, 157, 158, 208, 291, 292, 296, 341, 387, 479
PC 3451 Burnett, 402, 448
PC 364 David Cole, 139, 147, 149, 155, 161, 163, 164, 292, 314, 318, 319, 341
PC 376 Stephen Matthews, 277, 278, 302, 303, 332, 348, 351, 352, 379, 380, 413, 415, 452, 456, 457, 458, 459, 460, 461, 462, 463, 464, 465, 489
PC 396 Andrew Harrison, 190, 361
PC 4 David Bishop, 315, 316, 497
PC 400 Adrian Girton, 144, 147, 159, 292, 341, 479, 684
PC 45 Robin Allard, 350
PC 468 Rodney Gooderson, 44, 45, 53, 54, 55, 60, 61, 70, 71, 72, 74, 76, 83, 103, 149, 253, 254, 323, 513, 547, 585, 592, 609, 691, 692, 693, 707, 708, 709, 734
PC 471 Paul Menarry, 315, 316, 497
PC 485 Barry Gotts, 129, 147, 149, 151, 155, 158, 163, 208, 209, 292, 294, 296, 341, 479, 597
PC 517 Christopher Jackson, 324
PC 543 Richard Mann, 130, 131, 135, 136, 138, 155, 171, 241, 268, 300, 314, 327, 328
PC 556 Richard Currie, 347

PC 566 Roland Smith, 309
PC 575 David Brammer, 62, 64, 65, 68
PC 588 Brian Lilly, 239
PC 656 James Welham, 103, 104, 105, 308, 428, 527
PC 677 Richard Walker, 213
PC 70 Andrew Coller, 329, 343, 344, 345, 716, 717
PC 754 Matthew Wright, 323, 347
PC 774 David Craske, 309, 352
PC 78 Lindsey Wakefield, 78, 415, 417, 486, 490, 491
PC 801 Jonathan Chapman, 321, 323, 527
PC 802 Graham Keeley, 177
PC 805 DA Davidson, 76
PC 816 Stuart Hooper, 176, 485
PC 837 Douglas Cracknell, 325, 379, 443, 565
PC 852 Paul White, 147, 149, 159, 216, 292, 296, 341, 342, 343, 479
PC 86 Ian Thexton, 172, 174, 175, 300
PC 868 Neil John Thompson, 78, 485, 490
PC 896 Kelvin Steward, 457, 467, 483
PC 9015 Powter-Robinson, 686
PC 9022 Alison Harvey, 288, 326, 420
PC 9034 Caroline Reid, 213
PC 9056 Tamsin Raines, 132, 136, 137, 155
PC 9059 Nichola Marshall, 173, 319
PC 9078 Carmel Fitzpatrick, 301, 302
PC 9094 Sally Hawkins, 85, 86
PC 9102 Cathleen Gore-Rowe, 239
PC 9118 Fiona Bowles, 374
PC 9130 Clare Smith, 144, 146, 162, 349, 388, 449
PC 935 Patricia Hooper, 136
PC 939 Keith Jones, 51, 60
PC 946 Gillian Murray, 323
PC 960 Andrew Plumb, 158, 278, 279
PC 979 Jennifer Elton, 332, 462
PC 988 Sandra Scarlett, 351
PC Emma Cross, 213
PC John Tacey, 348, 349

PC Karen Girton, 685
PC Keith Manship, 81
PC Robert Bush, 463, 632
PC Sloan, 213
PCSO 8692 Biggs, 686
Pead, Alan, 768
Pead, Shaun, 757
Penfold, Peter, 453, 454, 455
Pettifor, Tom, 685, 711
Phoenix, Pat, 231, 232, 409
Pierrepont School, 24
Platts, Philip, 361
pneumothorax, 571, 652, 664, 665, 666, 667, 668, 736, 742
Police National Computer, 547, 749
Porteus, Christine, 604
Portham, Janet, 431, 782
Portham, Richard, 390, 432, 434, 587, 781
Posner, Richard, 736, 737
post-mortem, 31, 198, 231, 233, 311, 312, 327, 409, 413, 434, 435, 436, 439, 441, 442, 534, 598, 663, 664, 666, 681, 682, 683
Pounder, Professor Derek, 679
POW Trust, 661, 662, 670, 673, 675, 676, 742, 743
Powell, William, 718
Prabhudesai, Ashish, 159, 160, 349, 383, 385
Protection from Harassment Act 1997, 416, 764
PS 3065 Ian Fletcher, 177, 309, 395, 396, 452, 460
PS 3093 Richard Davidson, 130, 131, 132, 135, 136, 137, 138, 151, 155, 171, 172, 174, 210, 240, 296, 300, 314, 318, 327, 328, 341, 342, 385
PS 3125 Michael Mizen, 319, 320, 323, 324, 326, 350, 352, 361, 395, 427, 462
PS 3262 Paul Watson, 103, 185, 355, 356, 527
PS 622 Terry Stevens, 346
PS Middlebrook, 191

Puaca, Steven, 654, 678, 679, 681
putrefaction, 202
Putterill, Roger, 173, 175, 368, 369, 375, 376, 377, 514, 597
QC Anthony Scrivener, 401, 415, 449, 469, 480, 508, 535, 536, 537, 538, 539, 540, 541, 546, 547, 548, 551, 552, 553, 554, 555, 556, 565, 567, 575, 624, 629, 630, 631, 632, 635, 637, 638, 639, 643, 644, 645, 646, 696, 697, 698, 734
QC Michael Mansfield, 688, 718, 719, 751
QC Michael Wolkind, 624, 637, 639, 643, 646, 651, 653, 715, 734, 735
QC Rosamund Horwood-Smart, 451, 501, 525, 528, 529, 530, 531, 532, 543, 545, 549, 550, 551, 554, 632, 637
R v Anthony Edward Martin, 278
R v Bird [1985], 520
R v Fearon & Bark, 278, 380, 457, 503
R v Scarlett [1994], 520
R v Williams (Gladstone) [1984], 521
R. v. McFadden [1976], 645
Racey, Jakki, 725
RAF Wyton, 127, 158, 278, 279
Ravnkilde, John, 247, 780
Read, David, 304, 362
Read, John, 303
Redman, Jayne, 782
Redman, Philip, 785
Redmoor House, 215, 557
Renshaw, Graham, 331, 459, 463, 468, 571, 629, 630, 639, 641, 643, 791
Renton, Alex, 754
Reverend Rachel Larkinson, 339
Reverend Richard Harlow-Trigg, 340
Rice, John, 492, 493
Riddington, Mark, 401, 402, 787
Righton, Peter, 689, 720
rigor mortis, 201, 202, 203, 235
Ripes House, 51, 62, 66, 543
Robertson, Bob, 362
Robertson, Sarah, 755

Rosenberg, Joshua, 768, 769
Rotherham child abuse, 15, 690
Rumble, Christine, 145, 349, 384, 449
Russell, Lynn and Megan, 681
Sainsbury, Peter, 610, 611, 618, 657, 658, 660, 661, 669, 673, 675, 676
Samuels, Gillian, 417, 418, 419, 420, 596
Sands, Derek, 132, 134, 135, 145, 348
Saunders, James, 611, 624, 637, 653, 654, 660, 662, 694, 695, 696, 697, 698, 699, 700, 723
Schooling, Christopher, 2
Schooling, David, 433, 444, 445
Scotland Yard, 15, 30, 32, 33, 34, 40, 41, 42, 416, 417, 699, 708, 711, 712, 714, 730, 732, 746, 749, 751
Scott, Andrew, 606
Scraton, Professor Phil, 160, 177, 377, 402, 447, 747
Scrimshaw, Michelle, 499
Sekar, Satish, 726, 742, 746, 751
Shankly, Bill, 727
Shaw Savill steamship company, 28
Sheridan, Constance & Janice, 5, 88, 89, 92, 93, 94, 96, 97, 100, 101, 104, 335, 593
Shirley Oaks children's home, 760, 761
sicut aquilae, 20, 606
Sir Bernard Hogan-Howe, 746
Sir John Owen, 92, 538, 539, 546, 547, 548, 549, 552, 558, 560, 561, 562, 563, 564, 565, 567, 569, 570, 571, 572, 573, 575, 583, 591, 592, 630, 637, 642, 651, 745
Sir Kenny Dalglish, 688
Skinner, Dr John, 235
Slaughter, John, 436, 437, 441, 537
Smith, David James, 726, 727, 728, 759
Smith, Hamilton, 733
Smith, Kerry, 246
Smith, Tracey Drindra, 453
SOCO Barry Wells, 103, 104, 105, 224, 288, 420, 478, 489
SOCO David Rowlands, 224, 231, 232, 275, 409, 434, 489, 490
SOCO Ian Bradshaw, 299, 356, 357, 381, 388, 458, 468, 641, 694
SOCO Laura Bishop, 160, 224, 231, 232, 233, 244, 274, 275, 302, 311, 312, 330, 339, 409, 434, 435
SOCO Theresa Bradley, 224, 231, 232, 409, 410, 413, 414, 455, 456, 466, 467, 640
Spalton, Christopher, 753, 783, 789
Spalton, John, 128, 295, 315, 332, 333, 334, 530, 537, 538, 753, 782, 785
Stanfield, Cherie, 232, 233
Starr, Malcolm, 306, 591, 624, 656, 706, 716, 739, 740, 768
Stevenson, Raymond, 761
Stiff Upper Lip, 754
Stokes, Andrew, 425, 426, 427
Stone, Barbara, 726
Stratton, Mick, 707, 709, 710
Stuart, Derek, 99, 359, 390, 398, 477
Subject Access Request, 684, 771
summing up, 38, 43, 548, 549, 558, 560, 561, 562, 563, 564, 566, 570, 571, 575, 634, 637, 642
Supreme Court, 654, 752, 767
Supt Hobbs (acting), 385
Supt John Richard Hale, 138, 162, 163, 192, 208, 294, 385, 386, 387
Sutton, Eileen, 173, 366, 367, 368, 596, 782
the *Bexley Times*, 732
the *Cardinal's Hat*, 169, 391, 392
the *Country Life*, 337
the *Daily Mail*, 306, 708, 714, 763
the *Daily Mirror*, 670, 711, 712, 713, 714
the *Daily Telegraph*, 584, 586, 675, 676, 682
the *Dog World*, 93
the *Eastern Daily Press*, 344, 592, 681, 743, 773, 777
the *Eelman Chronicles*, 783
the *Fenland Citizen*, 313
the *Glasgow Herald*, 536
the *Guardian*, 43, 609, 653, 669, 715, 755

the *London Evening Standard*, 760
the *Lynn News*, 30, 31, 32, 33, 34, 35, 36, 37, 38, 39, 92, 549, 551, 592
the *Metro*, 684, 689
the *Newark Advertiser*, 677
the *North Otago Times*, 41, 416
the *Scotsman*, 587
the *Sun*, 265, 591, 673
the *Sunday Express*, 671
the *Sunday Times*, 746, 750
the *Times*, 42, 540, 543, 545, 587, 600, 690
the *UK Shooting News*, 716
the *Wisbech Standard*, 339, 601, 602, 716, 725, 728, 730, 732, 791
the *Yorkshire Post*, 621
Thompson, Jean, 226, 348
Tidey, Peter, 588
Tindsley, Jacqueline, 654, 678, 679, 681, 682
Toms, Christopher, 193, 194
Tony Martin Action Group, 2, 779, 780
Townley, Rodney, 21, 23, 29, 254, 446, 649, 697, 755
Turner, John, 433, 474
Vinodkumar, Narayanan, 142
Virgo, Wallace, 30, 32, 33, 34, 36, 37, 38, 39, 42, 43
Vittadini, Anthony, 82, 84

Walker, James, 761
Walker, Les, 298
Walley, Michael, 201
Warburton, Chris, 765
Ward, Hugh, 100, 101, 335, 705
Warden, David, 33, 36, 37, 38, 39
Watchdog, 675
Watts-Russell, Peggy, 373
Webb, Arthur, 418, 419, 420, 433
Webster, Christopher, 103, 218, 219, 315, 316, 379, 423, 496, 498, 500, 507, 510, 512, 513, 528, 529, 541, 585, 596, 600, 618
Webster, Pauline, 103, 273
Western, Roger, 422, 423, 424
Whittleton, Karen, 160
Widdecombe, Ann, 670, 705, 734
Wilkie, Stuart, 787
Williams, Kenneth, 445
Wilson, Alastair, 663, 742, 745
Wise Buddha, 765
Woods, Carol, 185, 269, 270, 355, 526, 527
written instructions, 576
www.10Prisons12Weeks.com, 694
www.barristerblog.com, 552
www.Justice4BrianPead.com, 694
www.LambethChildAbuse.org, 694
www.nicmadge.co.uk, 560
Wylie, Ian, 304